THE CONFLICT BETWEEN
THE CALIFORNIA INDIAN AND
WHITE CIVILIZATION

THE CONFLICT BETWEEN THE CALIFORNIA INDIAN AND WHITE CIVILIZATION

by

SHERBURNE F. COOK

University of California Press
Berkeley and Los Angeles, California

University of California Press
Berkeley and Los Angeles, California

University of California Press, Ltd.
London, England

ISBN 0-520-03143-1 (paperbound)
Library of Congress Catalog Card Number: 75-23860

Printed in the United States of America

CONTENTS

NOTE REGARDING PAGINATION: The original pagination from the Ibero-Americana volumes has been retained at the top of the pages for the convenience of readers familiar with the earlier publications. A new, consecutive pagination for this combined present volume has been added at the foot of the pages. The page references in both the Contents and Index listings are to this new pagination.

Contents

Contents

FOREWORD

The six essays reprinted here were written in the late 1930s and published as volumes of the Ibero-Americana series between 1940 and 1943. At that time the authorities for the study of the California Indians in their relations with people of European culture under the missions and during the years of secularization and the disasters of the Anglo-American settlement were Hubert Howe Bancroft and Father Zephyrin Engelhardt. Both were careful scholars who, after collecting and scrutinizing vast amounts of material, wrote detailed accounts that remain basic. Both attempted a limited tabulation of data; in both there was an underlying view that emphasized the romance of the missions and ranchos of the Spanish and Mexican periods. The essays by Sherburne Cook, with due credit to Bancroft and Engelhardt, made use of the library collected by the former and the decades of impressive ethnographic work of A. L. Kroeber and his students, for a far broader approach employing more nearly universal categories and applying statistical analysis.

Cook came to these studies as a biologist and, despite his sympathy for the underdog, examined the Indians with objective detachment as though they were an animal population in a laboratory. His introduction to *The Indian versus the Spanish Mission* is explicit: "The present work consists of an examination of the reaction of a primitive human population to a new and disturbing environment . . . ." For him the resort to historical evidence was a substitute for observational or experimental methods made necessary by the fact that the events occurred in the past:

The latter [the field or observational method] is, of course, the one universally favored by the animal biologist, but it is very rarely available for the study of the human species over a long period of time. Still more unutilizable is the experimental method, in the course of which the

[ix]

organisms may be deliberately subjected to all sorts of treatment and in which controls for comparison may be maintained. Nevertheless, the fact that these two avenues of approach are closed to us should not prevent us from using the sources of knowledge which are open . . . .

Cook brought further to these studies, as to all his work, a thorough and systematic examination of evidence, using statistical analysis as far as possible. The much debated matters of punishment and adequacy of food in the missions as well as Anglo-American treatment of the Indians, he handled with formidable thoroughness. Every instance of punishment in the mission records as well as discussions of discipline in contemporary records was painstakingly brought together. Food production and consumption in the missions were carefully related to numbers of people and their nutritional needs. Anglo-American treatment of the natives was reconstructed by exhaustive examination of local newspapers and the remarkable range of memoirs and other records in the Bancroft Library. Cook's findings were a series of astringent observations that both revealed and emphasized aspects of Indian-white relations in ways that upset many people at the time. If the California missions emerged as having power dimensions beyond mere exercise of Christian charity, Anglo-American dealings with the Indians were shown to be not far removed from systematic destruction.

Initial reactions to the essays were seldom neutral. They varied from anger at what was regarded as denigration of the Franciscan missionaries to enthusiasm for an array of brilliant new approaches and perceptions. With time much of the initial upset has dissipated as students and public have come to understand that European ethnocentrism is but one approach among many possible. The initial enthusiasm has persisted and deepened, for the studies have proved themselves both as pioneering explorations in the emerging field of ethnohistory and as works of fundamental importance in California anthropology and history. They have won wide and increasing use by the new generations of scholars in these and other fields.

The small initial editions of the essays have long been out of print. The present edition makes the essays available without change in text but has rearranged the order. The four volumes of Ibero-Americana (21-24) on the Indian and the whites are reprinted first. They were written as a unit and had remarkable impact when they appeared. Two earlier volumes, *Population Trends among the California Mission Indians* and *The Mechanism and Extent of Dietary Adaptation among Certain Groups of California and Nevada Indians* (Ibero-Americana: 17-18), represent examination in which the author came to the formulation of idea in the later writing. In material and analysis they are complementary to the four essays and therefore have been placed at the end.

The University of California Press is to be commended for its willingness to reissue these important contributions to the history of California. They have the timelessness of fundamental scholarship which opens new doors to understanding. In short, they have become classics.

Berkeley, California

WOODROW BORAH
ROBERT F. HEIZER

PART ONE

The Indian versus the Spanish Mission

originally published as *Ibero-Americana* Volume 21, 1943

I. INTRODUCTION

THE PRESENT WORK consists of an examination of the reaction of a primitive human population to a new and disturbing environment. As such it constitutes a study in human ecology, the word ecology being used to denote all the relations of a biological group with its physical and social surroundings. In other terms, it concerns itself with the factors and responses inherent in, and resulting from, the interaction of two civilizations, the one old and static, the other new and dynamic. In particular, those factors are considered which lend themselves to at least semiquantitative treatment.

The investigation concerns the disintegration of the aboriginal Indian stock of the middle Pacific coast of the United States under the influence of Spanish and American culture. This particular example has been selected for various reasons.

1. The effect of racial impact and competition was here unusually complete. It resulted in the substantial disappearance of the primitive population and the utter extinction of its civilization. The weaker established race gave way with little opposition to the stronger invading race. This response may be advantageously contrasted with two analogous biological competitions which occurred on our continent, the Spanish-Apache contact in the Southwest and the Spanish-Aztec contact in Central Mexico. In the former, the primitive race suffered little diminution of population and no weakening of culture in the course of three centuries. In the latter, there was but a moderate effect on population, although the civilization was radically altered. In the Mexican area, however, in contrast to the other two regions, the established race, largely through interbreeding, extensively assimilated the invader, with the eventual emergence of a new, composite race and civilization. We have thus before us examples of three fundamentally distinct types of human adaptation to a newly introduced and in all respects similar invading civilization.

2. The replacement, historically, of the Spanish by American political control affords the opportunity of comparing the response on the

part of one human group to contact with two other quite different groups. This situation has not been duplicated elsewhere in North America except, perhaps, in the southwestern states.

3. There is a relatively large body of information readily available in the libraries and archives of California.[1]

4. The extensive number of individuals concerned makes it possible in certain connections to utilize large enough masses to warrant employment of statistical methods. This could not be done if the populations were small or their approximate numerical value unknown.

The wide field for investigation presented by any comprehensive problem in human biology with its physical, social, and psychological ramifications, obviously makes it necessary to restrict discussion and detailed consideration to various specific topics, particularly to those which lend themselves, at least partially, to concrete treatment. Facility in handling factual material, if nothing else, demands that certain perhaps artificial restrictions be imposed for the sake of clarity in presentation. Consequently, this study has been arranged along the lines of a few leading ideas even at the sacrifice of omitting or suppressing matters which might otherwise appear pertinent.

Finally, it should be pointed out that, since we are dealing with events which occurred in the past, it is necessary to employ what may be termed the historical method rather than the field or observational method. The latter is, of course, the one universally favored by the animal biologist, but it is very rarely available for the study of the human species over a long period of time. Still more unutilizable is the experimental method, in the course of which the organisms may be deliberately subjected to all sorts of treatment and in which controls for comparison may be maintained. Nevertheless, the fact that these two avenues of approach are closed to us should not prevent us from using the sources of knowledge which are open, that is to say, the records of what human beings, the organisms concerned in our study, have actually done and how they have reacted under definite conditions.

---

[1] All citations to manuscripts, unless otherwise stated, refer to documents contained in the Bancroft Library of the University of California, Berkeley. Many of these are in the form of transcripts. The "Bancroft compilation" referred to in connection with mission population is a tabular compilation of annual statistics taken by Hubert Howe Bancroft from original sources now lost.

II. POPULATION DECLINE

THE MOST OBVIOUS and impressive result of white settlement upon the aborigines in California was the profound diminution in numbers suffered by the natives. Population decline is therefore the central phenomenon of our investigation and the point of origin from which any discussion of causative factors or subsidiary biological relationships must proceed.

The simple fact of this decline is so far beyond question as to need no emphasis. Its exact numerical course, on the other hand, is very difficult to compute. The methods employed to determine the initial factor, the aboriginal population, cannot be utilized except in very local instances, for we are dealing with an essentially dynamic rather than a static condition. Consequently, it is preferable to present no more than a general survey of the population decline in the region.

The aboriginal population, that is, the numbers of Indians at the beginning of the Spanish period, can be estimated with a reasonable degree of accuracy. Since, however, the analysis of the existing data together with discussion of methods constitutes a topic of investigation somewhat apart from the problem of interracial conflict, the material bearing on these matters has been incorporated as an appendix. This appendix presents the conclusion that in the year 1770 the native population in California, exclusive of the Modoc, Paiute, and Colorado River tribes, amounted to approximately 135,000.

During the next seventy years, or more exactly until 1834, the losses were confined to the missions and the territories subservient to them. There is no reason to suppose that the tribes outside mission influence suffered any diminution in this period. The tribes within the mission sphere were either aggregated completely in the mission establishments or suffered losses owing to the secondary disruptive effects of forcible missionization. The groups actually in the missions underwent a decline which can be determined with some accuracy and which has been discussed elsewhere.[1] The secondary losses can only be conjectured.

---

[1] S. F. Cook, *Population Trends among the California Mission Indians,* Univ. Calif. Publ., Ibero-Americana, No. 17 (Berkeley, 1940). See below pp. 395-446.

The mission losses, as indicated by the record of deaths, include, of course, gentiles and mission-born Indians. The index to statewide depletion is actually the total number of gentiles baptized minus the population living in the missions at the time of secularization. This

TABLE 1

POPULATION DECLINE

Year	Population	Source
1770	133,500	Appendix, p. 194.
1823	100,000	A. S. Taylor, *Indianology* (1864), Pt. I, p. 1.
1832	98,000	See text, p. 5.
1848	88,000	See text, p. 5.
1849	100,000	C. H. Merriam, "The Indian Population of California," *Amer. Anthro.*, n.s. (1905), 7:594–606.
1850	100,000	T. B. King, *Rept. to U. S. Govt.*, 1850. King says less than 100,000.
1851	73,000	J. D. Savage, in H. Dixon's "California Indians," MS, 1875. Savage gives 59,000 for northern and central California, to which may be added an estimated 14,000 for southern California.
1852	85,000	C. H. Merriam, *loc. cit.*
1856	61,600	T. J. Henley, *Repts.*, *Commr. Indian Affairs*, 1856, p. 245.
1856	50,000	C. H. Merriam, *loc. cit.*
1860	35,000	*Ibid.*
1865	30,000	D. W. Cooley, *Repts.*, *Commr. Indian Affairs*, 1865, p. 115.
1866	24,500	Supt. Maltby, letter to L. V. Bogy, *ibid.*, 1867, p. 133.
1867	21,000	L. V. Bogy, *ibid.*, p. 132.
1870	30,000	C. H. Merriam, *loc. cit.*
1870	20,000	E. S. Parker, *Repts.*, *Commr. Indian Affairs*, 1870, p. 81.
1873	22,000	*Repts.*, *Commr. Indian Affairs*, 1873, p. 344.
1880	20,500	C. H. Merriam, *loc. cit.*

in turn is contingent upon the assumption that withdrawals from the wild state for purposes of conversion constituted a dead loss. In other words, during seventy years there was no increase in population among the tribes in contact with the missions which would tend to restore the aboriginal number and to compensate the draining-off by conversion. This assumption seems reasonable in view of the apparent aboriginal equilibrium between birth and death rates existing prior to 1770. In fact, far from a restoration of losses, the whole trend appears to have been toward a decline among the unconverted remnant.

If the methods referred to previously are applied to the Bancroft transcripts, these records indicate approximately 54,000 gentile baptisms; but from this figure must be deducted the mission population at the end of the period of active missionization. The latter date was actually 1834, but for this purpose it is perhaps better to anticipate by two years and say 1832, at which time the mission records show a population of approximately 17,000. We may then take the difference, 37,000, to represent the decline from 1770 to 1832. The total native population in 1832, therefore, may be set at 98,000.

From 1832 to 1848 two disturbing processes were at work. The first was secularization, which very rapidly wrecked the missions economically and at least dispersed the neophytes. To what extent it was mere dispersal and to what extent actual loss of life or reproductive capacity was concerned it is impossible to say at the present juncture. Perhaps 5,000 would adequately cover the actual population reduction involved. The second process was the ever-increasing encroachment of the Mexican and American ranchers and agriculturists upon the non-Christian tribes, especially in the central valley and the northern Bay region. Here again we cannot assess accurately, but considering both prior and subsequent events, it would not be too liberal to postulate the loss of another 5,000. This would mean a native population of 88,000 in 1848.

The system of government now changed as the gold era began. The incursions of explorers, miners, and farmers began to take terrific toll of life among the Indians. The losses were very great, but we cannot be sure of figures until the 'sixties, at the end of which decade the Indians certainly numbered no more than 30,000. However, in the intervening time independent parties and government agents made a number of close estimates. No claim to perfection in their enumerations can be made, but in the aggregate a fairly clear picture is presented. Furthermore, the study made by Merriam[2] is doubtless quite reliable for this period even though his estimate of the aboriginal population seems too high. In table 1 appear the data from several independent estimates, Merriam's figures subsequent to 1848, and the censuses of the United States Bureau of Indian Affairs.

---

[2] C. H. Merriam, "The Indian Population of California," *Amer. Anthro.*, n.s. (1905), 7:594–606.

Despite minor discrepancies, it is apparent that the great decline began with the discovery of gold and the opening up of hitherto virgin territory, particularly in the foothill strip of the Sierra Nevada and the Eel, Trinity, and Klamath watersheds, and continued with the rapid extinction of the aborigines or their segregation on the reservations. Meanwhile the old mission population utterly disappeared, except for a few scattered individuals in the north and the desert peoples of the south. By 1870 all the surviving natives of northern and central California (except those east of the Sierra Nevada and the Cascade range) were on reservations or under government protection. The nonreservation Indians south of the Tehachapi, numbering perhaps 5,000, were living a semi-independent existence in the sterile mountains and deserts which offered little inducement to white settlement.

Subsequent to this time, conditions were more stable. The population continued to decline slowly until a minimum of approximately 15,000 was reached. Meanwhile there had been some interbreeding with the white stock. In recent decades there may have been a slight increase, for the United States census for 1930 lists 19,212 Indians in California. In other words, a leveling-off process has been apparent in the last two generations, and a more or less final equilibrium has been reached.

In assessing and evaluating the factors which contributed to decline of the aboriginal population certain difficulties arise. These involve primarily the problem of orderly investigation and presentation. The entire field is so vast and complex, its ramifications so wide and often obscure, that a sharp, clear segregation of individual components becomes not only difficult but perhaps undesirable. No phenomenon of this type ever depends upon a single factor or cause, or even upon a precisely distinguishable group of factors. Moreover, when such a factor appears to emerge as a concrete unit, one invariably discovers that it is related to other factors, these to still others, and so on almost without limit. Indeed, a philosophy of human ecology or environmental relations must of necessity concern itself with complexes rather than discrete units; it must attempt to see the picture as a whole rather than as individual strokes of the brush. Nevertheless, for the purpose of the analysis or the detailed study of a general situation, one is forced to consider specific phases and aspects of the problem as if they were independent, instead of interdependent as they actually are. Practical considerations of space and time demand a consecutive, rather than a simultaneous, treatment.

A preliminary attempt to organize our knowledge of the factors involved in population decline would first require a classification along certain broad lines. Since we are dealing with the impact of a new civilization, there must be concerned, at the beginning at least, the direct effect of pure physical contact between the two races. Two phases of this contact are distinguishable. The first involves the direct personal shock of conflict, which may take many forms varying from slight to extreme. For example, in this particular instance there is a range from mild exploration and conversion to a new religion with its accompanying modification of Indian daily life, through forced conversions, actual kidnaping, and punitive expeditions, to the direst state of slavery and massacres or wars of extermination. The second phase concerns the dislocation and disturbance of the finely adjusted native life with particular reference to displacement of sedentary populations and reduction of the natural food supply.

Following immediate contact, there occurs a long train of indirect consequences which affect every aspect of life. For convenience these may be grouped into four primary categories.

1. Dietary effects. Here we include changes in type of food, taste and distaste, deficiencies of various sorts leading to malnutrition, and often partial or complete starvation.

2. Disease. Apart from malnutrition may be distinguished epidemic diseases, usually newly introduced by the incoming race, together with venereal disease.

3. Social factors. Here must be considered a host of influences of the most diverse types, some of little consequence, others of the most profound significance. Thus there might be mentioned the question of forced or free labor with its economic ramifications, crime and punishment, urbanization, vagrancy, alcohol, and sex delinquencies.

4. Genetic factors. These do not follow so directly from the first interracial contact, but in subsequent years, during the period of adjustment, they possess great weight, since the nature of the final

equilibrium will be determined in large measure by the degree of interbreeding and by the character of the hybrids.

It is proposed to follow somewhat the lines suggested above, first considering the more concrete data and eventually discussing, so far as feasible, the bearing of the nonmaterial social and genetic aspects of the problem. However, it must be borne in mind that, when we speak of impact of civilizations or contact of races, we are using only the most general terms. Actually, we encounter a series of impacts and conflicts, each presenting different characteristics and involving different groups of individuals. In California, as has been mentioned in the introduction, the Indian was first confronted with the Spanish-Mexican civilization. The framework of that contact embodied two quite distinct elements. Of these, the first concerned the relation of whites to Indians after the latter, or at least many of them, had been incorporated in permanent establishments, the missions. The second involved the relation between the Spanish-Mexican secular—that is, military and civilian—groups and the wild Indians, a relation which, with some modification, continued into the American period.

Since the type of contact, together with the factors concerned, was quite different in the secular than in the clerical relationship, it is advisable to consider the two separately. Consequently, the discussion which follows is concerned only with the mission environment and its influence on the Indian.

The mission environment.—The mission status represents a type of interracial relationship which has been of frequent occurrence throughout Latin America but which has had few examples in English America. In motivation, it is unique in human history, since it was in large measure conditioned by the desire of the invading or dominant race to convert the other to a new way of thinking, that is to say, to a new religion. Economic and political factors were undoubtedly involved, but the driving force was provided by a group of men inspired primarily by religious, not material, zeal. The purposes were, consequently, not the deliberate social or military subjugation of the weaker race, although this may have been an inevitable by-product, but were those of religious conversion. Since the means to this end were inevitably material and practical, it was through their employment that the strictly biological and behavioristic effects were exerted during that period of contact when the strictly spiritual ends were being accomplished.

We have therefore to eliminate in this study the purely moral aspect of the problem. In the course of conversion it was considered essential to remove the native from his normal ecological niche and to transport him to a completely new environment. Indeed, an organized effort was made to eradicate in his mind many of the distinctive cultural traits which had been an integral part of himself and his ancestors for generations. As a result, in California a number of large groups of animals (using the term with no invidious connotations) were suddenly forced to make a really violent adaptation to a strange environment. Already delicately adjusted to the ancient habitat, they were obliged, in two or three generations, to accustom themselves, not only to new material surroundings, but to a whole series of quite profound cultural and psychological changes. Since the element of active physical conflict was largely absent, it is possible for us to analyze in some detail the economic, social, and cultural factors concerned in the unsuccessful effort of the Indian race to maintain itself under the particular external conditions imposed by the white man.

According to the classical conception, when the environment of a species changes, the species either undergoes certain parallel changes or "adaptations" which enable it to persist or, in default of such adaptations, it disappears. The rapidity and effectiveness of the adjustive process depend in turn upon a host of considerations involving the structure, functional activity, and genetic composition of the species. In general, the older, more exactly adapted and genetically stable the species, the less the facility with which it is capable of meeting changes. This is a very broad principle and must be applied with caution to such a complex type as *Homo sapiens,* but I think it may be held that the aboriginal California variety of the species belonged to the more stable, less flexible category. Consequently, one would expect the process of adjustment to be slow, difficult, and attended by great sacrifice on the part of the race as, indeed, it seems to have been.

During the course of adaptation, with most species, the intimate mechanism is not clear. In other words, what goes on in the group or the individual frequently escapes our observation, particularly when highly complex animals or man are involved. On the other hand, there are invariably manifestations that something is happening. These phenomena may be termed, for lack of a more descriptive word, "responses." In the invertebrates and lower vertebrates, such actions may be of the order of simple tropistic or neuromuscular acts. In the higher invertebrates and the vertebrates, such elementary activities may become increased in complexity to include conditioned reflexes, instinct, and all that the psychologist understands by "animal behavior." In man, the higher mental faculties of choice, judgment, and reason are superadded, with the result that purely observational or experimental analysis is extraordinarily difficult. Nevertheless, certain activities may be abstracted, so to speak, from the whole complex and mentioned, even though no complete discussion can be attempted.

In the animal and plant kingdoms in general, not only does the individual react or adjust to external changes, but there is also a very definite group response when the change is of sufficient extent to affect many individuals simultaneously. Group behavior, group function, or group physiology has been noted by natural historians from the most ancient times, but only recently has a competent scientific attack on the problem been developed. Students of the social life of animals have led the way and are opening up new fields as each year passes. Aside from simple description, their most valuable tool has been the analysis of population changes. An environmental change affects a group composed of individuals, and a fundamental characteristic of the individual is that he differs from all others in the group; thus one succumbs when another does not; one reproduces when another does not. By means of the sum of the effect on individuals the mass effect on the group may be ascertained.

To return to the situation of the mission Indian, it is possible to study the effect of the contact between Indians and whites by investigating the responses of the individuals and the group to the change in environment superinduced by that contact. Having set forth what those responses were, we may then attempt to discover the factors which gave rise to them, and, so far as feasible, attempt quantitative assessment.

[10]

Since no structural or functional adaptations could occur in the short space of two or three generations, the actual responses of the Indians to the mission system are restricted to visible activity by individuals or small groups and to population changes in the whole group. The visible activity with respect to the mission system could take but one of two forms: obvious opposition or acceptance. The positive aspect was manifested in an entirely unsensational manner, merely in carrying on the routine of daily life in the mission. The negative aspect, i.e., opposition, was made evident through either flight or rebellion. The extent of fugitivism and rebellion is then the key to the response of the individual, whereas population trends indicate the response of the group.

Population changes in the missions.—In a recent paper[3] the data bearing on this question have been examined and critically analyzed. The chief conclusions were set forth as follows (p. 48):

Primarily, as a result of consistent wholesale addition by conversion, the total population rose rapidly until approximately 1800. Thereafter the increase continued, but more slowly, up to an equilibrium point near 1820, subsequent to which a definite decline set in. These observed changes, which were based upon a large gentile immigration, mask the true situation with respect to the converted population. The latter was subject to a very great real diminution from the beginning. This is clear from the falling birth rate and the huge excess of deaths over births which was present throughout the mission era. Actually the critical and determining factor was the death rate, for it has been shown that the decline in gross or crude birth rate may be accounted for largely by the constantly increasing sex ratio (males to females). Since the latter was invariable at unity for children under ten, the change must have been due to a differential death rate between males and females during adolescence and maturity, which would result in a relative decline in the number of child-bearing women. The death rate as a whole was always remarkably high, even, for some as yet unexplained reason, at the very start of the missions. It tended definitely, however, to fall during the last thirty years and, at the existing rates of change, would probably have come into equilibrium with the birth rate ultimately. These aspects of the total death rate were due primarily to the state of the child death rate, since the adult death rate did not alter so materially in sixty-odd years.

The chief conclusion of a more general nature is that the Indian population, which presumably had been in a more or less steady equilibrium

[3] S. F. Cook, *op. cit.* See below, p. 446.

prior to missionization, underwent a profound upset as a result of that process, a process from which it was showing signs of recovery only at the time of secularization. The indications are, indeed, that several further generations would have been necessary to recast the race, as it were, and bring about that restoration of biotic equilibrium which eventually would have occurred.

Eliminating all detail and rounding off numerical values, the data upon which these conclusions were based are the following. The total mission population in 1770, 1780, 1790, 1800, 1810, 1820, 1830, 1834 respectively was: 100, 3,000, 7,400, 13,100, 18,800, 21,100, 18,100, 15,000. The sex ratio (male/female) in the decade 1770–1780 was normal, approximately 1; by 1834 it had risen to 1.35. The crude birth rate per thousand in 1780, 1800, 1820, 1830 was respectively 45, 40, 35, 32. At the same time the value of 540 children per 1,000 adult females remained constant throughout. For the total population the mean values for the death rate per thousand in the decades centering around 1778, 1788, 1798, 1808, 1818, 1828 were respectively 70, 70, 85, 83, 76, 70; for children 140, 145, 177, 167, 143, 102. Finally, the percentage of newly converted gentiles, which represents the proportion of immigration to the missions, expressed as number of gentile baptisms per thousand total baptisms was, for the years 1776, 1790, 1800, 1810, 1820, 1830, the following: 27, 12, 8.5, 6.0, 4.5, 2.5.

The group response of the natives to the mission environment was therefore a very marked decline in numbers, referable primarily to the high mortality rate and secondarily to a reduced birth rate and altered sex ratio.

III. DISEASE AND NUTRITION

IT IS NECESSARY now to consider what might have been the factors responsible for the observed changes. When any population undergoes a sudden and profound diminution, it is, of course, customary to investigate first the three most probable causes: war, famine, and pestilence. If these will not account for the decline, then search must be made for more obscure reasons, perhaps of an economic, social, or cultural nature. In the present instance, as far as the internal population of the mission is concerned, war may be excluded at the beginning, since the number of neophytes who died by violent means was negligible. Certain uprisings did occur and various recalcitrants, rebels, or criminals perished in fighting or by execution, but armed conflict on a large scale did not enter the picture. There remain, then, disease and starvation as effective factors which require extended consideration.

DISEASE

That disease was important cannot be doubted. Indeed, its existence would be postulated purely on the basis of the physical conditions: large numbers of natives brought together in contact with newcomers who were the carriers of numerous maladies to which the older population was unaccustomed and hence not immune. The result should be high incidence of the imported diseases and consequent high mortality, frequently reaching epidemic proportions. From the first entrance of the Europeans into the new world the aboriginal inhabitants suffered one sweeping epidemic after another, each segment of the population undergoing in turn a cycle of devastating pestilence followed by gradual immunization and recovery. Among the Indians of Lower California it has been estimated that disease was responsible for nearly one-half the observed reduction in population.[1] One might therefore assume that in the neighboring province of Upper California a similar decline occurred.

Mortality in the missions.—Since disease is the proximate cause of many deaths under all human conditions, we may begin with a con-

[1] S. F. Cook, *The Extent and Significance of Disease among the Indians of Baja California, 1697–1773,* Univ. Calif. Publ., Ibero-Americana, No. 12 (Berkeley, 1937).

sideration of the mortality figures in the missions.[2] Certain points merit particular emphasis.

From the earliest birth records and also from the results of careful extrapolation of the graph of the mission birth rate it appears highly probable that the gentile, or wild Indian, birth rate was approximately 45-50 per thousand per year. Now there is no reason to suppose, on any grounds whatever, that the premission or aboriginal population was suffering a material decline in numbers. Therefore the premission death rate must have equaled the birth rate. At least, it can have been no higher. This would imply a death rate of, let us say, 50 per thousand. But from the data it appears that the earliest mission death rate was definitely greater: approximately 70 per thousand as a mean for the decade 1774-1784, with the rate for the lowest year 54 per thousand. Granting some statistical inaccuracy due to relatively small numbers and possible errors of count and record, it is evident that the mortality jumped during the process of missionization. Part of this increment, but not all, was due to disease.

Throughout the life of the missions the mean death rate mounted steadily, reaching a peak in the decade 1800-1810, then gradually declined so that at the end it was the same as, or perhaps slightly lower than, at the beginning. The annual rates show, furthermore, a series of marked fluctuations, reaching in 1806 a maximum of 170 deaths per thousand. These annual fluctuations are of great significance because they indicate relatively rapid changes in death rate which can be referred most plausibly to health conditions. No other factor—aside from war, which did not exist, and natural calamities, of which there were none—can induce such swift and reversible increases in mortality. The years of minimal mortality, if this argument is valid, represent the most healthy years, those in which major or minor epidemics were absent. We may, then, draw an arbitrary line on the graph, connecting these minima, and say that the mortality shown above this line certainly represents the effect of disease.

On the other hand, even in the best of times there was considerable illness—endemic, residual, or chronic—which raised the death rate.

---

[2] The data are those used in Cook, *Population Trends* (1940), *ibid.*, No. 17. They were derived in turn from the records of mission censuses in the Bancroft Library, Berkeley. See below, pp. 395-446.

In fact, in the wild state itself a large proportion of the deaths was due to disease. But what we may term the "natural" component—the amount of illness to which any race is subject under the most ideal conditions—is included in the probable basic death rate of approximately 50 per thousand. The remainder may be called the "artificial" component: the excess over the wild or original mortality directly referable to the new conditions imposed by the unnatural environment, in this instance, the mission. The artificial component here is represented quantitatively in the difference between the minimum mission death rate, and the wild death rate.

Let it be noted particularly at this point that the artificial residual disease component is represented *in* this difference and not *by* it. If the latter expression were employed, the implication could be that the mortality involved was due entirely and exclusively to disease, whereas there is no evidence, at present at least, for assuming that this was so. There undoubtedly were numerous nondisease factors which, operating steadily over long periods, increased the mission death rate directly or indirectly. It is impossible to determine at the present juncture, or perhaps ever, the exact fraction of the difference which may be ascribed to the effects of bad health. Nevertheless, some numerical expression is highly desirable. A conservative, but purely arbitrary, estimate would be one-third, or, say, 35 per cent. Since we possess no rigid information like that available in studies of contemporary epidemiology and vital statistics, this value may be employed with the assurance that it does not too greatly misrepresent the actual situation.

We may, then, break down the data for each year as follows:

Causes of Death	*Death Rate*
Wild or natural incidence of disease and other causes	50 per thousand
Mission or artificial incidence of disease and other causes	Excess over 50 per thousand
Endemic or residual disease plus other long-term causes	Average of the minimum for the period minus 50
Endemic or residual disease, 35 per cent	
Other causes, 65 per cent	
Epidemics plus local or temporary intensifications of endemics	Excess over the average of the minimum for the period

Under ordinary circumstances, with a geographically stable population the decline over a certain period is simply the numerical difference between the total number of persons living at the beginning and end of the period. Here, however, we are dealing with an aggregation of individuals which arose *de novo* in the year 1769–1770, increased from zero to a maximum, and then diminished slightly until the end of the period in 1834. At this date the population, as a mission group, suddenly ceased to exist. The actual census figures for the period therefore show, not a diminution, but an augmentation from 0 to 14,910. It is necessary therefore to use the difference between the number of births and deaths to demonstrate what was happening to the population in the missions.[3] From the available data we find that from 1779 to 1833, there were 29,100 births and 62,600 deaths.[4] The excess of deaths over births was then 33,500, indicating an extremely rapid population decline.

If now, according to the suggestions made above, we arbitrarily set the most probable wild or natural birth and death rates each at 50 per thousand (see tabulation above), then for the number of persons involved there should have been 40,000 births and 40,000 deaths. The fact that only three-quarters of the predictable births actually occurred is referable to the low and declining birth rate (32 per thousand in 1833). Of the 62,600 deaths, 40,000 correspond to the expected wild or natural mortality, leaving 22,600 to be accounted for as due to the effect of mission life. If we utilize the periodic minimal death rates as set forth above and calculate for each year the difference between the minimum and 5 per cent of the population, we get the figures for the mortality due to endemic, residual disease and other causes. The total number of deaths for the 64-year period amounts to 11,300; 35 per cent of this total is 3,950.

The remainder, likewise 11,300, represents the results of epidemics or recurrent intensifications of commonly present illness. The total

---

[3] The increase, apart from births, was due to conversion of wild Indians, or really to immigration. There were approximately 83,400 Indians baptized, of whom only 29,100 were actually born under mission auspices, leaving 54,000 immigrants.

[4] The figures prior to 1779 involve relatively small numbers of persons, for whom the births cannot be calculated with much accuracy. It has seemed better, therefore, to omit the first decade entirely. Furthermore, in all calculations the numbers are rounded off to the nearest hundred since the last two digits have no statistical significance.

which may be definitely and directly attributed to disease is 15,250, or 45 per cent of the net population decrease. No claim is made to absolute accuracy, but if the underlying assumptions are in any measure correct, this value must indicate at least the order of magnitude of the disease effect.[5]

The time curve of the disease effect, in particular the nonepidemic component, is also of interest. If we examine the absolute numbers of deaths annually to be ascribed to this factor, we find a steady increase to a maximum in the decade 1800–1810, followed by a decline. Thus the course of the total death rate is quite closely approximated. It is probable that two closely related factors were operative: the high susceptibility of new immigrants and the selective action of the disease itself on the population. In the beginning, all or most of the mission inhabitants were nonimmune recent converts. As time went on, however, the number of converts in relation to the total mission population decreased, almost to the vanishing point in the years 1830–1834. On this basis alone one would expect the incidence of chronic disease to be at a maximum at first and to decline steadily. But the absolute number of new conversions increased consistently until about 1805, and then fell off rapidly. From 1770 to 1805, therefore, the number of susceptible newcomers increased more rapidly than the selected, partially immunized survivors of the old population. Subsequently the situation reversed itself, and from 1805 to 1834 the mission Indians as a group were consistently gaining resistance to the common imported diseases. Yet whenever a new disease, such as measles, smallpox, or cholera, arrived, it swept through the entire population irrespective of individual origin.

With these general conclusions derived from examination of the population records, we may turn to the contemporary documents for detail regarding certain other points.

Epidemics.—Of true epidemics carrying off hundreds or thousands in a few weeks or months there were remarkably few in Upper California. In fact, there was only one of really great extent, and perhaps

---

[5] With respect to disease Upper California seemed to resemble Lower California. Thus the estimated proportion of deaths attributable to disease in both regions was probably somewhere between 35 and 50 per cent. In both, epidemics and chronic or endemic ailments were of approximately equal weight as lethal factors.

two of moderate intensity. This situation contrasts forcibly with that in Lower California where at least five serious epidemics occurred within a comparable period of time.[6] Perhaps one might be tempted to fall into conventional ways and ascribe the relative immunity of California to the salubrity of its far-famed climate. At the same time one must remember that commerce with the outside world was very small, that the West Coast was for many years almost completely closed to immigration, and, finally, that a watchful military government together with a competent and vigilant clergy closed the door to every obvious source of infection.

The first notice of epidemic diseases in Upper California was contained in the works of Father Palóu who mentions one in the vicinity of Santa Clara in 1777:[7]

By the month of May of the same year (1777) the first baptisms took place, for as there had come upon the people a great epidemic, the Fathers were able to perform a great many baptisms by simply going through the villages. In this way they succeeded in sending a great many children (which died almost as soon as they were baptized) to Heaven.

However, no details are given of the territorial extent, the numbers affected, or the type of disease.

No other record of a real epidemic occurs until 1802, when the inhabitants of the missions from San Carlos to San Luis Obispo were affected by some respiratory ailment. The children were the victims, to the almost entire exclusion of adults.[8] The illness was variously

---

[6] All these were of insignificant proportions when compared with what took place on the mainland both in early days and more modern times. One need think only of the terrific scourges of the sixteenth century to appreciate the difference: smallpox, *matlaza-huatl,* typhoid among the Aztecs killed literally millions. In 1779 and 1797 in Central Mexico smallpox alone must have accounted for half a million deaths. On the Atlantic Coast, in New England, prior to 1620, smallpox is estimated to have reduced the Indian population by 90 per cent.

[7] Francisco Palóu, *Life of Junípero Serra* (Mexico, 1787), translated by C. S. Williams (1913), p. 213. Also cf. Palóu, *Historical Memoirs of New California,* Bolton translation (Berkeley, 1926), IV:161.

[8] Carrillo to Arrillaga, Monterey, Jan. 20, 1802, Prov. St. Pap., 18:194; Carrillo to Arrillaga, Monterey, Feb. 27, 1802, *ibid.,* p. 190; Carrillo, Monterey "Diario," Feb. 28, 1802, *ibid.,* p. 193; the governor to the *comandante* of Monterey, Loreto, Apr. 9, 1802, Prov. Rec., 11:167; Carrillo to Arrillaga, Monterey, June 30, 1802, Prov. St. Pap., 18:170; "Informe de San Carlos," 1804, Arch. Mis. Pap. Orig., 1:306; Tapis to Arrillaga, Santa Bárbara, Mar. 1, 1805, Sta. Bárb. Arch., 6:28–35.

described as *"fuertes dolores de cabeza," "cerramiento de garganta,"*
"pulmonía y dolor de costado," "dolor de costado," "fuertes calenturas,
toz y dolores de cabeza." Clearly pneumonia and apparently diphtheria (*cerramiento de garganta*) are indicated. The greatest mortality
was at Soledad with "many Christians and gentiles" and "more than
seventy dead in that mission." "Great havoc" was also caused at
Monterey and San Luis Obispo. At the peak of the epidemic at Soledad five or six died each day. Perhaps two to three hundred was the
mortality at all the missions involved.

In 1806 occurred the first measles epidemic, by far the most serious
witnessed in mission days. This was a clear example of a newly introduced malady attacking a fresh, unprotected population. Its mode of
introduction is unknown (probably from Mexico by an incoming
ship), but its spread was very rapid, and the damage very great among
both children and adults. It was reported from San Francisco that
from April 24 to June 27 the deaths had reached 234 in number, 163
adults and 71 children.[9] In Santa Bárbara during December, 44 neophytes died in 15 days.[10] The total mortality may be reckoned from
the general censuses. In 1806 the deaths in excess of the mean of the
years 1805 and 1807 were 1,800. If we allow 200 as being due to other
causes, we may still ascribe 1,600 to measles. The total population for
1806 was given at 18,665, a decrease of 1,693 from the previous year.
But in 1806 there were 1,572 baptisms. Hence the effective reduction
was 3,265. Granting half this as being due to measles, we again have
a mortality of about 1,600. Although the adults were hard hit, the
children suffered most. The mean child death rate in 1806 for all the
missions was 335 per thousand. In San Francisco alone it was 880, the
population under ten years of age being almost completely wiped out.[11]

[9] Abella, in the *libro de misión* for San Francisco, June 27, 1806 (extracts by Savage
in Bancroft Library).

[10] Carrillo to Arrillaga, Santa Bárbara, Dec. 31, 1806, Prov. St. Pap. Ben. Mil., 35:14.

[11] At about this time or a little earlier occurred a queer disease called *"el latido,"*
which apparently was not widespread or particularly fatal. According to Bancroft (*California Pastoral* [*History of California*, vol. 34], p. 617), who took his information from
Langsdorff, it began with pulsation in the lower belly followed by cramps and pain in
the neck region. Cephas Bard (*Contribution to the History of Medicine in Southern
California* [1894], p. 28) says it was "palpitation of the heart" but "was always referred
to the epigastrium." Many guesses have been made as to what *"el latido"* really was,
but its nature has never been ascertained satisfactorily.

For the next twenty years no outstanding epidemic occurred, although the diseases already present flared up occasionally. About 1827, however, there was a recrudescence of measles, which, although of moderate intensity, did not approach the severity of the first outbreak. From the census figures it may be estimated that the mission mortality amounted to several hundred, perhaps a thousand. The incidence was spotty, the child death rate, which reached 577 per thousand at San Juan Bautista and 524 at Santa Clara, being quite low elsewhere. At San Diego it was noted that the measles had caused "some" deaths among the white population and "more damage" among the Indians.[12] At San Buenaventura measles appeared at the end of 1827 and lasted till March, 1928. Many adults and children died, but "many more adults died of syphilis."[13]

By the end of the decade 1820–1830 California was coming into much closer contact with the outside world; probably associated with this increased external intercourse, several new diseases appeared, which at times became epidemic in their scope. Since the missions were secularized in 1834 and for practical purposes ceased to function, the effects of these recent introductions cannot be considered with respect to the missions themselves. They may, however, be mentioned. In 1833 for the first time there was an alarming amount of smallpox.[14] Scarlet fever may have been introduced along with other "contagious fevers,"[15] and it is certain that cholera reached menacing proportions in 1834.

Even though the missions were only lightly touched by large-scale epidemics, they suffered heavily from general illness and periodic semi-epidemics. Wholly aside from the evidence of the census reports discussed previously, we have many contemporary statements which tend to support this conclusion.

As early as 1787 it was recognized officially that there was much illness in the missions. Governor Pedro Fages wrote in that year regarding Mission San Antonio.

[12] Census, Aug. 26, 1827, St. Pap. Mis., 5:25.

[13] Ordaz, "Informe Anual," San Buenaventura, Dec. 31, 1828, Archb. Arch., 1:48.

[14] S. F. Cook, "Smallpox in Spanish and Mexican California, 1770–1845," *Bull. Hist. Med.* (1939), 7:153–191.

[15] G. D. Lyman, "The Scalpel under Three Flags in California," Calif. Hist. Soc., *Quarterly* (1925), 4:142.

It is this climate, in which are observed particularly extremes of heat and cold, which may be responsible for the frequent illness and deaths which have been experienced . . . [and concerning San Carlos] many and frequent are the deaths occurring among the neophytes.[16]

In 1794 Arrillaga pointed out that the increase in the size of the missions was more apparent than real, because "some of the missions are suffering from sicknesses which are causing considerable damage."[17] Two years later Borica commented that the bad state of the neophytes was partially due to the *"efluvios pestiferos"* which spread from one to the other in their villages and the buildings where the unmarried men and women sleep."[18] It is thus clear that before the missions were twenty-five years old illness had become sufficiently noticeable to attract the attention of the governors.

Beginning in 1797 we have an incomplete series of annual reports from presidial commanders to the governor. These usually contained a statement on the community health. Thus for 1797 Grajera from San Diego said, "there have been no unusual or epidemic diseases."[19] Goycoechea reported from Santa Bárbara "many cases of typhoid and pneumonia . . . many have died of consumption, which misfortune is very common and principally among the Indians."[20] From San Francisco Argüello reported ". . . an epidemic among the neophytes of whom several died."[21] The following year there was an appearance of *"catarro"* at Santa Bárbara[22] which did not appear to be particularly fatal. Fatalities from dysentery, however, occurred at San Diego. Three years later "contagious fevers" are described from Los Angeles "which are doing great damage to the natives at San Gabriel and San Juan Capistrano."[23] In 1803 there were "unknown diseases which killed various Indians,"[24] followed by "colds and fevers"[25] in 1804 and "diarrhoea, vomiting, and other ailments such as belly ache and fever."

---

[16] Fages, "Informe general sobre misiones," St. Pap. Mis. and Col., 1:124.
[17] Arrillaga, "Informe," Sept. 9, 1794, St. Pap. Mis., 1:127.
[18] Borica, "Estado general de las misiones ... en 1795," Aug. 24, 1796, *ibid.*, 2:73.
[19] Grajera to Borica, June 30, 1797, St. Pap. Sac., 6:102.
[20] Goycoechea to Borica, Dec. 31, 1797, *ibid.*, p. 100.
[21] Argüello to Borica, Dec. 31, 1797, *ibid.*
[22] Borica to Goycoechea, Feb. 11, 1798, Prov. Rec., 4:99.
[23] Rodríguez, "Statement," San Diego, Jan. 10, 1801, Prov. St. Pap. Ben. Mil., 29:3.
[24] Argüello, "Informe," Dec. 31, 1803, St. Pap. Mis., 3:40.
[25] Carrillo, "Informe," June 30, 1804, *ibid.*, p. 50; also Prov. St. Pap. Ben. Mil., 34:12.

The year 1805 was a good one but nevertheless there appeared "severe constipation with fever and headache . . . from which several Indian children died";[26] also "consumption, bloody dysentery, and other unknown diseases among the neophytes from which they die with frequency."[27] In 1807 Argüello again stated that the "predominant diseases are syphilis, dysentery, and tuberculosis,"[28] which accounted for the extremely small increase in population. Fathers Miguel and Zalvidea in their reply to certain charges made against the missions affirmed that "the missions have three times as many sick as in other times," that the hospital at San Gabriel contained from three to four hundred patients and that

. . . granting that in all the missions there are many more patients than formerly, nevertheless it is certain that the Physician of Monterey said that in no other mission—even without having seen half the patients—were there so many as in this one.[29]

In subsequent years similar reports were made with monotonous regularity describing the death of the neophytes from consumption, dysentery, and pneumonia (or perhaps influenza). A few samples will suffice to establish the trend through the remainder of the mission era. In 1811 the president of the missions, Father Señan wrote: "The most dominant diseases are syphilis, tuberculosis, and dysenteries."[30] Again, regarding San Francisco:

The births scarcely correspond to a third part of the deaths, even in years when there is no epidemic. But in a year like 1806, when there was a simple epidemic of measles, more than three hundred died and twenty-three were born.

Six years later the succeeding president, Father Sarría, discussed the alarming population decrease which he said was going on "without there being recognizable any particular pest or epidemic apart from the regular diseases which are almost always present."[31]

Syphilis.—Without doubt the most important single component of

---

[26] Carrillo to Arrillaga, Santa Bárbara, June 30, 1805, *ibid.,* p. 27.

[27] Argüello to Arrillaga, San Francisco, Dec. 31, 1805, *ibid.,* p. 22.

[28] Argüello to Arrillaga, San Francisco, Dec. 31, 1807, *ibid.,* 37:38.

[29] Miguel and Zalvidea, San Gabriel, May 24, 1810, Sta. Bárb. Arch., 9:191–196.

[30] Señan, "Contestación al interrogatorio del ano 1811," *ibid.,* 7:112–216.

[31] Sarría, "Informe sobre frailes de California," November, 1817, *ibid.,* 3:39–93.

this entire disease complex was syphilis. Indeed, so widespread and so devastating in its effects was venereal disease that it merits extended consideration. Among the natives of Lower California, and in direct contrast with the inhabitants of the west coast of the mainland, syphilis was universal in its occurrence and extremely severe in its effects.[32] Upper California seems to have resembled Lower California rather than the mainland in this respect, although in the Franciscan missions of the north the disease may not have been so fatal, or its external manifestations so striking as in the older Jesuit missions of the southern peninsula. In both regions one might be inclined to discount the severity of the disease on grounds of exaggeration by those on the scene, were it not—and this is particularly true of Upper California—that there is absolute unanimity of opinion and emphasis on the part of priest and layman, soldier and civilian, contemporary reporter and later raconteur. After reviewing the evidence, one is impelled to the conclusion that venereal disease constituted one of the prime factors not only in the actual decline, but also in the moral and social disintegration of the population. These effects cannot be strictly assessed in numerical terms, but their weight can be appreciated if some of the evidence is reviewed.

Syphilis appeared in Upper California certainly within the first decade of settlement.[33] The conventional story, which may or may not have been true, attributed its introduction to the Anza expedition to Los Angeles in 1777. Thus Miguel and Zalvidea state that this "putrid and contagious disease had its beginning with the time Don Juan Bautista de Anza stopped at the mission San Gabriel with his expedition."[34] However, it may not be fair to lay the blame entirely on Anza's troops since there were numerous other means of introduction. The expeditionary force of Portolá in 1769 and other troops entering the country were without doubt heavily infected, not to speak of the early civilian settlers. Indeed, irrespective of the social status of the immigrants, it would have been a miracle had the country

[32] Cook, *Extent and Significance of Disease among the Indians of Baja California*, pp. 29 ff.

[33] In Lower California the disease was successfully excluded for at least forty years after the first mission was founded. Once introduced, however, it spread with extreme rapidity through the well-organized establishments.

[34] Miguel and Zalvidea, San Gabriel, Mar. 17, 1810, Sta. Bárb. Arch., 9:184–187.

escaped the pest.[35] Once introduced, the spread was an easy matter. The relations of the soldiers with the Indian women were notorious, despite the most energetic efforts of both officers and clergy to prevent immorality. In fact, the entire problem of sexual relations between the whites and the natives, although one which was regarded as very serious by the founders of the province, has apparently escaped detailed consideration by later historians, both Californian and American.

The very first expeditions were characterized by disorderly conduct with the Indian women on the part of the soldiers. The following significant excerpts are from the diary of Pedro Font in 1776.[36]

The extortions and outrages which the soldiers have perpetrated when in their journeys they have passed along the Channel, especially in the beginning (p. 252).

[The Channel Indians] are displeased with the Spaniards, because of [the latter's] taking away their fish and their food to provision themselves ... now stealing their women and abusing them (p. 256).

The women [at San Luis Obispo] are affable and friendly ... a reason why the soldiers were so disorderly with them when they remained in this vicinity for a time [i.e., during the halt of the Portolá expedition] (p. 271).

There were also numerous desertions, the soldiers going away to live among the natives and, of course, carrying their venereal disease to spread among their hosts. Thus Junípero Serra in his representation of 1773 asks a general pardon for all deserters:

... if any of them should yet be found scattered among the heathen, so that the danger of inquietude among the heathen and the perdition of the wretched wanderers and Christian renegades may be avoided. ...'[37]

In 1773 a case of rape occurred in San Luis Obispo and in 1774 there were two cases at Monterey. By 1777 conditions had become bad in the south.[38] The soldiers at San Gabriel and San Juan Capistrano "go

---

[35] In 1798 Governor Borica wrote the viceroy (Prov. Rec., 6:92) that "there arrived at Monterey the new settlers for the town of Branciforte—destitute and some afflicted with syphilis."

[36] Fr. Pedro Font, *Diary of an Expedition to Monterey ... 1775–1776*, translated by Bolton in *Anza's California Expeditions* (Berkeley, 1930), Vol. IV.

[37] Palóu, *New California*, Bolton transl., Vol. III.

[38] Ortega, San Diego, July 11, 1777, St. Pap. Sac., 8:31–52.

at night to the nearby villages to assault the heathen women." Four men confessed to several of these delinquencies, and the missionaries of San Juan Capistrano charged that the soldiers of the guard went so far as to beat the gentiles to make them disclose where their women were hidden. A few years later Governor Fages issued an order to the effect that:

The officers and men of these presidios are conducting and behaving themselves in the missions with a vicious license which is very prejudicial on account of the scandalous disorders which they commit with the gentile and Christian women. I adjure you to prevent the continuance of such dangerous behavior . . . inflicting severe penalties upon those who are guilty.[39]

The civilian settlers were no better. For instance, with respect to the founders of the city of San José:[40]

From that time (1782) the evil influence of the settlers began to be felt . . . the disgraceful conduct with regard to the heathen and bad example to the neophytes because of the brutality and violence exercised by these settlers on their women.

Even to the end of missionization complaints continued. In 1839 Inspector Hartnell remarked upon a certain white man "who had given venereal disease to many women of the mission."[41]

There is no need for further multiplication of instances. From those already given it will be clear that from the time the Spanish first set foot in California there was ample opportunity for the introduction of syphilis to the native population, not at one but at very many places. Indeed, since there were soldiers stationed at every mission, since the troops were continually moving around from one place to another, and since this military group was itself generously infected, the introduction may be regarded as wholesale and substantially universal.

Given the conditions of contact just outlined, a steady and rapid infiltration of venereal disease among the mission Indians was no more

---

[39] Fages to González, Monterey, July 1, 1785, *ibid.*, 2:43.

[40] Fr. Tomás de la Peña to the viceroy, "Detalles sobre la fundación ... el pueblo de San José," Colegio de San Fernando, July 27, 1798, St. Pap. Mis. and Col., 1:45.

[41] Hartnell, "Informe," San Antonio, Aug. 7, 1839, Hartnell "Diario," p. 37.

Other accounts will be found in the following: Prov. St. Pap., 9:107 (1789); *ibid.*, p. 121 (1789); *ibid.*, 10:151 ff. (1791); *ibid.*, 13:42 (1795); Prov. Rec., 4:145 (1796); Archb. Arch., 5:101 (1833). These by no means exhaust the list.

than might be expected. This undoubtedly occurred, but it apparently took a full generation for the situation to become really serious. It is noteworthy that in 1791, at least twenty years after the disease first arrived, Fages was able to contrast the "decadent condition" of the old missions (i.e., those in Baja California), which he ascribed to syphilis, with the "flourishing and progressive" state of the new ones.[42] However, Governor Borica, in his report for the year 1793–1794, mentions that there is much syphilis in the missions.[43] From this point on few statements of health conditions failed to mention syphilis. The precise extent of the malady with respect to numbers of persons involved is difficult to estimate; here, as in so many other instances, we are forced to rely upon the word of contemporary witnesses, who were much impressed but who may have been prone to some exaggeration. The following statements are pertinent and have a cumulative value even if their individual reliability may not be high:

Most Indian deaths are due to syphilis.[44]

The dominant diseases of the Indians are syphilis, of a very malignant type, and dysentery . . .[45]

The most dominant disease is syphilis, of which a considerable number die. . . .[46]

They are permeated to the marrow of their bones with venereal disease, such that many of the newly born show immediately this, the only patrimony they receive from their parents, and for which reason three-quarters of the infants die in their first or second year, and of the other quarter which survives, most fail to reach their twenty-fifth year.[47]

There are [in San Francisco] no good Indian boatmen—those who might be available are in great part attacked by syphilis . . .[48]

. . . according to his opinion the Indians are dying of syphilis; many have the lesions, and others have it internally . . .[49]

. . . That to the question he has been asked as to why the Indians die: he

[42] Fages, "Papel de varios puntos concernientes al Gobierno de la Peninsula de California," Feb. 26, 1791, Prov. St. Pap., 10:151.

[43] Borica, July 13, 1795, St. Pap. Mis., vol. 2.

[44] Carrillo, "Informe," Santa Bárbara, June 30, 1804, St. Pap. Mis., 3:50.

[45] "Contestación al interrogatorio del ano 1811," Sta. Bárb. Arch., 7:112–216.

[46] *Ibid.*

[47] *Ibid.*

[48] Abella to Argüello, San Francisco, Sept. 30, 1815, Archb. Arch., 2:102.

[49] Abella to Solá, San Francisco, July 31, 1817, *ibid.,* 3:146.

will reply, as a priest that he does not know, but as a physician he will say that they are very much contaminated and this malady syphilis is incurable among them.[50]

He speaks of a syphilitic Indian and says that in his opinion one of the reasons why they are practically all dying of this terrible malady is that the missions lack all medicines and there is no other physician than the Providence of God.[51]

. . . there are twenty-seven fugitives; of the others some are afflicted with chronic ailments and the rest mostly infected with the venereal virus.[52]

Perhaps as a result of the fine climate and small population epidemics and contagions are little known, except that among the neophytes venereal diseases are devouring them horribly . . .[53]

From these and many similar documents one receives the impression that syphilis among the mission Indians might be described as a totalitarian disease, universally incident. Perhaps this would be an extreme view. Perhaps there were some who were able to avoid the infection, but this must have been rare in communities so generally unsanitary, so crowded, and so characterized by sexual promiscuity as the missions. Even granting a fair number of exceptions, the mass effect of venereal disease upon the population must have been tremendous and must have made itself felt in a multitude of ways.

The number of those whose death was directly attributable to syphilis may not have been great, although there is some divergence of opinion concerning this point.[54] Some of the citations quoted previ-

---

[50] Abella to Solá, San Francisco, Jan. 29, 1817, *ibid.*, p. 125.

[51] Gil to Solá, 1818, *ibid.*, p. 43.

[52] "Informe de Santa Cruz," Dec. 31, 1825, Arch. Mis., 1:852.

[53] Victoria, "Informe general sobre California," Monterey, June 7, 1831, Dept. Rec., 9:132.

[54] There has been a certain amount of confusion in the minds of some modern historians regarding the precise effects of syphilis. Bancroft (*California Pastoral,* chap. 20) states that by 1805 syphilis "with scrofula and consumption" killed hundreds annually. Cephas Bard, a physician himself, ascribed the high mortality to such causes as "zymotic diseases, syphilis, tuberculosis and intemperance" (*op. cit.,* p. 12). Hittell (*History of California,* Vol. I) holds syphilis responsible for the very high death rate (p. 743) and then declares (p. 787) that "it had not among the Indians the terrible character which it has assumed amongst civilized peoples . . . nor was it until the introduction of spirituous liquors that it became aggravated into the deadly scourge which decimated and in some cases *almost of itself* exterminated whole tribes." Before the advent of spirituous liquors, he says, "the affected aborigines were able to continue their usual avocations without any great inconvenience . . ."; truly a remarkable situation, particularly since, until 1834, intoxication was held by the missionaries at a very low level indeed.

ously and various others which might be adduced seem to suggest many deaths from syphilis. But it is probable that often, when a syphilitic person succumbed for any more or less obscure cause, the demise was uncritically attributed to the venereal disease. However, many Indians may actually have died as a result of the disease itself. It is rather difficult to discount completely eye-witness accounts, even though they may be made by uninformed and possibly prejudiced individuals. Some credence must be given the repeated assertions that the Indians were *dying* from syphilis.

Though the direct mortality from this cause may not have been as high as might be implied by contemporary statements, the secondary effects were undoubtedly of great significance. A population thoroughly saturated with venereal disease will fall easier prey to other maladies, whether the latter be chronic or epidemic, and there can be no question that this increased susceptibility accounts for at least part of the virulence displayed by pneumonia, tuberculosis, and other ailments. If we allow for the debilitating action of syphilis, we may ascribe to it responsibility for much of the mortality included in the category of endemic or residual disease discussed above, together with their sporadically epidemic outbursts. It was pointed out that roughly 45 per cent of the net population decrease, or 15,250 deaths, might be attributed to disease. Of this number, no more than 3,000 can have been due to the measles and other swift, clearly recognizable epidemics. The remainder, say 12,250, were caused by the standard general maladies, consumption, dysentery, typhoid, and the like, including syphilis. To formulate the problem in concrete terms, we might refer between 1,000 and 5,000 of these deaths directly or indirectly to venereal disease. This would mean 1.5–8 per cent of the total mission deaths, 4.5–22 per cent of the effective population reduction, and 6.5–33 per cent of the reduction due to disease. Although these figures can in no wise be considered accurate in the mathematical sense, they probably fairly represent the scope of syphilis as a factor in destroying the mission-Indian population.

Although the primary and immediate effect of venereal disease was on the death rate, the question arises of its influence on the birth rate. The relationship here, if any, appears to be somewhat complex. As mentioned previously, although the crude birth rate steadily declined during the mission period, the fertility rate (i.e., the number of births per thousand women) remained very constant. This was obtained by relating the number of mission births to the number of adult women as given in the annual census reports. Now if syphilis, or any other factor, seriously reduced the actual conceiving or bearing capacity of the women, the fertility rate should have diminished in conformity. The observed facts were explained by means of the falling sex ratio. The latter, after some irregularities in the first decade, due probably to unequal conversion of the sexes, underwent a very steady and consistent increase until 1834. At that date the ratio of men to women was between the limits 1:35–1:50. Therefore, the relative number of women in the population decreased at substantially the same rate as the unadjusted number of births, a finding entirely consistent with the unchanging fertility rate. In view of these facts, we are almost forced to conclude that venereal disease did not reduce reproductive power among the mission Indians. Such a conclusion is of rather striking significance. It is at variance with general opinions, both contemporary and modern, since it implies that actual conception and delivery were not materially affected by widespread and severe incidence of syphilis. The additional explanation has been offered (based also upon the census records) that, since the sex ratio among newly born infants and children was invariably near 1:00, the shifting sex ratio among adults was due to a differential death rate, the women dying younger or in greater numbers than the men. Such an unequal mortality might be ascribed to a greater susceptibility among women to common ailments, to a possible difference in living conditions, or to a higher incidence and greater virulence of syphilis in women. If this last theory were true, then syphilis might be considered as having contributed, in a secondary and remote fashion, to the declining crude birth rate.

Though it is not possible to assess the importance of venereal disease, as opposed to other diseases, in its effect on crude birth rate, nevertheless we may form a general estimate of the significance of disease in this connection. As previously pointed out, the net diminution of population, as expressed in terms of excess of deaths over births was 33,600. As contrasted with the probable state of the population, had it not been missionized, it was computed that of this number there were 22,600 more deaths and 11,000 less births than there would have been in the aboriginal condition. Of these, 15,250 deaths were attributed directly to disease of all types. This, then, accounts for 45 per cent of the net population decrease. But if the indirect influence of venereal and other disease on the birth rate, through the differential sex mortality, be considered, the estimate must be revised upward. The birth deficiency of 11,000 amounts to approximately 30 per cent of the total. Purely arbitrarily, let us assume that one-half this deficiency may be ascribed to the effect just noted, whereas the other half was due to other causes. Then disease immediately and remotely may be held responsible for not 45 but 60 per cent of the net population decrease.

Environmental factors in disease.—We may regard disease as a basic factor in the contact relation between any two races or species, such as those with which we are here dealing. This is particularly true of new maladies introduced by the new, invading race with which the established race has had no experience. Yet, aside from the lack of immunity thus assumed, the intensity of the disease factor may and will be conditioned by subsidiary or secondary factors contingent upon the new environment. Although most of these, in the missions, cannot be discussed in detail at the present juncture, their existence merits at least cursory mention.

1. Sexual relations. This matter has already been touched upon in connection with the introduction and spread of venereal disease. It was pointed out that personal contact of this type was very common between whites and natives. It need only be added that, aside from the marital status, promiscuity was extensive among the Indians themselves. In fact, there was no obstacle whatever, except the unfortunately futile zeal of the missionaries, to the wholesale dissemination of the pest.

2. Aggregation. With respect to nonvenereal disease, contagion was enormously facilitated by the custom of gathering large numbers of Indians in one place. Under aboriginal conditions the native group was seldom larger than one hundred, and frequently less. In the missions several hundred or even one or two thousand were congregated

in a single set of buildings. They ate together, worked together, and even slept together, in close quarters. Once a microörganism was introduced, the chances for infection were vastly greater than under the gentile system.

3. Intercommunication. In contrast to the wild state, there was a great deal of moving around from one mission to the other, from the mission to the outlying villages, from the mission to the nearest presidio, and finally up and down the whole length of the coast. Infection could thus be transported with the greatest ease from one center of population to the other.

4. Change of climate. Although at the outset most mission inmates were natives of the adjacent territory, as the establishments expanded, many were brought in from considerable distances. As a rule, with the exception of those in the Salinas Valley, the missions were located on or near the coast, and were hence subject to the cool, damp, foggy seashore climate. Indians brought here from the hills and valleys of the drier and warmer interior would doubtless have to become acclimated in the purely literal sense. During the process they would be somewhat more prone to infection than normally. Even the Spanish were impressed by this fact. Again and again in their reports they ascribed the unhealthy state of the neophytes, particularly with reference to tuberculosis, to the climate and pointed out that the maximum illness appeared to coincide with the rainy season of late winter and spring. In a very general way, although no rigid correlation is possible, one may detect a higher mean death rate in those missions situated near the shore than in near-by establishments farther inland. A few specimen opinions concerning the role of the climate with respect to disease may be cited:

[The climate] is generally healthy, more for the Spaniards than for the innumerable heathen who inhabit it . . .[55]

According to observation this climate is remarkably extreme with respect to both cold and heat from which may result the frequent illness and death which we are wont to experience.[56]

Most of the summer there were heavy fogs and when they departed the

---

[55] Author unknown (probably Fages), "Relación del temperamento de 1785," Monterey, Dec. 31, 1785, Prov. Rec., 2:116.
[56] Fages, "Informe general sobre las misiones, 1787," St. Pap. Mis. and Col., 1:124.

sun shone with excessive heat, from which extremes, in my judgment, originated many ailments . . .[57]

. . . but since April the north and northeast winds blew more frequently, very dry and sickly, causing severe bowel complaints and fevers . . .[58]

5. Bad sanitation. Apart from the factor of simple crowding, the life in the missions must have been anything but sanitary. In the independent family huts adjoining the mission the Indians were probably no worse off than when living in their own villages. However, the large rooms or compounds, where the unmarried men or women slept, must have been breeding-places for disease. With little ventilation, no heat, no protection from dampness in the rainy season, with the occupants packed in as closely as was humanly possible, it would have been amazing if respiratory infections had not been rampant. Thus a survivor of the period wrote:[59]

The Indians in their wandering life as savages enjoyed good health . . . Afterward very harmful to them was enclosure within infected walls, according to the system adopted by the missionaries . . . The walls usually were a yard thick and lacked necessary ventilation: imagine the odor which would emanate from those never-washed bodies, without being able to change the air.

Perhaps the above is an overstatement, and certainly the missionaries repeatedly and earnestly repudiated the idea that unhealthful or unsanitary conditions obtained in the enclosures. But the facts cannot be denied that scores of persons were kept at night in general rooms and that few hygienic measures were taken for their protection.

The neophytes received their food from large containers daily. Complaints were made, perhaps without justification, that the kitchenware was not kept clean. However, we must remember that the cooking and scullerywork were performed by neophytes, and it is altogether too much to imagine that the strictest supervision could induce these semisavages to maintain modern standards of cleanliness. Despite attempts to localize its distribution, sewage was disposed of according to the methods now prevalent in rural Mexico, that is, anywhere and everywhere. The water supply usually came from small streams

[57] Goycoechea to Borica, Santa Bárbara, Dec. 31, 1797, St. Pap. Mis., 2:103.

[58] Carrillo to Arrillaga, Santa Bárbara, June 30, 1805, Prov. St. Pap. Ben. Mil., 34:27.

[59] Antonio M. Osio, "Historia de California," MS, 1878, p. 216.

(which might disappear in a very dry season), small ponds, or wells. A more perfect arrangement for the spread of gastrointestinal disorders could scarcely be devised.[60]

6. Poor diet. The significance of diet will be discussed at length in a subsequent section. At this point it will suffice to say that, if the diet was actually defective, its deficiency undoubtedly operated as a factor predisposing to infectious disease.

7. Lack of treatment. Considering that from 1776 to 1825 there was only one qualified physician in all California and that the missionaries had no particular medical training, it is not surprising that the neophytes received treatment only on the rarest occasions.[61]

Included in the mission regime, to be sure, was an infirmary or hospital, which served actually only as a space for sick Indians—where they might rest and be made comfortable, to a limited extent. But since there were no supplies or medicines, real treatment and nursing could not very well be given them. The following excerpts probably give a substantially just picture of mission hospitalization:

Each mission had its infirmary, which consisted of a porch and some straw mats where the Indians might recline. Sometimes the Fathers themselves prescribed medicines . . .[62]

In the Mission of San Luis, at the request of the Reverend Father Fray Luis Martínez, in a hospital which he has for his neophytes, in which I found about thirty patients, the greater part being women, I found tuberculosis and syphilis . . .[63]

Many times [each year] I took the female, and some male, patients of the mission [San Diego] to Agua Caliente . . . and stayed there bathing and treating them for two months.[64]

---

[60] In justice to the missionaries it must be stated that the military and civilian establishments were just as bad as the missions, perhaps worse. Furthermore, sanitary science as we know it was unheard of at that day. In spite of the criticism by the military, it is remarkable that the missionaries were able to accomplish as much as they did, considering the scanty means at their disposal.

[61] The only specific instance known to me of a physician's giving any but the most casual attention to the disease problems among the Indians is that of José Benites in 1804 and 1805. He made a rather careful survey and administered relief to many patients. Cf. S. F. Cook, "California's First Medical Survey," *California and Western Medicine* (1936), Vol. 45, No. 4.

[62] A. F. Coronel, "Cosas de California," MS, 1878, p. 224.

[63] Benites, quoted in Cook, "California's First Medical Survey."

[64] Apolinaria Lorenzana, "Memorias," MS, 1878, p. 48.

In San Gabriel, San Juan Capistrano and San Luis Rey they have built mortuaries in the hospitals for the better accommodation and administration of the sick. We say hospitals because, all the Fathers realizing that the Indians are rapidly disappearing, mainly from dysentery and syphilis, they have taken the most energetic measures to halt the rapid spread of the evil. In many of the missions these hospitals have been set up in proportion to the means available to the priests who are using such facilities as are at hand. In spite of all this it is observed with grief that the results are not commensurate with expectations.[65]

. . . lack of fundamental treatment by a physician, for there is none. In all the missions there is an apothecary shop but this resource, managed without knowledge or method, far from being of use may be of harm, in a word it is of no value . . ."[66]

Summary.—To summarize, the mission Indians' lack of immunity to introduced infection and their possibly inferior physique predisposed them to whatever new diseases happened to attack them. The effect of these diseases, in terms of population decline, was undoubtedly greater under the mission system than it would have been in the wild or natural state. This in turn was at least partially due to the unfavorable factors which characterized the physical and social environment imposed by the missions.

NUTRITION

A faulty or insufficient diet over a short or a long period can affect the welfare of a population in three ways. It can render the group increasingly sensitive to bacterial infection or disease through lowered general resistance. It can be accompanied by specific deficiency diseases, such as the avitaminoses. Finally, it can kill by pure lack of quantity or direct starvation. Over several generations, where a relatively slow but consistent decrease in numbers is observed, acute starvation may be ruled out, except in very unusual individual cases. At the same time a condition of either quantitative or qualitative inadequacy may exist, the influence of which is felt only slowly and obscurely. A priori we have no right to assume any inadequacy to have been present in the mission population, for a poor diet is not in the same category as infectious disease, which is almost certain to be

---

[65] Anon., "Tabla estadística," Dec. 31, 1818, Sta. Bárb. Arch., 10:302.

[66] Victoria, "Informe general sobre California," Monterey, June 7, 1831.

present following racial contact of this sort. The mode of attack on the problem, in a broad sense, must be twofold, involving the questions: (1) What was the diet of the neophytes, and would it be considered by modern criteria adequate; and (2), is there any evidence, immediate or remote, that the population suffered from nutritional deficiency. To answer these questions, it is necessary to examine with care all available information pertaining to food supply.

The entire food supply of the neophytes was derived from three primary sources.

1. The largest and most important was the grain raised by the missions themselves. Although there was some variation from one mission to another, four basic materials were included, corn, wheat, barley, and beans, with the first two always predominating in quantity. There was absolutely no importation of these crops; hence the Indians' supply was strictly limited to what the missions could produce.

2. The missions supplied all animal food, in the form of beef, tallow, and lard, from their own resources.

3. To an undetermined extent the neophytes continued to utilize their primitive or wild food: acorns, small seeds, grasses, insects, shellfish and the like. These materials, however, were invariably used as a supplement rather than as a staple dietary component.

Mission diet.—There are two primary sources of knowledge relating to mission diet. The first consists of annual crop and livestock reports or censuses, the second of numerous statements by contemporary observers. The former is fundamental and merits detailed consideration.

Each mission submitted annually a statement of the quantity of staple foods produced, primarily wheat, corn, barley, and beans, together with a scattering of minor crops. The returns were in the form of *fanegas* sown and fanegas harvested in each crop. There was also submitted a census showing the number of cattle, sheep, goats, pigs, horses, and mules in possession of the mission at the end of each year. The crop reports are more valuable for present purposes than the livestock censuses, since they give a better index to total diet.[67]

---

[67] These reports, which formerly existed in the California Archives, were destroyed in the San Francisco fire of 1906. However, they had been previously copied and tabu-

The mission grain crop, which, as previously stated, formed the primary component of the diet, can be determined from the crop reports with considerable accuracy, since the annual harvest in fanegas is stated for each type of plant. The total, then, for a given period of time represents the maximum available to a single mission or all the missions for that period. In other words, it is impossible that the Indians could have received more corn or wheat than was produced or harvested by the missions.[68] Starting then with the gross harvest, we must first deduct the amount, for each year, which was used the following year as seed. This will give the net harvest—that which could be used for food purposes. As might be expected in any agricultural community, there were enormous variations from year to year owing to the innumerable factors which make for success or failure in a crop. Hence the net harvest for any one year in a mission, or even for any one year in all the missions, has little significance. Presumably— and this is borne out by many statements—on the one hand, in good years reserves were built up and, on the other hand, in poor years shortages were made up by gifts or loans from more fortunate missions. It is necessary therefore to base conclusions on averages of large numbers of missions and years.[69] This enables us to arrive at certain broad generalizations, although we are forced to concede the possibility of all sorts of local and individual exceptions.

The first column of table 2 gives the means for the annual net crop by missions; the net crops for presidios and pueblos are also included for comparison. These numbers in themselves are of secondary significance, because we wish to know how much food was provided for the neophytes rather than the total crop as such. It is, however, possible to obtain some idea of the diet if the volume of grain is expressed in terms of calories. From the population tables we may first determine

---

lated carefully by the workers under H. H. Bancroft. These tabulations or transcripts, made in the 1870's, are still available in the Bancroft Library of the University of California and may be considered essentially accurate copies of the originals.

[68] The question might be raised of the possibility of contributions from the military or civil establishments to the missions, but there is no record of such a contribution. Indeed, the trend was exclusively in the other direction. The missions supplied large amounts of grain to the presidios and perhaps some to the pueblos.

[69] It may be stated here that attempts to show correlations between annual crop variations and vital statistics have been uniformly unsuccessful.

TABLE 2
FOOD SUPPLY OF THE MISSION
(Each item represents the annual mean from 1783 to 1834)

Establishment	Mean annual crop in fanegas (net)	Mean quantity per person in fanegas (net)	Mean calories per person per day
Missions			
San Diego........................	2,875	2.18	955
San Luis Rey....................	5,685	3.49	1,530
San Juan Capistrano.............	2,905	3.81	1,670
San Gabriel.....................	4,820	3.62	1,585
San Fernando....................	2,490	3.24	1,420
San Buenaventura................	3,310	4.20	1,840
Santa Bárbara...................	2,600	2.55	1,115
Santa Ynéz......................	2,435	4.47	1,955
La Purísima.....................	2,475	2.95	1,290
San Luis Obispo.................	1,890	3.21	1,405
San Miguel......................	1,540	1.98	865
San Antonio.....................	1,580	1.63	715
La Soledad......................	1,705	3.51	1,535
San Carlos......................	1,885	4.10	1,790
San Juan Bautista...............	2,000	2.47	1,080
Santa Cruz......................	1,910	4.57	2,000
Santa Clara.....................	3,070	2.67	1,165
San José........................	3,195	2.98	1,305
San Francisco...................	2,525	3.47	1,520
San Rafael......................	1,260*	....	.....
San Francisco Solano............	1,316*	....	.....
Mean............................	2,680	3.21	1,405
Presidios			
San Diego.......................	2,360	8.05	3,410
Santa Bárbara...................	850	2.48	1,015
Monterey........................	622	1.82	640
San Francisco...................	1,125	5.80	2,075
Mean............................	1,240	4.54	1,785
Pueblos			
Los Angeles.....................	3,850	10.35	4,540
San José........................	2,455	14.95	6,550
Branciforte.....................	610	13.68	6,000
Mean............................	2,305	12.99	5,700

* San Rafael, 16 years; Solano, 10 years. These missions were omitted in computing the average.

[37]

the annual grain production of each mission per person. These values are given in the second column of table 2. It will be noted that there is great variation among the missions, the range extending from 4.57 fanegas per person at Santa Cruz to 1.63 at San Antonio, the mean for all the missions being 3.21 fanegas. The presidios show even greater variations (8.05–1.82; mean, 4.54), whereas the pueblos are consistently higher (14.95–10.35).

To convert these means to terms of calorific value, certain approximations must be made. The unit of one fanega may have been somewhat variable, depending upon local conditions and the complete lack of standardized weights and measures. Nevertheless, taken over a long time and in numerous localities, it may be considered equivalent to 1.6 bushels. Under modern conditions, furthermore, the weight of a bushel of any cereal crop varies, depending on the type of grain and the conditions of preparation, moisture, and so on. Therefore it is impossible to assign an exact and accurate weight to a "bushel of wheat" or a "bushel of corn." Thus a bushel of barley will weigh perhaps 46 to 50 pounds, husked corn 68 to 72 pounds, shelled corn 52 to 56 pounds, corn meal 48 to 50 pounds, wheat somewhere near 60 pounds and beans also near 60 pounds. Converting and using mean values, we should ascribe the following weights for a fanega of barley, corn, wheat, and beans respectively: 77, 88, 96, 96 pounds. Not a great deal would be gained by converting to pounds each individual crop item in the mission reports (nearly 15,000 items). It is simpler to convert the total annual crop per mission. The true factor, of course, lies somewhere between 75 and 100 pounds, but in view of the general uncertainty it is necessary to assign a purely arbitrary value. It seems desirable to keep the inevitable error on the side of overestimate rather than underestimate, in order that the mission diet may be presented with the maximum liberality consistent with the facts as we know them; hence it will be appropriate to regard a fanega of any crop as containing 100 pounds.

The final approximation must come in assigning the calorific value of a unit weight of these foods. Such a value varies considerably, depending on the plant species and also on its physical state. Thus the Okey-Huntington tables give the following values (in calories per pound):[70] whole wheat, 1,633; corn meal, 1,613; beans (dried red), 1,574. Most cereals therefore approximate 1,600 calories per pound. According to this estimate, the fanega has a calorific value of nearly 160,000. It is possible now to express the mission-Indian grain diet in terms of calories per person per day (third column in table 2). The range was from 2,000 in Santa Cruz to 715 in San Antonio, and the mean value for the nineteen old missions was 1,405. Before discussing the adequacy of this diet it is necessary to consider what deductions must be made.

It is very clear from the general information which has come down to us from the mission period as well as from contemporary sources that by no means all the produce of the missions was fed to the neophytes. Naturally, every possible pathway of leakage cannot be ascertained, but certainly there must have been included the food supplied to the missionary staff and the garrison, the supplies furnished the presidios, the grain exported in exchange for trade goods, and wastage due to accident and deterioration in the storehouses. Of these, the last source of loss, together with unidentifiable factors, cannot be evaluated at all. The grain exports are extremely difficult, if not impossible, to determine. The amounts consumed by non-Indians and those supplied to the presidios can be estimated within reasonable limits.

Every mission from the beginning had a garrison of several soldiers and their families, and the garrisons comprised from two to twelve men. The documentary series in the Bancroft Library contains numerous statements with respect to the number of persons in garrisons and the amounts of grain provided for their consumption. I have been able to tabulate 135 such statements from the years 1826–1833 in the missions San Francisco, San José, Santa Clara, Santa Cruz, and Solano. Since the garrison system was always very uniform and since the supplies necessary were always essentially the same regardless of geographical location or year, these 135 records may be considered a fair sample for all the missions throughout their existence. The mean

---

[70] *Okey-Huntington Allowances for Adequate Food at Low Cost,* California State Emergency Relief Administration, University of California (1933). The table of calories is taken from M. D. Rose, *Laboratory Handbook for Dietetics* (New York, 1937). Similar tables may be found in the standard texts on human nutrition.

number of garrison soldiers was 5.86 and the mean value of supplies per man per month was 0.975 fanegas, or 11.7 fanegas per year. For 5.86 men this amounts to 68.5 fanegas per year.

The quantities supplied to the presidios were more variable. In theory, each presidio grew enough crops to feed its own population and according to the data shown in table 2 this was actually the practice. Nevertheless, particularly in the last part of the mission period, the presidios were continually calling on the missions for supplies, which were provided on credit. It is significant that, even though the presidios raised as much corn and wheat per capita as did the missions, this quantity was regarded as inadequate for the white population of the former, although the missionaries seemed to feel that it represented an abundance for the Indian inhabitants of the latter.[71]

With respect to the actual quantities involved there are at hand in the documentary material of the Bancroft Library sixty-six statements in which the supplies furnished are listed and itemized. The period included is from 1808 to 1830, and nearly all the missions are represented. Although this sample is not as complete as might be desired,

---

[71] It is stated (Archb. Arch., 4[1]:24) that at San Diego in 1820 the annual need was 1,300 fanegas of corn and 286 of beans. For 1819, 1820, and 1821 the corn crop was respectively 2,531, 939, and 2,250 fanegas and the bean crop 304, 298, 274 fanegas. Nevertheless, the presidio in 1820 was asking for food from the four southern missions. Similarly, at Santa Bárbara in 1823 the annual requirement was placed at 1,100 fanegas of corn and 270 of wheat (*ibid.,* 4[2]:4). The production was 440 fanegas of wheat and 418 of corn.

In San Diego for 1778 the total food consumption of the "72 men of the presidio" (plus, of course, their families) was given as follows (St. Pap. Pres., 1:55) with the units converted approximately to pounds. (Numbers in parentheses give number of pounds per person annually.)

corn	58,500 (254)	crude sugar	2,330 (10.1)
beans	14,800 (65)	chili	1,500 (6.5)
lentils	1,150 (5.0)	meat	695 (3.0)
peas	1,300 (5.7)	flour	385 (1.7)
rice	860 (3.7)	biscuits	720 (3.1)
tallow	1,535 (6.7)	dried fish	240 (1.0)

In that year the presidio produced only 36,500 pounds of corn and 5,350 pounds of beans. For the balance, even at this early date, the presidio was dependent upon the missions and perhaps upon imports from Mexico. The establishment at the time had an approximate total white population of 230. The food supply per person for the year may thus be calculated. The result is approximately one pound per day per person, certainly an inadequate diet according to modern standards. Although it is probable that this strictly military ration was liberally supplemented by private sources of supply such as truck gardens, hunting, and fishing, these data are illuminating as showing what was regarded by the army as a reasonable base ration for white troops.

particularly for the earlier decades, it is reasonably comprehensive and may be utilized in default of any better data.[72] Examination of the sixty-six records indicates that the mean annual contribution of each mission to its presidio was 227.5 fanegas of grain.

Some foodstuffs were subministered to the ships which plied regularly with freight and passengers from San Blas and Acapulco to California. According to one record[73] the supplies of this sort from 1797 to 1804 amounted to a total of 250 fanegas (100 in 1799, 150 in 1804). If these years are representative, then throughout the entire period a rough proration would indicate 2 fanegas annually per mission.

Much greater were the quantities sold to foreign trading vessels. A fairly exact estimate might be made by collecting the miscellaneous items scattered through hundreds of thousands of documents in the Bancroft Library and elsewhere. But even if such a procedure were possible, any general averages computed on the basis of such data would not possess a high degree of validity. Foreign commerce, even of the smuggling or bootleg type, did not exist at all prior to 1815 or 1820. Hence no deductions from the mission produce figures could be made for the first fifty years. Subsequent to 1820, when trading increased greatly, the quantities of withdrawals for sale from the mission stores are largely conjectural. Though the records of general commerce are very numerous, they are usually in the form of customs receipts (i.e., imports rather than exports). Furthermore, the primary export items were hides and tallow rather than grains. In addition, it must be remembered that not only the missions sold such material,

---

[72] That this sample is satisfactory for the later period at least is demonstrated by the following calculation. The statements in the Bancroft Library list 19 contributions of the four missions—San Francisco, San José, Santa Clara, and Santa Cruz—for the decade 1821–1830 inclusive. According to these entries, the amount of cereal crops furnished the San Francisco Presidio was 4,420 fanegas. Interpolating on the basis of these figures, we get as the quantity supplied by the four missions in ten years (40 contributions) a total of 9,305 fanegas.

Now there is also a summary (Vallejo Docs., 20:251) of the monetary value of the credits advanced to this presidio in the same decade, amounting to $41,171 (41,171 pesos). We may safely assume that one-half the money was for cereal crops, the balance being for meat, fats, and manufactured goods. The prices for grains at this time were (Arch. Mis. [1824], 1:272): wheat, $2.00 per fanega; corn, $1.50 per fanega; and beans, $2.33 per fanega. Let us say, $2.00 per fanega as an average price. Then one-half the total sum, at this rate, would imply a purchase of 10,290 fanegas, which corresponds quite well with the estimate of 9,305 obtained by the first method.

[73] Subministrations to the ships, 1805(?), Sta. Bárb. Arch., 9:494.

but also the presidios and private individuals. Even Bancroft, who made a fairly complete survey of trade relations listing nearly every ship which touched at a California port from 1820 to 1845, nowhere gives data pertaining to the grain export of the missions. Consequently, in default of really adequate quantitative information, it is best to leave the question open and deduct nothing from the mean annual harvest of the missions, recognizing that, although some error is introduced by this omission, it is on the side of overestimating the food supply of the neophytes.[74]

The last cause of loss was deterioration and spoilage subsequent to the harvest. There are no data available concerning this point but it is safe to assume that at least a small part of each crop was thus eliminated.[75]

In sum, it is possible to deduct from the mean annual crop per mission 68.5 fanegas used for the garrison, 227.5 fanegas subministered to the presidios and perhaps 5 fanegas supplied to ships or sold in trade. Let us say, 300 fanegas in all. Deducting from the general mean in table 2 and converting units, the conclusion would be that the maximum dietary value of the grain crops to the neophytes was 1,205 calories per person per day. It must be emphasized that this is a maximum figure. It would be entirely in order to follow modern procedure

---

[74] Another factor involved is geographical location. The missions closest to the principal seaports (San Francisco, Monterey, and San Diego) probably disposed of more of their crops commercially than did those at remoter points.

One or two accounts at hand are suggestive. In 1823 (Arch. Mis., 1:580) a Russian ship put into San Francisco. There were sold to it 535 fanegas, 50 fanegas, and 500 fanegas of grain respectively from San Francisco, Santa Clara, and San José. If this rate applied generally to all the missions, the exports would have reached a tremendous volume (more than 300 fanegas annually per mission). Probably, therefore, this represents an exceptional transaction.

In the Vallejo Documents (1830) 1:213, there is a summary of the trading done in San Francisco from 1821 to 1830 inclusive. There were 32 ships involved and the value of the total imports amounted to $21,579. Since trading was almost entirely by barter, the exports may be assumed to have been of equivalent value. Now, wholly gratuitously, let us assume that one-third of the exports were cereals, and that one-half of these were from the missions. Further, let us assume that the average price per fanega was $2.00. Then the mission sales would have been 1,800 fanegas, or for the four Bay missions (including San Rafael but not Solano) 45 fanegas per year per mission. This estimate appears much too high.

[75] Father Durán (Archb. Arch., 3:71) reported from Santa Cruz in 1816 that between three and four hundred fanegas of corn could not be sent to the presidio because it spoiled on the ground owing to lack of transport. Such incidents may have occurred with some frequency.

and reduce by 10 per cent for domestic wastage and deterioration. Likewise, the assumed weight of grain per fanega is almost certainly 10 per cent too great. If these corrections are allowed, the calories per person per day would not exceed 1,000.

The principal type of animal food consumed by the mission Indians was beef, with perhaps some mutton and pork. An estimate of the quantities involved is difficult to obtain, since the mission records do not specify food consumption. There were, to be sure, annual live-stock censuses through which one might arrive at an approximation of the maximum food supply as was done for the cereal crops. How-ever, such a determination would have little, if any, significance; rela-tively few stock animals were consumed as food. The mission herds were enormous—adequate to supply meat bountifully to thousands of neophytes. However, a large proportion of the animals were slaugh-tered for hides and tallow, the principal export commodities, many of them were lost by theft, and many others strayed off the ranges or were killed by drought, frost, or wild animals. Even if these factors could be gauged in a semiquantitative manner, the results would be of doubtful value because the balance remaining for consumption as food could not be estimated without very large error. It is necessary therefore to rely upon the written statements of the missionaries.

The most comprehensive statement is that contained in a general report[76] for 1796 to the effect that of 50,000 head of cattle owned by the missions 6,000 were annually slaughtered for food. There were at the time thirteen missions with a total population of approximately 11,000. Six thousand cattle per year means 460 per mission per year or 9 per mission per week (18 every two weeks).

Other data of a numerical character are as follows.[77] In 1800 at Santa

[76] Salazar, "Informe," College of San Fernando, May 11, 1796, Sta. Bárb. Arch., 2:63–83.

[77] There are also semiquantitative records: "one piece per person per week" (Grajera, Mar. 2, 1799, Prov. St. Pap., 27:91); "cattle are killed during most months" (Argüello, Dec. 11, 1798, *ibid.,* p. 58); "meat for one or two days is given weekly" (Goycoechea, Dec. 14, 1798, *ibid.,* p. 70); "usually meat was given" (Perez, "Una vieja," MS, 1877); "every two weeks they slaughtered cattle" (Lorenzana, "Memorias," MS, 1878); "there was a daily ration of meat" (Coronel, "Cosas," MS, 1878); "a certain number were killed every week" (Solá, Apr. 3, 1818, Prov. Rec., 9:176–195). Furthermore, every missionary who expressed himself on the subject asserted that, as a universal procedure,

Bárbara 170 steers were slaughtered between January 1 and October 1.[78] At San Francisco in 1814 Langsdorff says that 50 to 60 steers a week were used.[79] Amador states that at San José 100 to 200 cattle were slaughtered every Saturday.[80] At San Diego, in 1814, the number killed every two weeks was 24.[81] If we reduce these estimates to the same basis as the first one (i.e., number killed per mission per week), the results are 4.4, 50–60, 100–200, and 12 respectively. Obviously the Langsdorff and Amador figures may be great exaggerations; at least, they are guesses. The three statements in which the missionaries themselves went on record show only 9, 4.4 and 12. In this connection it should be pointed out that the missionaries, perpetually on the defensive in matters of mission administration, were not likely to underestimate the food they gave to their Indian charges; furthermore, they were in a much better position than outsiders to know the actual number of beef slaughtered. We may, then, tentatively at least, accept the estimate of 9 animals per mission per week in 1796.

A modern range steer in good condition will weigh something over 1,000 pounds. The mission cattle were the old, unimproved Mexican and Spanish breed and moreover may not have been fed very heavily. Let us assume an average weight of 900 pounds. A dressed carcass today represents between 53 and 63 per cent of the total weight. Under mission conditions it is probable that not only the muscle and fat were utilized, but also much of the visceral material, such as heart, liver, and stomach. On the other hand, we should deduct the nonedible bones. A reasonable estimate would then be 60 per cent of the weight of the animal on the hoof or, say, 550 pounds. Nine animals per week would then amount to 4,950 pounds, or 710 pounds per day per mission. Since there were 13 missions in 1796, with a total population of 11,000, this means a daily individual allowance of 0.84 pounds of meat per day per person. In order to determine the exact calorific equivalent, it

---

numerous cattle were slaughtered for food. This was admitted, at least in principle, by all the military writers. There can therefore be no doubt whatever that meat, to a greater or lesser extent, was a fixed item in the mission dietary.

[78] Tapis and Cortes, Oct. 30, 1800, Sta. Bárb. Arch., 2:86–143.
[79] G. H. von Langsdorff, *Voyages and Travels in Various Parts of the World,* translated by T. C. Russell (1927), p. 151.
[80] J. M. Amador, "Memorias," MS, 1877, p. 102.
[81] Martín and Sánchez, 1811, Sta. Bárb. Arch., 3:27–37.

would be necessary to know the precise proportion of muscle, fat, liver, and so on which was eaten, as well as the type of cut. This is manifestly impossible to discover. The closest approximation is to assume a value of approximately 1,000 calories per pound, thus indicating an individual intake of 840 calories per day.

Aside from cereals and beef the missions produced small quantities of truck crops, principally legumes like lentils and peas. The total quantity of these may be determined from the annual reports. In the entire province from 1783 to 1833 there were produced in all 74,200 fanegas per year, allowing 5 per cent deduction for seed (see table 2), or 0.845 fanega per person per year. On a daily basis this is equivalent to .00023 fanega, or .00037 bushel per person. If the average weight of these crops is assumed to be approximately 60 pounds per bushel and the energy value to be 1,500 calories per pound, then the calories per day per person from this source amounted to 30.

There were perhaps other foodstuffs supplied in very small quantities by the missions. The invoices of ships and records of goods received by the missions show inconsiderable imports of chocolate, sugar, chili, vinegar, and various condiments. Some of these doubtless found their way to the infirmaries for the benefit of the sick, but the rank and file of the neophytes never saw them. There may have been other minor food items. Although there were few, if any, dairy cattle, and consequently there was no material supply of milk, butter, or cheese, there may have been some poultry. Such items can have been of little or no significance in energy production, yet they were undoubtedly valuable as accessory sources of food.

Wild Food.—Wholly apart from the mission economy itself, there was one food source available to the Indians, the aboriginal wild food. This consisted of scores of plants and animals, utilized according to season and location and in varying amounts by the Indians prior to missionization. In the aggregate these wild sources made up a fairly complete diet or, at least, one upon which a good many thousand persons had subsisted for generations. If the aboriginal food sources had remained entirely available to the neophytes, and if to this the mission dietary of grain and meat had been added, the Indians should have enjoyed an excellent nutritional environment. But the policy of the missions was opposed to the utilization of this supply. In theory—and the problem was subject to endless debate—it was felt that the material and spiritual welfare of the newly converted savages would be better served by keeping them confined strictly within the mission influence and by preventing any reversion to their old habits of life. This question of policy, with its social and religious implications, does not concern us here. The crux of the matter is that the neophytes were prevented from utilizing their aboriginal food sources, even though these were abundant.

However, no prohibition can ever be complete, and there were many exceptions to this rule. In the first place, mission policy by no means condemned the use of wild foods per se provided they could be obtained without detriment to the main objectives of the system. In the second place, whenever the mission production of foodstuffs fell below maintenance standards, as occasionally happened locally, the priests were compelled to allow their charges to find food wherever they could. This expedient was deliberately resorted to in the first decade, before agriculture and the stock industry had become fully established. Despite attempts to avoid such a predicament, conversion frequently outran cultivation. In the third place, throughout the entire history of the missions there was a continuous stream of fugitives leaving the establishments and subsequently returning, either voluntarily or by compulsion. The net result of all these factors seems to have been a steady flow into the missions of wild foods, in particular, seasonal herbs and tubers, acorns, and fish. It is manifestly impossible to gauge the extent of this importation in numerical terms; but it must have constituted a very material contribution, both in absolute quantity and as a source of vitamins and other nutritional elements.

Simply for the sake of comparison, there may be cited the dietary habits of the California Indians today. It has been shown that under modern conditions and after a century of so-called civilization, up to 10 per cent of the dietary regimen of the Sierra Nevada Indians still consists of wild food.[82] What may we then expect of the diet among

---

[82] S. F. Cook, *The Mechanism and Extent of Dietary Adaptation among Certain Groups of California and Nevada Indians,* Univ. Calif. Publ., Ibero-Americana, No. 18 (Berkeley, 1941).

similar people not one generation removed from their aboriginal surroundings? Considering the complete lack of concrete data, it may be permissible to base an estimate on the dietary in the missions upon our modern observations and to ascribe to wild sources approximately 10 per cent of the total, or, let us say, a statistical mean of 200 calories per person per day.[83]

Calorific value of the mission dietary.—To summarize the foregoing discussion, the average neophyte in the mission period received or obtained food having an energy value of 2,320 calories ($\pm$ 20 per cent) per day. It must be remembered that this figure represents the probable maximum diet and that the actual nourishment of any one individual at any particular time may have been much less. Indeed it has been suggested that a 20-per cent reduction in the estimate for grain intake would be legitimate. Moreover, the allowance of 840 calories per person per day from meat alone seems excessive. The actual energy value is therefore more likely to have been from 2,000 to 2,100 calories rather than the theoretical maximum of 2,320. Granting that our preliminary estimate is correct within reasonable limits, the question now arises whether this diet was adequate.

With respect to the number of calories included in the diet certain modern data may be used for comparison. It is considered that for the civilized white races the available food supplies should be sufficient to provide 3,300 calories "per man per day."[84] An allowance of 10 per

[83] A fairly clear statement of mission policy is contained in Lasuén's "Representación" of 1800 (Sta. Bárb. Arch., 2:172): "Even the most important tasks of the mission are left undone when there is not sufficient food for the workers. They are then permitted freedom to go out into the woods, but no one is forced to go. Nevertheless on such occasions sufficient provisions are bought and brought from other places to sustain all those, sick and well, who remain in the mission."

This statement is confirmed by several of the foreign visitors in the later mission era. F. W. Beechey records (*Voyage to the Pacific* [1831], 2:22): "If it should happen that there is a scarcity of provisions, either through failure in the crop, or damage of that which is in store . . . the Indians are sent off to the woods to provide for themselves, where, accustomed to hunt and fish, and game being very abundant, they find enough to subsist upon." Beechey (*ibid.,* p. 20) also describes a scene at San Francisco: ". . . others were grinding baked acorns to make into cakes, which constituted a large portion of their food. . . ." However, I find no other mention of acorns as an important dietary constituent.

[84] See Graham Lusk, *The Elements of the Science of Nutrition* (4th ed., 1928), pp. 756–758, for a discussion of the food supply to populations. The figures cited in the text are taken from Lusk.

cent is included for domestic wastage, making the required net intake 3,000 calories. In prewar Germany the value was 3,640 and in England 3,410. Our estimate of roughly 2,000 to 2,100 calories as the probable daily nourishment of the individual mission Indian appears therefore to be considerably below the optimum level. However, certain additional factors should be considered.

The estimates for modern civilized nations are based upon the supposition that the diet is wholly adequate with respect to quantity and quality. It is nevertheless possible for a population to exist with fair success on a maintenance diet of much lower level. Thus Lusk (*op. cit.,* p. 756) places the actual requirement of the people of prewar Germany at 2,285 calories per man per day, whereas the quantity used was 3,640 calories. Another factor is the character of the population with respect to size and age-sex composition. The Indian was, as a rule, somewhat smaller than the white man, perhaps sufficiently smaller to warrant a reduction in calorific necessity from 3,000 to 2,700. The age-sex factor is significant since the infant mortality of the mission group was high and the number of children consequently small. Furthermore, the sex ratio was high. The effect of these factors may be approximated by computing the dietary requirement. For this purpose we may use the values for the civilized white population of 2,000 calories for the average child up to fourteen years, 2,800 calories for a woman, and 3,600 calories for a man. The last two values are applicable to active, not sedentary, individuals, but it must be remembered that the mission Indians were active in the physical sense. This method yields 2,950 calories "per man per day" as compared with 3,000 for modern white races. Again, reducing by 10 per cent to account for average size difference, we get 2,655 calories. It therefore appears doubtful whether the probable maximum caloric supply of the mission Indians met the requirement for adequate diet in the quantitative sense and whether there was sufficient food for maintenance purposes.

Even if we were to concede the mission diet to have been quantitatively sufficient, there remains the question of the adequacy of its protein, mineral, and vitamin content.

As indicated previously, the food supply was predominantly grain. This means the presence of a moderate amount of plant protein. If the meat supplement was as extensive as the few data we possess seem to indicate, then we cannot regard the combination as being too low in total protein. Even if the meat supply was less than we have supposed, the population would still have had access to a maintenance level of the essential amino acids.

With regard to minerals doubts may arise. The grains and legumes would ensure sufficient phosphorus but perhaps might induce a calcium deficiency. However, calcium might have been obtained from other sources, such as the animal food. Moreover, there is some evidence that lime was incorporated with the cooked grain.[85] If so, it is unlikely that a serious calcium deficiency existed. Sodium chloride was, of course, present in the meat, although the grains contributed little. It is alleged by Governor Solá that the cereals were fed "without salt or any condiment."[86] A more explicit statement comes from Tapis and Cortes, two missionaries who were defending the system against charges of negligence and corruption. They assert:[87]

Neither salt nor lard is added to the *pozole,* for experience has shown us that they do not agree with most of them [the Indians] and to the minority with whom they agree neither one nor the other is denied, if they ask for them.

It is fairly clear therefore that salt was not regarded as a necessary dietary constituent and was not purveyed on an extensive scale. Whether an actual sodium chloride deficiency existed cannot be determined with certainty.

The adequacy of vitamins is similarly a matter of opinion. If the neophytes had been restricted rigidly to corn, wheat, beans, and beef, we might conclude that they received a fair supply of vitamins A and B_1, that vitamin C was low and that B_2 (or G) was doubtful. This would raise the possibility of the occurrence of scurvy and pellagra. However, there are no records which support this supposition. The Spanish and

---

[85] Coronel ("Cosas," p. 221) states that "el atole era maíz cocido con cal. ..." Furthermore, since the white population utilized extensively the *tortilla* which is invariably cooked with lime, it is highly improbable that the missionaries would neglect to include this substance in the standard dietary of the Indians.

[86] Solá to viceroy, Monterey, April 3, 1818, Prov. Rec., 9:176–195.

[87] Tapis and Cortes, Sta. Bárb. Arch., 2:86–143. Substantiating evidence comes from Lapérouse (*A Voyage Round the World* [translation, London, 1798], 2:215) who refers to "*atole* ... which is seasoned neither with salt nor butter."

Mexicans of the time were thoroughly familiar with scurvy and would have reported its presence.[88] Pellagra was of course unknown, but there is no definite, indirect evidence of its presence.[89] Furthermore, there were available small quantities of foodstuffs which would have no quantitative significance but which might have been of value as vitamin sources. A few cows supplied a little milk; there were some fresh vegetables in the mission gardens.[90] In the south a small citrus industry was established. In addition, the Indians must have procured a certain amount of wild green plant material. It is impossible to say to what extent these sources were utilized, but it is reasonable to assume that they did not provide the entire population with a completely balanced diet in the modern sense. On the other hand, there was probably enough material of this nature to prevent severe incidence of deficiency disease. Surveying the field a century afterward, one is apt to incline toward the belief that the accessory food factors were marginal and that the Indians as a whole lived continuously on the verge of clinical deficiency.

[88] Scurvy did occur seriously in the Portolá expedition of 1769 and at San Diego among the soldiers during the following winter; but there is no mention of its having attacked the natives.

[89] The only indication, and it is but an indication, that extensive deficiency diseases were present, lies in the descriptions of venereal disease. The frequent references to skin affections (pustules, sores, rashes, etc.), which ascribe the latter universally to syphilis, suggest the remote possibility that some of them may have been associated with dietary deficiencies. However, the descriptions are too general and inexact to use as diagnostic criteria.

[90] It is difficult to ascertain just how much fresh plant material was actually available. All observers testify that gardens existed generally and that a certain amount of fruit was raised. Opinion varied as to the actual production. Beechey (*op. cit.,* 2:37) states that ". . . beans, pease and other leguminous vegetables are in abundance, and fruit is plentiful." Choris, who saw California in 1816 with the Katzebue expedition, says (see A. C. Mahr, *The Visit of the Rurik in San Francisco in 1816* [1932], p. 93): "In their free time the Indians work in gardens that are given them; they raise therein onions, garlic, canteloupes, watermelons, pumpkins, and fruit trees. The products belong to them. . . ." However, Vancouver, writing at an earlier date, thought otherwise. With respect to San Francisco he says: (*A Voyage of Discovery to the North Pacific Ocean* [London, 1801], p. 23): "[The garden] contained about four acres . . . and produced some fig, peach, apple, and other fruit trees, but afforded a very scanty supply of useful vegetables." Of Santa Clara he writes (p. 33): "The extent of it, like the garden at San Francisco, appeared unequal to the consumption of the European residents"; and of San Carlos (p. 62): "With these advantages it generally produces a great abundance of the several kitchen vegetables and some fruit." However, owing to sales to passing ships ". . . the productions of this and the only other garden at San Carlos were nearly exhausted."

The foregoing discussion is based upon purely statistical considerations and refers only to general conditions. There are, however, certain purely individual and local data which have definite significance.

Contemporary accounts.—Among those interested persons who commented at that time on the status of the mission Indians or in later years wrote down their impressions, there existed two divergent schools of opinion. One held that the Indians were satisfactorily fed, the other maintained the opposite. Naturally, opinions were highly colored by current political and social controversies, such as the perennial contest for power between the missionaries and soldiers. Sometimes personal considerations—racial or religious prejudice, political or business ambitions, or pure like and dislike—entered the picture. It is therefore unwise to rely completely upon the unsupported opinion of any one individual, no matter how superlative his ability or integrity.

On the positive side we find the great missionary presidents, Serra and Lasuén, who were beyond any question fully convinced that everything necessary was supplied to their converts. Thus Lasuén[91] avers:

Besides their three meals ... they are rarely denied anything that they come to ask for in order to eat. ... This ... is done according to the means of each mission. This is not uniform but every effort is expended on the neophytes. It is not to be denied that among the missionaries there are some more and some less solicitous and liberal regarding the convenience of their spiritual children just as there are good fathers of families. ...

The inference here is plain that, although it was the intention to give the neophytes all they wanted, it was not always within the means of the missions to do so.

Tapis and Cortes contend as follows:[92]

That this food is sufficient to sustain them and enable them to withstand their work ... may be observed by anyone who is possessed of eyes and wishes to see.

... He may observe that certain neophytes who raise chickens do not feed them on their wild seeds ... but on the *pozole* left over after eating all they want. Besides this daily consumption of provisions, during the

---

[91] "Representación," San Carlos, Nov. 12, 1800, Sta. Bárb. Arch., 2:154–240.
[92] *Loc. cit.*

wheat harvest the fourth part of an *almud* is given daily to those engaged in the harvest. The same practice is pursued on Sundays and during Lent as well as on the principal holidays of the year.[93]

Eulalia Perez,[94] who spent her youth in San Diego, states that breakfast consisted of chocolate with *atole* of corn with bread on holidays; on other days usually *pozole* and meat. At noon there were *pozole* and meat with greens, and at night *atole* with meat or at times pure *atole*. She goes on to describe her experiences in carrying refreshment to the workers in the fields. "This refreshment was made from water with vinegar and sugar or with lemon and sugar, so that the Indians should not become sick." The custom of giving fruit juices as a beverage seems to have had a rather wide vogue, particularly toward the end of the mission period.

Amador in his recollections describes all the meals as consisting of *atole* (a gruel made by boiling ground corn, wheat, or barley) and *pozole* (a cooked mixture of barley, beans, corn, pigs' feet, squash and chili).[95] He also says that "the Indians at San José never went hungry." Coronel thus describes the diet:[96]

Food was given three times a day.... It consisted of beans and corn or wheat cooked together, which was called *pozole;* sometimes *atole* and meat were given in the morning. . . . To the married men were given weekly a ration of grain, that is corn, wheat and beans, and daily a ration of fresh or dried meat, generally fish.

---

[93] Regarding actual quantities given the neophytes, there are two statements which are worthy of mention. Romero ("Memorias," MS, 1878, p. 19), who worked as a servant for eleven years at San Fernando, says that each married man was given 3 *cuartillas* of grain a week and each unmarried man 2 *cuartillas*. Since a *cuartilla* equals 6 pounds and since each family had on the average one child, the net grain ration would have been equivalent to 1,320 calories per day per person for families and 2,740 calories for single men. However, the latter were expected to distribute their ration among relatives. Hence the result is approximately the same.

Tapis and Cortes (Sta. Bárb. Arch., 2:86–143) state that each neophyte who ate at the general mission mess received about three-quarters of an *almud* in the form of *atole* or *pozole*. Since an *almud* is approximately 800 cubic centimeters or 1.6 pounds of corn or wheat, this would imply an equivalent of 1,930 calories. But since Tapis and Cortes estimate that one-quarter of the neophytes were always absent from any particular meal, the average equivalent would be 1,450 calories.

These values come definitely within the range predicated on the basis of general crop statistics.

[94] "Una vieja," MS, 1877, pp. 17–18.

[95] J. M. Amador, "Memorias," p. 102.

[96] A. F. Coronel, "Cosas," p. 221.

Langsdorff in 1818 described the mission diet as follows:[97]

The principal food of the Indians is a thick soup composed of meat, vegetables and pulse. Because of the scarcity of fish here [San Francisco] the missionaries obtained a special dispensation from the Pope allowing the eating of meat on fast days. The food is apportioned three times a day . . . in large ladlefuls. At meal times . . . each family sends a vessel to the kitchen and is served as many measures as there are members. I was present once at the time the soup was served, and it appeared incomprehensible to me how anyone could consume so much nourishing food three times a day. . . . Besides this meal, bread, Indian corn, peas, beans and other kinds of pulse are distributed in abundance, without any stated or regular allowance.

The above quotations and many other similar accounts give the impression of abundance and liberality, of easy-going pastoral richness, an impression which has crept into the secondary literature and colored many of the more popular and less critical works on early California. With this in mind, it is only reasonable to present the opposite side of the picture.

He charged the Ministers of that mission of San Francisco to exercise greater care with the cleanliness of the great copper tanks or kettles from which the *atole* and *pozole* are given to the neophytes. The latter [*atole*, etc.] are composed some days of wheat and others of peas . . . with none of the corn or wheat bread known as tortillas.[98]

In 1806 the crops failed at San Diego[99] and there was scarcely enough food to maintain the neophytes. In 1819 the crops were destroyed[100] at Santa Ynéz, and the missionary feared there would be a famine. In the same year the Bay region suffered.[101] The minister at San Francisco reported that the stock were dying and the crops poor. He undertook to plant crops in the region of San José "to alleviate the great misery in which these unfortunate neophytes find themselves."

Until 1779 at San Diego the neophytes were left at their native villages because there was no food at San Diego.[102] Of four hundred converts only twenty were living at the mission. By 1787 about one-

---

[97] *Op. cit.,* p. 51.
[98] Solá to the viceroy, Monterey, Apr. 3, 1818, Prov. Rec., 9:178.
[99] Rodríguez to Arrillaga, San Diego, June 20, 1806, Prov. St. Pap., 19:140.
[100] Uria to De la Guerra, Santa Ynéz, Apr. 26, 1819, De la Guerra Docs., 5:263.
[101] Cabot to Solá, San Francisco, Oct. 30, 1819, Archb. Arch., 3:116.
[102] Fages, "Informe," 1787, St. Pap. Mis. Col., 1:129.

half were at the mission, and the crops were large enough so that "they all can be fed."

In 1821 Father Prefect Payeras wrote Governor Solá, referring to San Francisco, that "this mission can supply nothing because for the last three or four months the neophytes have had nothing to eat."[103]

The following three opinions were expressed by the military commanders of the presidios in 1798 in answer to a questionnaire submitted by the governor:

... I consider the quantity [of food] so small that in the course of the year it does not amount to 22 fanegas of grain per individual, and it is likewise observed that it is insufficient for their sustenance and much less to resist the arduous strain of the labors in which they are employed.[104]

Although sufficient to sustain life it [the ration] cannot suffice for him who works from morning till night.[105]

Without being prompted by pity, but only using common sense, I deem this food insufficient with which solely to maintain themselves and to resist the hardships to which they are subjected.[106]

At about the same time the governor wrote the viceroy that conditions at San Francisco had improved and that the Indians "now get three hot meals a day."[107] This was owing to the efforts of Fray José María Fernández, who opposed the methods of his colleague, Fray Landaeta. Apparently under the Landaeta regime they did not get three meals a day.

In 1826 Father Zalvidea wrote that "these unfortunate Indians lack fat ... beans and corn."[108] At the other end of the colony Argüello complained that "the soldiers are in no wise different from the Indians and the worst is that they are all feeling starvation. May God intercede in all this!"[109]

The multiplication of further instances is unnecessary. It will be

---

[103] Payeras to Solá, San Francisco, Aug. 5, 1821, Archb. Arch., 4:76.

[104] Sal, Monterey, December 15, 1798, Prov. St. Pap., 17:63. Note that the opinion of Sal is not borne out by his figures; 22 fanegas per person per year amounts to 5 pounds per day, a far greater quantity than the missions could have provided. Possibly some error is involved in the original or in the Bancroft transcript.

[105] Grajera, San Diego, March 2, 1799, *ibid.*, p. 191.

[106] F. Goycoechea, Santa Bárbara, Dec. 14, 1798, *ibid.*, p. 70.

[107] Borica to the viceroy, Monterey, July 1, 1798, Prov. Rec., 6:97.

[108] Zalvidea to Echeandía, San Juan Capistrano, July 15, 1826, Archb. Arch., 5:25.

[109] Argüello to De la Guerra, San Francisco, Apr. 21, 1820, De la Guerra Docs., 4:136.

clear that there was no unanimity of opinion concerning mission diet. This divergence may be partly, but not entirely, explained on the grounds of personal ignorance, political bias, or religious prejudice. The truth seems to lie, as it so often does, between the extremes. There is no doubt that the missions intended to produce and to give the neophytes what would be regarded today as a fairly adequate ration. This policy was carried out in general through the years; there were, however, many local exceptions. Evidently considerable want and suffering were caused by crop failure, indifference and neglect on the part of certain missionaries, and numerous other factors. Thus in the aggregate the quantity and quality of the diet fell below the theoretical standard set up by the missionary administration. On the other hand, the evidence does not warrant the contention that the neophytes were subjected to conditions of really acute malnutrition or starvation over more than brief intervals of time.

To return now to the primary question concerning the significance of food in the population decline, we are again obliged to adopt a middle ground. It cannot be stated categorically that the whole group suffered direct losses from starvation. Nor, despite the doubtful adequacy of the vitamin and mineral intake, is there unimpeachable evidence that immediate damage was done by an acute lack of any accessory factor. Conversely, it does not appear that the neophytes universally and consistently received entirely adequate and nutritionally complete food. The tremendous incidence of disease, especially continuous, nonepidemic disease, suggests a level of nutrition probably insufficient for ordinary maintenance and certainly below the optimum necessary to provide a high resistance to infection. The low resistance implicit in a high-disease incidence and mortality is in definite conformity with the only moderate caloric intake and marginal vitamin supply which undoubtedly existed. A suboptimal diet may therefore be regarded as one factor which operated indirectly to check any population increase through its tendency to predispose to disease. It is, of course, manifestly impossible to assign any numerical value to the relative significance of such a factor.

IV. NEGATIVE RESPONSES TO THE MISSION ENVIRONMENT

THE POPULATION CHANGES induced by disease and perhaps by faulty diet must be regarded as purely mass effects operating on the aggregate without respect to individuals. To be sure, illness is a personal matter, and the total mortality must be viewed as the sum of the individual deaths. Yet these processes contain an element of inevitability. A man becomes infected when he comes in contact with the appropriate bacteria; he survives if his innate resistance is sufficiently high, he dies if he is constitutionally unable to cope with the disease or if external conditions over which he has no immediate control are such as to render his recovery impossible. He himself has no latitude for response; his fate is in a certain sense predetermined.

On the other hand, there are many factors which may be racially and personally unfavorable, which in the long run and including many persons may affect the numbers and vitality of a population but which are not directly and necessarily lethal to one single person. In a very broad sense some of these factors may be regarded as stimuli, capable of evoking a response in the individual. Then his response (or lack of it), its manner and extent will determine his status with respect to the environment of which such factors are an integral part. Further, if the responses of a sufficient number of persons are of the same type, the biological status of the whole group may be affected. It is difficult and probably unnecessary to attempt any sharp differentiation between individual and group responses of this pattern. The primary thesis is that, if enough separate units are observed to behave in a definite manner in the face of a given set of conditions, then we may think of such behavior in terms of group reaction. Furthermore, the factors which give rise to this particular type of group behavior may be conceived as operating first on the individual to induce his response. The final group response, or in ecological terms "adaptation," will then represent the statistical trend of the aggregate, and the latter may be affected at any time by changes in the nature and intensity of the stimulating factors.

Individual human responses may take very different forms. There may be first utter indifference, then mild like or dislike, stronger like or dislike, until there is some overt act. Aside from a few written opinions we have no means of assessing the reaction of the individual Indian to the mission system until the stage of action is reached. But action, as far as the Indian was concerned, was pretty definitely circumscribed. If his feeling was one of indifference or satisfaction, he would remain a neophyte and live and die unnoticed in the historical annals. If the reverse were true, he might pursue a sullen and discontented existence, indulging perhaps in a certain passive resistance to the system. In this event his unhappiness might be reflected in a thousand little ways which, although quite apparent to an observer on the spot, would not cause sufficient excitement to warrant official attention or comment. Nevertheless, if a large number of fellow neophytes shared his attitude, the result would be seen in the material and moral degeneration of the entire system. Since the system, even before secularization, was in this condition, it cannot be doubted that a great deal of general discontent was present, perhaps more than is obvious from the written record of the times. Now if the negative response evinced in a mild form by mere passive resistance became intensified to the point of physical action, there were only two possible lines of procedure. The Indian might exhibit one of the two universal modes of response to an unfavorable environment, flight. He might leave the missionary environment bodily and betake himself elsewhere. On the other hand, he might attempt the other mode of response, active, physical resistance, which would necessarily take the form of armed rebellion and warfare. Either mode of response could be embarked upon by an individual or by a group of any dimensions.

We have therefore to examine the extent to which the Indians gave evidence of negative individual and group responses to the mission environment by these two tangible methods. Subsequently we have to consider the factors inherent in that environment which could give rise to such extreme behavior.

Fugitivism.—Apostasy began as soon as conversions began, although it was some years before official notice was taken of it. By 1781, however, Junípero Serra[1] was able to list fifteen persons whom he described as being "confirmed apostates." Subsequent to that date no year passed without some mention of fugitives in the official correspondence. The problem became continuously more acute as more and more neophytes ran away, until secularization converted practically all the mission population into fugitives.

Generally speaking, and regardless of original motive, there were two categories of fugitives, temporary and permanent. The criterion between the two categories is whether or not a person was dropped from the mission rolls. On many occasions, undoubtedly thousands, neophytes ran away. Of these, a very large proportion returned to the fold after absences varying from a few days to several years. Some of these, probably the majority, came back of their own volition. Perhaps they went out only for the purpose of a temporary vacation; perhaps they changed their minds with reference to the desirability of the wild as opposed to the mission environment. The reasons leading to such voluntary return are as manifold as human nature. Others, quite a large number, were forcibly brought back by the many expeditions, large and small, which went out for this exact purpose. There was a residue, however, of determined souls who ran away, stayed away, and eluded all attempts to recapture them. After an indeterminate period, which may be estimated as approximately two years, they were given up for lost and dropped from the records as standing members of the mission community. These formed the group of permanent fugitives.

The number of permanent fugitives has been already estimated in a previous publication.[2] As explained there, the clue lies in the difference between the mission population as calculated from baptism-death data, and that stated in the annual censuses, the so-called "unaccounted depletion." It was shown that this source of loss represented about 4 per cent of the total losses (i.e., 96 per cent were by death) and that up to 1831 the cumulative desertions were 3,464. In 1832, 1833, and 1834 the desertions increased very greatly, bringing the final total to 5,428. This figure has significance as an index of response as discussed above. It means specifically that up to 1831 the mission environment had

---

[1] "Padrón," San Carlos, Dec. 22, 1781, St. Pap. Ben. Mil., 3:27.

[2] S. F. Cook, *Population Trends among the California Mission Indians,* Univ. Calif. Publ., Ibero-Americana, No. 17 (Berkeley, 1940), pp. 27–28. See below, pp. 425-426.

affected the neophyte population so adversely that out of about 81,000 individuals (the actual total baptisms were 81,586) 3,400, that is, one out of every twenty-four, resorted actively and successfully to flight. If we eliminate from the total baptisms those who because of infancy, senility, illness, or death were physically unable to escape, the ratio will be very much higher. But to gauge the true extent of this response we must consider those who attempted escape and subsequently gave up the attempt or failed. The only evidence of a quantitative nature pertaining to this matter consists of a series of reports or notes scattered at random through the documentary material. I have collected such items as I have been able to find and have embodied them in table 3. The source of each item is on record but has not been appended to the table. In addition, in table 4 will be found the only specific and complete data covering a single year.

Although the data contained in table 3 constitute a rather inadequate sample, certain deductions can be made. As a mere approximation, let us take the entries in the table in which specific numbers of fugitives are given and compute the proportion of the mission population represented. The numbers which are listed as "caught" may be used for this purpose with the full realization that those caught by no means represent all who ran away. The mean value is 8.3 per cent. If the mean is restricted to those fugitives not labeled "caught" or "returned" the result is almost the same: 9.8 per cent. Now there exists a statement[3] giving the total number of fugitives for each of fifteen out of the nineteen missions up to the year 1817 (see table 4). From the censuses incorporated in the Bancroft compilation of vital statistics it may be calculated that the percentage of fugitives per mission, based on cumulative baptisms up to that year, ranges from 0.1 to 15.6, with a mean of 5.95. The total number was 3,205, but that represents all fugitives, permanent and temporary, up to the end of 1817. The two groups may be segregated within this total by the method outlined above, since the permanently missing persons were dropped from the census rolls; the discrepancy between the cumulative baptisms minus cumulative deaths on the one hand and the current existing population on the other represents the permanent fugitives. This value, for the nineteen

[3] "Estado," 1817, St. Pap. Mis., 4:44.

TABLE 3
Fugitives from Various Missions, 1781–1829

No.	Year	Mission	Number of fugitives	Remarks	Percentage of the mission population
1	1782	San Carlos........	15	All adults.........	2.9
2	1782	San Diego........	2	....	0.29
3	1782	San Carlos........	...	"Several".........	...
4	1783	San Diego........	2–4	....	0.4
5	1786	San Buenaventura.	...	"Frequent".......	...
6	1787	San Buenaventura.	...	"Several".........	...
7	1787	San Diego........	30	More than 30 caught	3.3
8	1787	San Carlos........	...	Several caught......	...
9	1793	San Francisco.....	21	....	3.0
10	1795	San Francisco.....	280	....	32.1
11	1796	San Francisco.....	21	Caught...........	...
12	1796	San Francisco.....	150	....	19.0
13	1796	Santa Clara.......	41	....	2.9
14	1796	San Francisco.....	200	....	25.3
15	1797	San José..........	83	Caught...........	...
16	1798	Santa Cruz.......	138	80 adults, 58 children	27.4
17	1798	Santa Cruz.......	90	Caught...........	17.9
18	1798	San Francisco.....	48	Returned voluntarily	7.4
19	1799	San Carlos........	50	Caught...........	7.0
20	1800	Santa Clara.......	21	Caught...........	1.7
21	1804	Santa Clara.......	32	Caught...........	2.6
22	1805	San Gabriel.......	40	....	2.5
23	1805	San Juan Bautista.	200	....	16.9
24	1805	San Francisco.....	13	Caught...........	1.1
25	1806	San Francisco.....	10	Caught...........	0.9
26	1806	Santa Clara.......	48	Caught...........	3.4
27	1807	San Francisco.....	62	....	6.7
28	1813	San Buenaventura.	2	....	0.2
29	1816	Soledad..........	19	....	3.8
30	1816	San Fernando.....	...	Fugitives increasing.	...
31	1816	San Francisco.....	6	Caught...........	0.5
32	1816	San Juan Bautista.	12	All male..........	2.1
33	1816	San Buenaventura.	1	....	0.07
34	1816	Santa Cruz.......	40	Returned voluntarily	11.2
35	1819	San Francisco.....	...	"All" ran away temporarily.........	...
36	1819	San Juan Bautista.	47	....	7.1
37	1819	San José..........	15	....	0.9
38	1820	San Francisco.....	30	....	2.4
39	1824	Santa Bárbara....	453	Fled after rebellion..	49.1
40	1824	Santa Bárbara....	163	Caught...........	...
41	1825	Santa Cruz.......	27	....	6.3
42	1826	Solano	13	....	4.5

missions in 1817, was 1,596. The probable total fugitives for the nineteen missions in 1817 (based on 3,205 for 15 missions) was 4,060. Then the temporary fugitives at the time of the 1817 count amounted to 2,464. Since the entire population of the missions at that time was 20,427, the percentage of current fugitives would have been 12.1, a value which

TABLE 4

Total Number of Fugitives up to 1817

Mission	Number of fugitives	Percentage of cumulative baptisms
San Diego..............	316	7.5
San Juan Capistrano......	254	7.1
San Gabriel.............	473	8.6
San Fernando...........	5	0.2
San Buenaventura........	27	0.8
Santa Bárbara...........	595	15.1
La Purísima............	52	1.8
San Luis Obispo.........	136	6.1
San Antonio............	167	4.3
San Carlos..............	431	15.6
San Juan Bautista........	174	8.0
Santa Cruz.............	60	5.8
Santa Clara.............	310	4.9
San José...............	3	0.1
San Francisco...........	202	3.8

checks reasonably well with that of 8.3–9.8 derived from the data in table 3. As a compromise, 10 per cent will not be far from the actual value.

The extent of fugitivism may be better appreciated if we translate the existing data into different modes of expression. It should be consistently remembered that the act of escape was the culmination of the response; it was the final gesture, arising from an urge which in many instances may have been frustrated. As suggested previously, a large share of the population was not in a physical condition appropriate to the arduous necessities accompanying the process of running away. Many persons were too young, too decrepit, too ill to attempt it. A great many more found themselves inhibited by the moral suasion or physical pressure exercised by the missionaries. Others were swayed by fear of the punishment which was often meted out to recovered apostates or by the desire for certain rewards, perquisites, and inducements held out to the faithful. As the years went on, many had been raised from childhood in the mission and had no haven of refuge outside to which to flee, even had they so desired. Escape was a serious and dangerous procedure fraught with innumerable perils and uncertainties. Numerous must have been the primitive Hamlets who preferred to bear those evils which they had, rather than fly to others they knew not of. And yet, in the face of all this, at any particular time approximately one person out of ten was undertaking to escape the mission environment. The escape response therefore constituted a biological phenomenon of very deep significance. It passes definitely from the category of the isolated individual and becomes a group movement, a mass tendency which was held in check only by the severest measures on the part of the dominant race.

Here we begin to observe an example of the action and interaction, the mutual interplay of factors, which so frequently arises at the point of contact of two species, races, or cultures. The escape response must be regarded as basic, the primary reaction to the inherent conditions of missionization. Once this process started, however, the situation changed because certain new problems were thereby engendered. First, from the moral and religious point of view the effect was very bad, since it advertised the fact that, so far as the neophytes were concerned, the mission system was not a success and that conversion to Christianity was not a force sufficiently powerful to hold the converts. Thus a bad influence was brought to bear upon the remaining, faithful Christians as well as upon the gentiles. Second, the material effect was disturbing through the disruption of mission administration and reduction in the necessary labor supply. Third, social problems were created among the troops and civilians by the presence of idle and impoverished Indians in their midst. Fourth, the only too acute danger existed that certain of the fugitives would inflame anti-Spanish sentiment among the gentiles, to the extent of armed uprising and attack. A very hazardous state of affairs thus came into being, one which could not be tolerated by the whites.

In responding to this new situation, which they themselves had created, the clerico-military administration had three courses open to them, all of which they pursued at one time or another: (1) by various means to prevent escape; (2) to punish those who escaped and were caught; (3) to send out armed forces to capture runaways and return them to their missions. However, the effect of the first two of these procedures was to intensify the original escape complex by adding new factors which exerted an unfavorable influence on the converted Indians. Physical restraint and confinement, as well as punishment of a corporal or any other nature, would render more violent the desire to get away on the part of a previous fugitive and would crystallize the urge in others who as yet had not gone the whole distance in this type of response. Moreover, it led to abuses on the part of individual soldiers and clergymen which were in no wise contemplated by the mission founders. This was followed by more widespread apostasy and thus a vicious circle was established. The final stages were witnessed after secularization, when the control and restraint of the church fathers was removed and the entire mission system went to pieces with terrific rapidity.

The third procedure operated somewhat differently but to the same end. Since many fugitives went to the wilderness and were harbored by unconverted gentiles, the expeditions necessarily followed them thither. This resulted in a rude awakening for the savages. They saw armed parties come among them and drag off the Christians to a fate which must have seemed like slavery. Their first impressions of the white men, therefore, can scarcely have been favorable. This in turn predisposed them against conversion. Consequently, when many of them in the later days were brought by strong moral pressure or even physical force to the missions, the desire to escape was already present in the minds of many of them, even before they saw their new environment. Obviously, this tendency to escape became increasingly intensified, the more such neophytes were brought under mission auspices.

A great deal could be written concerning the details of administrative policy toward fugitivism and the methods used to combat it, but such extensive consideration, although of historical interest, does not appear necessary at the present juncture. The primary thesis is clear: fugitivism as the first active response of the neophytes to the mission environment was of such wide scope as to constitute a mass reaction to certain elements in that environment.

Rebellion.—The second mode of response was active resistance. Customarily among the animals—apart from sex or food competition between individuals—physical combat is the last resort when flight or escape is prevented. It must be regarded as the extreme response, to be utilized when all else has failed, a response the appearance of which requires a stimulus of maximal intensity. The analogy of the animal can, of course, not be pressed too far, since the response of the animal is always with reference to other individuals. One cannot conceive of a wolf or a lion attempting to bite or claw a set of circumstances or a complex of environmental factors as he would a tangible enemy of his own or some other species. Nevertheless, there are points of similarity. The human being would not attempt to take physical action against a political or economic system, but he might do so against a person whom he regarded as being responsible for that system. Furthermore, a group of human beings, unable to flee from such an environment, might pool their individual responses and organize a joint effort against the system through resistance to those persons or groups who were regarded as upholding it. Active resistance or rebellion therefore becomes a group response rather than one in which individual units are concerned. It is naturally not essential that the entire population be involved, although in extreme examples it may be. What is necessary is that the stimulus become sufficiently intense to pass the threshold of reaction of several individuals simultaneously, so that the response of all occurs at the same time. If the stimulus—be it of whatever nature, physical, economic, social, or moral—arises suddenly and with great force, the response will be equally quick and strong. But if the stimulus, as represented in the general environment, is relatively constant and perhaps at a low level of intensity over long intervals of time, there will be no large-scale group response. The response will then take the milder form of attempted flight rather than resistance. Occasionally, however, and apparently almost at random in the statistical sense, the threshold of reaction will be passed simultaneously in a number of persons, and, if the number is great enough, there will be a sudden and seemingly inexplicable local outburst of active physical rebellion. Thus we may explain the periodic uprisings which disturbed the even tenor of mission days. For rebellion was not a continuous performance, as was apostasy, but appeared now and then, on a few occasions when the cumulative influence of mission environment reached a point where some small group of neophytes could no longer find release in flight and could no longer restrain the antipathy which they felt toward the mission routine.[4]

Many of the so-called uprisings or rebellions noted by the missionaries or subsequent historians were little more than personal quarrels or family feuds, such as might arise in any community. Frequently they spent their force in a single homicide or other act of violence. Several cases of attacks on priests are on record, of which the most noteworthy was the murder of Father Quintana at Santa Cruz. But these cannot be regarded as revolts, fundamentally, against the system. Frequently also small struggles took place between mission Indians and adjacent heathen or between heathen and the Spanish, in which certain neophytes participated. These likewise must be left out of consideration. It should be noted, however, that, whenever a strictly internal uprising did occur, the tendency of the rebels was to enlist the sympathy and material support of any available gentiles. This was clearly true in the first noteworthy insurrection, in 1775 at San Diego.[5] This affair is significant in numerous respects. In addition to its extent—for several hundred Indians were concerned and the material damage inflicted was great—its effect on the Spanish was profound, so that it colored their entire Indian policy in subsequent years. Al-

---

[4] It should be emphasized that no moral or ethical connotations are here intended. The mission Indians for present purposes are to be considered in the light of organisms only, and their behavior is to be investigated by the same methods as would be employed with an entirely nonrational species of animal. Whether missionization was good or bad for them, or whether civilization for them was desirable on spiritual or cultural grounds, is completely aside from the question.

[5] For details concerning this famous revolt any of the standard works may be consulted (e.g., Bancroft, Hittell, Englehardt). For contemporary records Palóu, *New California*, 4:37–38, may be mentioned, as well as Ortega, "Account of Insurrection," Nov. 30, 1775, St. Pap. Ben. Mil., 1:1, Carrillo, "Evidence taken," 1776, Prov. St. Pap., 1:221 ff., and Rivera y Moncada, "Statements," June 18, 1776, St. Pap. Ben. Mil., 1:22.

though it occurred only six years after the arrival of the first expedition of Portolá and Serra and the founding of the mission, it was a distinct reaction to missionization on the part of converts. The latter at the time had not been aggregated into the mission establishment proper but, owing to lack of accommodations, were permitted to remain in their own villages. The full force of the mission environment had therefore by no means affected them. Nevertheless eight Christian villages participated, as well as an indeterminate number of heathen villages. As a matter of fact, aside from having gone through the formal process of religious conversion, the Christians differed in no essential respect from the heathen. The reasons offered for their action were very simple but illuminating. According to the testimony recorded by Rivera y Moncada the neophytes revolted because the fathers baptized them, and they wanted to kill the fathers and soldiers "in order to live as they did before."

The rapidity and intensity of this San Diego response designates these Yuman Indians as being endowed not only with considerable energy and drive, but also with unusual perspicacity in recognizing the hidden dangers of missionization, racially speaking, even before they had acquired any degree of practical experience with it. Indeed this tribe was always troublesome. In direct nonconformity with conventional mission policy the administration was compelled indefinitely to allow them to a very marked extent to live in their own villages. They were never tractable as laborers. Beyond the distance of one day's march they remained unconquered and predominantly unconverted through mission history, and after 1834 they caused enormous trouble by repeated attacks on white settlements.

In 1785 an attempt was made to murder the missionaries at San Gabriel,[6] and the following year there was an abortive conspiracy at San Diego.[7] Trouble broke out in 1794 at San Luis Obispo which was termed an "uprising" (*levantamiento*).[8] Further minor disturbances continued for several years, often in conjunction with the stock-raiding activities of the surrounding gentiles, but nothing of real significance

---

[6] Fages, Dec. 5, 1785, Prov. Rec., 2:131.
[7] Zuñiga to Fages, San Diego, August 15, 1786. Prov. St. Pap., 6:35.
[8] Arrillaga, 1794, *ibid.*, 12:187.

happened until the Purísima rebellion[9] in 1824. Early in March of this year the neophytes at Santa Ynéz, Purísima, and Santa Bárbara initiated a well-organized revolt. At Santa Ynéz and Purísima they took over the missions with some loss of life and much property damage. However, troops were immediately dispatched, and the insurrection was crushed after a brisk battle in which the Indians incurred numerous casualties. The survivors, to the number of hundreds, fled in a body to the valley and were recovered with the greatest difficulty. This is the only instance where the converted Indians, north of Los Angeles, organized and carried out a really serious rebellion. Although the proximate reasons advanced by the culprits were inadequate and even fantastic, there is no doubt that the ultimate cause lay in years of dissatisfaction and discontent, which increased steadily and finally exploded in open warfare.

To summarize, there were no more than two really important examples of active physical resistance by the Indians, and in both these the outcome was complete failure. In this respect, the contrast is indeed significant between the aborigines of California and those of the Southwest, like the Yuma and Apache.

Contemporary opinion.—That the neophytes were not all completely happy and contented in their new environment was entirely obvious to those who lived with them and watched over them.[10] Indeed the failure of the converts to appreciate the efforts made on their behalf

[9] The documentary material concerning this affair is voluminous. The political and ecclesiastical background as well as the military events have been adequately treated by Bancroft and other historians.

[10] Exceptions to this statement are to be found in the early reports of missionaries during the first years of conversion. Since the original neophytes came in on a voluntary basis, and since the routine of the mission had not yet been established in full force, there probably was a higher degree of contentment in the early years than afterward. It must be remembered also that the first accounts of mission work are likely to be optimistic and enthusiastic.

Some individuals in later years made similar statements. The following excerpt from Benjamin Morrow (*A Narrative of Four Voyages* [1832], p. 212) shows to what absurd extremes some persons could go, for there is no single phrase or expression in the quotation which is not essentially false: "These converted Indians have a very smart, active, friendly, and good-natured demeanor. Their features are handsome and well proportioned; their countenances are cheerful and interesting; and they are generally a very industrious, ingenious and cleanly people. The sins of lying and stealing are held by them in the utmost abhorrence, and they look upon them as two of the most heinous crimes of which a man can be guilty, murder alone excepted."

was a continual source of perplexity and sadness to the missionaries. Likewise, the soldiers and civilians, long after the missions had disappeared, could not understand why the natives failed to adopt their new mode of life with enthusiasm and to thrive under it. The problem also drew comment from strangers who chanced to visit the territory as explorers or traders. Finally, the Indians themselves on a few occasions expressed their own ideas. It is of interest to set forth some of these comments and opinions, not because they throw much light on the underlying factors, but because they constitute an excellent example of the operation of the human mind when confronted with a problem in human behavior or biology and of the doubtful value of personal testimony relating to a rather abstract proposition. With respect, then, to the question: Why did the Indians seek escape from mission life, the following answers may be cited as illustrative of contemporary thought.

1. Opinion of White Men.

Notwithstanding all this, an irresistible desire for freedom sometimes breaks out in individuals. This may probably be referred to the national character. Their attachment to a wandering life, their love of alternate exercise in fishing and hunting and entire indolence, seem in their eyes to overbalance all the advantages they enjoy at the mission, which to us appear very great.[11]

. . . after they [the Indians] became acquainted with the nature of the institution and felt themselves under restraint, many absconded. Even now, notwithstanding the difficulty of escaping, desertions are of frequent occurrence, owing probably, in some cases, to the fear of punishment—in others to the deserters having been originally inveigled into the mission by the converted Indians or neophytes . . . in other cases again to the fickleness of their own disposition.[12]

Parmi les Indiens, dont la plus grande partie paraissent si soumis, il y en a qui connaissent tout le prix de la liberté, et qui cherchent à se la procurer par la fuite. Ils réussissent facilement a s'évader, mais ils sont souvent repris ... et, sans considérer que ces hommes n'ont fait qu'user du

---

[11] G. H. von Langsdorff, *Voyages and Travels in Various Parts of the World,* translation by T. C. Russell (1927), pt. 2, p. 171.
[12] F. W. Beechey, *Narrative of a Voyage to the Pacific and Bering's Strait* (London, 1831), 2:170–171.

droit le plus naturel, ils sont ordinairement traités en criminels et mis en fers impitoyablement.[13]

And if they alleged, as proof of cruelty, the number of Indians who have fled . . . I had the satisfaction of replying that they were already coming back and that they assured me that none had gone for fear of work, nor of punishment, but because of fear of the disease, contagious and mortal, which was actually prevalent in the mission at the time; also on account of their natural preference for the wilderness.[14]

Let the more intelligent Indians be asked why they run away and they will reply: "The same things happen to us as to every son of Adam. Naturally we want our liberty and want to go to hunt for women . . ."[15]

The neophytes during their period of probation see mission life as it is. They are not compelled to stay but most wish to do so and become baptized. Thereafter, however, they are prone to run away for no other reason than "innate fickleness."[16]

. . . they go astray for no other reason than that they are Indians.[17]

2. Indian Opinion.

[A certain Indian of San Antonio ran away] because he wanted to live away from the mission. He did not get a bit of land to farm and also he could not stand the oppression under which they live, and the many floggings they are given.[18]

[Many Indians have run away saying they are now a] free nation. They cry with one voice: We are free and will not obey or work.[19]

[Some Indians came to San Carlos saying that many were running away from San Francisco Solano] because the Indians do not like Father Altimira.[20]

The following items constitute the testimony of certain Indians who escaped but were caught. On their return each was asked to state why

---

[13] Auguste Bernard du Hautcilly, *Voyage autour du Monde* (Paris, 1835), 2:5. Most Frenchmen who visited California were unfavorably impressed by the aspects of compulsion characteristic of the mission system.

[14] F. de Lasuén, "Representación," San Carlos, Nov. 12, 1800, Sta. Bárb. Arch., 2:206.

[15] R. Abella to Solá, San Francisco, Jan. 29, 1817, Archb. Arch. 3(1):125.

[16] Paraphrase of statement of E. Tapis to Arrillaga, Santa Bárbara, Mar. 1, 1805, Sta. Bárb. Arch., 6:28.

[17] J. Cabot to De la Guerra, San Miguel, Mar. 6, 1818, De la Guerra Docs., 7:89.

[18] Echeandía to alcalde of Monterey, Monterey, Jan. 17, 1831, Dept. Rec., 9:81.

[19] Portilla to Figueroa, San Luis Rey, Dec. 20, 1834, St. Pap. Mis., 9:49.

[20] Sarría to Argüello, San Carlos, Oct. 18, 1823, Archb. Arch., 4(2):86.

he absconded. The arabic numerals below indicate the individual reasons given:

1. He had been flogged for leaving without permission.
2. The same reason.
3. The same reason. Also, he ran away because he was hungry.
4. He had been put in jail for getting drunk.
5. He had run away previously and had been flogged three times.
6. He was hungry. He absconded previously and, when he returned voluntarily, he was given twenty-five lashes.[21]
7. He was frightened at seeing how his friends were always being flogged.
8. Because . . . of the great hunger he felt.[22]
9. When he wept over the death of his wife and children, he was ordered whipped five times by Father Antonio Danti.
10. He became sick.
11. His wife and one son died.
12. Because of hunger; also, he was put in the stocks while sick.
13. He wanted to go back to his country.
14. His wife, one son, and two brothers died.
15. His wife and a son had run away to their country, and at the mission he was beaten a great deal.
16. Because of a blow with a club.
17. They beat him when he wept for a dead brother.
18. He went to see his mother.
19. His mother, two brothers, and three nephews died, all of hunger, and he ran away so that he would not also die.
20. Lorenzo went away.
21. His father died.
22. Being bad, they whipped him.
23. His wife sinned with a rancher, and the priest beat him for not taking care of her.
24. They made him work all day without giving him or his family anything to eat. Then, when he went out one day to find food, Father Danti flogged him.
25. His wife and two sons died, and he had no one to look after.
26. His little niece died of hunger.
27. He was very hungry.

---

[21] Nos. 1–6 inclusive are from a letter by Gutiérrez at Monterey, March 7, 1836, Prov. St. Pap. Ben. Mil., 81:44. Note that these incidents occurred after secularization when the mission (San Antonio) was in charge of an administrator.

[22] Nos. 7–8 from a *relación* by Argüello *et al.*, San Francisco, Aug. 9, 1797, Prov. St. Pap., 16:71. These Indians were new converts and ran away in a body shortly after conversion. They also participated in armed resistance to parties sent out to bring them back.

28. After going one day to the presidio to find food, when he returned, Father Danti refused him his ration, saying to go to the hills and eat hay.

29. When his son was sick, they would give the boy no food, and he died of hunger.

30. Twice, when he went out to hunt food or to fish, Father Danti had him whipped.[23]

Much of the above-cited Indian testimony will obviously be heavily discounted. Several of the accusations are absurd, and many of the reasons advanced are trivial and irrational. Yet they ring true to the primitive psychology of the Indian, as most persons who have had dealings with this and similar races will admit, and they merit at least a fair examination.

If we examine the opinions expressed by competent white observers, we find that they exhibit a uniform trend. They all ascribe Indian aversion to mission life to love of liberty, distaste for their surroundings, longing for their native home, or revolt against all forms of restraint or compulsion. In other words, the white man, thinking of the Indians as a group, conceives their responses in terms of pure abstractions. These abstractions are those in which his own thoughts are likely to be cast. In the early nineteenth century the rights of man and human liberty were dominant among politico-social ideas. Hence the emphasis laid on them by the white commentators.

The Indian neophyte, on the other hand, possessed no such philosophical background nor such a ready-made system of concepts to which he might refer his condition and his actions. The new convert had no comprehension of liberty as opposed to servitude or slavery because he had known only one type of social status and had no basis for comparison with anything else. Furthermore, aside from small family or tribal affairs he had never encountered a situation which demanded expression in terms of abstract social concepts. Consequently, when called upon to give an account of his reasons for a specific line of conduct, he was totally unable to go beyond the concrete events of daily life. We must, therefore, regard Indian testimony as rationalization of underlying discontent in terms of sharp personal experience with definite environmental factors. Viewed in this light,

---

[23] Nos. 9–30 were with the same group as Nos. 7–8. Argüello, "Relación," San Francisco, Aug. 12, 1797, *ibid.*, p. 74.

Indian testimony makes sense. Moreover, it is no longer incompatible with the testimony of the white man. Both groups approach the same solution of the problem, but they approach it by different pathways and in different modes of expression. Where the Frenchman or the American assigns love of liberty as the cause for flight or resistance, the Indian says he ran away because he was put in jail. Where the white man talks about slavery, the Indian says he objected to being made to work by some individual, for instance, some particular father in the mission.

From the statements given here and many more which might be adduced certain factors emerge as possessing definite weight in the mission environment. The most important, and yet by far the most difficult to assess, is that called loss of liberty, by which is meant the restriction of the Indians' freedom of action, particularly with respect to the freedom they had previously enjoyed. Under the missions they were under no greater physical restraint or social compulsion than many civilized groups today; yet with their background the loss of personal license was a severe blow. Perhaps the best analogy is not that of slavery, which implies rigorous physical exactions, but captivity.

Since it is not feasible to attempt analysis of the whole general concept of what we might call captivity, it is necessary to limit discussion to those more material aspects which can be treated from an objective, or at least semiobjective, point of view. The environmental factors concerned which are sufficiently concrete to warrant discussion here relate to such tangible aspects of mission life as aggregation or crowding, bodily confinement in restricted areas, reaction to the type of food furnished, forced labor, delinquency and its punishment, restricted sex relations, and certain cultural factors such as religious beliefs and language. To put these factors in terms of liberty or freedom, they relate to restriction of freedom in space, restriction in diet, restriction in type of physical activity, restriction of sex relations, and restriction of social and intellectual expression. Be it remembered that the word "restriction" as here used does not necessarily imply a reduction or diminution in the scope of any of these categories but rather implies their redirection in new and unaccustomed channels.

Responses Based on Spatial Restrictions

The initial act of contact between the mission organization and the Indian was one involving spatial relationships. The process of conversion itself took the native from one region, the ancient environment, and placed him in another. Thenceforward he was restricted rigidly to the latter. Now his reaction to the new environment, his entire frame of mind concerning it, would necessarily be modified by the manner in which he was brought into the fold. If he came gladly and willingly, then he would be predisposed in its favor. If he were driven to conversion against his desires, then he would be prone thereafter to dislike or hate the system under which he was obliged to live. Compulsory migration, or in the term of the times "forced conversion," becomes the initial factor of restrictions imposed in space.

Resistance to compulsory conversion.—At the outset it must be stated unequivocally that neither the plans of the Franciscan hierarchy nor those of the political government of New Spain contemplated conversion of the heathen on any other than a voluntary basis. Hence it is not at all surprising that the theory endorsed by Serra, Palóu, Lasuén, and the other early missionaries and the routine actually practiced by them employed no other means of conversion. Any pressure was restricted to legitimate moral suasion, spiritual arguments, and social or economic inducements extended without recourse to threats or physical compulsion.

The method of kindliness and persuasion sufficed to bring in large numbers of heathen during the first twenty years of the missions. In 1787 Captain Goycoechea of Santa Bárbara, a bitter enemy of the missions, was able to say, ". . . we still do not solicit heathen, only receive those who voluntarily offer themselves for baptism."[24] The motives which prompted these voluntary conversions were undoubtedly various. In the light of centuries of experience the missionaries very skillfully played upon every conceivable natural desire. They emphasized the externals of their religion—the ceremony, the music, the processions. They also sought to make mission life as attractive as possible by holding out the inducements of clothing, shelter, and food. Accord-

[24] Goycoechea to Fages, Santa Bárbara, June 27, 1787, *ibid.*, 7:58.

ing to any moral or ethical standards, these methods were entirely proper and laudable.[25] However, inevitably, after the adjacent natives had been assimilated in their entirety and it became imperative to broaden the field of conversion, mild methods gradually became inadequate. Instead of waiting for the heathen to come in (Serra was obliged to wait months for his first converts at San Diego), the fathers began to go out after them. These expeditions took the form, in the beginning, of peaceful little trips to neighboring villages, where perhaps the local chieftains could be persuaded to undergo baptism. Frequently neophytes were sent out to proselyte among the heathen brethren; occasionally soldiers were employed for the same purpose. Obviously, troubles arose; some gentiles were recalcitrant, some were even hostile. This in turn called for stronger methods. Mild, sober exposition of the beauties of Christianity and the charms of mission life no longer sufficed. Meanwhile the grim threat of the military had long been in the background. It was entirely natural that the missionaries, when simple persuasion began to lose its power, should turn to the soldiers for support. The latter, jealous of the missions and seeking to advance the political power of the state, were only too willing to cooperate. The entrance of the military into the active field of proselyting ended the era of true voluntary conversion. The terms *conquista* and *reducción* lost completely their original spiritual connotation and came to signify little more than the subjugation of the natives in the strictly material sense.

The shift in practice and its accompanying alteration in policy occurred during the decade 1790–1800, principally under Governor Borica. As early as 1787 Governor Fages reported:[26]

We find that the gentiles who are gathered in these missions are regularly those which inhabit their vicinity and that on passing six or seven

[25] The opinion of the laity was that the mundane inducements were more potent than the spiritual. Thus Beechey, who was generally quite fair in his estimates, says (*op. cit.*, 2:23), "When these establishments were first founded, the Indians flocked to them in great numbers for the clothing with which the neophytes were supplied. . . ."

Jesús J. Vallejo, a violent partisan of the missions, states ("Reminiscencias," p. 27): "I am of the opinion that most of the Indians abandoned their savage life animated more by the desire to improve their social condition than impelled by religious sentiments. . . ."

[26] "Report on the Missions," 1787, St. Pap. Mis. Col., 1:150.

leagues distance from their native heath they either will not be baptized or will not remain long in the mission.

He went on to say that it was impossible to reach these natives because of the labor involved in getting them and recovering them when they ran away.

In 1794 the governor was memorialized by the missionaries of San Francisco.[27] They wished permission to hunt new mission sites north of the Bay and reported that neophytes had been sent by boat to the Bay islands, "para que conquistaran Gentiles." Subsequently the governor refused such requests, commenting as follows:[28]

The zeal of the Religious for the salvation of souls stimulates them to attract to our religion by all methods the unhappy heathen who live in darkness and so they use whatever means they judge appropriate although some of these methods are fruitless. There is no doubt in view of what has just happened to the Christian Indians whom they sent by sea to catechize [heathen] that in the future they should abstain from such conquests and impressments.

The following year the governor wrote that guards would be furnished missionaries to confess or baptize Indians who could not get to the mission but "never to capture fugitives or above all gentiles."[29] Again in 1798 orders were issued to the effect that gentiles must be handled carefully and not be brought by force to the mission.[30]

It is clear from the tenor of the official correspondence, as well as from much other evidence, that the missionaries near San Francisco were recruiting heavily by means of private parties and expeditions from the Costanoans and the Coast Miwok. The great increase in baptisms shown in the San Francisco baptism records at about this time substantiates such a presumption. Several hundred were baptized, so many, in fact, and from such a distance, that purely voluntary conversion could not be assumed even if we did not possess voluminous evidence of definite physical resistance on the part of the gentiles.[31]

[27] Fernández to Borica, San Francisco, Nov. 30, 1794, Prov. St. Pap., 12:28.

[28] Borica, Monterey, Dec. 3, 1795, Prov. Rec., 5:31.

[29] Borica to the *comandante* at San Francisco, Monterey, June 9, 1796, *ibid.*, p. 86.

[30] Argüello to Borica, San Francisco, Mar. 30, 1798, Prov. St. Pap., 17:97.

[31] As an example, the "Raimundo affair" of 1797 may be mentioned. Raimundo was a mission Indian who went out with a party of neophytes in search of fugitives and new converts. The party was cut to pieces in the East Bay region by gentiles.

By 1810 extensive expeditions in search of fugitives were established policy. At the same time many prisoners were taken and brought back to the missions. Often some of these were criminals and raiders and were treated as prisoners of war. Others were innocent of wrongdoing but were caught in the general net. Frequently they were released, but the temptation was strong to baptize them and retain them as neophytes. As time went on, the friction between wild Indians and whites increased, until toward the end of the mission period all pretense of voluntary conversion was discarded and expeditions to the interior were frankly for the purpose of military subjugation and forced conversion. It is not feasible to cite specifically all available data bearing on this matter. The following samples of events and opinions should suffice to establish the general validity of the contention that large numbers of gentiles, subsequent to 1800, were converted by coercion.[32]

1805. Luis Peralta went on a punitive expedition from Santa Clara.[33] After he had caught up with the Indians the latter began to fight. He fired on them and killed "five of the bums (*gandules*)." The survivors fled to the brush, where he attacked again and killed five more. The Spanish then "beat the bush" and captured "twenty-five head (*piezas*)," all women. The prisoners were then brought to Santa Clara for conversion.

1806. After a rumored conspiracy at Santa Clara, Gervasio Argüello went out to catch the culprits. He brought back forty-two Christians and forty-seven gentiles.[34]

1806. The governor's instructions to presidial commanders contained the statement concerning the Indians: "By frequent expeditions on

[32] Much detail will be found in the works of H. H. Bancroft and Father Zephyrin Englehardt (*Missions and Missionaries*). The former inclines to be unsympathetic with the missionaries; the latter is a strong proponent of the mission system. Although he does not deny the facts, Englehardt seeks to justify the activities of the fathers on the ground that their intentions and motives were above reproach but that their policy of conciliation was nullified by a hostile and often brutal military element. It must be admitted that he presents a strong case for the clergy.

[33] Peralta, "Diario," 1805, Prov. St. Pap., 19:33. The contemptuous tone which characterizes his references to the Indians is very typical of the soldiers and civilians subsequent to 1800.

[34] Arrillaga to *comandante* of San Francisco, Monterey, July 17, 1806, Prov. Rec., 12:266.

the part of the Commanders we might be able to achieve their total conquest or reduction."[35]

1816. Father L. A. Martínez made an expedition to the tulares. Although the "fruit of his expedition" was only five persons, the incident called forth comment by the prefect, Father Sarría, who protested vigorously forced conversions made with the aid of troopers.[36]

1819. Father Amoros reported that they had just baptized in San Rafael one hundred Indians from the region of Tamales, "the remnants who had survived the conquests of San Francisco Mission."[37]

1823. Amoros reported:[38] "It seems that the Guiluc nation is remaining quiet. The gentiles brought by Sergeant Herrera were baptized and are very contented." However, since the seventeen men from Livantolomi did not wish to come, he advised a small expedition to collect them.

1823. The following account represents what was probably an extreme example, but it is sufficiently graphic in detail to merit reproduction in full. This is contained in a personal letter from Father Altimira to the prefect.[39] He had uncovered excesses committed by a group of Indians from San José who had been permitted to go out hunting gentiles for conversion. The gentiles from the rancheria Lybaitos deposed as follows:

Several days ago there came here an Indian from San José called Ildefonso with many mission Indians armed with bows, spears, and 2 guns, saying that they had come to hunt fugitives. They went to Ululatos and the Indian Ildefonso told them that they must come to San José and be made Chrisians, that Farther Narciso [Durán] was summoning them, and if they did not respond, the Father from San Francisco would come to get them, and they would suffer much because they would be severely chastised. The Ululatos, Christians and gentiles, resisted, saying they did not want to, whereupon they [the San José Indians] held them [the Ululatos] up, robbed them, and beat them. We [the Lybaitos] being afraid, ran away and escaped. They then went to the rancheria of the Chemo-

[35] Arrillaga, San Diego, Dec. 22, 1806, Prov. St. Pap., 19:109.

[36] Martínez to Solá, San Luis Obispo, May 30, 1816, Archb. Arch., 3(1):33, and Sarría to Solá, *ibid.*, p. 119.

[37] Amoros to Solá, San Rafael, Sept. 26, 1819, *ibid.*, 3(2):111.

[38] Amoros to Argüello, San Rafael, April 10, 1823, *ibid.*, 4(2):84.

[39] Altimira to Señan, San Francisco, July 10, 1823, *ibid.*, p. 21.

coytos, fought, killed five men, and wounded one other. Afterward they went to another rancheria, called Sucuntos, and killed all the people[*sic*]. They carried off many gentiles by force and shipped them away. They went to another rancheria on an island called Ompimes, and then we saw no more of them. They were here three days and nights. Your Christians, Ululatos, Suisunes, and the gentiles unbound each other and set out for the Tulares, for which reason they are here. All of us are fatigued and dispersed.

Altimira then protested strongly against such measures and exhorted the prefect to correct the situation. He mentioned Father Amoros and, referring to Father Durán, said:

It is already an old scandal the way he operates in this matter. A thousand times I have heard mentioned his outrageous and arbitrary sorties, in which he goes out, or sends a large body of neophytes.

The following opinions of contemporary observers are significant and representative.

Ein Soldat ging noch weiter und beschwerte sich gegen uns dass der Komandant ihnen nicht erlauben wollte, sich dort drüben Menschen einzufangen um sie, wie in den Missionen, für sich arbeiten zu lassen.[40]

Empero esto se salvará con conoser que California tiene incalculable numero de Indos selvaticos y estos cubrian las bajas y aun aumentaban el numero anual de cada mision porque con frequencia ó se prestaban voluntariamente a recibir el bautismo y quedaban en la mision ó se hasian espediciones militares en las cuales se conducian porcion de Indios que se obligaban a ser Cristianos y a quedar agregados por total a las comunidades establecias.[41]

The Indians were captured by the military who went into the interior in pursuit of them, detachments of soldiers being frequently sent out from the Presidio and other military posts in the Department on these expeditions to bring the wild Indians into the missions to be civilized and converted to Christianity. Sometimes two or three hundred would be brought in at a time, men, women, and children. They were immediately turned over to the padres at the different missions.[42]

The Indians who were brought into the fold of the missions were either induced through persuasion, by force, or enticed by presents.[43]

---

[40] Adelbert Chamisso, "Diary, 1816," in A. C. Mahr, *The Visit of the Rurik* (1932), p. 34.

[41] Juan Bandini, "Apuntos para la historia de la Alta California," MS, 1847, p. 100.

[42] William H. Davis, "Glimpses of the Past," MS, 1878, p. 6.

[43] Charles Wilkes, *Narrative of the United States Exploring Expedition* (1844), V:183.

Referring to parties of neophytes who were permitted to spend vacations in their home territory, Beechey says:[44]

On these occasions the padres desire them to induce as many of their un-converted brethren as possible to accompany them back to the mission, of course implying that this is to be done only by persuasion; but the boat being furnished with a cannon and musketry, and in every respect equipped for war, it too often happens that the neophytes and the *gente de razón,* who superintend the direction of the boat, avail themselves of their su-periority, with the desire of ingratiating themselves with their masters, and of receiving a reward. There are, besides, repeated acts of aggression which it is necessary to punish, all of which furnish proselytes. Women and children are generally the first objects of capture, as their husbands and parents sometimes voluntarily follow them into captivity [p. 23].

The expenses of the late expedition fell heavy upon the mission, and I was glad to find that the padre thought it was paying very dear for so few converts, as in all probability it will lessen his desire to undertake another expedition; and the poor Indians will be spared the horrors of being butchered by their own countrymen, or dragged from their homes into perpetual captivity [p. 31].

As for the various methods employed for the purpose of bringing prose-lytes to the mission, there are several reports, of which some were not very creditable to the institution: nevertheless, on the whole I am of opinion that the priests are innocent, from a conviction that they are ignorant of the means employed by those who are under them [p. 17].

From the above-cited evidence and from much more which might be adduced, it appears incontrovertible that mission policy under the pressure of various uncontrollable circumstances, underwent a pro-found change whereby conversion, instead of being entirely volun-tary, was, with a few exceptions, a compulsory procedure. As suggested before, this forced translocation of large numbers of Indians could not fail to engender in many of them a conscious antipathy to their new environment, an antipathy which found an outlet in apostasy, fugitivism, and physical resistance. Particularly is this true of the con-verts made during the second half of the mission period. Not only were the newly baptized gentiles affected by this factor, but the "old Christians" as well. The latter, who had been born in the missions or who had been voluntarily converted years previously, were inevitably impressed by the treatment afforded other members of their race.

---

[44] F. W. Beechey, *op. cit.,* Vol. 2.

This must have been true despite the fact that the neophytes themselves were often the actual agents of coercion. Great masses of sullen, discontented newcomers, introduced against their will, were certain to modify the entire mission atmosphere and to contaminate with the virus of their hatred many racial brethren who otherwise would have been at least partially satisfied with their lot.

Homesickness.—We may now turn to another aspect of what has been designated restriction in space, an aspect which is very closely related to and associated with the factor of forced conversion and which, for lack of a more precise term, may be called "homesickness."

Homesickness was one of the most subtle and elusive of the imponderables in the Indian–mission complex, and yet perhaps one of the most universal. The word is used here in its broadest sense: the nostalgic urge which drives a human being toward some place, group of persons, or mode of life with which he has been familiar—an urge which, unsatisfied, gives rise to profound mental and physical disturbances. It is not necessary to assume that this feeling was at all times acute. Indeed, it may well have been absent in many neophytes, particularly those born in or brought at an early age to the missions. In many others the memories of early days and old friends or places doubtless grew dim and indistinct with the passage of time, until the longing fell below the level of the conscious and was revived only occasionally in connection with some incident or word which called up half-forgotten associations.

The evidence for the existence of widespread homesickness is presumptive rather than explicit, intuitive rather than objective. There is very little in the written documents covering the matter; the missionaries and soldiers were by no means psychoanalysts and, furthermore, had relatively little interest in the private emotions of the Indians. There are, to be sure, numerous scattered remarks by the clergymen with reference to the eagerness and desire of the neophytes to get out into the country again, away from the mission, but as a rule they did not specifically emphasize the factor of nostalgia. However, there are a few reports having a direct bearing on the problem which may be cited as illustrations.

In the autumn of 1823 numerous neophytes were moved from San

Francisco and San Rafael to fill up the new mission at Solano. There was a good deal of difficulty in persuading some of these to go, particularly those who originated on "the coast of Bodega" and other places in Marin County.[45] At the same time there was an agreement that certain neophytes at San José who did want to go might do so "because they are natives of the region around the new mission."[46] It is very clear that members of each tribe wished to be situated as close as possible to the ancestral home.

An interesting point is raised by W. H. Davis concerning the Indians who were Christianized in the later mission years:[47]

Sometimes two or three hundred would be brought in at a time, men, women, and children . . . After they had become adapted to their new condition, their influence on the new arrivals of Indians brought in was very marked, and they yielded much more readily to the civilizing influences exerted upon them than those first captured.

Evidently the presence of old friends and acquaintances or of any fellow tribesmen made life much more bearable under the strange new conditions.

Lasuén relates the following anecdote as characterizing the Indian temperament. After describing how the neophytes continually begged leave to hunt and fish because they were hungry, he goes on:[48]

On one of these occasions to some of those greedy people who requested permission to go to the woods I answered with certain annoyance: "Well, you make me realize now that, although you were given a steer, a mutton, and a fanega of grain every day, you would, despite all this, long for your woods and your shores." Then the keenest-witted Indian of those who had heard me replied, somewhat shamefacedly, "It is so Father, as you say, it is so."

Finally, the following graphic, although probably overdrawn, description by Katzebue may be quoted:[49]

---

[45] Sarría to Argüello, San Juan Bautista and San Carlos, Sept. 5 and 12, 1823, Archb. Arch., 4(2):56, 70.

[46] Altimira to Argüello, San Francisco, Oct. 4, 1823, *ibid.,* p. 25.

[47] W. H. Davis, "Glimpses of the Past," p. 6.

[48] Lasuén, "Representación," San Carlos, Nov. 12, 1800, Sta. Bárb. Arch., 2:174.

[49] Otto von Katzebue, in A. C. Mahr, *op. cit.,* p. 61. The reports of Chamisso and Choris, both of whom were with the Katzebue expedition, relate the same incident in almost the same words. Either the affair was one which made a great impression on all three travelers or else there was close collaboration in writing the three accounts.

Twice in the year they receive permission to return to their native homes. This short time is the happiest period of their existence; and I myself have seen them going home in crowds, with loud rejoicings. The sick, who can not undertake the journey, at least accompany their happy countrymen to the shore where they embark and there sit for days together mournfully gazing on the distant summits of the mountains which surround their homes; they often sit in this situation for several days, without taking any food, so much does the sight of their lost home affect these new Christians. Every time some of those who have the permission run away, and they would probably all do it, were they not deterred by their fears of the soldiers. . . .

Suggestive statements, hints, and inferences might be gleaned in much greater number from the documentary collections, but those given above may be accepted as adequate indication that homesickness existed among the mission Indians and may have been significant among the factors conducive to fugitivism.

Whatever the weight of this factor in the entire mission environment, it is certain to have operated less intensively among the earlier converts from territory adjacent to the missions than among those brought in later from distant regions. Each mission started with a group of neophytes who actually lived at or very near the mission site, and these subsequently continued to live literally in their home territory. Since the converts came from the same or closely related villages they all spoke the same language, had more or less the same cultural background, and understood each other thoroughly. As the radius of conversion lengthened with the years, however, people were brought in from a great distance. They came from different terrain, spoke a distinct language, and were thrown into a well-developed community of indifferent and possibly hostile strangers. Among such Indians the desire to return to their old country was vastly stronger than among those who had been raised almost on mission property itself. The missions around the Bay illustrate this principle quite clearly, particularly the mission of San Francisco. From 1770 to 1790 the converts were drawn exclusively from the peninsula, down as far as San Mateo. During these two decades fugitivism was not serious, because the Indians, if they did run away, went no farther than a few miles' or a few hours' travel from the mission. In the 'nineties the East Bay was overrun, and the Bolbones and Sacalanes, with other Costanoan tribelets, were carried wholesale to San Francisco. Precisely at this time escape in masses began. Repeatedly the apostates from this mission are specified as being Sacalanes or similar tribesmen, thus indicating that the foreigners from the *otra banda* were dissatisfied with existence as mission Christians. In the next decade, 1800–1810, large numbers of Valley and Delta Yokuts, Miwok, and Wintun, as well as Marin County Miwok, appeared at the San Francisco mission. These gave even more trouble and rendered the fugitive problem acute as long as the missions lasted. It cannot be maintained that simple yearning for the ancient habitat was the dominating reason for this augmentation of apostasy, but it must have been of some significance among the Yokuts, Wintun, and Miwok who were brought into the missions.

As indicated, the drive toward the escape-response became intensified (among all the neophytes) following the conversion of large numbers of distant gentiles. Now this intensification gave rise in turn to counterresponses on the part of the dominant white civilization which were of importance to both races. No longer was it possible to await with some confidence the return of neophytes who wandered off into the woods and the fields for a few days or who went over the hill to visit their gentile relatives and friends. No longer could a corporal with a few men go out in the morning and round up the forgetful ones before evening. It now became necessary, if the mission system was to be held intact and the proper discipline and morale were to be maintained, to send out large, elaborate, and expensive expeditions comprising scores of soldiers, who would penetrate far into the interior and conduct real campaigns. In other words, we have here the immediate cause of the great expeditions which began shortly after 1800 and lasted till 1845. The effect of these was threefold: (1) they recaptured many or most of the runaways; (2) they captured and brought back many new converts; (3) they antagonized the interior tribes and disrupted their whole natural existence. The results now became cumulative. The "forced" conversion of numerous new gentiles reintensified the powerful desire to escape already existing among those who had been "voluntarily" converted, and the further increase of apostasy induced more expeditions. Moreover, the rough treatment given the heathen decreased the possibility of their peaceful conversion and magnified their physical, or even military, resistance. This situation in turn carried with it a train of evils such as robbery, murder, and stock-raiding, which eventually became intolerable to whites and Indians alike; these evils, even if no other factors had intervened, would ultimately have spelled the doom of the entire mission regime. We see here, therefore, another example of that action and reaction which is so likely to characterize a racial or cultural contact: missionization → restriction in space (and many other causes) → flight or escape → pursuit, recapture and new conversion → intensification of the restriction → increased escape → more extensive and violent pursuit → . . . etc. Provided no other factors act to modify the chain of events, the final result is inevitably open warfare and the physical (not spiritual) conquest of one race by the other.

Revolt against overaggregation.—A third factor in the space-relation complex pertains to the population density or state of aggregation. It has been known for many years and recognized by naturalists as an established empirical fact that most animal species show favorable or adverse responses, either as individuals or groups or both, depending upon how many individual units are gathered together in a limited volume or area. The range of phenomena concerned is very wide, extending from a colony of bacteria or protozoa in a test tube to populations of large mammals. Naturally, the secondary factors involved—such as reproductive habits, available food, presence of predators or parasites, and so forth—are extremely variable, and the situation of one species is never exactly duplicated by that of another. In recent years the whole problem of space, density, and crowding with respect to individual and group welfare has been attacked from an experimental and quantitative standpoint. As a result, the importance of the purely spatial element has been established beyond question. One need mention in this connection no more than the work of Allee on goldfish and various invertebrates, Park on flour beetles, Gause on protozoa, Pearl on fruit flies, and Retzlaff on mice, to appreciate the extent of this trend of investigation.[50] Quite uniformly it has been proved that

---

[50] It is manifestly impossible to cite the entire literature in this field. Complete bibliographies will be found in the standard ecological texts and the monographs of Shelford, Chapman, and Elton. More specific references, as well as extended discussions of crowd-

for every population in any habitat whatever there is an optimum number of individuals. If the number is too great, the reproduction rate falls off and mortality from all sorts of causes increases. If the number is small, there tends to be an increase to the optimum.

Human beings are no exception to the general rule. Sociologists and historians can point to innumerable instances of overaggregation or overpopulation of a given restricted region, and our modern cities constitute a proving ground and laboratory for studies in human population density. In studying the responses of the California Indians we must therefore take cognizance of the shift in grouping which occurred during the process of missionization. In the aboriginal state, as has been repeatedly stressed by Kroeber and his colleagues, the coastal and valley Indians were spaced very exactly in conformity with the food supply. In regions of prolific sustenance the general density of population was high, whereas in barren areas it was low. Condensations of population were found along rivers, in coast lowlands, and in small fertile valleys. In the missions were likewise large aggregations within restricted territories. There was also satisfactory equilibrium with available food supply, since this could be adjusted through agriculture to any population level. The difference between the two habitats lay in density, not with reference to an extensive region or territory, but with reference to the numbers congregated for living purposes in a single small spot. In the native environment the actual number of individuals living in close physical contact was defined by the village or rancheria, and the latter was always strictly limited in extent. According to our present information, the village population never exceeded 200 (Channel Chumash), infrequently reached 100–150 (Valley Yokuts), and as a rule was below 100. Among many tribes not more than 30–50 constituted the habitat unit, a value which might decrease to the limits of one or two families. Wherever, for reasons of concentrated food resources, a large population could be supported, the whole aggregate exhibited a decided centripetal tend-

ing and aggregation, are given by W. C. Allee in his works: *Animal Aggregations, a Study in General Sociology* (Chicago, 1931); "Recent Studies in Mass Physiology," *Biological Reviews,* 9 (1934):1–48; and *The Social Life of Animals* (Chicago, 1938). Finally, all papers of consequence which have appeared since 1920–1925 have been abstracted in *Biological Abstracts* and *Berichte über die wissenschaftliche Biologie.*

ency, that is, it broke up into groups of uniform small dimensions, all of which might be close together, while each kept its territorial and social integrity. Indeed, this trend toward disaggregation, toward establishment of numerous units of 100 or less individuals, was a fundamental trait of the primitive social structure and must have represented a powerful species urge.

The tendency in the missions was in the opposite direction, toward forcing the Indians into larger and larger aggregates. As compared with the normal group of 30–100, the mission population averaged 500–600 and frequently was much greater. Aggregates of over 1,000 were common and occasionally a population of 2,000 and more was reached. This centrifugal mission trend naturally conflicted violently with the innate Indian centripetal preference, generating controversy, not only between missionaries and neophytes, but between two schools of Spanish opinion. The issue was not drawn, to be sure, in modern biological terms. The converts simply expressed repeatedly a desire to "live in their rancherias," in which matter they were supported by certain civilians and ecclesiastics. But the weight of missionary authority was against it.

The arguments against leaving the Indians scattered in their native homes after baptism were numerous and, from the standpoint of the missionary, unquestionably cogent. They were well summarized by Lasuén in 1802 and are worth repeating here. Lasuén pointed out:[51]

1. Wherever tried, the method had not worked. He cited the Colorado River disaster of 1783, although it might be answered that the causes of that fiasco were to be found elsewhere. He also pointed to the bad conditions in San Diego and the Dominican missions of Lower California. However, in this instance the missionaries really had little choice in the matter, for the Yumans of the regions flatly refused to come into the missions and nothing effective could be done to compel them.

2. The neophytes would revert to their original barbarous customs, which was undoubtedly true.

3. The neophytes would forget their catechisms and tend to apostacize from the Christian religion. This was also quite true and is a

---

[51] Lasuén to the guardian, Santa Clara, June 16, 1802, Prov. St. Pap., 18:269.

rather sad commentary upon the depth and sincerity of the process of conversion.

4. All the Christians now under the direct supervision of the missions would run away to the rancherias again and this would mean tremendous religious and economic loss. As a matter of fact, Lasuén might well have stated in so many words that it would have disrupted, in the material sense, the entire mission system. This argument is in itself a powerful bit of evidence of the existence of a centripetal drive on the part of the Indian communities which had to be counteracted in order to hold the missions together.

5. It would be necessary to baptize each rancheria *in toto,* for the existence side by side of gentiles and new converts would breed much friction and trouble.

We find thus a direct collision between two forces, each characteristic of, and inherent in, its own type of civilization: the disintegrative predisposition of the Indian culture and the integrative or fusing tendency of the white mission-military culture. The two are mutually exclusive; no compromise is possible. The weaker culture or race must give way and surrender to the stronger, to the probable detriment of the former.

The effects of this involuntary condensation of population were no doubt manifold. There must have been a general mental or psychological factor operative, which found expression in attempts of individuals to get away from the central aggregation or perhaps in a mass resistance to centralizing measures. However, we have no way of assessing or evaluating the extent and quality of such a factor. As a more concrete effect, the increased susceptibility to epidemics has already been mentioned, for it is obvious that the chances of spread of infections were enormously enhanced by bringing so many persons into close physical relationship. In much the same way the spread of ideas was facilitated. Purely by the laws of probability, if there is a group of 10x persons in a single physical aggregate, the chance of random contact between individuals is greater than if the same number of persons occur in 10 groups of x units each. Thus the condensation of population increases the possibility that an idea, say of escape, will travel through the whole population or that a conspiracy to revolt or to take some other joint action may be brought to fruition. There might well have been also an intensification of day-to-day wear and tear on the nervous system of the individual neophyte since, with the denser immediate population, he came in contact with a greater number of his fellow Indians than he ever did in his natural state. This in turn would have meant more stimuli per unit of time, more mental and emotional activity, and more quarrels and hates, as well as more friendships. On the whole, the entire tempo of his existence was accelerated by the mere physical presence of so many of his fellow men. A broadening of the field of stimulation is likely to be followed by a corresponding intensification of response, and it is probably safe to consider that apostasy and resistance would have been noticeably less in the missions, had the neophytes been segregated in relatively small groups.

This quickening of central nervous activity was particularly effective in the later converts who were brought in as adults from outlying tribes. The sudden transition from the settled, customary existence in a small rancheria to life amid the almost urban conditions of a large mission establishment must have come as a deep mental shock to this class of Indian. Not particularly facile and adaptable as a race, the converts must have found it extremely difficult to make the change. It is not surprising, therefore, that the immediate flight response was most highly developed among the latecomers and that the majority of the fugitives were among those most recently converted.

Resistance to confinement.—Before leaving the problem of spatial relationships one rather minor aspect of the problem merits mention. This relates to the enclosure of individuals within extremely narrow confines, i.e., incarceration. Imprisonment in the missions consisted of two types: jailing for civil or criminal offenses and shutting up in buildings for social or moral reasons. Concerning the former little need be said. In all cultural societies it frequently becomes necessary to curtail the liberty of the criminal, and mission society was no exception. But the number of persons involved was not great.

The other type of confinement was probably of greater biological and psychological significance. It affected not simply the socially maladjusted individual, but the solid citizen, the whole sober and working community. Reference is made to the widespread custom of shutting up and locking in every night large numbers of both females and males. There has been much bitter controversy respecting this practice by both friends and enemies of the missions, a controversy based primarily on humanitarian considerations. The idea of wholesale confinement was repugnant to numerous soldiers and civilians who were not otherwise noted for their gentleness and charity in dealing with Indians. The missionaries themselves regretted its necessity but supported it on grounds of pure administrative expediency in the control of community morals. It must be admitted that they advanced some extremely strong arguments. However, from the standpoint of this discussion the effects of the measure are of more consequence than its justification. Descriptions of the *monjerio,* or women's sleeping quarters, vary little. That given by Father Tapis of Santa Bárbara may be considered accurate and typical.[52]

The room of the single women is 17 *varas* [a *vara* equals roughly a yard] long by 7 wide, is of brick and has a high, wide window for light and ventilation. It has its sewer for corporeal necessities during the night. Along the walls is a platform, 20 *varas* long by 2¼ wide, with two stairways of brick and mortar at the ends for those who want to ascend and sleep upstairs. In the evening they have a fire for heat and every night they are given a tallow candle to illuminate the room.

Lasuén's description is almost the same.[53]

It is 17 *varas* long, more than 6 in width and of equal height; walls of one and one-half *adobes,* plastered with mortar [*mezcla*] and whitewashed, a strong and well-made movable platform [for bedstead] along both sides and a seat [*testera*] of more than one *vara* in height and two in width, three large windows with bars on one side and four loopholes on the other. Its toilet facilities are separate and everything made of good timber covered with planks and a roof of tiles.

Accusations were made that conditions in these rooms, as well as in those of the unmarried men, deteriorated in certain missions in such a way as to become nearly unbearable. The lack of ventilation and the odor were stressed particularly by certain political opponents of the missionaries. Although these charges were doubtless grossly exag-

---

[52] Oct. 30, 1800, Sta. Bárb. Arch., 2:99–100.
[53] "Representación," 1800, *ibid.,* p. 181.

gerated, there must have been some residue of fact. Assuming the *vara* to be equivalent to an English yard, then, according to Tapis, the floor area would have equaled nearly 1,100 square feet. The sleeping platforms along the walls, 17 by 2¼ varas (Tapis must have erred in giving 20 varas as the length), would have provided approximately 700 square feet. Although we have no precise data, it is probable that in the medium and larger missions at least fifty to one hundred women must have slept here. The smaller estimate yields a probable space of 14 square feet, or an area 7 by 2 feet, for each person. There can be no doubt that the women were packed in tightly, and that accumulation of filth was unavoidable. But let us ignore the possible physical effect of such crowding, the disturbances of rest, the spread of infection, and the inadequate ventilation. There still remains the mental and emotional strain caused in a group of adolescents and young men or women who were used to the utmost freedom of personal movement in their native state. It is unbelievable that they should not have resented years of being confined and locked in every night in a manner which was so alien to their tradition and their nature.

To summarize some of the foregoing discussion it may be stated that, apart from demographic changes, the missionized Indians responded to their environment primarily by numerous individual attempts to escape from it, or to resist it, in the physical sense. One group of factors which was at least partially responsible for the observed response was associated with the spatial restrictions imposed by the missions. In particular one may distinguish within this group: (1) emotional or material resistance to any type of compulsory conversion; (2) the emotional tendency to return to the familiar ancestral habitat which we have termed "homesickness"; (3) a revolt against over-aggregation in the missions which ran counter to a centripetal drive on the part of the Indians or urge to reëstablish the pristine, lower population density; and (4) a probable resistance to any confinement, especially to the custom of mass incarceration of both sexes at night. Further resolution of the components in this group of factors might be achieved if an exhaustive study were attempted.

V. LABOR, SEX, AND PUNISHMENT

LABOR

IN HIS REPORT on the state of the missions for 1795–1796 Governor Borica assigned as one of the causes for the bad condition of the neophytes "the labor which until recently they have performed ... without regard to their feeble constitutions."[1] Others also have repeatedly expressed or implied the idea that manual labor was one of the outstanding factors in the downfall of the mission Indians. Some examination of this theory is therefore desirable.

The labor problem, as it pertains to the neophytes, presents two aspects, the first relating to the extent and severity of the effort undergone and the second to the degree of compulsion exercised by the authorities. In other words, was the actual physical exertion detrimental to the Indians and was the compulsion of sufficient severity to induce a generally unfavorable response on their part?

Concerning the type, amount, and hours of labor in the missions we have several statements which are definitely reliable. During the early years of Borica's tenure as governor there was a good deal of agitation with respect to the condition of the neophytes. In the course of the controversy lengthy statements were issued by the four presidial commanders, and detailed rejoinders were submitted by the clergy, in particular the "Reply" of Tapis and Cortes and the great "Representación" of Lasuén. Among the matters discussed was labor, a very clear picture of which may be obtained from these documents. It must be remembered that as a group the soldiers were unfriendly to the missions, whereas the clergymen naturally were attempting to put up a strong defense of their institution. Some of these statements merit quotation *in extenso* since they constitute the basic source material on the question.

At the San Gabriel, San Juan Capistrano, and San Luis missions the number of hours of work in which the neophytes are employed is regulated. They begin their labors at six in the morning and work until almost sunset. In this one, the San Diego Mission, a certain excess of hours has been noted. . . . The Indian women are employed in every masculine oc-

---

[1] June 30, 1797, St. Pap. Mis., 2:98.

cupation, precisely as the men, but those in an advanced stage of pregnancy, those who are nursing, and the old women are assigned to carrying wood, and the children are used to frighten away birds from the gardens and orchards and to perform other light tasks.[2]

The time that the Indians regularly go to work is an hour or more after sunrise until close to noon and after two in the afternoon until almost sunset. Those who work by piecework (*tareas*) quit more or less early, according to when they finish. . . . The Indian women who are pregnant are put to work at the *metate* to grind *atole*, flour, etc.; the work of those who are nursing is not reduced as I am informed by those not in this condition. All those who are considered useful participate in hauling adobes, rock, bricks, and the like for construction. The small children are employed in driving the birds away from the vegetable gardens and orchards and other light tasks, according to their age and sex.[3]

The customary time that the Indians work in the missions, excepting piecework during the winter, is daily, in the summer until nine o'clock, unless some indispensable work presents itself such as freeing the season's grain from mildew or guarding adobes and tiles. I have seen several Indian women with children at the breast carrying adobes, also some pregnant but not in an advanced stage. The children are assigned to clearing the gardens, that is, pulling grass and weeds and other work that they are capable of enduring. Only the old people who are not strong enough for any task are exempted from work.[4]

In winter they work scarcely three hours in the morning and another equal period in the afternoon: in the summer about four hours now and then, leaving the trivial and light tasks to the pregnant Indian women, those nursing, the old people and the children.[5]

The customary hour for ringing the bell to go out to work is more than an hour after sunrise. At the stroke of the bell the people gather slowly in the quadrangle (with the exception of those doing piecework) and they jointly divide the duties of the day. After the tasks are distributed, many return to their homes and leave of their own volition to begin their work, which is unquestionably two hours after sunrise, and which terminates at the hour when the priests eat. It is absolutely certain that they never work more than one hour and a half in the afternoon, because it never occurs that Indians are found at work at the conclusion of the Divine Office, which is performed when the sun is midway to the horizon and lasts three-quarters of an hour, unless they are engaged in planting, weeding, culti-

---

[2] Grajera to Borica, San Diego, March 21, 1799, Prov. St. Pap., 17:191.

[3] Goycoechea to Borica, Santa Bárbara, Dec. 14, 1798, *ibid.*, p. 70.

[4] Sal to Borica, Monterey, Dec. 15, 1798, *ibid.*, p. 63.

[5] Argüello to Borica, San Francisco, Dec. 11, 1798, *ibid.*, p. 58.

vating or harvesting grain. On such occasions they are delayed somewhat as their fields are rather more distant. Then, however, they are excused from vespers.

In order that the so-called "great labor" that the commandant ascribes to the piecework system may be understood, we shall explain this clearly and distinctly. To the women no other piecework is given than that of grinding, and each grinds two *almudes* of wheat per day for *atole,* and when it is for bread eight and sometimes nine women grind seven *almudes* of soaked wheat. The men are given a piecework contract; nine men making 360 adobes two *tercias* long and one wide, which, divided among nine men makes 40 adobes a person. The soil is soft and water is close at hand. Those engaged in this piecework never work after eleven o'clock, neither on Saturdays, and often even not on Fridays because they had advanced the work during the early days of the week. Those who make tiles operate by piecework. Sixteen young men and, at times, an equal number of fairly old men who happen to be in the village, are designated. All these people, together with two women who haul sand and cow dung to them, make 500 tiles a day . . . These Indians finish the task at eleven, and even at that they have always advanced Saturday work so that they have the day free for going out or to rest.[6]

Then follows a description of weaving and spinning, also a discussion in acrimonious vein of the hardships suffered by neophytes who are loaned as laborers to the presidio.

The pregnant Indian women have never been, we repeat, have never been, assigned to the *metate* for grinding *atole,* flour, and other arduous tasks. And so that this may never happen they are very careful to advise us when they find themselves in a state of gestation so that their names may be entered on the register we have of the pregnant women. They are employed in finishing wool, pounding oak bark for the tannery, and accompanied by other women who assist them, cleaning wheat on the threshing floor after threshing . . . Sometimes they are employed in the garden and orchard pulling up weeds and grass. . . . After parturition they remain at home all the time they wish and when they feel that they may be of use or possess inclination to work they present themselves with the others whose duty it is to supply the *pozolera* with wood, having as associates in this task the old men who are able to work. During the wheat harvest the women who are nursing prepare the meal for *atole,* each one being given an *almud* of wheat which they grind on the *metate.* All the women who

[6] Reply of Tapis and Cortes to Goycoechea's statements, Santa Bárbara, Oct. 30, 1800, Sta. Bárb. Arch., 2:86–143. This is probably the most specific and detailed firsthand account of mission labor we possess. Lasuén's discussion is as authoritative, but is less concrete and much more prolix and argumentative.

are considered useful participate in carrying adobes, when the cart assigned to this work does not suffice . . . These same women also take part in the conveyance of brick and tile, and very rarely rock, the latter being small and for the purpose of leveling off the foundations. The hauling of other construction material is the duty of the ox-driver and his oxen and the mule-driver and his mules. Of the children, nine years of age and over, some are employed in combing wool for the looms and passing the shuttles to the weavers, others in watching the tiles and bricks so that the animals do not tread on them, others in chasing the birds away, but most of them in diverting themselves with their childish games.

In spite of individual differences arising from personal experiences or political bias all observers, not only those cited above but others as well, are agreed with respect to certain essential points. There can be no doubt that the standard working week consisted of from 5 to 6 days at 6 to 8 hours per day, let us say, 30 to 40 hours per week. Nowhere do we find any claims that more than 40 hours were required, except under extreme provocation. The actual tasks were those characteristic of rather primitive agriculture and strictly home industry. Much of this work would be classed today as light labor. It is very significant that even the bitterest opponents of the missions never accused the clergy of giving the Indians work which might cause either excessive fatigue through extremely long hours or physical injury through intense exertion and occupational hazard. The worst they could do was the charge that pregnant women were too severely treated. There is no doubt that by modern standards the work was very reasonable both as to hours and nature. One need only compare the mission labor condition as set forth in the excerpts quoted with modern civilized labor conditions such as are encountered by the average farmer or worker in heavy industry. We may conclude immediately therefore that, as far as the adult neophyte was concerned, he was not obliged to perform labor which could in any way be injurious physically in either the individual or racial sense.

The only possible exceptions were the pregnant women and the children. Respecting the latter, all presidial commanders are in agreement that nothing more arduous was required of them than a little gardening and bird chasing. Overburden of pregnant women would be a serious charge, were it not for the fact that because of the low birth rate, as well as for religious reasons, the missionaries were exceedingly anxious for pregnancies and deliveries to be successful and would be most unlikely to jeopardize the issue. Finally, it must be remembered that in the California "Arcadia" no one did any really strenuous work, and what would be regarded by the Spanish white population as onerous labor would have been considered quite ordinary by the average American of the period. The purely physical effects of manual labor may therefore be dismissed as a factor effective in the racial disintegration of the mission Indian.

The mental and moral aspects of labor, however, belong in an entirely different category. The compulsion placed on the Indian, the restriction upon his daily activity through obligatory physical effort is important. But it is not the whole story. His reaction to labor itself, in the abstract, must be considered, since mental or bodily exertion of the type demanded by white civilization was completely new to him. It constituted an environmental factor, of the nonmaterial type, with which he had never come in contact and which therefore required an emotional and intellectual readjustment or adaptation very difficult for him to make. Labor, with its associated complex system of rewards and penalties, has perhaps constituted a more serious obstacle to the racial reorientation of the Indian than brutal but quite comprehensible physical conflict. We may focus attention on the aspect of compulsion in labor among the mission Indians, keeping continually in the background the idea that labor in any form was alien to their disposition, their social heritage, and their biological environment.

Despite innumerable lamentations, apologies, and justifications, there can be no serious denial that the mission system, in its economics, was built upon forced labor. Any coöperative system of support, any organization which is economically self-sustaining, as were the missions, must of necessity be founded upon the productive toil of its members. This very necessity is the primary compulsion, but if the corporate members are of sufficient intelligence, the compulsion becomes rationalized and there is an appearance of willingness and volition. On the other hand, if the mass is stupid and ignorant, then the hierarchy of authority at the top must exercise force, moral or physical, to obtain the essential effort on the part of the mass. Compulsion then becomes personal, and we begin to speak of "forced labor." Thus in its essence the mission system predicated forced labor by the neophytes. Understanding all this, the missionary fathers did their utmost to enlighten the neophytes, but with little success. The next step was moral suasion, and it must be admitted that, in general, such measures were adequate. When, however, they failed, physical means became necessary,[7] for the economic discipline of the community had to be maintained at all costs. It was very natural that many neophytes, not in the least comprehending the ideals of the Church and its servants or the complexities of administrative theory, should regard necessary "forced labor" as directed personally at themselves and should rebel against it. On the other hand, it is noteworthy that of all the complaints and grievances of the neophytes, relatively few were directed against the work itself.

One certain adjunct to the mission labor system, and one which was repeatedly deplored by the priests, was the diversion of workers to the presidios and other army posts. Abuses grew up here which did not affect the main body of neophytes seriously but which became enormously magnified in their moral implications. It was at first contemplated that the construction and care of military establishments should devolve upon the army itself, but the soldiers were few and the officers negligent. Military effort was directed mainly toward garrisoning and protecting the missions. It was also a great temptation to the not overly industrious soldiers to tap the great reservoir of substantially free Indian labor. Hence a system soon came into effect whereby the clergy loaned their charges for work in the presidios as manual laborers and as domestic servants. It was fully understood that all such services should be paid for, the Indians to receive a fair wage, payable in money or commodities. Not only neophytes might be permitted to work at the presidios but gentiles as well, provided they came voluntarily and were paid in full.

---

[7] The term slavery has been uncritically applied to the mission social system. It should be pointed out that there was no implication of personal ownership whatever. Furthermore, in theory always, and in practice usually, the fruit of Indian labor was devoted to the welfare and improvement of the Indian himself. Any selfish enrichment of the mission was incidental and contrary to the tenets of the Church. The system was much closer to socialism or communism, in the Marxian sense, than slavery.

The wages were not high but perhaps were adequate. The daily wage rate was 1½ *reales* a day,[8] in 1787. This amounts to about six American cents. In addition, food and clothing were furnished. An appreciable number of Indians was involved. In 1790 Governor Fages used about 70 in Monterey over a period of six months. The workers were employed in groups, each group remaining some two months at the presidio.[9] From 1786 to 1789 inclusive a total of 1,184 pesos was contributed by the company at Santa Bárbara[10] as compensation for Indian helpers. This amounts to an average of 396 pesos annually, or at 1½ *reales* a day, 2,110 man days per year and, assuming a five-day week, 8 men continuously at work. In 1794 Sal reported[11] that 78 men were working at San Francisco: 40 neophytes and 38 gentiles. The same year Arrillaga stated that at Santa Bárbara the pay was 1½ *reales* per day plus an *almud* of maize per week.[12] At Monterey the remuneration was a strip of cotton cloth and a blanket per month. Very shortly afterward complaints began to arise that the stated pay was not forthcoming. Borica wrote to this effect[13] to the *comandante* of San José in 1795 and in 1804 the viceroy himself directed the governor to pay the Indians from San Juan Bautista who, in 1800, worked at Monterey.[14] Tapis and Cortes, as well as Lasuén, were very bitter concerning the failure of the soldiers to compensate the neophytes, and in 1825 the guardian, Fr. López, set forth a long argument to the effect that the missions were feeding the colony by Indian labor.[15] He also maintained that the neophytes had not been paid since 1810, fifteen years previously. There is thus no doubt that subsequent to 1790 the attempt to pay for Indian labor was abandoned and the work was done under unmitigated compulsion.[16]

---

[8] Fages to Lasuén, Monterey, July 10, 1787, Prov. Rec., 3:63.

[9] Fages to Castro, a series of letters, April to September, 1790, Dept. St. Pap. San José, 1:28–40.

[10] Goycoechea, Santa Bárbara, Dec. 30, 1792, Prov. St. Pap., 12:61.

[11] Sal to Arrillaga, San Francisco, Apr. 30, 1794, *ibid.*, p. 73.

[12] Arrillaga to Sal, Monterey, May 7, 1794, Prov. Rec., 2:147.

[13] Borica, Monterey, Dec. 23, 1795, *ibid.*, 4:241.

[14] Iturrigaray to Arrillaga, Mexico, 1804, Prov. St. Pap., 19:7–8.

[15] López to Alaman, Mexico, July 5, 1825, Archb. Arch., 3(2):141–148.

[16] In justice to the military it should be stated that they themselves were grossly underpaid, months and years often elapsing during which they received no compensation whatever.

Although, as with normal mission labor, that which was performed for the military was not over-severe physically, yet it no doubt served to intensify the aversion with which all labor was regarded by the Indians. It was a particularly offensive example of compulsory activity which was incessantly kept before the eyes of the Indians. The latter, who found it sufficiently difficult to comprehend why they should be required to work for their own economic advantage in the mission, were completely at a loss to see any justification for their being obliged to donate the sweat of their brow to the soldiers. As the guardian López put it, "The Indians are complaining bitterly at having to work that the soldiers may eat . . ."[17] Furthermore, the unjustifiable forced labor at the presidios probably served to create greater dislike for the draft upon their services at the missions, which was socially more or less reasonable. Since the neophytes were incapable of drawing fine distinctions, their tendency would be to charge the responsibility for abuses to those in direct authority over them, that is, to the missionaries.

Turning now to a more fundamental aspect of the labor problem, we observe that the California tribes shared with other Indians the characteristic, or the vice, of whole-hearted aversion to physical labor. Whether the labor was compulsory or voluntary, the Indian—at least at the time of his first contact with the white man—preferred not to perform it. Hence he has been universally termed lazy and indolent. Now there is very little to be gained by applying opprobrious epithets to a race or a group without analyzing, at least in a cursory fashion, the reasons for such inherent traits as call forth the epithets.[18]

In their wild state the Indians underwent extensive physical exertion. Even in California, where life was easier than in the eastern

---

[17] See fn. 15.

[18] A very restrained description of mission-Indian work habits is the following, taken from Lasuén's "Representación": ". . . besides those who have escaped or are away on leave, the sick and their caretakers. Those who are well are prone to offer some indisposition as a pretext, knowing that they are generally believed and that even in case of doubt the missionary always excuses them from work. Nobody hurries them; they sit down, they lie down and often leave to return whenever they see fit. When they work by the job [*tarea*] they are permitted to leave it unfinished and others, generally the majority, are urged not to exceed it. These *tareas* are customarily very moderate so that without more than the time necessary for common work and with only a little less indolence or with fair activity many are able to finish a whole day's work in the morning, and in three or four days that of a whole week to obtain recompense and have the rest of the time free."

forests or on the central plains, much hard work was devoted to the obtaining of food, whether through fishing and hunting or by gathering acorns, nuts, and other plant materials. The processes involved in preparing the food were likewise laborious and tedious. Furthermore, the building of shelters and the manufacture of clothing, utensils, and weapons demanded much time and effort. No Indian group ever survived a year in a state of complete indolence and inactivity. Indeed, among numerous tribes extraordinary exertions and hardships were necessary for simple survival. It is therefore inaccurate to assume that the Indian disliked to work simply because muscular exercise was involved. He disliked it because of the conditions under which it was performed. The whole basis of the aboriginal labor system was the idea of intermittent effort rather than steady, consistent exertion. This, in turn, was associated with the facts that, first, the food supply was highly seasonal and, second, no preparative measures were required. The fish ran at a certain time, the acorns were ripe in a definite month. Hence the native worked hard to accumulate these materials when they were available. He strove mightily and without stint for a brief period. Then he rested and loafed until his environment demanded another expenditure of energy. Even the women, upon whom devolved the domestic tasks, operated on much the same basis. Hence there was developed a tremendously powerful tradition of labor only when necessity demanded. There was no concept of continuous effort over a long period of time, directed toward a consistent production of commodities or an end to be achieved in the relatively distant future. In a sense the Indian style and method of labor was admirably adapted to his environment and to the needs of his way of life.

Now, place him in a so-called civilized environment, surrounded by a race with an utterly different tradition, that of the value of labor performed throughout the year. In order to conform to the new type of culture he is forced—in the widest sense—to alter his inherited method of work. Whether in a mission, on a reservation, or as an independent agent he is obliged to work every day, a certain number of hours, at tasks the immediate value of which are obscure to him. Since he sees no direct necessity for ploughing the wheat field or weeding the vegetable garden, he feels no internal compulsion to perform these tasks. He is thus regarded as lazy and improvident, and pressure is brought to bear from without. Since he cannot appreciate the value of the work, it becomes irksome to him, and he resents the pressure which forces him to do it. In other words, he tends to carry over into the new environment the habits of thought and the methods of labor which served him adequately under aboriginal conditions. As a result, not only the external compulsion but the labor itself acts as a stimulus which generates negative or adverse responses.

At this point a vicious cycle, similar to those already discussed, begins to form. In response to disinclination toward the new type of labor and to either impersonal economic compulsion or personal moral and physical pressure, the mission Indian takes one of two courses. He exercises passive resistance by stalling or "soldiering" on the job or by malingering and inventing all sorts of excuses for not working. Alternatively, he avails himself of the flight mechanism and runs away. No matter which course he adopts, he is regarded by the white race, clerical and secular alike, as indolent, improvident, and exasperatingly oblivious to his true economic welfare. To correct this failure in racial, social, and environmental adjustment, the missionaries, soldiers, and civilians respond by doing exactly the worst possible thing under the circumstances; increasing the extent and severity of the pressure, which in turn forces a little more labor from the Indian but also intensifies his own trend toward refusal to work or toward escape.

Thus we see in seventy years of mission experience an irreconcilable conflict between the inborn, almost instinctive tendency of the Indian to work in his ancient way and the necessities of the European and American economic system. Although, urged by compulsion of various categories, the Indian did perform a great deal of labor, this native, original tendency was substantially unaltered. Its tenacity was demonstrated by the fact that, when all compulsion was withdrawn at secularization but the opportunity for volitional labor and self-support was provided, the neophytes reverted in a body to their ancestral methods and disintegrated completely as an economic unit. As individuals, they either returned to the wild life among the heathen or subsisted miserably upon the thin charity of the white men, indulging in manual labor only to ward off acute, absolute starvation.

Apart from the strictly mission enterprise, as well as including it, the California Indian race proved itself a total failure as far as the labor system was concerned. From the point of view of population changes the race was doomed to severe depletion, if not extinction, in free competition with the whites simply because it could not sufficiently rapidly and successfully adapt itself to the labor system basic to white economy. This in turn is referable to the inherent attitude of the Indian toward consistent, long-continued physical exertion, an attitude built up through generations of adjustment to the wild environment, not to any genetically ingrained moral turpitude or reprehensible intellectual backwardness.

Sex Relations

It is generally admitted that the instinct controlling sex relations, together with those governing food and protection, underlies the welfare of any human race or animal species. Moreover, the behavior patterns of groups and individuals are motivated by sex perhaps more than by any other single factor. It follows very naturally therefore that, in surveying the interrelations between the California Indians and the mission social system, some consideration must be devoted to the element of sex.

This subject has two aspects, which, although they may be separated for purposes of discussion, are very closely associated. One concerns the strictly biological, reproductive instinct, the other, the cultural superstructure erected upon the basis of reproductive urge and necessity. It is felt preferable here to dissociate these two aspects, even at the risk of setting up an unwarrantably artificial distinction. At the present juncture certain considerations pertaining to the more material phases of sex relations are set forth, the cultural and moral phases being deferred for subsequent treatment.

One of the greatest difficulties encountered by the missionaries was the regulation and control of sex relations among the neophytes, and between the neophytes and outsiders, whether white or Indian. Even if such matters as polygamy, divorce, property rights, purchase of wives, puberty rites, menstrual customs, and the like are left out of consideration as being predominantly cultural in nature, there still remains the problem of sex drive and its satisfaction. In brief, was normal (or customary) sexual satisfaction reduced among the neophytes, and, if so, would such inhibition induce unfavorable reactions among those concerned?

There is no generic reason to believe that the sex drive was more powerful among the Indians than among any other large segment of the human species. Certainly those proclivities were not reflected in an unusually large number of offspring, nor does a survey of the anthropological literature yield such an impression. Moreover, there is no reason to suppose on anatomical or physiological grounds that the gonadic hormones are of greater potency or are produced in larger quantities in an Indian than in a white man, an Oriental, or a Negro. It is legitimate therefore to assume that any differences existing between the California Indian and the California white man were referable only to the extent and manner of release of the sex desire.

In the aboriginal state very definite laws and customs prevented the unlimited indulgence in and satisfaction of the sex instinct. These are not considered in detail here, because they concern the cultural aspect of the problem. However, it must be pointed out that, in general, more license was permitted in the Indian community than under the Spanish civil code or the code of Christian morals. The extent of promiscuity may be estimated from the written statements of the missionaries and other persons interested at the time in Indian habits. For illustration the following may be cited.

The failure of the mission Indians to increase more may be attributed to their great incontinence . . .[19]

The vice of sodomy among the Indians of the north is quite common . . .[20]

The principal vices of the Indians included *impureza* (San Diego), *luxuria* (San Miguel), *luxuria* (San Antonio), *impureza* (San Gabriel), *luxuria* (San Luis Obispo).[21]

There is a tradition that these Indians were very virtuous and rarely fell short in their wifely duties, but if one may judge by what has been

---

[19] Lasuén, "Census," San Carlos, March 1, 1795, St. Pap. Mis., 2:4.

[20] Martínez, "Causa Criminal," March 10, 1829, St. Pap. Ben. Mil., 68:5.

[21] From the "Contestación al Interrogatorio," 1811, and 1811–1814, Sta. Bárb. Arch., 3:27–37 and 7:112–216.

witnessed since the white man came into this part of the world, we should be justified in believing that their morality was at a very low ebb.[22]

Stephen Powers was much impressed by the licentiousness of the native Californians. In his work he refers in this connection specifically to the Karok, Hupa, Pomo, Maidu, and Yokuts.[23] Thus he states (p. 412) that the Californians are a "grossly licentious race, none more so, perhaps" and (p. 22) : "Before marriage virtue is an attribute which can hardly be said to exist in either sex, most of the young women being a common possession. . ."

The situation among the Yuma was described by Pedro Font in these terms:[24]

In the matter of incontinence they are so shameless and excessive that I do not believe that in all the world there is another tribe that is worse. The women, it might almost be said, are common, and the hospitality which they show their guests is to provide them with a companion.

Contemporary observation is definitely corroborated by modern anthropological research. The existence of general premarital promiscuity as an accepted type of behavior has been noted among the Mojave,[25] the Wappo,[26] the Tübatulabal,[27] the Wintun,[28] the Paiute,[29] and the Pomo.[30] The practice of "courtship" prior to marriage seems

---

[22] Salvador Vallejo, "Origin of the Indians of California," MS, 1875, translation by E. R. Hewitt (1935), p. 3.

[23] Stephen Powers, *Tribes of California* (1877), Contr. No. Amer. Ethnol., Vol. 3.

[24] The diary of Pedro Font, translated by H. E. Bolton, *Anza's California Expeditions,* IV:98–109. Quoted by C. D. Forde, *Ethnography of the Yuma Indians* (1931), Univ. Calif. Publ. Am. Arch. and Ethn., 28:95.

[25] Kroeber, *Handbook of California Indians,* p. 747. Also, G. Devereaux, "Institutionalized Homosexuality of the Mojave Indians," *Human Biology* (1937), 9:498–527.

[26] H. E. Driver, *Wappo Ethnography* (1936), Univ. Calif. Publ. Am. Arch. and Ethn., 36:208.

[27] C. F. Voegelin, *Tübatulabal Texts* (1935), *ibid.,* 34:191–246.

[28] C. A. DuBois, *Wintu Ethnography* (1935), *ibid.,* 36:36. The author comments that "several informants insisted that in former days sexual immorality was very severely punished, which certainly today no longer holds. Whether morals were ever as strict as some informants implied is doubtful . . . There seems to have been a very considerable gap between theory and practice in this realm of culture . . ."

[29] J. H. Steward, *Two Paiute Autobiographies* (1934), *ibid.,* 33:423–438. Voegelin (*op. cit.*) gives another autobiography, and Paul Radin (*Winnebago Autobiography* [1920], *ibid.,* 16:381–474) still another. Of these four all but one (Steward's second) recount long adventures in promiscuity. The impression one derives is that such behavior is regarded as quite customary.

[30] E. M. Loeb, *Pomo Folkways* (1926), *ibid.,* 19:280.

in certain instances to have been little more than an excuse for sexual relations.[31] Numerous examples are on record where festivals, dances, rituals, and celebrations of various descriptions were attended by a general community orgy.[32] The Indian attitude seems to have been quite definitely indifferent to or favorable toward sex license.[33] In fact, no real obstacle existed to a full, unrestrained exercise of the reproductive function, nor within the framework of tribal custom and regulation was there any real inhibition placed upon the sex impulses of man or woman.

It was this liberal and plastic tradition with regard to sex which ran squarely up against one of the most rigid and uncompromising inhibitory codes the world has ever seen. To the missionaries such candid acceptance of sexual freedom appeared the worst form of viciousness, and from the very inception of the missions the clergy fought against it with the strongest zeal and fervor, using every device known to them to eradicate the unwholesome tendency.

---

[31] Loeb (*ibid.*, p. 275), says, "Courting women played an important part in the lives of young Pomo men. Courtship and marriage, however, had nothing to do with one another . . . Courting was almost entirely for the purpose of enjoying illicit sexual intercourse. These statements might be applied to most primitive peoples, for the idea of combining courtship and marriage is distinctly Anglo-Saxon in tone." The last sentence would probably be disputed by many California anthropologists, for it has been shown that in many tribes courtship did actually precede marriage. However, among the Kato and Wailaki Loeb found conditions similar to those among the Pomo (*The Western Kuksu Cult* [1932], *ibid.*, 33:52 and 94).

[32] Such examples include ceremonies and practices of the following tribes: the Shasta, girls' adolescent ceremony (Kroeber, *Handbook*, p. 300); the Maidu, girls' adolescent ceremony (Kroeber, *Handbook*, p. 428: "General license was not only tolerated but almost obligatory during each night of the dance"); the Karok, salmon dance (Powers, p. 31); the Maidu, erotic dance in the spring (Powers, p. 286); the Wappo, cohabitation before marriage was frequent and matches often resulted from philandering at "big times" (Driver, p. 208); the Paiute, fiesta (Voegelin, p. 220: "Many women: much copulation").

E. W. Gifford and A. L. Kroeber (*Culture Element Distributions, IV: Pomo* [1937], Univ. Calif. Publ. Am. Arch. and Ethn., 37:150) list general sex license as an accompaniment to puberty rites as present in two, absent in five, and doubtful in eight of the fifteen Pomo subtribes. Kroeber (*Elements of Culture in Native California, ibid.*, 13: 312) lists the same culture trait as present among the Yuki, Shasta, and Maidu. No data are given with respect to the other tribes. It is probable that more intensive investigation would yield generally positive results.

[33] Powers repeatedly expresses or implies the total lack of reproach. Kroeber (*Handbook*, p. 747), referring specifically to the Mojave, says, ". . . there seems to be no serious criticism of either men or women on the score of conduct dictated by sex feeling. The old do not exhort the young to be continent but urge them to enjoy themselves while they may . . ."

In addition to the traditional attitude of the neophytes among themselves, further difficulties were encountered in enforcing moral standards as between the neophytes and adjacent heathen. As a rule, particularly in the early days of the missions, the heathen were the aggressors. Thus Fages wrote in 1790:

When gentiles steal the wives of other Indians [presumably Christian] and are escaping, they should be reasoned with and made to see the evil of their ways.[34]

Grajera said:

It is not generally understood how the natives of these parts hate the mission Indians. The former should not be allowed to hang around, in order to prevent the illicit commerce which they are accustomed to carry on with the women.[35]

Or witness the statement of Estudillo that the wild Indians were accustomed to the systematic stealing of women and that even in Christianity they traded women with each other.[36] But the aggression was not all on one side. In the numerous expeditions conducted by the soldiers—and even in private raids—the neophytes went after the women. Much resentment was thereby generated among the wild tribes, who reciprocated in kind whenever possible.

More serious socially, although not so difficult to control, were the relations between the Indians and the whites. Morality and discipline both demanded that the Spanish soldiers and civilians should let the Indian women strictly alone. Yet, as has been mentioned in connection with the spread of syphilis, there was a great deal of illicit intercourse, dating from the first explorations of 1769–1770. Most of this was clandestine,[37] but numerous cases of prosecution are on record and much official attention was devoted to the evil. Thus disciplinary measures were taken in 1777 with respect to the soldiers at San Gabriel and San Juan Capistrano "who are those who go by night to the nearby villages

---

[34] Fages to Castro, Monterey, Jan. 2, 1790, Dept. St. Pap. San José, 1:26.

[35] Grajera to Borica, San Diego, July 17, 1797, Prov. St. Pap., 16:172.

[36] Estudillo, San Francisco, Apr. 15, 1809, Prov. St. Pap. Ben. Mil., 40:1.

[37] A very free admission concerning such affairs is that of Valdes ("Memorias," 1878, p. 18): ". . . we were not permitted to go to the Indian villages, but we went when we had an opportunity, being careful that the corporal should not see us. I have no doubt that some went to seek the favors of the women . . ."

for the purpose of raping the native women."[38] It is clear from the testimony that the soldiers frequented the rancherias, obtaining the women by force or bribery.

Fages, in 1785, issued an order as follows:[39]

... observing that the officers and men of these presidios are comporting and behaving themselves in the missions with a vicious license which is very prejudicial because of the scandalous disorders which they incite among the gentile and Christian women, I command you, in order to prevent the continuation of such abuses that you circulate a prohibitory edict imposing severe penalties upon those who commit them ...

Ten years later the viceroy Branciforte issued a decree forbidding the troops to remain overnight away from the presidios because, among other reasons, such procedure carried with it "considerable prejudice to good discipline and Christian morals."[40] Another order was issued the following year by Borica in the same vein:[41]

... there being repeated complaints made to the governor concerning the excesses committed by various individuals of the companies with both Christian and gentile Indian women ...

In 1823 Father Durán complained to Figueroa of the bad state of affairs at San Luis Obispo and San Diego.[42]

Some of this he attributes to the immorality and bad example of the soldiers at San Luis Obispo; it is said that prostitution, drunkenness and gambling with the Indians are continuous.

If the state of affairs between the more or less disciplined white soldiers and Indians was as bad as these and many other records indicate, the condition among the neophytes themselves must have been much worse, and from the standpoint of the clergy no measures would have been too severe for the maintenance of moral decency. But such measures are notoriously difficult to put in effect, as social workers have invariably found. Aside from religious teaching and moral sua-

---

[38] Ortega, "Diligencias practicadas por Sargento Francisco de Aguilar," San Diego, July 11, 1777, St. Pap. Sac., 8:31 ff.

[39] Fages to Diego González, Monterey, July 1, 1785, *ibid.*, 2:43.

[40] Branciforte to Borica, Mexico, Oct. 5, 1795, Prov. St. Pap., 13:42.

[41] Borica to commanders of presidios, Monterey, April 11, 1796, Prov. Rec., 4:145.

[42] Durán to Figueroa, San Gabriel, June 17, 1823, Archb. Arch., 5(1):78.

sion the missionaries had no other recourse than physical repression of the unbridled sex inclination of the Indians.

Mission policy embodied two procedures which affected the Indian sex life directly. The first was enforcement of strict monogamy with no possibility of divorce. Although divorce had always been easy in the wild state and adultery had perhaps, among the men, been somewhat common, monogamy was an inherent cultural trait of the natives. Its continuation in the missions, even if unrelieved by divorce, could not have constituted an unfavorable factor. Moreover, extreme penalties for adultery coincided with Indian law, if not perhaps with their practice. It is probable, therefore, that normal adult sex function was not seriously interfered with, and any ill effects resulting from the rigid application of the Christian marital code were felt within the cultural rather than physiological sphere.

The other procedure was the very drastic separation of the sexes from puberty to marriage. This was accomplished simply by constant oversight and watchfulness during the day. At night the young men and particularly the young women were locked up in separate quarters. This attempt at almost monastic continence must have exerted a profound effect upon the neophyte youth. The mass deprivation of all normal outlet for sex impulses to the entire population between, let us say, fourteen and eighteen years old inevitably had repercussions upon the psychology of the group as a whole and the younger component in particular. It is hard to escape the conclusion that, in addition to aberrant outlets like homosexuality, the repressed sex drive must have become manifest in neuroses, appearing in both individuals and the group. Certainly the untrammeled freedom of generations and the impulses of youth could not be cleanly obliterated by the mere exercise of forcible segregation. It is furthermore doubtful whether the measure was completely successful from the practical point of view. With several hundred neophytes in each mission perfect supervision was impossible. Many clandestine love affairs must have occurred.

It is impossible to assess the damage done the neophytes from the point of view of psychopathology. But it is quite clear that the community response to such a fundamentally adverse factor must have been powerful. Unfortunately, aside from subterfuge and homosexuality, there was no way in which such a response could take definite form as long as the neophytes remained in the missions. Passive resistance could accomplish nothing. Flight, however, was a solution. Even a few days in the wilds would serve to release the pent-up sexual energy on the part of a group of men and women. It may be suggested therefore that the sexual motive in fugitivism was strong—even though it is not obvious in the documentary sources or in the historical discussions of mission affairs. Curtailment of sex function must therefore be included with restrictions in feeding habits, spatial freedom, and physical activity as an adverse factor in the mission environment.

That the sex urge was too deeply rooted in the nature of the mission Indian to be eradicated or materially modified by mere repression is indicated in many ways. Indeed, it is to be doubted whether any permanent change at all was brought about by the moral or physical efforts of the missionaries. Reports of immorality and licentiousness continued as long as the missions endured. Toward the end of the period the infractions became, if anything, more numerous and flagrant. When at last secularization released the neophytes from any serious restrictive influence, all witnesses agree that a continuous orgy of promiscuity began and continued unabated as long as any neophytes were left. The civil authorities agreed with the clergy during this epoch in a chorus of denunciation of the neophytes' utterly dissolute habits. Evidently a strong reaction set in against the rigid mission discipline, which perhaps carried the Indians to greater extremes than were characteristic of the original primitive state.[48]

Wholly apart from inhibition of promiscuous sexual intercourse, another phenomenon was noted in the missions which was of a serious nature. This was the prevalence of abortion and infanticide, with the obvious implications as to reproduction and population decline.

---

[48] An illustration of Indian behavior following release from mission inhibition is afforded by the testimony of recaptured fugitives after the Purísima rebellion of 1824. Light is also shed on events which probably occurred frequently when the mission Indians escaped to the interior. It was agreed by five witnesses that a general debauch took place. "When the Christians arrived in the valley they exchanged their women for those of the gentiles without distinction as to married and unmarried women, for they were all mixed up among the Indians" (Testimony, June 1, 1824, De la Guerra Docs., 7:142–150). A great celebration took place, with twenty-five stolen steers slaughtered for the feast, but with no liquor because the fugitives had drunk it all on the way.

Abortion by physical means and infanticide by strangulation at birth were by no means unknown before the arrival of the Spanish, although the extent of the practice was probably not very great. Elimination of unwanted young is known to have occurred among the Yurok, Pomo, Wappo, Wintun, Yana, Sinkyone, Kato, Klamath, Hupa, and Yuma. Undoubtedly it was a general procedure among all California tribes,[44] although its frequency may have been somewhat less in the south. Reasons for the killing of young were various, ranging from ritualistic taboos to basic biological instincts. Thus it was usual to kill one of a pair of twins, and deformed infants were similarly disposed of.[45] Quite generally, abortion was used to prevent the arrival of illegitimate children.[46] As Kroeber writes with reference to the Yurok:

As a girl's property value was greatly impaired if she bore a child before marriage, and she was subject to abuse from her family and disgrace before the community, abortion was frequently attempted . . .[47]

Finally, and most significant, there is a body of competent opinion which holds that these methods were utilized as a primitive attempt at birth control and population check. This idea was first advanced in 1877 by Powers, who had in mind particularly the difficulties between the Indians and the Americans. Referring to aboriginal abortion among the Pomo he avers (*op. cit.*, p. 178):

. . . neither was it [infanticide] caused, as in later years, by that deep and despairing melancholy which came over the hapless race when they saw themselves perishing so hopelessly and so miserably before the face of the American.

In more general vein he says (*ibid.*, p. 416), "The very presence of the

---

[44] Although widely present, these customs are not universally admitted by modern informants. Thus Gifford and Kroeber (*Pomo*, p. 150) found abortion admitted by six Pomo subtribes and denied by ten. Infanticide was admitted by seven and denied by nine. It is possible that formerly abortion and infanticide were common to all the subtribes but that contemporary Indian citizens are hesitant about admitting it or else are ignorant of the facts. Such a possibility is suggested by E. M. Loeb (*Pomo Folkways*, p. 255) who states that "the majority of informants were somewhat reticent on the subject of abortion and infanticide."

[45] See Powers, *op. cit.*, pp. 17 –178.

[46] According to L. Spier (*Klamath Ethnography* [1930], Univ. Calif. Publ. Am. Arch. and Ethn., 30:57) the Klamath aborted children in cases of adultery. The Hupa did likewise to avoid bastardy (P. E. Goddard, *Life and Culture of the Hupa* [1903], *ibid.*, 1:55).

[47] Kroeber, *Handbook*, p. 44.

crime of infanticide points to an over-fruitfulness and an over-population." More recently Driver[48] has advanced the same thesis regarding
the Wappo:

Infanticide seems to have been common but may have been accentuated by
the uncertainty of the future and the trying conditions resulting from
exploitation by the whites.

The most complete study of aboriginal birth control has been made
by Aginsky on the Pomo.[49] After pointing out that in prehistoric times
there was doubtless some population pressure owing to a limited food
supply, he indicates methods of control, ranging from ritualistic con-
traception[50] to abortion and infanticide. This tendency toward control
of numbers was, he thinks, a purely individualistic reaction.

They strove to control the population of their territory individually, not
by means of tribal policy. It was a traditionally accepted pattern of behavior
and an integral aspect of this culture.

It is by no means surprising that such a "traditionally accepted
pattern of behavior" should be carried over into the missions, nor is it
remarkable that it should have inspired the missionaries with horror
and alarm. For example, Lasuén wrote in 1795:[51]

The failure of the mission Indians to show a greater increase may be attributed to their great incontinence and the inhumanity of the mothers,
who in order not to become old and unattractive to their husbands manage
to abort or strangle their newly-born children. Little by little these grave
evils are being corrected.

Again, five years later, he referred to

... the inhuman cruelty to which the Indian women are too much addicted
... to abort and strangle their children. To remedy this all means are
being employed ...[52]

In 1809 Argüello reported:[53] "Among the women there are many

---

[48] *Op. cit.,* p. 198.
[49] B. W. Aginsky, "Population Control in the Shanel (Pomo) Tribe" (1939), *Amer.
Sociol. Rev.,* 4:209–216.
[50] C. D. Forde (*op. cit.,* p. 158), describes a variety of contraceptive measures among
the Yuma, including abstinence during certain phases of the menstrual cycle. The Pomo,
according to Aginsky, employed *coitus interruptus.*
[51] Lasuén, Monterey, Mar. 1, 1795, St. Pap. Mis., 2:4.
[52] Lasuén, "Representación," Monterey, Nov. 12, 1800, Sta. Bárb. Arch., 2:187.
[53] Argüello, "Informe y Padrón," Santa Bárbara, Dec. 31, 1809, St. Pap. Mis., 4:1.

abortions and miscarriages." In the report of 1811, the missionaries from Santa Clara stated that "the dominant vice among the women is abortion."[54] Governor Solá, referring to the northern missions, wrote that:[55]

The greater part of the Indian women are pregnant because many are accustomed to abort very easily by means of certain seeds, herbs and pills which they take for this purpose. They are imbued with the idea that if they deliver at their normal time they will become old . . .

As late as 1829 Ignacio Martínez stated as follows:[56]

The vice of sodomy among the Indians of the north is somewhat common; likewise rape and infanticide. There have been several public instances and many which have remained secret.

It is difficult to estimate the precise extent of abortion and infanticide in the missions, since there are no specific and concrete data available. The Church and civil authorities in their statements imply that the evil was very widespread but they, in their concern over the situation, may have been prone to exaggeration. Such overemphasis may, however, have been partially balanced by abortions which were performed in secret and not permitted to come to the attention of the missionaries. It is true that the practice was not reflected in a noticeable reduction in birth rate, for, as has been pointed out elsewhere[57] the apparent reduction can be accounted for fully by the rising male–female sex ratio, and the fertility rate did not materially alter. Nevertheless the testimony of such men as Lasuén cannot be dismissed lightly, and the probability is great that the abortion rate increased very definitely over the aboriginal value, thereby becoming a serious, even if not critical, factor in the racial status of the Indian.

Quite aside from any possible direct effect on population numbers, the phenomenon of abortion has implications of general biological and sociological interest. It may be regarded as a clear-cut response to unfavorable environmental circumstances, that is, an act on the part of an individual which is performed under definite and usually extreme

---

[54] "Contestación al interrogatorio del ano de 1811," Sta. Bárb. Arch., 7:195.

[55] Solá to viceroy, Monterey, Apr. 3, 1818, Prov. Rec., 9:176.

[56] "Causa criminal," San Francisco, Mar. 10, 1829, Prov. St. Pap. Ben. Mil., 68:5.

[57] S. F. Cook, *Population Trends among the California Mission Indians,* Univ. Calif. Publ., Ibero-Americana, No. 17 (Berkeley, 1940). See below, pp. 395-446.

provocation. It therefore takes its place with escape and physical resistance in the pattern of Indian reaction to the mission system. Indeed,
in a certain sense, it is itself escape and resistance: escape for the child
from the environment of the progenitor, resistance to the system which
seeks to augment the number of individuals in the environment. It is
doubtful, naturally, whether any Indian mother in the missions ever
thought in terms of racial or social abstractions. She evidently rationalized her act by maintaining that she did not want to become pre-
maturely old, and so made herself absurd in the eyes of the white man.

As with fugitivism, each individual functioned as a unit through
her personal initiative. But if the contemporary evidence is to be
credited, a sufficient number of women joined in a common or parallel
reaction to warrant considering the phenomenon as a whole, in the
entire population, a mass or group response. We have thus a situation
analogous to that described by Powers and analyzed by Aginsky
among the Pomo, but doubtless on a far larger scale. In short, abortion
and infanticide developed among the mission Indians from an occasional, sporadic cultural item into a serious, although primitive and
haphazard, attempt to check population growth through birth control.
We find, therefore, along with the flight and resistance responses a
birth-control response. The environmental factors which led to this
type of behavior were not in themselves necessarily sexual in nature
but were the sum total of all those factors inherent in the mission complex—the generally bad conditions which manifested themselves in
disease, unsatisfactory diet, and the various restrictions on physical or
cultural expression.

It has been mentioned that, with certain aspects of flight and resistance, vicious cycles could be established wherein there were generated
on the part of the white civilization counterreactions which in turn
intensified these primary Indian responses. Attempted, even if unsuccessful, birth control did not lend itself to the establishment of such a
chain of events. For abortion and infanticide did not directly affect
the welfare of the white man, nor did these practices in any way
impede the progress of his civilization. Their repercussions were solely
upon the Indian himself. In the nature of the case, any countermeasures
were feeble and were of necessity preventive rather than retaliatory.

Race suicide, therefore, would not of itself become intensified, independently of other circumstances, but would vary in direct ratio with the general status of the Indian in the environment which was imposed upon him.

DELINQUENCY AND PUNISHMENT

In the preceding pages several factors characteristic of the mission environment have been discussed which were injurious to the Indians in the racial and population sense or which engendered responses of a type contrary to the interests of the mission system. In order to establish the system itself and, after establishment, to counteract the failure of the neophytes to make group and individual adjustments favorable to the smooth operation of the system, restrictions and compulsions were resorted to. The setting-up of such restrictions may be regarded as adjustments of the second order, or counterresponses to the Indian adaptation pattern. Furthermore, it has been shown that compulsions of all types intensified and crystallized the primary flight and resistance reactions. We may now inquire just how these measures were applied in a physical sense. The initial act was conversion, forced or peaceable; once accomplished, it could not be repeated. Other means were necessary to enforce over the years the social and economic corollaries to Christianization, and these means—when moral influence failed, as it was found to in many instances—could be no other than material. Compulsion and restriction were thus universally enforced by physical acts, and since the specific occasion for enforcement was inevitably engendered by some particular individual or small-group reaction on the part of the Indians, the enforcement was invariably applied to persons in the form of punishment. Since, therefore, chastisement was the point of application of the entire disciplinary system of restriction and compulsion, and since chastisement of its very nature had to be personal and tangible, it became the focal point of individual disaffection and resistance. In the process of rationalization previously alluded to, the Indian who comprehended only dimly the real factors undermining his racial virility and personal morale could center his attention on and understand thoroughly an experience with severe corporal punishment. For these reasons it is necessary to examine the character and extent of the physical disciplinary measures employed under the mission system.

The offenses which were punishable, apart from inconsequential misdemeanors, were of two primary types which, for purposes of the present discussion, may be designated "criminal" and "political." The former includes those derelictions, universally recognized as contrary to the welfare of any community, which indeed were acknowledged as beyond condonement by the Indians themselves, whether in their own primitive or the introduced white society. This category includes the usual range of offenses against the person—such as murder, assault, and rape—and those against property—theft, armed robbery, arson, and the like. To these might be added a third group consisting of sex delinquencies, such as fornication, adultery, incest, and sodomy, which were particularly offensive to the Church. There is nothing in the documentary records to indicate to an impartial observer that crime in this sense was much more frequent among the converted Indians than among the white population. As would be expected the actual number of Indian crimes was greater, but it should be remembered that the Indians outnumbered the whites by several hundred per cent. Furthermore, the moral deterrents to crimes of impulse and passion were more highly developed among the white population. On the whole, although the Indians may not have appreciated the full enormity of certain types of criminal act, there is no reason to feel that the punishment of such behavior, of itself alone, would ever have induced a profound moral revulsion against white society.

The other chief category includes offenses against Spanish mission society through failure to conform to its specific or general requirements or through overt acts contrary to its interests. Here would be included all forms of fugitivism, apostasy, refusal to complete set tasks, conspiracies to overthrow the existing regime, theft or destruction of army or mission property (as contrasted with the robbery of personal goods), and finally armed opposition to the missionaries, soldiers, or even civilians. In short, the political offenses committed by the neophytes were of the same species as are perpetrated by every racial, political, or religious group which is at odds with the governing order at the time. Furthermore, it was as difficult for the Indian as for the members of any other repressed group to perceive the immorality or essential sinfulness of his behavior. His reaction to chastisement for such acts was a normal, healthy resentment, directed chiefly against the individuals who were personally instrumental in applying the chastisement, whom he endowed, by extension, with responsibility for all his woes, of whatever nature.

Punishment for offenses of both criminal and political categories was often carried out by the soldiers, in particular by imprisonment. This was natural, since the only quarters for confinement were in the presidios. Furthermore, the secular arm was entrusted with authority over ordinary criminal delinquencies. Moreover, actual military operations and expeditions were carried on by the armed forces. Since these frequently resulted in punishment meted out to gentiles as well as to renegade neophytes for acts of war or insurrection, stock stealing, and general raiding of the frontier, the soldiers functioned in a disciplinary capacity for the entire community. For these reasons it is difficult as well as unnecessary to dissociate the presidios and missions with respect to crime and punishment among the Indians.

Although it is clearly impossible to form any quantitative estimate of the actual number of persons punished for all offenses during the mission era, there are a sufficient number of reports on record to furnish a clue to the relative frequency of various types of delinquency, as well as to the punishments accorded. This material has been consolidated in the form of a table, arranged chronologically (see table 5). The table shows 94 cases of disciplinary action involving a total of 362 persons, scattered more or less at random through the mission period from 1775 to 1831. The causes of delinquency may be grouped with moderate exactitude according to whether they were "criminal," "political," or doubtful. Homicide, assault, robbery, and incest clearly belong to the first category, and fugitivism, conspiracy, and armed resistance to the second. Somewhat doubtful is stock stealing, because the nature of this offense depends entirely upon the circumstances governing each separate offense. If an Indian went from his mission to a neighbor's range, killed and ate a steer, the criminal element predominates. If, however, a group of neophytes and gentiles raided a rancho and drove off a herd of cattle, the operation may be regarded as an act directed against white society as a whole rather than against a single person. Particularly is this true if some of the perpetrators were fugitives or gentiles

TABLE 5

PUNISHMENT FOR CRIME

Year	Place	Number of persons	Offense	Punishment	Source
1775	San Antonio	2 g.[a]	Stock stealing	Flogging	Palóu, *New Calif.*, IV:37
1775	Santa Clara	2 g.	Stock stealing	Flogging	*Ibid.*, p. 161
1778	San Diego	4 g.	Conspiracy + armed resistance	Death	Prov. St. Pap. Ben. Mil., 1:41
1782	San Diego	1 n.	Fugitivism	Imprisonment, hard labor	Prov. St. Pap, 3:79
1782	San Diego	5 n.	Stock stealing	Flogging (25)[b]	*Ibid.*
1783	Monterey	2 g.	Stock stealing	Flogging (25)	Prov. Rec., 3:170
1783	Monterey	15 g.	Stock stealing	Imprisonment, hard labor	*Ibid.*
1785	Monterey	1 n.	Stock stealing	Imprisonment, hard labor (1 mo.) + flogging (15)	*Ibid.*, p. 32
1785	San Gabriel	7 n.	Conspiracy	Flogging (15 to 20)	*Ibid.*, 2:123
1785	San Gabriel	4 g.	Conspiracy	Flogging (15 to 20)	*Ibid.*
1786	San Diego	10 n.	Stock stealing	Flogging (10)	*Ibid.*, p. 134
1788	Santa Bárbara	1 n.	"Incorrigible"	Imprisonment, hard labor (2 mos.)	Prov. St. Pap, 8:116
1794	San Francisco	4 n.	Stock stealing	Imprisonment	*Ibid.*, 12:49
1794	Santa Clara	8 g.	Stock stealing	Imprisonment, hard labor	Prov. Rec., 2:147
1795	Monterey	1 g.	Harboring fugitives	Imprisonment (1 mo.)	*Ibid.*, 5:41
1795	San Francisco	1 n.	....	Imprisonment, hard labor (4 mos.) + flogging (25)	*Ibid.*, p. 44
1795	San Francisco	3 n.	Robbery	Imprisonment (1 mo.) + flogging (12)	*Ibid.*

Year	Place	Status	Crime	Penalty	Source
1795	San Francisco	1 n.	Fugitivism	Imprisonment (1 mo.) + flogging (25)	Ibid.
1796	Monterey	3 n.	Fugitivism	Flogging (25)	Ibid., 6:174
1796	San Francisco	1 n.	Throwing stone at soldier	Flogging (25)	St. Pap. Sac, 5:82
1796	Monterey	2 g.	Homicide	Imprisonment (4 yrs.) + flogging (50)	Prov. Rec., 4:84
1796	Monterey	1 g.	Homicide	Imprisonment (4 yrs.) + flogging (100)	Ibid.
1797	Monterey	1 g.	Armed resistance + homicide	Imprisonment in chains (1 yr.) + flogging (75 × 3)	Prov. St. Pap, 16:76
1797	Monterey	2 g.	Armed resistance + homicide	Imprisonment in chains (2 mos.)	Ibid.
1797	Monterey	3 g.	Armed resistance + homicide	Imprisonment in chains (4 mos.) + flogging (25)	Ibid.
1797	Monterey	1 g.	Armed resistance + homicide	Imprisonment in chains (8 mos.) + flogging (50 × 2)	Ibid.
1797	Monterey	5 g.	Armed resistance + homicide	Imprisonment in chains (2 mos.) + flogging (25)	Ibid.
1798	San Diego	1 n.	Homicide	Imprisonment, hard labor (4 yrs.)	Prov. Rec., 5:275
1799	San Francisco	11 n.	Robbery	Flogging (30 × 3)	Prov. St. Pap. Ben. Mil., 27:4
1800	San Francisco	7 g.	Armed resistance	Flogging (15)	Prov. St. Pap, 18:31
1800	San Diego	3 n.	Murder of gentiles	Flogging (25 × 27)	Prov. Rec., 7:4

a The following abbreviations are used: g. = gentile; n. = neophyte.
b The figures in parentheses following the penalty of flogging indicate the number of lashes administered. If this figure is followed by another, the second indicates the number of times or consecutive days the penalty was applied.

TABLE 5—*Continued*

Year	Place	Number of persons	Offense	Punishment	Source
1802	Monterey	2 n.	Homicide	Death	*Ibid.*, 9:165
1805	San Diego	1 n.	Striking a missionary	Flogging (25 × 9)	*Ibid.*, 12:35
1805	Santa Bárbara	3 n.	Homicide	Death	Prov. St. Pap., 19:45
*1808	San Diego	8 n.	Fugitivism + bad character + stock stealing	Imprisonment, hard labor	
*1809	San José	3 n.	Assault on missionary	Imprisonment, hard labor	
*1809	San José	2 g.	Bad character	Imprisonment, hard labor	
*1809	San Juan Bautista	1 n.	Bad character	Imprisonment, hard labor	
*1809	San Juan Bautista	6 n.	Fugitivism	Imprisonment, hard labor	
1810	Santa Bárbara	21 n.	Conspiracy + armed resistance	Imprisonment, hard labor + flogging (25 × 9)	Prov. Rec, 11:10
1810	Santa Bárbara	12 g.	Conspiracy + armed resistance	Imprisonment, hard labor + flogging (25 × 9)	*Ibid.*
*1810	San Francisco	1 n.	Conspiracy + robbery	Imprisonment, hard labor	
*1810	San Juan Bautista	11 n.	Fugitivism	Imprisonment, hard labor	
*1810	San Miguel	3 n.	Robbery	Imprisonment, hard labor	
*1810	San Luis Rey	1 n.	Bad character	Imprisonment, hard labor	
1811	San Buenaventura	10 n.	Fugitivism + stock stealing	Imprisonment, hard labor + flogging (25 × 9)	Prov. Rec, 11:10
1811	San Diego	1 n.	Assault on missionary	Imprisonment, hard labor (8 mos.)	Prov. St. Pap. Ben. Mil., 49:2

1811	San Diego	1 n.	Robbery	Imprisonment, hard labor (5 yrs.) + flogging (20 × 4)	Ibid., p. 9
1811	San Diego	6 n.	Robbery	Imprisonment, hard labor (4 yrs.) + flogging (20 × 4)	Ibid.
1811	San Diego	2 n.	Robbery	Imprisonment, hard labor (2 mos.) + flogging (50)	Ibid.
1811	San Diego	1 n.	Assault + homicide	Flogging (50)	Ibid.
*1811°	San José	2 n.	Fugitivism	Imprisonment, hard labor	Ibid., p. 7
*1811	Santa Clara	1 n.	Fugitivism + bad character		
*1811	Santa Cruz	2 n.	Fugitivism	Imprisonment, hard labor	
*1811	San Juan Bautista	5 n.	Fugitivism + bad character		
*1811	La Purísima	5 n.	Bad character	Imprisonment, hard labor (2 mos.)	
*1811	Santa Bárbara	1 n.	Fugitivism	Imprisonment, hard labor	
*1811	San Gabriel	5 n.	Conspiracy	Imprisonment, hard labor	
*1811	San Francisco	2 n.	Stock stealing	Imprisonment, hard labor	
*1811	San Gabriel	6 n.	Homicide	Imprisonment, hard labor	
*1811	San Gabriel	6 g.	Homicide	Imprisonment, hard labor	
*1812	San Francisco	2 n.	Conspiracy + robbery	Imprisonment, hard labor	
*1812	San Carlos	2 n.	Robbery	Imprisonment, hard labor	
*1812	La Soledad	8 n.	Fugitivism	Imprisonment, hard labor	
*1812	La Soledad	1 n.	Robbery	Imprisonment, hard labor	
*1812	La Soledad	2 n.	Fugitivism + robbery	Imprisonment, hard labor	
1815	San Diego	1 n.	Assault	Flogging (25 × 9)	Prov. St. Pap. Ben. Mil., 45:8

° An asterisk preceding the date indicates the source of the item as the "List of Indians Held Prisoners at the Presidios," Estudillo Docs., 1:218. The offenses are listed in most of these cases, but apart from imprisonment at hard labor the penalties are not given. The date is that of the year of entry. The duration of prison terms is not given.

TABLE 5—Concluded

Year	Place	Number of persons	Offense	Punishment	Source
1815	San Diego	1 n.	Adultery	Flogging (25)	Ibid.
*1815	Santa Clara	2 n.	Fugitivism	Imprisonment, hard labor	
*1815	Santa Clara	7 n.	Fugitivism + bad character	Imprisonment, hard labor	
*1815	Santa Clara	11 g.	Bad character	Imprisonment, hard labor	
*1815	San Juan Bautista	11 n.	Failure to report fugitives	Imprisonment, hard labor	
*1815	San Juan Bautista	2 n.	Stock stealing + homicide	Imprisonment, hard labor	
*1815	San Juan Bautista	1 n.	Bad character	Imprisonment, hard labor	
*1815	San Juan Bautista	2 n.	Stock stealing	Imprisonment, hard labor	
*1815	San Juan Bautista	7 n.	Bad character, no specific charge	Imprisonment, hard labor	
*1815	La Soledad	4 n.	Fugitivism + bad character	Imprisonment, hard labor	
*1815	La Soledad	1 n.	Stock stealing	Imprisonment, hard labor	
1816	San Fernando	1 n.	Fugitivism	Flogging (4 × 10)	De la Guerra Docs., 1:123
1816	San Fernando	3 n.	Fugitivism	Flogging (6 × 10)	Ibid.
1816	San Fernando	4 n.	Fugitivism	Flogging (9 × 10)	Ibid.
1816	San Gabriel	6 n.	Fugitivism	Flogging (2 to 9 × 10)	Ibid.
*1816	San Juan Bautista	7 n.	Stock stealing	Imprisonment, hard labor	
*1816	San Juan Bautista	2 g.	Stock stealing	Imprisonment, hard labor	
*1817	San Juan Bautista	8 n.	Fugitivism + stock stealing	Imprisonment, hard labor	

[120]

*1817	San Francisco	1 n.	Incest	Imprisonment, hard labor	
*1817	Santa Cruz	1 n.	Stock stealing	Imprisonment, hard labor	
1824	La Purísima	7 n.	Conspiracy + armed resistance	Death	Prov. St. Pap. Ben. Mil., 57:36
1824	La Purísima	4 n.	Conspiracy + armed resistance	Imprisonment, hard labor (10 yrs.)	Ibid.
1824	La Purísima	7 n.	Conspiracy + armed resistance	Imprisonment, hard labor (8 yrs.)	Ibid.
1829	San Diego	3 n.	Conducting medicine dances	Imprisonment, hard labor (1 yr.) + flogging (25)	Ibid., 66:69
1830	Monterey	1 n.	Homicide	Imprisonment, hard labor (10 yrs.)	Ibid., 72:7
1831	Monterey	1 n.	Robbery	Death	Dept. Rec., 9:14
1831	Monterey	1 n.	Robbery	Imprisonment, hard labor (6 mos.) + flogging (100)	Prov. St. Pap. Ben. Mil., 73:8

more or less on the warpath. Therefore it appears reasonable to place solitary offenders under the classification of "criminal" and groups under "political." The persons denoted "bad characters" (*malevolos*) were general troublemakers and rebels against the system. It seems preferable to call them political offenders rather than criminal. On the basis of these qualifications, then, of the 362 persons disciplined, 284 were political offenders, 60 were criminals, and 18 were of doubtful category. Omitting the doubtful cases, 82.5 per cent of the persons were punished for political offenses. Even though the data here presented are far from complete, they may be regarded as a reasonably representative sample of the legal and punitive cases which passed through the hands of the military. If this is true, and if we bear in mind that most of the criminal cases (robbery, murder, etc.) went to the secular authorities, whereas the vast majority of the political cases (fugitives, etc.) were taken care of by the missions, then it is apparent that punishments for resistance to the social order far exceeded those inflicted for genuine crimes. It would be conservative to place the chastisement for the former type of dereliction at a minimum of 90 per cent of the total. In other words, the punishment of not more than one Indian in ten would be regarded by his fellow countrymen as the truly merited expiation of evil-doing.

The type of disciplinary measures was frequently degrading and offensive to the Indian. Corporal punishment, or flogging, was of course standard practice in the eighteenth century among all white civilizations, particularly when used upon so-called inferior races. Nevertheless it has been singularly ineffective for, unless the physical effects are so terrific as to break down utterly the spirit of a man, the result is usually to inspire him with an undying, implacable hatred, which in turn communicates itself to all his friends. Imprisonment, or other curtailment of liberty, if properly carried out, does not result in bodily harm, and is much more dreaded by a race to whom freedom means the breath of life. It was therefore unfortunate that the lash was so quickly resorted to by the Spanish administration and applied with such severity. The relative frequency with which corporal punishment was employed may perhaps be gauged by the data in table 5 (although the absolute frequency would have to be determined from more extensive information). The items in the table which were taken from the prison records of the years 1809–1817 (Estudillo Docs.) must be omitted from any such calculation, since they state no more than that the offenders were in jail. These persons, therefore, constitute a selected group. Moreover, many of these culprits may have been flogged in addition to incarceration. Apart from this group there were 209 persons. Of these 71 were flogged, 46 imprisoned, 75 both flogged and imprisoned, and 17 executed. That is, 70 per cent suffered corporal punishment, 57 per cent imprisonment, and 36 per cent both.

Granting that discipline was often necessary and inevitable and that it took the form, as a rule, of confinement and whipping, we must inquire as to the extent and severity of the punishment inflicted. Quite obviously disciplinary measures of a conservative type, inflicted fairly and justly without personal spite for offenses generally conceded to be flagrant, would not be likely to affect the mass of the neophytes as adversely as irrational chastisement, administered for no good cause, in excessive amount, or by cruel methods. Now it so happened that this particular point was seized upon by the enemies of the mission system (both at the time and subsequently) as an argument against the missionaries. Consequently, the verbal testimony, from documentary sources, is conflicting in the extreme. In fact, some of the generalities set forth by the missionaries on the one hand and by some of the military men and civilians on the other are mutually exclusive. Moreover, individual cases have been cited which, perhaps, may have occurred but which alone by no means prove any rule. Since the factor of punishment was quite important in the neophyte environment, it is necessary to quote a sufficiently representative range and body of evidence.

As witness that the neophytes were subjected to a mild and reasonable discipline, we have in the front rank Lasuén, who was at great pains to disprove all charges and imputations of cruelty. Some of his remarks are as follows.[58]

The treatment generally accorded the Indians is very gentle. In the mission of San Francisco too much indulgence is shown. Indeed a missionary of the said San Francisco mission, associated with the priest himself, at

[58] "Representación," San Carlos, Nov. 12, 1800, Sta. Bárb. Arch., 2:199–211.

the time the misrepresentations regarding the accusation of cruelty were formulated proved them all false and malicious. . . . That missionary told me on October 30 last: "For not knowing their lesson in school, the pupils are chastised more than [the neophytes] here for concubinage." If they say that former times are referred to, the same missionary of former times is still there . . .

Then follows a blanket denial of all general charges of cruelty and a repudiation of numerous libelous and malicious allegations. Specific instances are given of these rumors, and the actual moderation and kindness of the missionaries is emphasized. He then proceeds:

It remains for me to speak (and I fear I shall not be able to do so as fully as I desire) of the very gentle treatment we generally accord the Indian. These are gentiles whom we are trying to show that they are men: a people of vicious and ferocious customs, who know no other law than force, nor any authority other than their own free will nor reason other than mere caprice, who watched the cruelest and most barbarous practices with an indifference entirely foreign to human nature, accustomed to punish offenses against them by death. They are a people without education or government or religion or dependence. They have no reluctance whatever in throwing themselves impetuously into anything that their brutal appetites might suggest. Their inclination to lasciviousness and thievery [in the missions] is on a level with that which they show in the wild condition. It is a duty imposed on us to correct and punish men of this kind for their misdemeanors. They commit them [misdemeanors] in all forms—against moral propriety, against tranquility or public and private safety with the greatest readiness and the most incredible repetition.

A discussion of corrective measures is now in order. It is evident that a nation which is barbarous, ferocious[59] and ignorant requires more frequent punishment than a nation which is cultured, educated, and of gentle and moderate customs. The penalties should be adjusted to the state of civilization and the receptivity of the people and should not be less (nor, I suppose, greater) than corresponds to the misdemeanor. The procedure should be such that it may not prove ineffective nor prejudicial. Repetition [of the penalty] is a circumstance that aggravates the transgression because the most perverted and obstinate soul becomes set in vice and the stage may arrive where the delinquent has become incorrigible. Take note! I do not

[59] Lest the reader be entirely carried away by Lasuén's picture of the terrible California Indian, it might not be unfair to call to mind the many statements made by the exploring missionaries when they first encountered the gentiles. Under such circumstances, the latter were usually characterized as being very mild, peaceable, and amenable to Christianizing influence. The truth seems to be that for wild Indians the California tribes were definitely less barbarous and ferocious than, say, the Apaches or Yaquis.

intend to imply that the treatment we generally accord these Indians is pitched at the maximum severity, but the contrary. Our actual method is as follows.

The first offense: patience. The second: patience. The third: patience, and always patience. The punishment in order to be effective must be strictly necessary. Despite their being humans of such low grade, they are poor wretched mortals and worthy of the best treatment; consequently the gentlest and mildest means should be employed by preference. In order to resort to severity (and then always to the minimum extent), it is requisite to have exhausted the ultimate efforts of kindness—in the manner of a gentle and discreet family father with his children. The penalty should only serve to correct effectively and not to torment the delinquent ...

The system of treatment we generally give these Indians is founded on these axioms and principles. From these originates the fact that however grave and serious the misdeed may be, it is never ordered to give anyone more than twenty-five lashes and with an instrument incapable of drawing blood or of causing notable contusions. . . . The fugitives, despite absences of long duration, and although they may have committed mischief during their absence, are forgiven if they voluntarily surrender. And finally, no penalties are ever applied other than those solely correctional, even though the Indian insists on manifesting himself as incorrigible ...

The regime which has been here expounded, and which is in effect, shows that the treatment generally given the Indian is very gentle. If some missionary should violate it, more violated is the order of fair-minded thinking by him, who for private reasons, says that the treatment generally accorded the Indians is quite severe.

The next paragraphs admit the possibility of variation in individual character among the missionaries but flatly deny that there are any who are very severe (*muy duro*). If there were such, he would be removed immediately.

Since the discussion of punishment by Lasuén is the fullest, most authoritative, and most reliable which we possess, it may not be inappropriate to point out that, whereas he very ably sets forth the guiding principles of mission conduct in this matter, he is specific on only one point. That is the statement that twenty-five represents the maximum number of lashes ever given. We know he must be in error because there are numerous instances on record of floggings amounting to fifty or even one hundred lashes. Furthermore, his answer to concrete charges of excessive punishments in general consists of a flat denial without examination of particular evidence.

Tapis and Cortes likewise emphasized the leniency of the missionaries.[60]

> The punishments that we missionaries of Santa Bárbara visit on the Indians, when corrective measures and reprimands are of no avail are: fetters, lashes, shackles, and the stocks. The women are rarely chastised by means of the devices mentioned with the exception of the stocks . . .

> A boy, a man, or a woman flees from the mission, or does not return until other neophytes are sent to bring him or her in. On arrival at the mission he or she is reprimanded for the offense by obliging him or her to attend mass on holidays. He is made to comprehend that he voluntarily subjected himself to this and other Christian obligations and is threatened with punishment if further lapse into delinquency is incurred. If he repeats the flight or again has to be brought back, he will then suffer punishment by lashes and in the stocks. If he is very recalcitrant, as some are, and does not take heed, he is made to undergo the punishment of the fetters . . . The same is done with those who live in concubinage, those who steal anything of importance, or fight, incurring the danger of causing injury . . .

> The delinquencies of the women are punished by one, two, or three days in the stocks, in proportion to the seriousness [of the delinquency]. However, if they persist in keeping bad company, or in escaping they are punished [i.e., whipped] at the hands of another woman in the quarters of the single women . . .

> The Indians have realized that they never are punished unless we are convinced of their guilt and that by the grace of God they are never punished on account of rancor toward anyone. They take this punishment with humility and after suffering it are still as fond of the fathers as before.

The following statements are from soldiers and civilians who saw the missions in operation and refer to the actual punishments used.

> The punishment that the Indians suffer in their missions, whatever the dereliction may be . . . consists of lashes for both sexes, with the difference that if the misdemeanor is of lesser import, it does not exceed five lashes, and if it is of greater degree, the punishment may be up to fifty, in addition applying shackles . . .[61]

> The customary punishment imposed on the neophytes consists of twenty-five, thirty-three, fifty lashes and a *novenario* of twenty-five lashes per day depending on the infraction. In the case of the women it is gentler on account of the weakness of the sex . . .[62]

[60] Reply to Goycoechea's answers to the fifteen questions, Santa Bárbara, Oct. 30, 1800, Sta. Bárb. Arch., 2:86–143.

[61] Sal to Borica, Monterey, Dec. 15, 1798, Prov. St. Pap., 17:63.

[62] Grajera to Borica, San Diego, Mar. 21, 1799, *ibid.,* p. 191.

Punishment is never to exceed twenty-five lashes at one time although, if the offense is serious, this may be repeated in one week, or seven to eight lashes per day may be given. The women are to be chastised by other women.[63]

If the offense was fairly serious lashes were given which rarely exceeded twenty-five and on many occasions were fewer.[64]

[At Mission San Fernando] the greatest number of lashes which were imposed by the priest for any serious offense was twenty-five. When the crime was very grave, such as murder, robbery, etc., it was customary to have a *novenario* given: twenty-five lashes daily for nine days—but this was on the sentence of the governor or military commander.[65]

The penalties imposed were the stocks, prison, and when the offense was serious . . . they were given twenty-five lashes and upwards, according to the crime.[66]

The treatment accorded the Indians was very stern. Their shortcomings were pardoned but rarely or through special consideration. A very minor dereliction was punished with fifteen lashes, a more serious one with twenty-five. A person who was absent from work over two weeks through laziness or anything else not thoroughly justified suffered fifty lashes. Other serious infractions, such as quarrels at the rancherias, fights, or the use of arrows brought one hundred lashes and a set of shackles at the guard house.[67]

At least two provincial governors, Fages and Borica, concerned themselves with the discipline of the neophytes in the sense that they repeatedly expressed the opinion that chastisement was too severe. Although the testimony of both these men must be discounted considerably in view of their known dislike for the missionaries, there is doubtless a residuum of fact in their statements.

Fages in 1783 complained bitterly against Junípero Serra,[68] saying that "chastisement by putting in chains is very frequent in all the missions, but principally at Carmel, and also forced labor is resorted to."

[63] Paraphrase of statement by Father J. Casal of regulations for the conduct of missionaries, College of San Fernando, Mexico, Oct. 1, 1806, Sta. Bárb. Arch., 9:341.

[64] Apolinaria Lorenzana, "Memorias," MS, 1878, p. 13.

[65] J. M. Romero, "Memorias," MS, 1878, p. 20.

[66] Perez, "Una vieja," p. 20.

[67] Amador, "Memorias," p. 103.

[68] To Inspector General, Monterey, March 1, 1783, Prov. Rec., 3:87. The bitter personal animosity between these two men colored all their relations. Serra, who, to be sure, was a strong supporter of the corporal punishment system (cf. his letter to Neve, 1780, Sta. Bárb. Arch., 10:94), denied indignantly all charges advanced by Fages.

In 1784 he stated his reflections concerning excessive chastisement of Indians and noted the moderate flogging (25 lashes) received by the Gabrielenos who confessed to a plot to murder the priests and soldiers.[69] He also ascribed the quietness of the gentiles near San José and San Francisco to the light punishment of the previous year. But in 1785 he was complaining again. Writing to Father Matías he said he had heard and had seen with grief "that this father is chastising Indians with chains for trivial offenses."[70] Meanwhile the presidial commanders were not too lenient, for there is a letter from the *Comandante General* to Fages cautioning him against too drastic punishment for fear it will stir up trouble among both Christian and gentile Indians.[71] The immediate occasion was the imposition of stiff penalties by Zuñiga at San Diego.

When Governor Borica came to California, he apparently was very deeply shocked by the wretched state of the neophytes. Even though some of his acts and utterances may have had political motivation and perhaps contained a little of the element of hypocrisy, his first reaction to the mission system was undoubtedly one of amazement and aversion. He seems, at least for a while, to have been genuinely solicitous of the welfare of the neophytes. In August, 1796, he wrote that the missionaries at San Francisco were chastising the Indians too severely and that the army was to have no part in it.[72] He referred to "the sad, miserable Indians who have suffered and are suffering so much in that mission." Later in the same year he made a strong representation to Lasuén to treat the Indians better,[73] averring that the chief cause of their running away was the harsh treatment they received. Imbued with this spirit, he sent to his presidial commanders the questionnaire on the missions, the answers to which have been quoted freely in this discussion.[74] The governor's interference, together with certain statements made by a disgruntled missionary, Father

---

[69] To Soler, Monterey, Feb. 10, 1784, Prov. Rec., 2:98.

[70] To Matías, Monterey, June 11, 1785, *ibid.*, 3:51.

[71] Ugarte y Loyola to Fages, Chihuahua, Aug. 8, 1786, Prov. St. Pap., 6:91.

[72] Borica to Alberni, Monterey, August 11, 1796, Prov. St. Pap. Ben. Mil., 24:8.

[73] Borica to Lasuén, Monterey, Sept. 15, 1796, Prov. Rec., 6:172. In this volume of the Provincial Records there are no less than nine letters of Borica written to missionaries for the specific purpose of securing better handling of the neophytes.

[74] Borica to commanders of presidios, Monterey, Dec. 3, 1798, *ibid.*, 4:167.

Concepción Horra, drew forth very lively retorts from the clergy, including the "Representación" of Lasuén. Whether much change was effected by the agitation and so-called "reform" is doubtful, because the conditions which so troubled Borica were inherent in the system. Only the excesses could be eliminated and, as very justly pointed out by the clergy, the excesses, more often than not, were committed by the soldiers rather than the priests. However, Borica did feel that something of a local nature had been accomplished for he wrote that the Indians at San Francisco "are not flogged or maltreated as previously, and are not worked too hard."[75]

Subsequent to Borica's administration, agitation subsided, except for a few isolated cases,[76] until in the last years of the mission period the question again gave rise to controversy. In 1831 a case of some notoriety came before the courts. The majordomo of Santa Isabel Farm, attached to San Diego mission, was actually prosecuted on a charge of unnecessary cruelty in flogging Indians for cattle stealing and was sentenced to five years in prison.[77] The same year a San Diego neophyte committed robbery. The prosecutor asked for a light sentence and took the occasion to make a bitter attack on the missions, particularly for their habit of flogging Indians.[78] During the same period Mariano G. (afterward General) Vallejo was conducting a bitter campaign against the missions. On several occasions he entered complaints of inhumanity against the priests.[79] In an attempt to meet the criticism of his enemies the prefect, Father F. G. Diego, ordered corporal punishment reduced to a minimum. He wrote, apropos of the accusations of Vallejo:[80]

The Alcaldes of the mission, seeing my just aversion to flogging, and which at my coming I began to abolish, said to me several times: "if they did not

---

[75] Borica to viceroy, Monterey, July 1, 1798, *ibid.,* 6:97.

[76] An illuminating incident occurred in 1808 (De la Guerra Docs., 3:125) when three Indians murdered their majordomo at San Diego. Captain de la Guerra urged the viceroy to leniency, stating that the immediate provocation was *"el mucho castigo"* and general maltreatment inflicted by the majordomo. Complaints were frequent against these household officials, who were the deputies of the missionaries. They were almost always Indians themselves and tended to be overbearing and cruel in the exercise of their authority.

[77] Gomez, "Proceso," San Carlos, March 11, 1831, Prov. St. Pap. Ben. Mil., 72:11.

[78] Victoria, "Causa Criminal," Monterey, Aug. 27, 1831, *ibid.,* 73:4.

[79] Vallejo Docs., 2:52, 124.

[80] Diego to Figueroa, Santa Clara, June 30, 1833, Archb. Arch., 5(1):80.

continue to chastise delinquencies as heretofore, the mission would be lost." I replied that I was going to alter nothing, that they should comply with their obligations. As a result they have done some flogging, as has the majordomo, but only a few times, for I have stopped them with convincing reasons. My reason, my ideas, my feelings together are opposed to this custom of which I have never approved. Already in this mission under my charge such punishment as revolts my soul is being abolished.

The prefect's views were not shared by Father J. M. Gutiérrez of San Francisco, who wrote that as a result of a more lenient policy the neophytes were becoming worse. He then advanced a long argument for the old system of corporal punishment.[81]

It is perfectly obvious that the sudden solicitude for the welfare of the mission Indians developed by Vallejo and others had an entirely political origin. It is beyond human credulity to believe that the man who was notorious for his savage military campaigns against the wild Indians should be overcome with pity for their sad condition in the missions, nor is it to be imagined that it was the pure milk of human kindness which prompted criticism by other army officials at a time when all these gentry had their eye on possible profit to be derived from secularized mission property. Regardless of motive, however, it is significant that the military coterie was able to put its finger on corporal punishment as a weak point in the mission defenses. Had the clergy really been lenient, had punishment really been mild, fair, and just, the issue never could have been raised. The fact that the prefect gave ground, that he undertook to mitigate or even abolish corporal punishment, indicates an attempt to correct a situation which, in his writings at least, he admits was abhorrent to him, and this action establishes as basically justified (even after being trimmed of exaggeration) the charge of severe and unwarranted punitive discipline.

Apart from clerical and military testimony and apart from the recollections of the white people we possess one statement by a mission Indian himself. This was Lorenzo Asesara, an ex-neophyte of Santa Cruz who dictated his memoirs to one of H. H. Bancroft's workers.[82] Although one might expect to find any degree of exaggera-

---

[81] Gutiérrez to governor, San Francisco, June 16, 1833, Dept. St. Pap., Ben., 2:12.

[82] These recollections are interpolated in the manuscript "Memorias," by J. M. Amador, pp. 58–77 and 90–113.

tion, vituperation, and distortion of fact in a statement by a mission
Indian, the story given by Asesara bears every indication of sobriety,
fairness, and adherence to the truth as it was known to him. The
internal evidence is strong that the author was telling the facts as he
had personally encountered them. Moreover, he remains strictly within
the scope of his own experience and hazards no generalities beyond
his personal horizon. The first part of his story deals with the Quintana murder at Santa Cruz, a detailed, circumstantial account, in
which it is stated without rancor that the murderers were incensed at
the chastisement Father Quintana administered. In the second section
are recounted certain extreme brutalities committed by Father Olbes
of the same mission, in the line of discipline. Having described these
affairs, to some of which he was an eyewitness, Asesara goes on to say,

. . . although Olbes was cruel in his punishments, on the other hand, he
was very careful to keep his people well fed and clothed. . . . The Spanish
padres were very cruel to the Indians; they treated them very badly; they
kept them well fed . . . and they made them work like slaves.

Despite his strictures against Fathers Quintana and Olbes, Asesara is
very careful to say that the other priests he knew at Santa Cruz were
consistently kind-hearted and moderate in their discipline. One derives
the impression, which is substantiated by much other evidence from
various sources, that the treatment accorded the Indians varied im-
mensely, depending on the personality in charge. This is as might be
expected and is no more than a general expression of the variability
inherent in human nature. The critical point is that the immoderate
individual, the relatively rare stern or cruel missionary, exerted an
influence on neophyte opinion far out of proportion to his actual power
to do physical damage. Just as Simon Legree became the prototype of
Southern slave overseer to the Northern mind, so did the Duráns and
the Olbes come to typify the system to the mission Indian. Thus the
excesses of a few tended to overbalance the sane and moderate policy
of the majority.

In addition to the testimony cited in the preceding paragraphs, the
data in table 5 enable us to arrive at some idea of the actual extent of
corporal punishment and imprisonment, although it must be admitted at the outset that any such calculation is subject to very great

error because of the paucity of material. Furthermore, the items included in the table may not be wholly representative since (1) they constitute only the most serious criminal cases, (2) the cases handled by the military are too heavily weighted with respect to those offenses which were taken care of in the missions, and (3) owing to gaps in the official records, some years are not included at all. With these reservations an estimate may be attempted. In the period 1794–1799 inclusive 17 cases are mentioned, with 49 persons, and from 1810–1817 inclusive there are 48 cases with 203 persons. The annual means of persons punished are 8.2 and 25.3 respectively for the two time intervals. These particular periods are selected because they show the greatest number of cases on the records. Now quite clearly, apart from other factors, the number of criminals will depend upon the total population. In terms of the latter, the first period had 0.7 per thousand and the second 1.4 per thousand persons undergoing punishment. But the data for the second period included many prisoners in the presidio which the first period did not. Deducting these, we find an annual mean of 0.45 persons per thousand. With respect to the presidial prisoners for this period the years 1813 and 1814 are omitted in the original list. Allowing for this omission, the mean value per annum, for presidial prisoners was 1.3 persons per thousand. But this list included only prisoners at Monterey. Allowance of at least as many more must be made for the other three presidios together—a total of 2.6. This is undoubtedly an underestimate, but it may stand. With respect to the other cases cited in the list, adjustments must likewise be made. In the first place, no claim to entire completeness can be made. There are, no doubt, other documents bearing on other cases from the years 1794–1799 and 1810–1817, which have escaped attention. But leaving this point out of consideration, we must remember that we possess records only of cases sufficiently important to warrant official attention and correspondence, that is, those which were so serious that the missionaries had to turn the guilty parties over to the military for discipline, or at least had to consult with them. It is impossible to know how these cases compared, numerically, with the regular run-of-the-mill disciplinary cases within the missions. It would certainly be conservative to assume that not one case in ten ever was heard of by the

[132]

secular authorities, and perhaps not one case in one hundred. If we establish these as the limits of probability, we find an annual mean of 7 to 70 per thousand for the first period and 4.5 to 45 per thousand for the second. Provided the two periods considered were representative of the mission era as a whole, we get, on the basis of the extreme values here indicated, a probable 5 to 70 persons per thousand subject to corporal punishment during a year. Finally, even allowing for repeated chastisement of certain incorrigible individuals, the number of neophytes who at some time during their career were subjected to discipline must have been very much greater. A factor of three cannot be excessive. This would mean that from 15 to 210 persons out of every thousand must at some time have felt the lash or endured imprisonment. Even if any exactitude on the part of these figures is disregarded, it is highly probable that a very material number of the neophytes acquired personal experience with mission chastisements.

The efficacy of the punitive code in preventing reactions against the social order is very difficult to evaluate, as for that matter is the efficacy of the punitive system enforced by any civilization or culture. The missionaries, according to their statement, felt it was essential and that in its absence their whole system would collapse. There can be no doubt that the neophytes reacted very adversely to chastisement insofar as their feelings and inclinations were concerned. On the other hand, the clergy were perhaps correct in thinking that it functioned as a deterrent to apostasy and resistance. The problem is one of degree rather than principle. But there is one further consideration which must be taken into account. Corporal punishment for running away, for armed resistance, and for general raiding could be effective only in conjunction with a stiff policy of pursuit and capture. Quite clearly, if a neophyte thought he could get away and avoid forcible return to his mission, any threat of retribution after his return would be meaningless, or if he could commit a misdemeanor in the mission and be certain of escape thereafter, he would feel no concern over that penalty for the crime which could be exacted only in the mission itself. Certainty of capture, therefore, was as vital to the effectiveness of the system as the actual chastisement. Throughout most of the mission period the probability of capture was very high, and relatively few neophytes made a permanent escape. Up to, let us say, 1830 the combination of pursuit and punishment must have been definitely effective. To what extent this was true may be judged in a general way by the events following secularization and the breakdown of all systematic attempts to pursue and recapture runaway neophytes. From 1834 to 1840, as is well known, the missions disintegrated. The neophytes scattered far and wide, despite the fact that corporal punishment was still kept in force by the administrators of the missions. The phenomena accompanying secularization thus afford strong evidence that physical chastisement, of itself alone, failed to prevent crime and disorder or to keep the Indians in the missions. Real felonies, such as murder, rape, and robbery, may well have been held in check by the punitive system as also may have been minor delinquencies of a strictly intramission character. But it becomes doubtful whether the reactions against the mission social order epitomized by escape and armed resistance were materially reduced by physical chastisement per se. If this was what happened, then chastisement must be regarded as acting only as an irritant to both the individual and group. As such, it constituted an environmental factor to which the mission Indian found great difficulty in making suitable adjustment. Furthermore, in the manner suggested previously, it served as a focal point of disaffection and strongly intensified all responses counter to the mission culture.

VI. CERTAIN CULTURAL ASPECTS

IN EVERY CONTACT between human groups the ultimate equilibrium is determined, not only by material and biotic considerations such as reproduction, death, and disease, but also by a complex of nonmaterial, purely cultural factors. Much of the conflict in ideas and ideals which extended throughout the mission period has already been considered, particularly with reference to those points at issue wherein the struggle on the cultural plane was reflected in changes in the material status of the Indian. Such, for example, were the aboriginal theories and practice with respect to labor conditions and sex relations, or to crime and punishment. This background was clearly the decisive influence in determining the mode of response to the introduced civilization, particularly in so far as that response involved reaction on the part of individuals. Even gross population changes, although immediately dependent upon physical and physiological factors, such as diet, disease, or climate, may be influenced secondarily by intangible forces which mediate choice of food, care of sanitation, type of shelter, or procreative tendency.

It is thus impossible to dissociate the more material results of racial contact from the contributing imponderables. Nevertheless, in this realm of the cultural, there are certain factors which are of interest in a special sense. They represent ideas or habits on the part of more primitive groups which affect only remotely its physical status or economic welfare with respect to competition with the dominant race, but which on their own plane conflict with the corresponding traits of the latter. The appearance and disappearance of such cultural traits come within the purview of the anthropologist rather than the biologist, or perhaps fall between the two fields of interest, yet such phenomena can scarcely be excluded from any comprehensive study of racial interaction. The problem in the present connection may be briefly formulated thus: to what extent did those Indian characteristics undergo in the missions modifications which were not vital to physical or economic survival?

Obviously, this question is not susceptible to numerical, quantitative treatment. The best one can do is to assess opinion and indicate tendencies. Moreover, relatively few actual traits can be investigated, and those few only in their broad outlines. An exact study of the changes occurring in a cultural pattern can be made only if the original situation is known in detail and the final result is similarly well worked out. We have at hand, to be sure, a very precise knowledge of the aboriginal culture of the California Indian tribes, and by careful field work an analogous picture of present-day conditions could be obtained. But the situation after seventy years of missionization is very obscure in detail, and the end product is very difficult to visualize. In fact, the available documentary evidence permits examination of no more than four primary, general factors, each of which is probably a complex rather than a single cultural trait or process. These are (1) the idea of law, including attitude toward property rights; (2) language; (3) retention of primitive customs, rites, cults, and religious beliefs; and (4) assimilation of a new ethical code, Christianity.

Property rights.—In a previous discussion, some consideration has been given to the question of crime and its punishment. The emphasis was there laid upon the aspects of fugitivism and the effect of corporal punishment on the flight response. It was suggested that "political" misdeameanors were of more consequence than "private" crimes in the social conflict of the Indians with the mission system. At the same time vast difficulty and misunderstanding was caused by the failure of the Indian to appreciate the white man's reverence for the sanctity of private ownership.[1] This failing as a rule took the form of petty theft, together with all manner of deception and subterfuge for the purpose of acquiring possession of personal property. As a rule, such operations were on a small scale, were confined to easily transportable items, and did not involve physical violence.[2] Nevertheless, the irritant effect was large and contributed to ill feeling between the races to an extent entirely out of proportion to the material damage inflicted.

As a result of many years' experience, the Spanish colonists in California, military, ecclesiastical, and civilian, came to regard the Indian

---

[1] This problem is far broader than the field of the missions. Theft and robbery have always been at the root of the difficulties between the red man and white wherever they have met. There is thus no reason except convenience for limiting consideration of the matter to mission society.

[2] An exception was, of course, the raiding of livestock, which, however, may be considered as a separate category of behavior.

as a confirmed thief and robber, afflicted with an inborn, constitutional proclivity for larceny and duplicity. This point of view was further intensified during and after secularization when thousands of poverty-stricken ex-neophytes roamed the country appropriating everything they could lay hands on. In thorough agreement were the Americans who arrived after 1845 and who had had their own experience along the frontier for generations. As a result, there has arisen the very deep conviction that the Indian, wherever found, is totally without principles respecting other people's possessions and the means of acquiring them.

It is very doubtful whether there is any greater inherent tendency toward thievery in the Indian than in the white man. Indeed, it is probable that this manifestation of so-called Indian character derives, not from any feature of genetic constitution, but from the clash of aboriginal cultural background and training with the corresponding civilized legal and moral code.

Modern ethnographic research has demonstrated clearly that the California natives had a very keen sense of ownership, and that several tribes, at least, had evolved a highly complex pattern of conduct and behavior toward property. The Yurok, among whom, perhaps, such codes of action were most elaborately developed,[3] not only held land under private ownership, but placed exact valuation in terms of monetary units on land, commodities, and rights or privileges of all kinds. In common with most other tribes, even a wife was the personal possession of the husband, and any failure in marital relations, such as desertion or adultery, was financially assessable. Any other invasion of property rights was, likewise, to be computed on a monetary basis, and the guilty party was invariably liable for compensation. As Kroeber puts it: "The Yurok concerns his life above all else with property." Although the remaining California tribes did not go to such extremes as the Yurok, there is no reason to suppose that in all of them there was not a very definite appreciation of the integral connection between an individual and what belonged to him. Indian law, or rather the framework of custom according to which the Indian regulated his

---

[3] Kroeber, *Handbook of the Indians of California,* Smithson. Inst., Bur. Amer. Ethn., Bull. 78 (1925), chaps. on the Yurok.

conduct, was very explicit concerning the point that ownership of at least certain commodities was vested in the individual and that violations were punishable by the individual. Since, now, in his original social state the Indian adhered to tribal custom with great fidelity, there is no ground whatever for the opinion that he violated the property rights of other persons to a material extent. Certainly he cannot have been a congenital thief, since the social structure he built is predicated upon the very opposite assumption. Why, then, did he develop, with such startling rapidity, a larcenous disposition as soon as he came in contact with the whites?[4] There are three possible clues to this clash in behavior. They all lie in the fundamental difference between the primitive Indian and the civilized European legal structure.

1. Indian custom, at least among most of the northern California tribes, was highly individualistic. Transgressions against property were a matter to be settled strictly between the persons involved, with little, if any, interference by outside agencies. In the Indian view the village or group was in no wise concerned. Nor was there any superior power vested in the community as a whole which could enforce a code of conduct or punish infractions. The chief deterrent to crime against property, therefore, was the power of the owner to exact compensation or other retribution. Against the white man, in the beginning, the Indian had no way of estimating such retributive power in the individual and had had no experience with retribution by the state. It was quite in accord with human nature, therefore, that he should try a little exploratory pilfering, particularly since the newcomers invariably carried with them an endless array of new, highly desirable articles. If the initial offenses were not punished swiftly and surely, as they often were not, a precedent would have been established whereby the aborigine might secure certain material benefits of civili-

---

[4] Numerous narrations of the early explorers and settlers in California indicate that the very first contact between wild groups and the white man were characterized by robbery on the part of the Indians. For example, Junípero Serra states ("Memorial" of 1773 in Prov. St. Pap., 1:101): "As to this [theft] there is adduced the curiosity and liveliness of the same Gentiles, in particular those of Santa Bárbara Channel, who want to see everything and, if they can steal some object of ours, principally if metallic, they will not forego the opportunity. This in turn will appear to our people a capital offense, as has occurred several times. Few have been the times when the soldiers have passed by without killing some or several."

zation which otherwise would be denied him. If punishment was inflicted, it was most effective if meted out by the injured party in person; as suggested previously, the Indian had little comprehension of the justice of impersonal enforcement of property rights by regularly constituted officers of the law or by society through its agents. Yet this was precisely the manner of procedure adopted by the Spanish ecclesiastico-military state. Doubtless the result was often a bewilderment which intensified the sense of injustice felt by the victim.

2. Indian society, in its original form was very close and self-contained. Tribal custom applied strictly and literally to the tribe, and to no other group. In its most extreme form, the rancheria or village became the tribal unit. With respect to the property of outsiders, the rules of conduct to which the Indian adhered quite faithfully in his relations with his own social unit, ceased to hold, or at least were more or less weakened. The possessions of the next village or of the tribe the other side of the mountain were thus in a sense legitimate booty. Hence the forcible or covert acquisition of such commodities was not theft at all, in the narrow sense: looting or pillage, perhaps, but not larceny. This loosening of restraint increased with distance from the local community until the code ceased to apply at all. Consequently, members of a strange and different race were fair game, totally beyond the scope of the tribal code. That the Indian maintained a double standard, one for his own people, the other for strangers, was recognized by the missionaries. In the "Contestación" of 1811 we find the following:[5]

They lie and cheat those who are not of their own color and class, but not their own people. —San Juan Bautista.

The old people say that among themselves, originally, there was no such lying and trickery. But now that they are among Christians they seldom tell the truth. —San Carlos.

They have always kept faith among themselves with respect to their agreements. They give, borrow and make contracts like brothers, not like strangers. —San Carlos.

These poor people are quite faithful in keeping their few and simple agreements. —The President.

---

[5] Sta. Bárb. Arch., 7:190–192. The statements quoted were written in direct answer to questions bearing on legality and morals among the neophytes.

3. The Indian custom law, as has been pointed out, was a code of conduct regulating everyday relations between individuals. As such, it represented what experience in village life had taught the Indian was the most expedient way of life. There was little, if any, tinge of morality or ethics, no connotation of right or wrong,[6] no implication whatever that any principles were involved which possessed general applicability. The systematized legal systems of the Spanish or American settlers, with their abstractions and concepts of the right of a man to his possessions, were utterly foreign to the Indian cast of thought and completely incomprehensible to him. The integration of such ideas in the ethical system of Christianity likewise lay beyond his imagination. The motive of morals and conscience was, therefore, entirely lacking.

The complete inability of the Indian, even after years of religious instruction, to grasp the substance of the concept of right versus wrong was appreciated by the Spanish officials perhaps more keenly than by the clergy.

For example, in 1822 at San Buenaventura, a neophyte killed his wife because of infidelity.[7] The case went to Mexico, where the *Fiscal de lo Criminal* held:

[The criminal] is very poorly instructed in the Christian religion. . . . It has been six or seven years since he was baptized; he has not confessed, nor does he know the meaning of Confession or any other Sacrament, for which reason I consider him without any understanding of the laws of our sacred religion.

On the occasion of another murder, Governor Borica rendered the opinion that the neophytes "accustomed in their heathendom to kill without scruple have not yet grasped the evil of this crime, nor the justice of our laws."[8]

---

[6] The amorality of Indian law has been stressed by Kroeber (*Handbook,* p. 683), who has developed this thesis at length.

[7] Antonio Olivera to the commandant at Santa Bárbara, "Causa Criminal," Prov. St. Pap. Ben. Mil., 53:64–67. There are numerous cases in the records (e.g., *ibid.,* 49:7–8 and 82–85) where neophytes were prosecuted for murdering their wives when the latter committed adultery. The right, under Indian law, to inflict this punishment on an erring wife is well recognized. The persistence of the custom to such an extent in the missions in spite of the teaching of the Church is good evidence of the tenacity with which the Indian held to his native habits.

[8] Borica to viceroy, 1798, Prov. Rec., 6:74, 122.

A very clear exposition of the Indian psychology when confronted with civilized concepts of legal morality was that of José Estudillo in connection with another trial for murder. In this instance, Estudillo was attorney for the defense. He said in part:[9]

Everyone knows that generally these Indians in their heathendom do not have the least scruple against robbery, kidnapping women from each other, having four, five, six and even more concubines at one time, or even murder. It is certain that the Indian, whether Gentile or Christian, covets what he sees and steals what he can without causing him any emotion for he considers it quite proper....

These [neophytes] cannot divest themselves so easily of the customs of their barbarism nor can the greatest sacrifice on the part of the missionaries rid them of those customs so quickly. For it is manifest that, if it took many years of labor to bring more highly civilized Indians to perfect instruction in our Religion [referring to Mexico itself], how much less can be accomplished with a people ... who know no more than they can retain in their minds from day to day.

From the foregoing, and from much other testimony, it is plain that in the mass, the mission Indians never assimilated the full significance of Christian ethics in so far as they pertain to social conduct. Indeed, one cannot conceive of a harder task at which to set a primitive and barbarous racial group. To accomplish this task would have demanded a complete reorganization of the Indian's intellect and reorientation of his emotional life. That such a process was begun and carried quite a distance by the missionaries cannot be doubted, but that it was largely unsuccessful is likewise apparent. Furthermore, the emotional disturbance and mental conflict induced by the clash of systems and its inevitable rewards and punishments must have been very great. As a result, it is quite possible that the very traits were intensified which the missionaries most deeply deplored and labored the hardest to eradicate.

If the preceding analysis is at all correct, we must conclude that the exaggerated tendency toward theft and other crimes observed in the converted Indians was not due to any inherent depravity but was a

[9] "Causa Criminal," San Francisco, 1809, Prov. St. Pap. Ben. Mil., 40:1–10. Although most of the statements of Spaniards concerning Indian reaction to Christian law were made with reference to serious crimes such as homicide, the opinions they express apply equally well to all legal infractions, including theft.

purely cultural phenomenon arising as the result of the collision between traditional Indian custom and superimposed civilized legal and
ethical systems.

Language.—A fair index to cultural adaptation and amalgamation is
language. It is a trait which does not in itself imply such conflict as
some other factors, since the acquisition of a new tongue by no means
necessitates the surrender of the old. Nevertheless, if the primitive race
adopts the foreign idiom extensively, such a tendency is an indication
that intellectual intercourse is lively, and it follows that cultural fusion
is proceeding with a reasonable rapidity. This acculturation may be
assumed to go on whether or not the aboriginal tongue is retained.
But if the primitive group for any reason refuses to learn and use the
new language, then it may be inferred that communication between
the two groups is restricted, that assimilation of new ideas is slow,
and that the native race is not adapting itself readily to the new
environment.

Whether or not the California Indian acquired Spanish in the missions extensively and with facility is difficult to decide. It will be
necessary to review such evidence as we possess, but previously the
point must be stressed that the mission, despite religious instruction,
is a very poor environment for the development of facility in a new
language. This is for two reasons. In the first place, the aggregation of
large masses of Indians in the presence of very few, perhaps no more
than one or two, white men would cut down enormously the physical
opportunity to hear the new language spoken. In the second place,
the normal channels of intercourse, trade, labor, warfare, etc., were
largely cut off. The neophytes dealt primarily from day to day with
each other. It was only on the relatively rare occasions when they went
to work at the presidios, or hired out in the civilian families or ranches,
or when they went to the pueblos that they encountered the free give-
and-take which makes for learning a foreign tongue.

Considering the total lack of objective data or even expert opinion,
we are obliged to fall back upon a few scattered and casual statements.
Fortunately, when the questionnaire was sent out in 1811 to the missionaries, a report on linguistic progress was requested. The answers
were very brief and unexplicit. Nevertheless, they are perhaps illumi-

nating in their very lack of uniformity.[10] A brief formulation is as follows:

... Some speak Spanish, although with much difficulty.

—The President.

... They also understand and speak our Spanish language, specially the youth.

—San Diego.

... Many of the Christians, specially the men, speak and understand Spanish, although not perfectly.

—San Luis Rey.

... The Indians speak their native tongue and many understand Spanish without comprehending it very well.

—San Juan Capistrano.

Those who consort most with other classes talk Spanish ...

—San Gabriel.

... There are many who understand Spanish, but they speak it imperfectly.

—San Fernando.

... Several neophytes understand Spanish somewhat ...

—Santa Bárbara.

... Some understand and speak Spanish.

—Santa Ynéz.

As yet they understand Spanish but little ...

—San Miguel.

... They understand much of the Spanish language and talk with considerable ease ...

—San Antonio.

Few are those who understand Spanish ...

—San Luis Obispo.

... Most of them understand and speak Spanish fairly well; the rest, although they speak little, understand something ...

—San Carlos.

Those of this mission speak Spanish regularly ...

—Santa Cruz.

Practically all understand and speak Spanish ...

—Santa Clara.

Among them are many who understand and speak Spanish adequately ...

—San José.

With the exception of the converted Gentiles, all the rest speak Spanish, and of the former, many speak it.

—San Francisco.

---

[10] It must be remembered that the missionaries undoubtedly made out as good a case as possible. In conformity with traditional Spanish colonial policy, every effort was to be made to introduce Castilian among the natives, and in so far as possible to suppress the local idiom. This policy had, indeed, been reaffirmed in a royal decree transmitted by Borica in 1795 (Prov. Rec., 6:143).

To complete the record a few more opinions may be added to those cited above. (The first three of the following statements are from the "Contestación" of 1811.)

It is not easy to find a means and method to teach the Indians to talk Spanish well, because it is extremely difficult to make them neglect their own idiom when the majority speak the native rather than the foreign tongue.   —San Juan Bautista.

. . . And if the Indians do not speak and understand more Spanish it is due to their extreme barbarism and great unwillingness to forego their own language. . . .   —Santa Clara.

. . . The reason why they do not know it [Spanish] is their frequent communication and intercourse with their relatives and countrymen, both Christian and heathen.   —Santa Bárbara.

. . . Great effort is made to teach them all Castilian but progress is made only among the men, very little among the women.[11]

They speak their *idiomas* but one can see that they are usually quite attracted to the Spanish language.[12]

I have frequently heard him [one of the missionaries] talking to the Indians in Spanish, and a few answering him in the same but most in their own tongue, sometimes the conversation in two languages between the missionary and Indians lasting a long time.[13]

. . . A few still remain whose whole stock of Spanish was contained in the never-failing address of *"Amar a Dios"* . . . This was because they totally lacked knowledge of Spanish and no priest knew theirs.[14]

If we examine the twenty-three statements given above we find, liberally interpreted, that nine are affirmative or doubtful, whereas fourteen are negative, at least by implication. Since all but one of the statements are by missionaries whose interest lay in emphasizing the cultural advancement of their neophytes, it appears a reasonable conclusion that the Indians did not assimilate Spanish as rapidly as could have been desired. The conditions which gave rise to this situation were doubtless inherent in the mission system of colonization, and were not the fault of any one individual or group, yet whatever the

---

[11] "Tabla estadística," 1818, Sta. Bárb. Arch., 10:303.
[12] Lasuén, "Estado general," 1795, *ibid.*, 12:60.
[13] Lasuén, "Representación," 1800, *ibid.*, 2:169.
[14] Hugo Reid, "Los Angeles County Indians," *Los Angeles Star*, 1852.

reasons, the fact remains. The general failure of the neophytes to become familiar with white civilization through its language, or at least their indifferent success, testifies to that more general failure to adapt themselves which has been demonstrated with reference to other factors.

Retention of customs and religion.—Apart from law and language there exists in any society, primitive or otherwise, a vast body of traits which may for convenience be grouped under the terms customs and religion. Herein will be included the entire complex of beliefs, myths, and superstitions, on the one hand, and, on the other, the activities associated with them, such as costumes, rites, dances, ceremonies of all kinds, together with the necessary social structure for their administration. Needless to add, the entire group life is based upon and bound up in this interlocking set of traits. Furthermore, as the experience of centuries has demonstrated, it is extremely difficult to eradicate such traits from the collective mind of any human racial unit, and if the process is successful, it will probably be accompanied by the spiritual and intellectual disintegration of that unit. A people may achieve adaptation to a new physical environment, they may overcome obstacles of war, economics, and pestilence, but they are very likely to retain a considerable amount of their original nonmaterial culture.

The mission Indians appear to have been no exception to the general rule, despite the fact that great and peculiar difficulties were placed in their path. Over most of the continental United States, there was no spiritual conflict of serious magnitude between the white race and the Indians. This was due principally to the lack of interest shown by the whites. They literally did not care what the Indians believed, thought, or did, provided none of their own interests were affected. To be sure, a few ineffectual attempts at religious conversion have been attempted, and the modern Indian Service has tried to promote some education among the red men, but no wholesale, serious effort has ever been made to eradicate and destroy the aboriginal culture as inimical to civilized society. The Spanish missions were very different. Based entirely upon the premise of total conversion to orthodox Christianity, it was vitally necessary to extirpate those individual beliefs and tribal customs which in any way whatever conflicted with the Christian religion. Not only did this necessity apply to the doctrinal sphere, but it also extended to the administrative. The missionaries needed to erase, not only pagan or idolatrous tenets of belief, but also external manifestations like ceremonial rites. Not only did many gentile customs have to be suppressed, but, more important, all persons had to be eliminated who, under the gentile system, had exercised the slightest spiritual authority. Since the missionary was a spiritual as well as material dictator, it would have been fatal to his regime to permit any competition on the part of native strong men of the shaman class. The operation of the mission system, therefore, involved an immediate, powerful restriction on the social and intellectual expression of the Indians comparable with those previously discussed which affected liberty, space, diet, and sex relations. One might expect that the responses to this restriction would follow the same lines of resistance or escape as characterized the other types of restriction. Although this was doubtless true to some extent, the situation was modified by certain factors which did not operate in the other cases.

The first of these was the possibility of a new avenue of escape. Physical, spatial confinement could be enforced by purely corporal methods. Spiritual confinement, so to speak, provided the Indian was genuinely obdurate, could not be enforced at all. It was impossible to prevent the converted gentile from thinking of his folkways, from respecting the fellow neophyte who was a former shaman, from clandestinely carrying on his ancient ceremonies. Nor could the missionary prevent the Christian mother from passing on to her child the unforgotten lore and tradition of the tribe. The most elusive, the most tenacious thing in the social order of the world is tradition, which can be kept alive in the face of the bitterest persecution and which constitutes a region into which the most oppressed can always escape with impunity.

The second factor was the form of the Christian religion. It is no accident that Catholicism has been uniformly successful among primitive peoples. Its effective, simple dogma can be readily taught to minds of limited comprehension, and its system of observances can be dramatized so as to appeal to the primitive emotion. Moreover, the proselyting orders in the New World, through their vast experience were wonderfully adept at presenting their religion in its most attractive form. Christianity, therefore, itself provided a line of escape from the restriction placed on the older gentile spiritual culture. It was the hope of the clergy that the Indians would all avail themselves of this resource, and it is to their credit that so many did. In theory, there was not a complete restriction but a redirection, a recanalization of social and emotional energy. Unfortunately, the process, actually, was too swift, too sudden, to be complete. The Indian mentality was too fixed and rigid to give ground, to make the shift and adapt itself within one or even two generations. Consequently, in many instances, the effect was one of absolute restriction rather than an easy redirection.

To what extent the course of conversion was complete—using conversion to imply conversion in the whole way of life rather than in the limited theological sense—can be judged only by those records of the missions which give evidence of tendencies to retain or revert to aboriginal custom. These records include only statements of opinion and overt acts of sufficient consequence to require official attention.

Concerning the general question of the retention of primitive belief and custom by the neophytes, we have two very authoritative sources. The first is Boscana, that thorough student of Indian religion. He says,[15] "Superstitions of a ridiculous and most extravagant nature were found associated with those Indians, and even now in almost every town or hamlet the child is first taught to believe in their authenticity." The second source is the "Contestación" of 1811. One of the questions asked was whether the neophytes adhered to their former customs. Six missions replied, the statements being unanimous that great tenacity in this respect was to be observed. Several other questions concerned specific cultural traits; the answers to these were, likewise, without exception in the same tenor. In fact, I know of no competent contemporary authority who vouchsafed the unqualified assertion that the neophytes had to a significant degree given up the primitive customs and superstitions. To support this thesis, further detail with reference to more specific cultural traits may be considered.

Perhaps the central point in Indian religious culture was the shaman

[15] Geronimo Boscana, *Chinigchinich,* translated by Alfred Robinson, edited by P. T. Hanna (Santa Ana, 1933), p. 61.

or medicine man. In him was vested the power over life and death through the treatment of illness. His was the final authority and control, through supernatural agencies, over the general welfare of the people. Upon the shaman, therefore, the attack of the missionaries was focused, for without his overthrow the priest could not hope to control the spiritual life of the neophytes. Superficially, the effort was successful. Fundamentally, perhaps, it was not. The existence of shamans was admitted unequivocally by the missionary at Santa Cruz in 1811, who said: "There are among them certain malignant old men who inspire them with an abject terror of the devil whom they consider to be the author of all evil."[16] Boscana was equally candid. Apropos of the miraculous death of some garden plants, he ascribes the phenomenon to the Devil "and the motive I have for believing so is that at this time there were many gentiles in the mission, principally sorcerers (some were catechumens and some were not) who night after night performed their heathen ceremonies."[17] Elsewhere in the same treatise the priest describes in vivid fashion a contest with one of these shamans for the privilege of curing a sick neophyte, an incident which scarcely could have occurred if the shaman had not possessed extensive influence in the mission.

Antonio María Osio has the following comment:[18]

... experience of many years demonstrated that catechists who were reasonably faithful to their duty were not as much heeded and regarded as those who had a reputation as medicine men. The latter were sought with more eagerness to hear them recount the bounties which the Devil dispenses to those devotees who serve him well.

The shamans in the missions participated in two activities; treatment of the sick and the conducting of semireligious rites. Since the process of treatment usually involved ceremonies, the two activities

[16] "Contestación," Sta. Bárb. Arch., 7:158. The persistence of influence by the military or political tribal chiefs is also indicated in this document: "They still have more respect and submission for their chiefs [*capitanes*] than for the overseers [*alcaldes*] who are put over them for their civilization" (San Carlos, *ibid.*, p. 205); "Here in the mission the native chiefs who are Christians remain equal to the others [i.e., gentiles]" (Santa Clara, *ibid.*).

[17] *Op. cit.*, p. 79. From the context of this famous document it is clear that Boscana himself was under no illusions concerning the close relationship between Satan and the Indian sorcerers.

[18] "Historia de California," MS, 1878, p. 81.

were closely interrelated. The missionaries naturally frowned upon the medical efforts of the shamans, because their methods smacked of witchcraft and because any therapeutic successes would enhance their prestige. There can be little doubt, however, that the neophytes still adhered to the time-honored methods of treatment, and indeed one is rather inclined to sympathize with them in view of the pitifully inadequate methods used in their behalf by the missionaries.[19]

The combination of witchcraft, disease treatment, and shamanistic authority which existed in the missions can be gauged by two rather dramatic examples which may be taken as illustrative.[20]

In 1829 three neophytes were charged with sorcery.[21] Part of the accusation read:

> They were found dancing in one of the houses of that rancheria [Santa Ynéz], and bringing to the said dance house those most dangerously ill. To each of the latter they said that it was necessary that everyone of the sick who had been dancing should contribute glass beads or some other thing, in order that by this dance which they were making to the Devil they should become cured of their illness. [One witness testified]: That being in his house José el Ventureño entered, and said to him that, being sick in his house the Devil appeared to him and counselled him to dance so that he and the other invalids might get well. Contrariwise they all would die. The Devil gave him some seeds and disappeared.

Clearly, José el Ventureño was setting himself up as a shaman, if he were not already such.

---

[19] There is indication that some missionaries, recognizing the failure of civilized medicine, covertly permitted the neophytes to get what benefit they could from their own methods, provided of course no unchristian elements were introduced.

[20] The question may be legitimately raised whether the few cases which reached the official records really indicate a widespread condition or whether they constitute flagrant exceptions to the general rule. It must be remembered, however, that the neophytes were forced to conduct such practices secretly and that the Indian has always been very adept in preserving his secrets. This was recognized by Boscana, who, after citing two extreme cases of apostasy, avers that such things happened more often than is generally admitted. "As all their operations are accompanied by stratagems and dissimulation, they easily gain our confidence and at every pass we are deluded" (*Chinigchinich*, p. 81). Or consider the following frank confession from the missionary at San Luis Rey: "In short, in the matter of their superstitions regarding sickness, idolatry and witchcraft, they are so rare full of deceit and reserved, that although I have been among them since the foundation of the mission, that which I can most readily manifest regarding these matters is my ignorance of them. They never confess more than what they cannot deny" ("Contestación," p. 177, translated by A. L. Kroeber).

[21] Echeandía, "Causa Criminal," San Diego, Prov. St. Pap. Ben. Mil., 60:69–74.

The second case involves also the action of a visionary and is note-worthy, not only for the large number of Indians affected, but also for the secrecy with which the whole affair was kept from the missionaries.

A single female neophyte was able to delude the Christians of Santa Bár-bara. The case was that after a feigned paroxysm she said there had ap-peared to her the God Chupu [a deity worshipped along the Channel] assuring her that the gentiles would die from the epidemic if they were baptized, and that the same would happen to the Christians who did not offer tribute to Chupu and did not bathe their heads with a certain water. The report of this revelation, within an hour, which was midnight, ran through all the houses of the mission, and almost all the neophytes, includ-ing the *alcaldes,* went to the house of the visionary to offer their beads and seeds and to attend the ceremony for the renunciation of Christianity. The extraordinary and serious part of this matter is that, whereas the rumor extended through all the rancherias of the Channel and the mountains, the missionaries were totally ignorant of it, for Chupu revealed at the same time that any persons who told the Fathers would immediately die. Ac-tually we were unaware of the occurrence for three days.[22]

Other outbreaks of witchcraft could be adduced, if necessary, to demonstrate that the Indians, despite a fairly uniform adherence to at least the forms of Christianity, still retained a substratum of credence in the primeval superstitions and their prophets. The neophyte lived in two worlds, as it were: the everyday, commonplace atmosphere of mission Christianity in the broad daylight of which he carried on his routine activities, and a silent, secret world within himself to which he might and did escape on frequent occasions.

One curious by-product of contact with white civilization, which deserves mention although its application is general rather than spe-cific to the missions, is the loss of prestige suffered on the medical side by the shamans. These practitioners seem to have been, at least by native standards, moderately successful in treating indigenous ail-ments. However, when the devastating new epidemic diseases were introduced, their arts were totally unavailing. The wholesale destruc-tion caused by smallpox, measles, and the like occurred with only too painful regularity in spite of the time-honored methods of the medi-cine men. As a result a revulsion of feeling became evident, which

[22] Tapis to Arrillaga, Santa Bárbara, March 1, 1805, Sta. Bárb. Arch., 6:33.

manifested itself in a tendency to hold the would-be doctors responsible for the death of the patients (a mental reaction perhaps not
altogether confined to aborigines). This loss of faith in the native
treatment and those who administered it was far more profound than
could ever have been brought about through argument or repression
exercised by any white men, even respected missionaries. Thus, in a
way, the diseases of the latter accomplished more than their ideas. The
situation at a later date was caustically summed up by Hugo Reid:[23]

The seers have declined very much in their ability both of predicting events
and doing harm; although instances of sickness occasionally occur of which
they stand the blame. In performing cures, however, they still take the
precedence of the other members of the faculty known as M.D.'s.

More or less apart from operations which had a supernatural tinge
or which involved allegiance to a chief or shaman, the California Indians, in common with most other members of the red race, were
deeply in love with rites, ceremonies, and dances of all kinds. The
specific occasions of these were as numerous as the events of life: birth,
puberty, marriage, death, war, the seasons, and so on. Naturally this
strong proclivity was carried into the missions with them and was
almost impossible to suppress in its entirety. Recognizing that some
form of native ritualistic expression must be allowed, the priests more
or less deliberately adopted a twofold policy. They first undertook to
redirect the instincts into what to them were proper channels by
emphasizing Church ritual—admirably adapted to the purpose. When
this was inadequate, they permitted the neophytes to retain a great
deal of the native ceremonial insofar as the latter did not conflict with
Christian morals and propriety. Nevertheless, such concessions were
made without much enthusiasm, and frequently it became necessary
to prohibit all native ceremonial, because of the excesses which characterized such occasions.[24] Frequent references in the records attest the
important function served by dances of various kinds in the life of
the mission Indians. Describing mission existence, Tapis and Cortes
said: "... but almost every night they put on some dance in the kitchen

---

[23] *Op. cit.,* Letter No. 22.

[24] In 1782 specific orders were issued prohibiting dances of all kinds to the Christian
Indians (Zuñiga to Fages, Dec. 17, 1782, Prov. St. Pap., 3:76).

or the main room of the mission."[25] Lasuén complained of the bad effect exerted by neighboring gentiles on the neophytes of San Carlos:[26]

It happens that they put on a heathen and abominable dance or *fiesta;* if the Christian who is present refuses to participate in that vile diversion, they mock him and laugh at him and persecute him until he gives in.

Governor Arrillaga objected to the abuse of furloughs on the part of the neophytes, saying that "some of them . . . keep up their heathen rites."[27] The instance of José el Ventureño has already been cited, when the Santa Ynéz neophytes danced to avoid illness. In the "Contestación" of 1811 the president reported[28] that "these poor people . . . still preserve some of their rituals, specially the old ones." He then described some of these, as did the missionaries from San Luis Rey (the bird dance), Santa Clara, and Santa Cruz. The latter stated that "sometimes they hold nocturnal, secret dances always running away so that the Fathers shall not know it." The priests at San Luis Rey and Santa Ynéz claimed that their neophytes were using the jimson weed, with accompanying ceremonies.[29]

At times these dances developed into orgies, particularly after white influence had been long felt and liquor was obtainable. García Diego stated that "in their nocturnal dances, if they get drunk, they commit horrible excesses."[30] Hartnell in issuing instructions to administrators said that the latter should consult with the missionaries "on the best way to prevent the Indians from having immoral and superstitious dances."[31] Gomez recognized the performance of many ancient funeral rites, adapted to burial instead of cremation.[32] At San Antonio a dance was held in the house of the dead. He also describes in detail "orgies" at that mission which seem to have been the *toloache* ceremony, embellished with local variations.

[25] "Replica," Oct. 30, 1800, Sta. Bárb. Arch., 2:101.

[26] Lasuén to Olmedo, San Carlos, Jan. 25, 1803, *ibid.,* 12:368.

[27] Arrillaga, Loreto, Nov. 10, 1804, Prov. St. Pap., 18:342.

[28] Sta. Bárb. Arch., 7:157–166.

[29] The jimson-weed or *toloache* cult was particularly strong in the missions. Reference may be made to the extended discussion of this ceremony by Kroeber (*Handbook*).

[30] Fr. Francisco García Diego to Figueroa, Santa Clara, Sept. 21, 1833, St. Pap. Mis. and Col., 2:78.

[31] W. E. Hartnell, Instructions, San José, Aug. 28, 1839, St. Pap. Mis., 7:42.

[32] V. Gomez, "*Lo que sabe,*" MS, 1876, pp. 63–69.

Toward the end of the mission period the neophytes, under the influence of loosening disciplinary bonds, were permitted, even encouraged, by the priests to put on displays of native dances for the amusement of the civilian population. One of these at Santa Clara is described by Alfred Robinson.[33] It included several dances in costume and was sponsored by the missionary. General Vallejo was much addicted to this form of entertainment for which purpose he used the neophytes at Solano.[34] Many other instances might be mentioned.[35]

The data cited as well as the general impression derived from all contemporary accounts lead to but one conclusion. Any attempt in the missions to repress or materially alter the social and cultural traits of the Indians met with failure. The most obvious manifestations were no doubt eliminated, and many modifications in detail were achieved, but the basic pattern of life survived without material disruption. This phenomenon was due to the ability of the neophytes to find an outlet—partially clandestine, to be sure—for the urge to social expression. Hence, it cannot be said that much adaptation occurred. The Indian did not surrender his ways in order to take on white ways as far as ritual and ceremonial were concerned. But this failure to adapt, despite some adverse pressure on the part of the mission system, resulted in no such serious psychological and social conflict as was observed in the field of law and morals.

Assimilation of Christianity.—Although, as has been stated, the Indian did not "surrender his ways" in order to substitute for them the introduced ritualism and religion, there is no a priori reason to assume that he may not have added some of the latter to his own system. The two are not mutually exclusive, as are Indian law and European law. Christianity of a sort can be superposed on a substratum of cultism and ceremonialism and indeed, in the long run, it can be incorporated with the primitive system.

---

[33] Alfred Robinson, *Life in California* (1846), pp. 97–98.

[34] M. G. Vallejo, "Historia," MS.

[35] Other examples of the retention of primitive custom might be cited, for instance, feuds between families (Goycoechea, 1787, Prov. St. Pap., 7:91; Hugo Reid, Letter No. 9); the vulture (*gavilán*) ceremony ("Contestación" of 1811); *temescals* (wellnigh universal); purification ceremony (Hugo Reid, Letter No. 22); transvestites and other perversions (Gomez, "Lo que sabe," p. 100).

Some criterion of conversion to or acceptance of Christianity must be established. No one can demand of a primitive people that truly profound insight into religious significance and theological abstractions which is reserved in any race for those of the most zealous faith and intellectual power. Most members of any church would be inclined to concede as a bona fide convert the man who faithfully observes the prescribed forms of the faith and who, in so far as his mental equipment allows him, subscribes to its cardinal tenets. Judged on this basis, there can be no question whatever that many thousands of Indians became genuine Christians. The most powerful evidence for the success of the missionaries has come to light in the era since 1840. During the past hundred years those mission Indians who survived, particularly in the south, have adhered faithfully to the teachings which their ancestors learned from the fathers. Moreover, among such groups as the Yokuts and the Sierra Miwok, to whom fled hundreds of neophytes after secularization, the miners of the 'fifties found many Indians who sincerely claimed to be Christians.

With most of these survivors, as with the great mass of extinct neophytes, the central problem is not the fact of their conversion or their nominal adherence to the Faith, but the depth of the conversion. Did the mission group really assimilate Christianity to the extent that it in any way altered their belief or their spiritual equipment? This is an exceedingly difficult question to answer, and in fact probably cannot be answered at all. Obviously, there are no objective criteria; mere observance of form is no valid index to the spiritual motive behind the actions. Written opinion is untrustworthy, since it was difficult for a contemporary to go below the surface and since at that period every observer was influenced by racial, national, and religious prejudices. For manifest reasons the missionaries were prone to be optimistic concerning the success of their spiritual endeavors, although they did deplore the extent to which apostasy showed itself. Most of the Protestant Americans were contemptuous of both the missionaries and neophytes and suffered from a tendency toward extreme superficiality in their observations. It is probably best to attempt no categorical answer but to suggest that the neophytes must have absorbed a great deal of the form and spirit of Christianity. Moreover, it is highly probable that the ceremonial of the Catholic Church went far toward satisfying the innate love of the Indian for ritual.

If this were true—and in default of any good evidence to the contrary we must assume it to be so—we still have to inquire concerning the dynamics whereby the new ideology took its place in the Indian mind without the complete surrender of the old. Hugo Reid suggested a solution many years ago.[36] He predicates a piecemeal absorption of items of the Christian dogma which fitted into a checkerboard pattern where, as it were, the Indian philosophy constituted the black squares and the Christian the red, but the two were forever distinct. He says:

They have at present *two* religions—one of custom and another of faith. ... They don't quarrel with their neighbor's form of worship but consider their own the best. The life and death of our Savior is only, in their opinion, a distorted version of their own life. Hell, as taught them, has no terrors. It is for whites, not for Indians, or else their fathers would have known it. The Devil, however, has become a great personage in their sight; he is called Zizu, and makes his appearance on all occasions. Nevertheless, he is only a bugbear and connected with the Christian faith; he makes no part of their own.

Nevertheless, the checkerboard theory does not seem entirely consonant with the normal operation of the human mind. No individual can easily retain two independent sets of beliefs. They imperceptibly but inevitably merge with each other until the result is a single philosophy compounded out of elements drawn from both. (This is, of course, based upon the premise that the person does not completely reject one in favor of the other.) We cannot pretend, naturally, that the average mission Indian or his descendant ever achieved a perfect philosophical union of Christianity and paganism. We suggest simply that a tendency existed in this direction which was probably never completely fulfilled. This might be termed the fusion theory as opposed to the checkerboard theory.

If such fusion occurred, the first step would be the appropriation of certain items of the new or introduced system and the fitting of these into the old pattern. In the process, the adopted items would necessarily undergo certain modifications in order that they might be made to fit the pattern. Such an evolution is indicated at two points in Reid's

---

[36] *Op. cit.*, Letter No. 22.

analysis. The first is the assimilation of the life of Christ as epitomizing their own life. The second is the magnification of the Devil as their personal enemy. This whole sublimation, even though not consciously formulated, is indicative of a really profound insight on the part of those often described as little above the level of beasts.

Further illustration of spiritual fusion is found in Boscana's work.[37] Thus in his discussion of the immortality of the soul he expresses the opinion that the Indians had no such idea as gentiles; that they were strict materialists. He then proceeded to cite examples from the late mission period wherein Indians had dreams or visions of Paradise, with Chinigchinich in place of the Lord. Boscana says of these:

The reader will compare this belief with the doctrine of the immortality of the soul. It was taught by the moderns undoubtedly, and since their conversion to Christianity, for the old men at the time of their gentilism had no such idea [*Chinigchinich,* p. 76].

In many other of Boscana's anecdotes it is apparent that the Indians were adopting some of the ideas of Christianity but were placing them in a pagan setting.

If the concept of assimilation of religion by fusion is valid, it follows that racial conflict in this particular cultural sphere was resolved by adaptation in the reverse sense. That is, the primitive group adapted the introduced culture to fit its own mold, rather than changed its own culture to conform to the other. The pattern of religion, therefore, constitutes a noteworthy exception to the usual rule in the relations between the mission Indian and the white man.

In summary, it becomes evident that with respect to cultural factors the interracial contact or conflict led to quite different results, depending upon the degree to which a given cultural factor involved material relationships. In the field of personal relationships, laws and codes of behavior, the two systems were mutually exclusive and irreconcilable. For purely pragmatic reasons, the Indians were forced to make a rapid and very difficult adaptation which cost them dear in lives and

---

[37] Boscana was one missionary who was a confirmed skeptic regarding the ability of the neophytes to acquire Christianity. He continually reiterates that the doctrines of the Church never secured a real foothold in the Indian mind. "How little is the faith of these Indians in the teaching of Catholic truths." But Boscana had in mind a total adoption of unmodified dogma, a substitution of Christianity rather than its addition.

suffering. With respect to religion (in its most general sense), ceremonialism, and shamanism, the opposite was true. Despite the most intensive moral suasion and pressure, the Indians retained the basic pattern of their culture intrinsically unaltered. Indeed, they went so far as to adopt and modify Christianity and to incorporate it in such a way as to conform to their own manner of thought. In this one respect, therefore, the Indians achieved an adaptational success, which stands unique in their history.

APPENDIX

THE ABORIGINAL POPULATION
OF CALIFORNIA

FOR ANY STUDY of population changes an assessment of the initial population is necessary. Furthermore, such an estimate should be as exact as the nature of the data permits. Where reliable censuses are available, the problem presents no difficulties. But when, as in the present study, no such information is at hand, every possible avenue must be explored in the search for pertinent facts of any type which will form a basis of estimate, and many indirect methods must be employed in order to arrive at an approximation of the actual numbers.

The population of California in 1770 has been the subject of considerable investigation by anthropologists, particularly those of the University of California, who have contributed numerous papers bearing on the subject (principally in the University of California Publications in American Archaeology and Ethnology). Kroeber in his *Handbook*[1] has summarized most of this work and has contributed much enlightening discussion. Indeed, it is to be doubted seriously if Kroeber's conclusions can ever be subject to fundamental or drastic revision. Nevertheless, it is desirable and even necessary to resurvey the data for the following reasons.

First, Kroeber's policy tends toward conservatism in estimating numbers. In certain instances it is possible that he has gone a little further than necessary and that the true values may be somewhat higher than he has assumed.

Second, by the elaboration of certain methods not explored fully by Kroeber it may be possible to revise the estimates for some individual tribes or regions.

Finally, by employing the few mission baptism records now available which list converts and villages, new light may be shed on the probable strength of the groups which came under mission influence. Thus in the mid-coastal region at least a fairly precise figure may be obtained where previous investigators have relied on general estimates.

The methods utilized are well standardized. The first three are

---

[1] *Handbook of the Indians of California* (1925).

suitable for any population study in a primitive area. The fourth is of value only in missionized regions:

1. Direct enumerations..Here must be included the official and unofficial counts or estimates by persons on the spot, such as government agents, explorers, ranchers, etc. These are usually unreliable in detail and suffer from a universal tendency toward exaggeration.

2. The village-house method. In theory if, from personal recollection or archaeological discovery, we knew the number of inhabited villages belonging to a certain people, if we knew the actual or mean number of houses in each, and finally if we knew the mean family size, then by multiplication we could derive the total population. However, the method is subject to error from innumerable sources, and great care must be exercised in its application.

3. The area method. If we were dealing with a large, homogeneous territory and possessed exact population data on a fraction of it, then by simple proportion we could calculate the total value. The difficulty arises from the fact that areas are not homogeneous with respect to population; therefore, to avoid large error, an extremely critical attitude must be maintained.

4. The baptism method. In California each mission first baptized the heathen in the immediate vicinity and then spread out in a roughly radial fashion seeking new converts. Sometimes the territorial limits of proselyting activity and the intensity of the latter can be determined with reasonable accuracy. Hence the population of such areas can be set within quite narrow limits.

These four methods have been employed in this study, and the details of their application will be set forth in connection with individual tribes.

For purposes of population study California may be divided into three primary provinces, although on other grounds such a separation might not be justified. First may be distinguished a northern province bounded by the coast from the Oregon line to the vicinity of Fort Ross, thence by an irregular line running eastward to the crest of the Sierra. This represents nonmission territory. Our information concerning it consists wholly of contemporary American estimates and modern ethnographic research. It includes all the tribes from the Pomo,

Wintun, and Maidu northward with the exception of the Modoc and the Paiute. Second, we have the group in the central coastal belt from Marin County to Santa Monica, together with the Sacramento and San Joaquin valley tribes extending to the crest of the Sierra and Tehachapi. These tribes came completely or partially under mission influence. Finally, there is the coast and desert region south of the Tehachapi. Despite some mission contact the whole ethnographic and ecological status of these peoples was so different from that of the other California Indians that for present purposes they are best considered apart from the latter.

TRIBES OF NORTHERN CALIFORNIA

The Yurok.—The original population of this tribe has received considerable attention from Kroeber and others, its value being placed by Kroeber[2] at approximately 2,500. His figure is based upon several contemporary counts which included the number of villages and houses per village as well as total population. He concludes that the most probable averages are: 7½ persons per house and 6 houses per town, or 45 persons per town. Now if these averages could be used directly to compute populations elsewhere, a great deal would be accomplished. However, it is doubtful whether such a procedure would be justifiable. With respect to number of houses per village, and indeed village size in general, it is well known that this value is quite variable and that it is determined locally by geographic, economic, and social factors. Extreme caution therefore must be used in deducing village size or house number for other regions unless there are direct observations in support of the theory.

The number of persons per house may be more stable. It might be assumed among the Yurok that the "house" represented the family, and specifically the "social" family, i.e., the parents, children, and relatives living together in one social unit. In a population which is maintaining itself, as the Yurok for instance undoubtedly were, the genetic family (i.e., parents and children) has a minimum value of 4. Ordinarily a value of 5 must be the average, to include deaths prior to the

---

[2] *Ibid.*, p. 17. It is also stated (p. 16) that "Yurok population can be more accurately determined than the strength of most other Californian groups. . . ."

reproductive age. The social family will ordinarily include, particularly in a primitive society, other members—grandparents, brothers, etc.—who would raise the average number to at least 6. If the tribe is fairly well off with respect to food supply and with no pressure from outside peoples, the number will be higher, and it is conceivable that 7½ might be reached.

However, there are considerations which render dubious any direct transfer of this number to other groups. In the first place, 7½ is quite a high value for the social family. Sauer places the number at 6 for the aboriginal population of the upper Mexican west coast.[3] The value appears to have been approximately 5 in Lower California before missionization and approximately 3.5 thereafter.[4] According to the censuses for the Franciscan missions of Upper California the family number there was less than 3, but this represents extremely adverse conditions. In the spring of 1939 a study was made of a primitive village of 1,000 inhabitants in southern Mexico,[5] where the population and economic conditions had been stable for some time. The social family there averaged 4.6.

Further light is shed on the situation in northern California by the careful study of the Clear Lake Pomo by Gifford.[6] In the village of Cigom he found that out of 20 houses, 18 were inhabited by two or more families, that the average family consisted of 4.25 living members, and that the average house content was 10.2 persons. If anything approaching analogous conditions existed among the Yurok, then 7½ does not represent the average social family size (which was probably smaller) but indicates simply the characteristic number of house inhabitants.

The Yurok may be subdivided into two groups, the riparian, along the lower Klamath River, and the coastal. The former included 37 villages, containing an estimated 1,800 inhabitants. Strictly, 37 villages at 45 inhabitants each would total 1,665, to which 135 have been added

---

[3] Carl O. Sauer, *Aboriginal Population of Northwestern Mexico,* Univ. Calif. Publ., Ibero-Americana, No. 10 (Berkeley, 1935).

[4] S. F. Cook, *The Extent and Significance of Disease among the Indians of Baja California, ibid.,* No. 12 (1937).

[5] Santa María Ixcatlán, State of Oaxaca.

[6] E. W. Gifford, *Clear Lake Pomo Society* (1926), Univ. Calif. Publ. Am. Arch. and Ethn., 18:287–390.

to account for certain doubtful villages. The coastal part included 19 villages, which on a direct multiplicative basis would yield 855 inhabitants. However, Kroeber regards these settlements as being "somewhat smaller" than those on the river and reduces the figure to 700. We may accept his estimate and regard his total of 2,500 for both groups as being very close to the truth.[7]

The Tolowa.—This is a small group in the extreme northwest corner of the state, along the coast. There were 10 known villages, which at the Yurok rate of 45 each would give 450 as the population. This is a reasonable estimate, for Waterman[8] states that there was no material difference between the Tolowa and Yurok in village size.

The Karok.—This tribe inhabited the middle reaches of the Klamath, and in most respects resembled the Yurok. In fact, Kroeber (*Handbook,* p. 17) states that "these data, so far as they relate to house and village population, probably hold with little change for . . . the Karok, Hupa, Tolowa, [and] Yurok . . ." On the basis of a house count made in 1851 Kroeber (*Handbook,* p. 101) assigned 1,500 as the number of inhabitants. In a later consideration of the matter[9] based upon detailed recent information he places the number at very close to 2,000. This estimate may be accepted as the most accurate obtainable.[10]

The Wiyot.—This tribe, which inhabited the coast around Humboldt Bay and the mouths of the Mad and Eel rivers presents considerable difficulty. Kroeber's original population estimate was between 800 and 1,000. This was revised later to "little over 1,000" or possibly 1,200. The latter estimate is based on a study of the Wiyot country by Nomland and Kroeber,[11] together with earlier work, particularly by

---

[7] T. T. Waterman (*Yurok Geography* [1920], *ibid.,* 16:206–207), gives a list of 64 Yurok towns. Of these 16 do not have the number of houses assigned. Of the remaining 48 the average house number is 6.81. The total probable number for all 64 towns would then be 436, which at Kroeber's value of 7½ inhabitants each would yield a population of 3,270. This estimate appears to be too large, but it indicates that 2,500 is certainly not too high.

[8] *Ibid.,* p. 200.

[9] A. L. Kroeber, *Karok Towns* (1936), Univ. Calif. Publ. Am. Arch. and Ethn., 35: 29–38.

[10] It is of interest that in the Karok towns, although the inhabitants per house are still taken as 7½, the houses average only 4 per village, instead of the 6 assumed for the Yurok.

[11] G. A. Nomland and A. L. Kroeber, *Wiyot Towns* (1936), Univ. Calif. Publ. Am. Arch. and Ethn., 35:39–48.

Loud.[12] However, an examination of the published data by these authors does not necessarily lead to their conclusions. The village–house–inhabitant method is employed exclusively. Nomland and Kroeber state that the average size of the towns is smaller ("perhaps 30" inhabitants per village) than among the Yurok (45 inhabitants). If this is true, then either the inhabitants per house were fewer or the houses per village were fewer. There are no data whatever to indicate that the former assumption is true. In fact, Nomland and Kroeber assume that the reduced size was a function of the latter variable. Yet the existing published information does not bear this out.

The standard house number among the Yurok is 6. If we examine the data of Loud (*op. cit.*, pp. 258–275), we find that he mentions some 32 sites of "leading villages." For 19 of these, estimated house numbers are given, aggregating 123–133 houses, or an average of 6.47–7.00 houses per village. If the other 13 villages were of the same size, at least 6 houses each are to be expected. The Yurok value would then hold, yielding for the 32 villages 1,440 inhabitants. To this must be added 20 "minor sites" of, say 1½ houses each, or 225 persons, making a total of 1,665.

A similar treatment of the data presented by Nomland and Kroeber shows some 82 recognized village sites. Of these, 31 have the house number specified, with a mean of 4.68–7.68, again approximately 6. It is thus rather difficult to assume a much smaller number in the face of the only quantitative information in existence. Further calculation of the Nomland and Kroeber data is as follows.

1. The 31 villages already specified would yield 1,395 persons.

2. There are 18 other villages to which the terms "many," "several," and "large" are applied, and 8 which are referred to as "few" or "small." For the former, at least the average number of houses (6) may be assumed, and for the latter at least 1½ houses. The remainder, 25 villages, are not described in any pertinent way, and although they may have had inhabitants, for the sake of conservatism they may be neglected. Using these figures, we get $(18 \times 6 \times 7\frac{1}{2}) + (8 \times 1\frac{1}{2} \times 7\frac{1}{2}) = 900$. The total population would then be 2,295.

---

[12] L. L. Loud, *Ethnogeography and Archaeology of the Wiyot Territory* (1918), *ibid.*, 14:221–436.

As has been repeatedly stressed by all investigators, not all these 82 sites were simultaneously occupied. The 25 for which no data exist and which have already been excluded take care of some of this shrinkage. If we arbitrarily reduce the remainder by one-third, the population value still is 1,530. Nomland and Kroeber (*op. cit.,* p. 45) set the number of villages simultaneously inhabited at a maximum of 35. At 45 persons per village the total is 1,575.

If the existing data can be trusted, therefore, the conclusion seems warranted that the Wiyot population was somewhat larger than has been hitherto supposed. The number taken here is 1,500.

The Chimariko.—This was a tiny tribe on the middle Trinity River. Kroeber (*Handbook,* pp. 109–110) assigns a population of "perhaps 250." He shows five villages and three "places." This would indicate the Yurok level of about 45 per village. Certainly no more can be ascribed to a people inhabiting this wild region. We may therefore accept his estimate without reservation.

The Athabascans.—Here are included various smaller units: the Hupa, Chilula, Whilkut, Mattole, Nongatl, Sinkyone, Lassik, Wailaki, and Kato. As a group they inhabited the coast between Cape Mendocino and a point somewhat below the Humboldt-Mendocino county line, extending inland thirty or forty miles so as to occupy the drainage basins of the Mad and Eel rivers, and part of the Trinity. Our information is best concerning the Hupa, Chilula, and Wailaki.

The Hupa lived in Hupa Valley on the lower Trinity. Kroeber estimates their population as 1,000, and lists 12 principal villages. This would imply a maximum of 83 persons per village, a high value which might be justified in view of the relatively favorable habitat and affluence of the tribe. He mentions also (*Handbook,* p. 131) a census of 1851 which gives a total of 99 homes in 11 villages, or 750 persons (evidently using again the factor 7½). He also cites a census of 1870, which gives 641 persons in 8 villages, an average of 80. To the 750 of the earlier census he adds 250 to account for unnoticed settlements. This may be slightly excessive but is likely to be balanced by some diminution in numbers prior to the year of the census. The high average house number (9 per village) is striking in comparison with that of the Wiyot and Yurok towns and illustrates the variability of this factor.

The Chilula, on Redwood Creek, are estimated by Kroeber (*Handbook*, p. 138) to have included a population of 500–600. There are 18 villages known, of which 6 apparently had an average house number of 7. This would give an average village size of 53 inhabitants and a total population of 950. A reduction by one-third might be desirable to account for unoccupied houses and villages, yielding a net value of 630—or call it 600.

The Wailaki, on the upper Eel River, have been thoroughly studied by Goddard.[13] In his investigation of the Pitch group he observed in all 37 village sites, in 22 of which he counted house pits. The average house number is 5.2. Using the Yurok factor $7\frac{1}{2}$, this gives approximately 1,440 inhabitants for 37 villages. To this must be added a small section which Goddard did not investigate thoroughly, say 160, making 1,600 in all. Goddard thinks all the villages were simultaneously occupied, but it is safer to adhere to Kroeber's policy of reduction by one-third. Thus the population is placed at 1,000.

The main Wailaki are listed by Goddard (1923) as being aggregated in 66 villages and 13 subtribes. If these were all simultaneously inhabited, the total obtained by the multiplicative method would be, after reducing by one-third, 1,720, making for the entire tribe, about 2,700. Now Goddard estimates 650–800 for the Pitch group and 1,000–2,000 for the remainder, or 1,650–2,800 in all. By the multiplicative method, therefore, we arrive at a figure approximating Goddard's maximum and very far from Kroeber's estimate of one thousand.

Since the method hitherto employed seems to lead, at least for this tribe, to divergent, if not dubious, results, it would be of much value if some quite different means could be employed as a check. A possibility is the area method, which, although it has to be handled carefully, warrants consideration. Particularly is this true because the direct data on the remaining Athabascan tribes are extremely scanty, when not completely lacking.[14]

The validity of the area method depends entirely on the compara-

---

[13] P. E. Goddard, *The Habitat of the Wailaki* (1923), Univ. Calif. Publ. Am. Arch. and Ethn., 20:95–109, and *The Habitat of the Pitch Indians, A Wailaki Division* (1924), *ibid.*, 17:217–225.

[14] Kroeber estimates the combined strength of the Chilula, Whilkut, Nongatl, Sinkyone, Lassik, and Kato at 4,000.

bility of the regions involved. This in turn depends upon the size and the geographical features. In the northern province of California the population was distributed primarily along the water courses and the coast, since the food supply was derived partly from fish in the streams and from plants growing along the streams. Waterways, furthermore, were a basic means of communication. The remainder of the food was obtained from the hill country back from the rivers in the form of game and plant materials. Hence, although the sites of habitation were located on the streams themselves, the territory actually drawn upon included the entire watershed held by the tribe. A small area consisting of nothing but rough hills and stream heads could therefore not be compared to another small area which included only the lower reaches of a river and adjacent lowlands. On the other hand, two fairly large areas, each of which contained several streams throughout most of their length, together with intervening mountain ranges and representative coast lines, would tend to support equivalent populations. This is true, provided, of course, that the two areas were similar with respect to climate, vegetation, and food resources, with no other factor present which would seriously affect the general population density. It would obviously be absurd to compare 1,000 square miles along the Klamath with an equal territory in the Colorado desert, but 1,000 square miles on the Klamath or Trinity should not differ profoundly from an equal area on the Eel or the Russian rivers.

Specifically, we may calculate the population density of the tribes in the northwestern corner of the state and estimate from this the density of those immediately adjacent to the south (i.e., the Athabascan group). The population of the southern tribes may have been somewhat less dense, owing to the heavy redwood belt and to the smaller fish run in the streams, but the difference cannot have been great. The data for the northwestern group are given in table 1. The densities per square mile vary considerably (0.6–3.6) among the individual tribes and indicate the unreliability of any single one of these as a criterion. But the mean value of 2.1 seems quite reasonable. The reasons for the discrepancies are also fairly evident. Thus the Tolowa and the Wiyot were both coast tribes, but the former held a strip of relatively barren coast with a wide, almost uninhabited hinterland in Del Norte County, whereas the latter were restricted to a relatively narrow coastal belt which included the estuaries of the Eel and Mad rivers as well as the rich low country around Humboldt Bay. The Yurok and the Hupa occupied quite fertile stretches of some width on the Klamath and Trinity, whereas the Karok were located along the relatively barren middle section of the Klamath. The entire area includes the small fertile regions together with those of low productivity.

TABLE 1

POPULATION DENSITY OF THE NORTHWEST COASTAL TRIBES

Tribe	Population	Area in sq. miles	Inhabitants per sq. mile
Yurok (total)....................	2,500	760	3.3
Tolowa.......................	450	750	0.6
Karok........................	2,000	1,175	1.7
Wiyot........................	1,500	460	2.3
Hupa.........................	1,000	280	3.6
Chilula......................	600	220	2.7
Chimariko....................	250	275	0.9
Total......................	8,300	3,920	2.1

The Athabascan territory, exclusive of the regions of the Hupa, Chilula, and Wailaki, contains approximately 2,560 square miles. If the country of the Wailaki is also included, the area equals 3,100 square miles. The northwestern area is about 3,920 square miles. If we reduce the mean population density of the latter from 2.1 to 2, then the Athabascans should have had a population somewhere near 6,200. Similarly the Wailaki, with 540 square miles, should have had about 1,080 tribal members. But the Wailaki on the upper Eel River may have had living conditions more favorable than some of the other groups in the dense redwood belt and along the barren Mendocino coast. Hence their numbers may have been somewhat higher, say 1,400 to 1,500, or definitely under Goddard's minimum of 1,650.

We might proceed somewhat differently by accepting Goddard's minimum of 1,650 for the Wailaki. Then the population density would be 3.05 per square mile. The value for the two best-known Athabascan tribes, the Hupa and Chilula, are 3.6 and 2.7 respectively.

The general Athabascan value might then be taken as 3 per square mile instead of 2, which would yield a total population of over 9,000. But such an assumption seems dubious, and it is probably better to adhere to the original estimate.

The area method therefore gives us a figure for the Athabascans somewhat higher than Kroeber's original guess but definitely more conservative than is obtained by the house–village method. It will certainly not be overestimating if we assign 1,500 persons to the Wailaki and 4,700 to the combined Whilkut, Mattole, Nongatl, Sinkyone, Lassik, and Kato.

The Yuki.—The Yuki held the drainage of the South and Middle Forks of the Eel River and extended to the coast north of Fort Bragg. In physical and biological characteristics their land resembles closely that of the Athabascans. In fact, the entire belt from the Oregon line to San Francisco Bay may be regarded as one ecological unit, although there are minor variations as one proceeds from north to south. There were seven geographic divisions of the Yuki, including the Huchnom and Coast Yuki. Accurate data exist for one of these, the Ukomnom, who inhabited Round Valley. Kroeber (*Handbook*, p. 163) has listed three tribal groups or communities, with 15 villages, which he states constituted "probably a small part" of the entire division. Now if we ascribe an average of 30 inhabitants to each village, then the total is 450, not an unreasonable number for the thickly settled valley. The surrounding territory must have been much more thinly populated, and the whole division may have amounted to 750 persons. If we take Kroeber's statement literally that " . . . the conditions deducible from these data no doubt applied to all the Yuki," then we might multiply by 7 and get 5,250 for the whole tribe, a value that far exceeds Kroeber's minimum estimate of 3,000. But it is clear that the Round Valley district was abnormal in its population density. Hence the crude number 5,250 should be much reduced, to between 3,000 and 4,000, or say 3,500.

The area method is also applicable here. If we apply the factor of 2 persons per square mile, as among the near-by Athabascans, we get population of the Yuki proper as 2,420, the Huchnom 640, the Coast Yuki 350 (Kroeber's values are 2,000, 500, and 500 respectively), or 3,410 in all.

The territory which includes the 15 known Round Valley villages is about 80 square miles, giving a population density of 5.6 persons per square mile. In view of the abnormally high concentration in the valley towns, the population density for the Yuki proper in the remaining 1,130 square miles can be regarded as scarcely half as much, say 2.5 per square mile. This would give a population of 2,820 for the balance. The Huchnom, and certainly the Coast Yuki, must have been even more sparsely settled, perhaps even less than the previously assumed 2 per square mile. If we use this number, however, we get again 990 for the two groups. The total then amounts to 4,260 (450 + 2,820 + 990). We thus get:

Kroeber's estimate	3,000
Uncorrected multiplicative method	5,250
Corrected multiplicative method	3,500
Direct area comparison (Athabascans, etc.)	3,410
Direct area, based on Round Valley	4,260

A fair compromise is a total population of 3,500.

The Pomo.—The Pomo organization differed from that of the preceding tribes, the central unit being the village community, rather than the village. The population of one community might live in one central village or be dispersed in several smaller ones. Hence the community, rather than the village, must be the ultimate basis for calculation. Gifford at Cigom, among the Clear Lake Pomo, found 20 compound houses and 235 living inhabitants. Although Cigom may be regarded as analogous to the ancient community, during white occupation a good deal of condensation has taken place, and this settlement is far larger than the average aboriginal settlement. Kroeber regards a population of 100 as a fair value for the latter. Some 75 of these communities are known, primarily among the northern, eastern, southeastern and central groups. The southern, southwestern, and northeastern groups are very imperfectly known. On the basis of 75 communities, the population would have been nearly 7,500.

It is possible to analyze the population figures in a little more detail. In the four best-studied groups we know fairly closely the actual number of communities. Taking Kroeber's value of 100 inhabitants each, it is possible to determine the density by area. (See table 2.)

The net density of 2.31 for 2,335 square miles seems reasonable despite individual variations among the component groups, and agrees fairly well with the value of 2.1 obtained for the northwestern tribes. If the figure 2.3 is used for the remaining three groups, a population of 2,550 is indicated, or a total for all the Pomo of 7,950. This agrees quite closely with Kroeber's estimate of 8,000.

Some further facts of interest may be derived from the baptism records of the San Francisco Bay missions.[15] In the lists for San Francisco, San Rafael, and Solano there are 444 names from villages identi-

TABLE 2

POPULATION DENSITY OF THE POMO

Group	Communities	Population	Area in sq. mi.	Density per sq. mi.
North..................	32	3,200	1,230	2.60
East..................	6	600	340	1.76
Southeast.............	3	300	95	3.15
Central...............	13	1,300	670	1.94
Total...............	54	5,400	2,335	....
Mean...............	..	.....	.....	2.31

fiable as Pomo. In addition there are 581 names which are doubtful but which are certainly Coast Miwok, Pomo, or Wappo. At least one-third, or approximately 175, were probably Pomo, making in all nearly 600 Pomo conversions. Now these were from the southern half of the southern group, in the vicinity of Santa Rosa, Sebastopol, and Healdsburg. Probably the Santa Rosa region was cleaned out entirely, although conversions along the Russian River near Healdsburg may not have been complete. According to Kroeber's map (*Handbook,* p. 356) this region embraced six tribal communities with a relatively dense population, for no less than 52 village sites are shown. From the mission record we know that at least 600 persons lived here. The number must actually have been much greater, because conversion along the Russian River was far from complete.[16] It is probably safe to double the number

[15] There are in the Bancroft Library at the University of California several records of this sort. They were copied by A. Pinart in 1878 from the originals, which have since disappeared. The records mention the converts by name and usually state the village.

[16] In the San Rafael records two villages alone contributed 237 neophytes, villages which are specified as being near Santa Rosa.

of conversions and allocate 1,200 to this part of the Southern Pomo, and perhaps between 1,500 and 2,000 to the entire group. This was perhaps the largest and most numerous of all the seven divisions. If so, a general average of 1,000 per group is permissible and conforms to the previous estimate of 8,000.

The Wappo.—This tribe inhabited a region east of the Pomo in the Napa Valley and to the north, including an isolated region on the south shore of Clear Lake. Barrett[17] and Kroeber list 19 villages, or rather village communities. At the Pomo rate of 100 each the population would have been 1,900. Similarly, if the Pomo value of 2.3 persons per square mile was used, the population figures would have been 1,680. The mission statistics for the entire tribe are not very reliable since only the southern portion, in the Napa Valley, was completely absorbed. (About 550 converts can be clearly ascribed to the Wappo.) However, certain village or community figures are of interest. Thus the village of Mayacma near Calistoga furnished 103 converts to Solano, and Loknome (Laoquiomi) near Middletown contributed 112. The indication is therefore that these communities contained at least the average 100 postulated for the Pomo. Kroeber (*Handbook,* p. 221) thinks that the Wappo population "may have reached 1,000," but he perhaps loses sight of the fact that this tribe suffered heavily from dispersion owing to the missions prior to 1835, that is, prior to any direct estimates made from 1840 to 1860. In general, it must be remembered that not only such estimates, but also computations based upon the memory of modern informants, tend to set population figures too low, since the Indians themselves in missionized regions had disappeared in the middle of the nineteenth century, and their villages and house sites are forgotten by the present generation of survivors. The mission records show baptisms of at least 550 Wappo, and it is much to be doubted whether this represents as much as half the tribe. On the basis of all data we may raise Kroeber's estimate to approximately 1,650.

The Lake Miwok.—The Lake Miwok were a small group on the south shore of Clear Lake and the headwaters of Putah Creek. Barrett[18]

---

[17] S. A. Barrett, *The Ethnogeography of the Pomo and Neighboring Indians* (1908), Univ. Calif. Publ. Am. Arch. and Ethn., 6:1–332.

[18] *Ibid.*, pp. 316–317.

gives seven villages and Kroeber shows eight (*Handbook,* p. 172). These cannot be regarded as tribal communities, for the population certainly was not 700–800. Kroeber (*Handbook,* p. 272) supposes there were two and possibly three such communities. This would give 200–300. Eight villages on the Yurok pattern of 45 inhabitants each would mean a total of 360. By area comparison, using the Pomo-Wappo factor of 2.2–2.3, we get 380. Kroeber himself says "not in excess of 500." Probably 400 is a liberal estimate.[19]

The Achomawi and Atsugewi.—We now turn to the tribes inhabiting inland northern California, those situated on the watershed and in the valley of the Sacramento. Here it is necessary to start anew with respect to population estimates. The social organization is different from that of the coastal tribes and the two habitats are so diverse that the area density value of 2.0–2.3 cannot be applied without strict revision and examination. Of all these tribes the best studied are the Achomawi, which have been very carefully investigated by Kniffen.[20] He bases his estimates of population mainly on native recollection, but since this region has been relatively unaffected by the invasion of the white man and since large numbers of Indians still inhabit the territory, the method may be regarded as entirely sound. His figure for the total is 3,000, which may be accepted. However, the situation merits anaylsis in more detail. Kniffen shows eleven subtribes, and indicates the village number and population of each. From his map the areas may be calculated, and hence the population density. These data are embodied in table 3. It will be seen that there are two general subdivisions, an eastern group with six subtribes and a western group with five. The mean density for the former is 0.31 and for the latter 0.73. This difference is easily explicable on the basis of habitat, since the eastern half of the territory is lava country, partly desert, with few water courses, whereas the eastern half is more broken, with numerous streams and with forests of conifer and oak. The latter region is thus able to support a much greater population. If we limit the range still

---

[19] The mission records show 21 baptisms from Tuleyome and Oleyome indicating definite penetration by 1835 as far as the shores of Clear Lake, but not indicating wholesale conversion in that region.

[20] F. B. Kniffen, *Achomawi Geography* (1928), Univ. Calif. Publ. Am. Arch. and Ethn., 23:297–332.

further to the Madesi, Ilmawi, and Itsatawi, we find that these three subtribes, inhabiting the most productive region of all, have a density of approximately 1.1. Now this represents too small an area and too

TABLE 3

KNIFFEN'S DATA ON THE ACHOMAWI

Subtribe	Number of villages	Inhabitants per village	Population	Area in sq. mi.	Inhabitants per sq. mi.
Eastern Group					
Hammawi...................	9	28	250	770	0.32
Kosalektawi................	3	43	125	275	0.46
Hewisedawi................	5	35	175	475	0.37
Astariwawi.................	4	50	200	575	0.35
Atwamsini.................	27	12	300	1,090	0.28
Aporige....................	12	33	400	1,430	0.28
Total....................	60	..	1,450	4,615	....
Mean....................	..	33.5	.....	.....	0.31
Western Group					
Achomawi.................	17	20	350	665	0.53
Atsuge....................	5	60	300	655	0.46
Ilmawi....................	13	27	350	315	1.11
Itsatawi..................	25	6	150	70	2.10
Madesi...................	11	36	400	415	0.97
Total....................	71	..	1,550	2,120	....
Mean....................	..	29.8	.....	.....	0.73

great a condensation of population to use as a criterion. However, if the Achomawi and Atsugewi are included, so as to take in the pine-oak terrain as opposed to the sagebrush-juniper terrain of the six eastern subtribes, we have an area which is fairly large and likewise representative of the entire northern Sacramento Valley. The value of 0.73 persons per square mile is, of course, only an approximation, and indeed it may be too low, since considerable tracts of wasteland are included. For working purposes the factor 0.8 may be used.

The great disparity in population density between these Indians and the coast tribes is striking. But to appreciate the difference one need only contrast the relatively humid Klamath and Eel River valleys with their copious fish supply with the drier Pit River Valley and its lack of fish food.

The Shastan tribes.—This group includes the small groups Kono-mihu, Okwanuchu and New River Shasta together with the Shasta proper. As a whole they held the territory inside the coast ranges and across the head of the Sacramento as far as the territory of the Acho-mawi and Modoc. Practically nothing is known of their villages or numbers, if we except an early government census cited by Kroeber (*Handbook*, p. 287) which gave 50 villages for the Shasta proper. Kroeber's estimate for the entire stock is somewhat under 3,000.

We may, however, employ area comparisons, based upon the figures for the Achomawi. The upper Klamath and Sacramento regions of the Shasta do not differ fundamentally, in the ecological sense, from the Pit and McCloud country inhabited by the western Achomawi. It might reasonably be expected, therefore, that the mean density of population over a considerable area would be similar. If the value for the five western Achomawi subtribes (0.73) is too low because of the fact that considerable tracts of pure waste land are included, neverthe-less the value for the three most western subtribes (1.1) represents too small an area and too great a concentration of people. An intermediate figure seems indicated, say 0.9. This gives us 3,380 for the entire Shasta group, with 2,370 for the Shasta proper. A slight reduction to 3,300 may be in order, thus coming quite close to Kroeber's estimate.

The Yana, Yahi, and Maidu.—These tribes inhabited a great block of territory covering the entire northern Sierra Nevada from Mt. Las-sen to the Cosumnes River. From west to east they ranged from the edge of the foothills to the Sierra crest and in the northeast spilled over into the rough counry between Quincy and Honey Lake.

The Yana and Yahi were two related tribes occupying the region south of the Achomawi and east of the Sacramento. There is no perti-nent information concerning their villages. Hence we must fall back on the area method. Since their terrain was very similar to that of the adjacent Western Achomawi, it is reasonable to use the density value of the latter: 0.9. This gives approximately 1,900. Kroeber's estimate is 1,750.

The Maidu present a much more complex problem, since their range was so vast—over 10,000 square miles. Kroeber places their population at 9,000. Direct application of the Achomawi factor, 0.9, gives 9,650. However, the region may be subdivided and examined more closely. The tribe as a whole is separated, on a dialectic basis, into three parts. The first of these, the Northeastern Maidu, covered the land southeast from Mt. Lassen, along the headwaters of the Feather River. This country includes a few fertile spots, such as Indian Valley north of Quincy, but is predominantly high-mountain forest or sagebrush desert. In fact, it very closely resembles the habitat of the whole Achomawi. In view of this fact, the mean density of the Achomawi (all eleven subtribes) may be employed: 0.45. This yields approximately 1,500 persons.

The other two subdivisions are the Northwestern and Southern, which may be considered together. Their territory is divisible into three ecological provinces, or belts: valley, foothill, and mountain. The latter is High Sierra, above approximately the 4,000-foot level. It is rough, inaccessible, covered with dense coniferous forest, and relatively incapable of sustaining a permanent population. In fact, the line between the mountain and foothill strips may be considered to run just east of the last permanent village sites, that is, from a point north of Downieville to a point some ten miles southeast of Placerville. It is possible therefore to eliminate the mountain strip from calculations based on density of settled population.

The foothill and valley strips were relatively productive. Large oak forests and swampy plains contributed generous supplies of acorns, seed plants, fish, and waterfowl. A fairly high population density might therefore be expected. In default of any better criterion we may use the coastal value of 2.0 persons per square mile. (Certainly the Achomawi factor is too low.) This yields an estimate 8,880 for the Northwestern and Southern Maidu, which, added to the 1,500 for the Northeastern division, means a total of 10,380.

Certain information pertaining to villages may also be used in connection with the Maidu. Exclusive of the Northeastern Maidu, Kroeber lists and indicates on his map (*Handbook,* p. 446) 65 villages. To these may be added 27 listed but not specifically located (*Handbook,*

p. 394), making 92 in all. This would imply at least 100–110 persons per village, much too high a number. Subsequently, however, Kroeber[21] compiled a new list for certain sections of the Maidu country which much increases the number of villages for the areas under consideration:

TABLE 4

MAIDU VILLAGES

	Number of villages (later estimate)	Number of villages (earlier estimate)	Ratio
On American River to Folsom.....	13	3	4.3:1
On Sacramento and Feather rivers to Marysville.................	30	7	4.3:1
On American River near Auburn...	6	1	6:1
On Sacramento River from mouth of Feather River to Butte City (the Patwin).................	21	17	1.2:1
Mean ratio.................	..	..	4.1

If the areas included by the foregoing village estimates are representative, then the entire territory should have contained 260 (65 × 4) inhabited settlements. Kroeber intimates that each village "might have" consisted of 6 or 7 houses (*Valley Nisenan*, p. 260). If the number of persons per house was the same as among the Yurok, i.e., $7\frac{1}{2}$, then the village population would have been 45, and the total 260 × 45, or 11,700. But some reduction is necessary to account for uninhabited houses and villages. Using the previous factor, $\frac{1}{3}$, we get 7,800, which together with the Northeastern group gives 9,300 for the whole tribe. The four estimates (viz., Kroeber's original, direct-area comparison, adjusted-area comparison, and house-village number) yield 9,000, 9,650, 10,380 and 9,300 respectively, all within quite close limits. A final figure of 9,500 appears consonant with what facts we have regarding the matter.

The Wintun.—This tribe inhabited a large territory west and north of the Sacramento River as far north as Redding and Weaverville. Subdivisions existed according to Kroeber[22] who has studied the tribe

---

[21] A. L. Kroeber, *The Valley Nisenan* (1929), *ibid.*, 24:253–290.
[22] Kroeber, *The Patwin and Their Neighbors* (1932), *ibid.*, 29:253–423.

exhaustively. These are the Northern Wintun or Wintu, the River Wintun, the Hill Wintun, the River Patwin, the Hill Patwin, and the Southern Patwin. The local organization was by tribelets, or community groups resembling those of the coastal tribes, rather than by villages. Consideration of population requires segregation into three main parts. The first is that of the Northern group of Wintu, living in the hill country of Shasta and Trinity counties. There are no facts available concerning villages here, and we are obliged to resort to area comparisons. The value derived from the Western Achomawi, and used with the Shastans is applicable here. However, it is probable that 0.9 persons per square mile is a little too high since the country is very rough. Hence 0.8 is better than 0.9. This gives a population of 2,950.

The remaining five subtribes inhabited much more favorable terrain, and undoubtedly had a higher density, although it seems probable that the hill tribes were somewhat more thinly spaced than those on the river. Fine distinctions are, however, of little use in view of our scanty knowledge, and perhaps it is better to assume the density as 2.0 per square mile, as was done in the calculations for the Foothills and Valley Maidu. But before we make this calculation the Southern Patwin should be separated from the other groups. This is because (1) the data on villages for this subtribe are very inadequate owing to the disruption by the missions, and (2) there are mission data which may be of some service.

The four intermediate subtribes (River and Hill Wintun, River and Hill Patwin) covered an area of some 4,550 square miles, indicating a population of 9,100. For the same aggregation of subtribes Kroeber lists 47 communities or tribelets. The average strength per community is unknown but it might have reached 150–200. If so, the total population would have been 7,050–9,400, thus checking roughly with the results obtained by the area method. We may tentatively assume 8,000.

By the area method the Southern Patwin had a population of 3,300. At this point the mission records become of service. Recognizable Wintun conversions are as follows: San Francisco (to 1822) 973, Solano (to 1834) 921, San José (to 1825) 156, giving 2,050 in all. Now these neophytes were drawn exclusively from that part of the Southern Patwin country from Putah Creek south to Suisun Bay, or perhaps two-thirds of their territory. To this number must be added some 200 doubtful cases and also those baptized in San José subsequent to 1825. A total of 2,300 is quite conservative. The population of the Southern Patwin must therefore have been at least 3,000 and probably nearer 3,500, for those who escaped conversion in the southern part plus those in the untouched part to the north must have amounted to at least 1,000. A value of 3,300 seems well within the bounds of probability.[23]

Taking the three main parts of the Wintun together, we get a total population estimate of 14,250 (2,950 + 8,000 + 3,300). The excess over Kroeber's estimate of 12,000 (*Handbook,* p. 356) is not great and may be referred to mission depletion prior to the recollection of modern informants.

TRIBES OF THE CENTRAL COASTAL BELT

The Coast Miwok.—With this tribe we enter upon the second population province, the province which was completely or partially subjected to mission influence and for which, with certain exceptions, the best sources of information are the mission records. These have been employed to a limited extent as corroborative evidence in the consideration of the lower Pomo and Wintun, but with the Coast Miwok, the Costanoans, Salinans, Esselen, Chumash, and the southern coast tribes they constitute primary evidence.

The Pinart copy of the San Francisco records show 813 baptisms from villages which can be identified with considerable certainty as Coast Miwok, together with 55 from villages which probably are of the same tribe. This includes many individuals who came from the "North Coast," but since Marin County was the only "North Coast"

---

[23] The designations employed by the missionaries are sometimes clearly referable to small villages, but in others to tribal communities or tribelets. Thus the "Karquines," "Ululatos," etc., are clearly of the latter category. In some of these instances the whole community was apparently moved bodily to the mission and the number of baptisms must therefore be a close index to size. There are six such tribelets which may be cited as examples, all from regions adjoining San Francisco or Suisun Bay: Karquines, Ululatos, Suisunes, Canicaymos, Libaytos, Topaytos. These showed 112, 362, 202, 231, 132, and 117 baptisms respectively, with a mean of 192. The standard tribelet number therefore cannot have been far from the assumed 150–200.

touched by San Francisco missionaries during the years cited, these individuals must have been Coast Miwok. San Rafael contributed 866. Here many of the village names are unidentifiable, but the conversions were all within the first two or three years subsequent to foundation (i.e., 1817–1820) during which time missionary activity was purely local in character. To the above must be added 48 from Solano and 140 from San José, making a total of 1,922. This figure represents a minimum. There were undoubtedly some who escaped conversion, but such a clean sweep was made of Marin County that their number could not have been great. Two thousand seems to be a fair estimate of the total.

Kroeber (*Handbook,* p. 274) shows 40 villages on his map of the Coast Miwok, indicating from the mission figure an average of 50 inhabitants. The records of the missions include by name seven towns which are noted on this map: Petaluma, Echakolom, Olemaloke, Likatiut, Olompolli, Echatamal, and Huchi. The numbers are, respectively, 155, 39, 177, 73, 73, 15, 20, with an average of 79. Very likely some of these, notably Petaluma and Olemaloke, included more than one actual village, and hence the average should be reduced. Nevertheless, if these names referred in actuality to ten or twelve villages, the average would still be nearly 50. The mission of the Coast Miwok was San Rafael, which began proselyting in 1817 after the San Francisco missionaries had been raiding the north shore for two decades. During this period the missionaries had converted some 850 of the tribe, and hence must have seriously depleted the southern half of the territory. The San Rafael record lists no less than 111 places from which converts were obtained in Miwok country plus 16 which may have been either Miwok or Pomo. The latter group may be neglected for present purposes. Of the 111 Miwok names 72 were places in which five or less converts were made. It is probable that these represent family names, or the names of small localities, parts of communities, and the like, which cannot be regarded as villages. The remaining 39 communities have an average strength of 18.8 persons. This is undoubtedly below the true average because (1) some of the inhabitants are probably included among the 72 family or place names which cannot be regarded as true villages, (2) many of the villages were reduced in numbers by previous conversions at San Francisco, and (3) other persons from some of these villages were baptized simultaneously or subsequently at Solano and San José. Indeed the San Rafael converts represented less than half the tribe. It is therefore justifiable to double the average given above and to conclude that the Miwok village size was about 35, a number quite comparable with that found among the tribes to the north. Since this would mean 57 instead of 40 villages, the discrepancy can only be resolved by assuming that Kroeber's list is incomplete, an assumption justified on the ground that many villages were completely lost, both inhabitants and name vanishing.

The Costanoans.—This tribe consisted of seven dialectic or linguistic stocks extending along the coast ranges from San Francisco Bay to a point south of Soledad. Since there have been no modern survivors and since very few of the villages are known, recourse must be had to other methods of computing the population.

As a first approximation, Kroeber's estimate of 1,000 per group or a total of 7,000 (*Handbook,* p. 464) may be cited. Also a rough area computation, based on the Pomo and Coast Miwok number 2.0, would give 11,000. This is undoubtedly too high, but just how much the factor 2.0 should be reduced to allow for the greater aridity of the inland coast ranges is not clear. We may, however, examine the mission data. There were seven missions in Costanoan territory, San Francisco, San José, Santa Clara, Santa Cruz, San Carlos, San Juan Bautista, and Soledad, which corresponded very approximately to the seven dialectic divisions. There are two sets of historical data which apply.

1. The Pinart copies of the baptism records in the Bancroft Library. These have already been utilized in connection with the Coast Miwok. For the Costanoans the record is incomplete. There exist only San Francisco, Santa Cruz, and Soledad, together with a census for San José (1825). For San Francisco the record is fairly clear. The population in San Francisco and San Mateo counties was cleaned up by 1790. Almost all the villages are located quite specifically, and considerable reliance may be placed on the figures. Conversions across the Bay in Alameda and Contra Costa counties are also quite clearly indicated. There were in these two regions 1,031 and 1,323 baptisms respectively.

The areas concerned are pretty definitely circumscribed. Furthermore, the baptisms must represent closely the actual population, since missionization was unusually complete and occurred over a relatively short period. The density values are 2.2 and 1.8, or very close to the previously assumed 2.0.

The baptism numbers for Santa Cruz and Soledad are also clear-cut. In the first few years of each mission a series of village names occurs which is obviously local in character and denotes the first spread of conversions among the Indians in mission territory, i.e., Costanoans. Then these names cease. There is a hiatus of approximately five years in the decade 1800–1810. Then an entirely new series of names appears, which have a non-Costanoan sound and which are specified in many instances as being from the "Tular," that is from Yokuts territory. Furthermore, this sudden shift coincides in time with the beginning of the great series of expeditions to the San Joaquin Valley in search of converts.

There were in Santa Cruz 1,506 baptisms and in Soledad 1,326 which may be ascribed to Costanoan stock. With reference to the San José census only a few, some 40–50, can be regarded definitely as Costanoan, and these may be neglected. If we regard the other three missions as representative, and omit San José for the moment, we might conclude that their total, 5,186, was half the Costanoan population, making 10,000 in all. Perhaps a few hundred ought to be added for San José, but these would have to be balanced by deductions from San Carlos which baptized heavily among the Esselen.

Very rough area computations for Santa Cruz and Soledad show densities of 3.75 and 1.8 respectively. The difference lies plainly in the relatively favorable coast of the former and the semiarid ranges of the latter.

2. In the Bancroft Library are complete transcripts of the mission census records, obtained from the originals, since destroyed, by H. H. Bancroft. These have formed the basis for a previous study on mission population.[24] The annual baptisms for each mission are given, but without distinction between mission and gentile births. However, the birth rate is known approximately, and from it may be calculated

---

[24] S. F. Cook, *Population Trends among the California Mission Indians,* Univ. Calif. Publ., Ibero-Americana, No. 17 (Berkeley, 1940). See below, pp. 395-446.

the probable number of gentile baptisms per year for each mission. There is considerable error involved, and no claim to real precision can be made. However, in the mass the results conform fairly well to those obtained with the Pinart copies. Thus for the missions San Francisco, Santa Cruz, Soledad, Santa Bárbara, and San Buenaventura the Pinart baptism lists show 11,702 gentile converts, and the indirect computation from the census transcripts 12,180. The latter may be used, with, let us say, a leeway of $\pm$ 10 per cent for random error.

With respect to the missions in Costanoan territory, as already stated, the Pinart lists show the following numbers of Costanoan baptisms: San Francisco, 2,354; Santa Cruz, 1,506; Soledad, 1,326: a total of 5,186. From the Bancroft transcripts we find in Santa Clara and San Juan Bautista a wave of conversion beginning with foundation and subsiding to a minimum in 1797 and 1807 respectively. This minimum may be taken as representing the point at which local (Costanoan) conversions ended and more distant ones began. The Costanoan number is 2,691 and 1,414 respectively. In Santa Clara the period 1797–1808 saw 1,566 probable gentile baptisms. However, we know from the San Francisco record that this was an era of great activity among the tribes of the north shore of the Bay. Consequently, the majority at Santa Clara were doubtless from this region. Perhaps there may well have been Costanoans included, but we have no way of computing their number. Similar considerations apply to San José, which in the same period baptized about 1,400 gentiles. It is certain that many Costanoans were brought to San José, but it is equally certain that large numbers of Wintun and Plains Miwok were baptized. As a pure estimate let us assign the value 1,000 to the Costanoans baptized in the two missions from 1797 to 1808. As to San Carlos, it has already been pointed out that here many of the converts were Esselen. Up to 1800 there were 1,660 gentile conversions, at which time the gentile conversions practically ceased. Again, as a pure estimate we may assume that half of these, or 850, were Costanoans. The total of the seven missions would then be 11,140, or preferably 11,000 to $\pm$ 1,000.

Three sources of data, therefore—area comparison, and two sets of mission records—give for Costanoan population 11,000, 10,000, 11,000. The lower value, 10,000, may be accepted for present purposes.

The Esselen.—This small tribe, inhabiting the coast range below Monterey has completely disappeared. Its population according to Kroeber (*Handbook*, p. 545) was between 500 and 1,000, with 500 as the better guess. An area of approximately 580 square miles was embraced by the tribe. At 2 per square mile the population would have exceeded 1,000, but the density, in the rugged mountain country along the mid-Californian coast, could scarcely have been so great. A more reasonable guess would be 1 per square mile, or perhaps a total of 600. According to the San Carlos Mission records, cited above, there might have been some 800–900 conversions from the Esselen, certainly no more. A few village names have come down to us. Kroeber (*Handbook*, p. 545) mentions six. Alexander Taylor[25] gives an additional six designated as "Escelenes" plus a few others of doubtful origin (Kroeber includes some in his list). At the most there cannot be more than ten or twelve. This argues a population of not more than a few hundred. A compromise figure, considering these various sources, would be 750.

The Salinans.—These people inhabited the coast-range region between King City and San Luis Obispo. Our information concerning them is nearly as scanty as for the Esselen. The Portolá expedition in 1769 passed through the territory and saw several villages.[26] Specifically, there were ten, with an average population of 113 (range 30–220).[27] This would give a minimum of 1,130 Salinans with but a fraction of the probable total included. Alexander Taylor lists several villages from this region.[28] A contemporary informant mentioned 4, and the balance, 24, were derived from the "mission books." If all these were names of bona fide villages and not family or mere place names, and the earlier rate of 113 per village held, then a population of 2,700 would be indicated.

---

[25] A. S. Taylor, *Indianology* (1864), Pt. I, p. 7.

[26] The best account of this expedition is Crespi's diary, edited by H. E. Bolton, *Crespi, Missionary Explorer* (Berkeley, 1927).

[27] Kroeber (*Handbook*, p. 546) says 30–400, but the number 400 is definitely stated to represent three villages. Kroeber suggests that Chumash, Esselen, or Costanoan villages were included, but the route is very clearly in Salinan territory, as Kroeber delineates it.

[28] A. S. Taylor, *op. cit.*, Pt. I (1864), p. 8.

Area computation shows a higher level of population. The Costanoan density was nearly 1.8 persons per square mile with the maximum in the Bay region. The Esselen density was approximately 1.3. The Salinan density must have been still lower, for their range includes the wild Santa Lucia Mountains, the dry interior ranges, and the rocky coast of Monterey and San Luis Obispo counties. The density could not have been more than 1 per square mile, if it reached even this value. With 3,600 square miles the population might have reached 3,500–3,600.

We have some data from the mission records. Kroeber (*Handbook*, p. 547) points out that the total baptisms at San Antonio and San Miguel (the Salinan missions) were nearly 7,000, from which he argues that the total gentile baptisms would have reached no more than 2,000. However, Kroeber, as well as other investigators, have not realized the tremendous death rate at the California missions[29] as a result of which the proportion of gentile to total baptisms is larger than otherwise might be expected. The Bancroft transcripts indicate more closely the gentile increment. Both missions show a steady, heavy increase in gentile conversions from foundation up to a minimum in 1808. According to the ideas advanced previously, this denotes the end of the initial phase of conversion, and probably includes at least most of the Salinans. The total for this period was 3,442, or say 3,400. Even if we draw the line four years earlier at 1804, the total is still 3,000. It may be argued that some of these may have been Yokuts or other valley Indians. However, there was very little invasion of the valley prior to the Zalvidea and Moraga expeditions in 1806, and in the year 1806–1807 less than one hundred gentiles were baptized at San Antonio and San Miguel. Furthermore, it may be suggested that some Salinans found their way, from 1770 to 1800, into the mission of San Luis Obispo, for it is less than ten miles from this mission over the Santa Lucia Mountains to Salinan territory. If this were true, the losses to San Luis Obispo would offset any gains from the Tulares.

The area and mission data, therefore, agree in giving at least 3,000 persons to the Salinan tribe, and possibly more. Accepting 3,000 re-

---

[29] The annual adult death rate for San Antonio and San Miguel was 41.5 and 47.5 per thousand, and the child death rate 167.5 and 137.

duces the density from the assumed 1.0 to 0.83 per square mile. However, the character of the terrain renders such a value quite probable.

The Chumash.—This important tribe inhabited the coast and hinterland from San Luis Obispo nearly to Santa Monica. It was extremely populous, primarily owing to the fine climate and abundant seafood along the Santa Bárbara channel.

For population estimates area computations are of no value, since most of the Indians lived along the shore, with relatively few in the interior. On the other hand, the village and mission data are fairly reliable. Several accounts have been left by early explorers, such as Cabrillo and Portolá, and tradition preserved until late in the nineteenth century the names and locations of villages. These sources have been carefully examined by Kroeber, who has set forth the information thus derived on his map of the Chumash territory (*Handbook,* pl. 48, p. 526). He shows in all 85 recognized villages. These may be divided for convenience into three groups: 41 on the coast or very near it, 25 in the interior, and 19 on the channel islands. If we knew the average number of inhabitants, we should have a good first approximation to the total population. Fortunately, the baptism records of San Buenaventura and Santa Bárbara give us the necessary clue. These records show numerous village names, many of which are unidentifiable but some of which clearly correspond to Kroeber's list. About 90 per cent of the baptisms do thus correspond. In each record the number of baptisms corresponds, in all probability, to the inhabitants, since the Chumash were completely incorporated into the missions. The essential data are as follows.

This value, 7,460, is subject to some modification. For certain reasons it may be too low. (1) Kroeber may not have listed all the villages, although most of those of any importance are probably on record. (2) There may have been some diminution in population between the first contact with the Spanish and the conversion by the missionaries. (3) Approximately 350 baptisms in the records cannot be assigned to any of Kroeber's villages. (4) Numerous Chumash were baptized in Santa Ynéz, La Purísima, and San Luis Obispo. On the other hand, the estimate of 7,460 may be too high. If all Kroeber's villages were of a size comparable to those identified, then they certainly should have appeared in a recognizable form in the baptism record. This indicates that either they were not inhabited during the era of conversion, or they were of extremely minor consequence. Since less than half Kroeber's villages contributed, with any certainty, to the baptism record, we might reduce the estimated 7,460 by one-half, to 3,730. Then we should have to add the 350 remaining recorded baptisms, making approximately 4,100 for the two missions. To this must be added the conversions in the other three missions, for which no direct

TABLE 5

CHUMASH VILLAGES

Group	Number of villages identifiable in baptism records	Mean number of inhabitants	Number of villages according to Kroeber	Population*
Coast...................	15	93	41	3,813
Inland...................	8	96	25	2,592
Island...................	9	55	19	1,055
Total..................	32	..	85	7,460

* The population is calculated by using the figures for the mean number of inhabitants, as given in column 2.

baptism records exist. Santa Ynéz and Purísima baptized only Chumash, and San Luis Obispo drew primarily on this tribe. Allowing a number equivalent to that of the two largest (Santa Bárbara and Buenaventura), we arrive at 8,000 for the entire territory.

Two additional sources of information are available.

1. The Portolá expedition in 1769 left a record of most of the villages encountered. The route included the populous channel region and the overland strip between Purísima and San Luis Obispo. Estimates of inhabitants vary according to the account (of which there are several), but the total number seems to have been between 5,200 and 5,800 from the mouth of the Santa Clara River to Point Concepción and between 720 and 780 from there to San Luis Obispo. If we allow 3,000 for the unobserved interior and another 750 for the northwestern section the total would have amounted to over 10,000 persons. However, the estimates of Portolá, Crespi, and the others may have been

inaccurate, erring probably on the side of exaggeration.[30] It would probably be safer to scale this value down 20 per cent to 8,000.

2. The indirect computation based upon the Bancroft transcripts for the five missions concerned shows a total of 9,105 gentile baptisms. Perhaps 400 should be deducted for Salinans at San Luis Obispo and another 100 for Tulare Indians brought to all the missions. But this may have been offset by scattering the figures for unreduced Chumash. We may then regard 9,100 as a maximum for the latter.

All the historical evidence seems therefore to point to the correctness of Kroeber's estimate of 8,000–10,000. It may be wise to accept the lower figure and put the population at 8,000.[31]

Sierra Miwok.—With this tribe we return to the interior valley and the Sierra Nevada, where the Miwok held the region south of the Maidu as far as the Fresno River. The computation of population must follow the general lines laid down for the Maidu.

Kroeber's estimate is 9,000. By area, using the Achomawi factor 0.9 person per square mile, the population would be 6,400. However, according to the principle of uninhabitability, approximately 2,000 square miles of high-mountain country may be deducted from the total area, leaving 5,100 square miles of foothills and plains. At 2 persons per square mile the population would have reached 10,200 for the plains section and the foothill strip.

---

[30] Four accounts of this trip are extant: Crespi's diary in *Crespi, Missionary Explorer,* H. E. Bolton, ed. (Berkeley, 1927); Portolá's diary in *Diary of the California Expedition,* D. E. Smith and F. J. Teggart, eds., Publ. Acad. Pac. Coast Hist., Vol. 1, No. 3 (1909); Costanso's two diaries, *Diario histórico de los viages* . . . , A. van Hemert-Engert and F. J. Teggart, eds., *ibid.,* No. 4 (1910); and *Diario del viage de tierra,* F. J. Teggart, ed., *ibid.,* Vol. 2, No. 4 (1911).

The statistical material differs in detail although it is quite uniform in general. Some additional material is of interest. From all evidence it is clear that the channel villages were very large, whereas those from Point Concepción to San Luis Obispo were much smaller. The difference is of course referable to the food supply. The average number of persons per house in both regions was nearly 8, that is, much the same as among the Yurok. The mean village population along the channel was 450, to the northwest it was 75. The latter figure is fairly large and the former enormous. In fact, it is quite probable that Portolá's "rancherias" were often two or more closely connected villages, and that the mean of approximately 100, obtained from the baptism records, more accurately reflects the individual village size.

[31] The crude density at this rate is 1.3. If the coastal belt is supposed to have included 4,000 persons in a strip 10 miles deep and 100 miles long, the density here was 4.0 per square mile. The inland territory, including the region from Purísima to San Luis Obispo, would then have a density of 0.7, a figure not inconsistent with the character of the terrain.

Kroeber (*Handbook,* pp. 444–445) mentions 109 villages, but includes only those identifiable with a fair degree of accuracy. At the assumed Maidu rate of 45 per village, the population would amount to 4,900, quite evidently an underestimate.

The mission data are somewhat scanty but nevertheless suggestive. In the census of 1825 at San José we find the names of 979 persons from identifiable Miwok villages, 236 from Yokuts villages, and 257 from villages which might have been either Yokuts or Miwok.[32] Practically. all these were from the lower Cosumnes, Mokelumne, and Calaveras rivers, that is, they were Plains Miwok. Now this list cannot include all conversions from this region, for active proselyting continued for another ten years after 1825. Furthermore, we may estimate one-half the 257 doubtful cases as Miwok and assign 1,100 Miwok to San José prior to 1826. Then it is safe to add another 400 to account for subsequent conversions, making 1,500 in all.

If the other three groups were of equal size, then the whole stock would have amounted to 6,000. But according to Kroeber's data the Plains group, by area and by village number, appears to have been the smallest of the four. Fifteen hundred inhabitants gives the Plains Miwok a density of 1.45 per square mile. Applying this factor to the foothill strip (and excluding the high-mountain sector) we get 7,400 persons, or a grand total of 8,900.

Kroeber's map shows 15 villages for the Plains Miwok, or an average of 100 persons per village. At this rate the 109 villages as a whole would indicate a population of 10,900. It appears from the application of these various methods that Kroeber's value of 9,000 must be as close as we can come at present.

The Western Mono.—This tribe inhabited the Sierra slope, between the Miwok and the Yokuts at the southeastern extension of the latter. Kroeber, on various grounds, sets their population at a maximum of 2,000. For example, he points out that there were six tribal groups, as compared to the Yokuts fifty. If we assume that the Yokuts numbered 15,000–20,000, by direct ratio the Western Mono might have reached 1,800–2,400.

An exhaustive study of this tribe has been made by Gifford who con-

[32] California MS 38, in the *Archivos de Misiones,* unbound documents, Bancroft Library, Berkeley.

centrated his effort on the Northfork group.[33] He estimates the aboriginal population as 300, with 67 known villages and camps. But as
he points out, these villages were ephemeral, and there existed no
fixed abodes. It is useless therefore to attempt any computation based
upon number of villages. Of course, if his estimate of the Northfork
group is correct and the other five groups were of comparable size,
the total would be 1,800.

The total area was about 3,500 square miles, from the Yokuts border
to the High Sierra crest, of which 2,250 square miles may be considered uninhabited high-mountain country, leaving 1,250 square
miles as the actual home of the tribe. If we use the density value, 1.45,
of the Plains and Foothills Miwok, we get for the Western Mono,
1,810 persons. A value of 1,800 seems therefore acceptable.

The Yokuts.—This tribe, inhabiting the entire San Joaquin Valley,
is regarded by Kroeber as the key to the Indian population of California. He has consequently examined all possible sources of information and as a result has concluded that the population amounted to
15,000–20,000, with a set figure of 18,000. There seems little justification for a revision of Kroeber's estimate, particularly since no new
evidence has been brought to light since the *Handbook* was published.
The mission records are not particularly useful, since the number of
Yokuts brought to the mission was but a small fraction of the total
population. Area computations are of some interest, although by no
means decisive. The total Yokuts area was approximately 12,500 square
miles. If we extend the Plains and Foothills Miwok factor of 1.45
persons per square mile we get 18,100 for the Yokuts, exactly Kroeber's
estimate. With regard to area it has been stressed by Kroeber, and it
is general knowledge, that the east side of the valley and adjacent
foothills were much more heavily populated than the more barren
west side. These regions may be roughly delimited by a line drawn
from near Tracy southward along the route of the Southern Pacific
to the latitude of Fresno, thence generally south-southeast along the
western margins of Kings River Slough, Old Tulare Lake and Buenavista Lake to the Tehachapi. If we ascribe a density of 2.0 per square
mile to the eastern part and a density of 1.0 to the western—this, of

[33] E. W. Gifford, *The Northfork Mono* (1932), Univ. Calif. Publ. Am. Arch. and Ethn.,
31:15–65.

course, purely arbitrarily—the population value is 19,300. If we assume the density in the western part of the valley to have been even smaller, say 0.7, then the value is 17,600. Although the accuracy of this calculation can by no means be insisted upon, it seems to indicate a reasonable correspondence with the more careful estimate of Kroeber.

Tribes of Southern California

The Shoshoneans and Yumans.—It is necessary now to pass to the great mountain and desert region of southern California. The methods hitherto employed for estimating population become of far less value. In fact, the entire environmental situation is basically different from that obtaining with the tribes of the center and north. Even toward the coast the location and size of villages are very poorly known; the habit of migrating or wandering great distances was a characteristic of the people. The terrain, except along a narrow coastal belt, was extremely arid and could not support a large permanent population. The mission records are not decisive, since it is usually impossible to determine how far into the interior conversions were carried on. There are no clear-cut blocks of missionization, as among the Costanoans or Chumash. Area computations have no meaning, since the land was diversified and since, furthermore, there is no sound basic area from which to proceed. There are no baptism records giving village names, which might afford a starting point for a local area estimate.

Kroeber has utilized what evidence there is, but in default of more exact data some of his figures admittedly represent little more than shrewd guesses based upon long study and close qualitative contact with the problem. Nevertheless, his estimates may be accepted as the best obtainable. For purposes of this study it is unnecessary to attempt computation of the subdivisions of the Shoshoneans. We may therefore say, following Kroeber (*Handbook,* p. 881) that the Shoshoneans, exclusive of the Eastern Mono, amounted to 18,000. Of these the tribes directly in mission territory, the Fernandino, Gabrieleño, Juaneño, and Luiseño, accounted for 10,000. Of the Yumans we need consider here only those which came under mission influence, the Diegueño and Kamia. The other groups, Yuma proper and Mojave, although territorially in California, were never missionized and, in fact, are oriented historically and environmentally with the tribes of the Southwest. It is perhaps somewhat arbitrary thus to exclude them, but we must draw the line somewhere and this seems the most appropriate place. Kroeber estimates 3,000 as covering the Diegueño and Kamia, which together with 18,000 Shoshoneans, makes 21,000 in all.

For the sake of completeness certain mission and area data may be added. From the Bancroft transcripts it appears that the five missions San Fernando, San Gabriel, San Juan Capistrano, San Luis Rey, and San Diego baptized approximately 15,200 gentiles. This figure seems to conform to Kroeber's estimates and must include all the inhabitants of the well-populated coast as well as many converts from the western edge of the Colorado and Mojave deserts, since Kroeber's figure for the strictly coastal groups is only 10,000. Now let us draw a purely arbitrary line, representing the interior limit of fairly complete missionization and totally neglecting tribal boundaries, from the Tehachapi at Tejon Pass along the northern edge of the Sierra Madre and San Bernardino ranges, thence south through Palm Springs and along the San Diego–Imperial county line to the border. There will be included in this area approximately 13,300 square miles, and the density, calculated according to the mission figures alone, would be 1.15 per square mile. If, alternatively, we consider only the mission tribes themselves, i.e., the Fernandino, Gabrieleño, Juaneño, Luiseño and Diegueño, we find that, occupying an area of approximately 7,000 square miles and with a population of 13,000 (Kroeber's estimate), they show a density of 1.85. These values are probably inaccurate but are within the range of the reasonable.

Summary of Aboriginal Population

From the foregoing discussion we arrive at these totals: for the northern province, excluding Modoc and Paiute, 60,000; for the central province, excluding the Washo and Eastern Mono, 52,550; for the southern province, excluding the Colorado River tribes and Mojave, 21,000; total 133,550. This is about 7 per cent higher than Kroeber's total (125,000) for the same tribes, but is, however, not a serious discrepancy considering the wide margin of error inherent in all such calculations.

PART TWO

The Physical and Demographic Reaction of the Nonmission Indians in Colonial and Provincial California

Originally published as *Ibero-Americana* Volume 22, 1943

I N A RECENT PAPER I have set forth at some length the operation of various factors concerned with the decline of the mission Indian population.[1] It was shown that from the social and cultural, as well as from the physical, standpoint the native stock underwent definite deterioration and failed to respond successfully to the new environmental surroundings.

In the present paper attention is directed, not to the missionized, but to the wild component of the California population, those tribes and portions of tribes which never came under mission influence but which were exposed directly to the shock of civilian and military contact. As would naturally be expected, the picture is different in several essential respects. Perhaps the most fundamental distinction lies in the mental attitude of the whites. The missionaries, whatever the shortcomings of their temporal system, were imbued with a powerful desire for the spiritual and material betterment of the native race. The soldiers and the civilian population, on the other hand, were actuated only by their own self-interest, and were friendly, indifferent, or hostile to the native depending on whether mutual interests coincided or clashed. The result was that certain factors and tendencies which were eliminated or mitigated in the missions were allowed to operate without restriction among the general population. Since the influence of these factors was unfavorable to the Indians even under mission protection, it is clear that their effect would be greatly accentuated among the wild tribes. Particularly does this consideration apply to unbuffered physical contact between the races.

A second point of distinction is geographical. Under earlier conditions the natives came or were brought from their aboriginal haunts

[1] S. F. Cook, *The Conflict between the California Indian and White Civilization: I. The Indian versus the Spanish Mission*, Univ. Calif. Publ., Ibero-Americana, No. 21 (1943).

to a new environment, creating the problem of Indian adjustment to a strange external situation. With the fall of the missions—and even earlier—the whites began to penetrate into the native territory of the Indians, thereby setting in motion somewhat different forces. In the third place, during the later Spanish and the American periods the religious motif was completely absent.

It is proposed to consider here only the more obvious material influences which were brought to bear on the Indians and which had an immediate effect upon the population. There is, first, the primary effect on population induced by forthright homicide. Although the data are rather scanty, one can arrive at a fair estimate of the losses sustained by the Indians through killing, whether the latter was conducted as a public or private enterprise.[2] But the effects of armed invasion and violence obviously were felt, not only by those who fell beneath the gun or the knife, but also by the survivors. They were subjected to numerous secondary influences which in the long run might prove just as fatal and which can by no means be neglected in assessing the decline in population. Chief among these are disease and starvation, factors which perhaps cannot be expressed in as clear numerical terms as can homicide, but the significance of which can be pointed out in detail. Disease and starvation were mediated and intensified by various tertiary factors, which in themselves would not directly cause death but which would render a population hypersensitive. These would include such concomitants of physical conflicts as destruction of homes, clothing, and tools of the chase, together with small- or large-scale forced removals.

CASUALTIES

Any consideration of physical violence inflicted on the wild Indians in the mission period narrows down to an examination of the well-known and numerous expeditions into the interior. These expeditions have received much comment from all the historians of California, who have been interested in them primarily from the standpoint of

---

[2] It is noteworthy that, despite endless verbal and written comment on the "killing-off" of the North American natives, there has been little serious effort to determine the actual numerical extent of such slaughter. Indeed, I know of no critical examination of the available evidence regarding any of the numerous Indian wars in the United States or Mexico.

exploration and expansionist politics. Consequently, it will not be necessary to discuss them here except with respect to their effect on the natives.

1800–1830.—These incursions into virgin territory began with the Portolá-Serra expedition of 1769, but for many years involved only the so-called "mission strip," i.e., the region from which the missions drew most of their converts. This includes, for central California, the coast ranges and littoral from Ventura to Marin County, embracing all San Francisco Bay and extending eastward to the western edge of the San Joaquin and Sacramento valleys. It does not include the valley proper except at one point, that where the rivers break through the coast range above Suisun Bay and the Delta region. Since this western area saw its population completely missionized, it may be excluded from the present discussion. Interest here centers only in those tribes which, as a whole, never came under mission control. Thus the Costanoans, Salinans, Esselen, Chumash, and Coast Miwok may be definitely eliminated. Of the remaining tribes all except six were entirely untouched by Spanish influence in the physical sense. These were the Pomo, Wappo, Wintun, Maidu, Sierra Miwok, and Yokuts. The last two, the Sierra Miwok and the Yokuts, constituted together the largest single block of natives, and, moreover, were the most active in their relations with Spanish civilization.

Very early there must have been some infiltration of the Spanish into the valley. Yet aside from the expeditions of Fages in 1772, Anza in 1776, and Garcés in 1776, which did little more than explore the fringes, there were no large-scale operations. In the account of Garcés there is evidence that individual travelers had penetrated the interior before his appearance, and there can be no doubt that this process continued in a random fashion during the following forty years. The influence of such contact was significant, but primarily in a social and cultural sense, for the visitors were too few to influence materially the population level.[3]

---

[3] The sources of our knowledge concerning expeditions are almost exclusively the abstracts of official correspondence from 1770 to 1835. To these may be added in a few instances personal recollections and historical accounts, such as that of M. G. Vallejo. In this paper all citations to manuscripts, unless otherwise stated, refer to documents contained in the Bancroft Library of the University of California, Berkeley. Many of

Subsequent to the time of Fages and Garcés the first recorded major invasion of the valley was an unauthorized foray by Father Juan Martín in 1804. At this date the era of great expeditions may be said to begin.⁴ The Appendix, table 2, lists 29 of these. This number cannot be said to represent all the expeditions, incursions, and forays into the Tulares which occurred from 1800 to 1830. They include only those of which I have been able to find an authentic record and concerning which there is more than mere casual reference or mention. Traces exist of many other expeditions, usually conducted under illegal or private auspices, which left no impress upon the official records. Several of these are mentioned in personal recollections written at a later date, but for purposes of quantitative examination they are valueless.

Looking at the 29 recorded expeditions, one notes the large number for which there are no apparent Indian casualties (15 out of 29). The reason may be that fatalities inflicted on the Indians were regarded as reprehensible and therefore not reported, but it is more likely that such affairs simply did not occur. This assumption rests upon the fact that there were two clearly distinct types of expedition. One was purely exploratory and propagandist, undertaken by and accompanied by missionaries who were inspired by the most peaceful motives. This type predominated up to approximately 1813. Thereafter the char-

---

these are in the form of transcripts. The "Bancroft compilation" referred to in connection with mission population is a tabular compilation of annual statistics taken by Hubert Howe Bancroft from original sources now lost.

In the official records there are a few hints of *salidas* which may have passed the border of the mission strip. Thus a party went out from Santa Bárbara in 1789 in pursuit of a fugitive and penetrated "acia los Tulares" (Goycoechea to Fages, June 26, 1789, Prov. St. Pap., 9:107). The next year, Sergeant Olvera pursued a fugitive to a rancheria five days' journey from Santa Bárbara, where he was attacked by the natives and forced to retreat (Goycoechea to Fages, Sept. 2, 1790, Prov. St. Pap. Ben. Mil., 9:6). The hostile attitude of the Indians implies previous acquaintance with the Spanish soldiers. In 1795, a troop penetrated to the north among tribes living "30 leagues from Bodega" (probably Pomo), tribes which were also hostile (Borica to viceroy, June 23, 1795, Prov. Rec., 6:48. In 1797, Briones went in pursuit of a fugitive to a rancheria at the "orilla del Valle de los Tulares" (Briones to Sal, Jan. 26, 1797, Prov. St. Pap., 16:214). Actually, many more such minor attempts may have been made. They have remained unrecorded owing to their unimportance and also because such adventures were strictly against official policy at the time.

⁴ Fr. Juan Martín, "Visita a los gentiles tulareños," 1815, Sta. Bárb. Arch., 6:85–89.
For much information and interpretation concerning the inland exploration of the Spanish I am indebted to an unpublished article by Professor Herbert I. Priestley, which he has kindly permitted me to consult.

acter of the leadership changed from clerical to military. Troops were sent to the interior not to convert or explore, but to capture fugitives and punish recalcitrants. An inevitable corollary was fighting and bloodshed.

Despite the predominantly military and punitive nature of these later raids and campaigns, the Indian losses were amazingly small, if the official and semiofficial statements are to be believed. There were a total of 133 natives numbered as killed, plus five cases where the casualties were described as "many" or "several." The value 133 includes six expeditions. Using the same proportion for the other five would give 107 deaths or a total of 240 for all eleven expeditions. We may add a certain number for unmentioned killings and conclude that not more than 250 represents the maximum for all the 29 expeditions. To these it is probably fair to add a tentative 150 casualties to cover sporadic raids by unlicensed soldiers, *vecinos,* and mission neophytes, making a maximum of 400 violent deaths up to 1830.

1830–1848.—Subsequent to the decline of the missions, the interior expeditions changed their character. The highly organized official exploratory or punitive campaigns were replaced by numerous small ones, which more and more partook of the character of private retaliatory incursions and slave-hunting raids. They likewise increased in brutality. The famous campaigns against Estanislao in 1829 ushered in an era of intensive cattle and horse raiding by the now aroused valley tribes, aided by apostate neophytes, American trappers, and the criminal element throughout the West. Almost continuous fighting back and forth resulted, wherein all semblance of real expeditions was lost. At the same time, the expanding economy of the private ranches demanded an increased supply of cheap labor, which was most easily obtained from the adjacent native tribes. Thus punishing stock thieves and capturing farm labor became almost the same in method.

The official records of this period are naturally far from adequate. Moreover, subsequent reminiscences, although copious, do not permit us to form a complete picture of all the parties, raids, and fights which occurred. General and vague statements concerning conditions at the time are worthless. The best we can do is to enumerate those clashes of sufficient magnitude or importance to have been accorded written recognition. In the Appendix, table 2, are listed 21 of these. It will be observed that they cover the period of only nine years, 1833 to 1841 inclusive. After 1841 the situation became so confused and the power of the Mexican administration so weak that even nominal control over the military activity of the citizens was lost. It is consequently hopeless even to attempt an itemization of raids and battles. Of the 21 expeditions listed, 19 involved valley Indians. The killings are recorded for 6 of them, with a total of 241. The average, 40, is too high, since one of the forays was that of Mesa and Amador in 1837, which was distinguished by the barbarous and inexcusable massacre of some 200 persons. (It should be noted in fairness to their contemporaries that this act on the part of two ruffians, one of whom has given his name to a modern county, was universally condemned and repudiated.) It is justifiable to exclude this single case and compute an average of 8 for the other 5 expeditions where the fatalities are recorded. This would also conform, in essence, to 3 other engagements in which "several" were said to have been killed. Using 8 as a basis, the sum for the 19 recorded valley encounters, excluding the two exceptions noted, would be 152, or, let us say for convenience, 150.

Now a careful examination of the documents of the period, as well as of the many personal narratives by pioneers, leads to the conclusion that not more than one-third or one-quarter of the actual fights and expeditions, especially against valley stock thieves were ever recorded. One-quarter would not be too liberal an estimate. This means that instead of some 20 such affairs there were at least 80, in the decade 1831–1841. At 8 casualties each, the deaths would reach some 640, to which would have to be added the 200 victims of the Amador-Mesa slaughter, making 850 in all.

Subsequent to 1841 and up to 1848, warfare became much intensified in the south, but tended to decline in the valley and in the coast range until, at the time of the gold discovery, hostilities had substantially closed in this area. We may, therefore, allow perhaps 20 expeditions in those seven years, with an approximate 150 deaths.

During the later phases of Spanish and Mexican domination, the interior valleys were subjected to continually increasing inroads by Anglo-Americans and other foreigners. These aliens were of two categories, those who entered as immigrants and naturalized under Mexican law and those who entered surreptitiously or by force and who were in general hostile to the constituted government. The first group included men who actually settled on the land. In the valley country should be mentioned Cordua at Marysville, Sutter at Sacramento, Weber at Stockton, and Savage at Fresno. Apart from their great cultural influence on the natives, they are of little significance here, since their policy was uniformly friendly toward the Indians and on only rare occasions did they resort to violence.

The second group included such well-known and even notorious characters as Jedediah Smith, McLeod of the Hudson's Bay Company, Ewing Young, Walker, "Pegleg" Smith, and Captain J. C. Frémont. Their influence in accentuating the turmoil among the valley tribes was definitely significant and will be discussed later. Their direct effect as homicidal agents, however, is very difficult to assess. Popular tradition and their own accounts give no indication that they were in any way inhibited with respect to killing natives when such action appeared desirable. On the other hand, we know of no outstandingly flagrant cases of butchery, at least up to the advent of the so-called "Oregon men" in the late 'forties. It is probable that the number of killings, among the Miwok and Yokuts at least, was relatively small, when compared to the fifty-year record of the Spanish.

I have at hand accounts of nine actions which occurred in the Sacramento and San Joaquin valleys prior to 1848. There were undoubtedly others, record of which I have not seen.[5]

In these nine affairs apparently there were killed some 25 Maidu,

---

[5] These were, briefly:

1. Hastings' expedition from Oregon, "several" killed (John Bidwell, "California 1841–1848," MS, 1877, p. 108).

2. Sutter attacks River Patwin near Colusa. Various estimates of the number killed. Sutter ("Personal Reminiscences," MS, 1877, p. 40) says 6. Bidwell (MS, p. 110) says "many." L. W. Hastings (*The Emigrant's Guide to Oregon and California* [1845], p. 68) says 20. J. H. Rogers (*Colusa County* [1891], p. 52) says "several." Sutter's estimate of 6 is probably closest to the facts.

3. Sutter is attacked by and pursues the Miwok of the Mokelumne (MS, p. 44). Forced to retire with many wounded. Indian casualties not mentioned—perhaps 5 or 10.

4. Sutter goes "up the valley" to protect Peter Lassen (*ibid.*, p. 44). Killed "some." The tribe is indeterminate.

5. Sutter, in 1847, charges that Armigo and Sam Smith attacked a rancheria "60

15 Wintun, and 60 Miwok, in addition to perhaps 20 of undetermined tribes. To extrapolate from these figures would be very risky. Although it is probable that much more Indian fighting took place in the valley than was ever recorded, yet we have no means whatever of assessing it numerically. A very conservative estimate would be 100 violent deaths among the Wintun and Maidu and 100 among the Miwok.

The preceding discussion has centered around the tribes of the central valleys, particularly the San Joaquin. However, some attention must be devoted to the group north and northeast of San Francisco Bay. The Coast Miwok and Southern Patwin were heavily drawn upon for converts during the mission era, as a result of which their numbers were greatly reduced and their tribal life practically obliterated. Consequently they cannot be regarded as wild tribes which came in contact with white civilization primarily through the medium of soldiers, explorers, and ranchers. The same considerations apply in large measure to the Southern Wappo and probably to some extent to the Southern Pomo. Nevertheless, these groups—the Wappo and Pomo—were by no means entirely missionized. The northern half of the Wappo and all the Pomo except the southern fringe were virtually untouched at the time of secularization, as were also the Clear Lake Miwok. These peoples, however, soon felt the impact of the Mexican regime, chiefly through the activity of General M. G. Vallejo, and of later American immigrants such as Yount and Kelsey. They suffered material losses through this conflict, losses which were in no way attributable to mission influence.

---

miles north" and killed 13 (Sutter to Mason, July 12, 1847, Calif. Arch., unbound docs., No. 89). The charges were not proved in court but were probably well founded.

6. A group of mission Indians attack a rancheria on the American River (Sutter, MS, p. 44) and murder "many." In retaliation, 14 of the mission Indians, no doubt Mokelumnean Miwok, were shot.

7. Lindsay murdered at Stockton. In the resulting punitive expedition, the casualties were "several" (J. D. Mason, *History of Amador County* [1881], p. 36) or "a few" (Lewis Publishing Company, *An Illustrated History of Amador County* [1890], p. 31) or 22 (Sutter to Pico, April 9, 1845, Dept. St. Pap., 6:173). Sutter's estimate was probably closest.

8. Weber and José Jesús punish the Calaveras Miwok for cattle stealing. "Some" Indians killed (Lewis Publishing Company, *op. cit.*, p. 39). G. H. Tinkham (*History of San Joaquin County* [1923], p. 51) says "most of the bucks." Estimate, 10–20.

9. One Myers, trapping in Stony Creek Valley (Hill Patwin) attacked a village and killed "a good many," say 10 (J. H. Rogers, *op. cit.*, p. 54, quoting Bidwell).

In 1833 the Southern Pomo were attacked by Father Mercado, with 21 killed plus many wounded.[6] In 1834 the Satiyomi, a subtribe of the Wappo, were attacked by Vallejo, and after two battles 200 were killed and 300 captured.[7] These figures might be written off immediately, were it not for the general reliability of Vallejo and the fact that his own casualties were admitted to have reached one killed and 63 wounded. The Wappo losses must have been greater and may have approached 200. In 1836 the neighboring Southern Pomo fell afoul of these same Wappo and lost 22 killed and 50 wounded. In retaliation, Vallejo with a large force chastised the Wappo, killing many, say 20.[8] In 1837 Vallejo was skirmishing with the Patwin under the "ferocious" leader Zampay, but no casualties are mentioned. In 1841 Vallejo is described by W. H. Davis as going to Clear Lake and slaughtering 150 persons as they emerged from a *temescal,* the so-called "Clear Lake Massacre."[9] Two years later Salvador Vallejo went to the "Gulf of Mendocino" and by means of rapidly constructed boats, attacked the natives on islands, slaughtering 170.[10] Judging by the timing, these were Pomo in the vicinity of Fort Bragg, although conceivably some of the more northern tribes may have been involved. Charles Brown, writing in 1878, refers to a big expedition "toward Oregon" which he places in 1835 and during which 200 to 300 natives were butchered.[11] However, he is doubtless referring to the Clear Lake affair of 1841 or the Mendocino expedition of 1843. To the list may be added the García-Castro raid near Fort Ross in which several, perhaps 10, were killed,[12] and the burning of a temescal with occupants near Yount's ranch in which a great many, perhaps 50 persons, perished.[13] The remarkable feature of these northern affrays was the relatively enormous mortality. Gross exaggeration is to be suspected; nevertheless, there is reason to believe that the figures were not excessively inflated. In

[6] See Appendix, table 3.
[7] M. G. Vallejo, "Historia," MS, 1875, 3:22 ff.
[8] M. G. Vallejo to *comandante* of Sonoma, April 8, 1836, Vallejo Docs., 3:105.
[9] "Glimpses of the Past," MS, 1828, p. 290.
[10] M. G. Vallejo to *comandante* of Sonoma, April 1, 1843, Vallejo Docs., 11:354.
[11] "Statement of Recollections," 1878, MS, p. 11.
[12] "Proceso," Sonoma, August 6, 1845, Dept. St. Pap. Ben. Mil., 5:383–393. Some 250 captives were made but were later liberated.
[13] C. L. Camp, *The Chronicles of George C. Yount,* Calif. Hist. Soc., *Quarterly,* 1923, 2:3–67.

the first place, these were very elaborate expeditions, or rather military campaigns, undertaken with large bodies of white soldiers and numerous Indian auxiliaries. In the second place, the Spanish losses, when recorded, are found to be commensurate with relatively large-scale engagements. In the third place, it was the policy of the Vallejo family to support a few really heavy attacks on the Indians rather than bother with mere bushwhacking tactics. In the fourth place, the large dependence upon friendly Indians for auxiliary troops meant that a defeated enemy was subjected to a real massacre. Finally, one must reflect that, even if the casualties in the few campaigns of record were exaggerated, such excess was doubtless more than made up by small skirmishes, knowledge of which is now lost.

From the data presented above we find the deaths distributed as follows: Pomo, approximately 225; Wappo, 270, plus 150 for the Clear Lake massacre, which may have included both tribes. For the two tribes together the total is 645. The actual number may have been higher, since there was undoubtedly some unrecorded fighting.

We may now attempt to evaluate the effect of physical violence upon the decline of the general population throughout the entire period. Using the data submitted above, we may distribute the losses thus:[14] Yokuts, 700; Miwok, 825; Maidu, 25; Wintun, 50; Pomo, 300; Wappo, 345. The total is 2,245. We may now relate these values either to the aboriginal number of each tribe or to the decline from 1770 to 1848. Calculating these relationships and expressing the result as a percentage, we get the results shown in the table on page 11.[15]

This tabulation shows that during the years of Ibero-American occu-

---

[14] The total loss for the Miwok and Yokuts to 1848 from Spanish or Mexican attacks is taken as 1400. Half may be attributed to the Miwok, for although the Yokuts were more numerous and territorially extensive, the Miwok were far more aggressive. To the Miwok have also been added 125 to account for the activity of Sutter and other immigrants to the valley.

The value of 50 for the Wintun is a pure estimate, which includes the losses due to American hostility as well as Vallejo's campaign against Zampay. It may be far too low a value.

The values for the Pomo and Wappo include 75 each from the Clear Lake massacre. This is obviously a compromise.

[15] The population figures are taken from Appendix, table 1. Where necessary, approximate interpolations have been made, so as to discern the order of magnitude, even if not the actual and exact number.

pation the native population suffered more extensively from personal violence than might perhaps be anticipated. Even if the completely missionized groups are included, as well as those untouched by white influence, nearly 6 per cent of the population decline can be ascribed to this direct cause. Among the wild tribes those which resisted incursion most stubbornly are seen to have suffered really apalling losses. Thus the Sierra Miwok and the Wappo underwent reductions

	Percentage of aboriginal population killed in warfare	Percentage of decline due to killing in warfare
Yokuts...........................	3.8	17.1
Sierra Miwok.....................	9.1	27.3
Maidu...........................	0.3	2.5
Wintun..........................	0.3	0.8
Pomo............................	3.7	10.0
Wappo...........................	21.0	40.5
All six tribes....................	3.8	12.5
All central and northern California...	2.0	6.3

from their aboriginal number of approximately 9 and 20 per cent, respectively. In general, it is clear that, although warfare was perhaps a minor factor in the disintegration of the native population as a whole up to 1848, it was nevertheless a critical element in specific instances.

DISEASE

Introduced disease was the single factor which contributed most effectively to the decline of the Indian population in the missions. One would normally expect, therefore, that the gentile population would not be spared its ravages. The rather complete data on mission mortality enable us to evaluate the disease factor among the converts, but such information is totally lacking for the unconverted Indians. We are forced, consequently, to fall back on a few general statements and casual descriptions, reinforced by a liberal measure of conjecture.

That disease would spread to the interior tribes was inherent in the entire situation. Indeed, it is remarkable that violent epidemics did not occur much earlier than they did. The sources of infection were numerous, but may be conveniently and briefly grouped in three categories.

The first was the Spanish themselves, who from the very inception of Californian colonization were penetrating beyond mission territory. Although the great expeditions did not begin for forty years after initial settlement, there was a slow stream of soldiers and civilians trickling over the coast range into the valley. Tales of the Indians lend weight to the idea that they were constantly exposed to white visitation all through the last decades of the eighteenth century. This influx was, of course, not of great volume, but the possibility of disease transport was there. After 1800 this invasion swelled rapidly until the intercourse between coast white men and interior Indians became substantially continuous.

The second category includes the American and New Mexican trappers, traders, and adventurers who penetrated the central valleys in small numbers throughout colonial times. The effect of their arrival would parallel that of the Spanish coming from the west.

The third group, and by far the most significant, was that of the Indians themselves. Very early in the mission period, dissatisfied neophytes of various tribal origins began fleeing over the mountains to find refuge in the country of the Tulares. By the turn of the century, this stream had swelled to a flood. Undoubtedly, hundreds if not thousands of mission converts poured into the valley, bringing with them the diseases of the coast. It was when this intermingling reached its climax after secularization that really serious epidemics began to afflict the interior tribes.

The earliest known diseases in the interior were of venereal origin. At least the first specific reference in the contemporary writings was to syphilis, a statement from the pen of Fr. Juan Martín[16] concerning his trip to the San Joaquin Valley in 1894. He said:

Lo que siento es que mueren muchos gentiles ya por las continuas guerras mutuas, ya también por las muchas enfermedades *presertim* el Galico de modo que si no se les pone misión luego ... no quedará conquista.

The presence of syphilis in the valley at about this time has also been asserted by P. M. Jones, who made excavations around Buenavista Lake in 1899 and found certain skeletons which seemed to show a

---

[16] Martín to Señan, April 26, 1815, Sta. Bárb. Arch., 6:85–89, a letter in which he describes his visit to the Tulares.

venereal pathology.[17] In 1818 Governor Solá stated with reference to
the Santa Bárbara district and the wild tribes to the east:[18]

... pero hallandose infecionados del mal venereo, el que ya se va estendiendo
en el territorio donde habitan los gentiles por el roce que tienen con
algunos cristianos fugitivos que han pasado a ellos llevando el contagio ... .

In 1833 or thereabouts, G. C. Yount remarked that the Napa Valley
Indians were thoroughly contaminated.[19] Duflot de Mofras asserted
that "none of these tribes is free from the ravages of syphilis."[20]

A similar opinion was expressed by Charles Wilkes, who said that
venereal disease prevailed among the wild tribes and that they had
caught it from escaped mission Indians.[21]

Without adducing further general assertions, the conclusion may be
reached that syphilis, which very early swept through the missions,
had reached the adjacent wild tribes by 1800 and thereafter increased
steadily in extent. Unfortunately, we have no information whatever
concerning the intensity of infection. We can merely argue by analogy
with the experience of other nonimmune Indian tribes that it must
have been severe. Since the gentiles were living under more nearly
natural conditions than their Christian relatives in the missions, perhaps the direct effects were less disastrous. Yet there can be no question
that the presence of the malady on a large scale must have increased
susceptibility to other diseases and may have adversely affected the
birth rate.

With respect to nonvenereal chronic and epidemic diseases, there
is remarkably little evidence to show that these were present to a
serious extent among the wild tribes prior to 1830. The only direct
and unequivocal statement I have found concerning the matter is that
previously quoted from Martín who mentions the "muchas enfermedades" he saw in the valley in 1804. His statement is doubtless to be
accepted as evidence that disease of some kind other than syphilis did

---

[17] Cited by E. W. Gifford and W. E. Schenck, *Archaeology of the Southern San
Joaquin Valley, California*, Univ. Calif. Publ. Am. Arch. and Ethn., 23:23 and 38.
[18] Solá to viceroy, April 3, 1818, Prov. Rec., 9:176.
[19] C. L. Camp, *The Chronicle of George C. Yount*, Calif. Hist. Soc., *Quarterly*, 10:56.
[20] *Travels on the Pacific Coast* (1844), translation by M. E. Wilbur (Santa Ana, 1937),
2:173.
[21] *Narrative of the United States Exploring Expedition* (Philadelphia, 1844), 3:193.

exist at that time. On the other hand, it is very significant, in a negative sense, that not one of the diarists who accompanied the big expeditions from 1805 to 1820 makes any mention whatever of disease. Had there been any serious mortality from illness, such a phenomenon was almost certain to have been picked up and recorded by these excellent observers. On the contrary, they make repeated reference to the dense population of the regions they traversed. Moreover, we have several explicit assertions that the health of the gentiles was good. For instance, F. W. Beechey wrote in 1825: "This state of ill health [in the missions] does not extend to the uncivilized Indians,"[22] and Osio said: "Los Indios en la vida errante de salvajes gozaban de buena salud."[23] Thus, in view of our present information, we must conclude that disease, with the exception of the debilitating effects produced by syphilis, was not a serious factor in population decline during the mission era. Since avenues of infection were wide open for many years, the explanation of the relative immunity of the Indians in the field, as opposed to those of the missions, must lie in the difference between the two environments. In the missions great masses of individuals were placed in close contact; in the native habitat they were widely scattered. In the mission natural resistance was lowered, for all sorts of reasons. Along the coastal belt the foggy climate was much more conducive than the warmer interior to respiratory complaints, and, finally, water and food contamination was more probable in the missions.

Although disease did not constitute a serious menace to the aborigines for several decades, the situation changed radically at the end of the mission period. Shortly after 1830, epidemic plagues did get into the interior with devastating results. The first outstanding epidemic was that of the so-called "pandemic of 1833." Just what was the infection has never been determined. It certainly was not smallpox, but was designated variously as "cholera," "fever and ague," "remittant fever." Dr. E. W. Twitchell, who has studied the visitation from the standpoint of a physician, rules out malaria and smallpox

---

[22] *Narrative of a Voyage to the Pacific and Beering's Strait* (London, 1831), 2:70.
[23] A. M. Osio, "Historia de la California," MS, 1878, p. 216.

and admits the possibility of cholera and typhus. Nevertheless, he finally refuses to commit himself definitely.[24]

As to the devastation inflicted, there can be no doubt that it was tremendous, even though we allow for a great deal of hyperbole and exaggeration on the part of contemporary writers. Omitting the more lurid rhetoric, we find that Duflot de Mofras puts the mortality at 12,000 in the San Joaquin Valley and 8,000 in the Sacramento Valley.[25] Wilkes (*Narrative,* p. 195) found skeletons in large numbers at the fork of the Feather and Sacramento rivers. A man signing himself "Trapper" says the Indians were "almost annihilated."[26] George C. Yount says the epidemic struck on the American, Feather, Yuba, Tuolumne, and Merced, and on the first two rivers "whole tribes were exterminated." The stench of the dead bodies was "almost intolerable," and heaps of bones were a common sight. The decimation was so

---

[24] *California and Western Medicine* (1925), 23:592. Twitchell's opinion may be subject to some revision. His arguments against malaria and smallpox may be accepted. But his suggestion concerning typhus and cholera is subject to some doubt. As to typhus there is no evidence that the valley natives, who wore very little clothing and lived in quite open brush dwellings, were ever infested with lice. Typhus, or what has been designated as such, had been known to inhabitants of Mexico since Cortes, as "matlazahuatl." Its presence has not been recorded in the missions, and if it appeared in the valley, the Californians probably would have recognized it.

The Indians did suffer from fleas. Hence it is barely possible that some rat- and flea-borne plague, such as bubonic, got into the valley. But against this may be argued (1) that such a disease would have struck the coast first and hence would have been recorded; and (2) that the domestic rat was not common, if present at all, in the interior. Any such epidemic would have meant that the wild rodents were the intermediate carriers, an extremely unlikely supposition.

Regarding cholera, Twitchell states: "It might easily enough have swept through a valley with a common water supply and the dirtiest tribes on the continent." He is wrong on both counts. The epidemic was current in both the Sacramento and San Joaquin valleys, which are a good many miles from having a common water supply. Moreover, the Indians were affected on the Feather, Yuba, American, and Merced—all entirely separate watercourses. Indeed by simple geography any wholly water-borne disease may be ruled out. Finally, the California Indians were not the "dirtiest tribes on the continent." Their sanitation was as primitive as that of any backward people, but otherwise they are known to have been reasonably cleanly.

Twitchell says "measles could be thought of." As a matter of fact, measles is a far more likely guess than typhus or cholera, particularly in view of the bad mission epidemics of 1806 and 1828. Yet the travelers in the valley in 1833–1834 might well have recognized the disease and recorded it as such.

The most likely solution seems to be some air-borne or contact infection with a high fever and rapid course. Since we possess not a single account detailing specific symptoms, any further attempt at diagnosis would be the purest speculation.

[25] *Op cit.,* 2:174.   [26] H. H. Bancroft, *Works,* 34:617.

severe along the rivers that the salmon increased because of the lack of fishing by the natives. The most sober and enlightening account is that of J. J. Warner[27] who went up to the head of the Sacramento in 1832 and returned to the upper San Joaquin in 1833. On his return he found the whole populous valley deserted.

From the head of the Sacramento to the great bend and slough of the San Joaquin we did not see more than six or eight.live Indians;[28] while large numbers of their skulls and dead bodies were to be seen under almost every shade tree near water, where the uninhabited and deserted villages had been converted into grave yards.[29]

Only at the mouth of the Kings River, far up the San Joaquin, did they find a live village, which "contained a large number of Indians temporarily stopping at that place." During one night in that village, a score of persons died, demonstrating that the epidemic was still rampant. Some ten years later L. W. Hastings reported that in coming down the Sacramento Valley he saw several abandoned villages with up to 100 houses each.[30] The houses had fallen in, indicating long vacancy, and were filled with skulls and skeletons.

From the Yount and Warner accounts it is probable that the disease was severe in its effects from the upper Sacramento Valley at least as far south as the Kings River. Its lateral extension may have been as far east and west as the bordering foothills, although we have no direct evidence on this point. Let us assume, however, that the primary devastation was confined to the valley floor. This would embrace the territory of the Wintun, the Maidu, the Miwok, and the Yokuts, and involve a population of conservatively 45,000 persons. The total mortality of 20,000 mentioned by Duflot de Mofras is obviously excessive, for it would have meant the practical extermination of the valley tribes. On the other hand, the large numbers of skeletons found certainly

---

[27] Quoted by Lewis Publishing Co., *An Illustrated History of San Joaquin County* (Chicago, 1890), pp. 28–29.

[28] The absence of Indians does not necessarily mean extermination. It is entirely natural that the survivors would flee to more remote spots in the mountains and hence be unobserved by travelers following the regular route along the main watercourses.

[29] Other writers also stress the fact that these skeletons were left without any indications of usual ceremonial burial and that they were not in mounds as was customary. This in itself argues a high mortality and great terror on the part of the survivors.

[30] *Op. cit.*, p. 116.

indicate a high mortality rate, at least in restricted localities. Among these was the region along the Sacramento from the American to the Feather River, for both Wilkes and Warner mention this territory specifically. The Yuba lies between and must have been equally affected. Yount's implication is that farther south the region of the Merced and Tuolumne was less seriously devastated, but did not escape. This is in conformity with Warner's statement that he found no "live" village north of Kings River. Moreover, although there is no direct evidence bearing on the point, it is likely that, if the disease was very active at Kings River during Warner's visit, it also extended somewhat to the southward. If we take at face value the stories of these witnesses—and in general they probably were not indulging in pure fabrication—we must conceive of the focus of the epidemic as lying along the lower Sacramento and San Joaquin. If in this region the death rate was as heavy as is indicated, perhaps one-half the inhabitants perished. To the north and south the severity so diminished that at the extremes it was zero. Thus for the whole area we might set a value of 10 per cent for the mortality of all the tribes concerned. If this be admitted, we may postulate a figure of from 4,000 to 5,000, say 4,500 as the number of persons who perished.

The second serious epidemic was one of smallpox which occurred in 1837, the so-called "Miramontes epidemic." Since the details of this visitation have been given elsewhere,[31] it will be necessary here to consider only the extent and losses involved. Coming from Fort Ross, the smallpox first attacked Sonoma and then spread north and east so as to include, according to Cerruti, the valleys of Sonoma, Petaluma, Santa Rosa, Russian River, Clear Lake, Suisun, and the Sacramento "as far as the slopes of Mount Shasta."[32] In this region the Indians were "almost exterminated." He puts the dead at 100,000. Alvarado says 200,000 to 300,000 and Fernández 100,000. All these are obviously wild guesses. A more conservative statement was made by Vallejo, who said that "hundreds" were dying in his district.[33] Other evidence is derived from certain survivors. The pioneer John Walker of

[31] S. F. Cook, "Smallpox in Spanish and Mexican California," *Bull. Hist. Med.,* 1939, 7:183–187.

[32] E. Cerruti, "Establecimientos Rusos en California," MS, 1877, p. 8.

[33] M. G. Vallejo to *comandante* of San Diego, May 23, 1838, Dept. St. Pap., 4:205.

Sebastopol, Sonoma County, told the county historian, Samuel Cassiday, that George C. Yount pointed out to him in 1846 an Indian girl who was the "sole survivor" of her tribe during the epidemic.[34] Another Indian stated that in his tribe, also on the Russian River, the death rate was 10 to 20 per day during the peak of the sickness, and that in some tribes "nearly all" died. In Sonoma, General Vallejo's private company of Indian auxiliaries was so decimated as to be utterly useless from the military standpoint.

The focus of this epidemic seems to have been in the territory of the Pomo and Wappo, with an extension among the Sacramento Valley Wintun. (Cerruti's reference to Mount Shasta may be dismissed as rhetoric.) If several villages ("tribes") were actually annihilated and if Vallejo was somewhere near the truth in his reference to the death of "hundreds," we may suppose the casualties to have been in the vicinity of 1,000 among the Indians close to the Sonoma Valley and the Russian River Valley. It is probably safe to add another thousand to account for the Clear Lake region and the western side of the Sacramento Valley. The total of 2,000, although vastly less than the contemporary guesses, would still constitute a serious blow to the Indian population.

There were later epidemics, but we know relatively little about them. In 1844 the Lindsay family, migrating to Stockton, brought smallpox with them and communicated it to the neighboring Indians. Thence it spread at least as far as the Hills Miwok of Amador County. The casualties are unknown. Stephen Powers refers to a "fever" epidemic among the Wintun in 1846[35] and to an epidemic of "chills and fever" (*op. cit.*, p. 393) near Kern Lake which was also "very destructive" on Poso Creek and White River. This may be the epidemic referred to by W. M. Morgan when he describes the finding of a rancheria near Tulare Lake at which many skeletons were strewn around at random, as if the population had been killed by a pestilence.[36] George Gibbs, after visiting Clear Lake in 1851 says:

. . . There is but little doubt . . . of the principal cause of the diminution

[34] Set forth in Cassiday's book, *History of Sonoma County* (1888). The same material is also quoted by E. L. Finley, *History of Sonoma County* (1937), pp. 61 and 244.

[35] *Tribes of California*, Contrib. No. Amer. Ethnol. (1877), 3:232.

[36] *History of Kern County* (Los Angeles, 1914), p. 30.

in the ravages of the smallpox, at no very remote period. Some old Indians who carry with them the marks of the disease state it positively . . .[37]

From these facts it becomes clear that, following the sweeping epidemics of 1830–1840, all sorts of diseases became established among the central California tribes. Such maladies probably claimed a continuous toll of lives during the 'forties and flared into epidemic form occasionally. From time to time, doubtless, new pests were introduced which further decimated the already enfeebled population. Of the actual number of deaths to be allowed, one estimate is almost as good as another. Subsequent to 1838 we have to deal with the six tribes— Pomo, Wappo, Wintun, Maidu, Miwok, and Yokuts—as a whole, since there is no conceivable method of evaluating strictly tribal losses. We might say 1,000 died of disease, or we might say 5,000. If we restrict ourselves to the few outbreaks sufficiently severe to be recorded, the lower value might seem appropriate. If we attempt to make allowance for chronic ailments and minor epidemics, the higher value would not be too great. Perhaps, on the whole, the latter course is justifiable. If so, the losses from disease from 1838 to 1848 may be said to approach 5,000.

That a very profound reduction in native population is to be ascribed to introduced disease was attested by several reasonably competent observers at the time. It may be possible to draw the lines a little finer and arrive at a somewhat more concrete expression of the extent to which the reduction was carried.

Neglecting entirely possible mortality, even from syphilis, prior to 1830, it has been estimated that 4,500 perished in the 1833 pandemic, 2,000 in the smallpox scourge of 1837, and 5,000 from endemic illness and secondary epidemics up to 1848. This gives a total of 11,500. If the estimated aboriginal population of the six major tribes be taken as 58,900 (see App., table 1), the diminution from all causes is 18,100.[38] The percentage of the aboriginal population killed by disease would then be 19.5 and the percentage of the diminution to be ascribed to

---

[37] *Journal of the Expedition of Colonel Redick M'Kee.* In Schoolcraft, *Indian Tribes* (Philadelphia, 1853), 3:107.

[38] To obtain the value 18,100, an estimate was made from the data in Appendix I of the probable population in 1848. This number was then subtracted from the estimate for the aboriginal population.

this cause would be 63.5. The corresponding percentages for the entire territory north of the Tehachapi and including the nonaffected tribes as well as the missionized tribes would be respectively 10.2 and 18.9. The effect of disease in destroying the wild native population was, therefore, approximately five times as great as the effect of physical assault, warfare, and homicide.

Allowing that, in accordance with the estimates given above, somewhat more than 70 per cent of the population reduction among the unconverted Indians subject to the influence of Ibero-American colonization was due to physical shock and introduced infection, there still remains a 30-per cent decrease to be accounted for. It must be admitted that we cannot close up this gap by means of an exact numerical analysis, since many contributing factors do not lend themselves to this style of treatment. However, they should receive mention.

MISSIONIZATION

The six tribes bordering on the mission strip which are being considered here lost materially by way of conversion to mission life, not only from deaths, but also from extensive withdrawals. The overall and permanent loss from this cause must be included in the net population depletion.

It is possible from the mission statistical data to derive with reasonable accuracy the number of conversions among the valley and northern tribes. The sources of data and methods have been set forth in previous papers[39] and will not be repeated here. The final value is very nearly 10,000 for the missions north of San Gabriel and San Fernando. This covers a period from 1805 to 1834, let us say 28 years. Now these 10,000 baptisms by no means represent the final net loss to the tribes concerned. In the first place, prior to 1834 (or secularization), large numbers of converts escaped and returned permanently to their old habitats. The Bancroft compilation of mission censuses shows quite clearly that for all the missions the number of escapes, or fugitives, from 1805 to 1834 was about 4,250. Of these, at least 3,500 were from

[39] S. F. Cook, *Population Trends among the California Mission Indians*, Univ. Calif. Publ., Ibero-Americana, No. 17 (1940), and *The Conflict between the California Indian and White Civilization: I. The Indian versus the Spanish Mission*, Ibero-Americana, No. 21 (1943).

the missions under consideration, for the south contained only one-quarter of the total population and for other reasons had much less fugitivism than the center and north. This value of 3,500 represents permanent escapes from the mission, because the original figure 4,250 is derived from the differential between existing population and cumulative baptisms. It does not include temporary escapes. Therefore, of the 10,000 gentiles baptized, 3,500 converts came back to the native habitat, reducing the actual loss of the tribes to 6,500.

The question next arises what became of these 6,500 and their progeny. Up to 1834 there was a clear reduction. It has been shown that, although the birth rate may be taken as 40 per thousand, the death rate, for newly baptized converts at least, was fully 80 per thousand. An annual diminution of 4 per cent is thus indicated. The conversion of the outer tribes was carried on progressively up to the end of the missions and, therefore, we have no alternative but to assume that the increment of 6,500 permanent members was spread out more or less evenly over the twenty-eight years involved. Thus, starting with zero in 1805, there was a mean annual increment of 230 with a mean annual decrement of 4 per cent. The probable number existing at the end of twenty-eight years would be very close to 4,000, the remainder, 2,500, being net loss due to mortality in the missions.

With the disintegration of the clerical establishments, various fates befell the converts. There is no doubt that very many returned to their former homes in the interior. Numerous others sought some kind of niche in the civilized environment to which they had been brought. A few remained in the missions themselves, and still others died off. It is impossible to make a rigid calculation of the numbers in each category. According to the census taken in 1842, there were 990 neophytes still remaining in the eleven missions north of San Luis Obispo. By 1848 there could have been scarcely more than 500. Of the 990 still present in 1842, the vast majority must have been "old families," i.e., descendants of the earliest converts who knew no other home than the mission and who had no affinity with the wild tribes. Indeed, the number of valley Indians among them must have been very small, perhaps none, except at Santa Clara and San José. San Rafael contained principally local Coast Miwok, and Solano still had some of the neighboring

Wappo and Pomo. Certainly 200 would cover the Wappo, Pomo, Wintun, Miwok, and Yokuts remaining in 1848. A larger number were probably hanging around the towns and working on the coastal ranches. Particularly in Marin, Sonoma, and Napa counties were they to be found. It seems likely that 750 would represent the maximum who failed to return to their original tribes. At the existing rate of decimation due to disease and social causes, it is safe to assume that at least another 750 died from 1834 to 1848, without having reached their home territory. The number of those returning after secularization would then be about 2,500. The final loss to the interior tribes as a result of missionization would thus come to approximately 4,000.

If we accept this value as being reasonably close to the truth, we find that it very nearly accounts for the losses among the interior tribes not ascribable to warfare and disease. The latter causes were considered to have been responsible for 13,745 deaths out of a probable 18,100. The balance of 4,335 is substantially taken care of by the 4,000 permanently lost to the missions, particularly when it is remembered that all these estimates are subject to a wide margin of error. It is doubtful if a closer check can be obtained using the existing data.

STARVATION

Under the conditions which existed in the central valley and the north Bay counties from 1805 to 1848, one might well expect the incursions of hostile expeditions and sweeping epidemics to be followed by severe destruction of food supply and perhaps by actual famine. There is, however, serious doubt whether an extreme scarcity ever arose. At least, there is small reason to believe that, before the miners came, the wild tribes ever suffered so greatly from a food shortage as to jeopardize to any great degree the lives of the natives. On the other hand, there are three lines of argument to the contrary.

The first type of evidence is purely negative. As far as I am aware, in the diaries and accounts of expeditions, as well as in the later descriptive literature, there are only two specific references to cases of famine. Both these refer to the same rancheria, Telamé, in the upper San Joaquin Valley. Ortega stated that this rancheria in 1815 had suffered a great mortality and a great famine.[40] Cabot, three years later,

[40] Juan de Ortega, "Diario," MS, 1815.

said the people at Telamé had been scattered and debilitated by famine.[41] This is clearly an isolated instance, because the same writers visited numerous other villages in the same region, where there was apparently no food shortage. Moreover, it is possible that there may have been an epidemic in Telamé rather than a famine. If there had been widespread starvation among the Southern Yokuts between 1815 and 1818, some reference to it would certainly have crept into the written accounts. But apart from Telamé, no village or region is stated to have suffered from lack of nutrition.

The second point is more general. Although there was serious reduction of population and very great disturbance to native economic and social life throughout those years, the Ibero-American conquerors did not actually enter the territory of the valley and north Bay tribes as permanent residents. Consequently, the primary sources of native food supply were not disturbed. The oak trees and the grasses grew as they always had. The game was not killed, nor were the rivers fished out. Not until ranching and agriculture invaded these regions extensively, were the natural food plants and animals driven out or destroyed. Even the cattle industry as practiced by the California rancheros was not seriously damaging to the native flora and fauna, since the stock ranged such a wide territory that overgrazing could not occur. Consequently, the invading whites did not deplete the native food supply. Local conflicts certainly took place, wherein the Indians were temporarily prevented from getting food and stored acorns were destroyed, but such encounters were more in the line of social or cultural irritants than a menace to the nutritional status of the people. The vast reservoir of primitive foodstuffs was undisturbed.

In the third place, the white man himself involuntarily contributed to the Indian larder. One need only read the correspondence of the time to appreciate what an enormous number of horses and cattle (not to mention other provisions such as grain) were stolen and presumably eaten by the natives of the interior. Literally thousands of such animals were thus consumed. Indeed, it is quite possible that certain segments of the native population, for example, some of the Yokuts and Miwok, acually let the native dietary go by default and came to

---

[41] Fr. J. Cabot to De la Guerra, May 23, 1818, De la Guerra Docs., 7:88.

depend in large measure upon the white man's domestic animals. At any rate, up to 1848 it is probable that white civilization gave more food than it took away.

If the above arguments are valid, then in this one respect the racial conflict was an advantage to the native. His situation on the fringes of a pastoral civilization enabled him to improve his dietary status. When the farming and mining Americans settled on his land, it was a quite different story.

SECONDARY FACTORS IN POPULATION DECLINE

Apart from the phenomenon of missionization, the factors which were directly lethal to the native or wild Indian in his conflict with Ibero-American civilization were warfare and disease. In the decline of a population, however, numerous forces are always at work which undermine the resistance to physical pounding and sickness. A strong, virile people can absorb terrible punishment and still make good short-term losses, but a group such as we are here considering cannot do so, for there is little recuperative power and every loss is a dead loss. In other words, in order for warfare really to destroy and disease to be permanent in its effects, the entire economic, social, and cultural foundation must be shaken. Taken as a whole, the process which the wild Indians underwent is best embodied in the term "disruption." By this is meant the upheaval, the turmoil, to which they were subjected, and the loosening and tearing asunder of their social framework. A thousand minor incidents and pressures contributed to the final result, items which frequently defy even classification. A complete analysis of this process cannot be undertaken here. However, it is possible to point out briefly certain aspects of the disintegration of native society insofar as they pertain to material welfare.[42]

Destruction of property.—The earlier expeditions to the valley and to the north were essentially peaceful. A definite effort was made not to irritate the inhabitants in any way. Before long, however, owing

---

[42] There seems to be no compelling reason for citing all the documentary literature covering the disruption of Indian society. There are not enough data to warrant any numerical analyses, and the mere piling up of citations becomes unnecessarily tedious. Therefore, only typical and illustrative cases are specifically mentioned.

to various causes, the general attitude changed. Soldiers, civilians, and missionaries began to assume a hostile attitude. This was reflected, not only in a more direct policy of actually capturing converts and fugitives, but also in various incidents involving property. If the souls of the natives were sacred, certainly their property was not. Moreover, if signs of hostility were encountered, simple military policy dictated the swift paralyzing of resistance by destruction of war implements, food supplies, and even houses. As time went on and the tenor of relations changed from attempted friendship to bitter enmity, full-scale campaigns were conducted, which included widespread annihilation of the native sinews of war. The few recorded examples of this procedure give us a glimpse of what was going on, but they are too few to make possible any estimate concerning the extent of damage. No doubt the natives, especially around Buenavista Lake and along the Mokelumne River, lost nearly all their material resources and may well have been pauperized by the repeated hostile incursions into their territory. The mass effect must have been to cause a great deal of confusion and actual suffering, owing, not only to the outright loss of capital goods and stored food, but also to the extra time and labor involved in restoring the disrupted economy.[43]

Desertion of villages.—It was a repeated observation that, subsequent to 1805, if not previously, the approach of any white men was marked by wholesale flight on the part of the natives. Large numbers of Indians were prone to vacate their villages and betake themselves to some point of safety, leaving many of their possessions to be looted. An isolated affair of this sort might not be followed by fatal consequences. The inhabitants, after the strangers' departure, could return and take up their life where they had left it. But in the aggregate, the situation was serious. It generated a perpetual refugee problem. The Indians had to leave their food-gathering, their hunting, their domestic industries for a matter of days, perhaps weeks—to the inevitable detriment of all these pursuits. The Indian economy was primitive,

---

[43] Reference may be made to the senseless burning of the rancheria Bulas by the expedition under Father Martínez in 1816, to the pitched battles and conflagrations which accompanied the 1829 Sánchez-Vallejo campaigns against Estanislao, and to the widespread havoc wrought by the Vallejo family in Sonoma and Mendocino counties.

yet finely adjusted to the locality and the season. Any long interruption was sure to disrupt it to some extent. Moreover, for a strictly sedentary people, dependent upon their own terrain for support, it was very difficult to find a secure retreat, unmolested by other tribes and unhampered by climatic or geographical restrictions. In the sum, the hardships thus inflicted must have been considerable.

The extent of these temporary flights can be guessed at from some of the explorers' accounts. In canvassing eight expeditions,[44] from 1806 to 1819, I found thirty instances mentioned when the natives were present in their villages and received the white men in friendly fashion. On the other hand, there were thirty-two cases when the village in question was practically deserted, owing to the flight of the inhabitants, or when some of the Indians were present but were hostile. Some of the accounts are not clear as to detail, and hence the figures just cited may not be precise, but the general trend of behavior is sufficiently clear. Subsequent to 1806, just about one-half the inhabitants fled from their homes when the Spanish arrived. Now the foregoing compilation concerns only eight expeditions and sixty villages. There may have been one hundred expeditions and forays, great and small, from 1805 to 1848, and there may have been anything up to fifty villages within striking distance of each such incursion. (The number of villages affected would, of course, be far greater than the number actually entered.) Without pushing the numerical estimate any further it is clear that the aggregate effect of refugeeism, as one might call it, must have been serious. The suffering, hardship, and indirect damage to both native economy and health cannot but have been a significant factor in weakening the population.

Captivity and removals.—Perhaps the most significant influence, not only in reducing and disintegrating the homogeneous Indian population, but also in wrecking its morale, was the incessant capture and removal of individuals. Here we must reckon captures made for all reasons, including conversions; the effect on the remaining population was the same, irrespective of the motive behind the capture.

It was shown in a previous discussion that some ten thousand per-

---

[44] Zalvidea, 1806; Muños, 1806; Viader (first), 1810; Viader (second), 1810; Abella, 1811; Pico, 1815; Ortega, 1815; Estudillo, 1819.

sons were withdrawn from their native habitat for conversion, of whom no doubt the majority eventually returned. In addition, a large but indeterminate number were taken prisoner and brought to the coast for labor purposes. Long before the missions collapsed, both public and private parties were making some inroad on the more remote natives for this purpose, and after secularization, when the christianizing motive had disappeared, practically all captives were utilized as day labor on the growing ranches. Consider the following statements as illustrative only:[45]

a) 1796. Governor Borica writes that measures should be taken to stop the stealing of gentiles at harvest time.

b) 1797. Twenty gentiles came in and were distributed among the ranchers.

c) 1797. A party of civilians "caught in the rancheria seven gentiles for labor."

d) 1826. The citizens of San José request permission to go to the valley to "persuade" Indians to return as laborers.

e) 1826. In the recent campaign Sánchez captured 44 natives plus women and children.

f) 1829. The governor hears that in the recent expeditions a great many small children have been brought back and distributed as serfs to the various ranchers.

g) 1835. In the last expedition, the members captured and parceled out among themselves seven small children.

h) 1839. Contract of Noriega with Prefect Castro to make expeditions. If he can "persuade" any Indians to return with him, he may use them as laborers.

i) 1839. J. Castro accepts 77 gentiles from an expedition to Kings River. He puts them to work on his ranch.

j) 1840. Sutter relates how some San José Indians raided a tribe near him and kidnaped all the women.

---

[45] Sources of these statements are as follows:

a) Borica, July 3, 1796, Dept. St. Pap. San José, 1:63.
b) I. Vallejo, Sept. 26, 1797, Prov. St Pap., 15:149.
c) I. Vallejo, July 9, 1797, *ibid.,* p. 137.
d) Echeandía, June 15, 1826, Dept. St. Pap., 1:146.
e) I. Martínez, Dec. 10, 1826, *ibid.,* p. 186.
f) Echeandía, Oct. 23, 1829, Dept. Rec., 7:240.
g) Figueroa, Jan. 24, 1835, St. Pap. San José, 4:164.
h) Noriega, Nov. 6, 1839, Monterey Arch., 16:25.
i) Castro, July 7, 1839, Vallejo Docs., 7:330.
j) Sutter, Oct. 15, 1840, *ibid.,* 9:279.

k) 1840. Amesquita reports how a small party caught three men and several women. One rancheria, having "voluntarily petitioned to go to the mission," was allowed to do so.

l) 1845. Castro and García raid the Pomo near Fort Ross. García got between 12 and 13 men with families and Castro got 150 persons.

m) 1846. Feliz Berreyesa raids in the valley. Captures one group which escapes. Returns and captures 40 more. He had a pass from Salvador Vallejo "to get some Indians to work for him."

n) 1847. Sutter reports that one Armijo with one Sam Smith attacked a rancheria 60 miles north of Sacramento and carried away 37 persons "as slaves."

From these and other instances the impression is gained that capturing, or perhaps better, kidnaping, had grown to the dimensions of a major industry by 1848. Hundreds of Indians were certainly involved and very likely thousands. It may be argued that here, as with the capture for conversion, the majority of the victims were able to escape and return to their homes. But even if they all had managed to get back, the effect would have been disastrous. It is not possible forcibly to uproot and carry away at least one-fifth of a population, even temporarily, without serious social repercussions. The disintegration of families, the mental torture inflicted by wholesale removal of children, the upset of normal community life is sufficient to rock the entire society to its foundation and to break up the established order. The cultural chaos will be even worse than the physical, but consideration of this very important aspect must be omitted at present.

Internecine struggle.—Prior to Spanish occupation the many small tribelets and other political units which composed the large Indian tribes or linguistic divisions were frequently at war with each other. However, such affairs are stated by modern ethnographers to have been cast in a definite pattern. Following some wrong or injury, arms were resorted to and an elaborate ritual followed. The actual fighting was negligible, with perhaps half a dozen casualties, or even none at all. A fact of even deeper significance was that rarely if ever was the *casus belli* more than an affair of tribal honor or a minor infringe-

k) Amesquita, Nov. 16, 1840, Dept. St. Pap., 5:31.
l) "Proceso," Aug. 6, 1845, Dept. St. Pap. Ben., 5:383.
m) Berreyesa, June 6, 1846, Vallejo Docs., 12:224.
n) Sutter, July 12, 1847, Calif. Arch., unbound docs., No. 89.

ment upon some territorial right. Never in California within the knowledge of living man did there occur a profound upheaval or military conquest which threw large numbers of Indians into prolonged and bitter conflict. Precisely this happened after the Spanish occupation.

Very early in the mission period, the clergy and soldiers both adopted a policy of using mission neophytes as auxiliaries in warfare with the unconverted heathen. As De la Guerra put it, "... para hallar Indios huidos no hay como otros Indios." First utilized in a small way locally among the coastal tribes, the system was later extended on a broad front when elaborate expeditions to the deep interior were carried out. On such occasions the number of Indian auxiliaries was frequently very large.[46]

Not only were both local and Tulare Indians employed as irregular troops under white supervision, but through a pernicious system introduced by the early missionaries neophytes were permitted to go out alone and unattended in pursuit of fugitives. These irresponsible children of the wilderness, intoxicated by the authority thus lightly vested in them, soon exceeded all bounds of caution and of humanity, not only bringing back fugitives, but attacking peaceful wild tribes and committing all sorts of atrocities. Occasionally these guerrilla parties either were badly mauled by the exasperated gentiles or them-

---

[46] The number of Indians involved may be judged by the following illustrations:

1806. In a party which went after fugitives, 11 Christian auxiliaries were killed. (Arrillaga, May 6, Prov. Rec., 12:271.)

1813. In the Soto expedition there were 13 whites and 100 Christian Indians. (Argüello, Oct. 13, Prov. St. Pap., 19:345.)

1819. Corporal Butron went out with 18 whites and 40 Indians. (Solá, Apr. 26, Dept. St. Pap. San José, 1:123.)

1829. The second Estanislao campaign included 104 whites and 50 Indian auxiliaries. (Piña, "Diario," MS, p. 4.)

1836. Vallejo's campaign against the Wappo included 50 white men and 100 local Indians. (Vallejo Docs., April 8, 3:105.)

1839. A party went out under Palomares with 15 white men and 55 Indians. (*Ibid.,* Dec. 10, 8:358.)

1840. An expedition left San José with 25 whites and 100 Indians. (*Ibid.,* May 16, 9:139.)

1841. An expedition by Estrada with 11 white men, 5 local Indians, and 14 Tulare Indians. (Jimeño, Feb. 29, Dept. St. Pap. Monterey, 4:31.)

1843. The expedition of Salvador Vallejo to Mendocino included 70 whites and 200 Indians. (Vallejo Docs., Apr. 1, 9:354.)

selves indulged in excesses which even the lenient clerical and civil authorities could not overlook. The situation was further confused by retaliation on the part of the heathen, particularly in the last years of the missions. Innumerable forays and assaults on mission property were made, usually for the purpose of carrying off stock but often involving bloodshed. Moreover, such raiding parties frequently included fugitives from the mission itself, friends or relatives of the neophytes who were attacked.

Thus it came about that a chaotic state of civil war emerged, but not a civil war where the demarcation was drawn clearly upon tribal, territorial, class, or religious lines. Family fought against family, tribe against tribe, Christian and gentile against Christian and gentile, purely according to chance. All sense of racial unity was lost and, although the white man could be hated as the root of all the existing evil, that hate included also other Indians as the white man's agents. Under such conditions the disintegration of all ordered political society over a great area facilitated and promoted the fatal inroads of exposure, want, and disease.

THE INDIAN RESPONSE

We have dwelt at some length upon the shock to the native welfare which followed contact with Ibero-American civilization. We have emphasized the biological effect manifested in the serious decline in population and have pointed out that this group reaction was mediated by three physical forces—homicide, disease, and forced removal of large numbers of Indians from the normal habitat. Finally, we have mentioned a few of the secondary factors which contributed to the lethal influence of these three forces. From this discussion one might gain the impression that the physical collapse of the interior tribes was complete, that the wild Indian was utterly unable to compete with the invading race and was doomed to early extinction. Such an impression would not be wholly justified.

In the first place, the actual numerical decline in population, although severe, was not as great as that suffered by the same or similar Indians either in the missions or under American domination. In a previous paper (*Population Trends* [1940]) I have shown that the total number of gentile baptisms in the missions was nearly 53,600. The neophytes living in the establishments at the close of the era were either these same gentiles or their descendants, and numbered 14,900. The difference, 38,700, denotes, therefore, the decline suffered by this group or segment of California aborigines. Using relative values, we may calculate the decline, or ratio of reduction to original population, as 72 per cent. During the American period the decline was even greater. It may be calculated from the data in table 1 of the Appendix that the estimated population of all California Indians north of the Tehachapi was 72,050 in 1848 and 12,500 in 1880. Hence the decline was about 82 per cent. For the six tribes affected by Spanish colonization from 1800 to 1848, the corresponding figures are 58,900, and 35,950, or a decline of only 31 per cent. Thus from the standpoint of population alone these tribes made a showing which, although in the absolute rather poor, was relatively better against the Spanish civil colonial system than against the mission system or the American settlement.

Not only in population changes do group reactions and group adaptation to new environmental factors become evident. Usually there may be observed physical activities carried on in unison by a sufficient number of individuals to warrant their being regarded as group responses. The direction of such an activity may be negative or positive, that is, tending to remove the affected group from the environment or, conversely, to remove certain components of the environment from the group. It has been pointed out with reference to the mission Indians that this type of response usually took the negative form. The Indians generally attempted to escape, thus generating the widespread phenomenon of fugitivism. Seldom was the activity positively directed, toward active physical resistance or insurrection. The wild Indians evinced a different type of behavior. With them the positive reaction predominated over the negative. With the exception of temporary flight to escape the ravages of an invading party, the interior natives held their ground and resisted the onslaught. Moreover, not only did they stand their ground over a large territory, but they actually, and with some success, took the offensive. Together with this active response they underwent considerable physical and military adaptation.

The evolution of the response of resistance or adaptation is quite clear cut. On their first appearances among new tribes and subtribes, the exploring expeditions found the natives peaceful and inclined to be friendly. The customary hospitality was shown, presents were exchanged, and the gospel was heard from the priests with sympathy. As party followed party, however, and the natives saw their people drawn off to the missions or heard more and more tales of mission life, their first favorable attitude changed to one of hostility and fear. At this stage, the explorers and convert hunters began to find the villages empty, or were greeted with showers of arrows as they approached. Retaliation and "chastisement" were then in order. Gentiles were carried off by force rather than persuasion, and atrocities began to occur. By the decade 1820–1830, the people of the interior valleys and hills had definitely embarked upon a policy of physical resistance, not through any political or cultural unification, but through a common response to a uniform style of treatment.

The general effect of these events was to bring about a shift in the entire social horizon of the natives, particularly that of the Yokuts, Miwok, and Wappo. The disruptive forces, previously discussed with reference to their influence on population decline, had also the effect of generating an entirely new kind of civilization. To put it in essence: a peaceful, sedentary, highly localized group underwent conversion into a semiwarlike, seminomadic group. Obviously this process was by no means complete by 1848, nor did it affect all component parts of the native masses equally. But its beginnings had become very apparent.

We notice the inception of the change in a few rather sensational events, events which are indicative of the more fundamental, although much less obvious, changes going on underneath. In 1797 occurred the so-called "Raymundo affair." This individual, "Raymundo el Californio," took some forty neophytes on a fugitive hunt in Contra Costa County. They were set upon by gentiles and virtually destroyed,[47] much to the horror and alarm of the local authorities. In 1807 over one hundred neophytes escaped from the missions to the rancherias of Carquinez Strait, where they were cut to pieces by gentiles, only

[47] The correspondence on this matter is found in Prov. St. Pap., 15:16–25.

thirty getting back to the mission.[48] In 1813 Soto with twelve soldiers and one hundred auxiliaries was fought to a standstill in the marshes of the Delta by the consolidated rancherias of the region.[49] At about this period, the Indians began to find leaders. Pomponio and Joscolo did excellently, and Estanislao, the Miwok, was a real genius. Expedition after expedition was broken up by this brave people, until Vallejo invaded their territory in 1829 with cavalry, artillery, and all the panoply of war. Even the final campaign, which took a heavy toll of life and did the Miwok great damage, utterly failed to subjugate them.

Meanwhile the Indians were learning new methods of defense. Their acquisition of firearms was slow. Indeed, it is doubtful whether they had secured any appreciable stock of firearms prior to 1848. Their failure in this respect is not to be ascribed to lack of knowledge or aggressiveness, but rather to the fact that there were no guns to be had. The Spanish themselves were very poorly outfitted. There were no large stocks which could be stolen and powder was such a rarity that at one time the governor had to commandeer all private supplies in order to fit out an expedition. On the other hand, the natives very quickly learned the tactics of defense. Their original method was to stand up in masses and try to overwhelm the enemy with the fire power of swarms of arrows. But experience soon taught them that this weapon was relatively useless against Spanish leather armor, and the range was too short to enable them to hold up against gunfire. They then resorted to hit-and-run tactics—a heavy assault from ambush followed by a retreat into the impenetrable tule swamps or the chapparal, or else systematic sniping from cover. The Miwok under Estanislao developed a defense almost European in character. Against Sánchez and also Vallejo in 1829, Estanislao fortified a hill with brush breastworks and, if the word "fossas" can be so interpreted, an actual system of trenches. Against these defenses Sánchez failed completely, and Vallejo, even with a cannon, was not able to penetrate them until he resorted to a flank attack and covered his front by setting the chapparal on fire.

[48] Abella to Arrillaga, Feb. 28, 1807, Archb. Arch., 2:54.
[49] Argüello to Arrillaga, Oct. 31, 1813, Prov. St. Pap., 19:345.

Considering that all available accounts of this early fighting come from Spanish-Mexican officialdom and from prejudiced survivors, it is clear that throughout the early decades of the nineteenth century the valley tribes put up a pretty good fight. Despite repeated small-scale incursions and full-dress campaigns by the military, in which they were often beaten, they held the Spanish settlement to the coast. This, after all, is the critical point, for the successful defense of an area demands that any permanent lodgement be prevented, rather than that every stabbing invasion be annihilated. Such relative success indicates that the Yokuts and Miwok were able, with sufficient rapidity, to make a drastic reorientation of their ideas of physical conflict.

But this reorientation did not stop with an improved defensive. By the time of secularization, the natives had begun to pass actually to the offensive. One reads in every general history of the times a great deal about the activity of the valley Indians, and to a lesser extent of those north of the Bay, in raiding and stealing domestic livestock, in particular cattle and horses. This phenomenon is one of great biological and cultural significance. It is mentioned here, however, only as it bears on offensive warfare.

Very early in mission history, outlying heathen began to slip in and run off stock. As the years went on, they learned two things, perhaps subconsciously. They learned that with the correct technique such raids were very easy to carry out, and that they were highly irritating to the white men. Furthermore, the acquisition of horses enabled the Indians to improve their methods by providing fast transportation. As the great herds of cattle and horses spread out from the coastal ranches, the opportunities increased, until by 1835 stock raiding was universal.

The acquisition of horses and the practice derived from years of experience wrought a further extension of their warfare, for it is but a short step from the quick dash to cut away stock to the serious armed cavalry assault on a fixed point, such as a ranch house or settlement. These developments follow rather naturally. The essential point in this discussion is that the valley people possessed sufficient mental agility and racial adaptive power to utilize their opportunity. Thus, from a race of slow, unwarlike, sedentary seed-gatherers, these tribes were evolving rapidly into a group of fast, shifty, quite clever cavalry-men. This was a physical response, an adaptation to new conditions of the first order of magnitude.

As a result of this process, by 1845 the valley Indians had made in-land expeditions and invasions very costly and dangerous, but, more important, they had also actually begun to drive in the Spanish fron-tier. The change of status becomes apparent from the official records after the Estanislao campaigns of 1829. During 1830 and 1831 there was a period of quiescence, but in 1833 complaints began to arise that the valley Indians were committing serious depredations. They seem in this to have been aided and perhaps organized by outside adven-turers—American trappers and, particularly, New Mexicans who pene-trated by way of the Colorado River. The following years saw an intensification of the same process. In 1834 M. G. Vallejo proposed an expedition to subjugate the Indians raiding San José and "lay a formal siege to the place where the natives are fortified."[50] In 1836 conditions in San José had become so bad that the citizens had to petition the governor for help. In 1838 several rancheros were killed in raids in the Monterey district,[51] and in 1839 the Indians attacked the grain storehouse at Santa Clara.[52] In 1841, Mission San Juan was attacked,[53] and hardly a ranch was spared from Santa Bárbara to the Strait of Carquinez. The most spectacular raid occurred in 1840, when a band of heathen penetrated as far west as San Luis Obispo and ran off a thousand head of stock.

Meanwhile the government adhered to the old policy of counter-attacking by expeditions. Dozens of these were sent out, but with very poor success. It is true that many Indians were killed and many vil-lages destroyed, but the raiding continued. Finally a change of policy was contemplated, although not carried out. In 1840, the governor by decree established a force of twenty men to remain permanently on the border to act as military police and prevent the Indians from entering the passes of the coast range.[54] Micheltorena, in 1843, pro-

[50] Vallejo to commandant of San Francisco, Jan. 8, 1834, Vallejo Docs., 2:210.
[51] Castro to Alvarado, Sept. 26, 1838, Dept. St. Pap., 4:231.
[52] Mesa to Vallejo, Aug. 1, 1839, Vallejo Docs., 8:4.
[53] Anon., Jan. 24, 1841, Dept. St. Pap. Monterey, 4:30.
[54] Alvarado, "Bando," July 4, 1840, *ibid.*, 3:85.

posed to build a stockade in Pacheco Pass, but the plan fell through. This shift in basic procedure from offensive to defensive is the best evidence we have that the Indian assault was really effective.

What would have happened if external conditions had not changed we can only conjecture. The Indian offensive reached its peak about 1845, or perhaps earlier, and then rapidly diminished. The reason for the diminution does not lie in any efforts put forth by the California government or its people (with the exception of the energetic action of Vallejo in the north). Indeed, the Spanish regime was showing no ability whatever to cope with the situation. Rather, the reason lies in the penetration of Americans and other foreigners into the valley itself on a basis of settlement, not mere expeditionary raiding. These men were able to attack the Indians from the rear, so to speak, and were present in numbers adequate to reduce the Indians' effectiveness. We see, therefore, that the adaptation of the natives to the Spanish type of colonization was not only sharp and clear in the qualitative sense, but was also of considerable magnitude. In fact, had the status of, say, 1840 remained unaltered, it is entirely possible that the response of the wild natives would have enabled them to esablish a permanent physical equilibrium with Ibero-American civilization.

To sum up the foregoing discussion, it appears that the first effect of white impact on the native California Indian was to reduce his numbers through warfare, disease, and forced removal. The native racial response, however, was subsequently sufficiently powerful to minimize these influences and permit the evolution of a type of behavior calculated to insure his ultimate survival.

When we survey the racial conflict between the Ibero-American and the Indian, we cannot but be impressed by the far better showing made by the Indian in the wild than by the Indian in the mission. From the demographic standpoint there is no doubt that the Indian in his native environment withstood the shock of the new invasion better than he did when transported to the surroundings characteristic of mission life. He did so in spite of the fact that his numbers in the missions were not depleted by homicide and warfare, and that indeed he was protected quite effectively from physical competition. But perhaps this statement gives the wrong impression. Perhaps he survived better in the field because he was not protected, because he was forced to utilize his best adaptive power. Subjection to severe hardship and social disruption may well have been more potent agents in bringing out his full capacity than the easy existence and stable social order of the missions.

Other factors, however, may have been preponderant. It has been set forth at some length in a previous essay (*The Indian versus the Spanish Mission,* Ibero-Americana, No. 21 [1943]) how the racial fiber of the native decayed morally and culturally in the missions, how confinement, labor, punishment, inadequate diet, homesickness, sex anomalies, and other social or cultural forces, sapped his collective strength and his will to resistance and survival. Any detailed consideration of such matters cannot be undertaken here, but the suggestion may be advanced, at least tentatively, that the cultural aspects of mission existence largely account for the difference in behavior between the two similar groups of Indians. If this line of reasoning be granted, then the extremely important bearing of the cultural on the strictly biological becomes apparent. Indeed, one may go so far as to maintain that it is impossible to secure an adequate picture of the mechanism whereby primitive human races react physically and demographically without taking account of the social and psychological factors concerned. For analytical purposes, some distinction must be made, for synthetic purposes no separation is possible.

APPENDIX

TABLE 1

Indian Population from the End of the Mission Period to Modern Times

Tribe or group	Aboriginal population	1832–1850		1851–1860		1861–1870		1871–1880		1881–1940	
		Year	Population	Year	Population	Year	Population	Year	Population	Year	Population
All tribes........	111,900 (1)	1832	83,000 (2)	1851	59,000 (6)	1865	27,800 (11)	1873	17,000 (16)	....	......
		1848	73,000 (3)	1852	60,750 (118)	1866	16,800 (12)	1880	16,500 (17)	....	......
		1849	85,000 (4)	1856	53,100 (8)	1870	25,000 (14)	1880	12,500 (118)	....	......
		1850	85,000 (5)	1856	42,000 (9)	1870	23,000 (15)			....	......
		....	......	1860	28,000 (10)	....	......				
Costanoans......	11,000 (18)	1832	1,942 (99)	1852	1,000 (97)	1865	570 (99)	1880	281 (99)	1920	56 (99)
		1842	1,287 (99)	1852	864 (99)	....	......	....	......	....	......
Salinans........	3,600 (18)	1832	1,065 (100)	1852	478 (100)	1861	50 (47)	1880	150 (100)	1912	41 (47)
		1842	712 (100)	....	......	1865	383 (100)	1880	12 (47)	1920	20 (41)
										1920	31 (100)
Chumash........	8,000 (18)	1832	2,471 (101)	1852	1,000 (98)	1865	659 (101)	1880	40 (52)	1920	74 (101)
		1842	1,656 (101)	1852	1,107 (101)	....	......	1880	336 (101)	....	......
Yokuts Below the Fresno River....	12,000 (64)	1848	6,000 (63)	1851	12,400 (62)	1870	1,200 (15)	....	......	1918	696 (70)
		1850	5,000 (91)	1852	8,400 (58)	....	......	1872	1,600 (63)	1930	271 (69)
		....	......	1852	9,400 (96)			1872	1,000 (77)	....	......
		....	......	1856	2,930 (8)			1873	1,600 (78)		
		....	......	1858	2,500 (73)			1875	990 (80)		
								1876	1,200 (81)		
								1878	720 (82)		
Entire tribe....	18,000 (18)	....	......	1852	6,000 (86)			....	......	1910	600 (40)
		....	......	1856	7,000 (92)					....	......

Western Mono	1,800 (18)	....	....	1858	600 (73)	....	....	....	....	1920	500 (42)
Wintun	14,250 (18)	....	....	1852	5,700 (102)	....	....	1880 1880	1,460 (84) 2,000 (103)	1910 1915 1918	1,000 (37) 701 (71) 940 (104)
Maidu, excluding Northeastern Maidu	8,000 (18)	1846 1850 1850	8,000 (105) 3,500 (90) 4,500 (109)	1852 1856	5,000 (106) 2,300 (107)	1865	1,550 (108)	1880	1,000 (84)	1910	900 (38)
Yana and Yahi	1,900 (18)	....	....	1852	1,800 (111)	....	....	1880	12 (51)	1884	35 (52)
Achomawi and Atsugewi	3,000 (18)	....	....	1860	2,000 (93)	....	....	....	....	1910	1,100 (36)
Tolowa	450 (18)	....	....	1856	316 (85)	....	....	1871 1880	35 (54) 214 (85)	1910	120 (24)
Wiyot	1,500 (18)	....	....	1853 1853	1,000 (23) 800 (48)	....	....	....	....	1910	150 (23)
Wintun	....	....	....	1860 1860	450 (48) 440 (93)	....	....	....	....	....	....
Yurok	2,500 (18)	....	....	1851 1852	2,250 (112) 2,500 (19)	1870	1,350 (53)	1875 1880	1,125 (80) 900 (20)	1910	668 (20)

NOTE.—Population values are given from estimates and records. The figures in parentheses refer to the numbered list of sources, pp. 44–48.

TABLE 1—*Concluded*

Tribe or group	Aboriginal population	1832–1850		1851–1860		1861–1870		1871–1880		1881–1940	
		Year	Population	Year	Population	Year	Population	Year	Population	Year	Population
Karok.........	2,000 (18)	....	......	1851	1,050 (61)	1866	1,800 (12)	1876	1,300 (88)	1910	775 (21)
								....	......	1915	870 (71)
Hupa.........	1,000 (18)	....	......	1851	920 (112)	1861	1,000 (95)	1871	725 (76)	1891	461 (52)
		....	......	....	......	1866	650 (25)	1875	571 (80)	1903	450 (27)
		....	......	....	......	1866	600 (46)	....	......	1910	600 (27)
		....	......	....	......	1870	641 (26)	....	......	....	......
Chilula.......	600 (18)	....	......	....	......	....	......	....	......	1914	20 (50)
Wailaki.......	1,500 (18)	....	......	....	......	1867	400 (114)	1876	115 (81)	1910	200 (29)
Chimariko.....	250 (18)	....	......	....	......	....	......	1877	6 (55)	1889	2 (52)
		....	......	....	......	....	......	1880	6 (45)	1906	2 (22)
Yuki.........	3,500 (18)	....	......	1858	3,000 (74)	....	......	1873	500 (79)	1908	250 (43)
		....	......	1859	2,250 (113)	....	......	1875	509 (80)	1910	100 (30)
Other Athabascans.....	4,700 (18)	....	......	....	......	....	......	....	......	1910	100 (28)
Shasta........	3,300 (18)	....	......	....	......	....	......	....	......	1920	100 (35)

Miwok											
Coast.........	2,000 (18)	1850	......	1851	250 (87)	......	......	1880	60 (84)	1888	6 (52)
										1908	11 (43)
										1920	5 (34)
Lake.........	400 (18)	1850	100 (115)	......	......	......	......	1800	20 (115)	1908	25 (43)
										1920	20 (34)
Sierra........	9,000 (18)	1850	......	1852	4,500 (110)	......	......	......	......	1910	670 (89)
				1856	3,000 (8)					1930	763 (69)
Pomo, excluding Southern											
Pomo.........	6,500 (18)		......	1856	473 (72)	......	......	1877	25 (57)	1908	705 (43)
Southern Pomo	1,500 (18)		......	1851	5,000 (33)	......	......	1880	1,450 (117)	1908	42 (43)
Entire tribe...	8,000 (18)		......	1851	3,500 (87)	......	......	......	......	1908	747 (43)
				1858	3,600 (116)					1910	1,200 (32)
										1923	1,318 (68)
Wappo.........	1,650 (18)		......	1855	750 (89)	1861	100 (60)	......	......	1908	20 (31)
				1856	188 (72)					1908	15 (43)
										1910	73 (31)

NOTE.—Population values are given from estimates and records. The figures in parentheses refer to the numbered list of sources, pp. 44–48.

SOURCES FOR TABLE I

1. S. F. Cook, *The Conflict Between the California Indian and White Civilization: I. The Indian versus the Spanish Mission*, Univ. Calif. Publ., Ibero-Americana, No. 21 (1943), Appendix.
2. *Ibid.*, p. 194. Minus an estimated 15,000 for southern California.
3. *Ibid.* Minus an estimated 15,000 for southern California.
4. C. H. Merriam, "The Indian Population of California," *Amer. Anthro.* n.s. (1905), 7:594–606. Minus an estimated 15,000 for southern California.
5. T. B. King, *Rept. to U. S. Govt.*, 1850. Minus an estimated 15,000 for southern California.
6. J. D. Savage in H. Dixon's "California Indians," MS, 1875.
7. C. H. Merriam. Minus an estimated 10,000 for southern California.
8. T. J. Henley, *Rept. Commr. Indian Affairs*, 1856, No. 100, p. 245. Includes reports of subagents.
9. C. H. Merriam. Minus an estimated 8,000 for southern California.
10. C. H. Merriam. Minus an estimated 7,000 for southern California.
11. D. W. Cooley, *Rept. Commr. Indian Affairs*, 1865, p. 115. Minus an estimated 6,000 for southern California.
12. *Ibid.*, 1866, No. 16, p. 94. Minus an estimated 5,000 for southern California.
13. L. V. Bogy, *ibid.*, 1867, pp. 126–132.
14. C. H. Merriam. Minus an estimated 5,000 for southern California.
15. E. S. Parker, *Rept. Commr. Indian Affairs*, 1870, pp. 81 and 330.
16. *Rept. Commr. Indian Affairs*, 1873, pp. 342, 344. Minus an estimated 5,000 for southern California.
17. C. H. Merriam. Minus an estimated 4,000 for southern California.
18. S. F. Cook, Appendix.
19. A. L. Kroeber, *Handbook of the Indians of California*, Smithson. Inst. Bur. Amer. Ethnol. Bull. 78 (Washington, 1925), p. 17.
20. *Ibid.*, p. 19.
21. *Ibid.*, p. 101.
22. *Ibid.*, p. 109.
23. *Ibid.*, p. 116.
24. *Ibid.*, p. 125.
25. *Ibid.*, p. 130, based on C. Maltby, *Rept. Commr. Indian Affairs*, 1866, p. 95.
26. *Ibid.*, p. 131, based on E. S. Parker, *Rept. Commr. Indian Affairs*, 1870, p. 82.
27. *Ibid.*, p. 130.
28. *Ibid.*, p. 883.
29. *Ibid.*, p. 154.
30. *Ibid.*, p. 168.
31. *Ibid.*, p. 221.
32. *Ibid.*, p. 237.
33. *Ibid.*, p. 237, based on McKee's report.
34. *Ibid.*, p. 275.
35. *Ibid.*, p. 288.
36. *Ibid.*, pp. 308, 316.
37. *Ibid.*, p. 357.
38. *Ibid.*, p. 395. Minus 200 Northeastern Maidu.
39. *Ibid.*, p. 445.
40. *Ibid.*, pp. 489, 883.
41. *Ibid.*, p. 546.
42. *Ibid.*, p. 586.

43. S. A. Barrett, *Ethno-geography of the Pomo and Neighboring Indians*, Univ. Calif. Publ. Am. Arch. and Ethn. (1908), VI:43.
44. P. J. Delay, *History of Yuba and Sutter Counties* (Los Angeles, 1924), pp. 223–224.
45. R. B. Dixon, *The Chimariko Indians and Language*, Univ. Calif. Publ. Am. Arch. and Ethn. (1910), V:297.
46. P. E. Goddard, *Life and Culture of the Hupa, ibid.* (1903), I:9.
47. J. A. Mason, *The Ethnology of the Salinan Indians, ibid.* (1912), X:117.
48. L. L. Loud, *Ethnogeography and Archaeology of the Wiyot Territory, ibid.* (1918), XIV:301–302.
49. J. A. Mason, *The Mutsun Dialect of Costanoan, ibid.* (1916), XI:470.
50. P. E. Goddard, *Notes on the Chilula Indians of Northwestern California, ibid.* (1914), X:265.
51. T. T. Waterman, *The Yana Indians, ibid.* (1918), XIII:35–102.
52. J. W. Powell, *Indian Linguistic Families of America North of Mexico*, 7th Ann. Rept. Bur. Ethnol. (Washington, 1891).
53. Stephen Powers, *Tribes of California*, Contr. No. Amer. Ethnol., III (1877):59. He says 2,700, but this is one-half the aboriginal number.
54. *Ibid.*, p. 65.
55. *Ibid.*, p. 97.
56. *Ibid.*, p. 127.
57. *Ibid.*, p. 175.
58. D. B. Wilson, Report in Hayes Coll., Bancroft Library, Vol. 38, No. 7 (1852).
59. J. Bidwell, McKinstry Docs. No. 12 (1846), Bancroft Library.
60. A. S. Taylor, *Indianology*, (1864), III:3.
61. *Ibid.*, I:4. Quotes G. W. Taggart, who says territory originally had 36 rancherias, now has 19. By proportion population would equal 1,050.
62. H. Dixon, "California Indians," MS, 1875. Quotes J. D. Savage (1851).
63. C. Maltby, "Indians," MS, 1872.
64. Estimate, taking this area as having two-thirds of the aboriginal population.
65. Anonymous, Vallejo Docs. (1848), XII:326.
66. J. Sutter, McKinstry Docs., No. 28 (1847).
67. M. G. Vallejo, St. Pap. Mis. Col. (1833), 2:97.
68. *Census Report for 1923*, Round Valley Agency, at office of Sacramento Indian Agency.
69. *Ibid.*, 1930, by counties, at Sacramento Indian Agency.
70. *Ibid.*, 1918, Tole River Agency at Sacramento Indian Agency.
71. *Ibid.*, 1915, Redding District, Roseburg Agency at Sacramento Indian Agency.
72. H. L. Ford, *Rept. Commr. Indian Affairs*, 1856, No. 105.
73. M. B. Lewis, *ibid.*, 1858, No. 105.
74. V. E. Seiger, *ibid.*, 1858, No. 104.
75. L. V. Bogy, *ibid.*, 1867, p. 128.
76. Anon., *ibid.*, 1871, No. 85.
77. B. C. Whiting, *ibid.*, 1872, No. 84.
78. E. P. Smith, *ibid.*, 1873, No. 77.
79. *Ibid.*, 1873, No. 76.
80. *Rept. Commr. Indian Affairs*, 1875 (reports of various subagents consolidated).
81. C. G. Belknap, *ibid.*, 1876, pp. 14–17.
82. *Ibid.*, 1878, p. 280.
83. *Ibid.*, 1880, p. 9.
84. *Ibid.*, p. 238, from census of 1880.
85. A. J. Bledsoe, *History of Del Norte County* (Eureka, 1881), pp. 44, 101.

86. S. P. Elias, *Stories of Stanislaus* (Modesto, 1924), p. 196.
87. George Gibbs, "Journal," 1851, in Schoolcraft *Indian Tribes* (Philadelphia, 1853), 3:112. His estimate for the Pomo, exclusive of Northern and Central Pomo, is about 2,500. Add an estimated 1,000 for these two groups, making 3,500. He says that from Fort Ross to the Bay there were 500. Estimate one-half of these Coast Miwok.
88. Based on Lucy Thompson (*To The American Indian* [Eureka, 1916], p. 12), who says 3,000 for Hupa plus Yurok plus Karok at Weitspu at a dance. Subtract 575 Hupa (No. 80 above) and 1,125 Yurok (No. 80 above).
89. C. L. Camp, "The Chronicles of George C. Yount," Calif. Hist. Soc., *Quarterly*, 1923, II:56.
90. G. H. Derby, "First Report on the Sacramento Valley, 1849," *ibid.*, pp. 106–123.
91. *Idem*, "Second Report on the Tulare Valley of California, 1850," *ibid.*, 1932, II: 247–265. Gives 4,000 from Kings River south. Add 1,000 for San Joaquin River making 5,000.
92. San Francisco *Bulletin*, May 8, 1856.
93. San Francisco *Bulletin*, Jan. 6, 1860. There were 1,500 at Big Bend driven down by the winter. Assume all the western group there and one-half the eastern, that is, 1,000 westerners and 500 easterners. Then add 500 for the remaining easterners, making a total of 2,000.
94. San Francisco *Bulletin*, Apr. 23, 1860. Quoting D. E. Buel, Agent.
95. Sacramento *Union*, Apr. 23, 1861.
96. Placer *Herald*, Dec. 11, 1852. Quotes census agent of Mariposa County.
97. Estimate. Based on: State Census, 1852, Contra Costa County, 278; *ibid.*, Santa Clara County, 990; San Francisco *Bulletin*, Nov. 12, 1856, Monterey County, 200; San Benito County, estimated, 200; Alameda County, estimated, 300; San Francisco and San Mateo counties, estimated, 50; total, approximately 2,000. Take half these as being Costanoans, making 1,000. Balance, Tulare Indians.
98. Estimate. Based on D. B. Wilson in Hayes Coll. Vol. 38, No. 7, Santa Barbara County, 600; Ventura County, estimated, 300; San Luis Obispo County, 100; total, approximately 1,000.
99. Estimate. Based on mission populations. Take the population at the end of local conversions for each tribe. Calculate probable population in any year on the assumption that the birth or replacement rate was 4 per cent per annum and the death rate was 8 per cent. Then if y is the population at the end of time t and y_0 is the initial population, $y = y_0 e^{-0.04t}$.
100. Estimate. Calculated as in No. 99 above. San Luis Obispo taken as half Salinans, half Chumash.
101. Estimate. Calculated as in No. 99.
102. Estimate. Based on: J. H. Rogers, *Colusa County* (Orland, 1891), p. 29, Colusa and Glenn counties, 1,000 and *The Western Shore Gazetteer* (Woodland, 1870), p. 5, Yolo County, 200. There are three methods of extension to the entire tribe: (1) pure estimate, 2,200; (2) proportion of villages according to Kroeber, 1,650; (3) proportion of area, 2,135. The average for the Hill and River Wintun and Hill and River Patwin is, therefore, about 2,000. To this add 3,500 for the Shasta and Trinity Wintun and 200 for the remnants of the Southern Patwin. The total is approximately 5,700.
103. Estimate. The population of Colusa and Glenn counties in 1880 according to McCornish and Lambert (*History of Colusa and Glenn Counties* [1918], p. 45), was 500. Cutting the 1852 estimate in half gives 1,000 for the four intermediate groups. By direct-area comparisons it is 1,150. If the former value is used and a

population of 1,000 is assumed for the Wintu, the total is approximately 2,000. The Southern Patwin may be regarded as extinct.

104. Estimate. McCornish and Lambert (p. 189) give 150 for Colusa and Glenn counties in 1918. By simple proportion the four intermediate groups would then amount to 300. The Patwin or Cache Creek, etc., according to S. A. Barrett (*op. cit.*, p. 43), had a population of 140 in 1908. The whole group would thus equal 440. Assume a reduction in the Wintu from 1,000 to 500. The total tribal count would then be 940.

105. Estimate. Based on a count by John Bidwell (McKinstry Docs., No. 12), who says the population from Sacramento to Honcut was 1,750. In this region, Kroeber shows 34 villages, which at 45 persons per village gives 1,530. Bidwell's count must, therefore, represent practically the aboriginal number.

106. Estimate. The state census of 1852 gives Sutter County 514, Sacramento County 80. *Alta California,* Apr. 20, 1855, gives 300 for the valley Indians in Yuba County. Estimate these as 500 in 1852. Then the total for the territory of the Valley Nisenan is 1,100. Bidwell in 1846 gave 1,750 for the same region. Assuming a proportionate reduction for all the Maidu, the total would be approximately 5,000.

107. Estimate. (1) *Alta California,* Apr. 20, 1855, gives 300 for the valley in Yuba County; San Francisco *Bulletin,* Dec. 5, 1856, gives 150 for Sutter County. Add 50 for Sacramento County. Then the Valley Nisenan region would total 500. By proportion the Maidu would equal 2,300. (2) San Francisco *Bulletin,* Feb. 23, 1857, gives 700 for Sutter, Yuba, and Nevada counties. Add an estimated 50 for Sacramento County, 300 for El Dorado County, 1,000 for Butte County, and 200 for Plumas and Sierra counties. The total is 2,250.

108. Estimate. T. T. Waterman (p. 43), says that in 1863–1864 there were 300 at Berry Creek and 350 at Yankee Hill. There were 200 at Stringtown according to San Francisco *Bulletin,* Aug. 1, 1865.

109. Estimate. P. J. Delay (p. 233), puts the Valley Nisenan plus the Hill Nisenan from Honcut to Bear Creeks at approximately 2,000. Assume 500 Hill Nisenan from Bear Creeks to Cosumnes River and estimate the Valley and Hill Maidu at 2,000. Total = 4,500.

110. Estimate. If we assume that the rate of decrease of the Miwok was the same as that of the Maidu and that the Plains Miwok were practically extinct at this time (let us say 300 for Plains Miwok), the total Miwok would be approximately 4,500.

111. Estimate. The Yana had scarcely been touched at this time. Arbitrarily assume a reduction from 1,900 to 1,800.

112. Estimate. G. Gibbs (Schoolcraft, *op. cit.*, pp. 135, 139), says the Yurok rancherias from 1848 to 1851 were reduced from 18 to 16 and those of the Hupa from 12 to 11. This would indicate a corresponding reduction of population.

113. Estimate. The *Report on the Mendocino War* puts 450 at Round Valley (*Repts. Special Joint Committee on Mendocino War* [1860], in Pamphlets on Calif. Indians, Bancroft Library, p. 15). There were 300 in Eden Valley (Sacramento *Union,* Jan. 10, 1859). Assuming these two valleys contained one-third of the Yukian population, the total would be about 2,250.

114. Estimate. There were 400 reported on Round Valley Reservation by L. V. Bogy, *Rept. Commr. Indian Affairs,* 1867, p. 121. This must have included nearly all the existing Wailaki.

115. L. L. Palmer, *History of Napa and Lake Counties* (San Francisco, 1881), pp. 34–36. Verbal communication by a Lakeport Indian.

116. Estimate. L. L. Palmer's informant gave 2,270 as the Pomo population of Lake County. This is excessive and may be reduced to 1,700 for 1850 and 1,500 for

1858. The Sacramento *Union,* Aug. 10, 1858, placed the population of Mendocino County at 3,820. From this may be deducted 2,250 Yurok (see No. 113), leaving 1,570 Pomo. Another 500 Pomo may be added for Sonoma County. The total is 3,570 or, roughly, 3,600.

117. Estimate. The U. S. census for 1880 (see *Rept. Commr. Indian Affairs,* 1880, p. 238), gives Mendocino County 1,181. Deduct 500 for Yuki, leaving 681 Pomo. Palmer's informant gives 440 Pomo in Lake County and the census shows 150 in Sonoma County. Total is 1,271 or, roughly, 1,300. However, Palmer (*History of Mendocino County* [1880], p. 173), gives 850 as the population of Mendocino County, the localities all being in Pomo territory. This would raise the estimate to 1,450.

118. Estimate. This estimate represents an attempt to get a cross check on the accuracy of the foregoing individual estimates or calculations. Two critical years were selected, 1852 and 1880. For each, the separate items for the tribes were added. Where no specific item was available, an interpolation was made so as to conform as closely as possible with the known tendency of the tribe. The results indicate a considerable degree of uniformity. Thus for 1852, the calculated 60,750 is definitely within the range of the figures of Savage and Merriam, 59,000 and 75,000 respectively. For 1880 the calculated 12,500 is less than Merriam's 16,500 for the same year, but is within the same order of magnitude.

TABLE 2

Recorded Expeditions to the San Joaquin Valley from 1800 to 1830

Year	Chief commander	Tribal region visited	Reported casualties*	Remarks	Sources†
1804	Fr. J. Martín	So. Yokuts		No fighting	1, 2
1805	Fr. Cuevas	No. Yokuts		Natives attacked party, which retired	3, 4
1805	Peralta	No. Yokuts	11 K	Punitive for the Cuevas affair	3, 4, 5
1806	Zalvidea	So. Yokuts	30 C	Exploratory	1, 2, 6
1806	Muñoz-Moraga	No. Yokuts, So. Yokuts, Sierra Miwok		Exploratory. Some hostility by foothills Indians. Many fled on approach of soldiers.	1, 7, 8, 9
1808	Moraga	No. Yokuts		Entered Maidu and Wintun territory	1, 10
1810	Viader-Moraga	Sierra Miwok		Some Yokuts "attacked our troops but were driven off"	1, 11, 12
1810	Viader-Moraga	No. Yokuts, Sierra Miwok	18 C	In No. Yokuts territory. Attacked a rancheria, recaptured 15 Christians.	1, 11, 13
1811	Abella-Sánchez	No. Yokuts		Exploratory. Many Indians were frightened and fled.	1, 11, 14
1813	Espiñosa	So. Yokuts		Not mentioned by Priestley or the California Archives.	7
1813	Soto	Sierra Miwok	Many K	Punitive, pitched battle. Several hundred Indians involved.	1, 15, 16

* In the casualty records, K=killed, C=captured, W=wounded.
† Figures in this column refer to the numbered list of sources, pp. 52–53.

TABLE 2—*Concluded*

Year	Chief commander	Tribal region visited	Reported casualties*	Remarks	Sources†
1814	Cabot	So. Yokuts	...	Some skirmishing. Indians fired on soldiers	1, 7, 17
1815	Ortega	So. Yokuts	...	Indians fled	1, 18
1815	Pico	So. Yokuts	5 K "Several" W 3 C	Attacked Cheneches, captured 50 fugitives, attacked a rancheria near Madera. Attacked Tapee. Tried but failed to attack 3 other rancherias. All but 9 of the prisoners escaped	1, 19
1816	Martínez	So. Yokuts	8 K	Galecto destroyed by the wars. Fight at Lihuahilame. Skirmish at Thuohuala. Village (Bubal) burned and food and crops destroyed. General mistreatment of the natives	1, 20, 21, 22, 23
1816	Unknown	So. Yokuts	4 K	Malimé abandoned. Attacked another village.	24
1817	Abella-Durán	No. Yokuts Sierra Miwok	...	Exploratory, natives fled	1, 25, 26, 27
1818	Payeras	So. Yokuts	...	Punitive, conducted by neophytes alone	28
1819	Estudillo	So. Yokuts	45 C	Most villages empty. Indians had fled	1, 31
1819	Sánchez	Sierra Miwok	27 K 20 W	Priestley says over 60 killed and wounded. Amador says about 50 killed and 50 captured.	1, 25 32
1820	Sánchez	Sierra Miwok	8 K	On the Cosumnes.	32
1824	Portilla	So. Yokuts	...	Punitive against Puríssma rebels. Evidently no fighting	33, 34
1824	Moraga	Sierra Miwok No. Yokuts So. Yokuts	...	Traversed valley from Marysville to Santa Bárbara. Mentioned by no one except Amador	35

Year		Tribe	Casualties*	Description	Source†
1826	Sánchez	Sierra Miwok	40 K 44 C	......	36, 37
1827	Soto	Sierra Miwok	Many K 100 C	Five hour battle	38
1827	Pacheco	Sierra Miwok	.....	Soldiers retreated after several casualties	39
1828	Noriega	Sierra Miwok	Several K	Three separate fights. Spanish defeated in all, with several casualties. Burned a temescal with occupants	40
1829	Sánchez	Sierra Miwok	"quite a few" K	First campaign against Estanislao; defeated with heavy casualties	41, 42
1829	Vallejo	Sierra Miwok	30 K	Second campaign against Estanislao. Two-day battle. Indians forced to retreat after an able defense. No prisoners taken. Vallejo says 9 bodies found. Several prisoners shot. Pina mentions 8 others hanged. Both think "many" were killed. Amador thinks Indian losses were small. Thirty killed seems to cover all probabilities	43, 44, 54

* In the casualty records, K = killed, C = captured, W = wounded.
† Figures in this column refer to the numbered list of sources, pp. 52-53.

SOURCES FOR TABLE 2

1. H. I. Priestley, "Franciscan Exploration," unpublished MS.
2. E. W. Gifford and W. E. Schenck, *Archaeology of the Southern San Joaquin Valley, California,* Univ. Calif. Publ. Am. Arch. and Ethn. (1926), 23:22.
3. W. E. Schenck, *Historic Aboriginal Groups of the California Delta Region, ibid.,* p. 126.
4. Arrillaga to viceroy, March 11, 1805, Prov. Rec., 9:63.
5. Argüello to Arrillaga, May 30, 1805, Prov. St. Pap., 19:42.
6. Fr. José María Zalvidea, "Diario de una expedición tierra adentro," 1806, Sta. Bárb. Arch., 4:49–68.
7. E. W. Gifford and W. E. Schenck, p. 23.
8. W. E. Schenck, p. 127.
9. Fr. Pedro Muñoz, "Diario de la expedición hecha por Don Gabriel Moraga ... ," 1806, Sta. Bárb. Arch., 4:1–47.
10. Gabriel Moraga, "Diario de la tercera expedición echa por el alférez Don Gabriel Moraga ... ," MS, 1808, quoted by Priestley.
11. W. E. Schenck, p. 128.
12. Fr. José Viader, "Diario a noticia del viage que acabo de hacer por mandado del Señor Gobernador y Padre Presidente ... ," Sta. Bárb. Arch., 1810, 4:73–84.
13. *Idem,* "Diario del P. José desde 19 hasta 27 de Octubre de 1810," *ibid.,* pp. 85–94.
14. Fr. Ramón Abella, "Diario de un registro de los rios grandes," 1811, *ibid.,* pp. 101–134.
15. W. E. Schenck, pp. 128–129.
16. Argüello to Arrillaga, Oct. 31, 1813, Prov. St. Pap., 19:345.
17. Fr. Juan Cabot to De la Guerra, May 23, 1818, De la Guerra Docs., 7:88.
18. Juan de Ortega, "Diario que forma el sargento ... Don Juan de Ortego ... ," MS, 1815.
19. José Dolores Pico, "Diario que forma el sargento José Dolores Pico ... ," MS, 1815.
20. E. W. Gifford and W. E. Schenck, p. 24.
21. Fr. Luis Martínez, "Entrada a las rancherias del Tular," Archb. Arch., 1816, 3:42–45.
22. Sarría to Solá, *ibid.,* p. 119.
23. Cabot to Sarría, June 1, 1816, *ibid.,* p. 46.
24. Marquínez to Solá, Dec. 13, 1816, *ibid.,* p. 97.
25. W. E. Schenck, p. 129.
26. Fr. Narciso Durán, "Diario de la expedition de reconocimiento hecha en el mes de Mayo de 1817 ... ," MS, 1817.
27. Abella to Solá, June 1, 1817, Archb. Arch., 3:136.
28. De la Guerra to Solá, May 18, 1818, De la Guerra Docs., 2:50.
29. Cabot to De la Guerra, May 23, 1818, *ibid.,* 7:88.
30. De la Guerra to Solá, Sept. 15, 1818, *ibid.,* 3:100.
31. José Maria Estudillo, "Diario de la expedición hecha a los tulares ... ," MS, 1819.
32. J. M. Amador, "Reminiscencias," MS, 1877, p. 8.
33. Pablo de la Portilla, "Diario de expedición a los tulares ... ," Dept. St. Pap., 1824, 1:40–50.
34. R. González, "Experiencias," MS, 1878, p. 21.
35. J. M. Amador, MS, p. 9.
36. W. E. Schenck, p. 130.
37. Martínez to Echeandía, Dec. 10, 1826, Dept. St. Pap., 1:186.
38. J. Bojorges, "Recuerdos," MS, 1877, pp. 4–7.
39. *Ibid.,* pp. 14–16.

40. J. M. Amador, MS, p. 13.
41. *Ibid.,* p. 22.
42. Sánchez to Martínez, May 10, 1829, "Diario," St. Pap. Mis. and Col., 2:15–20.
43. J. M. Amador, MS, p. 23.
44. M. G. Vallejo to commandant of San Francisco, June 4, 1829, St. Pap. Mis. and Col., 2:11–15.
45. J. Piña, "Diario de la expedición al valle de San José ... ," June 13, 1829. Copy, MS, 1876, Bancroft Library, pp. 1–24.

TABLE 3

RECORDED EXPEDITIONS AND BATTLES FROM 1833 TO 1841 UNDER MEXICAN ADMINISTRATION

Year	Identifying commander	Tribal region concerned	Reported casualties*	Remarks	Sources†
1833	Mercado	Pomo	21 K "Many" W 20 C	The massacre by Father Mercado of San Rafael	1
1833	M. G. Vallejo	Pomo	...	To pacify Indians attacked by Fr. Mercado	2
1833	Chabaya	No. Yokuts	...	Pursuit of thieves	3
1834	?	No. Yokuts	8 K	Pursuit of thieves	4
1835	Larios	Sierra Miwok	...	Pursuit of thieves	5
1837	J. J. Vallejo	No. Yokuts	...	Pursuit of fugitives	6
1837	Burton	...	"Several" K	Battle resisting stock raiders	7
1837	J. Sánchez	No. Yokuts	"Several" K	Battle resisting stock raiders	8
1837	Arncho	...	...	Pursuit of stock raiders	9
1837	Mesa	Sierra Miwok	...	Attacked rancheria on Tuolumne. Ambushed and badly beaten	10, 11
1837	Mesa-Amador	Sierra Miwok	200 K 160 C	Went out with 70 men. Captured an entire rancheria. Butchered 100 in cold blood. Then massacred a second hundred. Amador claims credit for the massacre, which engendered a bitter controversy with the Vallejos.	12
1838	Noriega	No. Yokuts	...	Pursuit of stock raiders	13
1838	Alvarado	So. Yokuts	"Several" K	"Chastised" 7 rancherias	14
1838	G. Vallejo	Sierra Miwok	...	Fight with raiders	15
1838	J. Vallejo	No. Yokuts	8 K	Attacked a rancheria	16
1839	Martínez	So. Yokuts	77 C	Fight with raiders, party badly beaten	17
1839	J. Castro	...	...	Attacked 2 rancherias. Natives generally fled, even crossing the mountains.	18, 19
1839	J. J. Vallejo	Sierra Miwok	2 K	Pursuit of stock raiders	20
1839	Palomares-Mesa	Sierra Miwok	...	Pursuit of stock raiders. Party badly beaten	21, 22, 23
1840	Amesquita	Yokuts	"Several" C	Expedition "in search of rancherias"	24
1841	Estrada	Yokuts	2 K	Pursuit of stock raiders	25, 26

* In the casualty records, K = killed, C = captured, W = wounded.
† Figures in this column refer to numbered list of sources, p. 55.

SOURCES FOR TABLE 3

1. Mercado et al, "Causa Criminal," 1833, Monterey Arch., 1:32 ff.
2. M. G. Vallejo to *comandante,* San Francisco, Jan. 1, 1834, Vallejo Docs., 2:200.
3. P. Chabaya to governor, Feb. 9, 1834, St. Pap. Ben. Pres. Juz., 1:15.
4. Figueroa to alcalde of San José, Oct. 3 and Nov. 28, 1834, Dept. St. Pap., San José, 4:155, 163.
5. J. Larios, "Convulsiones," MS, 1878, p. 31.
6. J. J. Vallejo to M. G. Vallejo, Aug. 21, 1837, Vallejo Docs., 4:301.
7. J. Burton to Alvarado, Mar. 6, 1837, *ibid.,* p. 205.
8. S. Estrada to M. G. Vallejo, Mar. 22, 1837, *ibid.,* p. 223.
9. F. Arncho to M. G. Vallejo, Aug. 20, 1837, *ibid.,* p. 300.
10. J. M. Amador, "Reminiscencias," MS, 1877, pp. 13–18.
11. J. J. Vallejo to M. G. Vallejo, Dec. 10, 1837, Vallejo Docs., 4:357.
12. J. M. Amador, MS, pp. 18–21.
13. J. Martínez to M. G. Vallejo, Mar. 28, 1838, Vallejo Docs., 5:62.
14. J. B. Alvarado to alcalde of San José, May 3, 1838, St. Pap. San. José, 5:48.
15. G. Vallejo to Alvarado, Aug. 7, 1838, Dept. St. Pap., 4:222.
16. J. J. Vallejo to M. G. Vallejo, Oct. 11 and 22, 1838, Vallejo Docs., 5:201.
17. W. H. Davis, "Glimpses of the Past," MS, 1878, pp. 49–51.
18. J. Castro to Vallejo, July 7, 1839, Vallejo Docs., 7:330.
19. Estrada to prefect of San Juan, July 7, 1839, Monterey Arch., 9:12.
20. J. J. Vallejo to M. G. Vallejo, Aug. 16 and 21, 1839, Vallejo Docs., 8:41.
21. J. J. Vallejo to M. G. Vallejo, Dec. 10, 1839, *ibid.,* p. 368.
22. Ximeno to Juez de San José, Dec. 13, 1839, Dept. St. Pap. San José, 5:68.
23. M. G. Vallejo to J. J. Vallejo, Dec. 13, 1839, Vallejo Docs., 8:373, 395.
24. R. Amesquita, Nov. 16, 1840, Dept. St. Pap., 5:31.
25. Prefect to Jimeño, Feb. 31, 1841, Dept. St. Pap. Monterey, 4:32.
26. Prefect to governor, June 10, 1841, Monterey Arch., 16:30.

PART THREE

The American Invasion, 1848-1870

Originally published as *Ibero-Americana* Volume 23, 1943

INTRODUCTION

WHEN THE CALIFORNIA INDIAN was confronted with the problem of contact and competition with the white race, his success was much less marked with the Anglo-American than with the Ibero-American branch. To be sure, his success against the latter had been far from noteworthy; both in the missions and in the native habitat the aboriginal population had declined, and the Indian had been forced to give ground politically and racially before the advance of Spanish colonization. However, the nonmission Indian had demonstrated a certain power of resilience and, in the realm of physical activity, had been able to evolve a new behavior pattern which, if he had been left alone, might have permitted him to cope on fairly even terms with the invading race. The valley and northern tribes were evincing a fair capacity for adaptation, in the strictly material sense, to the new environment imposed by the entrance of a new biological group. Furthermore, the native culture had by no means utterly collapsed. To a certain extent in the missions and predominantly in the aboriginal habitat the Indian had retained his primitive social and religious character and, indeed, had appropriated a few features of the white civilization, modifying them and incorporating them into his own system.

When the Indian was forced to withstand the shock and impact of the Anglo-Saxon invasion, his failure in all these respects was virtually complete. In the physical and demographic spheres his competitive inferiority was such as to come very close to bringing about his literal extermination. His social structure was not only utterly disorganized, but almost completely wiped out. Culturally, he has been forced to make a slow, painful adjustment, ending with the adoption of the alien system, and he has now lost all but fragments of the aboriginal pattern. The present study undertakes to describe some of the processes involved in this racial failure and some of the factors determining its extent.

Without embarking upon any attempt to analyze the differences between the Anglo-American and Ibero-American personality, social order, or culture, certain points of divergence between the two groups may be mentioned briefly in so far as they affected Indian relations in California. Perhaps these points may be allocated to two prime categories: differences in mode of colonization and differences in economic and social attitude toward the aborigine.

The divergent Indian reaction to Spanish clerical authority, as demonstrated by the mission neophytes, and to Spanish civil authority, as shown by the unconverted interior tribes, is clear evidence that the two modes of interracial contact were fundamentally different. The opinion may be advanced that the determining factor was aggregation versus dissemination. The fatal effects of the altruistic mission lay, first, in the removal of the native from his original habitat and, second, in his subjection to continuous close association with the foreign environment and race. The relative preservation of the gentile element was due to the failure of the Spanish actually to occupy the territory of the Indian. This same distinction in the type of interracial contact appears when the Spanish system as a whole is contrasted with the American.

The great interior of the state was penetrated many times by the Spaniards. Repeatedly they entered the lands of the Indians, but they did not settle and stay on these lands. Between the frequent but still temporary foreign incursions the natives were able to maintain their life and social order more or less unaltered. At least they were not called upon to make any continuous and permanent adjustment to a change in their own environment. When the Americans arrived, they took over the Indian habitat and made it their own. The aborigines were forced, therefore, to adapt themselves, on their own ground, to a new environment. The final effect was precisely the same as if they had been bodily removed and set down in a strange region. They were subjected not to invasion but to inundation.

Another factor of significance here is that of numbers. Other things being equal, the intensity of conflict and the weight thrown against the primitive group will roughly follow the numerical strength of the new or invading species. This general principle has been demonstrated repeatedly with the lower organisms in their parasite-host or predator-prey relationships, and it holds similarly for human beings. The Spanish type of colonization was such that the invading and ruling caste or race was always small in numbers. In California, for example, the whole coastal strip was taken and held by little more than one hundred persons. By 1845 the entire population of the *gente de razon* did not exceed 4,000. Against this may be set the native population of over 100,000. The Americans, on the other hand, entered the region in great numbers. Undoubtedly they would have continued to do so, for by 1848 they were already coming in by the hundreds. Owing to the fortuitous discovery of gold in that year, however, they poured in by thousands to flood the country. Furthermore, because of the nature of mining, they swarmed in hordes into those hill and mountain retreats which the Spaniards had never even penetrated. The Indians, therefore, were overwhelmed by tremendous numbers of aliens at all points and at much the same time. The conversion of their vast primitive range and habitat into a group of civilized communities was thus accomplished in an incredibly short period.

Both branches of the white race arrived on the Pacific Coast with a heritage of long experience with the Indian; both had developed a well-formulated mental attitude and a definite policy with respect to the natives. But these attitudes and policies were conditioned by the widely differing pioneering and colonial experience of the two branches in the preceding centuries. Both Anglo-Saxons and Spanish had pursued an avowed course of exploitation of New World resources. The Spanish, however, had systematically availed themselves of human resources, whereas the English had tapped only material wealth. Whatever the causes of the divergence, by the nineteenth century the Ibero-Americans consistently followed the procedure of utilizing the natives and incorporating them in their social and economic structure, whereas the Anglo-Americans rigidly excluded them from their own social order. It followed, therefore, that in opening up California the Spanish system undertook as far as possible to employ the Indians, even by force, in useful pursuits. This in turn meant that the aboriginal race was an economic asset and as such was to be conserved. Destruction of individual life occurred only when and if the Indian actively resisted the process of amalgamation or definitely failed to conform to the conqueror's scheme of existence. Wholesale slaughter or annihilation was definitely undesirable.

The Anglo-American system, on the other hand, had no place for the Indian. If the latter could of his own initiative find subsistence within its framework, there was a priori nothing to prevent such adjustment. But if there was any conflict whatsoever with the system, the native was to be eliminated ruthlessly, either by outright extermination or the slower method of segregation in ghettolike reservations. Accompanying this economic difference was another divergence of great social significance. The Spanish colonial system always envisaged the retention of the native as the basis of the population and simultaneously encouraged racial mixture. The result was naturally widespread hybridization, especially among the lower classes. Thorough and complete mestization, as in some parts of Spanish America, would have resulted in the disappearance of the California Indian as a pure line strain but would not have destroyed his race or eliminated it as a factor in the body politic. Nor would it necessarily have involved long and bloody physical conflict during the period of racial reorganization. The American civilization, on the contrary, viewed miscegenation with the greatest antipathy and relegated the mestizo, or half-breed, to the same status as his Indian parent. Consequently, no blood bond could ever become established which would mitigate the indifference and contempt with which the Indians were regarded.

These, and other differences, were reinforced by a powerful tradition relating to the Indian. Among the Ibero-Americans, the Indian was regarded, if not with definite attachment, at least with tolerance and sympathy, as perhaps not yet an equal but as a human being entitled to the rights and privileges of his class. His life was almost as sacred as that of a white man; his soul was entitled to salvation. He was permitted to testify in court. Theoretically, his property was inviolate. At best, he could participate in civic and political activity; at worst, he was deemed a child before the law. This fundamentally friendly attitude was seldom manifested by the Anglo-Americans. The latter, coming fresh from two centuries of bitter border warfare and intolerant aggression, brought with them an implacable hatred of the red race, which made no discrimination between tribes or individuals. All Indians were vermin, to be treated as such. It is therefore not surprising that physical violence was the rule rather than the exception. The native's life was worthless, for no American could even be brought to trial for killing an Indian. What little property the Indian possessed could be taken or destroyed at the slightest provocation. He had no civil or legal rights whatever. Finally, since the quickest and easiest way to get rid of his troublesome presence was to kill him off, this procedure was adopted as standard for some years. Thus was carried on the policy which had wiped out *en masse* tribe after tribe across the continent.

In comparing the objective effects wrought by the Ibero-American and Anglo-Saxon civilizations on the native population, it must not be supposed that the differences just mentioned were absolute, for human nature is much the same everywhere, despite policies and tradition. The Spanish at times certainly resorted to barbaric physical violence, and the Americans frequently treated their Indians with humanity and justice. Nevertheless, the broad tendencies were apparent and were reflected in the details of the two types of racial contact.

MILITARY CASUALTIES, 1848–1865

During the early years of American occupation, the Indians were subjected to constant attrition through direct physical conflict. It would serve no useful purpose to recount in detail the multitude of minor wars and skirmishes which occurred in central and northern California. Some study of these, however, is necessary in order to derive an idea of the actual losses suffered from this cause.

The first stage of conflict lies between 1847 and 1852. During these five years, settlers began appearing in the interior valley and along the north coast. Their number was rapidly augmented by the hordes of adventurers during the days of '49. Action against the natives consisted almost entirely of small personal combats and fights between individuals and little groups. The only record they have left is in a few early newspapers, in diaries and reminiscences, and in such secondary works as county histories. A few affairs of sufficient magnitude to cause general comment found their way into these accounts. As for the rest, they are covered by unspecific statements concerning the general state of affairs. Such incidents as can be actually localized have been included in the present compilation, but it is obvious that homicide was vastly more extensive than is indicated here. Subsequent to 1852 we are able to draw extensively on the contemporary press accounts. Indeed, the newspapers provide the principal source of information on Indian affairs for this period.

The use of diaries, later histories, and particularly newspapers as a basis for setting up a numerical compilation of Indian losses will be immediately subjected to the criticism that the information supplied by white men on the scene at the time or afterward from memory is likely to be highly inaccurate. It must be conceded that this is frequently true with respect to detail and to individual encounters. But this objection may lose some of its force when we deal with an aggregate covering a large territory and a long time.

Let us grant that usually the reported number of Indians killed, whether in private raids or military campaigns, was in excess of the actual immediate deaths, and let us further assume that the exaggeration amounted on the average to 100 per cent. Then the apparent total over a period of years would be double the real total. But here the compensating factors enter. In the first place, by no means all encounters were recorded in writing at the time or subsequently. Particularly in the confused days of the mining rush hundreds of natives must have perished without trace at the hands of lawless miners in the Sierra foothills or along the Trinity and Klamath rivers. Even later, countless small parties of farmers and other settlers fought off raiding Indians or attacked their villages. We have no means of estimating the mortality thus caused, but it must have constituted a material proportion of the total. In the second place, the reports invariably mention the Indians killed on the spot. There is never any reference to those who afterward died of wounds. In most military operations by civilized armies the fatalities from wounds equals those on the battlefield. Hence, this cause alone would compensate for most of the exaggeration. For these reasons it is justifiable to accept the aggregate recorded deaths as representing somewhere near the true mortality inflicted by force of arms.

The statistical data have been assembled in a series of tables, placed in the Appendix. Table 1 has been taken from a previous study which dealt with the Indians during the Spanish period.[1] It includes such figures as are available with reference to the population of the Indians from aboriginal times to 1880. To reports derived from the written literature have been added personal estimates by the author. Table 2 shows estimates for the population in 1848, 1852, and 1880. Statements or calculations from other writers have been used, when such exist. Most of the items, however, represent personal estimates, based upon outright interpolation. Although these estimates can lay no claim to absolute accuracy, they have been made with care and with reference to the known course of tribal history. They are the best we can obtain under the circumstances, and we may employ them with the assurance that they are sufficiently close to the facts to serve as indices to the general trend of events. In table 3 are placed the Indian losses from 1847 to 1865 for which specific record exists. The sources of these figures are also appended. The table includes only those stated to have been killed. Only those engagements are included for which there is at least one clear reference in the available literature. When more than one account exists, the estimates have been cross-checked. Under these circumstances, the lowest figure has been accepted, or else the statement from what appeared to be the most reliable account. When the report reads "few," "several," "many," it has been necessary to assign a numerical value. When other information has been lacking, a uniform system has been adopted: a "few" is taken as 5, "several" as 10, and "many" whatever a conservative evaluation of the circumstances has seemed to warrant. This is a makeshift method at best, but it is believed that the error in the final result lies on the side of understatement rather than overstatement. In table 4 certain parts of tables 2 and 3 are combined, in order to show the losses in relation to the population decline. The dates for population are 1848 and 1880, whereas the mortality by homicide is given for the period 1848 to 1865 inclusive. The error involved in attempting a population estimate for 1865, by interpolation in table 1, appears too great to warrant such

[1] S. F. Cook, *Conflict between the California Indian and White Civilization: II. The Physical and Demographic Reaction of the Nonmission Indians,* Univ. Calif. Publ., Ibero-Americana, No. 22 (Berkeley, 1943).

an attempt. On the other hand, since all acute fighting had ceased by 1865, it is not worth while to add the few scattering deaths from then to 1880. Therefore, the percentage of the diminution from 1848 to 1880 ascribed to warfare was actually incurred in the first half of this period.

From table 4 of the Appendix it may be observed that over the entire territory somewhat more than 4,000 Indians lost their lives in physical conflict with the Americans and that this number denotes approximately 7 per cent of the entire population decline up to 1880. Although we can attempt no detailed calculation by tribes of the population in 1865, we have two rough estimates of its value (see Appendix, table 1).[2] These are 27,800 and 16,800 for 1865 and 1866 respectively. If we use the average (22,300) as a rough approximation, the proportion of the decline due to warfare is found to be only slightly higher, 8.6 per cent. The corresponding value for the Spanish period (1800–1848) is somewhat, but not materially, greater, between 11 and 12 per cent.

The overall value for the entire territory, as thus presented, is not, however, a complete index to the severity of the losses suffered by the Indians in restricted regions. Table 4 of the Appendix includes certain tribes—in particular the Chumash, Salinans, Costanoans, and Coast Miwok—which were in an advanced stage of decay by 1848 and which were not so situated as to incur any American hostility whatever. They might, therefore, be omitted entirely. The Yokuts, part of the Sierra Miwok, the Southern Patwin, and the Pomo had been decimated and enfeebled by missionization and a long struggle with the Spanish. Consequently, they offered but a modicum of resistance to American settlement. Concerning the Western Mono, the Wappo, and the Lake Miwok we have no definite data, which accounts for the absence of any mortality records for these tribes. If we exclude all the tribes which for various reasons are doubtful or of marginal value, we may focus attention on those which had not been subjected to much or any Spanish influence and which encountered the American invasion in the fresh, aboriginal condition. These give the best index to the effect of the powerful physical blows struck by the American pioneer. Among the Maidu, Wintun, Yana, Achomawi, Shasta, and

---

[2] Made by D. W. Cooley in his reports to the Commissioner of the Bureau of Indian Affairs in 1865 and 1866.

the northwestern tribes, 12 per cent of the losses was due to homicide, rather than 7.

It is noteworthy, and perhaps significant, that the relative loss in population was substantially the same among those tribes which first encountered American invasion as among those which first met the Spanish. If any conclusions may be drawn from this fact, they are (1) that pressure exerted by force of arms was very much the same regardless of what race wielded them, and (2) that the more rapid and complete collapse of the native population when opposed to the Americans was due to factors other than purely physical assault.

SOCIAL HOMICIDE

The mortality discussed in the previous section pertains strictly to armed conflict between the races. It includes casualties sustained in formal campaigns and informal expeditions in which the avowed purpose of the whites was to kill, chastise, or otherwise subdue the natives. It also includes operations of a joint or individual character conducted for the purpose of defense against Indian raids and general native depredations.

There occurred, however, throughout the period we are considering, a continuous series of violent deaths among the Indians of a type which cannot be designated as military, but which is better regarded as social. To this category would be allocated killings directly attributable to the social conditions under which the natives were obliged to live and which would normally not occur either in aboriginal surroundings or, to a measurable extent, in a peaceful and well-ordered white community. Among such direct causes of death would be murders of Indians committed by whites or Indians as the result of quarrels, brawls, liquor, women, or revenge for injury, to which would be added executions or lynchings for various crimes, and internecine fighting among Indians arising immediately from the social conditions imposed by the whites. Sometimes it is pretty difficult to draw a clear line between military and social homicide but, if we eliminate obvious borderline cases, the two categories are reasonably distinct.

In absolute numbers, the significance of social homicide in reducing the Indian population was not great. The chief value in studying it, however, rests upon the fact that it provides an interesting yardstick by which racial conflict can be measured and from which certain basic principles can be derived.

A total of 289 social homicides have been included in table 5 of the Appendix, covering the years 1852 to 1865 inclusive. Although this list cannot be regarded as definitive, it is representative and reasonably complete. The source in all cases was the daily press for the years studied. Whatever may be said concerning the unreliability of newspaper accounts of battles and raids, there is no good reason to question the accuracy of reporting in connection with purely local incidents, at least as far as the main facts are concerned. If an Indian was killed in a barroom brawl or was lynched by miners, that fact itself may be accepted, even though we eliminate all embroidery of detail. Moreover, if the participants were drunk at the time or quarreling over a squaw, a statement to that effect has a high probability of truth. It seems legitimate, therefore, to use the contemporary press as a running history of small, concrete events of social importance.

A further criticism of the method might be that many of the newspapers then printed have since been lost and that to get a complete picture covering the entire area is now impossible. To a certain extent, this objection has validity. However, it may be answered in the first place that the lack of completeness in our present files should not inhibit us from using what we have. In the second place, it should be pointed out that we have unbroken files of a few very important newspapers. These were the *Alta California,* San Francisco *Bulletin,* Sacramento *Union,* and Marysville *Appeal.* These journals, as was the habit with large city papers of the time, made a practice of systematically copying nearly every item of interest from the small country weeklies. As a result, we have remarkably good coverage of the local news in central and northern California. Since in the 'fifties and 'sixties any happening of a violent or fatal nature was of interest to readers, such occurrences were among the first to claim space. It is the belief of the writer, therefore, that a sound and adequate sampling of social killings has been secured from a careful page-by-page examination of the four journals mentioned. In addition, some papers of smaller circulation, which are available in the Bancroft Library and the State Library at Sacramento, were examined, and it may be noted that very few additional items were thereby obtained.

It is now possible that these social homicides may be used directly to study the degree of conflict between the white and red races. Certain preliminary assumptions must be made. It may be postulated that interracial homicide[3] is an outward manifestation and a tangible product of racial conflict and competition. Such a phenomenon could not occur if the two races were separate spatially from each other, nor would it occur if they were living together in a state of unanimity and concord. If this premise is allowed, then it follows that the more intense the conflict, the more extensive will be the social maladjustment and the greater will be the tendency for the latter to become manifest in deeds of violence.

To reinforce this train of reasoning and to place it upon more than a theoretical basis it would be desirable if some concrete relationship could be established between intensity of conflict and social homicide. For the latter variable we have moderately acceptable data, the material in table 5. We still need an expression for intensity of conflict. Obviously, many factors will be concerned here, not all of which can be formulated quantitatively or numerically. However, it is possible to make a very simple general assumption which will include most of the inherent factors: that the intensity of conflict depends upon both the number of white men and the number of Indians which compose any given social unit or community. Since the magnitude of the group contact is equivalent to the sum of the individual contacts and these depend upon the number of individuals present, it follows that the intensity of conflict may be represented by the arithmetical product of the two populations.

The reasoning employed here is at least superficially similar to that underlying the principles of chemical kinetics. According to classical physical chemistry, in a bimolecular reaction the velocity is a function of the product of the concentrations of the two reactants: i.e., the number of active particles of each per unit space. The analogy is carried still further by the implicit assumption that, as molecules or ions are

[3] This would include also killing of Indians by other Indians as a result of social, moral, or economic conditions imposed by the propinquity of white men.

conceived by the kinetic theory to be in a constant state of vibratory motion, so the active units in a social test tube are likewise considered to be in continuous motion. Hence, the chemical reaction depends upon the probable number of collisions of particles, and, by analogy, the observed effect of the social reaction, here homicide, is a function of the collisions between personalities. The analogy, of course, breaks down in detail. In particular, with social kinetics the effect of collision is not equal and opposite but unilateral. The white man affects the Indian, but the Indian does not affect the white man. Since this is so, a simple product of populations is doubtless not an exact expression of the relationship. However, it is worth a trial as a purely empirical mode of expression and as a first approximation in a quantitative sense.[4]

The homicide data in table 5 includes the period from 1852 to 1865. The corresponding population data should, therefore, cover the same period. However, owing to the scattered and rather uncertain population statistics, this arrangement is not feasible. In the table, the killings are divided into eight groups, more or less along tribal lines. The Maidu, Miwok, Shasta, Wintun, Yokuts, and Pomo are designated by their tribal names. In the entries for the natives of northwestern California, the dislocation of ethnic units during the 'fifties makes it impossible to assign specific incidents to the proper tribes. Consequently, the area is considered as a whole. The same considerations apply to the former mission Indians of the central coast. Now from table 1 there can be derived a reasonable estimate for the population of each of these eight groups in 1848 and 1880. Since the intermediate values are not subject to close calculation, the best we can do is to take the mean of the 1848 and 1880 values, although this is admittedly unsatisfactory. For the white population the United States census for 1860 may be used. A good deal of error is introduced here also, because the population shifted considerably in many localities from 1852 to 1865, and the returns for 1860 do not necessarily signify mean values. However, no better data are available. Finally, it is necessary to allocate from the

---

[4] Another possible approach would be that of the predator-prey relationship, which has been studied recently by biologists. However, this type of conflict includes an indirect effect on the predator through reduction of food supply. In the Indian-white complex, there is no reverse effect on the whites as a result of the reduction of Indians.

county census reports the proper number of white inhabitants to the area occupied by each of the eight groups. This must be a frank estimate in certain instances when the tribal boundaries did not coincide with county lines.

By means of the procedures here outlined, the totals for Indian and white populations were established as closely as possible. Then the products were tabulated. Finally, the social homicides were correlated with the population products. The value of the coefficient, r, was then determined by the customary method and was found to equal 0.906. Such a high value, which certainly possesses statistical significance,[5] is remarkable in view of the relatively crude means of setting up the variables. It certainly indicates—although, of course, it does not prove—that the assumptions here made are reasonable. Until a more precise formulation can be advanced, we may conclude that intensity of conflict may be expressed in terms of population product and that at least some social and biological phenomena were a direct function of contact intensity.

The direct effect of social homicide on the Indian population decline was not great. For the eight groups tabulated, the percentage of the diminution from 1848 to 1880 attributable to this source was as follows: Maidu 2.1, Sierra Miwok 1.1, Shasta 0.73, Wintun 0.28, northwestern tribes 0.23, Pomo 0.34, Yokuts 0.10, mission Indians 1.45, the eight groups collectively 0.58. Since the general average is less than 1 per cent, it cannot be regarded as particularly significant when contrasted with the much greater mortality due to other causes.

DISEASE

The second primary or proximate cause of the high native mortality was undoubtedly disease. The present writer has had occasion to investigate the influence of disease on the population of three other groups. For the natives of Lower California from 1697 to 1773, this factor was found to account for approximately 35 per cent of the popu-

---

[5] According to G. W. Snedecor (*Statistical Methods* [Ames, Iowa, 1937], p. 125), for a set of variables having 8 degrees of freedom, the value of r at the 5-per cent level is 0.602, and at the 1-per cent level is 0.735. A coefficient of 0.906 would, therefore, be regarded as "highly significant." The same data have yielded a chi-square value of 5.03, which is likewise definitely significant.

lation decline.[6] In the missions of Upper California, the value was placed at 45 per cent for acute and epidemic disease, with a possible 60 per cent if the indirect effects of syphilis are included.[7] Among the wild tribes in direct contact with Spanish colonial California, at least 60 per cent of the mortality was referable to sickness.[8] It would be expected, therefore, that in the American period a similar ratio would hold.

Our evidence concerning illness among the Indians consists, as is common in such circumstances, of casual references by persons writing on other subjects, or of very general statements. In addition, there are a few news items in the daily press and a number of more or less specific comments by Indian-reservation agents. In order to adduce and organize the existing information, it is not practicable to consolidate data in the form of a comprehensive table, as was done with military and social killing. Numerous verbal statements must be abstracted or quoted.

We may consider first syphilis and gonorrhea, since these maladies were universal and since, in their social implications, they stand apart from ordinary contagions. Venereal disease had already established a foothold among the native tribes before the advent of the Anglo-Americans. The mission Indians were very heavily infected—almost 100 per cent, if we may lend credence to the lamentations of the mission fathers. Carried by white men and neophyte fugitives, the infection had spread to the interior, possibly by 1800 and certainly by 1830. The central valley peoples and those of the north Bay country were well impregnated before 1845. The effect of the American influx, then, was merely to extend and intensify the existing condition by bringing in fresh sources of infection and spreading it, particularly in the north and northwest, to tribes which had previously escaped. No new principles would be brought out by following this process in detail. The primary consideration here is the intensity of the infestation.

Apart from numerous casual and uncritical persons, several highly

---

[6] S. F. Cook, *The Extent and Significance of Disease among the Indians of Baja California, 1697–1773,* Univ. Calif. Publ., Ibero-Americana, No. 12 (Berkeley, 1937).

[7] S. F. Cook, *The Conflict between the California Indian and White Civilization: I. The Indian versus the Spanish Mission,* Ibero-Americana, No. 21 (1943).

[8] *Ibid.: II. Reaction of the Nonmission Indians,* Ibero-Americana, No. 22 (1943).

competent observers and students have left us their impressions. One
of the earlier travelers, Bryant, says:

All these Indians . . . are weak and unvigorous. . . . But what most injures
them, and prevents propagation, is the venereal disease, which most of
them have very strongly.[9]

The modern ethnographer, Loud, thinks that these pests were introduced shortly after 1850 in the northwest.[10] Gonorrhea, according
to him, was particularly bad[11] and was assertedly very widespread.
Stephen Powers describes the introduction of syphilis among the
Karok, and adds an interesting cultural note.[12] When the disease first
appeared, the Karok deliberately infected themselves in order to com-
municate it to their enemies. The result of this novel method of warfare was, as Powers puts it, "disastrous in the highest degree." The
full-blood Yurok Lucy Thompson, writing in 1916, thus describes the
effect of syphilis on her people:

I have today looked among my tribe . . . and am deeply grieved to find but
very few babies born of good, pure blood, that is not tainted with the virus
of venereal diseases.[13]

T. T. Waterman in his careful study of the Yana states that in 1858,
when the Southern Yana were removed to the Nome Lackee Reservation, "most of them were diseased, presumably with venereal ailments, judging from the phraseology used."[14] The New York *Century*
for May 12, 1860, printed an article on the California natives in which
the following statement appeared:[15]

A gentleman who has spent much time in Mendocino County informs us
that the intercourse of the whites with the Clear Lake Indians . . . has laid

---

[9] E. Bryant, *What I Saw in California* (1846), p. 282.

[10] L. L. Loud, *Ethnogeography and Archaeology of the Wiyot Territory*, Univ. Calif.
Publ. Am. Arch. and Ethn. (1918), 14:302.

[11] Curiously there is no reference whatever to gonorrhea in the Spanish literature. Venereal complaints are frequently mentioned but invariably as "el mal Galico," or syphilis.
It is rather beyond credence that the Spanish should not have known the disease both
from experience and by name, and that they should not have introduced it along with
syphilis.

[12] Stephen Powers, *Tribes of California*, Contr. No. Amer. Ethnol. (1877), 3:23.

[13] Lucy Thompson, *To the American Indian* (Eureka, 1916), p. 131.

[14] T. T. Waterman, *The Yana Indians*, Univ. Calif. Publ. Am. Arch. and Ethn. (1918),
13:44.

[15] Quoted in the San Francisco *Bulletin*, June 18, 1860.

the foundation for the ultimate extermination of the race by disease ... Of five or six hundred squaws, from ten years old and upwards, he was assured not a solitary individual was exempt.

The reservation agents made such repeated reference to syphilis that reading their reports becomes monotonous. The following excerpts are merely samples:[16]

The odious disease syphilis ... has long been the destroyer of their health and numbers. (M. B. Lewis, 1858.)

In truth the troops ... are a great curse to the Indian Service, for in spite of the vigilant efforts of their own officers and of the officers and employees on the reservation, soldiers will clandestinely mix and cohabit with the squaws, thereby spreading disease and death among them. (W. P. Dole, 1863.)

What were the prevailing diseases among the aborigines in northern California previous to the coming of the whites I have not had an opportunity of ascertaining, but that some of the diseases from which they suffer most at present, and which are fast working their extermination, were unknown to them prior to the advent of the Caucasian race, is firmly attested by the older Indians and corroborated by early observers. The disease to which I have reference is venereal in its various forms ... The different forms and stages of venereal diseases embrace in one contaminated mass old and young, male and female. The sufferings entailed upon these wandering savages from this cause alone are atrocious, and beyond description ... The adage "prevention is better than cure" they know not, they heed not, and their rude practice of the healing art makes no pretension to curing these maladies ... As to the cause of death among the Indians I may make the general statement that syphilis destroys many of the newly born and very young and also causes many abortions. (Charles Maltby, 1865.)

About 50 per cent of the whole number [on Hoopa Reservation] have venereal disease in some form. (J. V. Farwell, 1871.)

It is ... a lamentable fact that a large number of grown-up Indians of both sexes have their system so tainted and poisoned with venereal disease that it is impossible for them to perpetuate their race. (C. G. Belknap, 1876.)

The diseases with which they are much affected are those of a syphilitic character ... No physician, I care not how skillful he may be, can successfully treat the Indians on this reservation [Hoopa], affected and situated as they are. (E. P. Smith, 1875.)

---

[16] All are from the U. S. Dept. Int., *Reports of the Commissioner of Indian Affairs.*

To the above qualitative assertions may be subjoined one item of actual statistical value. From 1885 through 1890 the reports to the commissioner included a detailed breakdown of the medical reports for Hoopa Valley and Round Valley.[17] Although this period is twenty-five years later than that which is under consideration, the figures can scarcely show a greater degree of infection than existed in earlier times. During these six years, the average population of the two reservations was 1,020 (the population was quite stationary). The average annual number of cases treated was, for syphilis 32, for gonorrhea 33. This would imply a total venereal incidence of 6 per cent annually. However, the medical reports distinguish between "primary syphilis" and "constitutional syphilis." The former category doubtless indicates fresh, new cases. Of these a total of 31 are recorded, or an average of about five per year. Now a record of 0.5 per cent for annual incidence and 3 per cent for advanced cases is certainly not bad. No civilized white nation can show a better one. The problem is whether the medical returns can be taken at face value. There is no doubt that they represent the number of Indians who went to see the doctor. But modern experience demonstrates that far from all our own afflicted citizens consult a physician. Furthermore, there is no reason to suppose that a reservation Indian would continue treatment after the period of active lesions passed. So we must increase these figures considerably, although we have no good guide to how much. Perhaps we may double the recorded value to account for cases which did not consult the reservation doctor and double it again to include those individuals in whom the disease existed in a latent form. This would yield a value of 12 per cent as the proportion of syphilitics in the population. Such an amount is certainly not excessive.

On the face of the records the incidence of gonorrhea would appear to be higher. Most of the cases listed were very likely initial, acute, infectious, although some may have been chronic and refractory. The unmodified returns would suggest an initial incidence of 3 per cent of the population annually. This is not an excessive estimate, particularly

---

[17] It is probable that a careful search of the records of the Indian Bureau in Washington would reveal much more similar data. Unfortunately, however, I have not had opportunity to make such an investigation and must rely upon the few reports published by the commissioners.

if we remember the notorious indifference and laxity of ignorant populations everywhere toward this disease. In fact, it is probable that only the most extreme and painful cases were ever brought to the attention of the doctor. If this is true, it would appear that practically the entire population on the reservations at one time or another suffered from gonorrhea. Another indication is derived from the category of "gonorrheal ophthalmia," which is listed through these years. This form of the disease almost invariably appears in the newly born, as a result of infection from the mother. Now a total of 37 such cases are listed. The total births in the same period were 137. Hence 27 per cent of the infants were infected. This is an enormous proportion, and the conclusion seems inescapable that gonorrhea was substantially universal among these particular people.

The question of the effect of syphilis on birth rate is always troublesome. That the disease can reduce fertility and cause abortions seems generally admitted. Considerable doubt may be raised, however, as to the severity of its influence. Many people in the nineteenth century, both educated and ignorant, probably overestimated the direct effect of the disease on the birth rate. Unfortunately, we have no good statistical method for solving the problem for a primitive population. The mean annual birth rate for Hoopa Valley and Round Valley during the six years from 1885 to 1890 was 23 per thousand, a very low value. But whether the low birth rate can be ascribed exclusively to syphilis is dubious in view of the many other factors which also were conducive to a reduction in fecundity. It is probably wisest not to attempt any numerical assessment but to restrict ourselves to the opinion that syphilis may well have been in part responsible.

May the data obtained from two reservations twenty-five years afterward be applied to the Indians at large in the 'fifties and 'sixties? It is possible to do so, with certain corrections. Conditions—moral, economic, and physical—were better at the later date. The Indians were moderately well protected against external influences. They had been given nearly a generation in which to stabilize their society. They had been sufficiently well nourished. They had been exposed to medical education, propaganda, and actual treatment for years. Consequently, the extent and severity of venereal disease must have been less than during the upheavals which immediately followed American occupation. Yet, under these relatively more favorable conditions, at least 10 per cent must have had syphilis and nearly all must have suffered gonorrheal infection. If we allow for only moderate improvement up to 1890, we have to admit an original incidence for syphilis of 20 per cent and for gonorrhea of well-nigh 100 per cent.

Such an onslaught by venereal disease constitutes a tremendous blow to the physical stamina and moral fiber of any race. The dismay voiced by contemporaries interested in the welfare of the Indian does not after all seem exaggerated. In essence, even if not in detail, their statements must have depicted quite accurately existing conditions.

Turning now to the common epidemic and chronic diseases, we find that many of these had been brought in and established prior to 1850. Smallpox, measles, tuberculosis, pneumonia, and various forms of dysentery were, of course, prevalent in pre-American days, and probably spread rapidly to the interior. Any which had not yet arrived were certainly imported by the miners in 1849–1850. During the first fifteen years of American settlement, the whites themselves suffered greatly from illness despite the salubrious climate of California,[18] and undoubtedly communicated all their diseases to the Indians.

One noteworthy aspect was the absence in this period of huge, sweeping epidemics such as the pandemic of 1833 or the smallpox epidemic of 1837. At least, there is no record of such universal devastations. Disease apparently attacked the Indians continuously, or at least frequently, in a chronic form or by small local flare-ups, thus exacting a steady toll of lives over a long period. This makes difficult the numerical assessment of the damage inflicted, particularly since no one ever undertook a serious estimate of mortality from the strictly numerical standpoint. There are, of course, many broad statements to the effect that disease was wiping out the native population, but these are of no value quantitatively.

---

[18] Two good surveys of health conditions written at the time are those of Henry Gibbons (*Annual Address before the San Francisco County Medical Society,* 1857, in Pamphlets by California Authors, Medicine, Vol. 3, No. 1) and of T. M. Logan (*Medical History of the Year 1868 in California,* 1869, *ibid,* Vol. 4, No. 6). Among the epidemics mentioned which afflicted the white population in San Francisco and Sacramento are cholera, 1851, bronchitis, 1851, scarlatina, 1851, smallpox, 1852, whooping cough, 1856, measles, 1856, smallpox, 1861, smallpox, 1868.

There are numerous references to the types of disease, other than venereal, which afflicted the Indians. Omitting as unnecessary the detailed citation of sources, we may summarize the types of disease as follows:

Dysentery was reported among the Wiyot, Hupa, Miwok, and at Round Valley and Smith River reservations.

Tuberculosis was found among the Wiyot, Hupa, Maidu, Miwok, and on all reservations. It seems to have been the most prevalent of all introduced diseases.

Cholera affected the Maidu in 1849.

Typhoid was reported by name among the Maidu in 1853.

Malaria was widespread, particularly in the valley, and was indicated by the symptoms described among the Yana, Maidu, and Yokuts.

Smallpox was noticed among the Maidu (1852, 1853, 1859), Miwok (1857), and Pomo (1853).

Whooping cough visited the Pomo.

Pneumonia was noticed among the Maidu.

Measles was found on the Round Valley and Smith River reservations.

Influenza and *diphtheria* were common among the whites and certainly must have afflicted the Indians.

It is evident that all types of disease were thoroughly established among the native population.

Apart from the reservation medical reports, we possess only fragmentary and isolated bits of information on the lethal and debilitating effects of disease. Of the individual tribes, the one for which health conditions are best recorded is the Maidu, which may serve as a type example. In 1849 the Indians below Yuba City were attacked by cholera[19] "to a fearful extent," and many of them died. There may have been 500 Indians in these villages, of whom, let us say, 100 died. In the same year, among the Indians "at Sutter's Farm, on the Feather River and at the Ranchos on the Yuba" several deaths occurred from "periodical fever" (probably malaria).[20] This was a large territory and, since most of the natives were affected, the term "several" may denote at least 50. In 1852, an unknown epidemic attacked the Indians at Hock Farm,[21] as a result of which in one month, according to General Sutter,

---

[19] K. Webster, *The Gold Seekers of '49* (1850), p. 170.

[20] G. H. Derby, *First Report on the Sacramento Valley, 1849.* Reprinted in Calif. Hist. Soc., *Quarterly* (1932), 11:106–123.

[21] Sacramento *Union*, Dec. 13 and 17, 1852.

40 had died, leaving only 8 survivors. The same year, smallpox struck around Nevada City and the "mortality is considerable."[22] If there were 500 Indians in the vicinity and the "considerable" mortality amounted to 20 per cent (a reasonable value for a smallpox epidemic), 100 persons perished. The next season these same tribes were visited again by smallpox and by typhoid.[23] The mortality from smallpox was stated specifically as 400 deaths, mostly of children. Typhoid may have accounted for another 100. In Butte County, Mansfield quotes a pioneer to the effect that in 1853 forty Indians died of pneumonia at a little rancheria near Cherokee,[24] and there was the same scale of mortality from this cause throughout the county. If this were true—and there is no particular reason to doubt it—and if we make a conservative estimate of twenty rancherias in the county, then nearly 800 Maidu must have perished from pneumonia plus, probably, influenza and tuberculosis.

Various other statements are to be found in the next ten years, but no actual figures are given till 1863. At that time, 600 Maidu were collected at Pence's Ranch, Butte County, for shipment to Round Valley.[25] It was noted that 50 were sick with "bilious intermittent fever," undoubtedly malaria, and 30 had died in three weeks. At that rate, at least 100 must have perished before the removal to the reservation was complete.

If we now summarize the few actual figures given for mortality among the Maidu, we find a total of 1,690. Disregarding the fact that nothing like all the illness and death was reported, we note that the cases cited cover only the region of the present Butte, Yuba, Sutter, and Nevada counties—only about one-half the territory of the Maidu (excluding the Northeastern Maidu). Sacramento, Placer, and El Dorado counties are not included, but this region must have suffered just as severely as the northern part. It is then certainly legitimate to double the total of 1,690 and ascribe approximately 3,400 deaths by disease to the Maidu through the year 1863, or let us say 3,500 through 1865. The population decline of the Maidu is estimated as 6,000 from 1848 to 1880. The proportion referable to disease would then be 58 per cent.

[22] Nevada *Journal*, Aug. 27, 1852.
[23] Sacramento *Union*, May 28 and July 23, 1853.
[24] G. E. Mansfield, *History of Butte County* (Los Angeles, 1918), p. 193.
[25] Marysville *Appeal*, Aug. 30, 1863.

There exists one other clue to the incidence of disease in the mid-nineteenth century. The reports to the Commissioner of the Bureau of Indian Affairs for certain years, as already mentioned, contain detailed medical reports. In addition, there are several other years for which the records give the number of Indians on the reservations who were taken sick and sought medical advice. In all, there are ten such reports from 1876 to 1890, inclusive. We may restrict the calculation to Round Valley, since that reservation contained many Maidu and since geographically and ecologically it is the reservation closest to the native Maidu habitat. The mean population from 1876 to 1890 was about 730. The total number of cases under care of the physician, for the ten recorded years, was 7,073, or an average of 707 annually. This means that 97 per cent of the Indians were ill every year. Since sanitary and health conditions were vastly better on a reservation in the 'eighties than in the wild state during the 'fifties, it is a safe assumption that among the Maidu in the earlier period the annual incidence of some kind of disease was 100 per cent; that is, every member of the community was at least mildly ill once a year.

Mortality is another matter. The mean annual deaths from all causes at Round Valley, as given by the same reports, was 22, or 3.1 per cent. This is a very good showing and indicates a definite control of disease. However, we may derive still further information from the medical reports. From 1885 to 1890, the diseases are designated by name. The serious communicable maladies may thus be segregated in a separate category.[26] When this is done, we find a mean annual incidence of 221 cases, or 31 per cent of the total cases seen by the physician. Otherwise expressed, 30 per cent of the population annually contracted a disease which in the wild state, under unfavorable general surroundings and with no medical attention, would be very likely to terminate fatally. Moreover, the annual incidence of these diseases among the native Maidu must have been much higher than 30 per cent. Without violating probability we may assume at least 50 per cent for the years 1850 to 1865. As for the morbidity of these diseases, apart from the illustrations known to us and cited previously, they must have been fatal in

---

[26] These include: cholera morbus, tuberculosis, pneumonia, pleurisy, other respiratory disorders, typhoid, typhus, malaria, dysenteries, measles, whooping cough, tonsilitis, influenza, and smallpox.

a large share of the cases. The population was nonimmune, the sanitary conditions were atrocious, the diet poor. Exposure and hardship were universal. It will not be violating any canons of epidemiology or commonsense, if we consider the death rate among those infected with these contagions to have been 20 per cent. Then, if 50 per cent of the population was annually infected, the net annual death rate due to disease would have been 10 per cent.

The value of 10 per cent thus derived may be applied to the estimated actual population. There were approximately 7,000 Maidu alive in 1848. If we disregard death from all other causes and apply a 12-per cent annual reduction beginning in 1850, we get 1,600 in 1865. The population of the Maidu probably became stabilized at or about this period. Since the estimated population in 1880 is 1,000 and since we must include a mortality of approximately 500 to account for homicide, we arrive at the conclusion that the decline of the Maidu was almost entirely due to disease. Actually, the value would be 90 per cent.

The two methods of calculation, one based on fragmentary statements of contemporaries, the other based on the Round Valley medical reports, thus yield respectively 58 and 90 per cent for the decline of Maidu population attributable to disease. Despite the many assumptions involved and despite a wide numerical disparity, both calculations agree with respect to the primary trend. There can be no question whatever concerning the tremendous influence of disease in the decimation of this tribe. As a compromise between the two values obtained, and in order to get a working figure for further calculation, we may put the weight of the disease factor at 80 per cent.

Considerable space has been devoted to the Maidu, first, because our best records pertain to them, and second, because, with the statistics for this tribe as a basis, it may be possible to formulate some conclusions for those tribes concerning which we have no actual data. We might invoke the general principle of intensity of racial conflict. However, the method of population products, which was useful in estimating the amount of social homicide, cannot be applied in an unmodified form. Homicide is a function of continued intercourse between the two groups. *Introduction* of disease is a similar function, but once established, disease exerts its effect quite independently of racial propinquity. The epidemics of the 1830's are examples. The Spanish had to be in contact with the Indians in order to get the infection going. Thereafter the pest ran its course among the Indians alone. We might expect, then, that during the American period those groups living in regions seldom or never entered by the white man would be relatively immune, whereas those which once came thoroughly into contact with him would suffer heavily.

The Maidu represent a people which was in close contact with the Americans. This is also true for the Yana, the Sierra Miwok, the Yokuts, and the valley divisions of the Wintun. In the same category might be placed also the Pomo, the Yuki, the Wiyot, and the Yurok. But the Hill Wintun, the Shasta, the Karok, many of the Athabascan tribes, and the Achomawi were very definitely less exposed, and undoubtedly felt to a lesser extent the ravages of disease. Just as a guess— for there is absolutely no basis for computation—we might say that in the latter group disease was responsible for 40 rather than 80 per cent of the population decline. Then, since the first tribal group was numerically the stronger, the general average over the entire region might be estimated at 65 per cent. It makes little difference whether we assign a value of 50 or 65 or 70 per cent. It is sufficiently clear that disease accounted for the vast majority of Indian deaths during the first years of American occupation.

At the outset of this discussion the prediction was made that at least 60 per cent of the population decline would be found to be due to disease. This prediction has been adequately substantiated. Thus we may conclude that in all the tribes from Cape San Lucas in Baja California to the Oregon line disease exerted much the same relative influence, irrespective of the type of civilization which introduced it.

There is, however, another line of approach. We should consider not only the relative significance of disease, but also its absolute striking power. To what extent did introduced contagions, of and by themselves alone, reduce the original population? A decline of, let us say, 1 per cent entirely due to disease would be far less serious to a species than a reduction of 50 per cent only one-half of which was attributable to disease. In the second reduction the significance of disease would be twenty-five times as great as in the first. In order to bring out this difference, we may express the effect, in terms not of percentage of decline in population, but of percentage of the original native population destroyed. This has been done in the following brief tabulation.[27]

The striking fact brought out by these figures is that, although the percentage of the population reduction due to disease did not differ very greatly, the annual absolute inroad on the native population due to the American contact was roughly three or four times as great as the decline due to any of the three types of Spanish contact. In other

Racial contact	Original population	Population decline	Number of years of contact	Percentage of decline due to disease	Percentage of original population killed by disease	Percentage of original population killed by disease per year
Lower California Indian–mission........	40,000	36,000	70	35	31	0.44
Upper California Indian–mission	53,600	38,700	75	60	43	0.58
Wild Indian–Spanish...	56,900	18,100	43	60	19	0.43
Wild Indian–American.	69,100	57,000	32	65	53.5	1.67

words, the relative importance of disease to the Indians was fairly uniform, but its absolute significance was far greater for those tribes among which the Americans settled.

This wide difference in the influence exerted on the native stock by the two civilizations can be explained only in terms of numbers. Even if no simple mathematical formulation is possible, such a device is not necessary for an appreciation of the divergence. The whole scheme of Spanish colonization on the west coast implied settlement and control by a ruling caste composed of very few people. On the contrary, the advance of the Anglo-American frontier was a mass movement. The ratio of Spanish to natives may have been as one to ten, that of the Americans to natives as ten to one. Although the introduction and propagation of disease is no strict function of any ratio, nevertheless such a huge disproportion in relative populations must have determined in large measure the long-term severity of the disease effect.

---

[27] The population data have been taken from previous papers dealing with the appropriate groups. For the wild Indian-American contact, the period used is from 1848 to 1880. Here, also, the missionized and nearly extinct coastal tribes have been omitted.

FOOD AND NUTRITION

Under American domination, the problem of food supply became acute. It had arisen, to be sure, in a mild form among the mission Indians and among the wild Indian tribes in close propinquity to the Spanish. But, as has been pointed out elsewhere, the missionaries raised large crops and prevented anything approaching actual starvation, whereas the natural, or aboriginal, food supply of the interior wild Indians was not materially interfered with. The Americans, on the other hand, seriously depleted the aboriginal food sources.

From the standpoint of racial conflict, the subject of food presents itself in several aspects, some of which involve population changes and some of which pertain rather to cultural alterations. The first and perhaps most critical phase of the matter concerns the question whether the total Indian dietary was depleted and, if so, how and how much.

The aboriginal food supply was copious and extremely varied, since it included every edible plant and animal within the confines of California. The quantitative adjustment of the Indian population, both generally and locally, has been shown to be very precise.[28] On general ecological grounds, therefore, one would anticipate that any disturbance to this organism-environment relationship would be followed by serious repercussions. Such a disturbance did occur as a result of American occupation, and consequent upon it the primitive reservoir of wild food available to the Indian was sadly depleted. The effect was induced in two ways: the Indian was driven away from his food source, and the food source was removed from the Indian by destruction or otherwise.

The removal of the Indian from areas supplying food was the result of several processes, all more or less interrelated. Settlement by the whites was the initial agency. It was not by chance that small fertile valleys or rich river bottoms were selected by the incoming Americans as the site of new farms and villages. These were the spots best adapted geographically to the support of a large population. But the Indians as a rule had already long established their own rancherias in those very places. Hence, according to the inevitable rule of pioneer-

---

[28] Kroeber elaborates upon this theme in his *Handbook of the Indians of California* (Washington, 1925).

ing, the aboriginal owners were confronted with the alternative of moving out or being driven out. No matter which course they adopted, the result was the same. They were forced to retire to less prolific regions, where the available food supply was inadequate for their support. This sequence of events was particularly characteristic of the valleys of the north Coast Range and the headwaters of the Sacramento River system. Notably along the Klamath, Trinity, and Eel rivers and their tributaries, the natives were so dependent upon the river itself for support that normally they scarcely left it from one year to the next. Similarly, in the San Joaquin and Sacramento valleys, numerous groups had come to depend upon the river itself and the riparian biotic associations. But, as already suggested, the towns and ranches of the white men were located in those precise spots. Indeed, if one follows on the map the development of early American agrarian and commercial activity, he will find it concentrated in the exact regions most thickly populated by the aborigines. There was a similar distribution in the mining regions, for all along the Sierra foothill belt and on the tributaries of the Klamath, the miners followed the watercourses, and in so doing, drove out the heavy Indian population.

Partly as a result of this uprooting and the consequent dietary stringency, the natives resorted to some type of resistance. Warfare followed inevitably. Then, as a concomitant to hostilities, the Indians were driven farther and farther back into the barren hills and forests, making it still more difficult for them to gain access to the only food sources which they were equipped to utilize. As a result, the shortage frequently became very severe. Numerous are the references to the hard circumstances under which these displaced populations labored.[29]

---

[29] The following items will give an idea of this condition:

"This river [Trinity] . . . is rated as the best in the country for salmon fish, which constitutes almost the whole subsistence of the Indians. The whites took the whole river and crowded the Indians into the sterile mountains, and when they came back for fish they were usually shot." (Gen. G. F. Beale to the governor, July 12, 1855.)

"Mr. Poole, a settler on Kings River, informs us that the Indians have recently been driven to the mountains and are not to be permitted to return, even if they showed an inclination to do so." (Sacramento *Union*, Sept. 5, 1856.)

Referring to the McCloud and Pit River Indians: "In winter they have great difficulty in procuring enough provisions to keep body and soul together." (Sacramento *Union*, Nov. 10, 1854.) It was admitted policy on the part of General Kibbe to drive these tribes into the mountains during the food-gathering season in order that they might starve.

Mere distance from food sources, however, was not the only factor involved in cutting down access to adequate subsistance. Perhaps an even more important by-product of warfare was the disruption of native food economy. As many ethnographers have pointed out, the Indians were dependent upon the natural supply of both plants and animals. Since this was available only for certain brief periods each year, the Indian method was to gather the material—acorns, salmon, grasshoppers, etc.—in bulk at the time of harvest and store it for future use. Most of the dietary items, furthermore, had to be processed both for immediate consumption and for preservation. Now it was vitally necessary that the entire man and woman power of a particular village devote itself without interruption to this pursuit while the season lasted. If, as frequently happened, the population had been driven off to some distance already and then, during the period of food preparation, was disturbed, attacked, or put to flight, the entire staple food supply for the year might be ruined. The loss of subsistence from this cause was particularly severe among the fish-and-acorn tribes of the northwest. To show the extent of such disruption of food economy, it may be worth while to introduce the following very sketchy paraphrase of events in the Klamath, Trinity, and Eel basins during the late 'fifties. This is taken direct from A. J. Bledsoe's *Indian Wars of the Northwest* (1885) and is correct in substance, if not in detail.

1855. Miners attack and burn "several" rancherias.
     Red Cap Rancheria attacked by miners.
     Volunteers attack two rancherias at Weitschpeck.
     A reservation is set up on the Klamath and all Indians of the region
     are removed to it.
1856. Hupa Indians under arms. Object to removal to reservation.
     A rancheria attacked on Redwood Creek.
     Another rancheria destroyed on Redwood Creek.
     A rancheria destroyed on Bear River.

(*Footnote 29 concluded*)
   Referring to the Miwok, many of whom had retreated to the mountains: "Some were found far up in the snows, starving and freezing." (J. D. Mason, *History of Amador County* [1881], p. 260.)
   In the Northwest: Some 200 to 300 Indians on the South Fork of the Trinity came in sueing for peace. They agreed to stop raiding in return for the right to fish and hunt in the vicinity. (Sacramento *Union*, Sept. 20, 1852.) "Some of the poor savages, who are now being hunted by Massey's men on the Humboldt trail, are begging of the ranchmen for permission to fish. They don't dare to fish, hunt or make fire without permission." (*Ibid.*, Dec. 29, 1858.)

The winter of 1856–1857 was hard. "It meant a struggle for self preservation by the Indians, a struggle against natural forces in which the whites were not a factor." Many whole tribes had been pushed into the mountains. The Indians were "chastened" by the winter and were quiet in 1857.

1858. The "Wintoons" on the headwaters of Redwood Creek, the Mad and Eel rivers begin depredations.
Three expeditions go out.
Rancheria attacked on Grouse Creek.
Two expeditions ambushed.
Indians withdraw entirely from the Mad River to the headwaters of Yaeger Creek.
Three rancherias destroyed on Yaeger Creek.
Indians are driven slowly into a small area on the headwaters of the Mad and Yaeger. There are seventeen camps. These attacked and destroyed.
A rancheria attacked on Redwood Creek.

1859. One hundred women and children sent to Mendocino Reservation.
A big storm occurs in January. "The hostiles, unable to hunt on the mountains and afraid to go down on the streams, were actually starved into submission within four weeks."
February: all rancherias raided; 160 Indians sent to Mendocino. Sporadic raiding on Eel River and in Mattole Valley, also on the Van Duzen and Mad rivers.

1860. Most of the Wintoons escape from the reservation. Indian Island massacre—the Wiyot practically destroyed. A rancheria destroyed on Mad River.
Four hundred and forty Indians sent to Klamath Reservation; in a few months all had escaped. They were now all dependent upon the whites for subsistence.

1861. A rancheria burned at Iaqua.
A rancheria destroyed on Boulder Creek.
Two rancherias destroyed on the Mad River.
A rancheria destroyed on Larrabee Creek.
Another rancheria destroyed on Larrabee Creek.
September to December: fifteen engagements in Humboldt County, at least four rancherias destroyed.

1862. Conditions much the same. "The marching and countermarching was continuous throughout the year ... The prisoners were mostly of friendly tribes, who willingly surrendered for the sake of temporary shelter and food."
Camp near Arcata attacked.

Camp on Little River destroyed.

Eight hundred captured Indians removed to Smith River Reservation. In two months all had escaped and returned.

1863. Conditions much the same.

Hupa destroy a friendly rancheria on Stone Lagoon.

A rancheria destroyed on north fork of Eel.

A battle on Redwood Creek.

A rancheria destroyed in Hoopa Valley.

A battle on south fork of the Trinity.

Another battle on Willow Creek.

Another battle, near Arcata, at Bald Mountain.

1864. Fighting on the South Salmon.

A rancheria burned in Hoopa Valley.

A battle in Mattole Valley.

A battle between Mad River and Redwood Creek.

Skirmishing now incessant. The policy was to wear down the Indians by "keeping them moving, and preventing them from laying in supplies of food and ammunition." Also by preventing the women and children from resting.

A rancheria destroyed on Elk River.

A "number" of rancherias destroyed in April.

A rancheria destroyed in July on the Mattole.

1865. By January, 1865, "Trinity County was cleared of all Indians who lived in rancherias and tribal relations.... The hostile tribes had been killed or captured, had been flooded by storms and driven by man, had been starved and beaten into absolute and final subjection."

This record speaks for itself. No further comment is necessary.[30]

Apart from the broad effects of settlement and warfare was the temporary disturbance accompanying wholesale removals to reservations. The press from 1855 to 1865 was filled with a most acrimonious controversy concerning the mismanagement and malfeasance in office exhibited by the Federal agents. One does not need to delve deeply into these charges and countercharges to discover that the officers entrusted with the care of the Indians on the new reserves were a pretty bad lot. Among their other derelictions was a tendency to neglect the food supply of their wards—either through crookedness,

---

[30] The general and social implications of disruption by warfare are discussed in connection with other topics. The significance here is solely with respect to the breakdown of normal food sources, the processing and preservation of foodstuffs.

neglect, or plain stupidity. Not until the middle 'sixties was any consistent scheme set in operation to ensure an adequate year-round food supply. Meanwhile, thousands of Indians had been gathered in droves and herded like cattle from their homesites to some unfamiliar and unpromising locality. Many of these people escaped at their first opportunity and made their way across the wilderness toward home. The minority remained. In either event there was inevitably a period of wasted time during which a food supply was not available and when, even if the raw materials could have been obtained, there was no opportunity to process and store them.

The epitome of Bledsoe's chronicle given above shows how the northwestern tribes fared. One might add equally sad accounts of the fate of the Achomawi and Maidu, who were hauled all the way to Humboldt County by way of San Francisco or driven across into Round Valley. Tales of want and suffering among these unfortunates are too numerous for extended mention. Simply as an example, consider the hegira of certain Achomawi and Maidu (Hat Creeks and Concows). They were a part of the large body of Indians who had been shipped in a body to Round Valley about 1860. In 1862 Agent Storms reported that the survivors, four hundred of them, had "left" the reservation, headed eastward.[31] Since there was no crop raised on the reservation, they had migrated to avoid starvation. We next hear of them at the moribund Nome Lackee Reservation, west of Tehama. The citizens thereabouts voted a set of resolutions requesting the removal of these Indians, "deposited at Nome Lackee by the authorities,"[32] who had left the Indians totally destitute, with no means of support and with no agent to look after them. From Nome Lackee they evidently moved, or were moved, to the "Old Landing" on the Sacramento River, whence they were again pushed on to Major Bidwell's ranch near Chico.[33] At this time, the summer of 1863, there were three hundred left and there was among the children, as the *Appeal* quaintly put it, a "temporary" epidemic due "to a change of diet." Finally, the Indian Service got around to assembling them and dumping them once more at Round Valley, where they remained thereafter.

---

[31] Sacramento *Union*, Sept. 30, 1862.
[32] San Francisco *Bulletin*, Nov. 6, 1862.
[33] Marysville *Appeal*, June 24, 1863.

The reverse of the removal of Indians from their normal food supply was the reduction or elimination of that supply for those who were fortunate enough to be relatively unmolested. Closely associated with this matter is the quantitative significance of such depletion. There were two general processes which contributed to the final result. One was the direct destruction of stored provisions through warfare or maliciousness, the other was the long-term ecological change caused by advancing civilization.

We have few means for estimating with any degree of precision the actual quantity of food materials burned, thrown away, or stolen by the whites. One possible guide would be the number of rancherias looted or destroyed, since the stores were customarily kept in the villages. We know that the custom of wrecking all Indian commodities, including food and food-processing implements, was begun by the Spanish in the times of the valley expeditions. The method was adopted and elaborated by the miners of 1849 and 1850 and was invariably practiced by all military and private Indian-fighting parties thereafter. Even the inoffensive Yokuts were repeatedly subjected to this treatment, and the tribes of the mountain sections suffered enormous damage. There can be little doubt that every tribe which indulged in a so-called war against the Americans lost practically every rancheria at least once in its history, and some groups were subjected to this process repeatedly. For example, the Bledsoe account specifically mentions the destruction of 32 rancherias (with stored supplies) from 1855 to 1863. In connection with other incidents "several" and "all" were destroyed. In addition are mentioned the destruction of 19 "camps," i.e., temporary stopping places. If we allow 18 to cover the "several" and "all" rancherias, we get a total of 50. But Bledsoe, even if his account is very circumstantial, does not include every incident of the sort. In fact, we may double his number and still be conservative.

Now Kroeber and other ethnographers have studied carefully the number of village sites for part of this region. Their total for the Tolowa, Yurok, Wiyot, Karok, Chimariko, Hupa, and Chilula is 177. Since these are sites, not simultaneously existing villages, and since many of the latter were deserted for other causes after 1850, this number may be reduced to 100. But there must be added those of the

Trinity River Wintun and the small Athabascan tribes in Humboldt and northern Mendocino counties, say 50. The total, 150, is not far in excess of the estimated 100 destroyed. Indeed, it would not be unfair to state that every permanent village in the northwest was sacked, if not burned, at least once. The stored food supplies per village in this region would normally amount to a good many hundred pounds of fish and an equal amount of acorns, etc. Perhaps a total of 2 tons would not be excessive for an annual average. This means the destruction of at least 300 tons of provisions in 8 years, or about 40 tons per year. If all the northern and central California tribes are to be included, we must account for the Shasta, the Pit River tribes, the Yana, the Maidu, the Miwok, and the Yokuts, not to mention the Yuki, Wailaki, and Pomo. The 40 for the Klamath and Eel territory must be multiplied by a factor of at least three, perhaps more. However, using three as a factor, we find an annual food-destruction rate of 120 tons. This perhaps appears a small figure when compared to our modern consumption of thousands or millions of tons of foodstuffs. But it must be remembered that the aboriginal food supply at its maximum was but marginal, just great enough to support the existing population. If we say that the average population through the period 1850 to 1865 was 40,000, then the loss per person was 6 pounds per year; not a great quantity in the individual sense, but an appreciable loss when spread over a large population for a long time.

Far more significant in the long run, however, than temporary losses through hostile acts, was the rapid change which took place in the availability of the raw food materials, a change which, although most noticeable at first, has continued to this day. The four basic staples of Indian diet were fish, game, acorns, and various seeds. With respect to fish, the salmon run in particular was very adversely affected. This was owing not so much to American agriculture or occupation per se as to mining operations. Into the salmon-bearing streams of the Sierra Nevada and north coast ranges dirt and silt began very early to be washed in immense quantities, with the result that comparatively few salmon could get up the rivers to spawn. This state of affairs was commented on by Bledsoe[34] (who, by the way, ascribed the Indian

---

[34] A. J. Bledsoe, *Indian Wars* (San Francisco, 1885), p. 149.

wars to interference with food supply) and by Powers.[35] Bledsoe also pointed to a complaint by the Chimariko that not only were the salmon fewer, but the muddying of the water lowered the visibility of the fish so that it was impossible to spear them. The Yokuts, who also had depended heavily on fish as well as on waterfowl and other aquatic animals, suffered in another way. As agriculture advanced in the San Joaquin Valley, the vast swamps were drained for farming purposes. Also, as time went on, the diversion of mountain water for irrigation lowered the water table to such a point that the original fauna almost disappeared. Thus the Yokuts were completely cut off from a very prolific source of food. Finally, as is well known, the introduction of hydraulic mining silted up great areas of bottom lands and changed the entire face of the country. Today the water-borne food of California could not support the remnants of the Indian population which still survive, not to speak of the aboriginal number.

The Indians never did depend greatly for food on the larger fur-bearing animals or the deer. Therefore the depletion of these animals was not, in spite of many complaints, a serious loss. However, the destruction and disappearance of small rodents was a real calamity. The rabbit, particularly, was utilized, and, to some extent, ground squirrels. It is doubtful whether agriculture has much reduced the number of these animals, but it has prevented the Indians from getting them. Their method was to organize great drives and sweep over a big area. This procedure was practically eliminated as soon as valley farms developed, because the Americans refused to permit the natives to move through standing crops or plowed fields.

Perhaps the greatest anguish was caused by the white man's own domestic animals, particularly cattle and hogs. Their influence was felt in two ways. The first, and lesser, evil was the fencing-in of the free range. This made trespassers of people who from time immemorial had gone wherever they wished in search of food, particularly acorns, seeds, and green plants. As a rule, the best food-bearing land was thus preëmpted, forcing the natives to search in poorer and more distant preserves. This in turn increased the difficulty and labor in getting a unit quantity of food and indirectly reduced the total amount available.

[35] *Op. cit.*, 3:73, 94.

The second, and greater, evil was the activity of the stock and hogs. Indeed, these introduced animals entered into direct ecological competition with the Indians—a kind of man versus animal conflict. For, under the stern protection of the whites, the cattle ate the grasses which produced the Indians' seeds, and the hogs ate the acorns. There is no question that the Indians were able to succeed in competition with the animals themselves, but when they were prevented from exercising their normal biological reactions, a very serious situation was created for them. This was recognized by the white men themselves, although they preferred to sacrifice the Indians rather than their livestock. Witness the following statements:

The stock . . . consuming the clover, grass, acorns and wild oats, which they have hitherto subsisted on . . . there is hardly any food in the mountains the Indians can get.[36]

. . . the hogs eat the acorns and roots, and the cattle take the clover, and therefore they kill the stock to subsist upon.[37]

. . . their hunting grounds are all occupied by the farmers, whose hogs destroy their acorns and manzanita berries . . .[38]

Their hunting grounds are destroyed, as game has been driven back to the mountains . . . acorns, their only dependence, now are scarce, and I think, on the whole, they are looking a rather hard winter in the face.[39]

. . . their supplies in plains and foothills, provided by Providence for generations back, have been consumed by the stock of the white man. . . .[40]

The acorns, the most important and most available breadstuff . . . are consumed by the hogs of the whites.

Their spring and summer food such as clover, wild lettuce, serrino, grass roots and various other kinds of vegetables . . . have [been] this season, and will hereafter be, consumed by cattle, horses and hogs before maturity.

The havoc raised by stock with the native food sources was of course but one manifestation of the larger racial conflict. Here, indeed, was a clean-cut focus of collision, the depletion of food supply, scarcely secondary to homicide or slaughter through disease.

[36] *Repts. Special Joint Committee on Mendocino War,* 1860, Pamphlets on Calif. Indians, Bancroft Library, testimony of W. T. Scott, p. 23.

[37] *Ibid.,* testimony of J. W. Burgess, p. 24.

[38] G. W. Applegate, Placer Co., 1856, in *Rept. Commr. Indian Affairs,* 1856, p. 243.

[39] G. H. Hoerchner, Calaveras Co. 1856, *Ibid.,* p. 240.

[40] This, and the following two statements are from M. B. Lewis, Fresno Indian Farm, 1856, *ibid.,* p. 254.

Naturally, the effect on population was largely indirect. It seldom happens that the immediate cause of death is complete lack of nourishment. Only following great famines does this occur, as it has for example from time to time in China, Russia, and the Near East. It is probable that seldom was food so scarce that the California Indians perished of actual starvation. However, partial starvation must have been quite common. The influence of this condition was to lower the vitality of the population in all respects. Particularly was resistance to disease so much reduced that many of the weaker members, such as children and old people, fell easy prey to whatever epidemic happened to strike them. Tuberculosis would also claim many victims in such a population. The physical weakness attending prolonged undernutrition would also contribute to mental and moral lassitude, thus preventing the group as a whole from bringing to bear its full energy in acquiring a new food supply. Moreover, the birth rate would tend to decrease, although we have no quantitative data concerning this matter. A very inadequate diet, as is well known, will prevent proper development of the fetus, make it more difficult for the mother to withstand delivery, and reduce the natural secretion of milk below the subsistence level of the newly born child. As a result of all these factors, the population would tend to decrease very rapidly.

As we know, the population did decrease materially during the years of most acute hardship, owing, among other causes, to the disturbance of food supply—a major environmental factor. Indeed, it is to be doubted whether the California Indian would have survived at all, if he had not been able, under this tremendous pressure, to evolve certain fairly effective responses to what may be termed the "starvation stimulus." Let us not forget that, with the exception of direct physical attack, starvation constitutes the most powerful biotic urge known to the individual. By extension, acute or merely mild and chronic hunger will drive an entire race or species into a path of aggression into which it can be led by no other means. (This thesis predicates, of course, that inanition has not proceeded to the point where all physical and moral fiber has been sapped and the group becomes utterly impotent.) The first response, therefore, to present hunger and the obvious probability of future hunger is to fight. The manner and form of the action are immaterial. The basic point is that the Indian, faced with the clear prospect of starvation, attacked the race responsible for his condition. The attempt was abortive in the long run, but for a period, until utterly defeated and exhausted, the Indians instinctively demonstrated the primitive, automatic struggle for *Lebensraum*. I think it may be maintained with assurance that the Indian wars and difficulties in California up to 1865 had as their basic cause the dislocation and depletion of the aboriginal food supply.

The battle to maintain primitive conditions failed. The strictly defensive reaction, that is, the attempt to drive out the invader and restore the *status quo ante* attained no measure of success, because of conditions beyond the defenders' control. Consequently, the Indian, if he were to survive at all, was forced to supplement the fundamental "fight" reaction by other responses better adapted to the circumstances. Some of these were tried, and some proved at least moderately effective.

We may look at the situation thus. Conceded that the aboriginal food sources were irretrievably diminished (not, of course, utterly eliminated) and that an irreducible minimum of food had to be obtained, then the Indian had but one recourse: to utilize the white man's supplies. The resistance or "fight" response, therefore, very quickly became coupled with a replacement response.

When first confronted with the problem of supplementing their diet with materials provided by the white man, there were two possible methods available. The first was simply to take the food, the second was to buy it. Let us grant that, in so far as the group response in general was concerned, considerations of expediency, not morality, were paramount. In terms of the individual, the Indian could feel no ethical objection to appropriating the white man's property when the white man had already forcibly dispossessed him of his original means of subsistence. Conduct, therefore, depended upon which course of action would most quickly relieve immediate needs and would be attended by the least severe retribution. In the long run the Indian found the method of purchase (by money or labor) the most satisfactory. At the beginning, however, normal economic channels were not open to him, and the starvation pressure was severe. As a result, within a very short time following the arrival of the heavy American immigration, the Indian began to appropriate to his use the white man's food. It was not until he had suffered vicious castigation that he relinquished this form of relief and universally adopted the second type of response. Although this chain of events did not follow any strict temporal continuity, it nevertheless represents almost an experimental adaptive procedure. Thus, if we disregard accuracy in time, we see first the major upset in the external environment, the reduction of food sources. Second comes the natural, instinctive response, to fight the causative agent. This failing, in the third place arises the theft, raiding, or appropriation reaction. This, too, failing to bring about a favorable adaptation, the Indian managed to achieve the final step, conformity with white methods for obtaining subsistence.

The details of this process may be read in the accounts of the Indian troubles of the mid-nineteenth century. When the Indian turned to the white man for food, he found one admirable source ready at hand, livestock. The problem of stock raiding, to be sure, was one which had existed since earlier Spanish times. It had been the cause of great difficulty between the heathen tribes and the Mexican immigrants, and no essentially new features were introduced by the coming of the Americans. The whole question with its many ramifications cannot be discussed here, but it is of interest to examine the extent to which the natives came to depend upon horses and cattle to supplement their own vanishing dietary. Although it is not possible to determine with any accuracy the number of domestic animals eaten after the innumerable stock raids, the following statements and abstracts may be cited to give some idea of the universality of this mode of behavior.

"The Indians, I think, kill stock for the purpose of using it for food."[41]

"I have never been on an excursion against the Indians but what I found more or less meat in their camp, either horse, beef or sheep meat."[42]

Referring to the Wailaki: "Much horse meat and pork was found and destroyed."[43]

A rancheria was attacked at Kettinshou, Humboldt County. "Several hundred pounds of fresh pork" were found there.[44]

[41] *Repts. on Mendocino War,* testimony of W. T. Scott, p. 23.
[42] *Ibid.,* testimony of C. H. Bourne, p. 48.
[43] San Francisco *Bulletin,* Oct. 23, 1861, letter from S. P. Storms, Round Valley.
[44] Marysville *Appeal,* July 4, 1861.

In Mendocino County Mr. Woodman lost 109 horses, 74 of which were found dead, "upon the bodies of which the Indians were having a good feast."[45]

Referring to a fight at Round Valley: "The unusual severity of the winter has doubtless reduced the Indians to a condition bordering on starvation and the consequence is, they are committing serious depredations on the stock."[46]

Horses stolen in Oak Run Valley. One horse returned, the others had been eaten.[47]

The Yuki are especially fond of mule meat. Large quantities of horse and mule meat are being laid up in their rancherias, judging by the number of slaughtered animals found.[48]

A band of Hayfork Indians (Hill Wintun) have raided cattle at Kenshaw's Flat. They jerked the meat and cooked it.[49]

The Indians were caught jerking beef at Kneeland's Prairie (Humboldt County).[50]

The Indians of Mariposa County "go in quest of mustang meat through necessity, as they must get that, or steal or starve."[51]

The Indians near Fiddletown shoot cows full of arrows. Then when the cows die, the Indians eat them.[52]

"A large portion of the time they were half starved. They sometimes had to steal cattle from the whites for self preservation."[53]

Referring to San Joaquin tribes: "These Indians ... have become so habituated to living on horseflesh that it is now with them the principal means of subsistence."[54]

"The Indians on the Trinity ... were very fond of mule beef and never failed to obtain a supply of it, when they had an opportunity to do so."[55]

Referring to the Sierra Indians, "[They] steal numbers of tame horses from the white settlers on or near the coast only to use for food—the Indian generally making no other use of the horse."[56]

The Indians "also are fond of horse meat, and when hard pressed with hunger will occasionally steal a bullock."[57]

[45] San Francisco *Bulletin*, Jan. 21, 1860.
[46] *Ibid.*, Jan. 26, 1861.
[47] Nevada *Journal*, Dec. 9, 1853.
[48] San Francisco *Bulletin*, March 1, 1861.
[49] Sacramento *Union*, Aug. 13, 1861.
[50] *Ibid.*, July 24, 1861.
[51] *Ibid.*, May 11, 1858.
[52] *Ibid.*, Sept. 18, 1854.
[53] R. T. Montgomery, "Recollections," MS, 1878, Bancroft Library, p. 8.
[54] E. Bryant, *op. cit.*, p. 435.
[55] J. Carr, *Pioneer Days in California* (Eureka, 1891), p. 119.
[56] J. W. Revere, *A Tour of Duty in California* (New York, 1849), p. 127.
[57] *Ibid.*, p. 121.

"If we had allowed the Indians to become accustomed to beef or horse meat, even capital punishment would not have held them in check." Speaking of the San Joaquin Valley people: "These ate mainly horse meat."[58]

"The Indians had a habit of stealing all horses and mules that they could lay their hands on, driving them into the hills and butchering them ... it always seemed to me as if they liked horseflesh better than beef and mule flesh better than either."[59]

The Yana "probably visited the valley and stole livestock to escape famine and actual starvation."[60]

One might easily find hundreds of references to stock raiding in the books, articles, and newspapers written between 1848 and 1870. Although many of the claims for losses advanced by the pioneers have been shown to be grossly exaggerated, no one can deny that an enormous quantity of stock was stolen or killed. Not all these animals were attacked for the purpose of obtaining food and by no means all were eaten, for stock raiding was carried on for many other reasons; but there can be little question that thousands of cattle, horses, mules, sheep, and hogs went to supply the Indian larder. It has been estimated previously that destruction of provisions by the white people reduced the annual individual food supply of the Indians by about six pounds. If we allow six hundred pounds of flesh to a steer, then this loss would be made up by only four hundred steers annually. The actual slaughter was probably far in excess of this figure. Consequently, the natives, on the average, more than made up the losses by destruction. Indeed, it is quite likely that on many occasions whole villages and tribes were saved from literal starvation by the livestock which they were able to steal from the whites.

Unfortunately for the natives, the devastation wrought by the whites in retaliation for stock thefts was so complete that this excellent replacement for the lost aboriginal diet served only as a temporary measure. In the long run it was far too costly. In making his final adaptation and in adopting socially recognized methods for obtaining food, the Indian was assured of a supply which, though inadequate at first, was ultimately sufficient for his support. In detail these

---

[58] T. Cordua, "Memoirs, 1855." In Calif. Hist. Soc., *Quarterly* (1933), 12:310–311.

[59] R. A. Anderson, *Fighting the Mill Creeks* (Chico, 1909), p. 7.

[60] T. T. Waterman, *op. cit.*, 13:43.

methods to which he eventually resorted were various, and, since they involve consideration of the entire cultural relationship between the races, can only be mentioned at the present juncture.

The most obvious and most peaceful means for obtaining food was for the Indian to perform labor, in exchange for which he would receive victuals or the money wherewith to purchase them. This in turn was contingent upon the existence of work for which Indians could be employed, and upon their capacity and willingness to do such work. A second method was mendicancy or dependence upon private charity, at best an inadequate and unsatisfactory source of steady support. Since both these devices together, in the early days, could not carry the Indian population, it was necessary for the Federal government to step in through the mediation of the Indian Service and undertake direct relief through food subvention on a large scale.

Although acceptance of food materials as a private or public gift may not appear on the surface an effective response to conflict with the invading race, it must nevertheless be regarded as such, for considerations of ethics and racial pride are totally extraneous when biological survival is concerned. If the native population can in any way maintain itself in conflict with the new civilization by forcing that civilization to support it, then the native population has succeeded measurably in adapting itself to its altered environment. Taking advantage of humanitarian scruples is entirely legitimate in the raw struggle for racial existence, for the underlying object is to meet the changed conditions imposed by racial conflict in the most effective Darwinian manner. Therefore, if the aboriginal population found by experience that making the whites give food was more conducive to ultimate survival than taking it from them by theft or physical force, then that population had worked out the best possible adaptation to the existing environment. Viewed in this light, the "slothful," "sinful" behavior of the California Indian becomes another of the not too numerous evidences that the Indian was able to compete adaptively with the white race.

The implication of these remarks is that after a period of hard adjustment the Indian was able to gain for himself a sufficient subsistence under the American occupation. A subsidiary question may be raised in this connection: whether, from the point of view of dietetics and nutrition, the new food supply was as adequate as the old. Quantitatively, the individual native was probably as well off as before the Americans arrived; that is, he no doubt maintained at least a minimum calorific intake. But was the new diet qualitatively as good? This question cannot be answered completely because we do not know the actual consumption of different kinds of foodstuffs. Certain points, however, are suggestive.

1. Despite the marked reduction of native food sources, these were by no means eliminated entirely. Even though the natural supply was, in the aggregate, below the minimum subsistence level for many years, it still formed the basis of the Indian dietary. There are repeated references in the early accounts to large quantities of staple foods gathered. The following items are indicative of the amounts involved:

A man hired Indians to exterminate grasshoppers on his ranch. At the end of six hours part of the killed animals weighed 42 pounds. (Nevada *Journal*, May 31, 1861.)

There is a big acorn crop this year. (Sacramento *Union,* Oct. 4, 1864.)

The Indians at Nome Lackee had a rabbit hunt lately. They caught several hundred. (*Ibid.*, March 29, 1859.)

The lower end of Shasta Valley is overrun with crickets as large as mice, and the Indians have collected a pile as large as any haystack in that vicinity. (*Ibid.*, July 22, 1858.)

At Nome Lackee Reservation, the Indians gathered 2,000 bushels of acorns. (*Ibid.*, Oct. 2, 1857.)

The Nevada County Indians are reaping a rich harvest of manzanita berries. (*Ibid.*, Aug. 10, 1855.)

At Hock Farm a visitor saw inhabitants preparing a large meal of boiled minnows and acorn mush. (*Ibid.*, July 10, 1852.)

The Indians are now catching salmon at Colusa. (*Ibid.*, April 13, 1852.)

At Clear Lake, the Indians eat fish and water fowl. They have an "immense stock" of these laid up on their island. They also eat at least one meal a day of tule roots, and the women were busy collecting grass seeds. (San Francisco *Bulletin,* June 1, 1865.)

At Knight's Landing blackberries are very abundant on Cache Creek. Many Indians picking them. (*Ibid.*, June 26, 1862.)

Starving Indians in Siskiyou and Shasta counties are living on the sap of the sugar pine. They strip off the bark and scrape off the sap. "Thousands" of trees are thus destroyed annually. (*Ibid.*, Feb. 21, 1859.)

The Indians on the south fork of the Merced, using "soap root," narcotized and caught 2,000 trout. (*Ibid.*, Aug. 1, 1858.)

Indians at Hock Farm are eating grasshoppers and manzanita berries. (Marysville *Appeal*, Aug. 31, 1861.)

The Indians near Grass Valley are all out hunting fresh plants for food. (San Francisco *Bulletin*, April 22, 1858.)

Several Indians from Placer County have been catching fish at Sacramento. "They have secured a large amount." (Sacramento *Union*, Sept. 29, 1862.)

Hoopa Valley Reservation: "Their main dependence for food, exclusive of that furnished by the Government, is salmon, acorns, berries, deer, grouse, and other game. Though not so plentiful as in former times yet ... they manage to have plenty." (J. V. Farwell, *Rept. Commr. Indian Affairs*, 1871, p. 157.)

One gets the impression that for perhaps twenty years after American settlement wild food constituted at least half the Indian dietary.

2. The great carbohydrate staple of the natives was the acorn, which took the place of the maize common to most other North American natives. As has been suggested, the supply of this vitally necessary food staple underwent progressive diminution as settlement and stock ranching increased. However, it is probable that its loss was largely superseded by the use of flour. There is much evidence to the effect that, when the Indians bought provisions or were given supplies by the government, the bulk consisted of flour, as the following accounts testify:

The Mariposa Indians are complaining that they are not receiving their flour according to the treaty. (Sacramento *Union*, Nov. 24, 1851.)

In Grass Valley in 1852, "the Indians came to town often to get flour, and occasionally a poor piece of meat." (D. C. Fletcher, *Reminiscences of California* [Ayer, Mass., 1894], pp. 41–44.)

Four hundred and eighty captives were brought by Kibbe to San Francisco in 1859. Their rations were beef and flour "which the Indians cooked as it suited them." (San Francisco *Bulletin*, Dec. 16, 1859.)

The Indians on Four Creeks are being fed by the agent. One thousand bags of flour and 1,200 cattle will be sent them. (Nevada *Journal*, Nov. 29, 1851.)

In the early mining days: "After a while the Indians would take a pan of flour and mix it up with water and ... eat it without cooking." (D. P. Barstow, "Statement," MS, 1877, Bancroft Library, p. 10.)

At a "grand cry meeting" near Stringtown the food consisted of one ton of flour as flapjacks and several barrels of acorn mush. (San Francisco *Bulletin*, Aug. 1, 1865.)

If this was so, then from the dietary standpoint there was no net reduction in food value. That the Indians themselves came to regard the white man's grains as an adequate substitute for acorns is indicated by several occasions on which thefts of such material occurred:

The Indians burned Pardee's ranch (Humboldt County). They also dug up the potatoes and threshed out the oats. (Sacramento *Union*, Nov. 8, 1858.)

Indians stole 15 sacks of wheat from Mr. Riggs's ranch. (Red Bluff *Beacon*, Aug. 25, 1858.)

"As soon as these fiends have eaten what flour they were able to carry away from Cooper's Mill [Humboldt County], it is expected they will make another attack." (Sacramento *Union*, August 12, 1861.)

Indians stole two horses, one cow, and some potatoes from Mr. Dersech, 25 miles north of Red Bluff. (Red Bluff *Beacon*, Feb. 4, 1863.)

The Indians raided the ranch of Mr. Cromby in Antelope Valley. They threshed out and packed off 20 bushels of wheat. (Red Bluff *Beacon*, July 24, 1862.)

Indians raided Mr. Bacon's barn near Red Bluff and stole 18 bushels of wheat and 500 pounds of shorts. (Marysville *Appeal*, July 15, 1865.)

Moreover, the quantities involved in such pilfering seem to demonstrate definite dependence upon cereal crops.

3. One of the most interesting dietary changes is related to stock raiding. It has already been mentioned that, for the purpose of getting food as well as for other reasons, the natives stole and ate tremendous numbers of domestic animals. Previously the Indians had been pretty largely vegetarians, although local groups at certain seasons had been able to obtain moderate quantities of animal food. Now, however,

large groups of them became, for a while at least, heavy consumers of flesh. As a result, the intake of protein and fat increased, as compared with that of carbohydrate. Moreover, the intake of animal protein was greater, as compared with that of plant protein. With our present state of knowledge on nutrition, we cannot make any categorical statement of the effect of such a dietary change on the character of the people. Nevertheless, the possibility remains that the reactions and the behavior of the Indians may have been modified by the great increase in meat consumption.

4. Regarding such accessory factors as minerals and vitamins, the opinion may be hazarded that there was little material change. The very wide variety of food sources in the aboriginal diet, which involved some animal food (fish, small game, insects) and many types of plants (nuts, acorns, seeds, grasses, tubers, leaves, etc.), must have ensured a pretty adequate intake of the common inorganic elements and the essential vitamins. After American occupation, it must be remembered, these sources were reduced but not cut off entirely. Therefore, the Indian still had access to a fair amount of vitamin-containing material. Furthermore, the addition of large quantities of fresh meat would tend to replace any accessory factors lost from the aboriginal supply.

In this connection, it is quite significant that the natives, in contradistinction to the whites, consumed the carcass of an animal *in toto*. They ate the liver, stomach, intestines, kidneys, and other viscera, which we now know to be an excellent source of many accessory factors. This habit of the Indians was the cause of much disgusted comment by the whites, who, as ignorant as the Indians of modern dietary principles, regarded the omnivorous tendencies of the latter as a mere manifestation of innate barbarism and brutishness. It is rather ironical as we look back on it now to see how the whites were actually promoting the welfare of the Indians. The following may serve as examples:

Four steers drowned in the Yuba River. They were given to a group of Indians who consumed every scrap of them. (San Francisco *Bulletin*, Sept. 22, 1857.)

"I butchered in Coloma one spring, and the Indians would hang around to get the offal. They would take the intestines ... and eat them with a great deal of gusto." (Barstow, "Statement," p. 10.)

"In Marysville, passing by one of the slaughter houses, I saw a collection of about twenty of these wretches waiting for the offal. They were in the habit of presenting themselves regularly every morning at the same place and at the same hour to gather the refuse of the slaughtering establishment." (H. R. Helper, *The Land of Gold* [Baltimore, 1855], p. 273.)

At dawn the Indians can be seen "prowling around in search of miserable offal for which they must compete with the dogs." (San Francisco *Bulletin,* Feb. 10, 1858.)

Indeed, the Indians who lived on the fringes of the settlements made a constant practice of collecting the viscera and other unwanted portions of slaughtered animals. On the whole, the evidence seems to indicate that in making the change from aboriginal to civilized diet, the natives suffered no material shortage in essential accessory factors.

LABOR

The preceding three environmental factors, homicide, disease, and diet, are those which determined in most direct and acute fashion the physical well-being and survival of the Indians as a race or biological entity. But with human beings, racial conflict and adjustment by no means end when the demands of pure physical survival have been met. In order for the final resolution of the competition to be successful, the group on the defensive must reconcile itself to the economic, social, and cultural changes wrought by the conquering order. It is to this group of relatively intangible factors that attention must now be directed.

Under modern civilized conditions the outstanding single problem confronting the individual, and by extension the group, is that of making a living. This naturally includes the entire range of phenomena embodied in the field of economics, a range so vast that it can scarcely be touched in a single brief survey. A good deal of reduction and simplification is therefore demanded. To this end the scope of discussion of these factors is narrowed to one primary aspect, labor. No clash between economic systems was involved, nor were any significant trade relationships or deep-seated financial considerations concerned. The Indian touched the white economic civilization only in the capacity of laborer. It has been pointed out in the matter of elementary food procurement that the native attempted several responses to the disturbance of the aboriginal environment before he met with more than transitory success. He was finally forced to adopt the white man's system of obtaining subsistence, that is, working for it.

To understand the background of the Indian labor problem in California one must go back to the colonial era, for the economic system established by the Ibero-Americans made a profound impression upon that of the later Anglo-Americans. It must first be remembered that the settlers from New Spain were few in number and that they had been trained by centuries of colonial experience to depend upon subject races for a labor supply. A further consideration of importance to the development of the California labor problem was that they simultaneously introduced three systems of labor.

The first may be termed the "communal" system. Its governing principle was that the labor contributed by the individual went into a common pool from the resources of which the individual received his support—food, shelter, clothing, and other necessities. The missions, which were operated entirely according to this system, were remarkably successful. In theory the component units, the natives, worked for their own benefit, since all products and all income were to accrue to them and ultimately they were to inherit jointly the capital structure which they had built up. In practice, the neophytes were reasonably well supported through the efforts of conscientious missionaries. However, the method carried with it one fatal defect. The Indians, converted direct from barbarism, were wholly unable to appreciate the complex theory involved and could not be persuaded voluntarily to donate immediate labor for remote benefits. Consequently, in order to set up a workable scheme, the church administrators were obliged to exercise a coercion which rapidly induced the development of a full-scale forced-labor system. Furthermore, most unfortunately, they also utilized labor as a punitive device for all sorts of delinquency. As a result, over a period of years, the mission neophytes came to confuse economically valuable labor with duress and punishment, an effect which further intensified Indian aversion to labor per se. This problem of mission labor has been discussed at length in another paper[61] and need not be mentioned further.

The second may be called the "peonage" system, developed by the ranchers and other large landowners. Here the motive of mutual benefit was completely absent. To be sure, large groups of workers might be aggregated in a single economic unit, but the fruits of their efforts, particularly as regards capital improvements, were almost completely absorbed by the overlord himself. The workers supposedly received wages, usually in the form of homes, food, and commodities; yet the size of the wage—and, indeed, its payment at all—was entirely in the hands of the employer. Moreover, in order to maintain the flow of undependable and transient Indian labor, coercion was usually resorted to. This might take the form of innocent persuasion, or economic pressure through control of food reserves, or out-and-out kidnaping and slavery.

These were the two primary forms of labor open to natives prior to American rule. There was, to be sure, in existence the third, or "free," system, but this was in effect only on a small scale, among the poorest ranchers and in domestic service. The free system, obviously, is that whereby the individual receives fair compensation and is at entire liberty to accept or relinquish employment in the open competitive market. It stands thus in direct contrast to the communal and peonage systems which prevailed prior to 1835.

When the missions fell, the communal system disappeared, but peonage and free labor remained open to the Indian. They had grown up alongside the mission system but in point of numbers and economic importance had been subordinate to it. Subsequent to 1835, however, first the peonage and then the free system came to predominate.

Very shortly following the establishment of the missions, a moderate number of civilian colonists were brought up from Mexico, and the towns of San José and Los Angeles were founded. These "pobladores" were expected to draw upon the native stock for labor. But most of the available Indians were converted and absorbed by the missions for their own purposes. This left only the gentile population to serve as a reservoir of man power. The seriousness of the situation being

---

[61] S. F. Cook, *The California Indian and White Civilization: I. The Indian versus the Spanish Mission.*

recognized, a rather elaborate code was formulated by the governors whereby, under certain restrictions, the colonists were permitted to employ unconverted Indians. In the beginning, the labor market thus created was free and competitive, since demand exceeded supply and inducements were necessary in order to get an adequate number of workmen. Moreover, at that stage the individual white men were on a more or less equal economic footing. Soon, however, two tendencies developed. The first was a growing reluctance on the part of wild natives to come in as day labor. This attitude was due to harsh treatment, lack of adequate remuneration, and fear of involuntary conversion. Insufficient voluntary labor meant that the civilian employers went into the field and compelled the natives to offer their services. After obtaining the workers desired the employers were obliged to detain them by force and to ensure competent performance by a system of punishment.[62] The early advantage held by the natives due to a labor shortage was by this means eliminated, and free employment reduced to a minimum.

The second tendency, which accompanied the universal introduction of force, was the unequal financial advancement of the civilians. Although during the first few years of settlement the colonists were more or less equal in status, later, by virtue of numerous factors—birth, intelligence, social standing, political influence, and the like—two classes emerged. One was the "poor white," the man who tilled a small acreage and owned a few head of stock. He was unable either to bring much physical pressure to bear on the Indian or to remunerate him satisfactorily. Consequently, particularly after 1835, there did exist a restricted free labor market among this group. The other class was that of the ranchero who received a really large grant of land from the government and who required a big staff to develop it. It was this class which not only furnished the color of the California social background, but developed the peonage type of labor system. For these men the use of force was easy, and the award of compensation pos-

---

[62] That a system of conscript labor was universally in vogue by 1790 is attested by the many official edicts and pronouncements, as well as by repeated protests on the part of missionaries. The abuses were recognized by all parties, but economic necessity as a rule took precedence over humanitarian considerations, in spite of formal decrees to the contrary.

sible. In short, the hacienda-peon society was introduced without much modification from Mexico to California and was impressed thoroughly upon the social thought of the state.

As a rule, the natives were brought to the ranches in large groups and maintained there in full-scale villages. Alternatively, they were left to inhabit their original rancherias and obliged to work whenever necessary. In return, they were kept supplied with food, clothing, and some useful utensils. The ranchero was the lord and master with full power of discipline. By 1840 there were some dozens of these feudal establishments, each maintaining from twenty to several hundred Indians—men, women and children—in all, perhaps from two to four thousand persons.

Now when, in the 'forties, foreigners began to drift in, they very characteristically fell into the ways of the country. Naturally aggressive, usually with a good business sense, they immediately began to imitate the ruling caste and to take out grants themselves. The very mention of such names as Sutter, Cordua, Savage, Yount, or Livermore calls to mind their vast estates and patriarchal way of life. More hundreds of Indians were gathered in, and it is highly probable that, had not the gold rush intervened, California would have become as thoroughly peonized as Old Mexico. It is indeed significant that well into the 'fifties nearly every wealthy American adopted without question the existing labor system. Bidwell and Redding, for instance, maintained serflike bands of Indian retainers until the Civil War period.

On the whole, the Indian adjusted himself with facility to the peonage system of labor. That he did so was demonstrated in two ways. In the first place, the retinue of servants and workers built up by certain rancheros was much larger than could have been held together by force alone. Consider for instance the examples furnished by M. G. Vallejo, Sutter, and Bidwell. The two former gathered around them, or controlled the activities of, entire tribes of natives. Their possessions included hundreds of square miles of territory. Their capital goods, primarily livestock, represented an enormous investment. In order to obtain and hold the necessary labor supply, they treated their peons well, kept them supplied with food and clothing, and paid them what cash they could. As a result their Indians were reasonably contented and labored faithfully. A vivid picture of the peonage system at its best has been drawn by Salvador Vallejo, and is worth quoting:[63]

... Many of the rich men of the country had from twenty to sixty Indian servants whom they dressed and fed ... our friendly Indians tilled our soil, pastured our cattle, sheared our sheep, cut our lumber, built our houses, paddled our boats, made tiles for our homes, ground our grain, slaughtered our cattle, dressed their hides for market, and made our unburnt bricks; while the Indian women made excellent servants, took good care of our children, made every one of our meals ... Those people we considered as members of our families. We loved them and they loved us; our intercourse was always pleasant ...

Now it is clear, and mission experience stands as testimony, that physical power alone could not have drawn together and held together a relatively harmonious aggregate of a few white people and a horde of Indians like that of the Vallejo estate. Had the natives been unhappy, discontented, and rebellious, their labor would have been worthless, and the entire project would have disintegrated. This is precisely what did happen to the Kelseys. These Americans, endeavoring to establish themselves south of Clear Lake, adopted the most brutal and repressive measures, starving, beating and murdering their Indian workmen. In the end, not only was their attempt an economic failure, but the exasperated natives finally resorted to murder. There can be little question therefore that, when administered in a humane and rational manner, the peonage system was reasonably satisfactory to the Indians. In the second place, we find that remnants of the Indians persisted in staying with certain wealthy rancheros long after it became impossible for the latter to exert any physical pressure whatever.[64]

[63] Salvador Vallejo, "Notas históricas sobre California," MS, 1874, Bancroft Library.

[64] The Marysville *Appeal* in an editorial on February 9, 1860, cited Major Bidwell of Chico, who maintained at least one hundred Indians on his ranch. They did good work, according to the editor, and were well cared for.

The Ukiah *Herald*, quoted by the Sacramento *Union*, Sept. 23, 1861, stated: "A good many Indians have heretofore been induced to retain their camps in squads of half a dozen to a dozen families on certain ranches so that the owners could have the benefit of their labor, making them such remuneration *as the Indians would accept*." (Italics mine.)

George Gibbs in 1851 (*Journal of the Expedition of Col. Redick M'Kee*, in Schoolcraft: *Archives of Aboriginal Knowledge*, 3:100) found numerous ranch Indians in the vicinity of Santa Rosa. He said: "These ranch Indians are ... perfectly under the control of the

After 1848, civil.law and public opinion completely put a stop to the practice of capturing masses of natives, of punishment by severe corporal methods, and of using military means to prevent escape. Nevertheless, for many years former Indian employees remained with the Vallejos. Sutter supported an Indian colony as long as he lived, and several other former "hacendados" maintained a semipeon establishment for one or two decades.[65] Obviously, if the particular natives under consideration had not become pretty well adjusted to their situation, they would simply have gone away.

For several reasons the peonage system, as administered by the more liberal landowners, seemed particularly well suited to the Indian.

1. In order to accomplish a successful transition from aboriginal society, no complex ideological adjustment was demanded, as it was for the communal system. The reward for effort was concrete and individual remuneration, presented in a form (commodities) readily comprehensible. No social consciousness was necessary, and no realization of the distinction between group and personal welfare.

2. No individual initiative was necessary, owing to the intrinsic compulsion of the system and to rigid supervision. Herein peonage differed from free labor, for with the latter the initiative and compulsion had to be generated within the person, rather than superposed from without. The Indian was thereby relieved of the arduous task of finding suitable employment in the first place and, subsequently, of acquiring sufficient skill to retain it. The often difficult process of learning new methods and handling strange tools was thus spared him because during his period of apprenticeship his material support was secure. His induction into the mysteries of the strange material civilization was made very easy for him, and strictly manual adaptation to new mechanical processes facilitated.

Spanish proprietors, who, in fact, have always treated them as peons and inculcated the idea of their obligation to labor."

In the 1870's Alexis Godey acquired a ranch in San Emigdio. He used all Indian labor. He gathered a group and formed a rancheria, which persisted as such for several years. (See F. F. Latta, "Alexis Godey in Kern County," in Kern Co. Hist. Soc., *Fifth Ann. Pub.* [1939], p. 38.)

[65] Major Bidwell retained his Indian rancheria till his death. Subsequently Mrs. Bidwell deeded in perpetuity to these Indians the rancheria lands on which they were living. Several families are still resident on this spot near Chico.

3. The type of work demanded was relatively congenial. All of it, for practical purposes, was outdoor manual labor. Although the California indigenes had never developed a complex agriculture, they had also never been far removed from the soil. They had depended upon wild plant products and were familiar with growth and seasons, drought and rainfall. The shift to simple agricultural procedures, such as ploughing, hoeing, and reaping, demanded no violent readjustment from the mechanical standpoint. Even more direct was the acquisition of knowledge concerning livestock. Here all testimony agrees that as a vaquero and stock tender the Indian displayed great natural aptitude. For the women, domestic service and household tasks were no more than an extension of the labor to which they had always been accustomed while in tribal relationship. The form was slightly altered, but the content was the same. In short, the peonage system almost automatically put the Indian at those tasks for which he was by nature and training best suited. Free labor, on the other hand, required him to explore a multitude of new avenues with which he was totally unfamiliar and to adopt many pursuits which he was at that time entirely unprepared to undertake. His ratio of actual success was, therefore, much higher as a peon than as a free agent.

4. The aboriginal living conditions were relatively unchanged. The custom of appropriating entire rancherias or of forming them where they did not already exist allowed the Indians to continue their home life undisturbed. Their dwellings remained the same, their families, and often their clans, remained united. Community life could proceed very much as it always had. They were not massed together as in the missions, nor were they split and scattered among an alien population.

5. The cultural, religious, ceremonial, and sexual life of the Indian was not disturbed to a material extent. As a rule, the white man who was lord of the domain permitted them to retain native custom, or at least he did not care if they did so, provided his own economic interests were unaffected. The Indian was thus relieved of the mental and emotional strain imposed by the necessity of suddenly acquiring a new religion and moral code, as in the missions. On the other hand, he did not have to force his ways into conformity with a host of new

customs and regulations as he was obliged to do when he lived in a town or a thickly settled farming district.

To summarize, it may be seen that peonage involved the least intense conflict of all three labor systems. The smallest degree of adjustment was necessary, and therefore the Indian found it the easiest road to economic adaptation.

The foregoing remarks apply to peonage almost in its ideal form. As previously pointed out, this ideal was most closely approached under most of the prominent California landowners who thoroughly understood the system and under the earlier, more enlightened foreigners. When the gold rush and Mexican War brought into California thousands of ordinary Anglo-Americans plus an enormous criminal element recruited from the scum of the earth, conditions changed greatly. Of primary importance was the disruption of the great landed estates and the disappearance of the pastoral economy which made them possible. A few survived for a while but, as the backbone of California society, the great estates vanished. The peonage system in its semi-ideal form likewise passed away, leaving essentially free labor as the only recourse for the native. However, the principle of forced labor, implicit in both the mission and pastoral labor systems, did not immediately die. It was absorbed and modified by the incoming Americans, perhaps subconsciously, and became manifested in certain phenomena of interest. These phenomena, although possibly not of vast quantitative importance, merit some consideration as showing how the Indian was the victim of the influence exerted by the Spanish on the American civilization.

The first manifestation was the typically Yankee attempt, through the California legislature, to legalize what amounted to the peonage system. The form of these statutes was derived from early American and English, not Iberian, sources. But the essence followed quite closely the tenor of Spanish and Mexican official decrees and public customs. There were three enactments of significance.[66] The first denied the right of Indians to testify in court, thereby shutting the door very effectively to any relief in the courts. The second decreed that

---

[66] The detailed process of lawmaking may be followed in the journals of the California legislature from 1850 to 1855. It does not appear worth while here to dissect this legislation from the legalistic standpoint.

any Indian, merely upon the word of a citizen, might be brought into court and declared a vagrant. Thereafter, he might be put up at auction and his services as a laborer sold to the highest bidder for a period not to exceed four months. No compensation, of course, was given, although the owner was expected to support the Indian. This act obviously made it possible for a native to be held not only as a peon, but as an actual slave, for any unemployed Indian could be proved a vagrant. The third statute was the so-called "indenture law," whereby any Indian adult or any child, with consent of the parents, could be legally bound over to a citizen for a long term of years. During this period his labor was available in return for subsistence.[67]

The extent of application of these laws is impossible to determine without a minute examination of all the court records prior to 1860. It is likely that their use was not very extensive among the general population. The contemporary press makes frequent mention of them but almost invariably in an unfavorable tone and for the purpose of pointing out abuses. Thus in 1861 the Humboldt *Times*[68] reported several cases of apprentices absconding from masters to whom they were indentured. The Marysville *Appeal* for March 22, 1861, complained that persons in Humboldt and Tehama counties were binding out Indians over age and under age. The Humboldt *Times*[69] stated that the former Indian agent V. E. Geiger got eighty natives apprenticed to him to work for him in the Washoe mines. "We hear of many others who are having them bound in numbers to suit." In the same year there was considerable scandal because certain men "recently connected with the Nome Lackee Reservation" had persuaded the county judge of Tehama County to indenture to them "all the most valuable Indians on the Reservation."[70] In some instances various persons even claimed chattel rights over these natives. A particularly offensive case occurred in Ukiah in 1865.[71] A man in that town hired an Indian to do a job. The latter met one Bob Hildreth, who claimed him as his property. When the Indian said he was work-

---

[67] The testimony law was subsequently repealed. The indenture law may still be in force. In a very cursory examination I have found no evidence of its repeal.

[68] Quoted by the Marysville *Appeal*, November 17, 1861.

[69] Quoted by San Francisco *Bulletin*, March 2, 1861.

[70] Marysville *Appeal*, January 4, 1861; Sacramento *Union*, February 4, 1861.

[71] Sacramento *Union*, August 19, 1865, correspondence from Ukiah.

ing for another man, Hildreth tied him to his horse and dragged him to death. Now Hildreth's claim was based upon the fact that he had bought the property of the late notorious Captain Jarboe from the widow. She stated she had set Jarboe's Indians free subsequent to his death. But Hildreth claimed they were part of the estate, and hence inalienable *under the apprentice law*.

It is probable that these cases were exceptions sufficiently flagrant to interest the newspapers. But the fact that the exceptions were so few suggests the probability that the practice of wholesale indenturing was not very widespread in the aggregate but was limited to a relatively few wealthier persons. Nevertheless, the effect on the Indians must have been injurious, for even barring the abuses the uncertainty and the injustice of the entire system must have exerted a marked moral effect.

More serious and more vicious in American hands was the second direct carry-over from colonial custom. This was the habit of out-and-out kidnaping of individuals for subsequent sale. For many years prior to American occupation it had been the habit of the landed proprietors to make "raids" upon unconverted tribes and villages in order to "capture" Indians. The latter were then brought to the ranches and established as peons. This practice was continued by the rancheros during the troubled period between 1845 and 1850, and even subsequently. The chief sufferers at this time appear to have been the group of tribes surrounding Clear Lake. Thus Revere reported that in 1846 the Indians on the southeast shore assumed that his party was hostile because they had been so frequently raided by Californians who kidnaped persons of all ages.[72] L. L. Palmer states that the Sanel and Anderson valleys were heavily raided for transient labor.

For instance the potato digging season was a time when help was most needed, and, as most of the local Indians were gone, assistance had to be had from some source, so a raid would be made on the upper valley tribes.[73]

It should be noted here that the problem of transient or migratory agricultural labor had already arisen and was being solved by methods inimical to the interests of the workers. The activities of the infamous

[72] J. W. Revere, *op. cit.*, pp. 88, 114.
[73] *History of Mendocino County* (San Francisco, 1880), p. 168.

Kelsey brothers have already been mentioned. The Kelseys' most sensational performance was the kidnaping of several score Clear Lake Indians, their transportation to Red Bluff to work in mines, and their desertion when the mining venture failed.[74] In 1855 Senator Sebastian read to the California legislature a letter from General E. F. Beale, written in 1852.[75] The general stated that numerous Indians were to be found at Rancho San Pablo in Contra Costa County who had been stolen from Clear Lake by Raymond Briones and Ramon Mesa. These persons "have for some time made a business of catching Indians and of disposing of them in various ways." This last statement is significant for it marks the transition from the earlier to the later system. The old Californian and to some extent early American ranchers captured Indian labor for their own use. The American variant which developed in the early 'fifties was to catch or kidnap the natives for sale. In other words, the boundary was at last crossed from technical peonage to actual slavery.

The extent of this Indian slave traffic, morally not one bit less offensive than the Negro slave trade, may have been greater than is now realized. It is therefore worth while to put certain evidence on review.

On October 2, 1854, the *Alta California* published an article in which it was stated:

Abducting Indian children has become quite a common practice. Nearly all the children belonging to some of the Indian tribes in the northern part of the state have been stolen. They are taken to the southern part of the state and there sold.

In the same year a Mexican, Marcus Vaca, was arrested in Sacramento on the charge of kidnaping Indian children for disposal in that town.[76] The case was dismissed because Vaca pleaded that he had no intention of selling the children. On May 23, 1857, the Butte *Record* noted the presence in Chico of a Mexican "who has been in the habit of stealing Indian children and selling them to Mexican rancheros in Southern

---

[74] There are numerous conflicting accounts of this episode, but the main outlines are reasonably clear. Probably between seventy-five and a hundred natives were taken to the valley, and probably not more than ten returned. The whole expedition was engineered with a brutality worthy of the *conquistadores* at their worst.

[75] In *Rept. Commr. Indian Affairs*, 1856.

[76] Sacramento *Union*, September 13 and 14, 1854.

California." The following year the San Francisco *Bulletin*[77] in an editorial claimed that the practice of enslaving Indian children was far from having stopped for there are "not a few of these servants in San Francisco today." Not long afterward W. H. Brewer averred:[78]

It has been for years a regular business to steal Indian children and bring them down to the civilized parts of the state, even to San Francisco, and sell them—not as slaves but as servants to be kept as long as possible. Mendocino County has been the scene of many of these stealings ...

In 1860 the Nevada *National*[79] stated that a band of whites had kidnaped a number of Washoe children on the Truckee and were bringing them into California. The Petaluma *Journal*[80] said:

The reason why the Indians on Eel River persist in killing the stock of the settlers is that children belonging to the Indians have been stolen and sold to the whites in the settlements below.

An editorial in the Marysville *Appeal* for December 6, 1861, contained the following full discussion of the problem:

But it is from these mountain tribes that white settlers draw their supplies of kidnapped children, educated as servants, and women for purposes of labor and of lust. ... It is notorious that there are parties in the northern counties of this state, whose sole occupation has been to steal young children and squaws from the poor Diggers, who inhabit the mountains, and dispose of them at handsome prices to the settlers, who, being in the majority of cases unmarried but at housekeeping, willingly pay fifty or sixty dollars for a young Digger to cook and wait upon them, or a hundred dollars for a likely young girl. Recent developments in this vicinity are sufficient proof of this. ...

Further enlightenment as to methods comes from Agent W. P. Dole in the same year:[81]

In the frontier portions of Humboldt and Mendocino Counties a band of desperate men have carried on a system of kidnapping for two years past. Indian children were seized and carried into the lower counties and sold into virtual slavery. These crimes against humanity so excited the

[77] January 2, 1858.

[78] *Up and Down California* (written about 1863; published in New Haven, 1930), p. 493.

[79] Quoted by Marysville *Appeal*, August 4, 1860.

[80] Quoted by Sacramento *Union*, March 7, 1861.

[81] Yuba City, July 15, 1861, *Rept. Commr. Indian Affairs*, 1861, p. 149.

Indians that they began to retaliate by killing the cattle of the whites. At once an order was issued to chastise the guilty. Under this indefinite order a company of United States troops, attended by a considerable volunteer force, has been pursuing the poor creatures from one retreat to another. The kidnappers follow at the heels of the soldiers to seize the children, when their parents are murdered, and sell them to the best advantage.

The Sacramento *Union*[82] made even more serious charges stating that there was a class of "pestilent" whites who systematically killed adults to get the children to sell. The latter brought from thirty to two hundred dollars and might be seen in every fourth white man's house. As late as 1867 L. V. Bogy, agent for Round Valley, found:

It was not uncommon for residents in want of a servant to buy, of a degraded class of mountaineers, known as "squaw men," children of tender years, who must have been stolen from their parents by these reckless outlaws.[83]

A few of these crimes reached the courts. What happened then exposes only too clearly the general attitude of white society. Three cases may be mentioned as examples.[84]

On October 16, 1861, two Marysville citizens found three men, Johnson, Wood, and Freak, with nine Indian children. They tried to sell the children (three to four years of age) for $50 apiece. Four had already been sold at prices ranging from $55 to $80. The citizens reported to the Indian Agent, who arrested the men and had them lodged in the Yuba County jail at Marysville (there being no jail in Sutter County, across the river). On the eighteenth, J. A. McQuaid, their counsel, applied for a discharge under *habeas corpus*. Judge Bliss then held that they were not legally held in Yuba County, since there was no evidence that there was any charge against the men. The sheriff of Sutter County laid claim to them, but McQuaid said the sheriff had no authority to make an arrest in Yuba County. They were again arrested in Yuba County, but the next day McQuaid argued for a discharge on the ground "that the papers were incomplete and informal and that the statute of 1850 under which they had been arrested was

[82] Editorial, July 19, 1862.
[83] *Rept. Commr. Indian Affairs*, 1867, p. 117.
[84] San Francisco *Bulletin*, October 21, 1861; Sacramento *Union*, October 18, 19, 1861; Marysville *Appeal*, October 17, 18, 19, 24, 1861.

repealed by the statute of 1860." Finally Judge Bliss held the men in $500 bail to appear before a magistrate in Humboldt County, where the kidnaping had actually occurred. The three then promptly left town, jumped bail, and were never heard of officially again. Meanwhile the nine little waifs were "provided with comfortable homes, most of them in Marysville."

On March 27, 1861, it was reported that settlers in Long Valley, Mendocino County, had been kidnaping children.[85] This was admitted by one G. H. Woodman, who claimed it was done with consent of the parents. The next year there was a warrant out for Woodman's arrest.[86] He had been seen in Ukiah with twenty children. This time he evidently escaped, but the following spring he was actually taken into custody for having kidnaped thirteen children.[87] However, when he came up for trial he was acquitted.

In 1864 two men named John were arrested in Colusa County for kidnaping two Indian children from Long Valley, Mendocino County.[88] They were taken to Ukiah and brought before a magistrate, who immediately proceeded to discharge them.

From these three acquittals and from the total lack of any convictions it is clear that kidnaping of the natives was very lightly regarded by the American settlers. Such ethical numbness can be explained only by the general dislike of Indians, by the feeling that perhaps Indian children were better off in white homes than with their wild parents, and by a purely selfish desire to get cheap labor.

Aside from the cases just cited we have one bit of concrete data relating to the numbers concerned. The *Alta California* of October 6, 1862, recorded a statement by one August Hess that one hundred Indian children had been taken through Lake County that summer. In the light of other evidence this figure does not seem excessive. Now if one hundred went through Lake County, another hundred certainly went down the Sacramento Valley and another fifty were taken along the coast. This would indicate something like two hundred fifty kidnapings in 1862. The practice began about 1852 and continued at least

[85] Napa *Reporter*, quoted by San Francisco *Bulletin*.
[86] Marysville *Appeal*, April 3, 1862.
[87] Sacramento *Union*, March 13 and 26, 1863.
[88] Marysville *Appeal*, December 17, 1864.

till 1867. During these fifteen years, then, perhaps between three and four thousand children were stolen. This estimate would not include squaws taken for concubinage or adults for field labor. The northern tribes must have suffered really heavy losses.

The effect on the Indians of this peculiarly Yankee kidnaping industry was exasperating to the highest degree, as is suggested by some of the contemporary reports.[89] It was not only an irritant which drove some of them to physical and violent retaliation, but it intensified and prolonged their aversion to the type of labor in which the kidnaped persons were employed. To that extent, therefore, whatever the reaction may have been, the Indian was retarded in his adoption of white labor customs.

It will be observed, in the outline given above, how the scope of physical compulsion changed with the coming of the Americans. Quite clearly, in the beginning the latter merely took over and utilized the existing practice of mass raids for farm labor. But in the early 'fifties this procedure altered to one of individual kidnaping, primarily of children for domestic and farm service—almost a bootlegging enterprise. The reason doubtless lies in the fact that the large-scale demand for Indian adult labor almost entirely ceased. This in turn was caused, first, by the replacement of the great cattle ranches by a vast number of small subsistence farms, on which Indian labor could not profitably be employed. Second, the labor market in the 'fifties was glutted by thousands of white ex-miners and particularly by Chinese. The demand for Indian labor, with the exception of domestic servants, thus disappeared entirely, and with it the profit of the slave trade.

One is tempted from this point to follow through the persistence of the forced-labor idea in subsequent years. It would be possible to show how the cheap labor market passed from the Indian to the Chinese and how the same rationale of peonage and compulsion was applied to the latter. One might then pass on to the new groups, each of which gradually replaced the other—the Italians of the 'eighties, the Mexicans and Filipinos of the early nineteenth century, down to the "Okies"

---

[89] One need only refer to the kidnapings of the past decade to appreciate the feeling of modern Californians with respect to this crime when perpetrated on themselves. In view of the strong current public opinion it is even more difficult to understand the callousness of the early immigrants toward wholesale stealing of native children.

of our own times. Simultaneously, one could trace the rise of great agricultural interests, dependent upon masses of unskilled, transient workers, which utilized these groups one after another. Finally, there could be delineated the thread of peonage or force in some aspect as applied by the landowners to all these systems. The influence of Iberian on Anglo-American civilization, as derived from primitive Spanish-Indian labor relations, could be demonstrated by such a survey.

A combination of circumstances—disintegration of large feudal estates, relative decline of the stock industry, reduction of native population, influx of new subservient races, and perhaps a more enlightened public opinion—all combined to destroy the preëminence of the peonage system and to force the Indian into free labor. His success or failure in this field must now be considered.

Since this essay is concerned primarily with the adaptation of the Indians to the conditions imposed by the white race, it is necessary to inquire briefly into the kind of employment utilized, the extent of such employment, and the difficulties encountered by the natives in taking advantage of their opportunities. The kind of work engaged in by Indians has always been determined, apart from sheer number of jobs available, by their capacity to do the work and by the opinion of white employers as to their capacity. In the early period, and indeed until recently, the opinion has been universally held that the native was fitted only for manual tasks and personal or domestic service. Such a feeling has been quite natural, since the transition from primitive economy to the more complex types of civilized labor was too great for the Indian race to encompass immediately. Nevertheless, quite early the Indians showed their ability to handle a great diversity of the less intellectual pursuits. In agriculture they quickly became familiar with most of the processes known to and employed by the whites. They did any kind of farm or ranch work, including planting, cultivating, and harvesting any crop. As stock tenders and vaqueros they were admittedly unexcelled. In the northern counties they were widely used as sheep shearers. As miners, in the 'fifties, they did very well, since they appeared able to assimilate readily the entire technique of both prospecting and panning gold. Freighters and expressmen found them very valuable as muleteers and packers, as well as guides in more difficult country. They found jobs on the river packets as deckhands and longshoremen. In short, Indians fully penetrated that segment of the labor field which included unskilled work out-of-doors. In addition, the natives frequently capitalized their knowledge of primitive crafts. Large quantities of fur-bearing animals were caught and the pelts sold by them, and they sold fish, game, and wild crops as well. To a small extent, for the demand was slight, they manufactured basketry and native drygoods. Finally, the women were widely employed in domestic service. It may thus be perceived that the field into which the Indians might fit was of considerable scope and was undoubtedly adequate to absorb all the labor which they were in a position to supply.

The degree to which these opportunities were utilized is difficult to determine. A more extensive investigation than is here possible might reveal the exact extent to which Indian labor was responsible for the progress accomplished between 1850 and 1870. However, a few facts may be cited to serve as a first approximation. With respect to general farm labor the majority opinion seemed to be that the Indians were quite widely employed. The following statements are representative:

Most of the able-bodied men from Mendocino Reservation worked for farmers.[90]

The whites would employ only one-fifth the Indians at Fresno Indian Farm, except at harvest time.[91]

In Mendocino County the men worked occasionally for farmers.[92]

The farmers needed them for labor and they worked well.[93]

In 1862 a "large number" of Clear Lake Indians came to the Napa Valley to harvest. The exodus to the northern mines threatened a scarcity of hands "but these Indians are helping to fill the gap." In 1865 it was noted that the "usual" number of Indians from Lake County were again in Napa.[94]

In Mendocino County the settlers employed "many" local Indians.[95]

---

[90] H. L. Ford, *Rept. Commr. Indian Affairs*, 1856.
[91] M. B. Lewis, *ibid*.
[92] T. J. Henley, *ibid*.
[93] San Francisco *Bulletin*, Oct. 21, 1861.
[94] San Francisco *Bulletin*, July 7, 1862; Sacramento *Union*, July 17, 1865.
[95] D. W. Cooley, *Rept. Commr. Indian Affairs*, 1806.

At Little Lake and Walker's Valley, Mendocino County, three to four hundred local Indians were engaged as harvesters.[96]

"Seeding and harvesting the crops are the periods of the year at which a large amount of Indian labor is required."[97]

"They already do a large share of the work that is done for the people of this vicinity."[98]

With regard to sheep shearing the following items may be added:

"The Indians can and do . . . render efficient service to the citizens of the vicinity [Tule River] as herders and shearers of sheep . . ."[99]

"The Indians of this vicinity [Round Valley] . . . form the 'laboring class' of that part of California. They are relied on by the citizens in the vicinity . . . especially in shearing sheep, in which, on account of their skill and carefulness they are decidedly preferred to white laborers and are sent for from far and near. They shear as many as forty thousand sheep semi-annually at five and six cents per head."[100]

"Sheap shearing in this part of the country [Tule River] is done almost exclusively by Indians and lasts nearly six weeks both in the spring and fall. It is not difficult for a good shearer to earn $100 at each shearing."[101]

It is possible from these statements—principally by reservation agents—to get an idea of the wage scale under which the Indians labored. The majority of the reports place the daily wage at from fifty cents to two dollars, depending on the skill required and the shortage or excess of workers. If we assume one dollar a day as a fair average, we find that this amount conforms quite closely to the usual standard of the time for unskilled labor. Certainly it is no less than that received by other racial groups for the same work and, allowing for differences in standard of living, is fully equivalent to that paid today.

In the field of mining, particularly during the first two or three years after the discovery of gold, the Indians participated to a very great extent. The natives worked the placers both as hired help and as independent operators. Frequently large groups of Indians were employed

---

[96] L. V. Bogy, *ibid.*, 1867.

[97] N. G. Taylor, referring to Tule River, *ibid.*, 1868.

[98] H. B. Sheldon, *ibid.*, 1884.

[99] E. P. Smith, *ibid.*, 1875.

[100] *Rept. Commr. Indian Affairs*, 1875. At five cents per head the total income would have been $2,000.

[101] C. G. Belknap, *ibid.*, 1886.

by white men, sometimes with the use of force, sometimes as a free venture. Many of these persons broke away and worked for themselves, or even hired others to work for them. The local foothill tribes operated as a rule independently, but often found employment with white miners. The distinction between hired laborers and independent miners was, therefore, so confused and so fluctuating that any attempt to segregate the natives into two classes appears both futile and unnecessary.

To convey some idea of the scope of Indian mining and also to bring out certain subsidiary points it appears desirable again to resort to the use of concrete statements and examples, although no exhaustive recapitulation is feasible.

Lieutenant J. W. Revere[102] says that Colonel Mason reported that Suñol and Company on Weber's Creek, American River, employed 30 Indians. Daly and McCoon on the same creek employed 100. Sinclair on the North Fork of the American employed 50 for five weeks. At that time (August, 1848) upwards of 4,000 men were working in the gold district (primarily the American River watershed) "of whom more than one half were Indians."

In August, 1848, C. S. Lyman says that on the Stanislaus there were "not many digging yet besides Indians."[103]

Earl Ramey deposes as follows: "The first miners on the Yuba in 1848, much more than is usually understood, depended upon the natives to do the actual extraction.... The natives at first were content to work by the day for negligible wages, but when they learned more about the real value of gold they began to mine it independently." He cites the case of one Sicard who married an Indian girl and received $75,000 in gold from members of the tribe.[104]

James Clyman asserted that in December, 1848, there were 2,000 white men, "and more than double that number of Indians" working gold at the rate of two ounces a day.[105]

C. W. Harlan mentions a certain trader who sold $1,200 worth of serapes to the Indians in exchange for their gold.[106]

---

[102] *Op. cit.,* pp. 230–240, quoting a letter from Col. R. B. Mason to the adjutant general in Washington, Aug. 17, 1848.

[103] *Around the Horn,* F. J. Teggart, ed. (New Haven, 1924).

[104] "The Beginnings of Marysville," Calif. Hist. Soc., *Quarterly* (1935), 14:211.

[105] In the James Clyman Docs., edited by Charles L. Camp, Calif. Hist. Soc., *Quarterly* (1927), 6:62.

[106] C. W. Harlan, *California, '46 to '48* (1888), p. 131.

According to L. L. Palmer[107] the Kelsey brothers, prior to their famous trip to Red Bluff, had taken out an expedition of 26 Indians, who had panned a great deal of gold in the summer of 1848. It was in an attempt to better this record that they took 100 Indians to starve at Red Bluff.

In 1848 Weber of Stockton trained 25 Siakumne Indians and sent them prospecting on the Tuolumne and Stanislaus.[108] When they found gold, he organized a mining company with "a small army" of Indians for laborers.

R. G. McClellan[109] stated that in 1848 there were "several thousand" Indians working as miners.

J. Q. Thornton in a letter to the *Journal of Commerce,* August 29, 1849, cited the case of seven white men on the Feather River who worked 44 days.[110] They employed on an average 50 Indians and panned a total of 275 pounds of gold. Another man is mentioned who had 60 Indians working for him.

Major James D. Savage, working the Big Oak Flat in 1849 hired every Indian who would work for him, a total which was said to reach between two and three hundred.[111]

R. G. McClellan (*op. cit.,* p. 143) mentions a trader who sold $50,000 worth of goods to Indians in exchange for gold in 1849.

Murphy of Murphy's Camp in 1850 got "many thousands" worth of dust from a "tribe" of Indians whom he forced to work for him.[112]

The Sacramento *Union* for June 24, 1851, contains an account of the tremendous business done at Sacramento in beads. The money was obtained by Indians digging gold on the Cosumnes.

Even allowing considerable leeway for exaggeration and misstatement, it is clear that in 1848 and 1849 the natives, either under direction or independently, worked in vast numbers and took thousands, perhaps millions, in gold from the streams. During these two years practically the entire native population of the Sierra foothills from the Feather to the Merced must have pursued the occupation of gold mining at least sporadically. To be sure, they derived little permanent

---

[107] *History of Napa and Lake Counties* (San Francisco, 1881), p. 59.
[108] Lewis Publishing Co., *An Illustrated History of San Joaquin County* (Chicago, 1890), p. 61.
[109] *The Golden State* (1876), p. 143.
[110] Quoted in J. Q. Thornton, *Oregon and California in 1848* (New York, 1849), 2:302–303.
[111] P. E. Vandor, *History of Fresno County* (Los Angeles, 1919), p. 77.
[112] Heckendorn and Wilson, *Directory of Tuolumne County* (Columbia, 1856), p. 96.

economic gain for they were universally robbed of their winnings, but the phenomenon, brief as it was, demonstrates that the natives could labor and did labor when the opportunity arose.

Their prosperity was short-lived. Practically no mention is made of them as miners after 1851. In fact, the decline of the industry was noted by contemporaries. Thus Dr. G. H. Hoerchner of Calaveras County wrote on June 22, 1856:[113]

Their condition at the present time is rather bad; from 1849 to the spring of 1854 their mode of living and condition were, all in all, tolerably comfortable; they then had facilities for digging gold and were doing remarkably well ... but since that time they are in a rather poor condition, as their gold mining is almost gone, surface diggings being scarce.

The analysis given by Dr. Hoerchner is probably correct. In the mid-'fifties all the easily accessible stream-bed gold had been exhausted. The white miners were free to move elsewhere. The local Indians were forced to remain in the region without benefit of gold.

It is noteworthy, in passing, that there is little record of mining operations by the natives on the Trinity and Klamath. There must have been some activity of the sort, but it seems to have been conducted on an insignificant scale. Perhaps the reason lies in the greater degree of hostility existing between the white miners and the Indians in the north than in the Sierra foothills.

On the whole, the Indian race gave evidence of considerable adaptability with respect to mining. Within a very short time they had assimilated not only the idea of the value of gold, but also the methods of obtaining it, and were able to make wide use of the new knowledge. From the standpoint of material culture it is of interest to note that the aboriginal implements and tools already available served the natives in this contingency. Several observers remarked upon the use of horn scrapers and shovels and crowbars of native manufacture. The earlier Indian miners used wicker baskets exclusively for panning, and not for some years did they adopt the tin or iron pan of the whites. The fact that their own existing industry supplied all the essential machinery for getting gold may have contributed to the ease with which they took up the pursuit.

---

[113] Quoted by T. J. Henley, *Rept. Commr. Indian Affairs*, 1856.

In the realm of business interprise we find that the Indian who could take advantage of the opportunities of the day was exceedingly rare. There were a few persons who made a living by selling wild products, such as fur or game.[114] Probably quite a number of the more intelligent and industrious natives acquired title to or squatted on small plots of land where they made a living of sorts by subsistence farming and gardening.[115] On the other hand, there were few if any individuals who engaged in an enterprise entailing the ownership of capital. In addition to cutthroat competition the native labored under the disadvantage of a lack of the requisite knowledge and experience to embark upon any such venture.

To recapitulate, under the free labor system, in the earlier years of racial contact, the Indian was limited to unskilled employment. With the exception of the brief gold-mining interlude this meant that he was forced into the field of agriculture, both as a permanent and tran-

---

[114] In 1858 (San Francisco *Bulletin*, Feb. 10, 1858) some Indians brought a boatload of furs to Stockton and soon sold them. Later that year (*ibid.*, May 27, 1858) certain strange tribesmen sold buckskins from door to door in Stockton. In 1861 a party brought two canoeloads of beaverskins to Sacramento and sold sixty pelts (Sacramento *Union*, April 20, 1861). This journal for July 12, 1853, mentions twelve natives, who were arrested and brought into court for violating the ordinance on selling fish. The judge discharged them. On several occasions the Indians are noted as selling wild berries of various kinds. There may have been more of this small-scale backdoor peddling than ever received attention in the press. Even so, it can hardly have amounted to much in the aggregate.

[115] Most of the examples of this type of endeavor which I have found have been from the period subsequent to the gold rush. It was not until the turbulent mining days had given way to more stable times that an Indian could settle down peacefully among white neighbors. The San Andreas *Independent* (quoted by San Francisco *Bulletin*, Sept. 1, 1860) commented on two families who were cultivating four acres and doing well. There was a rancheria on the Mokelumne (San Francisco *Bulletin*, October 21, 1861) where fifty Indians "purchased" eighty acres whereby they supported themselves. The Marysville *Appeal*, for Nov. 18, 1865, carried an obituary of Chief Olas of the "Olas" tribe near Nicolaus. He was described as "the proprietor of a small vineyard and orchard which he cultivated with industry and skill." These instances were, however, the exceptions which emphasize the rule.

In connection with independent industry on the part of the wholly uncivilized natives a curious item may be mentioned which is contained in the Los Angeles County Archives (I:410). This is a decree by the prefect of Los Angeles in 1841 granting a petition by certain gentile chiefs of Castac to be allotted horses "as property" and to "establish crops" in the Tejon. The decree states that these chiefs are reliable and the prefect considers it an unusual but valuable experiment, "y así pueden civilizarse aunque gentiles a ser utiles a la sociedad." Perhaps if the Anglo-Americans of 1860 had possessed the breadth of understanding of some Ibero-Americans of 1840, the problem of existence for the natives would have been easier.

sient laborer. In the physical, material sense, his adaptation to the new economic order may be regarded as adequate, even if not brilliant. At least he mastered enough of the new methods to permit him an existence in white society. That he did not exploit this advantage to its fullest and that he did not become suitable for employment in the skilled trades, professions, and business is referable to a failure to carry out an intellectual adaptation comparable to the physical response. This failure in turn may be traced to certain features of the aboriginal cultural background and to certain traits of Indian psychology.

1. It must be remembered that the majority of the nonmission Indians were obliged to make their economic transition from the aboriginal to the civilized with extraordinary rapidity. Varying with the locality, the period they were given in which to effect a complete reorientation was not more than ten years and sometimes less than one year. In such a brief interval no primitive race can be expected to achieve perfect success. Indeed, had it not been for the buffers provided by the peonage labor system and for the small aid afforded by the Indian Service, the Indians' failure would have been worse than it actually was.

The first, and possibly the basic obstacle to a quick adaptation was psychosocial: the inability to grasp the necessity, under the white man's system, of steady, consistent labor coupled with sufficient foresight to perceive the need for saving and accumulation of assets. This defect was immediately due to mental habit, which in turn was derived originally from the primitive social structure.

As has been frequently pointed out by students, the Indian in the wild state worked hard. But he worked only at intervals, those intervals being determined by the seasons of the year and the cyclical appearance of natural food crops, both plant and animal. Under the capitalistic system as the Indian met it, the average individual was forced to labor continuously for a daily stipend or was obliged in times of plenty to accumulate sufficient goods to provide a period of idleness. The Indian fresh from the native background failed to comprehend this inherent difference between the two economic orders. Partly through the power of long custom and training, partly through lack of instruction he tended to carry over into white society the methods which had served him in his own community. Hence is derived much of the comment concerning the so-called "fickleness" of the native disposition. Thus De Lambertie might remark:[116] "... étant peu laborieux, ils ne travaillent guère qu'au fur et à mesure de leurs besoins," and one reservation agent says, "They take no thought about provision for the future ... the great majority of them are idle, listless, careless and improvident."[117]

2. A closely related characteristic derived from prehistoric times was the tendency to spend wages for any commodity which appealed to the fancy, irrespective of its ultimate social worth. It would be pointless to quote from the scores of comments and lamentations which have come down to us describing how the natives poured out gold for articles of clothing, trinkets, decorations, and liquor. Whenever primitive man has encountered European civilization, this has occurred, and the California Indian thus stands merely as another illustration of a universal human trait.

Looking at the matter a little more closely, one perceives without difficulty that the entire phenomenon, as exemplified by the Indians, is derived from a divergent system of values. Here is a series of material items, arranged in a row: bright cloth, beads, a gun, a bottle of whiskey, a sack of flour, a pair of trousers, a banking account. An experienced white man knows which of these will be the most valuable to him now and in the long run. The raw native knows which are the most valuable to him now, but he has no concept of the long run. Each accordingly chooses; each derives satisfaction from his choice; each thinks the other is a fool. Given the millenium and rigid racial equality in all respects, each turns out to be right. But in the situation we are considering no millenium was in prospect, and the white man controlled the Indian. Consequently the latter, following the tastes and desires and artistic values of his forefathers, turns out to be wrong after all. For it is the white man's standards of value which are imposed upon the Indian.

Particularly in the realm of property and exchange medium the Indian was deficient. Take, for example, gold. In 1849, let us say, an

---

[116] *Voyage Pittoresque en Californie* (Paris, 1853), p. 271.
[117] E. P. Smith, *Rept. Commr. Indian Affairs*, 1875.

ounce of gold was worth x dollars. Therefore at prevailing prices an ounce would buy t pounds of flour. Just what did the Indian have to assimilate by way of new ideas in order to consummate this simple transaction? (1) He had to learn the meaning of "ounce" and "pound." This included familiarity with weights and measures of which he was totally ignorant. (2) He had to discover the meaning of "dollar," an intangible concept with which he had never had the slightest acquaintance. (3) He had to transmute weight of gold into weight of flour by arithmetic, using a yardstick the significance of which he could not comprehend. The mental processes involved, which seem to us childish in their simplicity, had to be developed *de novo* by the Indian, under the most adverse conditions. As a result, he was forced to a method of trial and error which appeared to spectators either comic or tragic, according to their emotions. During the trial-and-error stage he was, of course, universally and beautifully cheated out of most of his earnings.

In essence, the Indian applied his own primitive standard of intrinsic value to material objects and at the same time was completely incapable of comprehending the theoretical principles underlying the simplest civilized economy. His reaction was absolutely in accordance with expectation. No primitive mind can make the transition in a moment. That the Indian did in so short a time achieve any measure of success is testimony to his innate intelligence.

3. Another difficulty encountered by the Indian which demanded intelligence for its solution pertained to the learning of new mechanical processes. His facility in acquiring the relatively easy technique of gold panning has already been mentioned. This alone stamps him as a person not without normal dexterity and mental agility, despite the simplicity of the process. Moreover, we have the testimony of farmers and reservation agents (the latter perhaps of doubtful value) that the natives, under favorable conditions, were able to operate agricultural machinery. Such procedures as pertained to the care of animals were also picked up with little effort. There seems no intrinsic reason, therefore, to hold that the Indian was constitutionally incapable of entering the skilled trades. (Indeed, more modern experience has utterly disproved any such theory.) Why, then, was he so

rigidly confined to unskilled lines of effort? I believe the answer lies
not in lack of ability on the part of the Indian, but in the refusal of
white society to permit him to develop along this line. Only in the
missions was any attempt made to provide an opportunity. Since
those institutions, both because of social policy and because of entire
absence of white labor, were dependent upon the Indians for all work
of every kind, an intensive effort was made to train them as carpenters,
tailors, shoemakers, metal workers, and the like. The opinion of the
church fathers was that the experiment was definitely successful. The
natives could be taught rather complex processes with relative ease.
American civil society, however, was adequately supplied with white
workmen of this type and hence felt no need for encouraging the
native. Moreover, racial prejudice and contempt on the part of the
whites for all things aboriginal prevented the Indian from learning
a trade in the first place, not to speak of practicing it after his apprenticeship. Any adaptation which might have been possible was thus
blocked at the start.[118]

4. Written and oral expression by all classes of white society, from
clergy and educators to the riffraff of the waterfront, has always been
replete with accusations against the innate moral and mental character of the Indian, in so far as it pertains to his habits of work. We
find most often repeated the words "laziness" and "unreliability." If
these charges are well founded, they constitute a very serious indict-
ment of the Indian and point to a constitutional flaw in his nature
which would predestine to failure any effective adjustment to civilized
economy. Such a problem perhaps admits of no definitive solution.
The present writer, however, holds an opinion in the negative, based
upon the thesis that the manifestations of Indian behavior which impressed the early white men so forcibly arose not from genetic traits,

---

[118] A very characteristic expression of opinion is that of William Kelly (*An Excursion
to California* [London, 1851], p. 189) who compares the Indian with the Negro much
to the disadvantage of the former. He considers the Indian to be incapable of "acquiring
any art or handicraft that involves the slightest exercise of mind and judgment." This
type of superficial evaluation was universal at the time, particularly in California, where
the indigenes were regarded as the lowest sort of two-legged animals in existence. Unfortunately, this view was inculcated by those who should have known better in the
minds of the mass of white settlers. Under such conditions, any effort to allow the natives
scope for development in the trades and professions was, and has been since, stifled by
public opinion.

but from the interaction of primitive tradition and American social compulsions. The Indian has been the victim of a clash between two social philosophies, his own and that of the Yankee. This clash occurs at two focal points: the abstract concept of work and the concrete method of work.

The aboriginal philosophy envisaged labor of all kinds as merely a means to an end, the end being, first, physical existence, and second, as comfortable and calm an existence as possible. Since manual labor—the only kind the Indian knew—involved in itself a certain degree of effort and discomfort, it was not cultivated for its own sake. Thus a feeling of the futility of exertion per se was ingrained in the native character through generations of instruction and practice. On the other hand, the dominant, invading civilization was represented by a pioneer element which had always been obliged to work hard and in which the old Puritan fetish of work for work's sake had been intensified through two centuries of stern necessity. "The Devil finds some mischief still for idle hands to do" was a proverb which carried almost the power of a religious creed. Coupled with this sentiment was an underlying intolerance of peoples and races which adopted any other point of view. The freely exhibited tendency of the Indian, derived from his forefathers, to do nothing at all unless some immediate need kept him busy appeared to these people positively immoral. The conflict on the economic plane thus became sublimated to the realm of ethics and intrenched firmly in the mind of the dominant race a misconception of the ideals of the suppressed race.[119]

With respect to the manner of performing set tasks it has already been pointed out how the Indian method, based upon cyclical natural changes and envisaging short spurts of very strenuous effort alternating with periods of complete idleness, was wholly foreign to the American doctrine of continuous, consistent labor. But perhaps a deeper and more significant divergence lay in the Indian concept of time. To the aborigine, with no specific social or economic goal beyond the satis-

---

[119] A modern and very unfortunate misconception of the same type colors the average American's notions concerning the habits of Latin Americans, again united with ignorance and intolerance. Much of the Indian philosophy of labor has persisted in Mexico and Central America. The American, perceiving only that the Mexican way of labor differs from his own, immediately concludes that the latter cannot and does not work; what is worse, the American expresses this opinion freely.

faction of current physical demands, time was not a factor of importance. Hence as slow a pace was maintained as was consistent with getting a job accomplished at all. Quite naturally, therefore, when the native began to work for hire, he could not appreciate the incessant pressure exerted by an employer for speed and quick results. His vision reached no further than the day's wages. It did not embrace such totally unfamiliar intangibles as constructing a town, developing a mine, growing an orchard, getting ahead in business, or repaying a loan in ninety days. As a result, he did not immediately recast his view of the time element in economy, and therefore acquired a reputation for indolence and laziness.

Some degree of intellectual and psychological adaptation was indispensable before the native could render the kind of service regarded as satisfactory by the great majority of white men. But for a group to achieve a complete reorientation of its traditional concept of the nature of labor and of time within a very few years implies superhuman responsiveness and superhuman analytical power and intelligence.

We may sum up briefly the ideas here set forth concerning the reaction of the Indian to the free-labor system during the 'fifties and 'sixties. Although adjustment to the peonage system was much easier for the native, he did make an adequate adaptation to an environment of free labor. In so doing he was limited to the simpler types of unskilled work, but here he filled a real need and carved out a definite niche in the social hierarchy. The obstacles which prevented a complete readjustment which would embrace all forms of economic activity were primarily historical and environmental, not inherent or genetic. These obstacles were (1) traditional unfamiliarity with any need for continuous labor and accumulation of means; (2) complete incomprehension of the mechanics of European economy; (3) a traditional set of values at variance with that of the invading culture; (4) lack of opportunity (due largely to race prejudice) to learn new mechanical processes; and (5) a traditionally inculcated philosophy of labor and of the time element which diametrically opposed the philosophy of Anglo-America. Such was the force of cultural background that he was barely able to readjust himself to the new economic conditions. In the earlier years he was thus able to survive, but even today his adaptation is far from perfect. The interracial conflict on the economic front is still in progress.[120]

SEX AND FAMILY RELATIONS

One aspect of interracial contact of both biological and social interest relates to sex.

I have pointed out in connection with life in the missions that a serious irritant was the imposition on the neophytes of rigid sexual restrictions, such as obligatory monogamy, insistence on the Christian marriage ceremony, and the virtual monasticizing of the young men and women prior to actual matrimony. The trend toward inhibition and compulsion, which gave rise to strong resistance and flight reactions among the converted Indians, does not appear to any marked extent in the conflict between the aborigines and the society introduced by the Americans. In fact the tendency was entirely in the opposite direction, toward complete disintegration of Indian sexual custom and unlimited license with respect to such relations both between the races and within the Indian race.

This process of disintegration became externally manifest in three phenomena sufficiently objective and universal to warrant description. These were common-law marriages, prostitution, and forced cohabitation or outright rape.

1. The term "common-law marriage" requires some amplification. When an aboriginal couple proposed to live together, even for a short period, with the possible intention of rearing children and assuming a familial status in the community, the union was sanctioned by the social organism, with or without various ceremonies, as an "Indian Custom marriage." The crucial feature of this procedure was public sanction and consent. Any promiscuous or casual intercourse which did not bear this sanction was regarded, in theory at least, as undesirable and reprehensible. At the other extreme, during the period of

---

[120] Certain aspects of this conflict have been presented in detail in a recent paper by the author, *The Mechanism and Extent of Dietary Adaptation among Certain Groups of California and Nevada Indians,* Univ. Calif. Publ., Ibero-Americana, No. 18 (1941). It is there shown how poor economic adjustment is correlated with poor dietary adjustment.

acute interracial conflict, there was the familiar white marriage, endorsed by the law and usually by the church. This may be termed "legal" marriage. Now, when large numbers of American men penetrated the Indian country, many of them began to consort with native women. The character of such relations varied all the way from pure promiscuity to the establishment of families and permanent homes. We are here concerned primarily with the latter form, that is, with those unions in which the white man and Indian woman lived together in the same abode as man and wife for a minimum of several weeks or months. It is impossible to draw any exact line, for the essence of the matter is intent, not time. These extemporized adventures in matrimony could follow any one of three patterns. The marriage could be solemnized by the rites of the law and church and hence be legal according to white standards. Such unions did occur, and some were eminently successful. However, in the early days legal marriage between whites and Indians was quite the exception.[121] On the other hand, the marriage could be consummated according to whatever custom was prevalent in the tribe concerned. There were certain difficulties here, however. On the native side, such a union demanded public sanction, which the Indian community, often in a hostile mood, was not always willing to grant. On the white side, neither the individual white man nor his society at large was disposed to recognize the validity of Indian custom or to regard such a relationship as a marriage at all. The net result was that the majority of Indian-white matrimonial affairs were of the third pattern, that is, they carried the approval of neither racial group. Owing to the exigencies of the time, however, they were admitted *de facto* and tolerated by both groups as an inevitable concomitant to the period of racial and social adjustment. This type of union has been designated, for lack of a better term, a "common-law marriage."

The numerical extent of common-law marriage is difficult to de-

---

[121] Prior to 1845 generally—and subsequently in unions involving persons of Latin descent—interracial legal marriage was not only customary but universal. This divergence from Anglo-Saxon habit was due first to the long tradition of mixed marriages running back to the sixteenth century in Mexico, second to the smaller number of white men and hence more rigid control, third to the powerful influence of the Catholic Church, and fourth to the general acquiescence of the white women. All these factors were absent in orthodox American society.

termine, but all the available evidence tends to show that it was very great. The contemporary and historical literature is replete with rather vague generalizations to the effect that there were at least a few thousand white men who consorted habitually with Indian women.[122] Thus, if we assume several hundred, or roughly one thousand, at any given time, then over the entire period of settlement, say from 1850 to 1870, there may have been a total of three thousand.

There are few reliable, concrete data on this subject. Apparently no one at the time or since has felt it worth while to attempt an accurate or complete enumeration. Mrs. Lucy Thompson, in discussing the problem, mentions four storekeepers at one spot on the middle Klamath, all of whom had Indian wives, and implies that this condition was typical of the whole Yurok part of the river.[123] At that time there were at least twenty similar small settlements from the mouth of the Klamath to the line between Karok and Shasta territory. The four storekeepers must be multiplied by at least three to account for other permanent residents, such as miners and ranchers. A sum of 240 such unions is then indicated for the Klamath, Yurok, and Karok. To this total there should be added that of the coast settlement between Arcata and Crescent City. A reasonable guess would be 100. If we add another hundred for the interior and the tributaries of the Klamath, we get 440 as a possible total. Now the aboriginal population of these two tribes was approximately 4,500. By 1878 this had dimin-

---

[122] Typical statements of this sort are the following. (Italics mine.)

a) "Indian women have intermarried with white men *quite frequently* in Fresno County." (Sacramento *Union*, Mar. 10, 1859.)

b) There are *"hundreds of white men* living with their Digger wives." (San Francisco *Bulletin*, Apr. 8, 1857.)

c) "In Humboldt County there are as many halfbreeds as pure-blooded children of both races together." (W. H. Brewer, *op. cit.*, pp. 545–546.) Mr. Brewer adds also the following enlightening comment: "It is a noteworthy fact that nearly all the 'squaw men' . . . are rank secessionists—in fact, I have never met a Union man living in that way . . ."

d) There were *"quite a number"* of these men. They were usually men of means. So says L. L. Palmer in the *History of Mendocino County*, p. 169.

e) "Living among them are *many* white settlers. . . . The settlers and Indians have *generally* intermarried, so a *considerable* part of the Lower Klamath population is of mixed blood." (W. E. Dougherty, *Rept. Commr. Indian Affairs*, 1894.)

f) "In the mining counties during the early years *hundreds if not thousands* of white men throughout the state took Indian wives." (L. L. Loud, *op. cit.*, p. 324.)

[123] *Op. cit.*, pp. 11–25, 130–131.

ished to nearly 2,000. If an intermediate figure, say 3,250, represents the mean population during the interval 1850 to 1870, we may assume one-quarter, or 800, to have been women between sixteen and forty years of age. According to this calculation, 55 per cent, or over half the available women, had been appropriated by white men.

Another item, which is suggestive rather than numerically specific, is the following:

The miners and ranchmen around Cottonwood, Shasta County, are in the habit, it is said, of taking their Digger Indian concubines and collecting once or twice a week at the houses about in the neighborhood, where they hold balls in imitation of white people.[124]

Utilizing the purest assumption, let us say that these people all lived within a half-day's ride, or ten miles, of Cottonwood, and that the entire group amounted to twenty-five couples. In 1858 the total Indian population of this area could not have exceeded 500. If so, there might have been 125 women. Hence the number attached to white men might have constituted 20 per cent of the total.

A third item is derived from an account which appeared in the San Francisco *Bulletin* on August 21, 1861, to the effect that the employees at Round Valley were having much trouble with "squaw men." About 50 such persons were at that time settled on the reservation. The Indian population at Round Valley was fluctuating considerably but tended to approximate 1,000. Again using one-fourth as the proportion of marriageable women, we get 20 per cent for those attached to white men.

From the three very shaky estimates given above we thus get values of 55, 20, and 20 per cent for the proportion of native women in mixed marriages. A possible compromise would be 30 per cent for the entire area. The general Indian population was roughly 80,000 in 1848 and 15,000 in 1880. If the available women at any moment constituted one-quarter of the whole population, then during one generation (taken as thirty years) the total number would have reached the vicinity of 40,000. If the 30-per cent proportion held, then 12,000 Indian women at one time or another lived as the wives or concubines of white men.

We have one other line of approach to the problem. This is derived from certain data contained in the probate records of the United States

---

[124] San Francisco *Bulletin*, Mar. 16, 1858.

Indian Service. Among these documents are several thousand reports on heirship, in each of which is a statement concerning the marital status of the individual. An examination of these reports shows that they mention 1,050 persons who died subsequently to 1895 and who had married between the years 1850 and 1880. Of these 1,013 married in accordance with Indian custom and 37 married legally. The sexes are about equally represented. Therefore 525 women are included. Of the latter, 75, or 14 per cent of the total, married white men. This gives us an absolutely definite figure, for the records are accurate as far as they go and the sample included, while rather small, is representative from the standpoint of both time and area. Fourteen per cent must be regarded as a minimum, however, for the complete marital history of those persons who died in old age was not always known to the descendants. Many of them had contracted unions of relatively short duration with white men, which resulted in no offspring. Furthermore, the records include only unions which were recognized by the families as being sanctioned by either Indian or white law. Numerous marriages of the "common-law" type must have been ignored or forgotten. If we allow for such unrecorded marriages, then we are entirely justified in doubling the sure minimal value of 14 per cent. This yields 28 per cent or very nearly the estimate derived from the three isolated bits of information discussed previously. Since it can be no coincidence that calculations based upon two widely different methods conform in their result so clearly, we may accept the proportion of Indian women consorting with white men as 30 per cent and the total number of these women as approximately 12,000.

The entrance of thousands of white strangers into the most intimate relations with Indian women could not fail to exert a really profound influence upon native society. The full extent of such an impact can never be fully appreciated, for its ramifications must have penetrated the physical and psychological life of nearly every individual. We can merely point out briefly certain of the more obvious effects.

a) Much of the native home life was destroyed. When the white men took Indian wives or concubines, they did not enter into and become members of the native community. Almost invariably the couple withdrew to a new locale, to a purely white circle, to some isolated spot, or to some group of similar mixed couples. No matter which course was pursued, the woman was effectively removed from the Indian group and thereby prevented from marrying a man of her own race. The net result was to reduce the number of reproducing females and ultimately that of full-blooded children, while the native males were forced into an abnormally keen competition for the remaining females. The aboriginal mating equilibrium was thus disturbed.

Further complications arose when, as frequently happened, the woman in question was already the wife of an Indian. The "squaw men" as a rule were totally indifferent to the previous marital state of the squaw and hesitated not at all to break up already established homes. Whenever such an event occurred, one more cohesive bond among the natives was broken, leaving the human fragments to drift at random. Even the threat of a white man was often sufficient to strain family ties to the point of open rupture. Thus a universal state of uneasiness and apprehension was created. No Indian family could ever be sure that the wife and mother would not run away with or be appropriated by some white man.

b) Insecurity of normal family life was associated with a disintegration of the binding force in marriage itself. When such vast numbers of Indian women entered into a kind of twilight relationship with white men, the validity of the true Indian Custom marriage disappeared. In its place arose the system of mere cohabitation, with no social sanction from either race. In the south, among the Luiseños and Diegueños the Catholic Church, through general clerical control and through the missions, was able to enforce a fairly complete transition from genuine Indian custom to full legal matrimony. Among these tribes the prestige of marriage as an institution, irrespective of ceremonial form, was maintained. But in the central and northern part of the state, the moral obligation inherent in tribal custom was swept away and nothing offered in its place. This loss of moral compulsion was attended, as would be anticipated, by an increase in divorce, adultery, and general sexual promiscuity. The evil was propagated by hundreds of semi-outcast, half-breed children, for whom no ethical or moral standards were ever set up. Indeed the universal laxness in sex morals so vociferously denounced by many righteous white men may be ascribed in large part to the destruction of uniform marital responsibility suffered because of the white men themselves.

c) A psychological, emotional effect of serious proportions was induced by the system of common-law marriage. This was based upon the loss of caste suffered by both parties. The contempt which his own people visited on the white partner was universal and severe. Even the solemnization of the union by legal wedlock did not entitle the couple to acceptance among the Anglo-Americans. Any other type of association was regarded as adulterous and sinful without qualification. On the other side, white men were rarely accepted unreservedly by the native community, although the latter was usually forced to accord respect to any white man, simply because he was white. As a result a very large outcast group was formed which incurred the social obloquy of both races.

d) One curious effect was observed which gave rise to much complaint on the part of the native male population. As a result of wholesale association of the women with white men a spontaneous feminist movement developed. Aboriginally, the woman was not only physically, but economically and spiritually, subservient to the man. The squaw performed most of the hard manual labor associated with village life while her husband and father loafed away their time. She was obliged to obey every command and whim of her lord and master. To do otherwise was to invite stern and inevitable retribution. With the influx of thousands of white men, unmarried and on the hunt for females, the situation altered. The woman was now to a certain extent vested with bargaining power. She could confront the Indian male with the choice of better treatment or loss of his spouse to some white suitor. Moreover, the Indian woman was undoubtedly influenced profoundly by the enviable position which her sex occupied in the newly established white communities. Although no contemporary sociologist ever gave the matter attention, we get inklings of a pretty formidable feminine revolt. The agent at the Fresno Indian Farm reported:[125]

Though the men are, or once were, absolute masters of the women, many of them at this time ... have found shelter among the whites, and are consequently independent of the men.

[125] M. B. Lewis, *Rept. Commr. Indian Affairs*, 1856.

A statement also appeared at about the same period to the effect that "white men have taken the Indians' wives from their lodges and taught them to despise the lazy creatures who used to make them slaves."[126] If this state of mind was characteristic of a large body of female opinion, it is easy to see how, although no vast social upheaval was involved, the change could act as an irritant and thereby serve as another factor in the disruption of aboriginal family life.

e) An extensive secondary effect of miscegenation in the early phases of American-Indian conflict was the creation of a large group of half-breeds. When any two races come into physical contact, a certain degree of interbreeding inevitably follows. In this particular instance, however, the social problems were intensified by the unusually large number of children who were born very soon after the initial invasion by the whites.[127] Almost without exception, these offspring were absorbed into the Indian, rather than the white, community. They there occupied the place so frequently reserved for the half-breed, a place definitely inferior in caste to that held by the full bloods. At the other extreme, they were generally repudiated by the white people. A formidable class thus grew to adulthood in the 'seventies and 'eighties, which was cursed with the usual inferiority complex of the mixed blood but which was attached culturally to the Indian race. Thus was generated still another strain upon the already weakened native social organism.

2. Prostitution, according to most ethnographers, was unknown to the California aboriginal peoples. Although much latitude existed in sex matters—at least according to our own standards—the actual sale of female favors was not in vogue. There seem to have been no formal ethical scruples against the practice. Rather, it was unnecessary in the Indian community; adequate satisfaction was provided by the normal operation of society. Since the demand was thus practically nonexistent, no economic end was served by attempting to furnish the supply.

When the white race entered, however, a demand was immediately

---

[126] Sacramento *Union*, March 4, 1858.

[127] The genetic aspect of miscegenation constitutes a problem in itself, which it is hoped will ultimately receive consideration. In the present connection only the social aspect is pertinent.

created. Both in colonial times and subsequently there was an excess of both unmarried males and males of other circumstances, who wished to take advantage of the opportunity offered by numerous native women. The very bad economic condition of the native furnished a powerful incentive, which was coupled with the total lack of traditional or religious social taboo. It is easy to appreciate, therefore, how readily the native race might adopt this new means of improving its material condition.

Prostitution was apparently common in the later mission period, although its origin is obscure.[128] R. H. Dana describes the situation at this time as follows:[129]

Indeed to show the entire want of any sense of morality or domestic duty among them, I have frequently known an Indian to bring his wife ... down to the beach, and carry her back again, dividing with her the money she got from the sailors.

Gomez, who appears to have been something of an expert in such matters, states that "Los indios no tenian escrupulo en traficar con sus mujeres, ni los vecinos en admitirselas."[130] He then describes in some detail the method of solicitation by Indian men with respect to the use of their women. The price was usually a small amount of money or some trivial commodity. Frequently, according to Gomez, the white men concerned took back by force the money they had given in advance, or even went so far as to rape the women outright.

It is clear that by 1848 prostitution by Indians was a well-established custom near all the settlements and other centers of white population. The Indians of the interior, although probably still not practicing the custom among themselves, were doubtless quite familiar with it. When the great mass of gold miners poured in, accompanied by other

---

[128] Some of the early correspondence of the missionaries and officials mentions immoral relations between the soldiers or *vecinos* and the native women. Indeed, the problem was one of deep concern to the Church. But whether technical prostitution beyond mere random promiscuity was involved is not very clear. It is a safe assumption, however, that, as soon as the soldiers and civilians began consorting with native women, they also sought to win the favor of the latter by offering inducements of a material if not pecuniary nature. From this stage to one of open sale and solicitation the transition is simple and rapid.

[129] *Two Years before the Mast* (Boston, 1873), p. 199.

[130] V. Gomez, "Lo que sabe," MS, 1876, Bancroft Library, p. 162.

unattached males of all social and racial complexions, the natives were fully prepared to supply the enormous demand for women. Beginning doubtless with the arrival of the first miners, the trade in sex did not reach sufficient proportions to excite much comment before 1854 to 1856. In the latter year and thereafter, it was noted by several individuals. After referring to the complete demoralization of the Yosemite Miwok caused by reservation life between 1850 and 1854, Galen Clark states:[131]

In these straitened and desperate circumstances many of their young women were used as commercial property and peddled out to the mining camps and gambling saloons.

In 1856 the reports of the Indian Service contained several references to the same condition. J. W. Gilbert of El Dorado County spoke of the "almost general prostitution of their women."[132] M. B. Lewis, of the Fresno Indian Farm, painted a very sad picture, perhaps somewhat overdrawn, as follows:[133]

They [the women] have no chance for employment of a praiseworthy character; consequently, from necessity and an inclination to gratify their craving appetite for food and their fancy for dress and trinkets, in the absence of all words of moral advice, at the same time sought for by white men, and encouraged by those who ought to be their protectors, they have been led astray at an early age, and soon thereafter become the sport and traffic of worthless Indian men. In one or two brief years they become diseased and at the age of twenty wear the features of thirty-five to forty; outcasts among their own people; and as a general thing before they arrive at the age of thirty, die a shameful and miserable death.

Robert McAdam of Yuba County reported that the Maidu supported themselves by prostitution "to a very great extent,"[134] and Alexander Taylor in an article in the *Golden Era* for April, 1856, made similar statements with reference to the Indians of the north coast.[135] The contemporary press also carried comment on native prostitution. The Butte *Record* for May 23, 1857, printed the story of an Indian who

---

[131] *Indians of the Yosemite Valley* (San Francisco, 1904), p. 19.
[132] Letter to T. J. Henley, *Rept. Commr. Indian Affairs*, 1856, p. 242.
[133] M. B. Lewis, *ibid.*, p. 253.
[134] R. McAdam, *ibid.*, p. 244.
[135] A. S. Taylor, *Indianology* (1864), Ser. II, fol. 6–F.

prostituted his squaw to a Negro for a bottle of whiskey. The San Francisco *Bulletin* for June 10, 1858, quoted a complaint by the Yreka *Union* against numerous "low-grade white men" who supplied the local Indians liquor in return for their women. The Shasta *Courier* (quoted by the Nevada *Journal* for Nov. 12, 1858) stated that in Redding the recent rains had brought to town a "great increase" in the number of squaws, who gathered along the sidewalks in the evening and who were "forced to procure their bread and clothing in a manner the most infamous." Even as late as 1871 the Indian agent at Eureka stated that "their women prostituted themselves to the soldiers and officers from sheer necessity."[136]

The foregoing citations are sufficient evidence of the widespread occurrence of prostitution. It is clear, furthermore, that the evil flourished primarily because of economic necessity, and not because the natives were any more prone to adopt the custom than other races under similar circumstances. Indeed, it is noteworthy that every recorded comment points to the Indians themselves as the direct beneficiaries. I know of no instance in which white men acted as procurers or used Indian women for their own pecuniary profit. The traffic was conducted as strictly individual enterprise by the Indians alone and apparently was utilized only as a last resort to avert want and starvation.

The effect of the evil was undoubtedly similar to that observed in any social group. Apart from the spread of venereal disease, it tended still further to loosen sex restrictions and added to the domestic demoralization already existing among the natives.

3. The point at which sex relations between the races became sharpest and most irritating to the natives was that at which promiscuity and prostitution graded into open violence. Frequently, white men could not obtain a squaw as a common-law wife or were unable to buy her services. Then the temptation arose to use outright force and compel submission. Such a procedure was rendered shamefully easy because the general bad feeling of the Americans toward Indians was so strong that no personal crime by a white man against a native was likely to result in punishment of the offender. As a matter of fact, ordinary human resistance to such outrages was usually followed by

---

[136] J. V. Farwell, *Rept. Commr. Bur. Indian Affairs*, 1871, p. 157.

further persecution of the offended parties. In view of the notoriously bad character of many early settlers it is not surprising that rape and rapine were common frontier phenomena.

Several statements have been placed on record which describe these conditions in general terms. They are of value inasmuch as they emanate from members of the white race who, on other grounds, were not necessarily friendly to the natives. In December, 1859, the *Shasta Courier*[137] deplored the state of affairs on the Upper Sacramento:

There is also a set of white men living with them, debauching the squaws on every occasion, often going to the rancherias at midnight and dragging the women from their hovels.

L. H. Irvine makes the following statement:[138]

They [certain white men] hunted down good-looking young squaws, as if the squaws had been mere animals created for their own enjoyment and often forced these young women to submit to their passionate desires. A number of half-white children resulted from the forays of the men who thus violated Indian maidens, who were often regarded as worthless creatures except for rapes of this character. It is said that bands of white men, consisting of three or four depraved wretches, would often catch a young squaw or two and detain them for several days or weeks at their cabins ...

Such accusations might be regarded as gross exaggeration were they not borne out by the universal testimony of many persons who were thoroughly acquainted with the situation, and by a long series of actual cases. One of the best evidential items is a series of resolutions passed by a citizens' meeting at Frenchtown, Butte County, on February 14, 1854, which read thus:[139]

Whereas the peace and quietude of this neighborhood has been disturbed by the frequent outrages committed on Indian women by lawless characters, and whereas the Indians have been driven from their ranches ... and whereas children from ten to twelve years of age have not been spared by these fiends in human shape; therefore we ... do resolve ...

Then followed the announcement that, if the forces of law and order did not punish these offenders, the citizens "would mete out to them

---

[137] Quoted by the Sacramento *Union*, January 3, 1860.

[138] *History of Humboldt County, California* (Los Angeles, 1915), p. 70.

[139] Quoted by H. L. Wells and W. L. Chambers, *History of Butte County* (San Francisco, 1882), p. 218.

the punishment they deserved." It is self-evident that, when murder and rape attained such proportions as to provoke action by the white people themselves, the situation must have become extremely bad.

I have collected from the local press twenty-seven cases of rape so flagrant that comment was evoked from newspapers (1851–1860) which were already surfeited with violence. Although actual citation of these would serve no useful purpose, it may be pointed out that for every instance so well known and so vicious as to justify a press account there were probably a hundred others which passed unnoticed by all except the victims. No concrete estimate is justifiable, but there can be no question that crimes of violence perpetrated on Indian women by white men were numbered by hundreds and very likely by thousands.[140]

The effect on the Indians of attacks on women was probably out of proportion to the damage actually inflicted. The extremely personal character of these clashes, together with the exasperating nature of the attendant circumstances, aroused hatred where nothing else would. Both the individual and mass response of the red race to this type of persecution, therefore, exceeded in intensity the response to more serious but less concrete factors.

The reaction of the Indians included both the white race and their own people. The most obvious and violent response was usually directed toward the white perpetrators of individual outrages. Quite naturally, when Indian males witnessed an attack on a wife, daughter, or friend, they resisted by every means available. No race, no matter how backward or primitive, could be expected to do otherwise, and by common human consent any group is regarded as within its legal and moral rights in so doing. Such resistance, however, usually entailed injury or death to the Indians concerned and also to the white attackers. From the tabulation of social homicide, introduced in a previous connection, it appears that out of 289 recorded Indian deaths of this type 18 were directly attributable to brawls involving attacks on native women. The unrecorded mortality was no doubt much greater,

[140] To the cases of actual rape should be added those involving the kidnaping of squaws for sale as "servants," a trade which flourished along with the kidnaping of children as laborers. Indeed, it would not be overstating the situation to say that during the decade 1850–1860 no single squaw in northern California could consider herself absolutely safe from violence at the hands of white men.

as were the injuries not resulting in death. The fact that more white men were not killed or wounded during attempted rape was due without question to the profound fear, on the part of the Indians, of stirring up a so-called war, which could only result disastrously to themselves.[141]

Although immediate, armed resistance was thus the primary instinctive response, it did not constitute the entire reaction pattern. Abortive or frustrated resistance and, more often, involuntary compulsory acquiescence did not relieve the feelings of the offended persons or their community. A long series of violations or an occasional single vicious crime was adequate to stir in the native soul the most bitter rancor and animosity. More often perhaps than is realized these emotions built up to a point where some individuals, or perhaps the whole tribe, could no longer inhibit them. Then a desire for revenge became predominant and manifested itself in depredations on the whites or even in open warfare. This secondary or delayed response was more significant to native welfare than blind resistance at the scene of the crime. For the majority of sober white men sympathized with the outraged sentiments of the natives when the latter were directly defending their homes and families against criminals. But this sympathy vanished very quickly when innocent white people began to suffer for the derelictions of the guilty. For the sake of immediate protection and by virtue of pure racial solidarity revenge upon the community at large was not tolerated, no matter how extreme the original provocation. The final result, inevitably, was further punishment of the natives.

These considerations apply, to be sure, to many other types of outrage committed on the Indians. But in this instance the initial cause of trouble was so flagrant, so inexcusable, and so offensive to social decency that its effect on Indian sentiment was much greater than the actual harm done would appear to justify. The failure of both intuitive responses—immediate resistance and subsequent revenge—left a permanent scar upon the Indian nature. It forced him back to a silent,

---

[141] Resistance through legal channels, that is by the arrest and trial of offenders, was completely eliminated by the refusal of any white jury to convict a fellow countryman of any crime upon the Indian. But no case, to my knowledge, ever reached a jury, for no officer would make an arrest under such circumstances, nor would public opinion support a prosecution. Finally, owing to the law throwing out Indian testimony, no native, even the injured party herself, could be heard as a witness. Physical resistance on the spot was therefore the only means open to the Indians for the prevention of assault on women.

ineradicable, suppressed animosity against all things American which was not forgotten long after other wrongs had passed into oblivion. As a focus for hatred and emotional conflict between the races the wholesale rape of Indian women stands unique.[142]

There is some evidence that the reaction of the native males was not directed exclusively toward the whites. When outright abduction or rape was involved, resentment probably was felt only against the perpetrator, not the victim. But on the frequent occasions when the circumstances were not wholly clear, the possibility of consent existed. Then jealousy might incite the husband or brother to take action against the woman. Even more serious was the reaction when the female was not directly assaulted but yielded to moral or financial pressure. Reference has already been made to the expression of M. B. Lewis that prostitutes were "outcasts among their own people," and the same idea is set forth in different words by the Yurok, Mrs. Lucy Thompson. A few extreme cases are on record, such as that mentioned

---

[142] In connection with offenses against Indian women it is pertinent to inquire briefly concerning the attacks by Indians on white women, for one might anticipate that the Indians would seek revenge in this manner. However, the facts do not bear out any such hypothesis. Molestation of white women by natives was a relatively rare phenomenon. In a survey of the press I have been able to find only five cases of the sort. The first was in 1852 (Sacramento *Union*, February 24), when Indians merely insulted a woman near Sacramento. The second was in 1859 (San Francisco *Bulletin*, July 2; Sacramento *Union*, June 28), when two drunken Indians made "insulting proposals" to a small girl at Yreka. The third was in 1861 (Sacramento *Union*, July 15), when a former mission Indian at San José attempted to rape a girl. The fourth, in 1861 (Sacramento *Union*, September 24), was a case of actual rape near Cache Creek. The fifth (Marysville *Appeal*, March 29, 1864) was an "attempted rape" on a woman on Bear River. Since an attack on a white woman was the most heinous crime an Indian could commit, every such case was certain to be reported in the metropolitan press. This means that in nearly fifteen years only four white females actually suffered sexual violence from Indian men, and it is not clear that in three of these the deed was actually consummated. (In the 1852 case, the woman was not physically disturbed.) This is a remarkable record, particularly when we consider the number of rapes by white men on white women during the same period and the number of Indian men who were in a position to perpetrate the crime. The fact that in three of the four cases the Indians were summarily lynched and in the fourth the attacker was shot by a parent might lead to the supposition that fear of consequences acted as a deterrent. However, Indians committed plenty of other crimes for which the punishment was just as certain, and must have foregone many opportunities for rape when escape was easy. The explanation must lie elsewhere. As a matter of fact, the entire long and bloody history of Indian warfare in the United States is remarkably free from accounts of Indian sex assaults on white women. Unless the chroniclers and historians have been deliberately suppressing the facts, the American Indian, who has been distinguished for his ferocity and cruelty, has shown himself singularly free from the urge to commit sexual violence on his enemies.

by Mason in which "a squaw was stoned to death in Sacramento County in 1850 for yielding to a white man,"[143] or that in which a jealous Indian husband murdered his wife for cohabiting with a white man.[144] Such actions were infrequent, but they are indicative of the deep animosity which burned in the hearts of many Indians and which could find partial release in retaliation on their own kind. The emotional strain engendered by all types of interracial sexual congress is impossible to evaluate in concrete terms, but nevertheless it must have constituted a serious obstacle to rapid adaptation by the native to the American social order.

Before we leave the field of sex relations, a brief consideration of abortion is desirable. This phenomenon, although not strictly sexual in nature, reflects a state of unrest among the female population which may be associated with sexual factors as well as with other elements of the social order.

There is a cumulative mass of evidence to show that both abortion and infanticide were known and practiced by many of the California tribes, prior to the coming of the whites.[145] It is not surprising therefore that the custom should have continued even to modern times. It is impossible to determine statistically whether the number of these crimes increased after 1848, for no quantitative data whatever are available. Nevertheless, the opinion may be held that such an increase did occur.

One tribe among whom the habit of abortion was rather highly developed was the Pomo. Thus when Gifford and Kroeber studied the northern valley tribes their informants for the River Patwin, Hill Patwin, Hill Wintun, and Lake Miwok denied the aboriginal existence of both abortion and infanticide, whereas for the Pomo, six out of sixteen groups admitted abortion and seven admitted infanticide.[146] Aginsky has made a detailed study[147] of the custom as a means of birth

---

[143] J. D. Mason, *op. cit.,* p. 258.

[144] Sacramento *Union,* May 30, 1859.

[145] Numerous recent ethnographic studies contain information on this point, particularly many of those which have appeared in the University of California Publications in American Archaeology and Ethnology.

[146] *Culture Element Distributions, IV: Pomo,* Univ. Calif. Publ. Am. Arch. and Ethn. (1937), 37:150.

[147] "Population Control in the Shanel (Pomo) Tribe," *Amer. Sociol. Rev.* (1939), 4:209–216.

control. He concluded that such procedure "was a traditionally accepted pattern of behavior and an integral aspect of their culture." The basis of such behavior he thinks was a somewhat limited aboriginal food supply and consequent mild population pressure. With the mechanism of control thus already in operation, it is entirely logical to expect its amplification and extension when the inflow of the white race further reduced the food supply and rendered existence precarious in all respects. At least two observers commented on the prevalence of these methods among the Pomo or their neighbors. Thus George Yount stated with reference to the Napa Valley Indians:[148] ". . . they murder their offspring at birth to rid themselves of the care and toil of nursing and raising them into life." Stephen Powers was even more explicit:[149]

Neither was it [infanticide] caused, *as in later years,* by that deep and despairing melancholy which came over the hapless race when they saw themselves perishing so hopelessly and so miserably before the face of the American. [Italics mine.]

Powers (*op. cit.,* p. 416) agrees with Aginsky in his opinion that "the very presence of the crime of infanticide points to an over-fruitfulness and an over-population." Regarding the effect of the white invasion, he also states (p. 207) that the Clear Lake Pomo asserted they had not known infanticide before the whites came. This tribe, moreover, during the early period of settlement killed all half-breed infants at birth (p. 214). In another connection Powers (pp. 183–184) maintains that the Russian River Pomo commit this crime "to this day [1877] for they say they do not wish to rear any more children among the whites."

It is quite apparent from these citations that at least one tribe, the Pomo, showed an increase in the abortion and infanticide rate and, furthermore, that they rationalized their behavior with respect to the presence of the whites. The killing of half-white children indicates that not only were general economic conditions responsible, but that sexual factors, through miscegenation, were also involved. A statement of

[148] C. L. Camp, "The Chronicles of George C. Yount," Calif. Hist. Soc., *Quarterly* (1923), 2:56.
[149] *Op. cit.,* 3:178.

Mason regarding the Sierra Miwok shows that similar factors operated:[150]

They did not hesitate to commit infanticide when the means of living was scarce, believing ... that an infant had better die than grow up to starvation.

Elimination of infants by murder or abortion must thus have been a material factor in population decline. Unfortunately, we have no way of determining its relative significance, nor can we set up regional or tribal comparisons. From the social standpoint, the prevalence of the custom must be regarded as a spontaneous response by individuals of the group to the unfavorable living conditions created through racial conflict.

SUMMARY AND COMPARISONS

In these pages, and in two previous essays, the attempt has been made to analyze the conflict between the California aborigines and the white race in terms of the material factors involved. From these studies certain similarities and differences in the Indian response emerge with respect to the mission type of culture, to the pre-American settlers of Latin extraction, and to the Yankee invasion after the Mexican War.

The fundamental clue to success in interracial competition is the change in population. Under the relatively favorable control of the missions the natives suffered considerable diminution. From the mission records it is ascertained that approximately 53,600 Indians underwent conversion. At the end of the mission period (1834) there were 14,900 left, a reduction of 72 per cent. This signifies a mean annual reduction of 0.9 per cent. The six wild tribes which came into direct contact with the California civil and military civilization between 1800 and 1848 were reduced from approximately 58,900 to 35,950, or 0.8 per cent annually. The surviving mission Indians together with the remainder of the wild tribes which were subjected to Anglo-American influence from 1848 to 1865 diminished from 72,000 to 23,000, a mean annual depletion of 2.9 per cent. From these figures alone, it is apparent that the impact of the settlement from the United States was three times as severe as that of pre-American colonization.

---

[150] J. D. Mason, *op. cit.*, p. 258.

The triad of factors which brings about a decline in population is war, disease, and starvation. In the missions, war was of negligible consequence. A study of expeditions and sporadic fighting shows that for the six wild tribes mentioned above, roughly 11.5 per cent of the decline may be attributed to casualties suffered in armed conflict. The corresponding value for the period after 1848 is 8.6 per cent. Hence, although the absolute effect of warfare was greater in the American period, its relative influence on population decline was substantially the same as in the years of Ibero-American domination.

The relative effect of disease was also quite uniform, since in the missions, in the valley before 1848, and generally after 1848, approximately 60 per cent of the decline may be attributed to this cause. Such a result is not surprising, since most of the mortality was due to introduced epidemic maladies and the action of these upon a nonimmune population is entirely independent of the culture which introduces them. It is probable that the spread of disease was intensified in the missions by the crowded living conditions there but, on the other hand, this factor may have been nullified by the hygienic, sanitary, and curative measures adopted by the missionaries.

The effect of dietary maladjustment cannot be evaluated in strictly numerical terms. This factor operates on both birth rate and death rate; moreover, very few persons actually died of direct starvation. In the missions the subsistence level seems to have been low, and, because of a tendency to rely upon cereal crops, there may have been vitamin and mineral deficiencies. The nonconverted Indians encountered the problem of depletion rather than alteration of diet. Until 1848, the reduction of food supply was not serious because the few settlers in the interior did not materially alter the natural flora and fauna. After the gold rush, however, the universal conversion of fertile valleys into farms, the widespread cattle ranching on the hills, and the pollution of the streams all combined to destroy the animal and plant species used for food. The transition to a white dietary, although ultimately accomplished, was rendered difficult by economic and social obstacles. During the interim a great deal of malnutrition was present. From the nutritional standpoint, therefore, the natives suffered most under Anglo-Saxon domination.

Certain quasicultural items were undoubtedly significant in intensifying the effect of the primary lethal factors. Among these were, in particular, labor and sex relations. In the missions a great deal of unrest and maladjustment was caused by the current system of forced labor and of drastically restricted liberty in sex matters. In both these, the basic difficulty was not physical but emotional and was derived from the compulsion which forced activity into new and unaccustomed channels. Under the Americans, compulsion was of a different character, but even more disruptive in its effects. The native was compelled to labor by economic necessity rather than by personal command. In acquiring the tools and the facility for work he was obstructed by a hostile society, rather than aided by a paternal government. Hence his progress was slow and his entire material welfare—diet and health—suffered in consequence. From the sexual inhibitions of the mission environment he was carried by the Americans to the most violent and brutal excesses and his women subjected to universal outrage. The hatred and despair thus generated found expression in still further retardation of his material adjustment.

On the whole, therefore, and for many causes, the conflict of the native with the settlers from the United States was characterized by far greater violence than the conflict with the invaders from Latin America. This violence was reflected in greater relative population decline and in more difficult adjustment in all material respects under the American occupation.

APPENDIX

Note: Table 1, on pages 96-104 of the original, can be found on pages 236-244 of the present volume.

TABLE 2

ESTIMATED POPULATION IN 1848, 1852, AND 1880

Tribe	1848	1852	1880
Costanoan	1,000	900	300
Salinan	500	500	100
Chumash	1,150	1,050	200
Yokuts	14,000	13,000	600
Western Mono	1,300	1,200	600
Wintun	8,000	5,700	1,500
Sierra Miwok	6,000	4,500	1,000
Maidu	7,000	4,300	1,000
Yana	1,900	1,800	20
Achomawi	3,000	3,000	1,500
Tolowa	450	450	200
Wiyot	1,400	1,000	200
Yurok	2,500	2,400	900
Karok	2,000	1,800	1,000
Hupa	1,000	900	500
Chilula	600	500	30
Wailaki	1,500	1,200	150
Chimariko	250	200	20
Yuki	3,500	3,400	400
Other Athabascans	4,600	4,300	200
Shasta	3,100	3,000	500
Coast Miwok	300	250	60
Lake Miwok	200	100	20
Pomo	5,000	4,200	1,450
Wappo	800	800	50
Total	71,050	60,450	12,500

TABLE 3
INDIAN LOSSES FROM MILITARY OPERATIONS, 1847–1865*

Tribe	1847	1848	1849	1850	1851	1852	1853	1854	1855	1856	1857	1858	1859	1860	1861	1862	1863	1864	1865	Total
Yokuts					97					107							8			212
Wintun	13			50	2	180	49	125	25		15	4			12	11	20			506
Miwok	15		30	74	49	1	33					1	1	3						207
Maidu			120	41		15	70		5		10		79	4			3			347
Yana							13	9		34		19	10			20	28	23	65	221
Tolowa							30	7			10									47
Wiyot				20		25				7		4		120						176
Yurok					6				26							2	30	3		67
Karok				5		15			75									3		98
Athabascans†				50								120	16	103	270	130	5	57		751
Hupa									8				1	11						20
Chilula	100						17													117
Wailaki												158	60	33						251
Chimariko					5							10								15
Yuki					40		25	75	125	300				8						573
Shasta	3	34	88	28	5	15	5				1									179
Achomawi‡					45			112	40	200			15							412
Pomo	68																			68
Totals	199	34	238	268	249	251	242	328	304	648	36	316	182	282	282	163	94	86	65	4,267

* Figures include recorded deaths from military operations, including private expeditions. All figures should be taken as approximate.
† For the Hupa, Chilula, and Wailaki only those casualties which can be clearly ascribed to these tribes are so recorded. Otherwise they are allocated to the Athabascans.
‡ Here are included deaths among the so-called "Pit Rivers," which consisted predominantly, if not exclusively, of Achomawi and Atsugewi.

SOURCES FOR TABLE 3

The following tabulation includes the sources not only for the entries in table 3 but all significant sources for the tribes discussed in this period.

YEAR	TRIBE	
1847	Wintun	Sutter, Calif. Arch., unbound docs., MS, No. 89, Bancroft Library.
	Miwok	Lewis Publishing Co., *An Illustrated History of San Joaquin County* (Chicago, 1890), p. 31; G. H. Tinkham, *History of San Joaquin County* (1923), p. 51.
	Pomo	*California Star*, July 24, 1847.
1849	Miwok	J. W. Connor, "Statement," MS, 1878, Bancroft Library, p. 2; *Placer Times,* May 5 and 12, 1849.
	Maidu	A. F. Coronel, "Cosas de California," MS, 1878, Bancroft Library, p. 173; T. T. Johnson, *California and Oregon* (Philadelphia, 1851), pp. 158, 180; *Placer Times,* Apr. 28, May 5, 1849.
1850	Wintun	W. Kelly, *An Excursion to California* (London, 1851), pp. 143–147; E. de Massey, *A Frenchman in the Gold Rush* (1927), p. 100.
	Miwok	W. Shaw, *Golden Dreams and Waking Realities* (London, 1851), pp. 101–112; Heckendorn and Wilson, *Directory of Tuolumne County* (1856), p. 91; *Alta California,* July 1, 1850, Jan. 21, 1851.
	Maidu	J. D. Barthwick, *Three Years in California* (London, 1857), p. 132; E. F. Morse, "The Story of a Gold Miner," Calif. Hist. Soc., *Quarterly* (1927), 6:235; G. C. Mansfield, *History of Butte County* (Los Angeles, 1918), pp. 185–188; A. Barstow, "Statement," MS, 1877, Bancroft Library, p. 5; P. J. Delay, *History of Yuba and Sutter Counties* (Los Angeles, 1924), p. 234; M. Angell, *History of Placer County* (Oakland, 1882), p. 359; *Placer Times,* May 20 and 29, 1850; Sacramento *Union,* May 27, June 2, 1850.
	Wiyot	H. D. LaMotte, "Statement," MS, 1878, Bancroft Library, p. 6.
	Karok	A. J. Bledsoe, *History of Del Norte County* (Eureka, 1881), p. 8.
	Athabascans	P. E. Goddard, *Notes on the Chilula Indians of Northwestern California,* Univ. Calif. Publ. Am. Arch. and Ethn. (1914), 10:269.
	Chilula	*Ibid.*
	Shasta	H. L. Wells, *History of Siskiyou County* (Oakland, 1881), p. 121.
	Pomo	L. L. Palmer, *History of Napa and Lake Counties* (San Francisco, 1881), p. 62; P. Campbell to Vallejo, Vallejo Docs., Bancroft Library, 13:38; *Alta California,* May 27, June 5, 1850.
1851	Yokuts	J. Outcalt, *History of Merced County* (Los Angeles, 1925), p. 851; E. L. Menefee and F. A. Dodge, *History of Tulare and Kings Counties* (Los Angeles, 1913), p. 8; *Alta California,* Feb. 14, 1851; Sacramento *Union,* Mar. 25, 1851.
	Wintun	Sacramento *Union,* Aug. 16, 1851.
	Miwok	F. W. C. Gerstäcker, *Narrative of a Journey round the World* (London, 1853), pp. 351–356; P. E. Vandor, *History of Fresno*

	County (Los Angeles, 1919), p. 70; *Alta California*, Jan. 26, Feb. 7, 1851.
Yurok	H. L. Wells, *op. cit.*, pp. 126–129.
Shasta	*Ibid.*, p. 127; Sacramento *Union*, June 27, July 21, 1851.

1852	Wintun	F. A. Buck, *A Yankee Trader in the Gold Rush* (Boston, 1930), p. 107; I. Cox, *The Annals of Trinity County* (San Francisco, 1858), p. 115; J. Carr, *Pioneer Days in California* (1891), pp. 195–197; *Alta California*, Feb. 29, May 4, 1852; Sacramento *Union*, Feb. 28, Mar. 9, May 3, June 28, 1852.
	Miwok	Nevada *Journal*, June 12, 1852.
	Maidu	Sacramento *Union*, Feb. 20, Mar. 21, 1852; *Alta California*, May 14, 1852.
	Wiyot	L. L. Loud, *Ethnogeography and Archaeology of the Wiyot Territory*, Univ. Calif. Publ. Am. Arch. and Ethn., 14:324; A. J. Bledsoe, *Indian Wars of the Northwest* (San Francisco, 1885), p. 186.
	Karok	Sacramento *Union*, Oct. 4, 1852.
	Shasta	*Alta California*, Apr. 5, 1852; Nevada *Journal*, Aug. 14, 1852; Sacramento *Union*, Mar. 9, Apr. 6, July 19, Dec. 4, 1852.

1853	Wintun	I. Cox, *op. cit.*, p. 122; H. L. Wells, *op. cit.*, p. 133; *Alta California*, Mar. 6 and 30, 1853; Nevada *Journal*, Dec. 2, 1853; Sacramento *Union*, Mar. 5, 29, and 30, 1853.
	Miwok	*Alta California*, Mar. 2, 1853; Sacramento *Union*, Feb. 3, 5, and 12, 1853.
	Maidu	H. L. Wells and W. L. Chambers, *History of Butte County* (San Francisco, 1882), p. 217; Nevada *Journal*, Dec. 9, 1853.
	Yana	*Alta California*, Mar. 6, 1853.
	Tolowa	*Ibid.*, Jan. 18, 1853.
	Shasta	Nevada *Journal*, Aug. 26, 1853; Sacramento *Union*, Aug. 9 and 18, Oct. 10, 1853.

1854	Wintun	I. Cox, *op. cit.*, p. 85; Nevada *Journal*, Mar. 10, 1854; *Butte Record*, Mar. 11, 1854; *Alta California*, Mar. 15, Apr. 12, 1854; Sacramento *Union*, July 24, Apr. 29, 1854.
	Yana	*Alta California*, Mar. 3, 1854; Sacramento *Union*, Feb. 25, 1854.
	Tolowa	*Alta California*, Feb. 1, 1854.
	Chimariko	*Ibid.*
	Yuki	L. L. Palmer, *History of Mendocino County* (San Francisco, 1880), p. 459.
	Shasta	Sacramento *Union*, Nov. 27, 1854.
	Achomawi	Nevada *Journal*, Feb. 24, 1854; *Alta California*, Apr. 12, 1854.

1855	Wintun	*Alta California*, Oct. 25, 1855.
	Maidu	San Francisco *Bulletin*, Dec. 29 and 31, 1855.
	Yurok	A. J. Bledsoe, *op. cit.*, p. 169.
	Karok	*Alta California*, Feb. 20, 1855.
	Shasta	H. L. Wells, *op. cit.*, p. 138; Sacramento *Union*, Aug. 3, 6, and 9, 1855.

YEAR   TRIBE

1856   Yokuts   F. F. Lattá in the Livingstone *Chronicle*, No. 3, July 29, 1937, and
                   No. 7, Sept. 2, 1937; E. L. Menefee and F. A. Dodge, *op. cit.*,
                   p. 23; San Francisco *Bulletin*, May 5, 7, 8, 16, 21 and 23, June
                   12, Aug. 25, 1856; Sacramento *Union*, Aug. 11 and 27, 1856.

       Yana   San Francisco *Bulletin*, Apr. 22, 1856; Sacramento *Union*, Apr. 19,
                   1856.

       Wiyot   A. J. Bledsoe, *op. cit.*, p. 209; L. L. Loud, *op. cit.*, p. 326; San
                   Francisco *Bulletin*, Nov. 29, 1856.

       Chilula   A. J. Bledsoe, *op. cit.*, pp. 207, 208.

       Yuki   *Butte Record*, Oct. 18, 1856.

       Shasta   *Nevada Journal*, Jan. 18, 1856.

1857   Wintun   A. S. Taylor, *Indianology* (1864), Ser. II, fol. 44; San Francisco
                   Bulletin, Apr. 9, 1857.

       Maidu   San Francisco *Bulletin*, Nov. 9, 1857; Sacramento *Union*, June 5,
                   1857.

       Tolowa   San Francisco *Bulletin*, Dec. 5, 1857.

       Yuki   *Majority and Minority Reports of the Special Joint Committee on
                   the Mendocino War*, Appendix to Journals of the Assembly of
                   the Eleventh Session of the California Legislature 1860 (herein-
                   after referred to as *Repts. Com. Mend. War*), testimony of B.
                   Arthur, 32:51.

       Achomawi   Sacramento *Union*, Apr. 28, May 12, June 20, July 20, Aug. 3,
                   1857.

1858   Wintun   I. Cox, *op. cit.*, p. 129.
       Miwok   San Francisco *Bulletin*, Apr. 6, 1858.
       Yana   *Ibid.*, May 8, 1858; Sacramento *Union*, May 21, 1858; Red Bluff
                   Beacon, Aug. 25 and 31, 1858.

       Wiyot   L. L. Loud, *op. cit.*, p. 327; A. J. Bledsoe, *op. cit.*, p. 282; San
                   Francisco *Bulletin*, June 22, 1858.

       Athabascans A. J. Bledsoe, *op. cit.*, pp. 233, 256, 257, 265, 278, 285; L. L. Loud,
                   op. cit., p. 319; Sacramento *Union*, Jan. 27, June 10, 1858; San
                   Francisco *Bulletin*, Jan. 5, July 26, Aug. 4, 1858.

       Yuki   *Repts. Com. Mend. War*, testimony of B. Arthur, p. 51; Sacra-
                   mento *Union*, June 7, Aug. 16, Dec. 7, 1858.

       Hupa   San Francisco *Bulletin*, Nov. 9, 1858.
       Achomawi   Sacramento *Union*, May 6, 1858.

1859   Miwok   San Francisco *Bulletin*, Feb. 10, 1859.
       Maidu   R. A. Anderson, *Fighting the Mill Creeks* (Chico, 1909), pp. 21–
                   24; T. T. Waterman, *The Yana Indians*, Univ. Calif. Publ. Am.
                   Arch. and Ethn., 13:44; San Francisco *Bulletin*, Aug. 6 and 8,
                   1859; Sacramento *Union*, Sept. 2, 1859.

       Yana   Red Bluff *Beacon*, Feb. 2, 1859.
       Athabascans San Francisco *Bulletin*, July 11, Dec. 31, 1859.
       Yuki   *Repts. Com. Mend. War*, testimony of the following persons: W.
                   Frazier, p. 19; W. T. Scott, p. 21; L. Bataille, p. 26; H. H.
                   Buckles, p. 29; J. C. Hastings, p. 29; W. C. Hildreth, p. 32;
                   M. Corbett, p. 34; S. P. Storms, p. 38; G. W. Henley, p. 39;
                   H. L. Hall, pp. 41–44; T. B. Henley, p. 44; Sacramento *Union*,

Jan. 10 and 21, 1859; San Francisco *Bulletin*, Nov. 7, Dec. 12, 1859, Jan. 4 and 21, 1860.

Achomawi   W. C. Kibbe, *Report to the Governor* (Sacramento, 1860); Sacramento *Union*, Oct. 19, 1859; San Francisco *Bulletin*, Aug. 31, Sept. 8 and 28, Oct. 5, 1859, Jan. 21, 1860.

1860 Miwok   San Francisco *Bulletin*, Aug. 1, 1860.

Maidu   Marysville *Appeal*, July 3 and 8, 1860; San Francisco *Bulletin*, July 1, 1860.

Wiyot   A. J. Bledsoe, *op. cit.*, pp. 307–308; L. L. Loud, *op. cit.*, pp. 329–334; San Francisco *Bulletin*, Feb. 28, Mar. 2 and 13, 1860.

Athabascans   A. J. Bledsoe, *op. cit.*, p. 318; Sacramento *Union*, Jan. 26, 1860; San Francisco *Bulletin*, Mar. 13, Apr. 11, June 23, 1860.

Shasta   San Francisco *Bulletin*, Oct. 11, 1860.

1861 Wintun   Sacramento *Union*, June 12, Aug. 20, Sept. 18, 1861; Marysville *Appeal*, June 12, 1861.

Athabascans   A. J. Bledsoe, *op. cit.*, pp. 338, 342, 344, 345, 357–359; San Francisco *Bulletin*, Jan. 17, Feb. 4, Mar. 2, Apr. 24, May 29, June 11 and 19, 1861; Marysville *Appeal*, July 3, 4, and 9, 1861.

Wailaki   W. P. Dole, *Rept. Commr. Indian Affairs*, 1861, No. 63; San Francisco *Bulletin*, Jan. 26, 1861; Marysville *Appeal*, Oct. 22, 1861; Red Bluff *Beacon*, Oct. 24, 1861.

Chimariko   Sacramento *Union*, Aug. 13, 1861.

Yana   Marysville *Appeal*, May 7, 1861; San Francisco *Bulletin*, May 15, 1861.

1862 Wintun   Marysville *Appeal*, Aug. 7 and 30, 1862.

Yana   R. A. Anderson, *op. cit.*, p. 54; Marysville *Appeal*, Aug. 9, 1862; Red Bluff *Beacon*, Aug. 21, 1862.

Yurok   San Francisco *Bulletin*, Apr. 22, 1862.

Athabascans   A. J. Bledsoe, *op. cit.*, pp. 394, 396; San Francisco *Bulletin*, Feb. 27, June 27, July 12, Aug. 6 and 30, 1862; Sacramento *Union*, May 10, 1862; Marysville *Appeal*, Apr. 16, Sept. 2, 1862.

Hupa   Marysville *Appeal*, Apr. 16, 1862.

Wailaki   W. P. Dole, *Rept. Commr. Indian Affairs*, 1862, Nos. 62, 65; San Francisco *Bulletin*, Aug. 18, 1862.

Achomawi   J. H. Rogers, *Colusa County* (Orland, 1891), p. 91; San Francisco *Bulletin*, May 6, 1862; Red Bluff *Beacon*, May 10, 1862.

1863 Yokuts   San Francisco *Bulletin*, Apr. 27, May 26, 1863.

Wintun   Sacramento *Union*, July 3, 1863; Marysville *Appeal*, Oct. 7, Nov. 28, 1863.

Maidu   Sacramento *Union*, Mar. 16, 1863.

Yana   R. A. Anderson, *op. cit.*, pp. 64–70; T. T. Waterman, *op. cit.*, pp. 35–102; San Francisco *Bulletin*, Aug. 6, 1863; Sacramento *Union*, June 11, 1863; Marysville *Appeal*, July 29, 1863.

Yurok   A. J. Bledsoe, *op. cit.*, p. 406.

Athabascans   *Ibid.*, pp. 409, 415.

Hupa   *Ibid.*, pp. 425–427; Sacramento *Union*, Sept. 30, 1863.

Wailaki   W. P. Dole, *Rept. Commr Indian Affairs*, 1863, No. 31; Marysville *Appeal*, Sept. 26, 1863.

Yuki   San Francisco *Bulletin*, Aug. 14, 1863.

YEAR TRIBE

1864 Yana   Sacramento *Union*, Sept. 26, Oct. 10, 1864; Marysville *Appeal*,
                       Sept. 30, 1864.
      Yurok   San Francisco *Bulletin*, Mar. 26, 1864.
      Karok   *Ibid.*, Feb. 19, 1864.
      Athabascans A. J. Bledsoe, *op. cit.*, pp. 441–444; Sacramento *Union*, May 18,
                       June 7, 1864; San Francisco *Bulletin*, Apr. 30, July 15, 1864.

1865 Yana   G. C. Mansfield, *op. cit.*, pp. 219–223; T. T. Waterman, *op. cit.*,
                       pp. 52–53; Sacramento *Union*, July 24, Aug. 16, Sept. 4 and 26,
                       1865.

TABLE 4
POPULATION DECLINE DUE TO MILITARY CASUALTIES, 1848–1880

Tribe	Population in 1848	Population reduction up to 1880	Mortality due to warfare		
			Losses	Percentage of population in 1848	Percentage of population decline
Costanoan	1,000	700	none*	00.0	00.0
Salinan	500	400	none	00.0	00.0
Chumash	1,150	950	none	00.0	00.0
Yokuts	14,000	13,400	212	1.5	1.6
Western Mono	1,300	700	none	00.0	00.0
Wintun	8,000	6,500	506	6.3	7.9
Sierra Miwok	6,000	5,000	207	3.4	4.1
Maidu	7,000	6,000	347	5.0	5.8
Yana	1,900	1,880	221	11.6	11.9
Achomawi	3,000	1,500	412	13.7	27.4
Tolowa	450	250	47	10.4	18.8
Wiyot	1,400	1,200	176	12.6	14.7
Yurok	2,500	1,600	67	2.7	4.2
Karok	2,000	1,000	98	4.9	10.9
Yuki	3,500	3,100	573	16.4	18.5
Other Athabascans†	7,950	5,990	1,154	14.5	16.5
Shasta	3,100	2,600	179	5.8	6.9
Coast Miwok	300	240	none	00.0	00.0
Lake Miwok	200	180	none	00.0	00.0
Pomo	5,000	3,550	80	1.6	2.3
Wappo	800	750	none	00.0	00.0
Total	71,050	57,490	4,279	6.0	7.4

* The notation "none" signifies no mortality of specific record.
† Includes the Hupa, Chilula, Wailaki, Chimariko, and "Other Athabascans" of table 2.

TABLE 5
Social Homicide, 1852–1865*

Year	Maidu	Miwok	Shasta	Wintun	Northwestern Tribes	Pomo	Yokuts	Mission	Total
1852	3 M 7 E 11 T	1 M 1 E	1 E			1 E 1 L		2 M 1 L 2 E	
Total	21	2	1			2		5	31
1853	4 M 2 M-i 3 E 10 T	1 M-i		2 M 1 M-i 4 E					
Total	19	1		7					27
1854	1 M-i 2 L-i 4 E 1 S	1 M			1 M-i	1 E	1 S	2 M	
Total	8	1			1	1	1	2	14
1855	2 M-i 1 E		2 M 1 S	2 E			1 E		
Total	3		3	2			1		9

1856..........	1 L-i 1 S-i 2 T	3 L-i 1 E 10 T					18
Total..........	4	14					18
1857..........	7 M 12 M-i 2 L-i 5 S 2 E	3 L-i	1 M-i	1 M-i 4 E		2 L-i	39
Total..........	28	3	1	5		2	39
1858..........	1 M-i 2 L-i 2 E 1 T	2 M 1 M-i 1 S 1 E		2 M	1 M 1 E	2 L-i 1 E	18
Total..........	6	5		2	2	3	18

* Data from newspapers only.

Note.—The following abbreviations are used in the table:

M	Murders of Indians by whites, cause unknown; total, 48.	S	Murders of Indians by whites, women involved; total, 18.
M-i	Murders of Indians by Indians, cause unknown; total, 42.	S-i	Murders of Indians by Indians, women involved; total, 3.
L	Murders of whites by Indians, liquor involved; total, 11.	E	Executions or lynchings after or during a crime or misdemeanor; total, 73.
L-i	Murders of Indians by Indians, liquor involved; total, 38.	T	Intertribal feuds and warfare; total, 56.

TABLE 5—*Concluded*

Year	Maidu	Miwok	Shasta	Wintun	Northwestern Tribes	Pomo	Yokuts	Mission	Total
1859	4 M 2 M-i 2 L-i 2 S 2 S-i 2 E	2 M 4 M-i 1 E	1 M-i 2 S 1 E	1 E	10 T	2 M	2 E	1 M	
Total	14	7	4	1	10	2	2	1	41
1860	1 L-i 3 E 1 T	2 M-i 8 L 1 E		1 M-i 1 S 1 E	1 S 2 E			1 L-i 1 E	
Total	5	11		3	3			2	24
1861	2 M-i 4 L-i 2 E 2 T	1 E	2 L-i 1 E 3 T	1 E				1 L-i 1 E	
Total	10	1	6	1				2	20

Year									Total
1862..........	1 M-i 1 L-i 2 E 2 T	2 L-i 3 E	2 M-i	1 M 2 L-i	1 M 2 T		1 L	1 M	21
Total..........	6	5	2	3	3		1	1	21
1863..........	1 M-i 1 E	1 M 1 L-i 1 E			2 S 2 T		1 E		10
Total..........	2	3			4		1		10
1864..........	1 M-i 1 E	1 L-i 1 E	1 M 1 E				1 M 2 L-i	1 L-i	10
Total..........	2	2	2				3	1	10
1865..........	1 M 1 M-i 1 E	1 M		1 S			2 M		7
Total..........	3	1		1			2		7
Total all years......	131	56	19	18	23	12	14	16	289

* Data from newspapers only.

NOTE.—The following abbreviations are used in the table:

M   Murders of Indians by whites, cause unknown; total, 48.
M-i Murders of Indians by Indians, cause unknown; total, 42.
L   Murders of Indians by whites, liquor involved; total, 11.
L-i Murders of Indians by Indians, liquor involved; total, 38.
S   Murders of Indians by whites, women involved; total, 18.
S-i Murders of Indians by Indians, women involved; total, 3.
E   Executions or lynchings after or during a crime or misdemeanor; total, 73.
T   Intertribal feuds and warfare; total, 56.

PART FOUR

Trends in Marriage and Divorce since 1850

Originally published as *Ibero-Americana* Volume 24, 1943

ACKNOWLEDGMENTS

THE AUTHOR wishes to recognize the generosity of the Committee on Research of the University of California for helping defray necessary expenses incident to the gathering of data. He also desires to express his appreciation of the coöperation and courtesy of the following superintendents and their staffs in making available the content of Agency records: at Sacramento, Mr. Roy Nash; at Eureka, Mr. O. M. Boggess; at Stewart, Mr. Don C. Foster; and at Riverside, Mr. John W. Dady.

INTRODUCTION

RECENT STUDIES concerning competition among groups of animals have emphasized the very important effects upon numbers and survival which attend any interspecific conflict or contact. The investigations of many biologists have extended to the realm of man some of the principles derived from observations of behavior in animal populations. Such advances have, however, been confined essentially to considerations of a physical or physiological nature. The reason for this restriction of effort has been primarily the desirability, if not the necessity, of confining attention to phenomena which are susceptible to strict and rigid statistical treatment. Nevertheless it is to be conceded without serious question that interaction between groups and races of human beings involves also a set of factors, social rather than purely biological, which is of very great significance and which sets man apart from all other organic species. Any data, therefore, which throw light on the social implications of intergroup relationships are of value in filling out the picture drawn by the general human biologist.

Specifically, the problem is that of the contact between a primitive social group, the aboriginal Indian population of northern California, and the more complex culture introduced by Anglo- and Ibero-American civilization. The fundamental question is: To what extent and how has the Indian reacted or responded to the change of environment brought about by the influx of white men? Certain material and physical aspects of the matter have been treated elsewhere.[1] Here it is proposed to deal with marriage and divorce, or, perhaps better, with connubial union and disunion. This item has been selected from the general cultural pattern because by chance we possess sufficient material of a numerical character to permit its quantitative study.

---

[1] S. F. Cook, *The Extent and Significance of Disease among the Indians of Baja California, 1697–1773*, Univ. Calif. Publ., Ibero-Americana, No. 12 (1937); *Population Trends among the California Mission Indians, ibid.*, No. 17 (1940); *The Mechanism and Extent of Dietary Adaptation among Certain Groups of California and Nevada Indians, ibid.*, No. 18 (1941).

SOURCES OF INFORMATION

Marriage, among the aboriginal tribes, was a definite, fully recognized social concept. Reference to the voluminous anthropological literature of the past four decades will show that the California tribes had worked out a set of customs, rituals, and mores, pertaining to marriage which, although presenting minor differences from group to group, was quite uniform throughout the territory. During and subsequent to the invasion by the white man, the Indian population was seriously reduced and the survivors were either segregated on reservations or tolerated as individuals among the white population. In either event the entire social environment was radically altered. The institution of marriage as it had existed previously was forced to compete with the European and Christian idea of strict indissoluble monogamy with its civil and religious ceremonial implications. Considerable moral pressure was thus exerted upon the Indian to abandon his traditional concept of marital relations and to adopt that of the white man. To what extent he has since yielded to such pressure and adapted himself to the altered social environment may now be discussed.

The data which permit us to form some estimate of the adaptive Indian response are to be found in the Probate Proceedings of the United States Bureau of Indian Affairs. These may be obtained at most of the established Agencies, and have been utilized here from the Sacramento, Hoopa Valley, and Mission agencies in California and the Stewart Agency in Nevada. In the 1890's the land allotment system was introduced, whereby Indians were permitted to take up unoccupied land. Many such allotments were made in the years immediately subsequent to 1895. At the demise of any allottee, thereafter, it was necessary to establish the heirs, as is the procedure with any other estate. For this purpose an Examiner of Inheritance was appointed, who investigated each case, heard witnesses, and made a formal report on heirship. Since the heirs, as a rule, were the spouse and children, the marital history was carefully investigated. We have, therefore, a body of direct evidence bearing on the conjugal habits of the Indians.

In judging the validity of the data contained in the agency records certain restrictions and qualifications must be set forth. It must be recognized that this source of information throws little light on the problem of random sex relations, or promiscuity. In determining heirship and family relationships it is of no interest to a probate officer how many casual sex affairs were indulged in by a man or woman, provided these were extramarital and resulted in no offspring. In other words, he deals only in the unions which are sanctioned and recognized by the community as being sufficiently binding to warrant application of the term "marriage." We now encounter the fact that these bona fide marriages have been of two types. The first is that endorsed by the ordinary American white society: marriage with the consent of the law and usually with the blessing of the church. This type is designated as "ceremony" or "legal" in the records. The other is the so-called "Indian Custom" union. Primitively, all that was necessary in order to establish a recognized Indian family or household was for a man and woman to take up a common abode. This act characteristically was accompanied by certain forms and rituals, differing somewhat according to the tribe but possessing considerable binding force. When the Indian was driven into economic and social competition with the white man, most of these subsidiary rites and ceremonies were eliminated, but the central act has always remained. Consequently, an Indian Custom marriage means simply open and admitted cohabitation, without benefit of civil or religious ceremony. The United States Indian Service, recognizing that these unions carried the full approval and public endorsement of the Indian community, has for purposes of possession and inheritance of property placed them upon a plane of complete equality with those contracted in conformity with American law. The probate records therefore, tell nothing of the *sub rosa* or casual sex relations of the Indians, but deal specifically with those alliances regarded as legitimate by either the Indian or the white social order.

Much the same considerations apply to divorce. The original method among the Indians was very simple—mere separation. No particular ritual was necessary. Mutual consent or even dissatisfaction on the part of either spouse constituted adequate grounds. Despite the extreme looseness of the marriage tie—a looseness offensive to the orthodox morality of the white race—these Indian Custom separations or divorces have been recognized by the Indian Service.

The accuracy of the records may be open to some question. In relatively few cases is there documentary or formal proof of matrimonial relations, such as marriage certificates or court proceedings; most of the evidence is in the form of verbal testimony offered by relatives and friends. Where the deceased has been a young person, with many individuals conversant with his or her affairs, this testimony appears to be on the whole quite reliable since, as pointed out previously, even an Indian Custom marriage or divorce is based upon community knowledge and consent. On the other hand, a person dying at an advanced age would be likely to leave few contemporaries who would know the details of his youth. Thus it is probable that early and childless marriages by older individuals may have escaped the memory of modern witnesses. To compensate for such omissions, however, there is the fact that the youth of such individuals was spent during the period prior to or simultaneous with white occupation of the region. Hence any marriages occurring then must have been of the Indian Custom type. With respect to the actual credibility of the witnesses, the internal evidence seems to indicate a reasonably high level of veracity coupled with a sincere attempt to furnish reliable information. Moreover, it must be remembered that, since the inheritance of money or property is at stake, a motive is provided which would induce witnesses to mention all spouses, children, grandchildren, and other possible heirs of the deceased.

The most serious source of error is one not of intent but of circumstances. A point of interest from the social standpoint is the mode of termination of these Indian marriages: Were the husband and wife living together when death claimed one of them, or had they previously been divorced by Indian custom? In many cases, particularly those of elderly persons, it is beyond the power of witnesses to establish whether the husband or wife who died long ago had or had not been divorced prior to death. Furthermore, once the fact of predecease is proven, the question of possible divorce becomes of secondary interest to the examiner himself. Therefore it is probable that, in certain instances where termination of the marriage by death is indicated on the records, the couple had actually separated before any death occurred. This possible source of error must be considered in evaluation of the data.

The probate records give us data pertaining not to the entire population but only a sample of it. Nevertheless it is probable that this sample is adequate numerically and that it is sufficiently representative of the population at large. The whole number may be taken directly from the reservation and agency censuses. The date of the particular census used is immaterial, because, since 1895, the time of first allotments, there has been no significant change in the number of Indians. The approximate population figures for the four regions studied are: Sacramento 4,300, Hoopa Valley 2,000, Carson 2,400, Mission 2,800, giving 11,500 as a total.[2] This value, therefore, represents the average number of persons from whom information on marriage could be drawn. However, the probate records began with deaths occurring in 1895 and continue up to the present, a period of approximately forty-five years. The age distribution of the population is such that somewhat over 50 per cent of the individuals are over twenty years old, and hence in the marriageable category. In 1895, consequently, there would have been 5,750 adults married or capable of marriage. Since the length of an Indian generation is about twenty-five years, 1.8 new generations have reached the age of twenty since allotments were made. Adding 1.8 × 5,750, or 10,350 to the original 5,750 alive in 1895, we get the round value of 16,100 individuals from whom a sample of married persons might be drawn. Actually the sample includes 2,800 persons, or 17 per cent of the total. Although the sample is purely a random one, it is of sufficient magnitude.

The unrepresented fraction falls into two categories. First, there are those who have reached the age of maturity but who have not yet died; hence their estates have not yet been probated. Consequently, the sample from the younger generation is not as large as might be desired. Since there has been no selective mortality among these Indians, death has introduced no serious error. The second category consists of those

---

[2] The total number of Indians enrolled at the Carson Agency is nearly 6,000. However, the probate records were studied only for the groups designated "Carson Indians," "Walker River," and "Fallon." The population in this territory is roughly that given, 2,400.

who did not take allotments and who have never inherited any. In other words, the probate records apply only to those who died possessing at least a small amount of property. These individuals and their descendants represent beyond question the upper economic stratum of the population. The relatively shiftless, unambitious, and migratory persons are as a rule excluded, and we are dealing, in the statistical sense, with only the socially solid and stable element. The implication is clear. This more stable and conservative group which would secure and operate land allotments would be that part of the whole population which, by and large, would evince the greatest conformity and stability in marital relations—responsible heads of families, housewives, children raised amid moderately favorable domestic surroundings. To express this situation in as quantitative a form as the circumstances permit, we may say that we have data pertaining to between 30 and 40 per cent of the most favored half of the population, or, let us say, the middle and upper classes of Indian society.

The data have been organized and presented in condensed form in tables 1 to 6. The first two of these show the trend in marriage. The Indian groups are segregated according to social and historical environment. Thus the Sacramento records are subdivided to show the difference between the Indians at Round Valley and those who were never reservationized. Similarly, for Hoopa Valley a distinction can be made between the Hupa tribe and the mixture of Yurok, Karok, and perhaps other northwestern peoples who inhabit the same reservation. Although the records include numerous Washo, they are grouped with the Paiute, because both tribes have been subject to the same influences. The Indians under the jurisdiction of the Mission Agency fall rather naturally into two groups, those designated "Old Mission," and "Cahuilla." The former are, in the main, descendants of the Diegueños, Luiseños and Juaneños who inhabited the Spanish missions and who have been subjected to strong Church influence for over one hundred and fifty years. The latter are predominantly, although perhaps not wholly, derived from the unconverted gentiles who infested the mission frontier and among whom the Church influence was very weak prior to 1850.

In these tables the Indian Custom and the legal marriages are shown

TABLE 1
Type of Marriage, According to Approximate Date of Marriage

Groups	Prior to 1880			1880–1895			1896–1919			1920–1940		
	I.C.*	L.	Percentage I.C.	I.C.	L.	Percentage I.C.	I.C.	L.	Percentage I.C.	I.C.	L.	Percentage I.C.
Round Valley	283	17	94	182	37	83	44	99	31	5	11	31
California nonreservation	443	8	98	499	11	98	328	43	88	23	8	74
Yurok-Karok	288	11	96	271	10	96	83	77	52	13	34	28
Hupa	34	1	97	42	12	77	13	19	40	2	13	13
Paiute	437	0	100	414	0	100	427	32	93	67	18	79
Old Mission	58	60	49	56	70	44	24	75	24	6	13	31
Cahuilla	42	7	85	55	9	86	40	52	43	6	12	33

* I.C. = Indian Custom; L. = Legal.

TABLE 2
Marriages According to the Birth Date of the Individual

Groups	Prior to 1849			1850–1879			1880–1909		
	I.C.*	L.	Percentage I.C.	I.C.	L.	Percentage I.C.	I.C.	L.	Percentage I.C.
Round Valley	263	31	89	238	87	73	11	60	18
California nonreservation	462	11	98	584	30	95	185	30	87
Yurok-Karok	281	11	96	330	42	89	54	63	46
Hupa	19	0	100	66	30	69	6	16	27
Paiute	455	0	100	677	10	99	239	36	87
Old Mission	58	59	49	81	117	41	9	38	19
Cahuilla	23	10	70	101	32	76	17	39	30

* I.C. = Indian Custom; L. = Legal.

as they occurred in different eras. Table 1 uses the date of marriage to establish the time scale. This is somewhat difficult, because the probate records do not specify as a rule the exact year of marriage. However, it is possible to set up three periods: prior to 1880, from 1880 to 1895, and subsequent to 1895. Although it is nearly always possible to allocate a marriage to its proper period, it was felt desirable to check and reinforce this tabulation by arranging the marriages (in table 2) according to the birth date of the individual. The records are sufficiently accurate to permit a segregation by decades, but if this is done, the number of cases per decade may become too small. Consequently three arbitrary periods were chosen, to conform roughly to those used in table 1.[3]

The divorce data have been handled in a similar manner. Here the point at issue is whether a certain marriage ended by the death of one of the parties or by a divorce. Moreover, the situation is complicated by the fact that there are two kinds of marriage, Indian Custom and legal, and two kinds of divorce, Indian Custom and legal, all combinations of which have occurred. In table 3 the complete data are set forth, with time based upon the date of marriage. With Indian Custom marriages only Indian Custom divorces are shown, since there is record of no more than three such marriages which were dissolved by a white tribunal.[4] For legal marriages, both Indian Custom and legal divorces are indicated, since both occur frequently. However, in calculating the percentage of divorces with respect to deaths, the total divorces, irrespective of kind, have been employed. In table 3 and subsequently, the term "separation" is used to denote the breaking apart of the wedlock by any cause other than death.

Table 4 presents the same material as table 3 with one alteration.

[3] In table 1 the third period has been split into two parts: 1896–1919 and 1920–1940. It was not feasible to do this in table 2.

[4] An interesting question of law arises in this connection. Can a marriage consummated by tribal custom be dissolved by act of court? Apparently in California it can, or it has been in the past, the court holding that a tribal marriage is equivalent to a common-law marriage and hence capable of dissolution by a court. Another thorny legal problem which has perplexed the Indian Service has been what to do when an Indian couple, after legal union, separate by Indian Custom and then marry other persons, perhaps by ceremony. The administrative officers of the Indian Service have uniformly handled these situations according to the dictates of common sense and the welfare of their charges rather than according to the strict letter of Federal and state law.

TABLE 3

Separations Based on Type and Date of Marriage

INDIAN CUSTOM MARRIAGES

Groups	Prior to 1880			1880–1895			After 1895			Entire period		
	D.*	I.C.	Percentage I.C.	D.	I.C.	Percentage I.C.	D.	I.C.	Percentage I.C.	D.	I.C.	Percentage I.C.
Round Valley	211	68	24	122	66	35	23	15	39	356	149	29.5
California nonreservation	329	95	22	381	105	22	229	109	32	939	309	24.8
Yurok-Karok	235	52	19	190	61	25	81	38	32	506	151	23.0
Hupa	29	4	12	28	11	28	8	6	43	65	21	24.4
Paiute	346	78	19	290	123	30	317	178	36	953	379	28.4
Old Mission	45	12	12	28	27	49	17	13	43	89	52	36.8
Cahuilla	33	7	18	45	11	20	22	23	51	100	41	29.1
All groups	1,228	316	20.5	1,084	404	27.2	697	382	35.4	3,008	1,102	26.8

LEGAL MARRIAGES

Groups	Prior to 1880				1880–1895				After 1895				Entire period			
	D.	I.C.	L.	Percentage S.	D.	I.C.	L.	Percentage S.	D.	I.C.	L.	Percentage S.	D.	I.C.	L.	Percentage S.
Round Valley	14	3	0	18	23	8	4	34	103	4	8	10	140	15	12	16.1
California nonreservation	7	0	0	0	6	0	1	18	42	4	5	21	55	4	6	15.4
Yurok-Karok	10	0	0	0	8	0	1	11	79	12	5	26	97	12	6	15.7
Hupa	1	0	0	0	13	0	0	0	26	3	2	16	40	3	2	11.1
Paiute	0	0	0	0	0	0	0	0	38	12	3	28	38	12	3	28.0
Old Mission	49	9	0	16	62	6	0	9	73	17	3	21	184	32	3	15.6
Cahuilla	10	0	0	0	5	1	0	17	53	9	2	17	68	10	2	15.0
All groups	91	12	0	11.7	117	15	6	15.2	414	61	27	17.5	622	88	33	16.3

* D. = Death; L. = Legal divorce; I.C. = Indian Custom divorce; S. = Separation by either I.C. or L. or both.

In the latter, people of all ages are included. As a result the period prior to 1880 includes very largely individuals well advanced in years, since they had to be surviving at least in 1895. Therefore, in order to secure a homogenous age group, in assembling the data for table 4 the records of all persons who died or were separated after the age of thirty years were deleted. Table 5 corresponds to table 2 in using the birth date as a basis of time, but, even at the risk of showing too few cases per group, ten-year intervals are employed.

MARRIAGE FORMS

On surveying the material presented in the tables one perceives clearly that two quite distinct cultural phenomena are involved, marriage and separation. What we are dealing with actually is the form of marriage and the fact of separation. (The type of separation may be neglected for the moment.) When the white man first encountered the Indian, the latter possessed a social system which envisaged the union of a man and woman for the purpose of rearing a family and establishing a social unit. It also envisaged the disruption of that unit if and when the contracting parties for any reason so desired. Both marriage and separation then, were matters to be decided by the individuals concerned and in no way did they involve formal permission of the state. Certain formalities and procedures, to be sure, were considered proper and were endorsed by community public opinion. But it was within the power of the persons concerned to determine whether there should or should not be a union or a separation.

Now, when the dominating civilization of the white race in both the Ibero- and Anglo-American forms impinged upon native society, pressure was brought to bear at two points. Marriage as an institution was not disturbed, but the rites, the ceremonies, the customs pertaining to it were to be altered. Separation, on the other hand, was to be thrown out almost completely, for separation without a legal divorce was not to be tolerated, and the difficulties in obtaining such a divorce, at least in the early days, were in effect insurmountable. The Indian, therefore, had to make adjustment in two directions if he was to fit into the new scheme of society. With respect to marriage, he had to alter certain ritualistic practices; in other words, he had to make a purely cultural and perhaps relatively superficial adaptation. With respect to divorce, he had to make a profound social, sexual, and psychological change if he were to yield his aboriginal and individual right to separate from his spouse according to his transitory desires. To what extent he has been able, in one hundred years, to achieve these adaptations may be ascertained from an examination of the tabulated data.

In all seven groups, despite quantitative differences among them, there has been a definite change of habit in the marriage ritual or ceremony. Among those born prior to 1840 the tendency was obviously toward Indian Custom marriage. Since most of these individuals had arrived at adulthood prior to the entrance of the whites, no legal marriages in their youth were possible. Indeed, the records show that, except for the mission Indians, all the legal unions consummated among this age group fall into two categories. The persons concerned either married during the later years of their lives after they had long been subjected to contact with the American social order, or they were the spouses of those few white settlers who were willing to legalize their relations with Indian women. With the passing of time the various groups diverged, but for all of them the proportion of legal marriages increased.

Looking at the matter broadly, we may say that the adaptation on the part of the Indians has been moderately effective. A good deal depends on the point of view. If one pictures the California aborigine as a hard and fast traditionalist, a person who never deviates from the system of his forefathers, then it may appear surprising that since the turn of the century nearly one-half the marriages have been according to white rather than Indian custom. On the other hand, if one remembers that great social pressure has been exerted to force the change and that, after all, only the form of the marriage is affected, then the adaptive process may seem slow. Today, one hundred years after heavy white settlement began, the Indian Custom marriage still persists even in certain very enlightened Indian communities and may characterize, throughout the entire territory, perhaps one-tenth to one-quarter of the marital unions. This argues a certain degree of flexibility in Indian habit, but at the same time a quite powerful conservative tendency.

On the whole, the records of past and present indicate a gradual but certain weakening of this tendency, which is sure to result in the total disappearance of tribal custom matrimony.

The variations between the groups are significant in that they are closely associated with the intensity of white cultural and social pressure. If we do not insist upon too great exactness in detail, we may classify the seven groups in three broad categories from the standpoint of the rapidity of their cultural adaptation. The first includes the Round Valley Reservation, the Hupa tribe, and the Old Mission Indians. Their marriages for the period 1896–1940 show respectively 31, 32 and 25 per cent Indian Custom. If we had the data for the past five years, we would probably find no more than 5 per cent. The Round Valley people and the Hupa in the earliest period married almost wholly by Indian Custom. The Old Mission Indians did not (49 per cent Indian Custom), quite obviously because of mission influence.

The second type embraces the Yurok-Karok of the Klamath and the so-called Cahuilla aggregate in the south. These have shown a quite marked change but no such profound alteration as the previously mentioned groups. Moreover, the shift in their adaptation has come later, for in the middle period they had deviated not at all from the earliest period. The third category includes the Nevada Paiute and the non-reservation tribes of central California. These numerically strong bands have demonstrated very little evidence of marital adaptation. The Paiute, since 1895, have on record 91 per cent Indian Custom marriages, and since 1920 there have been 79 per cent such unions.

The cause of these differences cannot lie in the genetic make-up or inherent character of these peoples, for they are, by and large, a fairly homogeneous race. It must then be looked for in the social surroundings to which the various tribes have been exposed.

The most powerful and most evident factor has been the subjection of certain Indians not to the social order at large, but to specific agents thereof. We immediately note that the Round Valley Indians and the Hupa have been, since 1860, under the direct guidance and supervision of the Indian Service. Moreover, unlike some jurisdictions, in these localities the Indians have been gathered together into a compact mass where they can be easily and constantly kept under the eye of the agent. The moral efforts of the Indian Service have always been directed toward the legalization of the marital status. In these instances, such efforts could be brought to bear directly and continuously. To the governmental must be added the religious influence exerted by the contiguity of church organizations, as well as by missionaries actually on the reservation.

The mission Indians show the effect of such moral pressure very clearly. Indeed, they constitute a special case. We may assume freely that in, let us say, 1835 every mission Indian among the Diegueños, Luiseños and Juaneños had been married legally (and in the Church). Since these tribes were almost completely missionized, we may assume not more than 2 or 3 per cent Indian Custom marriages from 1800 to 1835. When the southern missions broke up, the neophytes scattered but remained more or less in their old territory. The great power of mission discipline was lost, and the natives underwent a reversion to their former habits. This is clearly shown by the fact that, of the marriages consummated from approximately 1850 to 1880, 49 per cent were Indian Custom. The tremendous cultural force of the mission organization and subsequent efforts of the fathers is shown, however, in the 51 per cent who married under Christian auspices. During the latter half of the nineteenth century a condition of static equilibrium apparently prevailed until, in the past forty or fifty years, the joint efforts of the Catholic Church and the United States Indian Service have reduced Indian Custom marriage almost to the vanishing point. The extraordinary tenacity of cultural tradition must be stressed nevertheless. Among the Round Valley and Hupa Indians, and even slightly among the descendants of the mission converts, tribal custom still persists.

The intermediate category shows the effect of church and reservation influence to a lesser degree. These people have been on the fringes, as it were. The Yurok and Karok were reservationized, to be sure, but they lacked the close tribal unity of the Hupa and always have been somewhat less accessible in their homes along the Klamath. The ideas of white society as carried by the usual political and ecclesiastical agencies have simply penetrated more slowly, and hence the results are not as striking.

The third category represents a far extreme. The nonreservation Indians of California have encountered official pressure only sporadically, and local religious effort has seldom been turned in their direction. Indeed, no consistent and organized effort has ever been made to alter their marital customs. The Northern Paiute and the Washo have, to be sure, been under Federal supervision for many years, and various religious bodies have been concerned with their welfare. But their population is large, whereas the white population is small. They are scattered over a vast extent of territory. Until recently, communication has been difficult. Moreover, they have in all respects retained their primitive outlook and customs to a far greater extent than any of the California tribes. For geographical and ethnic reasons, therefore, it has been substantially impossible for the Indian Service to exert that continuous, consistent pressure which is necessary for the conversion of deep-seated cultural traits.

Despite the great potency of direct propaganda, as shown in the missions and elsewhere, other factors are also of significance in determining marital trends. One of these is purely economic. In most sections of California and Nevada, an Indian couple, in order to marry by white ceremony, must make considerable exertion. This was even more true prior to the advent of the automobile. As a rule, they must travel to the county seat, file application for a license, and pay fees. All this may entail financial sacrifice, as well as inconvenience. In this respect the Paiute and California nonreservation Indians are most adversely affected, for they live in relatively thinly settled country. On the reservations, however, the agencies, as well as various religious organizations, have striven to facilitate the procedure of legal marriage. Indeed, the agents themselves have often officiated. Among the mission descendants, the difficulties of time, space, and money have been solved by the priests, who are always among their people and who have always brought the ceremony to them rather than making them go to the ceremony. It cannot be maintained that the factor of convenience and financial sacrifice has had great weight, particularly when any other real motive was involved. But one can appreciate that, other things being equal and human nature being what it is, an Indian couple would resort to the easiest and simplest manner of marrying.

A third factor concerns the social relations between natives and whites apart from any agencies or organizations specifically interested in the natives. After all, for a hundred years the Indian in the West has had to live his daily life not in the shadow of the superintendent's office or of the parish house, but among the average run of white people of both Latin and Nordic extraction. The character of the mutual relationship would be certain to influence the behavior of the native. Furthermore, the relative density of the two populations would be critical.

The Hupa and the Round Valley Indians were, in the eighteen-fifties, extremely hostile to the whites. Nevertheless, after the transition period had passed, these communities, although perhaps not entirely happy, were for decades on reasonably peaceful and felicitous terms with the neighboring white people. In addition, they were shielded by the government from contact with the more vicious and criminal white element. Hence they were in a condition relatively receptive to cultural infiltration. At least, there was no emotional barrier to American ideas. Finally, there were enough whites in the immediate vicinity to bring these ideas constantly to the attention of the natives. The situation of the mission Indians was still more favorable. Barring the transitory disturbances over land problems, there was never any open conflict between the ex-mission Indians and the whites. Furthermore, the character of the white population was different owing to the large Spanish and Mexican element present in southern California. The Ibero-Americans have always had a facility for assimilating the native which was not possessed by the Anglo-Americans, and this characteristic made it much easier for the mission Indians to merge with the general population, not only politically and economically, but culturally. Another strongly favorable influence has been the Catholic Church, not because of its propagandizing activities but because it brought the Spanish and Indian components of the population together on a common ground of faith and ritual. The transition of marital custom, therefore, has proceeded here in a definitely friendly rather than indifferent or hostile atmosphere.[5]

---

[5] The merging of the native into the general population has proceeded farther in coastal southern California than anywhere else in the state and perhaps on the west coast. The Mission Agency files, from which the present data were drawn, carries on its census

The Yurok and other Klamath River tribes have had much the same history as the Hupa in so far as their relations with the white settlers are concerned. The observed difference in their marital response, therefore, must be referable to other factors. The Indians of the interior of southern California entered the American period of colonization with no background of Christian culture such as the missions had given to their brethren of the coastal strip. On the contrary, their adherence to primitive customs was probably intensified by half a century of sporadic armed conflict with, first, the Spanish civil and religious authorities, and then with the American. By 1860, however, this hostility had died down, and the refractory Shoshoneans and Diegueños of the desert began to amalgamate materially and spiritually with the remnants of the mission neophytes. As soon as they did this, they fell under the same influences which were so effective with the latter. As a result, subsequent to 1895 the relative number of legal marriages increased with great rapidity until at present there is little to distinguish between the two groups. The nonreservation Indians and the Paiute have had a very different history. The nonreservation aggregate consists of the remnants of former large tribes—Pomo, Achomawi, Maidu, Miwok, Yokuts—who persisted in their native habitat and who for three generations have fought a long, tough fight for survival. They have been surrounded by busy, aggressive Americans with whom they have had unfriendly and often hostile relations. There has been no inclination on the part of the farmer or miner or businessman to alter Indian tribal custom and very little desire on the part of the Indian to make his ways conform to those of the whites. Economically and politically, these Indians have been a submerged caste. Culturally, they have been let alone, as long as their habits and behavior did not bring offense to the whites. Thus there has been no motive supplied by either side to induce a change in marital custom. Indeed, apart from very mild governmental pressure, the only purely cultural factors which could have operated to bring about a conversion to American

---

rolls some 3,000 persons who are recognized as government wards. There is another group of substantially the same size which is not under the jurisdiction of the agency at all. These people have passed over into American life almost completely and are indistinguishable from other elements in the citizenry. It is doubtful whether among these assimilated natives any tribal custom whatever exists. The only type of marriage common to them is that which is sanctioned by the state and church.

matrimony have been the force of example, the gradual conditioning to the new type through years of observation and acquaintance, and the final tendency to adopt new manners through pure imitation and familiarity. Obviously, these forces will be exceedingly weak if any contrary motive or drive is in existence, and it is only within comparatively recent years that the antipathy to the whites and all their ways has receded sufficiently to permit imitativeness of itself to become at all effective. Furthermore, the degree to which the latter force can accomplish results depends also upon the relative population densities. If a large body of Indians is situated in a remote region containing only a few white people, even though mutual feelings are neutral or even friendly, white custom cannot impress itself upon the Indians, simply for lack of opportunity. On the other hand, if a few Indians live in the midst of a heavy white population—as in a well-developed farming community or in a town—the Indians fairly quickly come to follow the example of their neighbors. The nonreservation Indians of central and northern California have lived in relatively remote regions and have never had contact with large bodies of white people. Hence the imitative tendency has been poorly developed. An even better illustration of adaptational failure due to lack of close interracial and social contact is that of the Paiute, who, in the great spaces of Nevada, see and observe only a few members of the white race. Isolation has contributed notably to their lack of progress.[6]

One other factor which has helped to determine the extent of cultural adaptation has been the degree of racial interbreeding characterizing a particular group. It is quite evident that, if one of the two parents in a family is white, he or she will use influence with the children on the question of marriage. This force becomes increasingly strong the greater the removal from pure Indian blood, until in families of one-quarter, one-eighth or less Indian blood, the white custom is quite irresistible. Added to the intrafamily influence is that of the

---

[6] It is worth noting that, in so far as one can derive an impression from the records, without careful statistical analysis being possible, those subdivisions of the Paiute and Washo, such as the Carson and Reno colonies, who have lived nearest to the larger communities have adopted legal marriage to a moderate extent. On the other hand, those bands which have lived at large over the state or who have been located at sparsely settled points, such as near Pyramid Lake or on the Walker River, have tended to retain the Indian Custom.

immediate community, which under these circumstances is usually essentially American in ideas and oulook, for families and individuals of very low degree Indian blood tend to gravitate to regions populated predominantly or exclusively by white people.[7]

We have not at hand now sufficient data on interbreeding to make possible any comparisons between the groups considered here, with the exception of the Old Mission Indians. Barring the latter, a purely subjective impression gained from examination of the probate records is that miscegenation has proceeded to substantially the same extent among all the natives concerned. Perhaps the Paiute and Washo have mixed less freely with the white race than the California tribes. If so, a further partial explanation would be afforded of the slow response of the former to cultural impressions. There is no doubt that the Old Mission Indians have in their veins far more white blood than any other west-coast natives. This is due first to the fact that they have been living among white people for a very long time and, second, to the fact that the particular branch of the white race with which they have been in contact, the Ibero-American, has always been socially well disposed toward miscegenation. From the earliest times the Spanish intermarried freely and on a status of equality with the natives, and in more recent times the heavy immigration of Mexicans and other Latin Americans has provided a huge and convenient reservoir of potential spouses. One need only examine the names carried on the Mission Agency rolls and the names of those white men or women who have married Indians to appreciate the tremendous degree of racial fusion in southern California between the Indian and the American of Spanish extraction. Since the latter is almost invariably a person of the Catholic faith and possessed of strong convictions on the subject of marriage, it is easy to perceive the weight introduced by this factor.

To summarize the foregoing discussion, we find that in its quantita-

[7] From this category of mixed-blood families must be rigorously excluded those which resulted many years ago from illicit affairs carried on by the so-called "squaw men," usually unattached white males of dubious social background who cohabited freely with Indian women. Undoubtedly, thousands of halfbreeds resulted from such unions between 1848 and 1870. From the purely social standpoint these progeny were essentially Indian. They were reared by their Indian mothers, with a few honorable exceptions, and lived in the tribe as Indians, thereby assimilating native culture in its entirety plus perhaps a superficial familiarity with white civilization.

tive aspect modification in form of marriage has been a function of four variables. The first has been the intensity with which the white race has consciously attempted by means of directive agencies to alter Indian habit or tradition. The second is the economic, spatial, and temporal convenience attending a potential alteration. The third is the character and degree of general cultural intercourse between contiguous segments of the two races, together with relative population densities. The fourth is the distance to which racial mixture has been carried within a particular group. In so far as the Probate Records are a test they show a close conformity between expectation and result.

DIVORCE OR SEPARATION

An examination of the data pertaining to divorce or separation demonstrates certain manifest trends. In the first place, from the tables it is clear that the tendency to dissolve unions is much weaker in legal than in Indian Custom marriages. Thus, throughout the entire period, over one-quarter of the individuals who married by the latter method separated from their partners prior to the death of either party. Of persons united by legal ceremony, only 16 per cent thus separated. Moreover, of this group approximately one-quarter went through the procedure of obtaining a court decree, rather than being contented with the extralegal, informal Indian method. These findings speak eloquently of the binding force inherent in the white institution of marriage. Several factors have probably contributed to this result. For example, those who sought legal marriage originally would be precisely those to whom the white culture was closest and to whom the inviolability of the marriage contract would make the greatest appeal. Furthermore, the social reaction of the white population would be much stronger against infraction of a ceremony marriage than an Indian Custom union, for the latter has never been seriously regarded by the community at large. But the application of primitive divorce ethics to a legal marriage, together with probable adultery and bigamy, is a situation which, if generally known, would invoke considerable adverse social pressure. Indian Custom divorces thus would be rendered rather difficult. Legal divorces, on the other hand, involve much red tape, inconvenience, and expense and would be resorted to only

TABLE 4

Separations Following Indian Custom Marriages

(Based on date of separation and pertaining to individuals thirty years of age or younger at the time of separation)

Groups	Prior to 1880			1880–1905			After 1905		
	D.*	I.C.	Percentage I.C.	D.	I.C.	Percentage I.C.	D.	I.C.	Percentage I.C.
Round Valley............	43	28	39	25	23	48	1	6	85
California nonreservation...	49	32	39	97	63	39	53	45	46
Yurok-Karok...........	23	15	39	42	39	48	17	16	49
Hupa..................	5	3	37	9	9	50	8	8	50
Paiute.................	34	14	29	74	79	52	61	60	49
Old Mission............	13	5	28	8	19	70	2	2	50
Cahuilla...............	7	2	22	17	11	39	5	6	55
All groups.............	174	99	32.6	272	243	47.2	147	143	49.0

* D. = Death; I.C. = Indian Custom.

[384]

TABLE 5
SEPARATIONS FOLLOWING INDIAN CUSTOM MARRIAGES
(Based on date of birth of individuals)

Groups	Prior to 1829			1830–1839			1840–1849			1850–1859		
	D.*	I.C.	Percentage I.C.	D.	I.C.	Percentage I.C.	D.	I.C.	Percentage I.C.	D.	I.C.	Percentage I.C.
Round Valley	53	7	12	66	16	20	85	36	30	102	64	39
California nonreservation	71	12	14	131	27	17	161	49	23	152	45	23
Yurok-Karok-Hupa	48	7	13	98	17	14	100	29	22	131	55	29
Paiute	76	3	4	98	23	19	167	49	23	217	80	27
Old Mission	22	3	12	6	3	33	19	4	19	19	13	41
Cahuilla	..	..	..	5	0	0	12	1	7	21	6	22
All groups	270	32	10.6	414	86	17.2	544	168	23.6	642	263	29.1

Groups	1860–1869			1870–1879			1880–1889			1890–1899		
	D.	I.C.	Percentage I.C.	D.	I.C.	Percentage I.C.	D.	I.C.	Percentage I.C.	D.	I.C.	Percentage I.C.
Round Valley	42	26	38	16	7	30	..	..	..	5	3	37
California nonreservation	163	53	25	112	51	31	91	45	33	30	20	40
Yurok-Karok-Hupa	101	38	27	46	16	26	19	19	50	10	9	47
Paiute	142	69	33	144	53	32	108	82	43	32	18	36
Old Mission	11	20	65	9	10	52	3	2	40	..	..	..
Cahuilla	21	17	45	23	11	32	6	3	33	3	2	40
All groups	480	223	31.7	310	148	32.1	227	151	40.0	80	50	38.5

* D. = Death; I.C. = Indian Custom.

in extremity. Both moral and practical considerations, therefore, have operated to strengthen the bonds of legal marriage.

The institution of tribal custom appears to have become somewhat less stable through the years. This is indicated in a general fashion by the data in all three tables. From table 3 it is evident that, when the separations following Indian Custom unions are grouped for individuals of all ages according to the approximate date of marriage, the ratio of divorces to deaths has increased. Thus the percentage of separations by Indian Custom divorce during the era up to 1880 was 20.5 for all seven groups, whereas in the period subsequent to 1895, the value was 35.4. Since these divorces occur most frequently in early life, the data were recast, in table 4, to include only persons of thirty years or less. In table 5 the data are presented with reference to the birth date of the individual. The same trend is manifest: an increase in the relative number of divorces. Assuming that these data express the general situation, it becomes evident that among the more conservative element in the Indian population the institution of tribal marriage has become less stable and is losing its cohesive power. Indeed, observation by the present writer and others indicates that in restricted regions, such as coastal southern California, Indian Custom marriage has already become synonymous with mere casual promiscuity.

The drift toward increase in separations, as compared with lifelong matrimony, is evident also within the legal marriage category. The data are difficult to assess in detail, owing to the necessarily small number of cases and their occurrence preponderantly since 1895, but it is probable that the same process is going on here as with Indian Custom marriage. The stability of legal marriage is greater on the whole, but its integrity continues to diminish. If this is true, then the conclusion is unavoidable that not merely tribal custom but the institution of marriage in its entirety has undergone serious relaxation since primitive times. This is a far more serious matter than mere disruption of an ancient custom since it implies a loosening of all family bonds among the Indians.

As suggested in a previous paragraph, we are dealing here with a much deeper social phenomenon than mere change in the formula for marriage. We are concerned with the fact of separation, whether by court or by tribal custom. This point of view is further justified by the data presented, for if the divorce percentages for each Indian group are noted, it will be observed that they are all substantially the same. Thus in table 3 the range for Indian Custom marriages in the period up to 1880 is from 12 to 24; in the period after 1895 it is from 32 to 51; for legal marriages after 1895 it is from 10 to 28. The other tables show similar results. In other words, and this is the crucial point, the various groups which evince such a disparity in adoption of legal marriage give evidence of almost complete uniformity in retention of divorce. An additional aspect of their behavior is that all seven groups show a rough correspondence in the rate of increase of divorce within the period covered by the probate records.

The inevitable corollary to these findings is that the cultural factors, relatively so potent in inducing changes in type of marriage, have been and are utterly impotent in modifying separation from matrimony. Not even the enormous moral power of the Church or the consistent efforts of agency superintendents have been able to alter the determination of the Indian to separate from his spouse if he felt so inclined.

The utter failure of cultural and social pressure to eliminate divorce, or indeed to prevent its actual increase, demonstrates clearly that marital separation is a phenomenon of a character totally different from method of marriage. Its roots lie not in custom or tradition or in tribal usage, but in the psychology and physiology of the individual and, since this is so, it is not susceptible of attack on a purely cultural plane. Even the most intense education and propaganda can be of little value unless supported by a deeper motivation. What social pressure has accomplished is to change somewhat the ceremonial of separation as well as of marriage itself and to generate a new set of cultural conflicts which the already perplexed Indian must resolve.

The fundamental difficulty from the standpoint of the Indian is that, whereas he has slowly been driven to give up the original tribal pattern of marriage behavior, no clear-cut, definite line of conduct has been offered him as a replacement. In other words, he is confronted with a confusion of standards, most particularly with respect to divorce. During the transition period, which for most tribes has extended to the present time, the white community, especially through its organized agencies, has recognized both types of marriage as being valid for the Indian, although consistent efforts have been exerted to accelerate the shift from Indian Custom to legal. In this aspect of the matter there is no material conflict. When it comes to separation, however, the situation is obscure. In theory, the basic tenet of white civilization has been the indissoluble nature of the conjugal union, a thesis very actively promulgated by all religious bodies and many welfare agencies. To carry out this idea to its logical conclusion would mean the total prohibition of all types of separation. But, as has been pointed out, the Indian has proved completely obdurate and has flatly refused to respond to this particular social pressure. Failing in its effort to eliminate separation from marriage as a whole, the American social order, primarily through the Indian Service, has attempted a secondary approach, namely, to introduce legal, statutory divorce as a substitute for mere informal separation or Indian Custom divorce. But in this the success has also been far from complete: since 1895 out of 502 legal marriages recorded in the probate files there have been 414 separations by death, 61 by Indian Custom divorce and only 27 by legal divorce. Realizing the futility of legal coercion and also the great practical obstacles to universal court divorce, the government and the social community at large have been obliged, during the transition stage, to grant social sanction to Indian Custom divorce. With Indian Custom marriage this is not so difficult, but with legal marriage it necessitates the violation of every established canon of Christian marriage. No stable modern society could allow such a situation to continue long or to become general in extent. The Indian has therefore been presented with a multiplicity of standards. He has been told that extra-legal divorce is wrong, but he has been widely permitted to indulge in it. Indeed, he has been presented for practical purposes with a free choice, and he has exercised this choice largely according to convenience and whim.

From the historical viewpoint it is evident that the old, simple tribal pattern has been broken up but that no equally clear and concrete procedure has been offered as a substitute. Some of the secondary effects of this anomalous state of affairs have been anything but conducive to an easy adjustment by the Indian to the American way of life. If one examines not only the final reports of the Examiner of Inheritance in heirship cases, but also the transcripts of testimony upon which the findings are based, he will not fail to be impressed by the profound confusion existing in the Indian mind concerning marital relations. For instance among the generation born approximately a century ago—as seen in the older heirship cases—there was a very clear concept of divorce by Indian Custom. These elderly witnesses distinguished with great distinctness between a bona fide divorce and mere casual separation. In the recent reports, and with young witnesses, great uncertainty frequently exists as to whether a certain separation was actually by tribal custom or not. Indeed, profound cleavage of opinion often arises between individuals as to what, after all, constitutes tribal divorce. The divergencies become very acute when the preceding marriage has been by legal ceremony rather than tribal custom. A group of perfectly sincere Indians may differ flatly among themselves as to whether a certain couple had or had not been actually divorced.

A very striking instance of the muddled state of Indian thought arises with the Hupa and other Klamath River tribes. Unlike the other tribes here considered, these people originally had the custom of buying wives. On marriage the bridegroom made a payment, in recent times of money, to the family of the bride. If the couple ever separated, this money was to be returned to the husband, the act of repayment constituting the tribal custom divorce. Here, then, is a concrete act or ceremony by which a genuine divorce could be recognized. In modern times this custom has more or less fallen into disuse. As a consequence, the Hupa are often highly perplexed when called upon to decide formally whether a certain separation was or was not genuine according to tribal standards. The bewilderment is increased when the marriage was legal, because a legal marriage, being nontribal, cannot involve the payment of a monetary token in the first place, and consequently it is impossible to make a repayment to validate a divorce. An impecunious Hupa couple who wish to separate are, therefore, caught in a serious dilemma. They cannot afford, or it is otherwise impossible for them to get, a court divorce and it is theoretically impossible to divorce according to correct tribal custom. The upshot naturally is that they separate anyway—and perhaps remarry—their actions being sanctioned or condoned by the community at large on grounds of pure expediency. The problems and views of these people are perhaps made most vivid by actual cases. Therefore the following samples are adduced for illustrative purposes. The questions and answers are taken verbatim from the records. Actual names, of course, are deleted.

CASE NO. 1 (1913)

A.B. lived with X.Y. in or near 1895. Affidavit by two old Indians:

They lived together for several years but were not married by either Indian or white man ceremony. A.B. never paid any money . . . they were not married but simply living together.

CASE NO. 2 (1933)

Witness No. 1, aged sixty-five.

Q. Was he [A.B.] married to her [X.Y.] in accordance with Indian Custom?

A. No, he just lived with her.

Q. Wouldn't that constitute a marriage in accordance with Indian Custom?

A. Not unless he paid money for her.

Witness No. 2, aged forty-four.

Q. Would you say that A.B. was married to X.Y. in accordance with Indian Custom?

A. I do not think he was married to her Indian fashion or legally.

Q. What constitutes an Indian Custom marriage?

A. The man pays some money for his wife.

CASE NO. 3 (1927)

A.B. married X.Y. legally and later separated.

Witness No. 1, aged fifty.

Q. Would the separation of A.B. and X.Y. constitute an Indian Custom divorce?

A. Yes. The old Indians used to buy their wives and when they separated or were divorced they got their money back. X.Y. did not buy my sister, he married her legally and there was no money to pay him back. His leaving would be a divorce among the Indians.

CASE NO. 4 (1923)

A.B. married X.Y. legally in 1918. In 1922 they separated. A.B. married R.S. by Indian Custom and X.Y. married C.D. A.B. had originally paid the mother of X.Y. the sum of $50. C.D. now paid A.B. the same amount which A.B. then paid to the aunt of R.S. According to the testimony of X.Y., this transaction established the tribal validity of both the divorce and the subsequent two marriages.

CASE NO. 5 (1932)

A.B. married X.Y. legally and later separated. Three witnesses were asked the following question:

Q. Would you consider that A.B. was divorced from X.Y. in accordance with Indian Custom?

Witness No. 1, aged thirty-two.

A. Yes, sir.

Witness No. 2, age twenty-seven.

A. Yes, sir.

Witness No. 3, aged thirty-seven.

A. When a man gets married Indian fashion he pays money for his wife and when they are divorced Indian fashion he is supposed to get his money back. A.B. was married to X.Y. legally and I do not think it would be an Indian divorce.

CASE NO. 6 (1933)

A.B. married X.Y. legally and later separated.

Witness No. 1, A.B. himself, aged forty.

Q. Would you consider that you were divorced from her in accordance with Indian Custom?

A. I do not know. I did not marry her in the Indian way. When a man marries Indian way he pays money for his wife and when they divorce Indian way he gets his money back.

Witness No. 2, aged forty-eight.

Q. Would you consider that X.Y. was divorced from A.B. in accordance with Indian Custom?

A. Yes, sir.

Q. Do you know what constitutes an Indian Custom marriage?

A. Just pick out the woman and live with her if she is willing.

Q. Is there any money transaction necessary in connection with such a marriage?

A. It may have been years ago but it is not so now.

CASE NO. 7 (1939)

A.B. married X.Y. legally and later separated.

Witness No. 1, X.Y. herself, aged twenty-four.

Q. Would you consider that you were divorced from him in accordance with Indian Custom?

A. If we had been married Indian way, after I left him I think I would have been divorced from him.

CASE NO. 8 (1940)

A.B. married X.Y. legally and later separated.

Witness No. 1, aged fifty.
Q. How was he separated, by divorce?
A. No, he never had money to get a divorce.
Q. Was she considered his wife at the time of his death?
A. Well, of course legally she was his wife, but he did not consider her as his wife.

Witness No. 2, X.Y. herself, aged thirty.
Q. Were you divorced from A.B. in accordance with Indian Custom?
A. Sure, I would think so, but I was not married to him in the Indian way. We were legally married but never legally divorced.

Witness No. 3, aged twenty-eight.
Q. Was he divorced from X.Y.?
A. They just separated in the Indian way.

CASE NO. 9 (1927)

A.B. married X.Y. by Indian Custom in 1888 and divorced by Indian Custom in 1918. After X.Y. died in 1924, A. B. claimed a share in her estate on the ground that he had not been divorced because his purchase money had not been returned to him.

It is clear from the cases cited and from many others in the records that extraordinary confusion of thought exists in the minds of the Hupa and Yurok as to just what does constitute an Indian Custom marriage and divorce. To this question are added the further complications following legal marriage. The other tribes studied give evidence of the same confusion, but perhaps in lesser degree owing to the absence of the purchase custom.

From the standpoint of cultural adjustment it is easy to see whither the argument must tend. In the matter of divorce, white society has been so uncertain and conflicting in its own aims that it has not exerted strong, unequivocal pressure on the Indians in any specific direction but has permitted the latter to respond in a variety of ways according to individual predilection. Now when, as with the form of marriage, the pressure of the dominant race is directed along a single channel, the response may be slow and painful but is consistent and eventually complete. But when the adapting group cannot as a whole perceive which of several possibilities constitutes the most effective response, then a permanent state of maladjustment inevitably results. A condition of mental uncertainty and confusion thereupon follows, which must be accompanied by all sorts of strain. When the cultural component is of such a fundamental character that it involves sex and family relations, then the initial maladjustment will bring in its train emotional disturbances almost amounting to neuroses. To just what extent these complexes based upon marital difficulties have influenced the emotional state of the Indians in recent generations is impossible to determine without the aid of mass psychoanalysis. It may be conjectured, however, that their effect has been considerable in weakening the stability of Indian marital and family life as a whole.

We may conclude that the steady increase in separations to be found, according to the probate records, among all groups of Indians and following both Indian Custom and legal marriages is in part, at least, due to the failure of white society to provide strong motivation in a single direction. The impossibility of developing a single consistent and favorable response with respect to both the fact and type of divorce may well be reflected in the tendency toward disintegration of the institution of marriage itself.

PART FIVE

Population Trends Among the California Mission Indians

Originally published as *Ibero-Americana* Volume 17, 1940

PREFACE

THE MATERIAL for this paper has been taken primarily from the Bancroft compilation discussed in the text. Certain numerical values, for instance those of actual births as opposed to baptisms, have been taken from numerous and scattered documents, a list of which is in the author's possession. The statistical methods are standard, and use has been made of texts by Fisher and Yule. Certain discussion is based upon the work of A. L. Kroeber (*Handbook of the Indians of California*, 1925) and C. H. Merriam (*Amer. Anthro.*, vol. 7 [1905], pp. 594–606).

The author wishes to express his indebtedness to Dr. Eschscholtzia Lucia for her suggestions regarding statistical methods, and to Dr. Herbert I. Priestley for his coöperation in making available material in the Bancroft Library.

Introduction

A GREAT MANY STUDIES have been made on the one hand of human populations in the more civilized communities and on the other of animal populations under natural or laboratory conditions. The former have been of value in solving sociological problems, the latter in the investigation of animal ecology. There exists, however, a borderline field which has not been explored with equal thoroughness, but which merits consideration. I refer to the more primitive human groups. Here we have aggregations of human beings subject to many of the social forces operating on civilized populations, but also, in certain of their ecologic relations, more nearly analogous to the higher animals. It is therefore of interest to determine, as far as available data permit, whether such groups behave like civilized races or like mammals and birds, or like both.

The American Indians, taken as a whole, form a group of this character. Although it is not feasible to study the entire race at once, nevertheless certain small, selected segments may be investigated. One such portion comprises the Indians of California who were assembled in the Spanish missions from 1769 to 1834. Certain aspects of this particular Indian population make it an unusually favorable type case. In the first place, although the data are relatively meager when compared with the prolific information obtainable for modern white communities, the available statistics are far superior to anything else we possess with respect to the North American Indians. This is because the Spanish administration caused actual censuses to be made annually throughout most of the mission period. In the second place, these Indians are of biological interest because they represent a large mass of individuals—a whole population, in fact—which was suddenly uprooted and transplanted from its natural and very wild environment to a foreign, artificial, and relatively civilized one. There should be here an opportunity to study the factors operating on this population and to study them in a more or less quantitative manner. In other words, there may exist the possibility of utilizing the methods of animal ecology to investigate a human population.

As an initial step in any such study it is essential to know as precisely as possible in numerical terms just what happened to the population during the process of environmental change and subsequent readjustment. The following pages represent an attempt to formulate an answer to this question, as far as the mission Indians are concerned, leaving out of consideration for the present any evaluation of causal or correlative factors.

THE AVAILABLE DATA

The basis of our information concerning the California mission Indians is the series of annual reports, or censuses, submitted by the Franciscan missionaries.[1] These reports varied somewhat with respect to the data given, but uniformly included statistics on existing population, baptisms (not births), and deaths. Occasionally other information was included, but only sporadically. They were filed as a group in the California Archives and seem to have been very complete. Unfortunately they were burned in the San Francisco fire of 1906 and hence as a whole were irretrievably lost. However, their content has been preserved, at least in essence. In the first place, there are a number of the reports from various missions, or copies of them, scattered through the manuscript files of the Bancroft Library. Although these fragments per se could not be used as a basis for any adequate analysis of Indian population, they serve two useful purposes: as a check on other data and as a source of scanty but valuable data concerning births (as opposed to baptisms) and sex distribution.[2] In the second place, there exists a very complete and thorough tabulation of all the mission reports in exist-

---

[1] The ultimate source is the *libro de misión,* or mission book, in which the baptisms, burials, and marriages were individually recorded for each mission, and from which the reports of the missionaries were compiled. Some of these may still be in existence but, if so, they are in a very fragmentary state. To assemble them and arrange the data in a usable form would involve a labor of extraordinary magnitude and the results would at best be incomplete.

[2] No attempt has been made, in this brief survey, to cite individual manuscripts or transcripts, for such a procedure would be very cumbersome. However, the writer has at hand a complete file of references to these individual mission reports in the Bancroft Library.

ence fifty years ago (that is, before the fire). These are also available in the Bancroft Library and will be referred to as the Bancroft compilation. One of Bancroft's collaborators, possibly Savage, went through the complete file of mission reports and copied them in tabular form, mission by mission. A faithful and accurate piece of work was done, since a comparison of the figures in the compilation with those in many of the still available reports shows no discrepancies of any significance. There is every reason to believe, therefore, that in the compilation we have a reliable copy of the essential data in the original reports. This compilation forms the basis of the present analysis.

For each mission there is given the following annual data: (1) existing population as of December 31, including adult males, adult females, children, and total (in some instances the total males and females are also given); (2) the adult, child, and total baptisms, together with the cumulative number; (3) the adult, child, total, and cumulative deaths. In some of the individual reports, but not in the general compilation, there are also listed such items as number of married persons, widows and widowers, and unmarried males and females, and number of births.

The accuracy of the censuses as given in the Bancroft compilation must be considered, for in drawing any conclusions with respect to changes and trends there are various sources from which error might arise.

At the outset it may be stated without reservation that in reporting the numbers concerned the missionaries made a sincere and honest attempt to give the actual facts. There has never been any internal evidence, nor any reliable external evidence, that deliberate falsification was ever attempted. Any error would have been due to the difficulty inherent in enumeration. The data—annual and cumulative—for baptisms, marriages, and deaths were taken from the written records of the mission, in which every such event was scrupulously recorded. Minor errors in counting were of course possible and undoubtedly existed, since the census takers were priests and not trained statisticians. But on the whole, these items (baptisms, marriages, and deaths) may be regarded as thoroughly reliable. More subject to question are the figures for existing population. For this the local priest had no recourse to written record but apparently was forced to make an actual count. This was not always easy for several reasons. Frequently neophytes were moved from one mission to another, many of them were farmed out to neighboring ranchos, many led a semiwandering life or lived on remote rancherias rather than at the mission proper. Finally—and a most important factor—there were always some who had absconded, fled to the wilds, or were otherwise absent without leave. There is no way of making an estimate of the absolute numbers of these in individual censuses, and the state of affairs just mentioned probably did cause numerous discrepancies in the annual reports. The figures for annual existing individual-mission population therefore are the weakest in the entire compilation, and it must be admitted that any such single item must be accepted with reservation and considered only as a fairly accurate estimate.

These intrinsic errors might tend to affect the general conclusions through their statistical influence. However, when we summate the annual mission figures to get the regional data, or when we take the mean of several missions, the errors tend to cancel. The only factor of serious import is the possibility of material loss of population by wholesale desertion. This matter is considered in a subsequent section in connection with death rates, and it is shown that for the whole mission population throughout the period the error thus introduced is not sufficiently great to invalidate the general results. The conclusion seems warranted on the whole, admitting the possibility of error in individual annual censuses, that these errors are primarily random in character, that there is no unidirectional major error, and that trends indicated through the use of large numbers of mission censuses possess a relatively high degree of validity.

Special mention should be made of the data prior to 1783. Up to that time no really accurate counts were made. The Bancroft compilation gives figures from 1769 to 1783, but these are openly stated to be estimates. During these years the only records kept were of baptisms (almost wholly gentile baptisms) and deaths. From these, and by frank extrapolation, the Bancroft compilers arrived at annual estimates which they considered to represent something approaching the truth. It is quite probable that they do approach the truth, but it must be clearly understood that it is only an approach. No single annual mission item can be accepted with any degree of certainty prior to 1783. However, when taken in the mass and considered in conjunction with the later data, the figures for these early years may be used with a reasonable probability that they do not seriously misrepresent the situation. At least no major discrepancies in general population trend can be attributed to their inclusion.

PRIMARY POPULATION TRENDS

The Bancroft data give the annual male, female, and child population of the missions. From this the trend of the total mission population, as well as that of subgroups, can be determined. In figure 1 the total

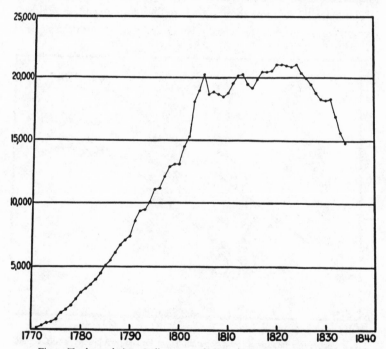

Fig. 1. Total population. Ordinate, population; abscissa, year of occurrence.

annual population is plotted against time in years. In figure 2 (p. 6) the total, the female, and the child populations are plotted as logarithms against the logarithm of time in years.

The simple curve merits consideration. From it can be seen that the mission population increased at a steady rate up till about 1798. Then, after a brief slowing, it increased very rapidly through 1805. This great increase was due to a vast influx of gentiles (a total of 8785 adults during the years mentioned). In 1806 the increase ceased very suddenly and, in fact, a decrease was observed. This was undoubtedly due to the destructive effects of the measles epidemic. However, subsequently, although a further increase occurred, the rate was quite small, never approaching the value of the years prior to 1806. In 1820 the population reached an effective standstill at about 21,100, a condition which lasted through 1824. Thereafter the decline began, rather slowly at first, more rapidly later, until the records close in 1834.

The logarithmic plots show substantially the same course as the direct curve. Up to 1800 the relation is definitely linear and the slope of

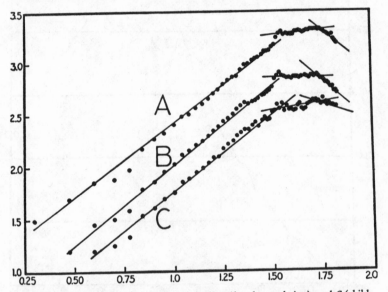

Fig. 2. Population data for *A* (total population), *B* (female population), and *C* (child population). Ordinate, log population; abscissa, log time in years from 1769.

the lines approximately the same. A simple equation might be used in the form $\log y = k \log x$, or $y = xe^{k}$, where y = population and x = time in years. This, of course, is the common exponential relation so generally found in population studies. In the curve of total population a definite discontinuity occurs around 1800. Thereafter the increase is slower, although still logarithmic up to 1825. Then there is a period of logarithmic decrease up to 1834. The changes thus tend to fall into three logarithmic phases of varying length.

The curves for females and children show the same general trend as the total curve. There are small quantitative differences between them, but these differences are not clearly enough defined to warrant ascribing to them any particular significance.

Certain points with respect to the population may be mentioned here. From the trend of the curve it is obvious that the great period of expansion of the missions was finished in 1805. At that time the population was approximately 20,300. Following the decline in 1806, it later (1820–1825) rose again to a somewhat higher value, but this rise was slow and erratic. The real maximum of what the ecologists would designate as biotic potential fell in 1805 and not in 1824, the year of greatest numbers. Probably the rate of increase would have fallen rapidly after 1805 in any event, but the trend was modified and intensified by the 1806 epidemic, which was appalling in its destructive effects, and from which, as shown by figures 1 and 2, the mission population never really recovered.

The figures quoted for maximum population in previous works on the California missions appear to be too high. Thus Merriam gives 30,000 in 1834. Kroeber, in his critique of Merriam, estimates 25,000 in 1830. From the present data it appears that the number in 1830 was 18,100, and that in 1834 it was 14,900. Since both Kroeber and Merriam have deduced the population of the entire state from their mission estimates, it becomes of some importance to point out that the figures as given here are probably the most accurate obtainable, since they are derived from the annual reports of the missions themselves. Furthermore, it should be stressed that any errors are on the side of magnifying the population. It is probable that some individuals reported in the censuses were in reality absent and that the number of Indians actually in the missions was somewhat smaller than as given here. Certainly there is no evidence of 30,000 being present in 1834.

In computing the original number in the area, Kroeber bases his calculation on a population of 25,000 in 1830. But in this connection it should be borne in mind that 1824 marked the maximum population, and that there had been a definite decline by 1830. Such a computation should therefore be based on 21,000 in 1824.

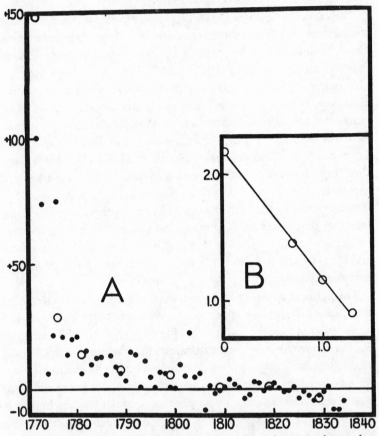

Fig. 3. Rate of change in population. *A:* ordinate, percentage increase or decrease from year to year; abscissa, year of occurrence. Dots represent annual change; circles five- or ten-year means. *B:* ordinate, log percentage increase or decrease using five-year means for the first twenty years; abscissa, log time in years.

It is even more illuminating to investigate the rates of increase or decrease in total population. In figure 3*A* are plotted the annual rates of change (that is, increase or decrease). At the beginning, of course, the rate of increase was exceedingly great since the start was at zero and each increment represented a very high percentage of the existing population. However, the rate of annual increase fell very rapidly. If we plot the logarithms of five- or ten-year means against log of age in years (fig. 3*B*), we find that there is an exponential fall in rate of increase up to about 1790. This is more or less what would be expected under the circumstances since the increase was due to conversion of gentiles and the latter process involved more or less constant numbers. But after 1790 the rate of increase falls in a very closely linear fashion (observe the ten-year means in fig. 3*A*). This fall continues until the increase becomes zero, in the neighborhood of 1820. Then an annual decrease begins which lasts to 1834 and which represents a linear continuation of the falling increase. In other words, two distinct processes are at work with respect to rate of change of population. The first is the inevitable decrease in rate of increase associated with the initial stage of building up the establishment. Now if this were the only factor concerned, and the population eventually reached a stable equilibrium where the additions equaled the losses, then the curve should sink exponentially to zero and remain there. But it does not. Some other, second, factor intervenes before the completion of the first cycle, and carries the curve in a linear fashion to the zero line and on below it. Thus, regardless of the discontinuities shown in figure 2, it is clear that this second factor began to operate more or less suddenly in the decade 1790–1800 and exerted a steady influence as long as the records were kept, interrupted only by minor fluctuations such as epidemics or sporadic wholesale conversion of gentiles.

So steady is the decline that one is almost tempted to extrapolate the increasing rate of decrease after 1820. But this would be dangerous because, as will be pointed out later, the death rate was rapidly decreasing in this latter period and it could not be expected that the linear relation shown in figure 3*A* would hold indefinitely.

In order to analyze the situation with respect to the mission Indian population—as with any population—and to determine the biological status, rather than the social or purely historical, it is essential to consider not so much the trend of whole numbers as the components which determine the trend. These are, of course, the sources and value of increments and the sources and value of depletion; in other words, the intensity of reproduction and of death. Now in a stable population these are given, as a rule, by the birth and death rates, and may be analyzed in a crude or refined manner, depending upon the completeness and accuracy of the data. In the present instance we are limited by certain peculiarities and defects in the primary data. The most serious of these limitations are the lack of information concerning age distribution and the complete lack of any record of births as such, for the missionaries made no consistent distinction with respect to age except as between adults and children and reported all child baptisms regardless of the source of children (but see the discussion in the immediately following section, pp. 10–18).

Increments to the population therefore are derived from (1) births among converted neophytes and (2) gentile baptisms. The latter include both adult and children baptisms. The first problem, then, is to estimate, if possible, the actual number of children born and then to determine the birth rate.

BIRTH RATE

The birth rate of the mission population has been estimated by three different methods. No one of these is completely adequate and each entails a considerable probable error. However, they check with one another rather closely and enable us to follow the trend of birth rate with a satisfactory degree of accuracy.

Method 1.—This is an entirely indirect method. It consists essentially in calculating the probable number of gentile child baptisms in each year for the whole area and for individual missions, and then in subtracting this value for each mission in a given year from the recorded child baptisms. Since all children born in the missions were immediately baptized, and the mission baptisms therefore equal the mission births, the remainder represents the number of births.

In order to derive the gentile child baptisms certain calculations must be made. We first need to know the approximate number of children in the population per unit number of females. Now in the missions illegitimacy was virtually nonexistent, owing to the rigid discipline. Therefore births occurred only to married women. Those females, however, actually or potentially capable of reproduction, together with those who had outlived their reproductive period, were virtually all married. Therefore the number of married women is a good index to the number of reproductively potent units. Now in the wild state these same women, although not married in the Christian sense, were associated in families, for monogamy was more or less the rule. When gentiles were baptized, furthermore, the male and female heads of each family were immediately brought into matrimony. Therefore the rela-

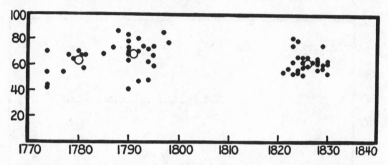

Fig. 4. Percentage married women in total adult female population. Ordinate, percentage; abscissa, year of occurrence. Dots represent annual figures for individual missions; circles the means of three groups centering approximately around the years 1780, 1791, 1826.

tive number of married women, in the first twenty years of mission existence, is practically identical with the relative number of reproductive and post-reproductive females in the wild state. If, then, we can determine the ratio of married women to total women and ratio of children to married women during these years, we would have an index whereby it would be possible to calculate the number of gentile children baptized annually.

With respect to the relative number of married women in the missions, I have been able to find sixty scattered annual reports in the manuscripts of the Bancroft Library in which the number of married women is given. These reports embrace the periods 1774–1798 and 1813–1830. Nearly all the missions are represented, and the sixty items may be reasonably considered a proper random sample. The data are shown graphically in figure 4. It will be seen that, although there is some dispersion of the individual points, there is a strong tendency toward a constant value. Three means are also shown (1774–1781, 1785–1798, 1821–1830) which lie within 8 per cent of each other, all between the values 60 per cent and 70 per cent. Throughout the mission period, therefore, the married women constituted approximately 65 per cent of the total female population. In view of this constancy, and since it is more advantageous to deal with larger numbers, we may relate the number of children directly with the total number of females, rather than with the married females.

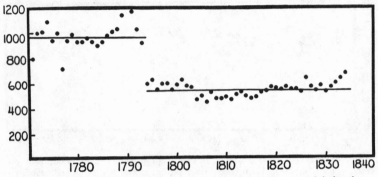

Fig. 5. Child-female relation. Ordinate, number of children per 1000 adult females; abscissa, year of occurrence.

Taking the combined figures of all the missions and plotting for each year the number of children per thousand females, we get figure 5. It will be observed that the number runs fairly constant with time up to the years 1792–1793. Here there is a sharp discontinuity. Subsequently the number again runs at a very constant level up to 1834. From 1794 on there is, without doubt, a straight-line relationship; that is, barring minor annual fluctuations, the ratio of children to total females remained the same throughout these forty years. Prior to 1792 a similar state obtained (allowing for the greater inaccuracy of the earlier censuses). Now, in view of the very consistent relationship over almost the entire mission period, it is difficult to conceive of a real shift such as is indicated on the graph. Actually it may be explained as due to a change in the method of enumeration by the missionaries.

Until about 1792 the category of children included everyone up to the age of puberty and even beyond. At this time the system was changed so that persons up to the age of ten years were listed as children, all others being classed as adults. Hence at this point (1792–1793) there was a sudden apparent reduction in children and an increase in adults—which could in no wise be accounted for by contemporary baptisms and deaths. For example, according to the Bancroft compilation, in 1793 there were 6488 adults and 3006 children, and in 1794 there were 8146 adults and 2471 children. During the intervening year the adult baptisms minus deaths were 644 and child baptisms minus deaths were 320. Thus the actual increase in adults was 644 and the apparent increase 1658. The difference, 1014, may be called the fictitious increase. Similarly the actual increase in children was 320 and the apparent increase −535. The difference here (−535 − 320) is −855, which represents the fictitious increase. The two values, +1014 and −855, correspond as closely as is to be expected.

It becomes necessary, therefore, to introduce a correction into the data to bring all the censuses into line with a common system. This may be done by taking the mean child/adult female ratio for the second period (value = 0.546) and using this to recalculate the probable number of females and children prior to 1792. The total adult figures may be used because at this period the sex ratio was very nearly unity and the child sex ratio certainly was practically 1.

These recalculated values for male, female, and child population cannot be considered more than a fairly close approximation, but they represent the best estimate under the circumstances.

We may now proceed to the calculation of the birth data. It may be assumed with safety, on the basis of the sex ratio figures in a subsequent section (see pp. 29–34), that the number of men and women gentiles was substantially equal. Furthermore, if the ratio of children to females throughout the mission period was 0.546, as given above, then the same ratio applies approximately to the gentile state. Then we may consider the ratio of children to adults to be about half this value, or 0.273. The Bancroft data show the annual baptisms of adults and of children. Hence we may say that 0.273 times the number of adult baptisms for any year represents the number of gentile children baptized during that year. This number subtracted from the total child baptisms gives the number of children born.

It should be borne in mind that this method leaves a great deal to be desired with respect to absolute accuracy. Particularly is this apparent if the method is applied to individual missions, for numerous discrep-

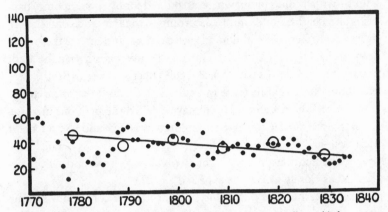

Fig. 6. Crude birth rate, based on total regional population. Ordinate, births per one thousand population; abscissa, year of occurrence. Dots, annual data; circles, means of ten-year periods.

ancies and anomalies are noted. However, if the number of individual missions be large, the errors are reduced, and the general trend at least can be determined. For the whole area two modes of applying

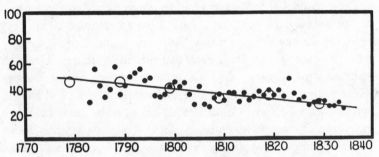

Fig. 7. Crude birth rate, based on annual means of individual missions. Explanation as in fig. 6.

the method may be used: (*a*) it may be applied directly to the population of the area as a whole (the result is shown in fig. 6, together with the means of ten-year periods); (*b*) it may be applied to the individual missions and then the results of all the missions for each year averaged. This method will of course give a somewhat different figure since the missions are not weighted with respect to difference in size. In figure 7 are plotted the annual means of the missions. This method was not used prior to 1783 because the number of missions was so small that the significance of the results did not seem to warrant including them. Ten-year means of the annual means are also shown in the figure.

The results of both modes of applying the indirect method (as ten-year means) are also shown in figure 9 (see p. 17).[3]

Method 2.—In the individual mission statistics it is observed that often in a given year, particularly in the latter years of mission existence, no adult baptisms are recorded. At the same time, however, children were baptized. Now it is exceedingly unlikely that any significant number of gentile children under ten were converted (that is, brought to the missions and baptized) apart from their parents. Therefore it can be very safely assumed that these child baptisms all represented births to women already living in the missions. From them, therefore, an index to the true birth rate may be obtained. (There are in all 245 child baptisms from twenty missions.) The results obtained are shown as annual means and ten-year means in figure 8 (p. 16); the ten-year means are also placed on figure 9.

Method 3.—A search of the manuscripts in the Bancroft Library yielded a number of annual reports in which the actual births were recorded. There are in all sixty-four reports, and these of course represent by far the most accurate direct clue we possess with respect to the actual birth rate. The data are scattered but nevertheless have been brought together in figure 9 as the annual mean when information

---

[3] There is a statement on baptisms (Cal. Arch. St. Pap. Mis., vol. 4, p. 37) entitled *Noticia de los Indios bautizados ...* , which covers the five years 1811–1815 inclusive. This document gives the total baptisms for the period as 8385, of which the baptisms of *Gentiles e hijos de estos* total 5062. The births (*Indios hijos de la Misión*) then equal the difference, or 3323. By means of the above-outlined method based upon the Bancroft compilation, the corresponding figures for the same period are: 8341 total, 4955 gentile baptisms, and 3386 births. The correspondence (within 2 per cent) is reasonably close.

In the comments on the general census for 1796 the total baptisms are given as 1230, including 603 adult gentiles, 236 children of the latter, and 391 children of converts. The corresponding figures according to the Bancroft data are: 1187 baptisms, 582 adult gentiles, 159 gentile children, and 446 births. In this document (*Estado de las Misiones ...* , 1796, Cal. Arch. St. Pap. Mis., vol. 2, p. 90) the total existing population is put at 11,216, whereas the Bancroft tables give it as 11,209, that is, practically identical.

from two or more missions is available, as the actual single value when there is only one mission. Also three approximate ten-year means are included.

When the net results of all these methods are plotted together, as in figure 9, it will be observed that from 1794 to 1834 there is a very close correspondence between the ten-year means obtained by each method. In fact, the correspondence is as close as could be expected considering possibility of error inherent in the original data and in the assumptions

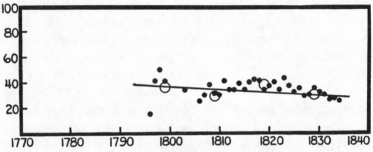

Fig. 8. Crude birth rate, based on annual mission data for those years in which gentile baptisms were lacking. Explanation as in fig. 6.

underlying method 1. It is evident that during this period the birth rate underwent a continuous and uniform decline. Methods 2 and 3 cannot be employed prior to 1794 owing to lack of data; but if the line representing the general trend subsequent to that date be continued backward, it is found to pass very close to the points actually obtained by method 1 (modifications *a* and *b*). This fact further substantiates the validity of method 1 and also indicates that the decline in birth rate dates substantially from the inception of the mission system and proceeded uninterrupted to the close of the system in 1834. The birth rate was about 47 per thousand in 1779 and about 30 per thousand in 1829, a decrease of approximately 35 per cent. At the end of the period there were no indications that the rate tended to stabilize, much less to increase. One more deduction may be made. Since the population in the earliest years was in few respects different from the gentile, unconverted type, the birth rate at this time may safely be assumed to be the normal wild birth rate. At least the latter must have fluctuated beween 45 and 50 per thousand.

One very important aspect of the birth-rate problem remains to be considered. The previous discussion has concerned what should actually be considered the "crude" birth rate, that is, the births per unit of the entire population. Of much greater biological significance is the number of births to each unit of the reproductive female population, a factor sometimes called the fecundity or fertility rate. It appears inadvisable to use the latter terms in this connection since we have no information concerning true fertility; hence this factor will be referred to by the more noncommittal term "adjusted" birth rate.

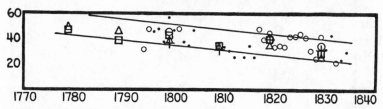

Fig. 9. Crude birth rate; comparison of data obtained by different methods. Ordinate and abscissa as in fig. 6. Squares represent ten-year means as in fig. 6; triangles, ten-year means from fig. 7; crosses, ten-year means from fig. 8. Dots indicate annual individual mission birth rates where such are available (see text); small circles, annual means of similar direct birth rates where two or more missions reported; and large circles, the means of all such reports approximately centering around the years 1799, 1819, and 1829.

It is commonly supposed, and has been widely stated, that in the mission Indian population the reproductive capacity of the females was very much reduced. That is, the actual mean number of young borne in a living condition by the individual female declined owing to natural and induced abortion, venereal disease, failure to conceive, and so on. In the data at hand I can find no grounds for believing that such a reduction occurred. Rather it appears that the child-bearing capacity of the females was unaffected and that the apparent reduction, together with the actual fall in crude birth rate, was the result of a diminished relative number of women in the entire population. This opinion rests upon the following evidence:

a) The decline in crude birth rate was concomitant with a rise in the male/female sex ratio (see subsequent section on sex ratio, pp. 29–34). The birth rate fell from about 47 to 30 per thousand population. Meanwhile the number of females per thousand males fell from 1000 to about 700. In other words, the fall in crude birth rate may be very substantially accounted for by the reduction in numbers of females.

b) It was shown previously that children were born, in the missions, almost exclusively to married women, and that the proportion of married women in the female population was constant. It was also shown that the ratio of children in the population to the total females was also constant—certainly from 1794 onward. Since most of these chil-

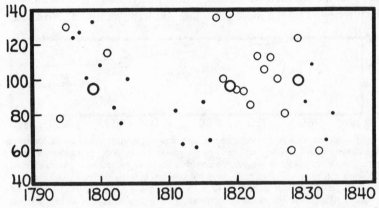

Fig. 10. Number of births per one thousand women. Ordinate, births per one thousand women; abscissa, year of occurrence. Dots indicate annual reports of single missions; small circles, annual means where two or more missions reported; large circles, means of all reports centering approximately around the years 1799, 1819, and 1829.

dren were born in the missions, the constancy of the ratio argues an approximate constancy in the number of children produced by a unit number of women.

c) The best direct evidence is given by the sixty-four reports (see method 3 above) in which the actual births per annum are recorded. In figure 10 these data are plotted, together with three ten-year means. It is obvious that there was no tendency for the ratio births/women to fall throughout forty years. And, if so, it is highly probable that there was no sudden, or even gradual fall in the twenty years previous. It may therefore be concluded tentatively that the child-bearing capacity of the Indian women in the missions did not materially alter during the mission period, and that the trend of the adjusted birth rate was neither up nor down but was essentially horizontal.

THE GENTILE INCREMENT

That the California missions did not very quickly show a decrease in population, in view of the declining birth rate and high death rate, was due to the constant infusion of new blood by conversion. First drawing in the adjacent heathen and then spreading out in an ever-widening circle, the missionaries, supported by the soldiers, cleaned up the areas within one or two days' march of each mission. Wherever serious gaps occurred, they were filled in by new missions. Finally, in the decade 1800–1810, it was necessary to go farther afield. Expeditions to the Colorado Desert, the San Joaquin and Sacramento rivers, and, toward the end, into the hill country of northern California served to recruit the diminishing population and maintain it until, as is indicated by the general population curve, the labor and expense of sending out long expeditions was incommensurate with the return in the form of convertible gentiles. The effect of this process on the total population of the state cannot be discussed here, although, as many have shown (cf. Merriam and Kroeber), it resulted in a general depletion from the start.

With respect to the mission population per se, although the general situation is well known, certain details are of interest. There have been calculated, and plotted in figure 11 (p. 20), as ten-year means, (*a*) the gentile baptism rate or the annual number of gentile baptisms per thousand existing population (the child baptisms are calculated as 0.27 times the adult number and deducted from the total child baptisms); (*b*) the absolute annual number of gentile baptisms; (*c*) the absolute annual number of births (for comparison with *b*); and (*d*) the annual ratio of gentile baptisms to births. The latter, of course, is a true index to the relative importance of the two sources as a means of maintaining or increasing the total population. It will be seen from figure 11 that the gentile baptism rate fell rapidly from 1000 per thousand population in the first year, since then, of course, the whole population consisted of converted gentiles, to a mean of about 270 per thousand in the period 1771–1782. (The first two years were omitted in calculating this mean.) In the next period, 1783–1793, the mean fell to 117 per thousand. Thereafter the decline was rapid and linear, until in

[417]

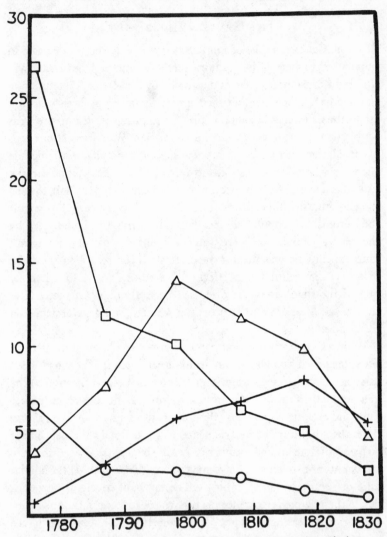

Fig. 11. Interrelations between sources of population augmentation. Abscissa, year of occurrence. Squares represent gentile baptism rate with the ordinate, baptisms per one thousand population; triangles represent the absolute annual number of gentile baptisms with the ordinate in hundreds; crosses represent the absolute annual number of births with the ordinate in hundreds; circles represent the annual ratio gentile baptisms/births expressed on the ordinate as units. All values are births plotted in terms of five- or ten-year means.

the last decade the mean annual rate was only 25 per thousand. Meanwhile the absolute number of baptisms, which is an index to the activity of the missionaries in securing converts, rose steadily to an annual average of about 1400 in the decade 1794–1803. Thereafter it fell consistently to an annual average of about 450 in the last decade. The great peak of conversion was around the year 1800. Thereafter a principle similar to that of diminishing returns apparently became operative. During the same time the annual number of births (although, of course, not the birth rate) increased very steadily up to the point of maximum total population (near 1820) and then fell off. Up to the decade around 1800, therefore, the absolute augmentation from both sources increased. Then the gentile increment began to fall off, whereas the birth increment still increased. The result was a net increase but of much diminished value. After 1820 the trend of both sources of augmentation was downward.

In figure 11 it will also be observed that the ratio of gentile baptisms to births was falling—rapidly at first, and then after 1785–1790 in a linear fashion up to 1834. This, of course, is simply a graphic representation of the decreasing relative importance of the gentile supply as contrasted with the native-born supply of human beings. Thus from 1771 to 1782 gentile conversion added 6½ times as many individuals as did births; from 1783 to 1793 it added 2½ times as many, and from 1824 to 1834, only ⅘ as many. Throughout the entire mission period there were recorded 83,407 baptisms, of which approximately 42,200 were gentile adults and 11,400 gentile children, or a total of 53,600, as compared with 29,800 births. Nothing can show more clearly than these figures the utter dependence of the missions upon wholesale gentile conversion.

Since we now know in a general way the two primary sources of augmentation, we may combine the two and derive the rate of augmentation from both sources. This is done by using the total baptism rate. In figure 12 (p. 22) are plotted the results (as five-year means up to 1784, thereafter as ten-year means), directly and also logarithmically. As has been indicated, the rate was very high at first, owing to relatively rapid conversion of adjacent gentiles (the mean annual rate for the first five years being 418 per thousand). It fell very quickly for

some twenty years, and then continued to fall more slowly, but steadily, up to 1834. In the curve we find the same two phases as with the
gentile baptism rate alone. First there is a logarithmic decrease in

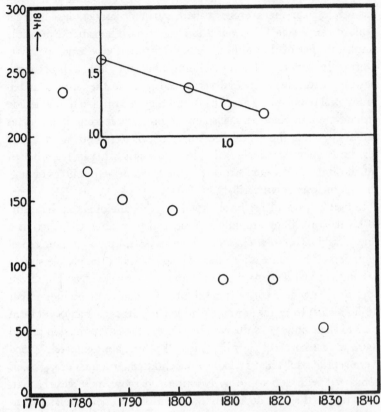

Fig. 12. Total baptism rate. Ordinate, baptisms per one thousand inhabitants; abscissa,
year of occurrence. Five- or ten-year means. In the inset are plotted the data for 1799–
1829 inclusive as the log of the baptism number per one thousand against the log of the
date, considering the year 1799 as the origin.

rate (up to approximately 1790). This is followed by a fairly consistent
linear decrease. The last decade shows a mean annual total baptism
rate of only 50 per thousand.

DEATH AND DEPLETION

Although the mission population was being augmented by birth and conversion, it was also being depleted.[4] This depletion, as will be shown, was due primarily to death, and secondarily, in the last few years, to desertions. It is the deaths which are of special interest.

The Bancroft tables enumerate the adult, child, and total deaths for each mission per annum. It is therefore relatively simple to establish the death rate directly by calculating the number of deaths per thousand population. In figure 13, *A, B,* and *C* (p. 24), the data for total, child, and adult deaths, respectively, are presented as annual rates and ten-year means. The general picture is clear enough. Certain points, however, merit emphasis.

1. The individual annual returns show an enormous variability. Most of this fluctuation is to be expected, since the conditions governing death are always more variable than those governing birth. However, such extreme rises as are found in 1806 and 1828 can mean only one thing, sweeping epidemics. And indeed we know that measles in both years were very destructive. With respect to the smaller fluctuations they cannot be discussed in detail here.

---

[4] The great excess of deaths over births and hence the real decline in population was appreciated by both the clerical and military administrations. As early as 1795 the following statement was made (*Población de Presidios y Misiones a fin de Dec. de 1794,* Cal. Arch. St. Pap. Mis., vol. 2 [1795], p. 11): "The spiritual conquest of California progresses in the number of gentiles reduced, but those established in the missions do not reproduce in conformity with their number." It was noted in the general mission census for 1799 (*Estado general de las Misiones ... en 1799,* Cal. Arch. St. Pap. Mis., vol. 2, p. 112) that the death rate was double the birth rate. (According to the Bancroft data, in this year the death rate was 96 per thousand, and the birth rate, calculated by method 1, was 44 per thousand.) In 1796 an anonymous document entitled *Cálculo de la Mortalidad en las Misiones ...* (Cal. Arch. St. Pap. Mis., vol. 1, p. 100) stated that the ratio of deaths to births was as 12 to 10. This was an underestimate, since the ratio was actually more than 2 to 1. In the same year the matter was discussed in the general census (*Estado de las Misiones ... , 1796,* Cal. Arch. St. Pap. Mis., vol. 2, pp. 90–92), where it was pointed out that although there was an apparent increase "the real and effective loss ... in this year is 629 persons." The excess of deaths over births according to the Bancroft data was 608. Arguello (Cal. Arch. Pr. St. Pap. Ben. Mil., vol. 42, pp. 2 and 6) puts the effective loss for 1811 at 651 and for 1814 at 675. The corresponding figures from the Bancroft compilation (using method 1) are 773 and 616.

Antonio Osio ("Hist. de la Calif.," MS, 1878) puts the ratio of deaths to births at 3 to 2; Juan Bandini ("Apuntos ... ," MS, p. 100, 1847), at 4 to 3; and Lucas Alaman (*Censo de la Rep. Mex.,* Cal. Arch. Dep. St. Pap., vol. 16, p. 1), at 10 to 9.

2. Apart from annual variation, there is a distinct trend in the means for longer periods. Considering total deaths, the initial rate was about 70 per thousand. By 1800 it had risen to approximately 85 per thousand. Then it fell gradually again to nearly 70 per thousand by 1830. Two aspects of the matter are of significance here. In the first place, the very

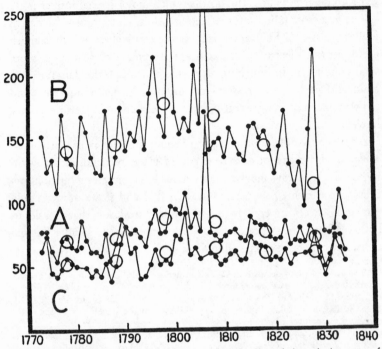

Fig. 13. Death rates. Ordinate, deaths per one thousand population; abscissa, year of occurrence. Dots represent annual totals; circles, ten-year means. *A*, total deaths; *B*, child deaths; *C*, adult deaths.

high initial rate is remarkable, for it raises the question whether it represents the natural, gentile, pre-mission death rate. From the annual data, and the fact that the very earliest years give a rate not far from 70 per thousand, it might be assumed that this was indeed the wild death rate carried over into the missions. However, it will be remembered that the birth-rate curve, even if directly extrapolated, showed a birth rate no higher than 45 or certainly 50 per thousand. If we assume, therefore, that the wild death rate was 70, then we cannot escape the conclusion that the Indian population of California was in a state of very rapid decline when the Spanish arrived. There is no other evidence showing that this was true, and on general grounds it must be regarded as highly improbable. The alternative explanation is that at the point of, and in the process of, missionization either the birth rate fell very sharply or the death rate rose very sharply—so suddenly that the change from the wild to converted rate was not reflected in the mission records. This in itself is a difficult conception, but it seems to me somewhat more reasonable than the previous alternative. If for lack of anything better we accept this assumption, then we have to assume further that the death rate suddenly rose rather than that the birth rate fell. The reason for this is that suggested above: the death rate always is far more labile than the birth rate. Factors such as nutrition, disease, and starvation can operate almost explosively on the death rate, whereas births and fertility are slow to change and shift over long intervals. It is therefore probable that some aspect of the change from wild to mission life increased the general death rate among the Indians to an abnormally high level.

The second aspect concerns the trend of the death rate. The increase was marked during the first thirty years. The causes were various and need not be discussed here. The subsequent fall is of significance in that it is an indication that certain conditions at any rate were improving as time went on. The worst period was over before the missions closed, and it is perfectly possible, although not certain, that, had not secularization and disruption occurred, the death rate might have fallen much lower.

3. The comparison between the adult and child death rates is rather striking. The adult death rate was always relatively low. It began at about 50–55 per thousand, rose slightly to 60–65 per thousand, and thereafter remained nearly constant, showing, if anything, a slight decrease to about 60 per thousand. It is likely that the initial rate was somewhat above the pre-mission value, although just how much it is impossible to say. However, the subsequent changes were relatively insignificant as compared with those involving children. The child death rate refers to individuals under the age of ten; hence the data cannot be construed as infant mortality, strictly speaking. Just how

many of the child deaths occurred at an early age it is difficult to tell, but the probability is that a great many of them were of this type. Because all infants were baptized at birth, the many who died very soon after birth appear in both the birth and death categories. Actual stillborn infants of course were not included.

Regardless of the relations within the group, the ·behavior of the whole shows at the beginning an enormous death rate, approximately 140 per thousand children. The annual fluctuations were very wide. much more so than with adults, thus demonstrating the greater suscep- tibility of the children (or the greater stability of the adult population). In fact, the death rate during the outstanding epidemic years was ap- palling. Thus in 1799 it was 26.5 per cent; in 1828, it was 22 per cent; and in the measles year of 1806, the mortality rose to 33.5 per cent. In each of those three years, therefore, from one-quarter to one-third of the total population under ten died off. (And it follows that the inci- dence of the diseases must have been nearly 100 per cent in the affected districts.)

Apart from sudden devastations the child death rate rose rapidly from the beginning to approximately 170 per thousand in the decade 1794–1803. This included the two high mortality years of 1796 and 1799, but aside from these the general level is seen to be relatively high. Subsequently, even in spite of the very bad epidemic of 1806, the next decade, 1804–1813, showed a lower death rate. This tendency became intensified in the succeeding two decades, until in the six years from 1828 to 1834 the death rate averaged only 86 per thousand, a rate not much higher than half the rate in the 'seventies and 'eighties. In other words, after passing through a maximum centering around the year 1800, the child death rate fell and was still falling rapidly when the mission period ended. To explain this great decrease various reasons might be suggested, such as the immunization of the population, nat- ural selection of a resistant strain, and so forth, but it is not necessary to discuss the matter here. It will be sufficient to point out that, arguing along the same line as with the total death rate, the child death rate in the early period of missionization was probably much higher than the corresponding rate under pre-mission conditions. This is further sup- ported by the later fall, far below the initial mission rate. For if the initial rate was an approximation to the pre-mission rate, then we would have to say that mission life so improved the inhabitants that the child mortality was cut in half in sixty years, a conclusion unjustified on any other grounds. It seems more reasonable, therefore, to suppose that the child death rate in the unconverted state was materially lower than in the early mission period, and that the rate in the later mission period came to fall toward or to the level prior to conversion.

Before leaving the matter of death rates, one more factor must be considered. It is known and recorded that frequently mission Indians deserted the missions and fled to the wild country. It is impossible to determine at present exactly how great this number was;[5] how many

---

[5] The contemporary correspondence contains a great deal of discussion of the matter of fugitive neophytes. They were a source of concern to the missionaries, who regarded them as lost souls, and to the civil authorities because of the numerous depredations they committed. Some idea of the number of runaways may be obtained from the representative data given in the table below.

Date	Mission	Number of fugitives	Source
1795	San Francisco	280	Cal. Arch. Prov. St. Pap., vol. 13, p. 147
1798	Santa Cruz	138	Cal. Arch. Prov. Rec., vol. 6, p. 69
1807	San Francisco	62	Archb. Arch., vol. 1, p. 37
1816	San Juan Bautista	12	*Ibid.*
1819	San Juan Bautista	47	Archb. Arch., vol. 3, p. 106
1819	San José	15	*Ibid.*
1820	San Francisco	30	Archb. Arch., vol. 4, p. 29
1824	Santa Bárbara	453	Cal. Arch. Dep. St. Pap., vol. 1, p. 53
1825	Santa Cruz	27	Archb. de la Mis., vol. 1, p. 852

It should be emphasized, however, that the movement was not all in one direction and desertions at any given time should not be regarded necessarily as permanent. The missionaries had a great deal to say concerning neophytes who absented themselves but relatively little concerning those who came back. Certain points should be borne in mind: (1) A great many neophytes wandered away during certain seasons but returned of their own accord. Thus in the census for 1828 we read (Hayes, *Mission Book,* vol. 1, item 214): "Many of the fugitive Christians ... who were mentioned in the last report have appeared, begging forgiveness, which has been granted them." (2) Numberless expeditions, large and small, were sent out to recover runaways. These usually were successful, particularly in regions adjacent to the missions. (3) At times, particularly in the south, a large number of neophytes lived, not at the mission proper, but in isolated ranchos or settlements. Since they were Christian they were included in the censuses. At the time of enumeration, however, many of them might be absent temporarily from their homes and thus escape numbering.

On the whole it is probably best to regard the mission population as not entirely static, but to some degree as moving in two streams, one away from, the other toward, the mission. If, as the data indicate, the outgoing stream was somewhat greater in volume than the returning, nevertheless the disparity was not as great as it seemed at the time to the missionaries. The net loss, as indicated by the cumulative figures, probably approaches the actual situation rather closely.

of the fugitives remained in desertion and how many returned or were brought back. There is no doubt that the missionaries tended to keep all converts on the books as existing population even when some had actually deserted. However, they were not kept on the books indefinitely, and any permanent desertions would ultimately be reflected in a diminution of existing population as reported in the censuses.

It should be possible to arrive at an approximation of the losses by desertion over a long period. The basis for such an attempt is the fact that, if the censuses were absolutely accurate and if all baptisms and deaths were recorded, the annual change in population should equal the difference between baptisms and deaths for the same period. On the contrary, if any significant number of converts deserted, were not added to the losses by death, and were not included in the existing population, then there should be a disparity between the totals for existing population and the totals as figured from the baptism and death data. In other words, there should be an unaccounted depletion. The situation may be analyzed by two similar methods:

1. When, for each two succeeding years, the existing population was compared with the difference between baptisms and deaths, it was found that errors existed in both directions (that is, unaccounted increases as well as decreases). When these deviations were averaged, it was found that the mean annual discrepancy from 1771 to 1831 inclusive was —0.036 per cent, an amount which for any one year may be regarded as negligible. In 1832, 1833, and 1834 the depletion due to desertion was significant, namely, 4.9, 4.4, and 3.1 per cent respectively. We know, however, that during this period the missions were rapidly going to pieces and neophytes were leaving in large numbers.

2. We have in the Bancroft compilation the cumulative figures for baptisms and deaths. Hence in any given year total baptisms to date, minus total deaths, should equal existing population. However, from 1795 on there is a discrepancy in that the computed value is always in excess of the recorded value. The difference can represent only the cumulative loss through desertion. This loss was as follows:

1795	— 341	1825	—2954
1805	—1263	1831	—3464
1815	—1927	1834	—5428

Adult Sex Ratio

From the statistics at hand it is possible to calculate the adult sex ratio for each year per mission. The adult age was assumed by the missionaries to be from nine years upward (beginning at ten). This of course does not conform to civilized ideas of adulthood, but, since the females underwent a very early puberty and were married often very young, this arbitrary age line does not introduce any great error.

In figure 14 there are plotted the ratios for the total mission population obtained by taking the ratio of the sum of the males in all the

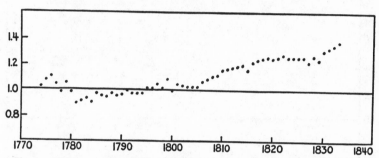

Fig. 14. Adult sex ratio: male/female. Ordinate, ratio; abscissa, year of occurrence. Based on total mission population.

missions to the sum of the females. The trend is perfectly clear. In the earlier years the ratio was normal or high, but fell rapidly to a minimum about 1780–1785. Thereafter it rose steadily to a value of about 1.35 in 1833–1834. The rise is linear, save for minor fluctuations. It is clear from the graph that a shift in sex composition began very early, not more than fifteen years after the start of missionization, and continued progressively throughout, even during the period of greatest growth in absolute population.

The method of summating the population of course tends to suppress individual mission differences. These may be given more weight if the separate annual mission ratios are calculated and then the mean annual ratio obtained, as is done in figure 15 (p. 30). Here the mean ratios are plotted, together with the standard deviation. Here substantially the same result is obtained. There is an initial decrease to a minimum in the years 1780–1785, followed by an approximately linear rise

to about 1.5 in 1833–1834. It will be observed that the standard deviations are very great and the probable errors of the means are, as a rule,
greater than the annual differences in the means. However, the trend
is manifest. In figure 15 the means for ten-year periods also have been
plotted. Here the standard deviations and the probable errors are very
much reduced, and the differences between the means of the ten-year
intervals become statistically significant. The same trend is evident.

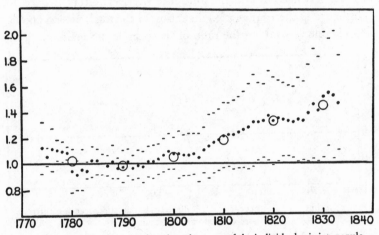

Fig. 15. Same as figure 14, but based on the mean of the individual mission population. Standard deviations also shown. Circles indicate means for ten-year periods.

It is clear, therefore, by whatever method of calculation, that the sex
ratio began to shift in favor of the males very early in mission history.
The significance of this shift is of course obvious as far as race survival
is concerned, for the reproductive power of the people is a function,
among other factors, of the number of females.

A more extended analysis was made by plotting the annual sex ratio
of the missions individually (the sex ratio as ordinate against the year
after foundation as abscissa). The curves themselves are not reproduced here but the essential data are embodied in table 1. The point
of outstanding significance is that all the missions conform to a general
pattern, although the individual variations are rather marked. This
general pattern is as follows. The first few years subsequent to foundation, irrespective of calendar year, show a decrease in ratio from an

initially high level to a minimum. The only exceptions are Santa Cruz, Soledad, and Santa Ynéz, which indicate an increase from the start. In order to get some basis for comparison, although admittedly purely arbitrary, the ratio

$$\frac{\text{sex ratio}}{\text{year prior to minimum value}}$$

was calculated for each point to the left of the minimum sex ratio on the graph. These values were then averaged, giving in effect the slope of the line representing the initial decrease or, in other words, the rate of decrease. This value for each mission is tabulated under the heading "initial decrease." After a variable number of years a minimum sex ratio

TABLE 1

SEX RATIO

Mission	Initial decrease, arbitrary constant	Years from foundation to minimum sex ratio	Value of minimum sex ratio	Final increase, arbitrary constant
San Diego..............	−0.442	24	0.75	0.356
San Luis Rey..........	−0.360	6	0.95	0.186
San Juan Capistrano....	−0.178	19	0.90	0.194
San Gabriel............	−0.202	23	0.95	0.213
San Fernando..........	−0.126	28	0.94	0.598
San Buenaventura......	−0.199	29	0.87	0.657
Santa Bárbara.........	−0.262	21	0.84	0.740
Santa Ynéz............	......	2	0.82	0.235
La Purísima...........	−0.444	17	0.82	0.595
San Luis Obispo........	−0.500	19	0.78	0.565
San Miguel............	−0.563	6	0.95	0.270
San Antonio...........	−0.488	15	0.87	0.472
La Soledad............	......	2	0.96	0.721
San Carlos............	−0.154	22	0.95	0.273
Santa Cruz............	......	2	1.02	0.656
San Juan Bautista......	−0.359	11	0.95	0.400*
Santa Clara...........	−0.198	12	1.03	0.356
San José..............	−0.730	7	1.13	0.149
San Francisco Asís......	−0.455	9	1.00	0.285†
San Rafael............	−0.548	16	0.87	.....
San Francisco Solano....	−0.521	10	1.01	.....

* Calculated value = 0.765, due to very high ratio, 3–14 years inclusive. Latter probably abnormal. Value above corrected.

† The constant from the ninth through the forty-sixth year was 0.238; from the forty-seventh through the fifty-ninth, 0.454 (removal to San Rafael in the forty-seventh year).

is reached, subsequent to which all missions show an increase which continues as long as the censuses were taken (1834). The slope of this line, or rate of increase, was calculated by the ratio

$$\frac{\text{sex ratio}}{\text{year subsequent to minimum value}}$$

and the results embodied in the table under the heading "final increase." In the table there are also listed the number of years required to reach a minimum value and that value itself.

An analysis of the data in table 1 indicates that there were two processes going on, one tending to reduce the ratio, one tending to raise it. There is, however, no correlation between the two processes, or between any two of the four variables listed, which can be regarded as statistically significant. The conclusion is warranted, therefore, that, whatever these processes were, they were mutually independent.

With regard to the initial decrease certain conjectures are possible. The period here represented was that of active conversion and reduction of the population near the mission. Since the average sex ratio for the first three years of establishment was greater than unity in all the missions except one (San Fernando = 0.97), two explanations are possible:

1. The missionaries at first converted more males than females from a given wild group. As time went on, however, they gathered in the remainder, until after a few years the mission population represented a true cross section of the group, and the sex ratio showed a value less than unity, as was in fact generally true. This would mean, then, that the normal wild sex ratio was less than unity.

2. The missionaries converted the entire population from the start, and continued to do so as long as any inhabitants remained in the region. This would indicate a wild sex ratio of much greater than unity.

Although there is no way of deciding the question definitely, short of scrutiny of the actual baptismal records, which are unavailable, it seems more probable that the first explanation is valid. One reason for this opinion is the general fact that sex ratios tend to be low rather than high among primitive peoples. Another is the extreme difficulty in explaining how any set of factors could operate continuously first to decrease and then to increase the ratio over several decades. It is much more reasonable to assume—and it must be emphasized that this is an assumption—that relatively more men were reduced in the early years of any mission, that soon the ratio tended to return to its original value, but that powerful factors were working in the opposite direction, that is, to increase the ratio. The existence of such factors is made clearly evident by the tremendous increase in sex ratio observed in every mission, and, although no strict and satisfactory correlations can be made, it is probable that these factors were operative in every mission from the very beginning.

The actual shape of the sex-ratio curves, the values of the ratios, and the other data given in table 1 would represent the interplay of unrelated factors: the rapidity and type of conversion in the early years, as opposed to the forces effective throughout which tended to increase the ratio.

It would be of considerable importance if we could determine the nature of these factors. Although it is not possible on the basis of the present data to go very far, certain tentative suggestions may be offered.

In tabulations such as those which we possess of mission population we might look for clues in connection with birth rates, gentile baptisms, and death rates. In view of the statements made above regarding the initial decrease, the effect of gentile baptisms has been examined. Thus, during later years, if there were any marked influence of new conversions on sex ratio, it should be possible to detect some relation between annual shifts in sex ratio and sudden large additions of gentiles by conversion. This point has been examined by determining the chi-square value of the association between the two factors. This value is —53.4, indicating a probability of less than one in one hundred that the association occurred by chance alone. Hence we may conclude that one factor which was involved, and the one which was predominantly influential during the first years of the missions, was the gentile baptism rate. In the middle and final decades the gentile baptisms ceased to be of outstanding importance, and some other factor assumed control and tended to increase the ratio just as the gentile baptisms had tended to reduce it.

With respect to birth rates it might be suggested that for some reason there came to be an excess of male births over female births, or perhaps a differential infant mortality in favor of the males. However, we have records of the sex distribution of the children in the missions. A search of the archives of the Bancroft Library has revealed a moderate number of annual census reports in which this particular matter is covered, and in this way a random sample has been secured consisting of 281 items representing all the missions at all stages of their existence from about 1775 to 1834. The age group is from birth to nine years inclusive and hence infant mortality, as well as actual births, is covered. The mean sex ratio is 0.992 (S.D. = ± .064, P.E. = ± .043). Since this sample is sufficiently broad and representative, it may be stated with some certainty that neither differential birth rate nor differential infant mortality was a factor in the sex-ratio increase.

Since it must be concluded that the factors involved were operative subsequent to birth, one might hope to find some clue in an examination of death rates. Accordingly the association between sex ratio and adult death rate and that between sex ratio and child death rate were studied. The chi-square values for the two associations were 33.6 and 44.6 respectively, thus demonstrating a very high probability that a definite relation exists. The evidence clearly favors, then, a differential death rate in very late childhood and adulthood which reduced the relative number of women.

We may conclude, then, that the initial phase, conditioned by a very great gentile influx, tended to bring the sex ratio to approximate unity, where it might have remained, had not the mortality factor entered the picture in such a manner as to nullify the previous influence and, as time progressed, to shift the ratio heavily in favor of the males. The significance of the changing sex ratio with respect to crude birth rate has already been mentioned and its bearing on other matters will be discussed subsequently.

Age Distribution

In the study of any population a great deal can be learned if the age distribution is known, particularly if changes in the distribution can be followed over any considerable period. With respect to the present analysis it is unfortunate that records appropriate to this purpose are almost entirely inaccessible. In fact, only the original baptismal and burial registers of all the missions would completely solve the problem.

However, some slight clue is afforded by two documents in the Bancroft Library. These are compilations or lists of neophytes, one for San Luis Obispo in 1794 and the other for San Francisco Solano in 1826, in which the ages of most of the individuals are given. (The former is to be found in the Vallejo Documents, vol. 28, pp. 2 ff., and the latter in the Archivo de las Misiones, vol. 2, pp. 85 ff.) The information has been taken from these lists and organized in simple fashion in tables 2 and 3 (pp. 36 and 37). The following points should be noted:

1. From the data involving one calendar year each in two missions no very far-reaching conclusions can be drawn. In fact, nothing whatever can be said concerning shifts in age composition with time.

2. Not all the persons listed were designated by age, and some of the figures when given were illegible. However, since only approximately 10 per cent of the population in each mission had to be neglected, the samples presented in the tables may be taken as fairly representative.

3. The Solano Mission in 1826 contained a very large proportion of newly baptized gentiles. Since of course there was no record of their births, the missionary fathers were forced to estimate their ages. Thus we find what would otherwise be considered a remarkably large number of persons precisely forty years old. If the data in table 2 are plotted on coördinate paper, the resulting figure shows abnormal peaks and valleys and cannot be considered of very great value with respect to detail. Since the San Luis Obispo Mission had been established nearly twenty-five years in 1794, its returns are much more steady and consistent.

4. The numbers are of course far too small to warrant any elaborate statistical analysis. However, if the data are plotted in graphic form, despite the irregularities mentioned above, there is a tendency for the fall in numbers with age to be fairly uniform.

5. The median age was substantially the same in both missions: approximately twenty-three years (see table 3).

6. In a comparison of the two missions, it may be observed that the group under five years of age at San Luis Obispo was smaller than that between five and ten years, whereas at Solano the former group was

TABLE 2
Age Distributions

Age in years	San Luis Obispo, 1794				San Francisco Solano, 1826				United States population, 1930
	Male	Female	Total	Total in percentages	Male	Female	Total	Total in percentages	Total in percentages
0–4..........	30	31	61	8.2	46	44	90	14.2	9.3
5–9..........	51	59	110	14.8	38	39	77	12.1	10.3
10–14.........	51	49	100	13.5	28	16	44	6.9	9.8
15–19.........	27	29	56	7.5	30	35	65	10.2	9.4
20–24.........	51	44	95	12.8	32	29	61	9.6	8.9
25–29.........	38	48	86	11.6	25	21	46	7.2	8.0
30–34.........	18	23	41	5.5	31	19	50	7.9	7.4
35–39.........	25	33	58	7.8	16	21	37	5.8	7.5
40–44.........	17	20	37	5.0	49	28	77	12.1	6.5
45–49.........	14	17	31	4.2	11	7	18	2.8	5.7
50–54.........	5	8	13	1.7	18	2	20	3.1	4.9
55–59.........	5	12	17	2.3	10	5	15	2.4	3.8
60–64.........	6	8	14	1.9	9	9	18	2.8	3.1
65–69.........	1	13	14	1.9	7	6	13	2.0	2.3
70–74.........	0	2	2	0.3	1	4	5	0.8	1.6
75–79.........	0	4	4	0.5	0	0	0	0.0	0.9
80–84.........	2	1	3	0.4	0	0	0	0.0	0.4
85 and over...	0	0	0	0.0	0	0	0	0.0	0.2
Total........	341	401	742		351	285	636		

the larger. This distinction may or may not be significant. If it is valid, it probably may be referred to the more stable composition of the San Luis Obispo population as compared with that of Solano. For, although the latter mission in 1826 contained a miscellaneous group of neophytes transferred from older missions, it had also, as mentioned above, a large number of very recently baptized gentiles, among whom one might expect to find many small children.

7. As a matter of general interest data are included in the tables for a modern population, that is, the total population in the United States

TABLE 3

MEDIAN AGES

	Males, years	Females, years	Total population, years
San Francisco Solano, 1826...........	25.4	21.4	23.4
San Luis Obispo, 1794..............	21.2	23.6	22.3
United States total white population, 1930...........................	27.2	26.7	26.9

for 1930 (data taken from the Fifteenth Census of the United States, 1930, II, 565–571). Inspection of the crude data (for naturally no refined methods can be applied here) shows a general conformity. The trend of the age-distribution curve of the American white population is very similar to that of San Luis Obispo and, allowing for the fluctuations already mentioned, to that of Solano. The slope of the American curve is more gradual and far more regular, as might be expected. This tendency is otherwise supported by the difference in median age (see table 3): Solano, 23.4; San Luis Obispo, 22.3; United States total, 26.9. Another indication is the difference in percentage of the population to reach an extreme old age. Thus, in Solano, 0.78 per cent of the population was over seventy years of age; in San Luis Obispo, 1.1 per cent; and in the United States, 3.2 per cent.

In making such a comparison we must not ignore the fact that the modern American population is changing rapidly with respect to age distribution. Thus (see Fifteenth Census, II, 568) the median age of the white population in 1900 was 22.9, essentially the value found in

TABLE 4
PERCENTAGE OF POPULATION AGED UNDER TEN YEARS

Total mission population		Total United States		United States total native white		United States Negro		United States native white, native parentage		United States native white, foreign or mixed parentage	
Decade ending	Mean annual percentage	Decade ending	Percentage	Decade ending	Percentage	Decade ending	Percentage	Decade ending	Percentage	Decade ending	Percentage
1782	22.7	1850	29.1								
1792	25.0	1860	28.7								
1802	22.5	1870	26.9								
1812	19.1	1880	26.7	1880	30.0						
1822	19.3	1890	24.3	1890	27.8	1890	28.6	1890	26.1	1890	32.5
1832	19.8	1900	23.8	1900	27.1	1900	27.4	1900	25.9	1900	30.2
		1910	22.2	1910	25.5	1910	25.6	1910	25.0	1910	26.5
		1920	21.7	1920	24.9	1920	23.0	1920	24.5	1920	26.1
		1930	19.6	1930	21.7	1930	22.8	1930	23.2	1930	17.6

the two missions, whereas the value for the Negro population in 1930 was 23.1. Furthermore, if one plots the distribution of the total American population for 1880, the correspondence with the two missions (always remembering the marginal reliability of the latter) is rather definite.

The statement may therefore be hazarded that what few direct data we possess concerning age distribution indicate that, in this respect, the mission population did not differ very materially from the American population of some sixty years ago.

Although it is to be regretted that a study based on full age-distribution data cannot be made, further comparison of the mission Indians and more recent racial groups in the United States can be made by a somewhat cruder and more indirect method. This consists of tabulating the percentage of children under ten years in these populations. For the United States the data are contained in the Fifteenth Census Report (II, 581–582) from 1880 or 1890 to 1930. For the missions this age group (0–9 years) is that denoted by the category "children." By calculating the annual percentage and averaging ten-year periods, values substantially equivalent to those in the census are obtained. The trend over a period of several decades for each population group may thus be ascertained and compared, although such groups may have existed in different absolute eras.

Such data are given in table 4 for the total mission population (1772–1832); total United States (1840–1930); total United States native white (1870–1930); United States Negro; United States native white, native parentage; and United States native white, foreign or mixed parentage (the last three for 1880–1930). There is a diminishing trend in all of these groups, the modern populations in fairly regular steps, the Indian more irregularly (the latter group was much more fluid, contained smaller numbers, and was much more subject to local influences). If the data be plotted and lines drawn to represent the general trends (extreme accuracy not being necessary), the resulting picture is quite clear-cut. The downward trend among the Indians, which represents the tendency toward a higher median age, has substantially the same slope as that of the total white population during the past eighty years.

We know that our white population consists of native- and foreign-born. The pertinent data on the foreign-born are not included in the table because only 1 or 2 per cent of these people, on the average, were under ten years of age, and hence represented less than 1 per cent of the total white population. Of the native-born, one category is of native and the other of foreign or mixed parentage. If the data for these (see table 4) and for the Negro group are compared, certain tendencies become evident.

1. The trend of the total native white and that of the Negro run very nearly parallel to each other and, within limits, parallel to the trend of the mission Indian.

2. The downward trend of the native white of native parentage is relatively gentle, whereas that of the group with foreign or mixed parentage is very steep.

Now the present significance of these observations lies in the fact that the mission Indian population was made up of precisely the same type of components as the recent American, at least as far as the environmental factor is concerned. Thus the original mission population was due to immigration, from no great distance to be sure, but involving a complete change of habitat. In the middle period there was a mixture of "immigrants" and first-generation "natives" (that is, mission natives). Toward the end there were still a few "immigrants" but an increasing number of "native-born," the latter partly of "native" and partly of "foreign" parentage. The analogy obviously cannot be pushed too far, particularly as it concerns quantitative detail, but the basic thesis is still tenable that in the total of the two ethnic groups (Indians and modern Americans) the same mode of aggregation is associated with a very similar trend in apparent age distribution.

In order to investigate somewhat more thoroughly the age-distribution problem among the mission Indians, wholly apart from any comparison with modern population, the ratio of children under ten to entire population was calculated for each year in nineteen missions (San Rafael and Solano were omitted because of their short life and atypical populations). The means were then determined for ten-year periods, from 1774 to 1833. The data show marked irregularity; in fact, no precise detailed analysis is possible. However, certain indicative aspects may be noted.

From the data for the whole region (see table 4) it is evident that the sharp decline occurred in the third and fourth decades (from 1792 to 1812). Thereafter a tendency is present for the value of the ratio to remain constant. Of the individual missions, eighteen out of nineteen show a decline during the same two decades, whereas only one (Santa Ynéz) rose from the start. Of these eighteen, eleven continued to fall, although perhaps irregularly, until 1833. The other seven reached a minimum in 1813 and then showed an increase up to 1833.

It is believed that this situation is correlated with two factors: the child death rate and the gentile baptism rate. In order to test this idea the chi-square values were calculated for the associations (using annual values for each mission) between the ratio of children under ten to total population and these two factors. With respect to both factors the probability that the relationship arose by chance was far less than one in one hundred. According to Fisher's table with $N = 1$, a chi-square value of 6.6 or greater indicates a value of P of 0.01 or less. The chi-square values here for child death rate and gentile baptism rate were -117 and 26.8 respectively. It is a fairly safe assumption, therefore, that both factors were operative and accounted, at least partially, for the general trend in age distribution as well as for individual mission differences.

Following this line of thought we see that during the foundation period (say up to 1793) the mission population consisted predominantly of newly converted gentiles and included approximately the normal proportion of children under ten years of age. The age distribution must have closely resembled that characteristic of the wild state. About 1795 a series of devastating epidemics began, which lasted intermittently for several years. The effect of these is very noticeable in the child mortality rates of the subsequent period and is undoubtedly reflected in the decided fall in number of children. The result was probably a moving of the age-distribution curve sharply to the right. Furthermore, this era saw the end of wholesale gentile conversion, and consequently no large new increments of children could be expected from this source. After 1810–1815 the period of great mortality was past (see fig. 13) and a recovery had begun. This is evident from the fact that the number of children maintained itself and possibly increased a little. Here also lies the explanation of the definite trend toward recovery shown by seven missions, as noted above.

Extrapolation of any tendency is dangerous, but the opinion may be offered that had not the missions been destroyed subsequent to 1834 the trend toward recovery might have become manifest during the next one or two generations by a return to the age distribution which apparently existed in the wild state prior to missionization.

THE POPULATION FACTOR

It has been maintained that the crowded conditions of mission as opposed to wild life should tend to intensify unfavorable influences, and these in turn would become manifest in the trends of birth and death. Since the degree of crowding is a function of absolute numbers, if the foregoing assumption is valid, the greater the number of persons the higher should be the death rates and sex ratio and the lower the birth rate. But the results obtained by the method used here do not demonstrate this proposition. In fact, the results are somewhat unexpected. There is no really significant association between population number and birth rate or child death rate, whereas there is a somewhat significant negative association with sex ratio and adult death rate. The chi-square values calculated for population against (1) adjusted birth rate, (2) child death rate, (3) sex ratio, and (4) adult death rate are respectively $-2.3, -1.4, -11.0$, and -7.1. These values indicate that the larger the population the lower the sex ratio and adult death rate. Thus the entire question is thrown open and no acceptable explanation is possible which can be based on data hitherto obtained. We are forced to take refuge in the unsatisfactory statement that, if crowding had an effect, this effect was completely masked by other as yet unexplored influences.

REGIONAL MISSION VARIATION

The chain of missions extending along the California coast were regarded by the Spanish as a single administrative unit. But at the same time they presented a picture of anything but homogeneity as far as environment and racial composition were concerned. In the warm, relatively arid south there were found such racial stocks as the Yumans and Shoshoneans. The cooler, damper north was populated by the Salinans and Costanoans. A problem of some interest, therefore, is that of variations and contrasts within the mission groups.

If the mission data are inspected even superficially, it will very soon become evident that there is a distinct geographical variation in the well-being of the mission population. Rather uniformly better conditions seem to prevail in the south than in the north, and, in fact, the change from better to worse seems to take a roughly linear course from San Diego up the coast. So definite is this rather subjective impression that it demands, as it were, some attempt at quantitative formulation.

It will be admitted readily that the chain-like arrangement of the missions, on the map, is not perfect, and that certain liberties have to be taken in order to examine the phenomenon graphically. Nevertheless the canons of common sense will not be seriously violated if we express the general geographical trend as a series of nineteen points, corresponding to the nineteen old missions, beginning with San Diego and ending with San Francisco. Reference to a map will show that from San Diego to La Soledad the missions were actually strung along the coast like a chain of beads. Above the latter there was some tendency to double up, but, although a linear arrangement must perforce be somewhat arbitrary, the series as here constituted conforms quite closely to the relative location of the missions.

As an initial step a graph was plotted with the series of missions on the abscissa, spaced at equal distances apart. (In point of fact, the spacing of the missions was quite uniform on the terrain itself.) On the ordinate there was then plotted for each mission the mean adult death rate, child death rate, adjusted birth rate, and sex ratio. With respect to each of these there was a great deal of fluctuation from one mission to the next, but for each factor there was also a distinct trend of the points upward from south to north. The figures are not reproduced here but the data[6] are presented in table 5 (p. 44).

In order to get a common basis for the comparison of the four categories mentioned above, the means of the nineteen missions with respect to each factor were calculated and value for each mission expressed as the deviation from this mean. The deviations then were

---

[6] Since the material was available, data for adult gentile baptism rate are included in table 5, although consideration of this factor is not essential to the present discussion.

TABLE 5

DATA TO SHOW GEOGRAPHICAL VARIATION OF DEMOGRAPHIC FACTORS

Mission	I			II			III			IV			V		
	Sex ratio	Deviation	Deviation in percentages	Adjusted birth rate	Deviation	Deviation in percentages	Adult death rate	Deviation	Deviation in percentages	Child death rate	Deviation	Deviation in percentages	Adult gentile baptism rate in last 48 years	Deviation	Deviation in percentages
San Diego..........	1.27	−0.07	− 5.2	74.5	−20.5	−20.1	53.6	− 8.0	− 13.0	94.0	− 86.1	−47.8	7.55	− 2.15	− 22.2
San Luis Rey......	1.09	− .25	−18.7	107.9	+ 8.9	+ 9.0	26.9	−34.7	− 56.4	76.9	−103.2	−57.5	8.70	− 1.00	− 10.3
San Juan Capistrano	1.19	− .15	−11.2	107.8	+ 8.8	+ 8.9	41.5	−20.1	− 32.7	145.5	− 34.6	−19.2	5.32	− 4.38	− 45.3
San Gabriel........	1.19	− .15	−11.2	114.4	+15.4	+15.6	56.3	− 5.3	− 8.6	121.0	− 59.1	−32.8	6.30	− 3.40	− 35.1
San Fernando......	1.01	− .25	−18.7	90.2	− 8.8	− 8.9	44.7	−16.9	− 27.4	78.8	−101.3	−56.2	12.40	+ 2.70	+ 27.8
San Buenaventura..	1.19	− .15	−11.2	69.8	−29.2	−29.2	58.9	− 2.7	− 4.4	152.0	− 28.1	−15.6	10.56	+ 0.86	+ 8.9
Santa Bárbara......	1.24	− .10	− 7.5	81.8	−17.2	−17.4	61.5	− 0.1	− 0.1	144.0	− 36.1	−20.0	9.80	+ 0.10	+ 1.0
Santa Ynéz........	1.00	− .34	−25.4	93.6	− 5.4	− 5.5	59.2	− 2.4	− 3.9	136.8	− 43.3	−24.1	4.79	− 4.91	− 50.3
La Purísima........	1.10	− .24	−17.9	72.1	−26.9	−27.2	60.6	− 1.0	− 1.6	170.6	+ 9.5	− 5.3	8.42	− 1.28	− 13.2
San Luis Obispo....	1.65	+ .31	+23.1	89.7	− 9.3	− 9.4	59.9	− 1.7	− 2.8	337.4	+157.3	+87.4	5.70	− 4.00	− 41.3
San Miguel........	1.14	− .20	−14.9	78.9	−19.1	−19.3	46.8	−14.8	− 24.0	143.4	− 36.7	−20.4	9.36	− 0.34	− 3.5
San Antonio.......	1.67	+ .23	+17.2	140.9	+14.9	+14.8	42.6	−19.0	− 29.2	220.0	+ 39.9	+22.2	3.74	− 5.96	− 61.5
La Soledad........	2.04	+ .70	+52.2	84.4	−14.6	−14.8	67.8	+ 6.2	+ 10.1	173.5	− 6.6	− 3.7	11.70	+ 2.00	+ 20.6
San Carlos........	1.27	+ .07	− 5.2	150.7	+51.7	+52.3	65.1	+ 3.5	+ 5.5	205.8	+ 25.7	+14.3	3.53	− 6.17	− 63.6
San Juan Bautista..	1.35	+ .01	+ 0.7	128.0	+29.7	+30.0	63.5	+ 1.9	+ 3.1	219.7	+ 39.6	+22.0	11.37	+ 1.67	+ 17.2
Santa Cruz........	1.93	+ .59	+44.1	97.4	− 1.6	− 1.6	81.2	+19.6	+ 31.8	231.7	+ 51.6	+28.7	12.02	+ 2.32	+ 23.9
Santa Clara.......	1.50	+ .16	+11.9	60.7	−29.3	−29.6	67.9	+ 6.3	+ 10.3	209.7	+ 29.6	+16.5	13.78	+ 4.08	+ 42.1
San José..........	1.27	− .07	− 5.2	78.2	−20.8	−21.0	84.7	+23.1	+ 37.5	209.8	+ 29.7	+16.6	21.90	+ 12.20	+ 125.8
San Francisco Asís.	1.40	+0.03	+ 2.2	159.0	+60.0	+60.6	128.4	+66.5	+ 108.0	353.3	+173.2	+96.2	19.24	+ 9.54	+ 98.4
Mean..............	1.34			99.0			61.6			180.1			9.70		
σ.................	0.274			26.6			20.1			73.0			4.74		
Var...............	20.4			26.9			32.6			40.5			48.9		

placed upon a percentage rather than an absolute basis (see table 5). When the deviations thus obtained are plotted against the mission series, there is again apparent a definite shift from south to north. This shift represents an association between magnitude of the factors under consideration and location in the mission series, and the chi-square value may be calculated if the four factors are divided at the line of zero deviation and the mission series separated into northern and southern halves. Since the series contains nineteen points, the middle one—San Luis Obispo—will represent the mid-line. The chi-square value equals +23.3, indicating a probability of less than one in one hundred that such a distribution could have arisen only by chance.

As an additional check the arithmetical sum of the deviations in percentages was calculated for each mission. These sums were then plotted and showed two clearly defined groups, north and south, the mean of the sums of the deviations for the south being −85.3 per cent and for the north +83.0 per cent. The chi-square value calculated here was +10.7, again indicating the probability of chance occurrence as being less than one in one hundred.

Other methods of treatment are no doubt possible but the most striking aspect of the situation may be regarded as established: a very great quantitative difference between the northern and southern missions with respect to death rate, birth rate, and sex ratio. Secondarily, these differences seem to take the form of an irregular but clearly evident progressive shift from one geographical extreme to the other.

It would be of considerable interest and significance were it possible to determine the conditions responsible for this situation. However, since the present study attempts only to set forth the actual changes in population without extended discussion of causes, the following brief statement must suffice.

Since the observed shift takes place along geographical lines, one would seek first to investigate geographical, that is, environmental factors. Aside from the obvious differences in climate, including rainfall, temperature, and humidity, there are secondary differences in soil constitution, fauna, and flora which might very well exert an influence upon the conditions under which the separate mission populations existed. But an extensive study of all these factors in detail would of necessity precede any hypothesis based upon ecological considerations, and such a study is an undertaking for the future.

Apart from environmental causes, the possibility must not be overlooked that a genetic—or phylogenetic—principle is also operating. Certain points in this connection are indeed very suggestive and merit at least mention. If we divide the missions according to tribal affiliation, we find that a series of well-defined groups appears. At the south we have San Diego, recruited almost wholly from Yuman stock. Then comes the series San Luis Rey, San Juan Capistrano, San Gabriel, and San Fernando, situated in territory of tribes belonging to the Shoshonean family. Next, along the channel and coast, from Buenaventura to San Luis Obispo, the Chumash are represented. Above the latter there occur two missions, San Miguel and San Antonio, which were populated by Salinans. Finally, all the rest (except San Carlos), beginning with Soledad, lay in Costanoan territory. San Carlos drew upon both the Esselen, a Hokan stock to the south, and the Costanoans to the north and east. These five divisions may again be grouped according to larger relationships. The Yumans and the Shoshoneans, as pointed out by R. B. Dixon (*Racial History of Man,* 1923), who has surveyed the literature on the subject, are both predominantly brachycephalic and, in common with many other southwestern tribes such as the Apache, Navaho, and Pima, appear to be a younger and more vigorous stock. Whether or not one agrees with Dixon's theory of origins, all the historical evidence indicates that these two families were relatively much more aggressive and tougher than the other California groups. Let us then, tentatively at least, combine them into a Yuman-Shoshonean stock. Similarly the Chumash and Salinans both are members of the Hokan family, which, according to Dixon, is largely brachycephalic and of relatively recent origin in California. Finally the Costanoans, in common probably with the other members of the Penutian family (Yokuts, Miwok, Maidu, and Wintun), are dolichocephalic and, if Dixon's idea is correct, are an older people.

Turning now to the population data, if we examine the critical items used in this paper, namely, adult death rate, child death rate, sex ratio, and ratio children to total population, we find marked differences between the family groups (see table 6). The distinctions are specially pronounced in the three major divisions. The death rates and sex ratio are very much higher among the Costanoans than among the others, and child–population ratio is much lower. The Chumash-Salinan stock is intermediate between the two extremes. Although absolute accuracy in detail cannot be insisted upon, the general picture is sufficiently

TABLE 6

POPULATION FACTORS IN RELATION TO TRIBAL AFFILIATION

Tribe or family	Mean value for the missions drawing upon a certain tribe or family			
	Adult death rate	Child death rate	Sex ratio	Children / Total population
Yuman.....................	44.0	108.8	1.08	22.7
Shoshonean..................	43.8	124.5	1.05	26.6
Chumash*....................	57.6	167.3	1.06	18.5
Salinan......................	44.5	152.4	1.25	19.5
Costanoan†..................	86.9	221.9	1.43	19.0
Yuman-Shoshonean............	43.8	121.0	1.07	26.0
Chumash-Salinan (Hokan)......	53.4	173.1	1.14	18.4
Costanoan (Penutian)‡........	86.9	221.9	1.43	19.0

* San Luis Obispo is omitted here since, although in Chumash territory, it probably drew a large number of Salinans from the north. It is included below under Chumash-Salinan.

† San Carlos is omitted both here and below since it drew from both Hokan and Costanoan stocks.

‡ The Costanoans in these northern missions were much augmented after 1800 by recruits from the San Joaquin Valley and to the north of San Francisco Bay. However, these were primarily of Penutian stock and were genetically similar to the Costanoans. Some Yokuts also went to the Salinan missions but it is impossible to determine the exact number.

clear, and the statement is quite justified that, whatever may have been the causes, the Yuman-Shoshoneans resisted the debilitating influences of mission life much better than any others, the Hokan stock was less resistant, and the Penutian stock tended to succumb most readily.

In conclusion, therefore, we have to admit the possibility that variation between missions and mission regions may have been conditioned by two very different sets of factors operating simultaneously: geographical, or ecological, and racial, or genetic.

CONCLUSIONS

From the foregoing analysis we may obtain a moderately clear picture of what happened to the mission Indian population. Primarily, as a result of consistent wholesale addition by conversion, the total population rose rapidly until approximately 1800. Thereafter the increase continued, but more slowly, up to an equilibrium point near 1820, subsequent to which a definite decline set in. These observed changes, which were based upon a large gentile immigration, mask the true situation with respect to the converted population. The latter was subject to a very great real diminution from the beginning. This is clear from the falling birth rate and the huge excess of deaths over births which was present throughout the mission era. Actually the critical and determining factor was the death rate, for it has been shown that the decline in gross or crude birth rate may be accounted for largely by the constantly increasing sex ratio (males to females). Since the latter was invariable at unity for children under ten, the change must have been due to a differential death rate between males and females during adolescence and maturity, which would result in a relative decline in the number of child-bearing women. The death rate as a whole was always remarkably high, even, for some as yet unexplained reason, at the very start of the missions. It tended definitely, however, to fall during the last thirty years and, at the existing rates of change, would probably have come into equilibrium with the birth rate ultimately. These aspects of the total death rate were due primarily to the state of the child death rate, since the adult death rate did not alter so materially in sixty-odd years.

The chief conclusion of a more general nature is that the Indian population, which presumably had been in a more or less steady equilibrium prior to missionization, underwent a profound upset as a result of that process, a process from which it was showing signs of recovery only at the time of secularization. The indications are, indeed, that several further generations would have been necessary to recast the race, as it were, and bring about that restoration of biotic equilibrium which eventually would have occurred.

PART SIX

The Mechanism and Extent of Dietary Adaptation Among Certain Groups of California and Nevada Indians

Originally published as *Ibero-Americana* Volume 18, 1941

Introduction

Studies of mass adaptation to a new environment by an animal species living under natural conditions have in the past been quite numerous. We also possess many valuable reports of investigations involving groups of organisms experimentally controlled and observed. Much rarer, however, have been attempts to treat in an analogous manner problems involving human beings. Obviously the strictly experimental method is beyond the scope of any natural or social scientist, but what might be termed the historical method offers a substitute of almost equal value. This method implies the utilization of factual material pertaining to the observed changes which have taken place and are taking place in a human population with reference to such tangible or material elements in the group culture as are susceptible of at least semiquantitative treatment. If all cultural elements are included in such a study, the complexity of internal relationships may become so great as to nullify the original purpose. However, if a single element or aspect is selected and considered as a unit, it may be possible to present a reasonably clear picture of adaptation as far as this one element is concerned. The present discussion represents an endeavor to scrutinize the adaptive mechanism and progress of one rather homogeneous human group with respect to such a single element.

The group concerned comprises the Indians of central California and western Nevada. The element studied includes the group's feeding habits and dietary status, which in the course of the past hundred years have undergone considerable modification.[1]

It is possible to set forth, without any intention of being dogmatic, certain guiding ideas in the light of which we may undertake an analysis of the specific element at hand. These ideas are by no means

---

[1] The general sources of information on early conditions include (1) the ethnogeographic literature of the past fifty years, (2) a large body of contemporary manuscript and documentary material available in the Bancroft Library, University of California, and (3) U. S. Dept. Int., *Reports of the Commissioner of Indian Affairs*. Also, the modern status of certain parts of the Indian population was directly observed during two field trips in the summer of 1938. There has been no attempt in this paper to quote exhaustively from the enormous mass of data at hand. Mention is made of specific sources for illustrative purposes only.

new, but may be expressed for present purposes in the form of the following propositions or principles.

1. A group of primitive human beings, when driven by external force or faced with the alternative of starvation, will eat anything they can get.

2. When forced to make a choice between two types of diet, they will select a diet in accordance with (*a*) its geographic and economic availability, (*b*) their own inherited or acquired taste, and (*c*) the social usage of the group.

3. When a freedom of choice exists between two types of diet, they will likewise select in accordance with the same limiting factors.[2]

4. During the process of adaptation the more available food will tend to become more desirable on grounds of taste and will finally come to be preferred socially. Conversely, the less available or original food will first lose desirability so far as taste is concerned, and, second, will be minimized or neglected in social usage or custom.

5. The process of adaptation in the change from one diet to a basically different one must therefore ultimately depend upon a simultaneous diminution in availability of the old and augmentation of availability of the new.[3]

With these principles in mind we may attempt an analysis of the mechanism and extent of the changes which have occurred among the Indian groups mentioned above, as a result of which they have come to regard a standard white diet as more or less normal.

Factors Governing the Availability of White Food

Although with human populations, to a greater degree even than with animal populations, no individual environmental factor ever operates entirely in independence of others, nevertheless to simplify discussion an attempt at segregation and classification must be made. Hence we

---

[2] The white man's diet has at times been forced upon the Pacific Coast Indians as a matter of policy (in the Spanish missions and American reservations). Such policies have definitely influenced the groups concerned, tending to modify the response of the Indian to the alteration in his environment induced by the advent of the white man. Hence to a certain degree restriction in freedom of choice in itself constitutes a factor of significance. This matter is set forth at some length in connection with the system of forced labor or peonage.

[3] The term "adaptation" here signifies a complete shift from one diet exclusively to another diet exclusively.

may regard availability as being dependent upon two sets of forces—spatial or geographic, and economic.

The geographic factor.—Aboriginally the population of the desert and coast regions of the West was in a condition of equilibrium so far as food supply was concerned. The food sources—unlike, perhaps, those of the Plains and Eastern Indians—were extremely varied and numerous. However, the natives depended upon certain staple natural crops, such as acorns, pine nuts, rabbits, and salmon, which in the aggregate constituted an adequate diet both qualitatively and quantitatively. In fact, the human population apparently represented the optimum, in each locality, for the available food supply. The expression "in each locality" is to be stressed because the general region concerned here included wide local differences in climate, flora, and fauna which were reflected in the density of the human population. For example, the relatively sterile Great Basin supported a small population, with quite limited means of sustenance, whereas the foothills area bordering the Sacramento and San Joaquin valleys produced enormous quantities of acorns, fish, game, and minor foodstuffs—a situation which in turn made possible the densest Indian population north of Mexico. These local variations seem to be correlated with the inhabitants' tendency toward a settled or sedentary life. Thus Kroeber and others have pointed out that over most of this area the individual tribes and subtribes showed little, if any, inclination to wander far from their home territory. A few miles along the course of some small stream might represent their entire horizon, although east of the Sierra the localization involved much larger territorial units. The significance of this situation is reflected in its result, namely, that when white civilization arrived, new foods and dietary habits had to be brought to the Indians. The Indians did not travel long distances and bring new customs back with them to the tribal home.[4]

The basis of the geographical factor is, then, propinquity of the white population. But propinquity here presents two aspects. First, the likeli-

---

[4] This statement is, of course, to be taken as relative, not absolute. In the confusion following white settlement, particularly in the gold and silver rushes following 1849, old tribal boundaries were upset and local populations tended to shift. A major exception, furthermore, is offered by the Spanish missions. However, the Indians dependent on the missions were primarily those of the middle and southern coast, who are not included in the present group.

hood or probability that a certain local Indian group would have access to white diet would depend not only upon the nearness of any white people at all, but also on the number of white people within effective range. In the second place, it was necessary that white influence be more than fortuitous or casual. Such an influence had to be exerted over an appreciable length of time in order to induce any significant change in Indian habits. We may therefore say that propinquity is a quantity which depends for its ecological value upon the product of its intensity and its duration.

So far as any local group of natives was concerned, the initial contact as well as duration of contact depended upon other and more remote determinants. Thus in the Central Valley–Sierra Nevada area the white influx was modified locally by the character of the land, the type of economic pursuit prevailing, and, in some degree, the hostility of the Indians themselves. From 1849 to 1860 the western foothills of the Sierra were overrun by vast numbers of gold miners; similarly, east of the Sierra from 1860 to 1865 the silver rush brought thousands of persons. In the mining regions, consequently, white civilization (if one wishes to use the term) struck the foothills tribes with a tremendous impact, utterly disrupting the native life and economy. The effect on dietary habits was relatively insignificant in comparison with the effect on simple survival. Nevertheless, the staple white foods were introduced and, in some measure, utilized by the survivors among the natives. When the wave of miners receded, it left small permanent white settlements which turned chiefly to agriculture and stock raising for a livelihood. The greatly diminished Indian population subsequently depended to an appreciable degree upon the white foods which had been introduced in large quantities during the mining days. Across the mountains, among the Washo and Paiute of Nevada, the white population which persisted after the silver rush was much sparser than in the California gold country. Hence we find that in general the Nevada group has depended definitely less upon white sustenance than has the foothills group in California.

Illustrating this point are field observations made, on the one hand, among the Carson Valley Paiute-Washo tribes, and on the other, among the scattered remnants of the foothills Maidu of the Feather

and Yuba watersheds. The latter at present are thoroughly American-
ized. They subsist exclusively on a modern mixed diet. All informants
affirmed that they could remember no other state of affairs, although
several of them mentioned aged friends or relatives, now deceased, who
in their youth had depended somewhat upon the native diet. In this
region, apparently, the overwhelming invasion of miners, followed by
a substantial permanent agricultural population together with a very
great reduction of Indian population, has caused the relative availability of white food to be very high over a long period.

In the Carson City–Reno sector, on the contrary, the Paiute-Washo
still subsist to a marked degree upon the aboriginal foods (acorns, wild
game, etc.). Furthermore, the condition of primary dependence upon
wild rather than cultivated foods lies within the memory of living
persons. One informant, forty-five years of age, said that her mother
as a child often lived for a whole winter on Indian food because it was
too hard to reach a town. Another, of seventy years, as a child ate wild
game except when white settlements could be reached. One very intelligent woman of seventy pointed out that although in her girlhood her
parents had flour, her grandparents nevertheless lived exclusively on
Indian rations. Beef was obtainable along with flour, but her family
continued to depend markedly on rabbit and deermeat. Canned goods
appeared in her locality about 1900. A Washo woman of sixty-eight
stated that her family had no white bread when she was a child but did
get flour to "supplement" acorns and pine nuts. The single town
known to them was Carson City, where they went only occasionally.
They had no coffee—and the American Indian is exceedingly fond of
coffee—and had not heard of bacon. Many other persons spoke in the
same tenor, declaring that in the late nineteenth century white food
was eaten sparingly, chiefly because it was relatively unavailable. In
this region, therefore, when the flood of miners during the decade
1860–1870 receded, it left only an impression upon the dietary habits
of the Indian, an impression which was not reinforced and intensified
by any permanent large-scale settlement.

In the nonmetalliferous sections of California and Nevada the process of adaptation was slower at the start but more uniform and consistent. Where agricultural development was easy, as on the floor of the

Sacramento and San Joaquin valleys, white settlers of the farming type appeared early and multiplied in numbers until all the arable land was under cultivation, or at least preëmpted by American ownership. In these regions the natives suffered one of three fates—they died off, they retreated to the hills, or they were absorbed into white society. The survivors in any event were closely dependent economically upon white society, and therefore the availability of the white diet was very high. Among those groups or families which did not adopt the latter *in toto* the deterring circumstances were not geographic but essentially economic (as set forth in a subsequent section).

Quite a different situation obtained among the inhabitants of the really remote nonmining areas. Of this type the Achomawi and Atsugewi of the upper Pit River watershed are good examples. Far off the direct line of communication with the east, surrounded by inaccessible mountains and deserts, these people lived more or less undisturbed until late in the past century. The Americans, beginning then to penetrate their territory, came in small numbers and slowly, setting up a ranch here, a sawmill there, with an occasional country store. The intensity of settlement was very low and accordingly the availability of the white diet was not great. There has been a corresponding tendency toward continued reliance on the wild diet, a tendency which persists noticeably today. Furthermore, the influence of individual Americans in molding native habits can be detected. Thus, for example, one informant, a man of seventy years, told how, when he was ten years of age, the first white settler appeared. Hitherto the Indian family had had no white food. This settler hired some Indian labor and paid in coffee and flour. The informant's family were so pleased with the new beverage that they regularly drank it several times a day. An Atsugewi woman of seventy stated that in her childhood the first store near her home on Hat Creek was opened, whereupon the local Indians began to patronize it.

Before we leave the subject of geographic availability, or propinquity of white civilization, we should consider two other elements which had at least an indirect bearing. Certain tribes, particularly in northeastern California and northwestern Nevada, adopted toward the white settlers a definitely warlike attitude. The usual result of an armed clash was the withdrawal of the natives to the most remote spots within reach. This would of course retard the introduction into the tribes of all new customs, among them the adoption of the dietary habits of the whites.

Moreover, those natives who came under the influence of the reservation system were subject to a strong external political pressure. From the inception of the reservations the agents as a matter of routine policy not only encouraged but actively assisted the Indians in establishing agriculure. Large quantities of crops were produced, most of which were consumed by the reservation inhabitants,[5] who thus early came under the influence of a very high availability of white foodstuffs. Although this high availability might be considered a possibly abnormal or artificial phenomenon, the fact of its existence must be admitted and its significance conceded.

The economic factor.—In general, granting that in any particular territory white food was present, and available for consumption to a reasonable degree, the ability of the native actually to obtain the food depended upon whether he could pay the economic or social price. In the aboriginal state the native's subsistence was obtainable free, in the sense that he did not buy it with money or goods.[6] However, he paid for it in labor, often strenuous and exacting. When he came in contact with the white man, however, he could not freely use his own labor to obtain a supply of meat or grain by the simple process of taking it. If he did so, he paid a social price in the form of some type of chastisement. Essentially he was obliged to contribute his labor to the white man and in return to receive his food supply, either directly, or indirectly in the form of wages. The economic availability of the white diet therefore depended upon the type and amount of labor he could give the white man.

Throughout his entire contact with the white race (including both

---

[5] The numerical information with respect to agriculture on the reservations is readily obtainable in the *Annual Report of the Commissioner of Indian Affairs* from the year 1856. Since this phase of the subject is discussed here in general rather than detailed terms, specific statistical data may be omitted.

[6] This statement is of course subject to the exception that barter or trade was frequently carried on between peoples living at a distance from each other. Often, however, this barter consisted of the interchange of foodstuffs which were originally obtained from the wild or natural condition.

Spanish and Anglo-Saxon branches) the California aborigine has existed, as far as subsistence and material welfare are concerned, in one of four categories. He has been either a free laborer, a serf or peon, a vagrant and mendicant, or an out-and-out criminal. These states or conditions merit some consideration with respect to the availability of white food.

The Indian as a peon or serf.—The Pacific Coast Indian, particularly in his labor relations, deserves a chapter in the social history of the United States. Although libraries have been devoted to the Negro and to the problem of slavery, very little attention has been paid to the serfdom once in vogue throughout many parts of California. The problem as a whole must be left for future consideration, but the general historical background may be outlined very briefly. As is well known, the entire colonial policy of Spain in the New World rested upon the cornerstone of native or Indian labor which supported the ruling class—the agricultural, military, and clerical population.[7] This policy was introduced into California in 1769 with the establishment of the missions and presidios. A lively controversy, some of it quite acrimonious, has arisen in connection with the labor policies of the missions, a controversy which is not germane to present purposes. However, it must be pointed out that, whatever the merits of the matter, many thousands of Indians lived for seventy years under a system whereby they were required by moral and physical suasion to perform manual labor in return for their material support, including the major portion of their food. The mission system, consequently, by precedent alone, exercised a profound influence on the entire social outlook of both the Spanish and the American inhabitants of California.

The mission system as administered by the clergy, with its generally humane and sensible provisions, collapsed in the period between 1830 and 1835. It was succeeded by the administrator system, controlled by the secular authority, which retained most of the bad and little of the good of the older organization. The former mission Indians be-

---

[7] Colonial Spanish economic policy has received attention from all the leading writers on West Coast history, for instance, Bancroft, Bolton, and Chapman. For an excellent modern treatment reference may be made to L. B. Simpson, "Studies in the Administration of the Indians in New Spain. III," *Univ. Calif. Publ. Ibero-Americana*, No. 13 (Berkeley, 1938).

came actual slaves, could not endure the life, and dispersed rapidly. Meanwhile the military had utilized Indian labor. In theory the missions loaned neophytes for work at the presidios, for which the Indians were to be paid fair wages in money or commodities. Actually these men were seldom paid anything, and the mission records are filled with just complaints by the fathers against the army administration. Besides this so-called paid labor, the soldiers drew upon two other sources: criminals serving time for various offenses, and wild Indians who, particularly in the later years of Spanish and Mexican rule, were gathered in from the interior by armed expeditions. As the missions decayed and the military power grew weaker, the extent and influence of the great private ranchers increased. The whole coastal region from San Diego to San Francisco passed under the control of individual capital and enterprise. Since the large ranchers depended essentially upon stock raising and since the natives made excellent cowboys and ranch hands, the Indians were employed in large numbers.[8] Although these Indians were technically free employees, in practice they were serfs or peons because, even though their labor was compensated, they were often forced to work against their will. In the letters and diaries of the period 1830–1850, as well as in recollections written later, there are numerous records of Indians who were actually kidnaped and of fleeing Indians who were brought back by force and chastised for running away. In fact, the practice of sending out armed expeditions to catch fugitive laborers or procure new aborigines was universal.[9]

[8] General M. G. Vallejo at Sonoma had at least two hundred in his employ, and at one time Sutter maintained six hundred Indians together with their families.

[9] From the scores of stories and statements the following are illustrative. J. A. Sutter ("Personal Reminiscences" [MS, 1877], p. 77), wrote: "It was common in those days to seize Indian women and children and sell them; this the Californians did as well as Indians." W. Murray ("Narrative" [MS, 1878], p. 75) said: "The Indians are the bond-men of the country. . . . The universal panacea for the cure of their idleness appears to be the hard blows which the Californians are by no means scrupulous about laying on." T. Knight ("Early Events" [MS, 1879], p. 16) recounts how the Kelsey brothers "went up into the Clear Lake region and got some 80 Indians and drove them down to Red Bluff to work . . . "

Illuminating from the legal point of view is a statement in 1849–1850 by the "Committee in Charge of Indian Affairs," a body representing the California Legislature (Vallejo Documents [MS], Vol. XIV, p. 187). The statutes and regulations concerning Indian labor on ranches are discussed. These regulations were very repressive and clearly placed the Indians in the position of indentured servants at best. They were required to

This precedent for forced labor by Indians was naturally very powerful when the earlier American settlers arrived. Many of these newcomers were not slow to adopt the established custom, although it must
be conceded that probably most of the American ranchers prior to
1849 treated their Indian employees as they would have treated white
laborers. With the gold rush, however, the situation changed for the
worse. During the decade 1850–1860, along with the general disintegration of law and order and the almost total lack of social restraint of
any description, the Indians fared very badly. Serfdom or forced labor
was the least of the abuses suffered by these unfortunates. In fact,
nowhere in American history do we find a blacker page than that re-
counting the wholesale atrocities committed by the mining population against the ineffectual and inoffensive natives.

At the end of this period some semblance of a policy began to
emerge, based upon the concept of free labor. The slavery question
and the Civil War settled the matter; as far as the nonreservation
Indians are concerned, they have ever since been permitted free
competition in the labor market.

Thus during the Spanish, Mexican, and very early American phases
of California history large numbers of the Indian population existed
in a state of peonage and were directly dependent on the white element
for their subsistence. This subsistence took the form not primarily of
money, but of clothing, shelter, and food. The food was of the type
common to the white society dominant at the time: cereals, corn, and
beef. The economic availability of white diet to this part of the population was therefore very high. In fact, the native diet was almost
completely superseded over extensive areas and for quite long periods
of time.

If other factors had not intervened, there undoubtedly would have
emerged numerous Indian groups fully adapted to the new dietary
conditions, as were the older mission populations at the time of secular-

---

work under a master who had complete authority over them, and they might even be
bought and sold.

Mention might also be made of J. P. McFarland, who introduced a bill ("McFarland's
Peon Bill") into the legislature of 1853. This bill proposed the apprenticing of all Indian boys up to the age of 21 and of Indian girls up to the age of 18. The proposal met
violent opposition in the press (cf. account by a contemporary, Horace Bell, in *Reminiscences of a Ranger* [new ed.; Santa Barbara, 1927], p. 282).

ization. However, other factors of a lethal nature did intervene. In the first place, those Indians who had been subjected longest to the forced-labor system suffered a sweeping diminution in numbers, and hence whatever adaptations they had achieved perished with them. Second, the forced-labor system, however undesirable on other grounds, did function as a protection or buffer, permitting the Indians to obtain enough food for at least minimum nutritional requirements. When, however, the mission system broke down, and when American constitutional rights were fully recognized, the Indians under peonage were forced into the free-labor market, where no subsistence of any kind was guaranteed and where no protection was afforded. They were thus placed on the same basis as the wild Indians who had never before come in contact with white civilization. The spurious or artificial economic availability of white food disappeared, and with it disappeared whatever tendency toward utilizing that food had resulted from the peonage or forced-labor system.

At this point some comment on the reservation system or policy is necessary, not because the number of Indians involved was ever very large, but because it entailed a type of pseudo-serfdom or peonage—which, indeed, has existed until very recently. As far as food was concerned, reservation policy from its inception in California envisaged the complete dependence of the Indians upon a white diet. This was to be derived from two more or less overlapping sources. The first was the community farm, upon which the group as a whole was required to expend labor and from which it obtained a food supply—an arrangement very much resembling that of the old mission system, but with the religious motive entirely absent. It was essentially a communistic scheme in which the compelling force came from above, not from the group members as individuals. The second source of production was individual gardens, orchards, and stock ranges. The Indians were thus encouraged to display individual enterprise and initiative, although it was recognized that this initiative could not be fostered by compulsion.[10]

---

[10] The exact degree of compulsion is difficult to estimate in the earlier period. In theory it was entirely moral in nature, the government assuming that, if the Indians wished the protection and support offered by the reservation, they should contribute their labor. The enforcement varied with the personality and ideas of the individual

The data given in the annual reports of the agents supply an index of the effect of this policy upon the dietary habits of the reservation Indians. It is not necessary here to attempt any elaborate discussion or statistical analysis, but tables 1 and 2 embody the primary information.

Table 1 shows the trend with respect to the amount of land cultivated by the Indians during the early days of the reservations as opposed to the amount of land communally cultivated under direct

TABLE 1

LANDS CULTIVATED BY THE GOVERNMENT AND BY INDIANS

Reservation	Percentage of total cultivated land operated by the Indians*			
	1866–1875	1876–1880	1881–1885	1886–1890
Hoopa Valley..........	2.3	7.9	36.5	85.6
Round Valley..........	5.1	22.0	24.2	48.0
Tule River.............	20.9	79.8	86.7	88.0
Average of the three reservations..........	9.4	36.6	49.1	73.9

* The distinction between government- and Indian-operated land first appears in the statistical reports of the Bureau of Indian Affairs for 1866 and is continued through 1891 (very incomplete from 1867 to 1872). Subsequent to 1891 virtually all land on the United States reservations was operated by Indians.

government supervision. It must be noted that only three reservations are included here, but since they were the largest and oldest they may be taken as fair samples. Irrespective of the precise values given (which are in any event subject to numerous sources of error), it is clear that

---

agent, as is indicated by the entire lack of unanimity with which the agents expressed their opinions in their reports. That the compulsion existed is clearly shown by the following excerpts, which, incidentally, are illustrative of the widely divergent views held by different agents. (Italics mine.)

"The Indians . . . perform the large amount of labor that *is required* of them cheerfully, and with a degree of skill and industry that is very creditable to them" (N. G. Taylor, U. S. Dept. Int., *Rept. Commr. Indian Affairs,* 1867, No. 28, p. 111).

"The Indians . . . would not work at all if they were not *compelled* to do so" (E. P. Smith, *ibid.,* 1875, p. 221).

"They were *made* to work, they do not know why. . . . I found, in fact, that the reservation was a rehash of a Negro plantation. The agent an absolute dictator . . . The Indians were the most degraded of slaves . . ." (J. V. Farvell, *ibid.,* 1871, p. 157).

" . . . we work the land by a community of interest, *requiring* all able to assist in raising the general crops of wheat . . . while each is *required* to work some ground as a garden . . . " (H. B. Sheldon, *ibid.,* 1871, p. 16).

from 1866 to 1890 there was a very definite increase in the proportion of Indian-operated land. In fact, after 1892 many of the community farms in California were discontinued and full reliance was placed upon individual agricultural effort, supplemented, if crops failed, by direct rationing or relief. Although since that time pressure has always been exerted to induce the reservation Indians to engage in agriculture, the forced-labor system may be said to have disappeared by the last decade of the nineteenth century.

TABLE 2

SOURCES OF SUBSISTENCE OF THE RESERVATION INDIANS

Reservation	Percentage of subsistence derived from nonagricultural sources*					
	1876–1880	1881–1885	1886–1890	1891–1895	1896–1900	1901–1904
Hoopa Valley.........	62.6	33.3	12.6	10.4	1.2	9.5
Round Valley.........	13.0	2.0	2.0	9.0	10.0	7.2
Tule River............	18.2	21.0	15.0	5.0	2.5	10.0
Average of the three reservations.........	31.3	18.8	9.9	8.1	4.6	8.9

* The statistical segregation of subsistence into three categories began in 1876 and was discontinued in 1905. These three were: subsistence obtained by (1) civilized pursuits, (2) hunting, etc., and (3) government rations issued. Since 1 and 3 represent white food and 2 represents native food, the data in the reports have been simplified here by citing only the percentage of the total included in category 2. The sources were hunting, fishing, acorn and root gathering, and so on.

The shift from compulsory to free labor did not mean, however, a diminution in economic availability of white food, such as occurred with respect to the nonreservation Indians, for the food derived from the individual garden or farm was of exactly the same type as that which had been grown as a communal enterprise. It was merely a shift in means of attainment. That there was little or no reversion to the primitive feeding habits is demonstrated by the data in table 2. Here is set forth approximately the percentage of total subsistence acquired by the reservation Indians from primitive sources. Although the figures, individually, are pure estimates made annually by the agents, in the aggregate they represent a clear trend. A steady diminution is apparent from 1876 to 1890, after which a constant level is approached.[11]

[11] It is clear that in table 2 we have the midsection of a curve which should begin in

Subsequent to 1890 there are no data in the published reports of the Bureau of Indian Affairs which are adapted to this purpose and any arbitrary extrapolation is out of the question. However, a personal investigation at Tule River in 1938 (Round Valley and Hoopa Valley were not visited) leads to the belief that the present percentage of wild food consumed is very low indeed—not more than 1 per cent.[12] If this is true, there must have been a slow reduction in the dependence on primitive diet in the past forty-five or fifty years. Now, since the rapid decline up to 1890 may be partly ascribed to the forced-labor system, and since that system was almost extinct[13] in 1890, it follows that the slow subsequent decline was dependent upon quite other factors, probably not connected at all with economic availability.

In summary it may be stated that some type of forced labor or peonage was in practice in California from 1769 until after the gold rush, and was continued somewhat later on the reservations than in other places. When peonage ceased generally, the increased economic availability of white food accompanying that system was in large part eliminated, for various reasons; but on the reservations it was carried over, in a continuous process, when they shifted to a completely free-labor basis.

The Indian as a free or competitive laborer.—There is no doubt that extensively in earlier times and predominantly in recent times the majority of California and Nevada Indians have depended for their subsistence primarily upon their efforts in the open-labor field. But a full discussion of the Indian labor problem as a whole is beyond the

---

the wild state and end at the present. There are no numerical data for the wild state, but obviously the total wild food consumed would be 100 per cent. The part of the curve prior to 1876 would then show a steep decline to approximately 30 per cent. This is followed up to 1890 by a further drop to somewhere near 10 per cent.

[12] No informant at Tule River would state that he or she consumed any Indian food at all. This statement applies primarily to acorns, since the latter have always constituted a key item in the wild Indian ration and have universally persisted when other sources of nourishment have been utterly forgotten. If acorns are eaten at all at Tule River, it is by the least fortunate of the inhabitants and by them to only a negligible extent. The situation is very different only a few miles away among the nonreservation Yokuts near Visalia, Lemoncove, Friant, Dunlap, etc. Acorns and small game still constitute a very definite part of their diet.

[13] In 1938 in western Nevada and eastern central California I found no trace of forced labor either on or off reservations. In fact, the general tenor of opinion among Indians was that any labor at all, forced or free, would be very welcome.

scope of the present paper, and hence many interesting avenues must remain unexplored while brief attention is given to those phases which directly concern food habits.

It has been intimated that most of the Indians who first came in contact with the white man—the coastal tribes and the valley and foothills peoples—suffered so extraordinary a depletion in numbers that few of them survived to enter the free-labor market. Contributions to that market came from the semiremote or quite remote hills—mountain and desert groups which partly or wholly escaped the devastation wrought among Indians in close proximity to the valley ranches and the mines. The latter include such tribes as the Washo and Northern Paiute in Nevada, the Eastern Mono, the Achomawi, the Atsugewi, the foothill Maidu, the Modoc, and the Klamath in California. Among many of these we find that the only purely economic relation they have ever maintained with their white neighbors has been that of employee-employer. Hence to them the economic availability of white food has been solely through the medium of compensation for labor.

The documentary evidence on nonreservation labor, particularly from 1850 to 1860, is voluminous but scattered. Casual references are made by several contemporary diarists and raconteurs, and the reservation agents also occasionally reported on conditions among the Indians not under their jurisdiction. But it is very difficult to ascertain even within wide limits just how much labor for wages was performed by Indians during this period.[14] Subsequently, after there had been

---

[14] The following excerpts from eyewitness accounts indicate the state of affairs:

R. T. Montgomery, "Recollections" (MS, 1878), p. 8, speaking of the period around 1850, says, "The white settlers would give them occasionally a little wheat or corn for working in the harvest."

T. Knight, "Early Events" (MS, 1879), p. 15: ". . . when I lived in Napa Valley (prior to 1850) I used to employ them to work for me. . . . other white men employed them also."

W. R. Grimshaw, "Narrative" (MS, 1872), p. 44: "Before the discovery of the mines . . . in the summer months these Indians would come to different ranchos . . . and work for the proprietors in harvesting their crops . . ." He then goes on to relate that after the gold discovery the Indians mined considerable quantities of gold.

E. Bryant, *What I Saw in California, 1846–7*, p. 240: "Their luxuries, such as bull beef and horse meat, they obtain by theft or pay for in labor . . ."

C. J. Couts, letter in U. S. Dept. Int., *Rept. Commr. Indian Affairs*, 1856, p. 240: "They . . . are the main dependence of our ranchers for vaqueros."

(*Continued on next page*)

several years of mutual intercourse, manual labor became the chief reliance of the Indian, and the status of laborer was definitely assigned to him by white society. But there was always a lag between first contact and final adjustment, a period of transition during which availability of white food was relatively low. The extent of the lag for any specific population group depended upon the rapidity of settlement. Thus a region quickly and heavily settled would see the Indian population put to work very soon, whereas if only a few white men entered and these came in slowly, the natives would not all become laborers for perhaps a generation.[15]

At present, after seventy-five or more years of existence in white so-

G. H. Hoerchner, Calaveras County, California, letter, *ibid.*, p. 240: "Their condition at the present time is rather bad; from 1849 to the spring of 1854, their mode of living and condition were, all in all, tolerably comfortable; they then had facilities for digging gold, and were doing remarkably well . . . but since that time they are in a rather poor condition, as their gold mining is almost gone, surface diggings being scarce."

In 1856 three reports were sent in from newly established reservation areas in California which give a fair comparative picture.

1. From Klamath Reservation. J. A. Patterson, *Rept. Commr. Indian Affairs,* 1856, p. 249: "On this river above the reserve . . . some few of them work for the white settlers."

2. From Mendocino County. H. G. Heald, *ibid.*, p. 243: "The men work occasionally for the farmers"; H. L. Ford, *ibid.*, p. 257: "Most of the able bodied men of this tribe work for the farmers on Russian River and about Bodega . . ."

3. From Fresno Indian Farm. M. B. Lewis, *ibid.*, pp. 253–254: "Nearly all the males who have been industrious have found employment among the miners and farmers until recently." But the mines are worked out and "I am quite sure that the white population of this section of the country will not . . . give employment to more than one fifth of the Indian male population . . ."

On the remote Klamath, therefore, there was very little employment, and on the more accessible Russian River and in the upper San Joaquin Valley, a fair amount.

[15] Considering the relatively small total of labor performed by Indians from 1850 to 1860, as indicated in footnote 14, it is instructive to follow the trend during the subsequent twenty years in certain specific localities in California, bearing in mind the parallelism between amount of labor and economic availability of white food.

1. Klamath region. (Cf. citation from 1856 in footnote 14.) U. S. Dept. Int., *Rept. Commr. Indian Affairs,* 1875, p. 66: "A great number of young men go out and work for white men, principally in the cultivation and digging of potatoes around Humboldt Bay." In twenty years there had been a change from "some few" to "a great number," in this relatively very remote region.

2. Mendocino County (Hoopa Valley and Round Valley), a relatively remote region. L. V. Bogy, U. S. Dept. Int., *Rept. Commr. Indian Affairs,* 1867, p. 117: a group of 300 to 400 Indians gathered at Round Valley "from different points, where they had been engaged as harvesters."

Rept. Commr. Indian Affairs, 1875, p. 81: "The Indians of this agency (Round Valley) are relied upon by the citizens in the vicinity for service . . . in all kinds of heavy

ciety, the California Indian regards his job as the normal mode of securing subsistence, just as does the white man. Aside from individual differences, to be discussed below, the chief variations still discernible are regional and pertain to general economic conditions rather than to any racial distinction. Thus, in those parts of the state (and of adjacent Nevada) where a fixed and fairly steady supply of crude labor can be used, the local Indians as a rule are reasonably well employed. In other parts, where steady employment is scarce, the local groups are in a bad condition.[16] For instance, the Yokuts at Visalia, Porterville, and Friant are at present in a marginal condition. As a group

---

farm work . . . and especially in shearing sheep, in which . . . they are decidedly preferred to white laborers."

C. G. Belknap, *ibid.,* 1876, p. 14: "Many others are herding sheep and doing other labor for citizens."

G. Winslow, *ibid.,* 1882, p. 10: "The Indians have . . . netted something over $2000 from the sale of deer, otter, fox, and bear skin."

H. B. Sheldon, *ibid.,* 1884, p. 16: "They already do a large share of the work that is done for the people of this vicinity."

3. Tule River, a very accessible region opened up to agriculture with the first American settlement. (Cf. citation from 1856 in footnote 14.)

N. G. Taylor, *Rept. Commr. Indian Affairs,* 1868, p. 135: "Many go out and find employment from outside parties as opportunities offer."

E. S. Parker, *ibid.,* 1870, p. 81: "The most of these Indians work as laborers . . . All the Owen's River Indians are employed by the farmers in agricultural pursuits, not only during harvest, but throughout the year."

E. P. Smith, *ibid.,* 1875, p. 229: "The Indians can and do . . . render efficient service to the citizens of the vicinity as herders and shearers of sheep, as vaqueros, and also as day laborers."

C. G. Belknap, *ibid.,* 1884, p. 17: "Nearly all of the able bodied Indians of the agency have for a month past been working in the harvest fields of the adjacent settlements."

4. San Bernardino County. This section was inhabited by the descendants of the southern mission Indians who had been in contact with Spanish and American influence for two or more generations. They lived independently and were only indirectly controlled by the Indian Service. As early as 1856 they are mentioned as being extensively employed as vaqueros, and consistently thereafter they are reported as doing well. In 1880 the agent stated that the demand for Indian labor was equal to the supply, although this was not the case every year. In 1882 the opinion of the agency was that their living was as good as that of the white laboring population. In 1885 he said that many of them were among the best laborers of the country. It is plain that the period of adjustment was already over by 1850 and that thenceforward this segment of the Indian population was a well-established element in the laboring community.

[16] Lumbering, mining, and stock raising are fields of endeavor to which the Indian is well suited, and as a rule these provide fairly steady employment. The valley agriculture, on the contrary, is seasonal and depends primarily on migratory labor, and since the modern Indians by custom and inclination adhere to fixed abodes, they are unable to participate materially in this kind of work.

they do not earn wages enough to meet primary nutritional require-ments. Hence for them the economic availability of a modern Amer-ican diet is very low. On the other hand, the Northern Maidu along the forks of the Yuba and Feather rivers may have recourse to a varied type of employment. They are in a much better condition. Unemploy-ment in general is relatively low, and as a result reversion to primitive diet seems to be unknown among them except for reasons wholly unconnected with availability. And yet this population probably en-countered white food and became accustomed to it later, chronolog-ically, than the Yokuts population in the San Joaquin Valley.

Free labor can be converted into food in two ways. The first is through subsistence farms which are personally operated. This point has been mentioned in connection with forced labor and it is sufficient to state that most of the Western Indians still carry on small-scale agriculture or gardening. In fact, a large proportion of their food today comes from this source.[17] The second method is indirect, through the sale of com-modities or services to the white population. The sale of commodities never has been large, since it has been confined to products of the chase, a few crops, and the product of skilled handicrafts. Hence it is services which have constituted the Indian's primary contribution to society, and it is upon the interplay of demand for and supply of services that he has stood or fallen economically. Now the wages he receives for his services (or commodities) have always been paid in materials or money. If in materials, part was in the white man's food, and if in money, the wages could be spent only for the same type of ration. Hence is derived the direct relation between free labor and the eco-nomic availability of a white diet.[18]

---

[17] Of the Indian families visited in 1938, more than half had some kind of garden, and many maintained poultry or even livestock. Naturally, individual practice is gov-erned by circumstances. Thus such factors as age, ability, inclination, and available time enter to confuse the picture. In general, those families which are situated at some dis-tance from urban centers, or apart from other white people or Indians, tend to maintain more extensive personal farming projects, as do also those which are directly under the influence of the Indian Service. A careful investigation would probably show that more than 50 per cent of the California and Nevada Indian population engage in some kind of individual small-scale agriculture and that the group as a whole may derive as much as 10 per cent of its total subsistence from this source.

[18] A thorough study of recent and contemporary labor conditions among the Indians would require very extensive treatment. It should include consideration of wages (rates

Since labor is always competitive, the Indians, as a group, have been forced to maintain their position against other races, in particular those imported into the West for the purpose of supplying cheap labor. Despite the protective effect of the reservations, the economically free Indian has always had to struggle against the inroads of the foreigner. Even in the mining days much employment which might have gone to the Indians was absorbed by the Chinese. Later, Mexican and Filipino labor was introduced, and in the last few years difficulties have arisen from the competition of white immigrants from the drought area. The Indian is not an aggressive laborer and tends to be driven out by other races wherever the latter penetrate. Individually he can and does do good work, but collectively he has had a very difficult time to hold his position in competition with whites, Orientals, and Mexicans. This situation would very likely have resulted in his complete disappearance from the economic scene in the West had it not been for a few counteracting influences. The first, of course, is the preservative influence of the reservations, to which he might retire for help if general conditions should become too unfavorable. The second has been the rather sentimental attitude which many white men have taken toward the Indian. At the beginning distinctly hostile, and all the way along having been the prime cause of the native's sad lot, nevertheless the white man has frequently extended a helping hand and given an Indian a job, some food, and a cabin to live in, when the representative of no other race would have been so treated. In the third place, the Indian has had one resource unavailable to any other race in competition with him; with his background of knowledge and habit, when faced with absolute starvation from poverty, it has been possible for him to revert to his primitive food supply and thereby keep himself alive. Therefore when free labor has supported him he has utilized the white dietary, but when the availability of the latter has diminished from lack of free labor he has had a substitute which could

---

and totals), extent of employment, types of labor, income from sale of land, crops, stock, natural resources, and manufactured goods. Furthermore, many intricate social problems are involved, such as cheating of the Indians by the whites, expenditure of income on liquor and gambling, and income from prostitution. All these have an indirect bearing on the question of how much white food the Indian could or would buy with the means at his disposal; but adequate discussion of these factors must be left to the future.

tide him over a period of distress, a substitute possessed by him alone of all the races on the Pacific Coast.

In conformity with this situation, we find today that those local groups which are the poorest are those which, other things being equal, tend the most to revert to the aboriginal diet.[19] An instructive comparison of today, with respect to group or regional poverty as a factor reducing availability of white diet, is the one, already mentioned, between the nonreservation Yokuts of the upper San Joaquin and the Northern Maidu of the Sacramento. Both these groups were introduced to white civilization at approximately the same era, and both have adopted white customs very generally. However, the Yokuts have suffered severe competition in the labor market and are extremely poor, whereas the Maidu have escaped these difficulties to a noticeable degree. The Yokuts live in or close to a great fruit and vegetable area in which most of the labor is performed by migratory Americans, Mexicans, and others. There is very little work for them in any other pursuit than agriculture, a pursuit in which the Indian is not at his best even without competition. The Maidu, on the other hand, are able to engage in lumbering, some stock raising, mining, power development, and other types of labor which are more strictly local in character and in which there is less of racial competition. Now, in striking parallel with the economic contrast we find a food contrast. The indigent Yokuts are relying heavily upon acorns and other wild foods, so far as they can obtain them. Several informants among these people stated that they had no money to buy ordinary food but still were able to get from two to ten sacks of acorns annually.[20] A sack of acorns, after shelling and grinding, will make about fifty pounds of meal. A large number of families among the Yokuts and neighboring tribes in the San Joaquin foothills therefore have the use of at least two

---

[19] In more recent times, when the availability of the primitive foods has become relatively low, particularly during the depression, many Indians have gone on local relief.

[20] One informant had in her possession two hundred pounds of acorns still unused from the 1937 crop. Another said she got "a lot of acorns," or "several sacks." Another got "about ten sacks." Another got from ten to fifteen sacks last year. Another said his wife made acorn bread every other week and that it lasted a week, if eaten "a little at a time." An informant at Northfork (chiefly a Mono district) said that, although the amount depends upon the crop, in a good year they brought in the acorns by the truckload. Another Northfork Mono, who was in very unfortunate circumstances, admitted that he and his wife existed almost exclusively on acorn bread.

hundred and possibly five hundred pounds of quite nutritious acorn meal annually. This item in itself represents a considerable food value, and, together with a few garden crops and some small quantity of wild-game meat, enables these Indians to obtain a minimum ration when otherwise they would have to depend wholly upon relief or starve.

Among the Maidu, acorn eating is almost unknown. These Indians live, as far as diet is concerned, on the same level as their white neighbors. All informants were unanimous in stating that not only were no acorns eaten now (except for ceremonial purposes) but that none have been consumed for many years.

Another effect of the competitive labor status is that poverty differences are reflected not only in collective or sectional food habits, but also in family or personal habits. Wholly apart from factors of private taste or social status, the better situated an Indian is economically, the higher the availability of white food and the greater the tendency for him to utilize this food. This statement applies without modification only to that class of Indian which relies exclusively upon income derived from free labor. Under the paternalistic regime of a closed reservation in the past, and to a great extent at present, the labor is more evenly distributed among all individuals and personal differences tend to be obliterated. Where, as is relatively common in California, civil relief agencies contribute to the support of the indigent, assistance is usually rendered in the form of provisions. This obviously raises the subsistence level of otherwise starving families and at the same time provides white food to persons who without relief would use an equivalent quantity of Indian food.

In table 3 an attempt is made to demonstrate in a semiquantitative manner the interrelation of poverty and food habits in thirty-six Indian families selected at random in east-central California and western Nevada. The data in the table are derived from statements by the Indians themselves, together with direct inspection of their living quarters. Although based upon personal observation and subjective evaluation of economic status and food habits, the data show an unmistakable general trend bearing out the previous statement that there is a definite positive correlation between material income and economic availability of the white diet. In fact, the conclusion cannot be escaped that, under present-day conditions at least, the amount of income of the individual family constitutes the most potent single factor with respect to its nutritional status and dietary selection.

The Indian as a vagrant and mendicant.—Although since the beginning of white settlement the Indians have derived their subsistence mainly through forced or free labor, there have always been a signifi-

TABLE 3
RELATION BETWEEN POVERTY AND PRIMITIVE DIET IN 1938

Economic status	Relative dependence upon white food	Number of families in each category
Poor........................	Low	5
Poor........................	Medium	0
Poor........................	High	0
Medium......................	Low	0
Medium......................	Medium	11
Medium......................	High	7
Good........................	Low	0
Good........................	Medium	4
Good........................	High	9

NOTE.—In the left-hand column is indicated approximate economic status, and in the middle column approximate relative dependence upon white food. There are, therefore, nine possible combinations. The distribution of the thirty-six families studied is given in the right-hand column.

cant number of them who for one reason or another have been non-productive members of the community. This group has been recognized as a burden upon society and has been treated varyingly with pity and contempt. In fact, it is unfortunately true that the begging, loafing vagrant has attracted far more attention than his brother who stayed upon the farm or reservation and earned his daily bread.

The problem of Indian vagrancy has been far more vexatious in California than in any other part of the United States, for several reasons. In the first place, there was originally a very great Indian population. In the second place, the California tribes differed profoundly from the eastern forest or western plains peoples in that they were sedentary and immobile and hence tended to congregate in large numbers around their former tribal homes. In the third place, the course of their history was unlike that of most American Indians.

Vagrancy and its concomitant, mendicancy, had its inception in the Spanish mission system. In 1830 there were in the twenty-one California missions approximately 20,000 Christianized and more or less civilized Indians. They had departed from their ancestral ways and were on the highroad to amalgamation with white culture. They were carefully watched and governed by the clergy, who saw to it that they were fed, clothed, and lodged. But with secularization in 1834 there came a sudden change for the worse. The mission establishments were turned over to civilian administrators whose primary motive, it must be admitted, was personal profit. As a result the economic basis of the missions disintegrated completely, the Indians were left to their own devices, and little serious effort was made to keep them in even a mere subsistence status. To put it crudely, in the half-dozen years following secularization nearly twenty thousand Indians were dumped for support onto California, the entire white population of which did not exceed a few thousand.[21] Obviously most of these Indians could neither return to the ways of their forefathers nor support themselves through the slim economic resources of the country. There was no alternative but to starve, and starve they did by the hundred. In the process, however, they flocked to every white settlement, begging, stealing, besieging the inhabitants for charity, and thus creating a serious social problem in every pueblo and on every ranch. The story of their ultimate decimation and disappearance cannot be dwelt upon here, but the outstanding fact cannot be overemphasized: the secularization of the missions created a vast population of wandering, vagrant Indians whose only economic hope lay in the inadequate charity of the white people and who formed the nucleus of Indian vagrancy for fifty years to come.

The situation was made worse by the gold rush, when the invasion of the hitherto untouched foothills tore loose further thousands and sent them drifting through the mining camps and the valley towns. It is no wonder, therefore, that the Mexican private and official correspondence from 1830 to 1845 and the American literature of the West

---

[21] The whole story of the secularization of the missions has been told and retold. A vast contemporary literature exists and has been preserved in substance in the Bancroft Library. Reference with respect to details may therefore be made to that archive, as well as to the well-known secondary works of Bancroft, Englehardt, and others.

from 1845 to 1860 are replete with comments, exhortations, lamentations, and abuse concerning the swarms of Indian beggars and thieves who infested every part of the country. Laws were passed and repassed, but to no avail. The evil continued until the vagrant horde had found asylum on reservations, had been absorbed by the growing labor market, or had gone to their graves.[22]

In the seventy years following the establishment of the reservations

---

[22] It is manifestly impossible to quote at length from the contemporary accounts. The following samples, however, will give an idea of how vagrancy was regarded by some of those who witnessed it. It is worth noting also that the phenomenon impressed each observer according to his own interests and prejudices.

A. F. Coronel ("Cosas . . ." [MS, 1878], p. 224) wrote: "Hay que advertir que este sistema ó manejo fué declinando con tanta rapidez que hacia el año de 1840 y casi habia desaparecido y junto con el la mayor parte de los indios . . . Los que se destruyo muchos indios fué el abandono en que quedaron sin la mas minima protección atenidos a sus propios arbitrios—de aquí las borracheras y la corrupción . . . Aquí en Los Angeles morian como animales sin quien mirara por ellos—lo mismo era en las demas poblaciones y en las ex-misiones que estaban algunas reducidas a pueblos."

Jimeno Casarin, the governor's secretary, issued an order in 1840 (Calif. Archives, Departmental Records, XI, 53) that all vagrant Indians should be collected and put to labor on the public works. Decrees of this type were repeatedly issued from 1830 to 1847.

J. D. Stevenson, the United States Army commandant, issued the following order to S. C. Foster in Los Angeles, February 24, 1848 (Los Angeles County Archives, II, 672): "The public peace requires that the Indian Rancherees in the vicinity of the pueblo should be broken up or removed to a greater distance from the town. You are therefore required to cause their removal or breakage up on or before the night of the 26th Inst."

The *Sacramento Union,* January 23, 1855: "The situation of the Indians in the northernmost part of this state is truly deplorable. They are reported starving and generally lacking in the ordinary necessaries of life. A recent meeting at Pittsburg, Shasta County, afforded positive evidence of their pitiable condition. Resolution One states the natives are in throngs continually on the streets begging for food, and compelling the whites either to support them or watch them starve. A second resolution calls for establishment of a temporary reservation to afford them immediate relief."

Lewis Stark, of Quincy, Plumas County (in *Rept. Commr. Indian Affairs,* 1856, p. 243): "There are about 450 Indians in this locality . . . having to depend during many of the winter months on the charity of the whites."

A. Wiley, *ibid.,* p. 125: "The Indians . . . became (at least a large portion of them) worthless vagabonds . . ."

D. N. Cooley, Indian agent at Tule River, *ibid.,* 1866, p. 98: "A cruel, cowardly vagabond, given to thieving, gambling and drunkenness, and all that is vicious, without one redeeming trait, is a true picture of the California Digger."

J. E. Culburn, Indian agent at San Bernardino, *ibid.,* 1877, p. 37: "The third class is rather small, and includes those who hang upon the outskirts of the towns, pass wistfully through the streets, seldom asking for anything but silently begging with their longing, pathetic eyes. . . . This, which I will call the vagrant class, is not so large as I was prepared to find it, and I believe, from observation and from general report, that vagrancy is not a state into which the mission Indians naturally or willingly fall."

and the adoption of at least the rudiments of a humanitarian policy toward the Indians, vagrancy has notably decreased. There is and always will be a small segment of any population which gravitates into this class. But it is very much to be doubted whether today, or in recent years, the proportion of vagrancy is any higher among the California or Nevada Indians than among the contiguous white population. It is true that the Indians enjoy sitting on the curbstones of the small towns or hanging around in front of the pool halls, or sleeping on the porches of the country stores. But it is questionable whether such activity can be called vagrancy, and, furthermore, it is indulged in by the local whites as much as by the local Indians. There certainly is little, if any, true vagrancy or mendicancy to be observed in the Indian centers at present.

The wholesale vagrancy which existed in the mid-nineteenth century, affecting as it did a large part of the existing Indian population, exerted a good deal of influence on the food habits of the time. For the vagrants the economic availability of white food was very low. Yet for many of them primitive food was unobtainable. This group was then faced with actual starvation and forced to accept any available nourishment whatever, all considerations except life and death being secondary. As a result these people received principally white food, but white food of the worst sort, offal from slaughterhouses,[23] garbage from cities, spoiled or rotted provisions from various agencies. They acted far and wide as scavengers, eating almost any organic matter they could lay hand upon.[24]

After the subsidence of the wave of vagrancy discussed above, a new class of Indian appeared which still exists. This class includes those persons of more or less fixed abode who cannot or will not acquire the

---

[23] With respect to offal, judging by contemporary accounts and present-day reminiscences and hearsay, the Indians did not always come off with the worst of the bargain. In the early days all the viscera of a slaughtered animal were eaten by the Indian, including such items as the liver, heart, kidney, and brain. These portions of the carcass are now known to possess high nutritional value and of course command high prices in the ordinary market. Even the intestines and sometimes their content were consumed, a food which, despite its unesthetic qualities, is not to be undervalued as nourishment.

[24] Some remnants of these customs still prevail. For instance, Indian women in the vicinity of hotels (e.g., at the colony near Reno, Nevada) make a practice of collecting residues from the kitchens. These residues are by no means necessarily garbage and may be food of definite intrinsic value.

necessary means to provide their own subsistence. They are not vagrants or vagabonds or beggars in the strict sense, but they do derive their subsistence without any outlay in the form of commodities or labor. The problem of supporting them is just as acute as in the days of unrestrained vagabondage, but it is now as a rule solved by organized effort on the part of the community. The causes of this modern indigency—as it should be termed, rather than vagrancy—are precisely those which contribute to the great problem of general relief among the white population. The matter has been already touched upon in connection with free labor, but certain aspects deserve further brief mention.

The primary source of indigency is of course unemployment. The latter has always been present, as was pointed out previously, but naturally it was vastly intensified during the depression. The factors contributing are generally recognized and need no discussion. Secondary and quite permanent sources are social rather than purely economic ones. Like most other races, the Indians include a number of persons constitutionally lazy and averse to labor. Many white men have indicted the whole race on this ground, but there is very little clearcut evidence that the Indians, as a whole and under favorable conditions, are any more shiftless and lazy than their white competitors. Nevertheless there will always be exceptions and these exceptions will loom large in the public view. Another social factor of undoubted potency and the source of much controversy is the paternalistic policy of the Federal government. It must be remembered that for decades during the era of "rugged individualism" the Indian was always on reservation relief. Both the forced-labor system and the allocation of provisions by army and Indian Service have imbued the Indian with the idea that the white man will not let him starve. As a matter of fact, the very status of the Indian as a nonvoting ward of the government has inevitably carried with it the latter's obligation to provide subsistence. Hence the great ease and readiness with which the Indians, when hit by any depression, will turn to the Federal agencies for aid.

The two sources of supply, then, for Indians unemployed for any reason have been private charity and some form of public relief. Of the two the more consistent and voluminous has of course been the latter. Relief until recently has been predominantly Federal, through the Indian Service. During the past few years, however, a great deal has been assumed by the counties with or without Federal subsidy.

The significance of relief of indigency to this discussion is that, throughout the entire period since white settlement, relief has meant direct subvention in the form of clothing, shelter, and especially food. In the earlier period army provisions were distributed, these consisting mainly of flour, beef, sugar, and other staples in bulk. No attention was paid to quality or to accessory nutritional factors. Partly through this channel the Indians early became well acquainted with the staple items in the white dietary. Employing the terms which have been adopted here, we may say that all organized relief has operated in the past to increase the economic availability of certain components of the white diet, but has not increased the availability of other components. This trend has been maintained in some degree even up to the present by the more recent extension of credit at stores, with definite restrictions on the type of material which the Indians may purchase.[25]

In concluding this discussion of vagrancy and relief, it may therefore be stated that private charity in the earlier period (where it existed) and modern relief measures have uniformly reinforced the free-labor system by increasing the economic availability of the white diet to the Indian.

The Indian as a criminal.—The word criminal is used here with a very particular connotation. It is not intended to include those individuals who commit ordinary crimes such as larceny, assault, or murder. It covers a type of lawless activity punishable by imprisonment or death which was engaged in by the Indians on a large scale in the Spanish and early American period. I refer to the theft of livestock, including horses. Wholly apart from its legal, political, military, or social aspects, stock raiding by the Indians constitutes a biological

---

[25] In Nevada the Indian Agency policy is at present highly enlightened. The reservation Indians are encouraged to eat a modern balanced diet and seem to be responding in an encouraging manner to these educational efforts on their behalf. Furthermore, the direct-relief rations are made up in accordance with current nutritional knowledge and leave very little room for criticism. In California the Agency is equally enlightened, but it distributes relatively little material itself. It is obliged to carry on its work principally through the county authorities, who are not always distinguished for intelligence or solicitude for the best interests of their Indian charges.

phenomenon, or biological response, of very great interest. Its roots go far deeper than a conscious desire to damage the white man, to obtain a military advantage in time of hostilities, or even to obtain food. Nevertheless, emphasis must be placed here upon this last aspect.

The historical background of stock raiding in California, like the background of vagrancy, was distinctly at variance with that of similar activities in the East, on the Plains, or in the old Southwest. In California the warlike motive was relatively unimportant. For nearly a century after the founding of California a real Indian war did not occur, and for fifty years after the founding there were no hostilities of even minor importance. Nevertheless, ten years had not passed since Junípero Serra's arrival at San Diego before the missionary fathers were complaining that the Indians were stealing cattle. Now it was not only the wild or gentile Indians who committed these depredations, but the converted or mission Indians as well. The evil spread, and throughout all mission history one of the most serious problems which confronted the fathers was how to deal with the perpetrators of such outrages.[26]

The Indians soon began to transgress against the herds of the civil authorities and powerful private ranchers. By the decade 1830–1840 the situation had come to be regarded as a menace to the public welfare, and retaliation was resorted to in numberless public and private war parties and expeditions.[27] By this time the secularized mission Indians, allied with the wild tribes of the interior valley and foothills, had organized widely and carried on systematic raids to the very gates of the pueblos. The quantity of stock stolen—cattle and horses—was enormous—a sizable portion of the total provincial resources.[28]

---

[26] The correspondence and reports of the missionaries from 1780 to 1830 are filled with discussion of this problem. No adequate solution was ever found. Moral suasion seemed to be entirely ineffective and corporal chastisement appeared only to aggravate the evil by creating a desire for revenge in those who were punished.

[27] There are, in the manuscripts of the period in the Bancroft Library, accounts of scores of such punitive expeditions, varying from small *entradas* by two or three persons to real military campaigns.

[28] Many accounts exist in which the stolen stock is estimated in hundreds. Frequently private ranchers lost everything, even to their own saddle horses. No accurate compilation of losses has ever been attempted, but it would be no exaggeration to estimate that between 1830 and 1845 the Indians removed or destroyed from 25,000 to 75,000 head of horses or cattle.

As suggested above, the causes of this wholesale thievery were manifold and complex, but certainly one basic factor was the urge to obtain a cheap, adequate food supply. Not all the stolen stock was consumed as food, but there can be no doubt that a large proportion of it was so utilized.

When the interior valley and the foothills of the Sierra Nevada began to fill up with American settlers, and herds of cattle began to multiply in these regions, it was a simple matter for the local tribes to prey upon them. In so doing, however, they ran squarely into the hostile, intolerant, profoundly anti-Indian sentiment of the Americans. The latter needed only the slightest provocation for armed attack, and thus a vicious circle was established. The more the Indians raided, the more Indians the white men killed. The more Indians were killed, the more the survivors retaliated by destroying animals. In a few years the Indians were utterly subjugated in a military and political sense and drastic policing finally put an end to the era of widespread cattle stealing. In the meantime, however, the Indians had made extensive extralegal use of the white food supply.

During the interval between the secularization of the missions and the final establishment of orderly society by 1860, as was pointed out in a previous section, California was overrun by vagrant Indians. The latter, on an exceedingly low subsistence level, were forced to utilize every possible food source, including what they could obtain from charity and scavenging, and, as we may now appreciate, what they could obtain by theft, principally livestock. Both mendicancy and larceny therefore were manifestations on a vast scale of the response of the Indian to the very low subsistence level to which, through a peculiar chain of circumstances, he had been reduced. The primary biological significance of the entire episode lies in the rapid mass adaptation of the Indian population to the new environment wherein the new diet became relatively more available geographically and economically than the old and the population turned to utilize the new by any and every means at its disposal.

With the stabilization of society and the easing of what may be called starvation pressure through decrease in numbers and through government assistance, the Indians turned to less drastic methods of obtaining sustenance. Through the forced-labor and free-labor systems they found a means of support better suited to the new environment and less in conflict with other forces. Although still perhaps necessitous of charity or relief, the Indians have never since the mining days been so wholly outside the pale of the law.

FACTORS GOVERNING THE AVAILABILITY OF INDIAN FOOD

In the preceding pages we have seen how the California and western Nevada Indians passed through a period of disruption during which they resorted to any means to obtain whatever diet was most available. We have also seen how, subsequent to this era, the white diet became more available in a more or less orderly fashion. The converse proposition must now be considered, that during this same span of years the primitive dietary has steadily diminished in availability. The factors concerned here do not lend themselves to a classification on the basis of geography or economy and therefore no attempt will be made to preserve such a distinction.

Propinquity of food.—The Pacific Coast Indians as a rule were a sedentary people. In a country where the plant as well as the animal food was uniformly distributed over the terrain, it was not necessary for local groups to move long distances. Furthermore, the seasonal climatic differences were so small that subsistence could be obtained almost anywhere throughout the year. Thus, as Kroeber and others have pointed out, the coast population was split up into almost an infinity of tiny communities, each dependent upon the local food supply. After the advent of the white man, provided a given Indian group was permitted to remain in its old home and provided the aboriginal food sources were not cut off, the Indian group could still draw upon the ancient source of nourishment; but if that food source was cut off, or if the group was moved, then the availability of Indian food might drop to a very low level.

This localization with respect to food source must not, however, be regarded as absolutely strict and static. In certain groups there was a clear tendency toward some degree of nomadism. Although static conditions prevailed almost exclusively in the San Joaquin and Sacramento valleys, on the eastern slope of the Sierra Nevada, along the coast, and in the valleys of the Humboldt, Eel, Trinity, Salmon, and Klamath rivers, there was relative freedom of motion among the tribes of the Mojave and Colorado deserts and the western Great Basin east of the Sierra crest. For these tribes no single item of subsistence was sufficiently concentrated in one spot to warrant a strictly sedentary existence. The population was sparser and individuals or small groups were obliged to move moderate distances in order to utilize scattered sources of supply. Thus any one family would tend to inhabit a range rather than a spot. The range, it is true, would be circumscribed and the native tribe would remain within its limits, but the limits were ordinarily much wider than the horizon characteristic of the tribal units found in central and coastal California. After white settlement, these arid-country tribes could still exist upon the old dietary, provided they were permitted a moderate degree of freedom to move about within their range and, of course, provided that the food supply was left essentially intact.

Within historical times there has been a certain amount of redistribution among the Indians of the Pacific Coast.[29] The first major upheaval occurred in Spanish times, when the missionaries assembled most of the coastal population in the missions. So far as availability of native food was concerned (without reference to any other effects), this was not a serious dislocation, because the Indians were never moved many miles from their accustomed abode and frequently were not moved at all. The natural plant products, as well as small game, were within fairly easy reach of the mission; provided the missionaries permitted, the neophytes could gather their acorns and wild cereals with relatively small effort. That the fathers did permit this is attested by the written records of the period. In fact, it was part of the established mission policy to allow the converts at least some access to the native diet.

The break was a little more harsh for persons brought in from the San Joaquin Valley to the coastal establishments, but even for them the change was not fundamental. The same type of material could be obtained on the coast as had been used in the valley and foothills. In

---

[29] It should be clearly understood that the Pacific Coast Indians never were forced to undergo uprooting and transplantation on a scale remotely resembling that suffered by the Cherokee or even by the Sioux or Apache. Tribes were never shifted as wholes, nor was there ever any concerted effort on the part of authorities to deprive entire populations of their homesites.

fact, the aboriginal coast dietary is indistinguishable from that of the valley except in detail. Missionization therefore created no profound disturbance so far as propinquity of native food was concerned.

The troublous mining decade saw great confusion resulting from local invasions by white men. Miners entering the valleys of central and northern California to pan gold in the streams invariably drove out the Indian inhabitants and forced them to take refuge in more remote places, where the native food supply may or may not have been as easy to obtain. But in general, although greater difficulty probably was experienced and there was much hardship, it is doubtful whether mere accessibility of native food was greatly reduced.

Since 1860 there has been very little involuntary transfer of population. The scattered remnants of the formerly populous California tribes have remained essentially where they were situated at that time; nor have the Washo and Paiute strayed far from their aboriginal ranges. During this period (1860 to the present) various factors have operated both to increase and to decrease accessibility of the native diet. On the negative side there has been a tendency toward decrease of mobility, owing fundamentally to the disappearance of free range. For an Indian family to obtain wild subsistence it was necessary to travel some distance, albeit a short distance, because the oak trees supplying acorns grow in a rather scattered fashion over the hills and canyons, pine nuts are found only in rather isolated stands of timber, jack rabbits, squirrels, and deer have to be hunted over several miles of territory. A century ago the Indian was free to wander where he chose in search of these products of the wilderness, but within the lifetime of the past two generations most of the land has come under private ownership for agricultural, stock ranging, mining, or lumbering purposes. The owners of this land are not always willing that the local Indians should trespass even in such harmless pursuits as gathering acorns, and if the Indians do trespass, they may be subject to legal action. In a sense, the Indians in their pristine condition resembled any species of wild animal which forages over a definite range. They were therefore affected just as the animal species is affected when its range becomes curtailed or restricted and it is confined to an area which does not produce enough food for its adequate support. The

Washo and Paiute of Nevada and tribes such as the Atsugewi of Hat Creek have suffered less in this respect than the Yokuts, Miwok, and Maidu of the Sierra foothills because the white settlement has been less intense in their vicinity, and more accessible land remains, but even they have suffered noticeable restriction of movement.[30]

However, the undoubted restriction on physical movement which has followed white settlement has been somewhat compensated by the mechanical improvements introduced by the white man. These concern communication and transportation, particularly. Before the white man came, the Indian was forced to travel on foot. Besides the physical obstacles, there were human obstacles in the form of hostile or competing groups. On the Pacific Coast an equilibrium or adjustment had been achieved whereby there was very little tendency for any group to move outside its own sphere of influence. Consequently, distant or remote sources of food were practically unattainable. In our day many of these obstacles have been removed. In those rather limited areas where white men do not forbid it, the Indian may still forage for

[30] The Indians themselves are keenly aware of this situation and lose no opportunity to express their opinions concerning it. One informant at Dunlap (upper San Joaquin Valley) ascribed the failure of the Indians to obtain both acorns and game to this cause in particular, saying that the local families had been pushed off the "good land" (i.e., regions of prolific acorn supply) to land where the supply was poor. Another very intelligent Indian on the Tule River Reservation explained that the acorn supply was reduced because the white people preëmpted the lands and used the acorns for stock fodder (for cattle and hogs). By enclosing the oak-bearing land in fences, the whites established a legal means of preventing the Indians from competing with the hogs. The specific complaint was voiced by others that the acorn supply had been utilized by hogs rather than Indians.

On the eastern slope of the Sierra, the Indians, according to some informants, have been prevented from availing themselves of the pine-nut crop by the United States Forest Service, for the rangers drive them off the National Forest land, when they go into the mountains to gather the nuts. The explanation given for the prohibition is that the Indians must spend several days on the ground and camp there. This apparently is regarded by the Forest Service as a fire hazard.

As another limiting factor there must be included the fish-and-game laws (restricted areas, closed seasons, hunting licenses, etc.), although these operate in a moral rather than strictly physical manner to prevent freedom of movement. The Indians, whether with or without reason, are universally bitter at what they regard as an unfair restriction on their foraging activity. Although most of them in conversation with a strange white man affirm stoutly their entire compliance with the game laws, a few are willing to admit that infractions of these laws are quite general. Irrespective of the ethics and legality of the matter, it must be admitted that the California game laws definitely circumscribe the Indians and in some degree inflict hardship by preventing their utilization of a potential source of subsistence.

acorns or hunt small game. There are no competing tribes to keep out the stranger. Furthermore, the Indian may now reach these areas by means other than a laborious journey on foot. If he wishes and can afford it, he may go by horseback,[31] but his greatest boon has been the automobile. Some future student will find a most fascinating and instructive topic for investigation in the relation of the twentieth-century Indian to his automobile; for if ever a group of people found their relief from bondage in a mechanical contrivance, it has been our Indians. The effect with respect to propinquity of native food has been striking. For the first time in his history the Indian may now transport his family with ease and facility from the well-populated valley up into the mountains to gather pine nuts or acorns. He may select, furthermore, those spots where the nuts are borne in abundance. One year he may go here, the next year somewhere else, with total disregard of space and time. In the aggregate, of course, the food he gets in this way is of no great significance, but the psychological effect is really profound.[32]

[31] The biological value of the horse to the Indian has long been recognized, and the profound influence of this factor among the Southwestern and Plains Indians has been the subject of much discussion. In Spanish California the influence of the horse was also very significant and was thoroughly appreciated by the missionaries and the military authorities. Strenuous efforts were made for years to prevent the Indians from getting possession of horses, but ultimately all efforts failed.

[32] Representative statements by Indians give some indication of the extent of travel as well as of variation in local conditions. The numbers refer to informants. These statements are selected with reference to the gathering of acorns, since these constitute the most important single item of wild food in use today. The mileages are approximate.

1. Atsugewi, Hat Creek, California. Goes south of Mount Lassen (50 miles).

2. Atsugewi, Hat Creek, California. Goes as far as Montgomery Creek, Shasta County (40 miles).

3. Atsugewi, Hat Creek, California. Gets acorns in vicinity.

4. Atsugewi, Hat Creek, California. Gets acorns sometimes near by, sometimes south of Lassen Park (50 miles).

5. Maidu, Greenville, Plumas County, California. Gets acorns in vicinity.

6. Yokuts, Friant, California. Uses only local supply.

7. Yokuts, Friant, California. Uses only local supply.

8. Paiute, Reno, Nevada. The Nevada Washo go over to California for acorns (50–100 miles).

9. Washo, Carson Colony, Nevada. Gets a supply from California.

10. Washo, Carson Colony. Gets an occasional supply from California.

11. Washo, Dresslerville, Nevada. Goes by car to California for acorns (100 miles).

12. Paiute, Bridgeport, California. Goes to Yosemite and Sonora (100 miles).

13. Paiute, Leevining, California. Gets acorns from Yosemite.

14. Paiute, Independence, California. Gets local supply. Does not go to Yosemite for

When we attempt to evaluate the factors of land utilization and legal restrictions on the one hand with greater personal mobility on the other, we are forced to conclude, in the absence of rigid statistical data, that the two forces probably pretty closely balance each other. If we neglect the period of confusion during the nineteenth century as a transitory phase, it appears that the sheer physical attainability or propinquity of native foodstuffs is not very much less than it was before the advent of the white man. If the Indian really wishes to, he can obtain a certain amount of these materials.

Volume or quantity of primitive food.—Assuming that it is possible to obtain primitive food, the question still remains whether the Indians could in the past and can in the present get enough of it to repay the time and effort consumed in the gathering. Obviously in the beginning, say in 1750, the wild-food supply was adequate to support a population (including the Washo and Paiute) of conservatively 100,000 souls. At present it is doubtful whether this supply alone could support the modern population of roughly 20,000. Hence, the critical limiting factor with respect to primitive diet has not been the capacity of the Indian to reach and obtain the material, but his ability to get enough when he had reached it.

That the total quantity of wild food has been tremendously reduced by white civilization is a self-evident fact, appreciated not only by the Indians but also by every white man who has ever had occasion to consider the depletion of our natural resources. The general phenomenon therefore needs no discussion here. It may, however, be of value to point out very briefly some of the special aspects of this wastage which relate to Indian life and dietary habits. The underlying cause is obviously the utilization of land for all purposes by the white men, which in turn has resulted in the disappearance of the original flora and fauna. Among these purposes is agriculture, which has meant the conversion of great areas of grassy plain and fertile river bottom into plowed fields and orchards. This again has driven out the native grasses, from which tons of seed were gathered. It has altered the character of the rodent population, a large item in the Indian dietary. It

---

acorns, because there is no road over the Sierra at this point; but gets pine nuts from the Panamint Mountains, Walker Pass, and other places from 100 to 150 miles distant.

has obliterated swamps and marshland, the home of inexhaustible supplies of wild fowl. Modern agriculture alone would account for the disappearance of the Sacramento and San Joaquin valley tribes, which originally were extremely numerous.

The oak tree still flourishes in the coast ranges and foothills, but its fruit, the staple acorn, is now fed to hogs or used by the range cattle which overrun the hill country. Similarly the small seed plants have been devoured, and not only by cattle, but in large measure by sheep also.[33] Furthermore, as has been observed in many parts of the United States, when once an area has been overgrazed, the vegetation which springs up is of a different type. Many of the old plants do not return after once being thoroughly depleted. An additional factor in heavily irrigated regions is a lowering of the water table to the widespread detriment of the plant life still remaining. In the upper San Joaquin a reduced bearing power of the oaks has been noticed, which is probably referable to what one Indian described as "the country going dry."[34]

Plant sources of food have been depleted by lumbering. The most important primitive food of the Washo and Paiute was the pine nut, which these Indians obtained from numerous stands of old timber. (Young trees do not supply good nuts in quantity.) Within the lifetime of the present older generation many of these old stands have been lumbered off, leaving only inferior small trees or second growth.[35]

Animal food sources in general depend upon the state of the flora, since most food animals are herbivorous and such carnivores as are used must depend indirectly on plant food through their prey, the herbivores. Therefore when the flora undergoes a radical change, the

---

[33] Reduction of acorn and other seed supply was noted by informants at Hat Creek, Tule River, Bridgeport, Bishop, and Greenville. These reports are representative of what has occurred universally.

[34] Apropos of aridity it is worth noting that not only the food supply of the Indians, but actually the water supply, has been seriously affected in certain sections. Near Friant the existence of an entire colony of Yokuts has been jeopardized by the failure of the springs and wells. These people, and many like them, depend upon a strictly local water supply because of custom and because they have no financial means wherewith to bring the water from a distance.

[35] This loss has been felt principally by the Indians living in Mono County and Inyo County, California, and Carson Valley, Nevada, although it was mentioned by one Indian living on the Feather River.

fauna will be profoundly affected. More directly, however, the fauna has been subject to devastating inroads by the white man in hunting and fishing for both sporting and commercial purposes. In fact, as is well known, severe legal restrictions are now placed upon the taking of fish and game by all persons, in order to prevent the extinction of many valuable animal species. At one time the San Joaquin and its tributaries supplied enormous quantities of fish. These are all gone. Once the Sierra Nevada forests were the home of an unlimited number of deer. There are very few left, and most of the survivors fall before the guns of sportsmen. The ubiquitous and nutritious rabbit has been widely killed off.[36] The salmon has almost disappeared from the rivers of the north coast. Even the insects used as food have been affected. Grasshoppers have become scarcer in the valley. The edible larvae living on the pine have been reduced by lumbering, and the fly larvae around the shore of Owens Lake, prized by the Paiute, have disappeared with the diversion of that lake into the water mains of Los Angeles. These various items, plant and animal, are perhaps insignificant individually, but in the aggregate, and we must remember that the Indian depended originally upon an aggregate, their diminution and disappearance have profoundly affected the availability of primitive food material.

The economic status of the Indian.—It was pointed out at some length in a preceding section how the availability of white food depended upon the purchasing power of the Indian. The same considerations do not apply to availability of Indian food, because, although the relation between individual financial means and availability is direct in the former situation, in the latter it is inverse. The better the economic status of the Indian, the less is his tendency to procure native foodstuffs. This is primarily because the acquisition of native food is independent of price. Acorns, wild game, and the like cannot be purchased in the open market. They can be obtained only by individual effort, time, and labor, and the well-to-do Indian

---

[36] A specific instance of the wholesale destruction of small mammals was related by an informant at Tule River. He stated that a general poisoning campaign against ground squirrels and other rodents had been so effective that the Indians at present could get none of these animals. This is but one instance out of probably a great number and is a fair sample of a certain prevalent type of unintelligent procedure characteristic of agricultural as well as other interests.

as a rule does not wish to use his time and energy in procuring food when it is simpler and easier to purchase it for cash or to receive it in the form of relief.

The time factor per se is of significance. To gather wild crops such as acorns and pine nuts, or to hunt even small game, consumes time, and although to the white man the Indian appears to have an eternity at his disposal, the Indian does not always regard the matter in the same light. Any man, Indian or white, who works on a job—even on W.P.A.—actually does not have the time for such activity, unless it be semioccasionally as a relaxation.[37] And it is precisely the employed class who can obtain all necessary non-Indian food. The ones who have the time are those who are unemployed, and often they do attempt to supplement their diet with wild food.[38]

Intangible factors.—Very closely bound up with the question of time and energy spent in collecting wild foods is the factor of inclination or disinclination. There are numerous individuals who can reach acorns, fish, or game, who have ample time to do so, and who enjoy eating these products, but who simply do not bother to go and get them. One informant says it is "too much trouble," another that "people are too lazy," another that store food is "easier to get." All these statements are but expressions of a state of mind, an outlook on life which has been building up over the years since the Indian was first submerged in a sea of white culture. Such a state of mind is extremely difficult to assess quantitatively and impossible to analyze in numerical terms. However, it must be reckoned with as a very powerful influence.

[37] The Indians themselves readily give lack of time as a reason for not using the wild foodstuffs. One informant from the Atsugewi on Hat Creek stated that her family could get plenty of pine nuts but that their work absorbs all their time. A Maidu, in Greenville, Plumas County, said that even in his youth (he is now about seventy years of age) the Indians got a relatively small amount of game—one or two deer annually in the fall—because they had to work and had no time for hunting. They get no more rabbits from Honey Lake, for the same reason.

[38] One interesting though minor anomaly in the relation between economic status and food status is a phenomenon which may be observed among the Washo and Paiute. Many of these people make a standard practice of gathering pine nuts, expending much time and effort at it. They then sell the product in the regular market, thereby obtaining cash which they may spend for the ordinary line of foodstuffs. Economically they are utilizing the primitive food, but nutritionally they depend on the other type. A similar situation is found among some of the California Indians, who gather acorns, feed them to their own hogs, and then eat the hogs or sell them in order to buy other white food.

Along with disinclination to make the necessary effort to obtain wild food there must be mentioned a continuously decreasing facility in the preparation of these foods. It may perhaps appear a simple matter to gather a sack of acorns and to shell, grind, and cook them, or to gather pine nuts, or to skin and roast a rabbit. But if one consults the numerous accounts in the ethnographic literature,[39] or better yet, if one watches a modern Indian at the task, he will realize that not only are time and patience demanded, but also a great deal of experience and skill. Even an Indian—not to speak of a white man—who has never tried, would have no success whatever in making acorn bread or in roasting grasshoppers. Since the Indians have turned to white cooking methods as well as to white food, they have lost in great measure the ancient art. We find uniformly today that it is the older women who prepare the acorn bread, seldom the younger. In some regions (e.g., in the territory of the Maidu) even the middle-aged and older people have forgotten the method. Again and again we hear the story, "My mother (or grandmother) knew how to do it, but we do not." A chain of instruction is necessary, and once this chain is broken it cannot be reunited.[40] The skill, the art, is dying out, and it would not be unjustified to predict that after the demise of the generation now approximately forty years of age, an Indian who can make acorn bread in the old way will be a rarity.[41]

To summarize, the availability of Indian food (in the broadest sense) has definitely decreased. The California and Nevada Indian can still get to some source of supply with moderate ease. But because of various activities of the white population the total quantity has

---

[39] Many exhaustive descriptions of methods for food preparation have appeared in the *University of California Publications in American Archaeology and Ethnology,* as well as in other journals and monographs.

[40] Among the Maidu of the North and Middle forks of the Feather River there is an old man who likes acorn bread once in a while. In order to get it, he has to call upon the services of an elderly woman who, once a year, goes to his house and makes it. This woman seems to be the only person within miles who is able to perform the service. I spoke to five housewives of advanced years in the same general locality, and not one of them knew how to prepare and cook primitive food of any sort, except to dress and cook game animals.

[41] This statement must be taken as strictly relative. Some groups, as for example the Maidu, have substantially reached this condition now. Others, such as the Atsugewi or the Paiute, will take a much longer time to reach it, probably two and possibly three generations.

fallen below the minimum need of the Indian population, assuming that the latter had to depend on wild food alone for support. Furthermore, the Indian now shows a much diminished drive, in the psychological sense, for wild food, and he has also lost a great deal of his original facility in handling the material once he has obtained it.

Thus in the past hundred years there has been simultaneously a diminution in the availability of Indian food material and an increase in availability of the white dietary. Meanwhile, still other factors have arisen to throw the balance even more heavily in favor of the latter.

The Problem of Taste

The word "taste" is here taken to signify palatability, like or dislike of dietaries as a whole or of individual items therein. In other words, if two types of food, or two specific food substances, are equally available, in the sense hitherto employed, which will the Indian select? We here embark upon consideration of a problem which has wide implications in animal ecology, human psychology, and human sociology. Obviously (as I have hinted in connection with the Indian's disinclination to expend time and effort) such purely subjective phenomena as like and dislike cannot be treated in an objective, analytical manner. It is necessary to call upon observation of behavior and the personal opinion of those directly concerned.[42]

As far as the gustatory sense itself is concerned, there is no inherent quality of unpleasantness unless a substance in the mouth gives rise to a clearly painful sensation. No ordinary food material is of the latter type; if it were, it would not be utilized as food. In everyday life, however, we all regard certain substances as disagreeable or bad tasting. But the criterion of individual taste cannot always be accepted as valid, because other persons may look upon the same substances as tolerable or even desirable. Thus the average western European dislikes very much any food seasoned heavily with pepper, whereas some

---

[42] In studying such phenomena the human biologist has an advantage over the animal biologist or natural historian. The latter two may observe that a certain animal in captivity or other new environment will accept or refuse specific kinds of food, or even refuse food of any description. The first may likewise observe and record similar responses, but he may also elicit a statement of opinion in explanation of why a response occurs. The statement may not be worth much, but at least it can serve as a basis for further study.

groups eat pepper with relish. Putrid meat is regarded with profound disgust by most civilized white people, but primitive peoples may esteem it a delicacy. Furthermore, an individual belonging genetically to one group may be brought up from infancy among a foreign group and in adulthood show the characteristic taste reactions of the latter. It must be concluded, then, that taste in the individual is acquired and is the result of experience and habit. The reactions of a group to taste stimuli may be regarded as the sum of the reactions of the individuals. Hence, if new tastes are acquired or old ones lost by large elements of a population, there may be observed a corresponding group trend. In this sense we may think of a racial taste, which is acquired, and not inherited in the genetic sense. However, since the individual components of a population change in an orderly, consistent manner, there will always tend to be a residuum of taste reactions which will persist over long periods. Similarly a new racial taste will begin on a small scale, will spread to more and more individuals, and will only gradually come to be characteristic of the group as a whole. Thus in an entirely nongenetic sense racial taste may be said to be inherited.

The California Indians of four generations ago were possessed of a well-stabilized taste complex, with reference to their wild diet as a whole. They were thoroughly accustomed to this diet and for them it possessed palatability. As the native diet diminished in availability and the white diet increased, a new taste complex had to be built up in conformity with the conditions imposed by geographic and economic factors. Conversely, the old taste complex has tended to disappear, with, of course, a multitude of minor variations depending on personal and small-group differences. To put the question in another form and on a contemporary basis: How well do the Indians like the white diet as compared with the native diet? This question can be answered only by statements of opinion on the part of the Indians themselves, and by impressions derived from observing the Indians at home. A fair sample of the type of information or data to be obtained is set forth in the footnote below.[43] It may be worth while

---

[43] (To the informants quoted below, numbers have been arbitrarily assigned. The figures following the tribal name refer to age.)

1. Washo, 68, Dresslerville, Nevada. She eats the old food still, but likes white food better. She said her mother used to get tired of wintering on the old food—dried deer-

to quote these statements and observations, together with brief comment on details, in order that the reader may understand fully the kind of evidence upon which any conclusions pertaining to relative tastes and preferences must be based.

As to absolute preference, wholly apart from geographic or economic considerations, it is difficult to reach any positive conclusion. The Indians consulted seemed to show a fairly equal division of opinion. But, without numerous reservations, this apparently equal division cannot be interpreted as applying generally. In the first place, almost all the informants were persons past middle age, and, as already suggested, the older people tend for many reasons to adhere to the

---

meat and acorns—and welcomed the springtime, when it was possible to get white food.

2. Washo, 45, Carson Colony, Nevada. Her mother told her that when she (the mother) was a small child her family spent the whole winter occasionally on Indian food because it was too hard to get into town.

These two records show the geographic unavailability of white food but a positive taste reaction to white food.

3. Washo, 50, Dresslerville, Nevada. She likes acorns for a change.

4. Washo, 65, Dresslerville, Nevada. She likes acorns and pine nuts better than store bread. She can get plenty of ordinary food, but seems to like native food when obtainable.

The general impression derived among the Nevada Paiute and Washo is that they prefer white food.

5. Paiute, 65, Bridgeport, California. The old people still like the old food and use it when possible, but the young people prefer white food.

6. Paiute, 60, Bridgeport, California. He thinks that the old diet was monotonous and that the Paiute were glad to get white food.

7. Paiute, 40, Leevining, California. She thinks the Paiute like Indian food but eat it mainly for variety while depending primarily on white food.

8. Paiute, 30, Independence, California. He says his family eats acorns only for variety. The young people as a rule do not care for acorns or any other of the wild-seed crops.

9. Paiute, 75, Independence, California. She likes acorns and eats them when she can get them.

10. Yokuts, 68, Visalia, California. "All Indians" like Mexican food.

11. Yokuts, 40, Friant, California. He says that if the local Indians had any money the young people would eat white food because they prefer it (note low economic availability of white food). The old people would still use the native food because they are accustomed to it and like it.

12. Yokuts, 60, Squaw Valley, California. Both she and her mother like acorns, also pinole (small seeds) and berries.

13. Yokuts, 68, Visalia, California. She likes acorns better than white bread. The children like everything, but the old people like the old food. (During this interview the old lady was chewing on dried wild berries and one of her grandchildren was eating a jam sandwich.)

14. Yokuts, 78, Tule River, California. He says the older people always liked and still like acorns and do not consider an acorn diet monotonous. This informant related a story of how, when he was a small child, his father learned to plant watermelons. The

primitive cultural pattern. Of significance are the repeated statements (not all of which are given in footnote 43) that the younger element in the population prefers white food. Hence, if a random selection were made of persons under twenty-five years of age, the majority would undoubtedly express this preference. In the second place, again neglecting the economic factor, the primary function of Indian foodstuffs with respect to liking or taste is to serve as variety. The conventional menu of the Indian includes relatively few items, and any additional foodstuff which can be easily obtained is welcome. Thus, in Nevada pine nuts are kept on hand to be eaten a few at a time, just as a city

---

wild Indians would come and pull up the vines until they got a taste of the fruit. Then they liked it. The same thing happened with respect to corn. He says, furthermore, that the people back in the hills would see and try out the new garden products but would not eat much. Those living near white families, however, got used to eating fruits and vegetables and gradually came to like them.

15. Atsugewi, 70, Hat Creek, California. She likes Indian food, and "doesn't care for white man's grub." She encourages the younger members of her household to eat acorns.

16. Atsugewi, 60, Hat Creek, California. She says the people here eat a considerable quantity of acorns, principally for taste and variety.

In general, it appears that the Atsugewi hold relatively closely to the wild-food diet. They are fairly well off economically and their predilection is best explained on grounds of preference only.

17. Maidu, 70, Greenville, California. He likes acorns very much. "The best food we got."

18. Maidu, 70, Greenville, California. He would eat acorns if he could get them, because he likes them.

19. Maidu, 50, Greenville, California. He eats no native food and has no desire to do so.

20. Maidu, 35, Brush Creek, Butte County, California. She does not care for acorns. Her grandmother used to like them. Some of the old people still like them, but even they are losing interest.

21. Maidu, 65, French Creek, Butte County, California. She does not care for Indian food. The Indians in general prefer white food.

Near Mono Lake I attended a peyote meeting, a modern religious ceremony which was held on a Saturday night. On Sunday three meals were served to approximately fifty persons. The viands set upon the table represented what the hosts regarded as the best possible in honor of the occasion. Cost was a secondary consideration. The menus of these meals may therefore be regarded as indicative of what the modern Paiute of that region considers the best and most appetizing food obtainable.

The ceremonial breakfast consisted of canned peaches, cold boiled rice, and cold beef stew, served in that order. The noon dinner included acorn "biscuit," fried fresh-water fish, fried potatoes, frijoles, canned peaches and pineapples, frosted cake, and coffee with sugar and canned milk. The supper consisted of a stew of beef, potatoes, and onions, acorn "biscuit," sliced cantaloupe, bread and butter, and coffee. The noon meal was not seasoned. The stew at supper was seasoned and pepper was on the table. I observed that many of those present ate none of the acorn biscuit. Of those who did partake, most were older persons and they did not eat very much of it.

white family might keep a store of walnuts. As one Paiute expressed it, "We eat pine nuts for dessert just as you eat cake or candy."

Finally, it should be noted that on many occasions when an Indian says he likes "Indian food" better than "white food" he is really referring to some single component of the aboriginal dietary. This must be so because few, if any, living California or Nevada Indians ever subsisted upon a purely Indian dietary and consequently no modern informant has any real basis of comparison. What the modern informant actually means is that he prefers some specific constituent of the old dietary to some or most of the specific constituents of the new. When these and other reservations are given their due weight, it becomes evident that no modern subjective data can objectively answer the question of the Indian's liking or not liking the complete dietary of the primitive Indian as opposed to that of the white man.[44]

Further consideration of the problem leads to the conclusion that, although the trend of taste preference has clearly been in favor of the white diet, that trend has followed the shift in availability. Thus the primary and initially determining factor has been availability, and taste has in the main been secondary. In fact, the shift in taste may be regarded as an adaptation to changing environment which is reflected in availability.

Although it is difficult to assess quantitatively tastes for entire or complete dietaries, it is possible to detect peculiarities affecting individual items. Sometimes these may repeat in miniature what has happened on a larger scale with respect to the whole complex. Two examples may be mentioned which are interesting in themselves, apart from any possible ulterior significance.

The first pertains to beverages.[45] Prior to white settlement, and indeed for many years thereafter, the principal if not the only drink of the California Indians was manzanita cider. Its use was very widespread; indeed, it seemed to coincide, as might well be expected, with the geographic range of the manzanita (genus *Arctostaphylos,* with

---

[44] The nearest approach to an answer would require a careful census of every Indian within a specified region, and even this would be of doubtful value.

[45] By beverage is here meant any soft or nonalcoholic drink. The alcohol or liquor problem is, of course, important in any broad study of Indian social relationships. Liquor, however, can scarcely be considered a food or dietary factor, and hence must be excluded from that general category.

numerous species), which is found in great abundance throughout the chaparral belt of the Coast Range, the northern mountains, and the Cascade and Sierra foothills. It is not common on the valley floor, nor on the deserts to the south and east.[46]

The berries of the manzanita are easily obtainable within its range. They are placed in a dish, crushed, and leached with water. The juice is then drunk directly without sweetening. One informant stated that it tastes much like lemonade, and all persons who had tried it in the past testified to its refreshing quality.[47]

Now the curious fact, so far as change in taste is concerned, is that despite its very high availability even today, its ease of manufacture, and its admittedly pleasant taste, manzanita cider should have utterly disappeared from among the Indians. Yet this seems to be the fact. In 1938 no fewer than eight responsible Indians among the Atsugewi, Maidu, and Yokuts stated that they had known and used the drink in the past, but had not seen any for many years. Not one person admitted having any at present or knowing anyone who had. The search was by no means exhaustive, but it indicates that the beverage is now used very rarely, if at all. Manzanita cider, therefore, must be regarded as an item of the primitive dietary which has completely lost its vogue on grounds of taste alone.

---

[46] It is mentioned as used by the Nisenan (R. L. Beals, *Univ. Calif. Publ. Am. Arch. and Ethn.*, Vol. 31, 1933), the Miwok (S. A. Barrett and E. W. Gifford, Public Museum of Milwaukee, *Bulletin*, Vol. 2, 1933), the Northfork Mono (E. W. Gifford, *Univ. Calif. Publ. Am. Arch. and Ethn.*, Vol. 31, 1932), the Hupa (P. E. Goddard, *ibid.*, Vol. 1, 1903–1904), and the Mendocino County Indians (V. K. Chesnut, *U. S. Nat. Herb. Contr.*, Vol. 7, 1900–1902). It was known to informants in the field in 1938 among the Yokuts, Maidu, Northfork Mono, and Atsugewi. It is absent, however, in the accounts of the Patwin of the lower Sacramento (A. L. Kroeber, *Univ. Calif. Publ. Am. Arch. and Ethn.*, Vol. 29, 1932), the Panamints (F. V. Coville, *Am. Anthro.*, Vol. 5, 1892), the Cahuilla (L. Hooper, *Univ. Calif. Publ. Am. Arch. and Ethn.*, Vol. 16, 1919–1920, and D. P. Barrows, thesis, Univ. Chicago, 1900), the Surprise Valley Paiute (I. T. Kelly, *Univ. Calif. Publ. Am. Arch. and Ethn.*, Vol. 31, 1932), the Klamath (F. V. Coville, *U. S. Nat. Herb. Contr.*, Vol. 5, 1897), and the Luiseño (P. S. Sparkman, *Univ. Calif. Publ. Am. Arch. and Ethn.*, Vol. 8, 1908). I also found no trace of it among the Washo and Paiute of Carson and Owens valleys.

[47] Although this juice must be readily fermentable there is no record, written or oral, of its fermentation by the Indians, an almost incredible fact in view of their extreme fondness for intoxicating liquor. The explanation offered was that custom demanded that the cider be drunk immediately and therefore it never had an opportunity to ferment. But since it has been in very wide use from time immemorial until very recently, one would suppose that by pure chance fermentation might have been discovered.

As manzanita cider has gone out of fashion, coffee has come in, and its consumption is as widespread among the Indian as among the white population. Storekeepers in Indian localities testify without exception to the large quantities purchased. The records of the Carson Agency in Nevada show corresponding amounts distributed as part of relief rations. Nearly every Indian kitchen has a can of coffee on the shelf, and examination of refuse piles and dumps leads to the conclusion that there are more empty coffee cans than any other kind. The Indians personally, even the poorest, testify to their liking for the beverage, and if for any reason local relief supplies do not include coffee, widespread complaint arises.[48]

The Indian liking for coffee was apparently spontaneous. Even during the transition period in the 'sixties and 'seventies they were using it. In the remoter regions where its geographic availability was low its introduction came at a later date, but in all regions its acceptance seems to have been immediate and complete.[49]

The decline of manzanita cider therefore coincided in a general way with the rise of coffee, and, as suggested above, the shift of consumption must be ascribed primarily to a change in taste.

The second example of the operation of the taste factor concerns the type of meat eaten by the Indians. Prior to civilization the Pacific Coast and Great Basin Indians, with relatively minor tribal variations, con-

---

[48] The actual quantity consumed could, if necessary, be ascertained from the sales records of local stores and the files of the California and Nevada Indian agencies. Since, however, there can be no doubt that the Indians in general are very fond of coffee, there is no compelling reason for an elaborate statistical analysis.

[49] The approximate time of introduction and the Indian reaction may be roughly gauged from the following ages and statements of informants:

1. Yokuts, 60 years. Likes coffee but had none as a child.
2. Yokuts, 68 years. Had no coffee as a girl. Now likes it.
3. Mono, 60 years. Had his first coffee when the first stores got into the hills.
4. Atsugewi, 70 years. Had his first coffee as a small boy.
5. Maidu, 70 years. Had coffee as a child.
6. Maidu, 65 years. Has always had coffee.
7. Washo, 68 years. Had no coffee in her youth, but likes it now.

From these few records it appears that coffee was generally introduced some fifty to seventy-five years ago, or possibly earlier. Apropos of the time of introduction it may be noted that the government contracts let in 1898 and 1899 for Indian rations on the Pacific Coast included 62,040 and 77,300 pounds of coffee for those years, respectively (*Rept. Commr. Indian Affairs,* 1898 and 1899). Since these figures take no account of what was privately acquired by gift or bought, they indicate a high consumption rate at least as long ago as forty years.

sumed the flesh of any animal they could lay their hands on—mammal, bird, reptile, amphibian, and invertebrate.[50] It would therefore be assumed, a priori, that these people would eat impartially the meat of all animals introduced by the white man. They have in fact done so, sheep only excepted.

In reading the correspondence and diaries of the mission period, I was struck by the fact that, although there are scores of references to the stealing of cattle and horses by both neophytes and heathen Indians, there is not the slightest mention of sheepstealing. The opportunity certainly existed, for the missions maintained large flocks throughout their history and in general it is easier to steel sheep than steers. In the early American period the same phenomenon is evident: many reports of cattle raiding and none with reference to sheep. The apparent conclusion from this evidence is that, although both sheep and cattle were available, the Indians selected cattle to the exclusion of sheep, and the basis for selection must have been the factor of preference or taste.

The reports of the Indian Commissioners tend to show that on the reservations of California few if any sheep were included among the stock owned by the Indians, and furthermore, that mutton was not included among the rations supplied by the government.[51]

The same trend is to be observed at present. Sheep raising is very rare among the central California and western Nevada tribes, and relief rations include no mutton.[52] In order to obtain a direct expression of opinion, several Indians in scattered localities were questioned on the point. A definite majority stated that they themselves and their acquaintances did not eat mutton and did not like it.[53]

---

[50] One cannot entirely neglect the interesting taboos on certain animals which were common to every tribe and which have been described at length in the ethnographic literature. Anthropological opinion has tended to ascribe such phenomena to social causes. The point is worth raising, however, concerning the extent to which pure taste, or palatability, may have been involved.

[51] The contrast with some other groups is noteworthy, for instance with the Navajo, who have always depended upon sheep rather than cattle.

[52] One informant among the Paiute stated that recently a truckload of mutton was distributed among the Indians in Carson Valley. The people either refused it or threw it away. This statement was not confirmed, but the incident may well have occurred.

[53] The following samples are representative:

1. Paiute, 65. Likes mutton.

2. Washo, 50. Sometimes eats mutton. Many others will not eat it.

(*Continued on next page*)

Other examples probably could be found showing definite taste or distaste for particular food materials in the white dietary (such as the high regard for canned peaches and candy). It is not necessary to press the details further in order to conclude that within the whole range of white food the Indians have adopted some items and rejected others apparently because the former did and the latter did not appeal to their palate. With respect to the origin of these taste differences, we must confess almost complete ignorance. We can go no further than to point out that, although taste changes on a large scale follow, and are determined by, availability, in detail taste may operate independently of availability.

Certain related matters might be mentioned here, although data are lacking to support an exhaustive discussion. We may begin with condiments (exclusive of salt), such as pepper, pickles, and spices. The Anglo-Saxon peoples have always regarded the Indian menu as flat, tasteless, and monotonous. The Latin nations, however, are prone to hold the same opinion of the Anglo-Saxon regimen. Conversely, many English and Americans cannot endure the highly seasoned food of the Spaniard or Mexican. The Indian, in the process of adopting the white diet in general, has had ample opportunity to satisfy any innate craving for highly spiced food. Yet, as a rule, in the districts here studied he has gone to no extreme in so doing. Informants questioned on the point were of divided opinion. Some did not care for condiments at all; others liked pepper; most of them liked onions. The impression obtained was one of individual likes or dislikes with no clear-cut racial preference in any direction. Some traces of geographic or cultural influence may be found in the fact that the tribes exposed to relatively pure American habits, as for example the Paiute or the Sacramento Valley groups, adhere to a lower level of seasoning in their food than do those of the upper San Joaquin which have been exposed to the Spanish-Mexican subtype of the white dietary. The difference, how-

---

3. Washo, 65. She and her daughter never eat mutton; they eat beef.
4. Washo, 68. Does not like mutton. Not many Indians like it.
5. Yokuts, 78. Indians have no sheep and do not eat much mutton.
6. Maidu, 70. Eats no mutton.
7. Atsugewi, 70. Mutton eaten once in a while. Many people do not like it. Some say they get a headache from smelling it.

ever, is not sufficient to warrant any far-reaching conclusions. On the whole, a study of the use of condiments, which in other localities might yield information of some significance, does not promise to be of great value here.

SOCIAL FACTORS

Aside from geographic and economic factors, and apart from individual or group preference or taste, there is a further complex of intangible influences which modify the culture pattern of a people with respect to diet. These influences cannot usually be assessed in a rigidly quantitative manner, nor even discussed on a strictly materialistic basis. Nevertheless, their existence must be recognized and their effect given due weight. Some of these, so far as the present Indian population is concerned, are the following.

Political relations with the white man.—In spite of animosities, the relations between Indians and whites in the Pacific Coast region have been relatively peaceful. At least there have been few major Indian wars. A prolonged state of open warfare inevitably prevents the physical contact of the Indian with civilization and its cultural components, such as diet, and thus reduces or entirely abolishes the availability of the latter; and on the contrary, physical contact is facilitated by a condition either of peace on equal terms or of complete military and political subjugation. A murderous fight to the finish engenders on the part of the savage population for their white enemies or conquerors a hatred which is reflected in their every thought and act, making difficult the voluntary adoption of any white institutions or customs whatever. Not only is the generation which bears the brunt of the conflict affected, but future generations inherit the animosity. In California (to a lesser exent among the Washo and Paiute) there is a subdued resentment today which goes back to the wholesale brutalities of the mining era. This resentment is perhaps less keen than it would have been if there had been a long period of open warfare, but nevertheless it still acts as a minor retarding factor.

Intermarriage.—More powerful than the memory of past wrongs or even than the sting of present injustices is the effect of sexual union. Legal marriage between members of the Indian and the white race inevitably results in the adoption of white customs. The same result may be observed of extralegal unions.[54] The reason lies in the fact that the member of the dominant race (white) by virtue of social habit and contact tends to impose his or her inherited taste and habit upon the family as a whole. No white man, to be specific, will live on Indian food if he can avoid it, and no white woman (in the few unions between a white woman and an Indian) will cook and serve her husband and children anything but the type of food to which she has been accustomed from childhood. Clearly, the extent of this influence is directly proportional to the degree of intermixture and in a thoroughly mixed population may become a very important factor.[55]

Education and propaganda.—In certain of the Indian agencies (in this area, particularly the Carson Agency) an organized effort is being made to give the Indians instruction in the nutritional fields. This instruction does not attempt to discourage the Indians from eating their primitive food, or any individual items thereof, but rather undertakes to encourage them to utilize a wider range of foods, within the general category of the modern white dietary. Particular reference is made to recent developments in the field of vitamin research, since the tendency of Indians has always been to select the cheaper staple components such as flour, sugar, bacon, and macaroni, etc., which, although of high calorific value, may induce avitaminosis if consumed exclusively.[56] The wide success of various commercial interests as well as of philanthropic agencies in bringing about dietary modification in re-

---

[54] A delicate question of civil law enters here. Concerning legal marriage there is no argument, but undoubtedly most unions in the past have not been solemnized by the state or church and even today there is extreme laxity. We may, I think, distinguish three types of union. The first is technically correct marriage. The second is common-law marriage, wherein the man lives openly with the woman, rears children, and otherwise conducts himself as the head of a family. These are the two categories of significance with respect to dietary status. The third is casual intercourse, which may produce illegitimate offspring but otherwise has little bearing on the present discussion. Since the great majority (at least 99 per cent) of casual matings are between a white man and an Indian woman, the children would be brought up by the mother as Indians and would be subject to purely Indian influences.

[55] This factor is doubtless operative in the foothill region of central California, where the original population has been excessively reduced and the survivors have extensively intermarried. Less miscegenation has occurred among the Paiute, Washo, and Atsugewi, and among these tribes the effect has been markedly less.

[56] An interesting experiment in this direction is the nursery school conducted in the Reno colony by the Indian Service during 1938. The school is intelligently administered, the surroundings congenial, and the food of high quality.

cent years among the white population indicates that similar large-scale methods, if applied to the Indian groups, might meet with similar success. The full force of contemporary education and propaganda has never been brought to bear on the Indian, but if it were, far-reaching results might be achieved.

Habit and tradition.—The mere force of cumulative experience is very powerful. A people which has always followed a certain course will, by a kind of ethnic inertia, continue to follow it until and unless deflected by more powerful forces. A new behavior pattern will not arise suddenly. It takes time to develop and the rapidity of development depends upon the intensity with which circumstances promote it. Thus in the absence of the differential availability discussed previously, one would not expect the Indian population to make any shift from primitive to modern food. Furthermore, granting differential availability, if the new diet were clearly and profoundly distasteful to the majority of the population, one would expect its adoption to be seriously retarded. Finally, availability and taste both being favorable, the rapidity of change would still be somewhat reduced by the sheer force of habit and tradition. To what degree this factor has been operative over the past hundred years in California it is difficult to estimate, but that it has been present is demonstrated by the tendency of older people to refuse white food or to use their influence with the young in favor of the primitive diet and by the retention of primitive items such as acorns on ceremonial occasions.

As the tradition supporting the old diet gradually dies out, the new diet becomes endowed with social sanction. First favored because of greater availability and ease of acquisition, simultaneously or subsequently favored on grounds of taste, it eventually comes to be accepted as the normal, the desirable, and the proper or correct diet. The old distrust and resentment fades, the Indian comes to regard the white man as his social equal. What is accepted by the white man is accepted by the Indian, and what was originally adopted from an alien race comes, in the process of adaptation to a new cultural environment, to be an essential part of the Indian culture. Thus the white diet today is regarded by those Indians who are more advanced economically and socially as their own. If by force of circumstances they must turn back to the old, primitive food, they consider it a substitute to be discontinued as soon as possible. This feeling, of course, is less pronounced among those who are, in general, backward or very poor, but it is to some degree shared by all.[57] Thus we see that the final phase in the adaptational process is the acceptance of the new element as a normal and integral part of the environment.

THE EXTENT TO WHICH DIETARY HABITS HAVE CHANGED

In the foregoing pages attention has been directed primarily to the theory and mechanism underlying the nutritional adaptation of the central California and Nevada Indians. As a complement to this study it is desirable to make some attempt to estimate the actual results. This can be done only approximately, but the broad facts can be determined.

It would be most desirable to determine the course of the change, as well as the end result. This would mean that a curve could be plotted showing the relative degree of adaptation at any time since the first American settlement of the Pacific Coast. However, the existing data are inadequate. Reservation reports offer some clues (such as the figures given in table 2), but the total reservation population has always been small and it would be very unsafe to assume that reservation conditions existed among the Indians generally. Information to be obtained from letters, diaries, newspaper reports, and such, of the period 1845 to 1870 is very scattered in both time and space and is at best qualitative. The students of ethnography have gathered a few facts pertaining to the era 1895–1920, but their interest has lain almost exclusively in the primitive food materials as such, not in the extent

---

[57] Little incidents sometimes indicate the movement of strong but imponderable forces. As an example may be mentioned the peyote meeting observed in 1938. In a study being made at present of the peyote cult among the Washo and Paiute by Dr. O. C. Stewart, of the Department of Anthropology, University of California, Dr. Stewart points out that in its ritualistic and religious phases there is a mixture of the pagan Indian elements with those of modern American Christianity (personal communication). In 1938 I noted that, although a primitive food (the acorn) was given prominence at the ceremonial meals and accepted as an integral part of such meals, still the item which caused the most comment and elicited the most outspoken approval was a frosted layer cake. This cake had been baked by some of the girls who had learned the art at an Indian school. Their success in a characteristically American line of cookery undoubtedly increased the social esteem accorded them by the older and more conservative Indians. This was demonstrated not only by the spoken words of those present, but also by the marvelous celerity with which the cake vanished.

to which they were used subsequent to civilization. It might be possible to obtain sales records of stores and trading posts for the past seventy-five years, but this source is of doubtful value. Contemporary statements of living Indians, even those of great age, have no quantitative value whatever, since their evidence is based solely upon hearsay or unreliable memory of former times.[58] Furthermore, Indian informants are decidedly unspecific with regard to the exact period in which events occurred. They are extremely likely to confuse conditions in their own youth with those described by other Indians who have long since died. Thus the standard formula, "the Indians used to" do a certain thing, may refer to any time from twenty-five to one hundred years ago. This looseness in temporal localization makes it inadvisable to use information about the past gained from native informants.

We therefore are confined to a study of the present. It is possible to observe the actual presence of a primitive food item in the menu of an Indian group. Thus statements concerning whether or not a certain item is used now, and, if so, how much of it is consumed, are likely to be substantially correct.

The most direct method is to estimate the quantity of Indian food now consumed rather than white food, since the former is certainly the smaller quantity. Indian food in general may be subdivided arbitrarily into four categories, depending upon the relative amounts used now rather than upon the amounts used primitively: (1) acorns, (2) pine nuts, (3) fish and game, and (4) all other items. The last category may be neglected because it is only very rarely that any item other than those specifically mentioned is utilized. The use, for example, of seeds or pinole, tule or other roots, insect larvae, wild greens, or wild berries has been almost completely discontinued, and any sporadic occurrence of these materials in the diet would not affect the general situation.

This analysis is based upon field observations and therefore confined to the groups actually seen. The groups fall into four divisions, the Paiute-Washo of Carson and Owens valleys, the Yokuts and North-

---

[58] It should be emphasized that the memory of living persons may be unreliable quantitatively but still be valid qualitatively. Thus an elderly person may be perfectly accurate in stating that his family ate acorns when he was a boy, but be entirely at a loss with respect to how much of this food was consumed per month or per year.

fork Mono, the Atsugewi of Hat Creek, and the Maidu of Plumas, Butte, and Yuba counties.

The Paiute-Washo.—Of twelve families selected at random, ten use acorns, two do not. Four families specified approximate annual quantities: 2 to 10 sacks, 4 to 6 sacks, 6 to 7 sacks, 1 sack. The others stated: "several," "a few," "occasional," "considerable," "special occasions only," and "get prepared acorn flour." Taking rough means for the four reporting numerically, we get an average of about 4 sacks. The others apparently use less, although the terms "several" and "occasional" might be construed as a similar order of magnitude. This would indicate a general mean of 2 sacks annually. However, the figures given above were based by most informants explicitly upon "good years," or "if the crop is good." Frequently the trees bear little fruit, and occasionally none at all. To account for crop failure the values must be reduced by at least 50 per cent. A fair estimate would then be 1 sack of acorns per family per year.

Ten families reported quantitatively on pine nuts, also a staple food of the Washo and Paiute. Nearly all these stated that the crop had been poor for two or three years, and based their number of sacks obtained upon the last good year. Five families got at that time respectively 10 to 20 sacks (but sold all but 4 to 5), 8 to 10 sacks, 6 to 10 sacks, 3 to 4 sacks, 3 to 4 sacks (but sold many of them). One family reported 1 sack in 1937, a poor year. Three reported the use of very few, and one did not use them at all. In this record we must deduct the sales from the total in order to estimate the quantity actually eaten. Fifty per cent seems adequate to account for this loss, since, although some families sold more than half their crop, others sold no pine nuts whatever. This would give for the first five families an approximate mean of 4 sacks per family actually consumed. Since the sixth family obtained 1 sack in a poor year, they probably would get more in a good year. The other four families get few, if any, pine nuts. Hence a conservative estimate for good years might be 2 sacks per family. This estimate must be reduced to account for years of poor crop, and recent experience indicates that these occur quite frequently. Thus an annual average of 1 sack per family must represent the maximum consumption.

Several families reported on fish and game. These reports indicated a general lack of hunting activity among the Paiute—aside from pure sport, which provides very little animal food. Some persons stated that they obtained no food from this source, a few admitted getting "a few" rabbits or squirrels occasionally, and one or two claimed a fair amount of game. Since these last were very indefinite concerning how many animals were killed, or how often, their evidence is best disregarded. The general impression is that the amount of food obtained in this manner by the Indians is no greater than among the neighboring white people, probably no more than twenty or thirty pounds per family per year.

The significant items with respect to bulk are, then, acorns and pine nuts. In a previous discussion the weight of a sack of fresh acorns was taken as 100 pounds and the weight of the utilizable meat, minus the shells, as 60 pounds. Pine nuts are structurally quite similar, and the same weight estimates will hold. Thus if the average consumption per Paiute or Washo family is 1 sack of acorns and 1 of pine nuts, then the available food material would amount to 120 pounds per year, fresh weight. However, fresh acorn meat contains a fair quantity of water, probably (by analogy with similar nuts) from 20 to 25 per cent at least. The water content of the acorn meal used for making bread is given by Chesnut[59] as 8.7 per cent. Hence if we are to use calorific values based upon the meal, we must deduct for water loss in the drying of the acorns and grinding of the meal. This will amount to approximately 15 per cent of the fresh weight. Consequently the meal which has been prepared from 200 pounds of acorns will weigh about 100 pounds.

The food value of the acorn has been the subject of some investigation. It has been determined that the food value of 1 pound of the meal (approximately equivalent to 1 pound of the shelled nuts) is 2180 calories. The modern Paiute and Washo subsist on somewhat better than a bare maintenance diet and probably obtain at least the requisite minimum of calories, due allowance being made for age, size, and activity. If we take the average family as consisting of two adults and two children and estimate the calorific requirement as

[59] V. K. Chesnut, *Nat. Herb. Contr.*, Vol. 7, 1900–1902.

approaching 10,000 calories daily,[60] then the annual requirement is
3,650,000. If we take the calorific value of shelled acorns at 2180 per
pound and pine nuts at probably the same order of magnitude, then
the combined 100 pounds will provide 218,000 calories. This means,
then, that if the foregoing calculations are based on anything approaching reasonable estimates, the Paiute and Washo as a group
derive somewhere near 6 per cent of their energy requirement from
primitive food. Because of the probability of overestimation, it would
be more conservative to place the value at somewhere between 3 and
6 per cent.

The Yokuts and Northfork Mono.—These tribes obtain very little
wild meat, according to their statements; possibly as much as the
Paiute. Pine nuts are seldom seen. Hence for primitive food they
depend almost exclusively upon acorns. Of three families reporting
in numerical terms, one obtained last year from 10 to 15 sacks; another
gets annually about 10 sacks; another had above 200 pounds (2 sacks)
left in July from the previous year and had been eating them consistently since that time. Another family "gets some," another "gets
several sacks a year," another "eats acorns all the time." One family
eats none whatever.

This group without question consumes more acorns than the Paiute.
If we take the maximum consumption of the acorn-using families
as 10 sacks per family in a good year and consider that much less than
half the families eat none at all, we may arrive at an estimated mean
of at least 6 sacks per family. This number must be cut in half to account for frequent crop failure, giving a final value of 3 sacks per
family per year. The calorific requirement of this group is the same
as that of the Paiute, but the general subsistence level is probably
lower. However, owing to lack of concrete data on this point, the subsistence level must be left out of the calculation. If the number in the
family is estimated as the same as for the previous group, the value
of 10,000 calories daily may be accepted as the family requirement.

[60] This is obviously a very crude estimate. It is based on the requirement for a
laboring man of average size of 3800 calories, a woman at home of 2700, and two
children of 2000 each. But many families have several or no children, and many include
relatives—grandparents, aunts, sisters, etc. The value of 10,000 calories is perhaps too
low; for many families, however, it must be too high.

Then the annual requirement will be 3,650,000 calories utilized, of which 327,000, or 9 per cent, will be supplied by acorns. Again allowing for the possibility of overestimate, the final range may be set at from 5 to 9 per cent.

The Atsugewi.—Four families reported numerically on acorns, and opinion was unanimous that virtually all the Hat Creek group consumes this food. The values given respectively were: 2 to 3 sacks, 5 to 6 sacks, 2 to 5 sacks, 1 to 2 sacks, all "depending on the crop." The mean here is approximately 3.25 sacks. Now since the use of acorns is substantially universal, it is not necessary to reduce this figure to allow for nonusing families, but it must nevertheless be cut in half to account for crop failure, giving 1.6 sacks per family. Pine nuts are known, but are sparingly used. One family said that "very few were consumed," and one other that they ate "sometimes one-half a sack." Perhaps it would be legitimate to estimate pine-nut consumption at one-tenth of one sack per family which would make a total, with acorns, of 1.7 sacks. Using the previously described method of computation, the result is a probable primitive-food consumption of from 3 to 5 per cent of the total diet.

The Maidu.—It has been pointed out repeatedly that the surviving Maidu exist almost exclusively upon a modern white diet. To be concrete, in Greenville, Plumas County, three families were interviewed. One of these never eats acorns, pine nuts, or game; the second eats "a few acorns" but not every year; and the third gets from 2 to 3 sacks of acorns annually but no other Indian food. In Butte County, on the lower North and Middle forks of the Feather River, five families were interviewed. None of these used any sort of Indian food, nor had they done so within a generation. Near Bullards Bar, on the North Fork of the Yuba in Yuba County, one family had eaten "some acorns" three years ago but none since. At Dobbins, also in Yuba County, some ten to fifteen families were known to responsible local white residents, who testified that within their memory of the past thirty years none of these Indians had eaten any acorns whatever. Thus, of approximately twenty families interviewed or reliably reported on, only one makes a practice of consuming Indian food. This one uses, let us say, 2 sacks of acorns a year. The average is, then, very close to one-tenth of one sack per year per family among the Maidu. On the basis of the previous method of calculation this amounts to three-tenths of one per cent of the total calorific requirement. Since the consumption is certainly no greater than this value and since whole segments of the population use no Indian food at all, the percentage range may be set at 0.0 to 0.3.

The probable percentage ranges for the four groups under consideration are, then, respectively, 3 to 6, 5 to 9, 3 to 5, 0.0 to 0.3. Obviously, local conditions underlie the observed variation and an exact general mean would not carry great significance. However, the conclusion may be drawn that at present, among these groups as a whole, (1) the consumption of primitive food varies from a minimum of 0 to a maximum of 9 per cent of the total diet, and (2) the average consumption over a wide range of territory is probably less than 5 and more than 2 per cent.

With respect to adaptation to white civilization these results show that, so far as food is concerned, the Indian has almost, but not quite, completed the transition from the wholly primitive to the wholly modern dietary.

SUMMARY AND CONCLUSIONS

At the beginning of this paper the thesis was proposed that in order to make effective a mass adaptation to a new physical and social culture, so far as the nutritional element is concerned, a certain primary category of factors must be operative, namely, geographic and economic availability. This study has set forth the way in which these forces did operate with respect to our east-central California and western Nevada Indians in such a way as to favor the shift from the primitive to the modern white diet. With availability at a maximum, it is still necessary that the new diet satisfy the conditions imposed by palatability or taste and, finally, that this diet should come to be accepted socially. The evidence here presented leads to the conclusion that, although there have been and still are counteractive forces, nevertheless the balance has been steadily shifting toward the satisfaction of gustatory and social requirements. In short, during the past hundred years the process of nutritional adaptation has followed in its general outlines the course predicated in the opening thesis. Today we are witnessing the final stages of this process, which began in the mid-nineteenth century and will require one or two more generations to complete.

INDEX

Achomawi Indians, 175-177, 178, 180, 190, 237, 262-263, 278, 285, 351, 352, 357, 380, 454, 463

Adaptation, 56, 255; human, three types discussed, 1; responses, 9-10; and population change, 10-11; group responses to environment, 64-65, 227, 230-231, 232-233; flexibility lacking in California Indians, 9, 88, 101, 144-145; and missions, 9; Indian adaptation in gold mining, 321; Indian adaptation to white economy, 323-329; and labor practices of Indians, 101; and disturbance of food supply, 291-292, 295; dietary adaptation, 449-450, 477; and Indian marriage and divorce, 374-376; acculturation and property rights, 136-142; acculturation and language, 142-145; acculturation and customs and religion, 143-153; assimilation of Christianity, 153-157; fugitivism and rebellion, 57-67, 228-233

Aginsky, B. W., 344-345

Agriculture: in missions, 35-51; horticulture in missions, 50n; crop failures, 53-54; on reservations, 455, 459-461; Indian labor, 317-318; Indians as farmers, 322n, 466; American settlement, 280-281; advance in San Joaquin Valley, 288; development of ranching, 302-303; decline of great estates, 308; effects on Indian food resources, 483-484

Alamán, Lucas, 421n

Alameda County, 183, 242n

Altamira, Fray José, 77, 78

Amador County, 214

American River, 179, 204, 211, 213, 319

Americans: contrasted to Spanish, 256-259; impact on Indians, compared to Spanish, 346; and Indian resistance to Spanish, 231; early inroads into San Joaquin Valley, 202-203, 232

Amoros, Fray Juan, 77, 78

Anderson Valley, 310

Antelope Valley, 298

Anza, Juan Bautista de, 23, 199

Apache Indians, 1, 67, 124n, 444, 479n

Aporige Indians, 176

Arcata, 283, 284, 331

Argüello, Gervasio, 77, 110-111, 421n

Asesara, Lorenzo, 130-131

Astariwawi Indians, 176

Athabascan Indians, 167-171, 238, 278, 287, 351, 352, 357

Atsuge Indians, 176

Atsugewi Indians, 175-177, 237, 352, 454, 463, 481, 482n, 486n, 487n, 491n, 493n, 494n, 496n, 498n, 505

Atwamsini Indians, 176

Auburn, 179

Avitaminosis, 34, 498

Aztec Indians, 1; epidemics among, 18

Bald Mountain, 284

Bancroft, Hubert Howe, 76, 184, 200n, 401, 456n

Bandini, Juan, 421n

Barrett, S. A., 174

Beale, General E. F., 311

Bear Creeks, 243n

Bear River, 282, 343n

Beechey, F. W., 210

Beef, raised by missions, 35

Benites, José, 33n

Berreyesa, Feliz, 224

Berry Creek, 243n

Bidwell, John, 304, 305n

Big Bend, 242n

Big Oak Flat, 320

Bishop, 484n

Bledsoe, A. J., 282, 285, 286, 287-288

Bodega Bay, 81, 200, 464n

Bogy, L. V., 313

Bolbone Indians, 83

[509]